Cloud Security:

Concepts, Methodologies, Tools, and Applications

Information Resources Management Association
USA

Volume II

Published in the United States of America by
    IGI Global
    Engineering Science Reference (an imprint of IGI Global)
    701 E. Chocolate Avenue
    Hershey PA, USA 17033
    Tel: 717-533-8845
    Fax: 717-533-8661
    E-mail: cust@igi-global.com
    Web site: http://www.igi-global.com

Library of Congress Cataloging-in-Publication Data

Names: Information Resources Management Association, editor.
Title: Cloud security : concepts, methodologies, tools, and applications /
  Information Resources Management Association, editor.
Description: Hershey, PA : Engineering Science Reference, [2019] | Includes
  bibliographical references.
Identifiers: LCCN 2018048047| ISBN 9781522581765 (hardcover) | ISBN
  9781522581772 (ebook)
Subjects: LCSH: Cloud computing--Security measures.
Classification: LCC QA76.585 .C5864 2019 | DDC 004.67/82--dc23 LC record available at https://lccn.loc.gov/2018048047

British Cataloguing in Publication Data
A Cataloguing in Publication record for this book is available from the British Library.

The views expressed in this book are those of the authors, but not necessarily of the publisher.

For electronic access to this publication, please contact: eresources@igi-global.com.

List of Contributors

Table of Contents

Volume I

Section 1
Fundamental Concepts and Theories

Section 2
Development and Design Methodologies

Section 4
Utilization and Applications

Section 5
Organizational and Social Implications

Volume IV

Section 6
Managerial Impact

Section 7
Critical Issues and Challenges

Preface

The constantly changing landscape of Cloud Security makes it challenging for experts and practitioners to stay informed of the field's most up-to-date research. That is why Engineering Science Reference is pleased to offer this four-volume reference collection that will empower students, researchers, and academicians with a strong understanding of critical issues within Cloud Security by providing both broad and detailed perspectives on cutting-edge theories and developments. This reference is designed to act as a single reference source on conceptual, methodological, technical, and managerial issues, as well as to provide insight into emerging trends and future opportunities within the discipline.

Cloud Security: Concepts, Methodologies, Tools, and Applications is organized into eight distinct sections that provide comprehensive coverage of important topics. The sections are:

1. Fundamental Concepts and Theories;
2. Development and Design Methodologies;
3. Tools and Technologies;
4. Utilization and Applications;
5. Organizational and Social Implications;
6. Managerial Impact;
7. Critical Issues and Challenges; and
8. Emerging Trends.

The following paragraphs provide a summary of what to expect from this invaluable reference tool.

Section 1, "Fundamental Concepts and Theories," serves as a foundation for this extensive reference tool by addressing crucial theories essential to the understanding of Cloud Security. Introducing the book is "Curtailing the Threats to Cloud Computing in the Fourth Industrial Revolution?" by John Gyang Chaka and Mudaray Marimuthu: a great foundation laying the groundwork for the basic concepts and theories that will be discussed throughout the rest of the book. Section 1 concludes and leads into the following portion of the book with a nice segue chapter, "Approaches to Cloud Computing in the Public Sector" by Jeffrey Chang and Mark Johnston.

Section 2, "Development and Design Methodologies," presents in-depth coverage of the conceptual design and architecture of Cloud Security. Opening the section is "A Multi-Dimensional Mean Failure Cost Model to Enhance Security of Cloud Computing Systems" by Mouna Jouini and Latifa Ben Arfa Rabai. Through case studies, this section lays excellent groundwork for later sections that will get into present and future applications for Cloud Security. The section concludes with an excellent work by Rekha Kashyap and Deo Prakash Vidyarthi, "A Secured Real Time Scheduling Model for Cloud Hypervisor."

Section 3, "Tools and Technologies," presents extensive coverage of the various tools and technologies used in the implementation of Cloud Security. The first chapter, "CCCE: Cryptographic Cloud Computing Environment Based on Quantum Computations" by Omer K. Jasim, Safia Abbas, El-Sayed M. El-Horbaty, and Abdel-Badeeh M. Salem, lays a framework for the types of works that can be found in this section. The section concludes with "Keystroke Dynamics Authentication in Cloud Computing" by Basma Mohammed Hassan, Khaled Mohammed Fouad, and Mahmoud Fathy Hassan. Where Section 3 described specific tools and technologies at the disposal of practitioners, Section 4 describes the use and applications of the tools and frameworks discussed in previous sections.

Section 4, "Utilization and Applications," describes how the broad range of Cloud Security efforts has been utilized and offers insight on and important lessons for their applications and impact. The first chapter in the section is "Cloud Computing and Cybersecurity Issues Facing Local Enterprises" written by Emre Erturk. This section includes the widest range of topics because it describes case studies, research, methodologies, frameworks, architectures, theory, analysis, and guides for implementation. The breadth of topics covered in the section is also reflected in the diversity of its authors, from countries all over the globe. The section concludes with "Necessity of Key Aggregation Cryptosystem for Data Sharing in Cloud Computing" by R. Deepthi Crestose Rebekah, Dhanaraj Cheelu, and M. Rajasekhara Babu, a great transition chapter into the next section.

Section 5, "Organizational and Social Implications," includes chapters discussing the organizational and social impact of Cloud Security. The section opens with "Impact of Technology Innovation: A Study on Cloud Risk Mitigation" by Niranjali Suresh and Manish Gupta. This section focuses exclusively on how these technologies affect human lives, either through the way they interact with each other or through how they affect behavioral/workplace situations. The section concludes with "Trust Management in Cloud Computing" by Vijay L. Hallappanavar and Mahantesh N. Birje.

Section 6, "Managerial Impact," presents focused coverage of Cloud Security in a managerial perspective. The section begins with "The Collaborative Use of Patients' Health-Related Information: Challenges and Research Problems in a Networked World" by Fadi Alhaddadin, Jairo A. Gutiérrez, and William Liu. This section serves as a vital resource for developers who want to utilize the latest research to bolster the capabilities and functionalities of their processes. The chapters in this section offer unmistakable value to managers looking to implement new strategies that work at larger bureaucratic levels. The section concludes with "Smart Healthcare Administration Over Cloud" by Govinda K. and S. Ramasubbareddy.

Section 7, "Critical Issues and Challenges," presents coverage of academic and research perspectives on Cloud Security tools and applications. The section begins with "A Comparative Study of Privacy Protection Practices in the US, Europe, and Asia" by Noushin Ashrafi and Jean-Pierre Kuilboer. Chapters in this section will look into theoretical approaches and offer alternatives to crucial questions on the subject of Cloud Security. The section concludes with "Privacy Preserving Public Auditing in Cloud: Literature Review" by Thangavel M., Varalakshmi P., Sridhar S., and Sindhuja R.

Section 8, "Emerging Trends," highlights areas for future research within the field of Cloud Security, opening with "Advances in Information, Security, Privacy, and Ethics: Use of Cloud Computing for Education" by Joseph M. Woodside. This section contains chapters that look at what might happen in the coming years that can extend the already staggering amount of applications for Cloud Security. The final chapter of the book looks at an emerging field within Cloud Security in the excellent contribution "Emerging Cloud Computing Services: A Brief Opinion Article" by Yulin Yao.

Although the primary organization of the contents in this multi-volume work is based on its eight sections, offering a progression of coverage of the important concepts, methodologies, technologies, applications, social issues, and emerging trends, the reader can also identify specific contents by utilizing the extensive indexing system listed at the end of each volume. As a comprehensive collection of research on the latest findings related to using technology to providing various services, *Cloud Security: Concepts, Methodologies, Tools, and Applications* provides researchers, administrators, and all audiences with a complete understanding of the development of applications and concepts in Cloud Security. Given the vast number of issues concerning usage, failure, success, policies, strategies, and applications of Cloud Security in countries around the world, *Cloud Security: Concepts, Methodologies, Tools, and Applications* addresses the demand for a resource that encompasses the most pertinent research in technologies being employed to globally bolster the knowledge and applications of Cloud Security.

Chapter 28
Role of Agents to Enhance the Security and Scalability in Cloud Environment

Manisha Malhotra
Chandigarh University, India

Aarti Singh
Guru Nanak Girls College, India

ABSTRACT

Cloud computing is a novel paradigm that changes the industry viewpoint of inventing, developing, deploying, scaling, updating, maintaining, and paying for applications and the infrastructure on which they are deployed. Due to dynamic nature of cloud computing it is quite easy to increase the capacity of hardware or software, even without investing on purchases of it. This feature of cloud computing is named as scalability which is one of the main concern in cloud environment. This chapter presents the architecture of scalability by using mobile agents. It also highlights the other main issues prevailing in cloud paradigm. Further it presents the hybrid architecture for data security which is also the one of major concern of it. This chapter mainly highlights the solution for scalability and security.

INTRODUCTION

Cloud Computing incorporates virtualization, on-demand deployment; Internet based delivery of services and use of open source software. In contrast to the use of already established concepts, approaches and best practices, Cloud Computing is a novel paradigm that changes the industry viewpoint of inventing, developing, deploying, scaling, updating, maintaining, and paying for applications and the infrastructure on which they are deployed. Due to dynamic nature of cloud computing it is quite easy to increase the capacity of hardware or software, even without investing on purchases of it. From last few years, cloud computing has become a promising business concept. All existing business applications are complicated in nature and much too expensive. To run these applications there is a need of data centers having supporting staff and infrastructure like bandwidth, networks and server etc. along with a dedicate team for

DOI: 10.4018/978-1-5225-8176-5.ch028

its execution. For deploying such kind of applications, organizations have to invest large amount of funds which makes it difficult for small businesses to establish themselves. Therefore, cloud computing provides a simple alternative to start IT based business organization with much less initial investment. Although cloud computing offers significant edge of the traditional computing methods but the data which is being continuously transferred to cloud is actually *Big Data* (Chen et al., 2014). In fact, in order to handle the data received cloud owners need to have skilled analytics and also they must ensure that all clients get their due resources well in time and should satisfy the need. In order to automate the data centers, cloud owners are now moving towards deploying mobile and intelligent agents. The current work has thus been motivated by the emergent requirements of improving resource scheduling and cost optimization algorithms in cloud computing. The work aims to exploit mobile agents to overcome the barriers.

The chapter is therefore structured into three major parts. It begins by providing brief overview of cloud computing and issues prevailing in the cloud computing. The promises of mobile agents have been highlighted justifying them as enablers to the barriers so far projected in the success of cloud computing. Finally, it provides the solution for stringent security in cloud environment.

CLOUD COMPUTING

Cloud basically stands for **C**ommon **L**ocation-independent **O**nline **U**tility service, available on-**D**emand. It supports huge amount of virtual workload of resources including communicative environment for user. Cloud computing thus offers computing technologies being offered at cloud. Cloud computing offer lots of advantages over traditional computing such as online resources, offline access, flexibility, savings, just to name a few (see Figure 1).

Cloud computing includes everything that already exists (Armbrust et al., 2009). It is distributed into three segments namely, applications, platforms and "infrastructure". Majorly, the definition of cloud computing specifically revolves round the terms like scalability, pay-per use model, and virtualization.

In fact, enablers supporting cloud computing are interoperability, portability, integration of components, ease of deployment, pay as per use, economic, rapid provisioning and elasticity and so on.

Figure 1.

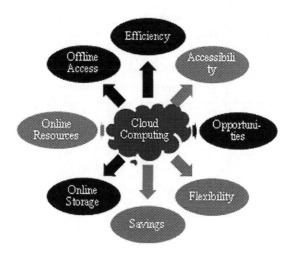

Because of the appealing features mentioned above, cloud computing is becoming a temptation for all business organizations.

Besides the various features that cloud computing supports, there are few barriers also that are acting as hurdles towards the complete adoption of cloud computing by the business community. For instance, cloud computing architecture (Armbrust et al., 2010) is service based architecture, i.e., it offers Software as a Service (SaaS), Platform as a Service (PaaS) and Infrastructure as a Service (IaaS). While SaaS allows the consumer to use desired software from the cloud infrastructure, the PaaS provides resources such as operating system and software development frameworks. On the other hand, IaaS provides the facility of virtual environment having virtual machines, storage, virtual networks and essential computing resources. Now, each service layer is equipped with certain inherent issues such lack of transparency about storage and security and integrity of data at software as well as platform level. Although IaaS provides primary security in the form firewall, load equilibrium. The design issues presented above majorly highlight the concerns related to security in cloud computing. Therefore, one of the prime objectives of this research work is to address these security issues pertaining to each layer.

ISSUES IN ADOPTION OF CLOUD COMPUTING

Referring to the literature (Armbrust et al., 2010), we could identify that there are many issues such as technological issues, business issues, performance issues and few miscellaneous issues are prevailing in the wide adoption of cloud computing. Figure 2 depicts the issues and are being discussed as follows.

Figure 2.

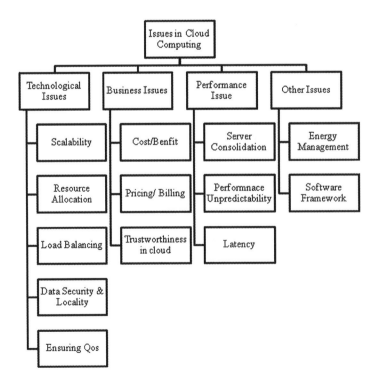

Technological Issues

This domain highlights on technological issues of cloud computing. The main focus is on some inherent issues which involve some following areas:

- **Scalability in Cloud Computing:** Cloud Computing delivers scalability platform. Cloud scalability has the capability to vigorously scale up and scale down the number of server instances which is assigned to a request depending on the demand of user. Whenever any cloud service will deploy on server, it can be extent on multiple servers.
- **Resource Allocation:** In cloud computing, according to user demands, the resources will provide as a service which is led by service level agreement (SLA) (Zhang & Cheng, 2010). Due to wastage of resource, there is a need of resource allocation technique because of high demand of resources which is definitely will share and most of requests are heterogeneous. Therefore, resource allocation and scheduling is one of the major issue of cloud computing.
- **Load Balancing:** Load Balancing is one of the key research areas which make resources effectively distributed. Many load balancing algorithms have been developed in this field; still there is need of improvement in lacking part.
- **Data Security and Locality:** Whenever customers use cloud application, his major concern is about the data storage and its locality. Data assurance must be there that no one accesses the customer's data without legitimate permission (Yang & Tate, 2009).
- **Ensuring Quality of Service by Migration of Virtual Machines:** It ensures that service providers deliver better quality of services. It mainly concerned about the allocation of virtual machines (VM) to job assigned by user. Effective QOS outcomes can be in the form of minimum processing time of the data center, virtual machine cost, data transfer cost and overall response time. There should be an optimized algorithm which considers minimum processing time and total VM cost.

Business Issues

As it is well known that cloud computing is the business model, so during its implication there are many issues which need to be considered. It mainly involves:

- **Return on Investment (ROI) Cost/Benefit:** It is mainly focus on user's side. The main of researchers is to optimize the cost and benefit for migrating computing tasks over the clouds (Yang & Tate, 2009). Such efforts can further help users while choosing cloud services.
- **Pricing/Billing:** It mainly focuses on providers' side. Researchers focus on developing pricing and billing models for cloud providers in order to retain customers at the same time guarantee profits for the providers (Armbrust et al., 2009, 2010).
- **Trustworthiness in the Cloud:** Cloud brokers are the bridge between the customers and cloud service providers. Customer depends heavily on the cloud broker and deciding the right cloud broker and evaluating its trustworthiness are major challenges.

Performance Issues

This issue is regarding the performance of a data center which further depends on servers and operators handling the requests.

- **Server Consolidation:** For taking maximum benefits of resource utilization, server consolidation is an effective way by minimizing the energy consumption. In case of single server, all VMs set to an energy saving state except the executing VM. Due to this, resource congestion takes place by changing footprints in VM on data center and by sharing of resources. It can be helps to select the effective server consolidation. Whenever the resource congestions are occurred in server, it works fast and effectively.
- **Performance Unpredictability:** In cloud computing with the help of virtualization, VM can easily share CPU, and memory, but it is quite difficult to share I/O. again using virtualization, I/O interrupts is the best solution to improve the performance of operating system. Multiple VMs are hold workload of I/O interrupts randomly. So, it is quite difficult to check the performance especially in a batch processing.
- **Latency:** It is also one of the important research issues of cloud computing that affect the performance of a server. Latency increases with the rapid use of cloud based applications.

Other Issues

- **Energy Management:** Performance of server depends upon the energy efficiency. Cost of powering and cooling is 53% of total operational cost (Foster et al., 2008). Infrastructure provider must reduce the energy consumption as well as cost for accounting energy. The main aim is to achieve the good performance of a data center by reducing energy.
- **Software Framework:** Cloud computing is the better option for hosting data intensive applications. It uses Hadoop architecture for scalable applications and use Map Reduce architecture for fault tolerance. Although Map Reduce architecture supports heterogeneous nodes but design of a suitable job scheduling algorithm which works for every node is still an open challenge.

All above unfolded challenges reveals that there is an ample of scope in the field of cloud computing. This chapter considers resource allocation, load balancing, data security issues and have made an attempt to propose solutions adjacent to these issues.

As already mentioned that business organizations i.e. the cloud providers are now making a shift towards deploying mobile agents to improve the performance of cloud technology. Next section provides an overview of mobile agents and also describes the feasibility of mobile agents in cloud computing.

MOBILE AGENTS: AN OVERVIEW

A Mobile Agent (MA) is a software module that performs a desirable task in a heterogeneous network by migrating autonomously from one machine to another. MAs are being used as mediators between users and devices (Danny, 1998). Figure 3 illustrates interaction of mobile agents with their environment.

Figure 3.

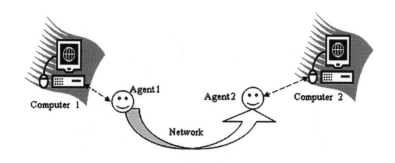

A mobile agent inherits features from distributed computing and artificial intelligence fields. Mobile agents have already been deployed successfully in many distributed and web based tasks because of their appealing attributes such as mobility, dynamic, portable etc. Table 1 delineates the features of mobile agents.

Characteristics of MAs reveals that these can be used anywhere in any technology. Some of the most pertinent applications of mobile agents in different fields are shown in Figure 4.

Multi agent system (MAS) referred as comprising of multiple interacting intelligent agents within an environment. MAS is used to perform difficult problems for an individual agent or a monolithic system. Intelligence may include some methodic, functional, procedural or any algorithmic approach. Agents in MAS may choose to cooperate, direct other agents and migrate from machine to machine.

Table 1.

Attributes	Description
Overcomes Network Delay	Only one time connection has to be established when agents have to migrate first time. Thus agents can work on limited bandwidth and reduce network delay.
Autonomous	Agents can operate without interference of user.
Asynchronous	Once mobile agents have been initialized and assigned a specific task, they leave their source location computer system and roam freely through internet.
Dynamic	They can initiate and destroy themselves.
Cooperative	Agents can cooperate with each other in cyberspace to achieve their goals and to provide services to their beyond their specified capabilities.
Robust	Agents can cooperate with each other in cyberspace to achieve their goals and to provide services to their beyond their specified capabilities.
Fault Tolerant	Due to usage of multiple agents, agent system has a tolerance for failure of limited number of agents. If an agent is being lost during execution then system can reproduce another copy of that agent or can assign the same task to another agent.
Protocol Encapsulation	Agents can make their own protocol and encapsulate the data.
Social	Agents interact with each other by agent technologies like Tool Command Language (TCL), Jade etc.
Reactive	Agents perceive their environment and react according to command given by user
Proactive	Agents can take initiative and make changes in their environment.
Veracity	Agents are expected to communicate with each other without floating false information.

Figure 4.

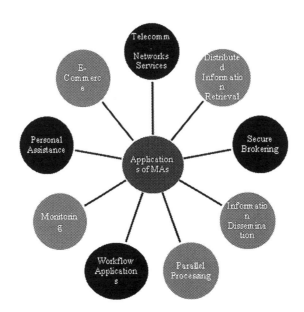

Due to the features and applications of mobile agents mentioned above, these are widely deployed in different field like distributed computing, grid computing, artificial intelligence, wireless sensor networks and semantic web. Incorporation of mobile agents improves the efficiency of system in different field as well as in different concerns. Authors have (Singh & Malhotra, 2012) amalgamated the mobile agents in cloud computing, since by deploying mobile agents the network traffic got reduced and at the same time response time could also be reduced. In contrast to this, in traditional system of cloud, every request is sent directly on WWW which leads to increase in network traffic, the amalgamated replica of mobile agent was created which could be migrated from one end to another. Figure 5 shows the amalgamation of mobile agents in cloud computing.

Figure 5.

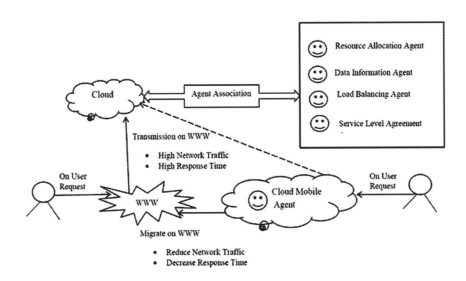

SCALABILITY IN CLOUD ENVIRONMENT

This work concentrates on guaranteeing adaptability in cloud computing in circumstances where either the assets of the cloud have been depleted or it cannot give administrations to more client or the asked for assets are not accessible with it. This work is being proficient in two sections: first is to look another group cloud to fulfill the demand close by and besides to scan for nearest datacenters with minimum reaction time of virtual machines (VM). The proposed system makes utilization of mobile agents to accomplish the objective. The proposed structure connects a mobile agent with every open/private cloud, which contains the data about that cloud, for example, different assets accessible with the cloud and it additionally monitors free and designated assets. Consequently, at whatever point an administration ask for lands to a cloud, agent checks the accessible free assets to choose whether the demand can be served or not. The proposed structure involves cloud mobile agent and directory agent as appeared in Figure 6.

- **Cloud Mobile Agent (MA$_C$):** It is related with each cloud and is in charge of keeping up asset data and also their status anytime, whether it is free or allocated.
- **Directory Agent (DA$_C$):** DA$_C$ keeps record of all MA$_C$ enlisted with it, alongside abilities of the mists. At whatever point a cloud is made its MAc should get enrolled with a DAc, which keeps up their database fundamental for giving versatility in administration.

Initially the MAc sends an enlistment demand to closest DAC alongside data of the cloud with which it is related, accordingly the DAC sends back an affirmation flag showing that the MAc has got enlist with it. Figure 7 clarifies this procedure.

Presently at whatever point a public/private cloud turns out to be excessively over-burden, making it impossible to deal with another client ask for then the versatility highlight is practiced to give administrations to the client through some other cloud. In such circumstance MAc gets enacted and sends demand to registry specialist requesting for the rundown of other MAc equipped for giving the coveted administration. The catalog operator on getting this demand seeks its database and gives the rundown of able MAcs. On getting the rundown from the DAC the initiator MAc sends benefit demand to them and sits tight for their reaction. In the event that some cloud having the required assets ends up notice-

Figure 6.

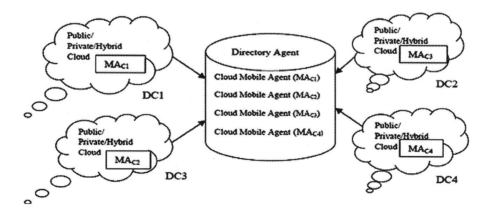

Figure 7.

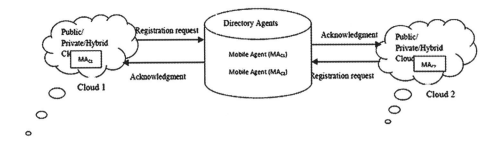

ably prepared to give the administrations, it reacts back to the initiator MAc. Initiator MAc checks all the got reactions, performs transaction with concerned MAcs and afterward at long last doles out the close in response to popular demand to the MAc most appropriate both, as far as less cost and quicker administrations.

As we know cloud computing research is still in its initial stages and there are many challenges still prevailing in it. The issues highlighted earlier need attention from research community and mobile agents may be instrumental in solving some of those issues. This research work has deployed mobile agents in cloud computing and this is unique contribution of this research work. Next section discusses the various security issues prevailing in cloud computing.

SECURITY ISSUES AND RESOLUTIONS

Infrastructure as a Service (IaaS), particularly data storage is one of important service given by a cloud. Single client and business associations are moving their data on cloud as a result of simple accessibility and lessened cost offered by it. Be that as it may, sparing information at a remote server is much the same as giving your cash to somebody, since in today's computerized period, information is the foundation of handling. In this manner, with all the adaptability offered by cloud, genuine security concerns

Figure 8.

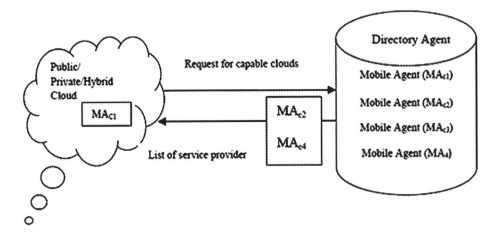

have additionally been produced. Security concerns are creating impediment for business associations to move altogether to open mists.

Recently, there is expanded consideration from research and business community towards developing an effective security measures in cloud environment. Some association like Cloud Security Alliance (CSA), European Network and Information Security Agency (ENISA) (Funmilade et al., 2012), Cloud Computing Interoperability Group and Multi-Agency Cloud Computing Forum are working towards giving viable and proficient controls to give data security in cloud condition. Some imperative security concerns winning in this area are information security, protection, data accessibility, trust management and so on. Be that as it may, as of late parcel of specialists have proposed systems for enhancing data security yet at the same time there is degree for research toward this path. This work investigates security issues in cloud paradigm and exemplifies existing algorithms for the same.

Security Issues Unveiled

Cloud is a web based administration worldview where clients get to different administrations from Cloud service provider (CSP) through web. At whatever point client signs in a cloud and begins getting to different administrations, data trade begins amongst client and CSP. To the extent security of data traded is concerned, just distributed storage is not concerned. There are in certainty different levels where security rupture may occur and trustworthiness of data might be bargained.

Figure 9 outlines different levels of security worries in cloud condition.

Each level focused on some key issues. All levels have their own significance and need measure up to consideration for guaranteeing general hearty security in cloud situations. Figure 10 highlights different levels requiring security alongside concerns basic.

- **Network Security:** While transferring data from one network to another, cloud service providers must ensure about robust and secure communication protocol to avoid network attack on data.
- **Interface Security:** It is concerned with the interface given by cloud suppliers and level of security offered by it. VM interface influences the inalienable security elements, for example, IBM Blue Mix is a cloud benefit in view of Linux and Microsoft Azure depends on Windows operating system. Linux working framework is more secure when contrasted with Microsoft Windows. In this way interface security would be better with Linux based interface. Hence interface offered by CSP ought to send secure working environment.

Figure 9.

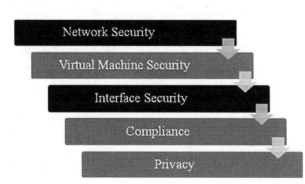

Figure 10.

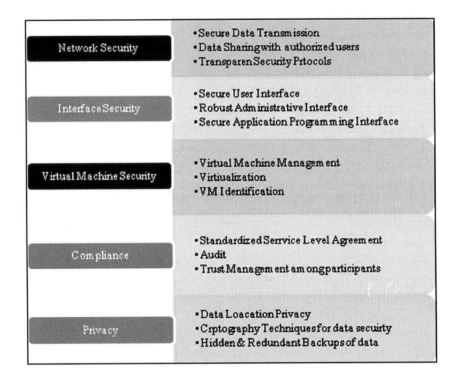

- **Virtual Machine Security:** VM security is of most extreme worry among all security concerns. Clients make utilization of VM for their processing assigned jobs. Further, a cloud makes utilization of Multi-tenancy strategy, i.e., same VM and assets are being utilized by various clients at various purpose of time to optimized resource utilization and VM cost. However, this builds plausibility of security breaks. Various clients of a solitary virtual machine must be detached to the degree so that secrecy of an individual might be kept up.
- **Compliance:** Compliance is directly related to service level agreement (SLA). SLA is the main legal certificate between the client and the provider which expresses the administration necessities of the client and administration benchmarks to be given by the supplier. Be that as it may, there is no institutionalization of SLA which is basic to make this plan of action dependable. Feeble usage of administration benchmarks by the supplier may prompt security defects.
- **Confidentiality/Privacy:** Confidentiality focuses on preventing client data from unauthorized users. In cloud computing all information is put away on geographically accordingly guaranteeing privacy of information ends up noticeably real issue. Applying different cryptographic techniques is the run of the mill arrangement being received. Information part is another method being utilized to guarantee security of information at supplier's end. In this procedure information is put away at different non-interfacing has. In any case, both above strategies have their own intrinsic issues.

All above recorded security concerns are of significance at various levels of correspondence with cloud. CSP needs to guarantee security at all levels, which is an extreme undertaking. Next segment investigates existing answers for above security concerns.

THE SECURITY ALGORITHMS: RELATED WORK

In concentrated on system mindfulness and reliable streamlining of asset allotment procedures and highlighted the exploration issues winning in this field. Creators stressed that more endeavors are required to make the current execution models prescient and responsive. Safiriyu et al. (2011) proposed a client character administration convention (UIDM) in cloud worldview. It suits all partners, i.e., end clients and suppliers. It gives validation, encryption and key administration component. They have tried frail, solid and extremely solid client personality and watched more disappointment if there should arise an occurrence of powerless IDM. Zhen et al. (2013) proposed a community oriented system security model framework utilized as a part of a multi-inhabitant server farm. They have utilized a brought together community oriented plan alongside bundle review at various levels of security. It shields the server farm from all conceivable system assaults. This unified security focus can convey security principles and gather information from the systems. In any case, the proposed model needs in recognition of system arrangement infringement.

Philipp et al. (2013) has built up a stage which guarantees the incorporated security and enhanced information handling known as Virtual Fort Knox. This item is reasonable for little and medium ventures. It gives physical security like get to control, assurance from altering of physical server and in addition insurance against disappointment of chairman.

The instrument introduced in a design which builds the security of virtual machine. The engineering is partitioned into two sections one is refresh checker design and another is online entrance suite engineering appeared in Figure 11. Refresh checker distinguishes the obsolete data introduced on virtual machine. Second one sweeps every single virtual machine and boot them if there is requirement for it. Assist, report generator is another part which produces the consequences of defects (as far as hazard level) in the wake of gathering all reports from scanner.

With the assistance of this report the blunder can undoubtedly be recognized and expelled. However, both these designs can be correlated just on Linux condition. Be that as it may, there is need of a non-specific engineering which can chip away at each condition.

Sapuntzakis et al. (2008) built up a component which allots virtual machines naturally. The proposed conspire has averted security breaks however does not permit updation of all bundles of virtual machines.

Figure 11.

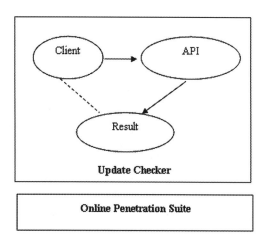

Qian et al. (2011) proposed a cloud information stockpiling engineering that gives open auditable cloud component which serves to looks at capability and capacities of information proprietor to survey the danger of outsource information with the assistance of outside review party. The proposed engineering involves four segments viz., information proprietor, client, cloud server and Third Party Auditor (TPA). It gives a component in which information proprietor delegate TPA to review the cloud server in successful and cost productive route for end clients, when it is required. With regards to security, it is not totally secure as it appears in light of the fact that the examining totally depends on TPA and information proprietors. Here the question emerge that if the proprietor and TPA are not conveying right answer to client, then will's identity in charge of that.

These systems (Yassa et al., 2012) proposed a dynamic information driven design which is equipped for limiting the SLA infringement by discharging asset arrangement. In the proposed design, the creators have concentrated just on asset discharging yet consideration towards security is lacking. Cloud Security Alliance checks all administration systems and review approaches for guaranteeing great security in distributed computing. It discharges new strategies with the assistance of National Institute of Standards and Technology (NIST) and Information Systems Audit and Control Association (ISACA).

Ryoo et al. (2013) exhibited a review on need of security in distributed computing. As of now, the greater part of the offices are chipping away at HDFS engineering which depends on ace slave hub. Ace hub is named as namenode and slave hub is named as datanodes. All information is recreated thrice and put away on datanodes. As per this review, all get to control of datanodes are overseen by a solitary point i.e. namenode which can be a reason for disappointment. They gave a model three lines of barrier as appeared in Figure 12. These are validation security at first level, encryption and security insurance at second level and quick recuperation at third level.

Authentication layer is utilized for client check with the assistance of advanced mark and encryption calculation is conveyed at second layer. Third layer utilizes quick recuperation calculation for recouping the information.

Huiqi et al. (2014) proposed Random Space Perturbation (RASP) strategy and Nearest Neighbor (kNN) which address the four primary perspectives information classification, inquiry security, proficient question handling and low preparing cost. Creators played out a trial under a danger model and found the outcomes giving more productivity at diminished cost. In any case, this strategy experienced information spillage and frail question security.

Figure 12.

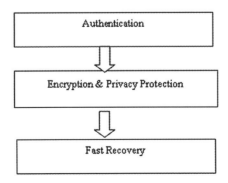

Hossein et al. (2013) introduced Encryption as a Service (Eaas) for guaranteeing the security at CSP. In this approach, a private cloud is being made by utilizing Message Authentication Code (MAC) for uprightness. This approach depends on multi-threading forms. Each single string hits proportionately on a parallel area and produces group of strings after encryption. Notwithstanding, this system works effectively just if the program had been composed in multi-threading style, generally the execution gets diminished. The portrayal of this model is appeared in Figure 13.

Xu et al. (2005) proposed an operator based trust display which guarantees the unwavering quality and validity. As appeared in Figure 14, the Trustworthy Agent Execution Chip (TAEC) engineering gives high security and deals with sensor hub by utilizing operator innovation. Before sending the information from hub A to hub B, it encodes the information by applying TAEC. Initially hub A gets the trust testament from TAEC Manufacturer (TAECM) which contains open key, security technique, and TAEC sort. After check of computerized mark, information is exchanged to hub B. Because of osmosis of specialists the proposed demonstrate moves toward becoming stage autonomous, however the use of advanced mark diminish the effectiveness of model.

Wang et al. (2013) proposed an examining instrument in cloud condition known as Public Auditing for shared information (PANDA) with productive client repudiation. The reason behind the client disavowal is that if a similar client would approach the cloud in denial period, the private key is produced and the information must be re-marked with private key. Due to this registering, time increments and productivity diminishes.

Authors have illustrated that with the help of virtualization (Quan et al., 2015) how we can increase the security of cloud. Virtualization protects the integrity of VM and IaaS components. A new intrusion

Figure 13.

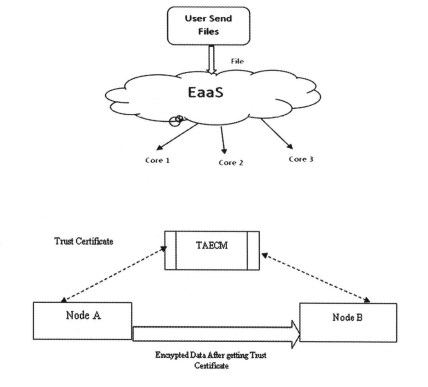

Figure 14.

detection system has been proposed as a security business flow language (Doelitzscher et al., 2012). It is the first prototype which provides the cloud security. This mechanism uses autonomous agents and made the SaaS architecture very flexible. The protocol that has been used for providing services is user identity management protocol (UIDM). It provided the security after checking the authenticity and authorization of user in networks.

Few other works concerning the security issues and solutions are available in Zissis et al. (2012). The authors have tried to mention all aspects of security that were need to be concerned. They have designed a framework which cures all kind of vulnerabilities and threats. They have migrated all kind protection to a third party which took care of all these things. Orellana et al. 2010 proposed a new transparent layer which encrypts the data before storing it on google server. The authors have presented a solution particularly for google server to store google docs. The user can select the security algorithm. After selecting the algorithm, the data would be converted into cipher text and would be stored in google server. Results shows that blowfish has smaller key size and faster speed as compared to other algorithms. However, all algorithms discussed are symmetric algorithms which are less secure than asymmetric algorithms.

Villalpando et al. (2014) proposed a methodology for detecting the different kind of attack that can be related to co-residency and network stress. These attacks could harm the kernel layer of cloud environment. To detect the above said attack, the method has implemented Smith Waterman Genetic Algorithm. Another author has proposed tracing the kernel layer of VM where each VM is traced simultaneously. The algorithm could detect the interaction between threads of VM on a core machine. For ensuring security, user authentication protocol is also quite promising. The protocol is based on identity based cryptography overcoming the weaknesses of its descendants.

A critical look at the literature reflects that there is strong need of a novel model which could address the open issues in cloud especially resource optimization, load balancing and a strong security mechanism to ensure security, integrity and authorization of user data stored on cloud. It also indicates that limited research had been carried out towards various security issues dominant in cloud. Thus, there is still ample scope of research in this dimension.

PROPOSED ARCHITECTURE

This architecture provides strong security of data placed in cloud and to ensure that even CSP can't breach this security. Literature survey highlighted that Blowfish and ECC techniques are best in symmetric and asymmetric key cryptography segments. These techniques make use of much small key sizes compared to existing techniques. This work proposes the combined use of above two encryption algorithms having smaller key sizes to provide stronger security than existing. Cryptography is traditionally accepted method of ensuring data security. It is the mechanism to secure data by converting it into non-readable form. There are two types of cryptography algorithms: symmetric and asymmetric key algorithms. Symmetric algorithms use only one key i.e. private key which is used for both encryption and decryption of data. In asymmetric algorithm, there are two keys, one is private and another is public key. Public key is used for encrypting the data and private key is used for decryption of data. Asymmetric algorithms are more secure than symmetric algorithm because in asymmetric algorithms both keys are different and leakage of one single key can't cause harm to the encrypted data. Presently cloud service providers are making use of triple DES technique for security which is symmetric key cryptography technique. There are two major agents used in this architecture whose description is as follows:

- **Crypto Agent (CA):** This agent is responsible for encryption and decryption of data at client end. It is equipped with user's set of keys. Whenever a user gets registered with a cloud service provider (CSP), CA exchanges its Elliptic Curve Cryptography (ECC) public Key with ECC public key of cloud service provider agent. When user sends some data to cloud data center, CA encrypts it using encryption mechanism adopted, on receiving some data from DC, CA decrypts it before providing it to user.
- **Cloud Service Provider Agent (CSPA):** This agent is responsible for interacting with CA of user. It receives encrypted data from the user, places it in cloud data base. It also keeps record of user ECC public key in server key log file. Whenever user requests for its data, it authenticates user, performs necessary encryption decryption process and then sends data to the user.

As far as threat of security breach from CSP is concerned, security mechanism must provide data decryption control to user only, even CSP should not be able to decrypt data in any way; it is possible with use of symmetric key cryptography; however, in case of symmetric key technique, algorithm complexity is less but security is also low. Whereas in case of asymmetric key algorithms complexity is more and security of data while travelling in network is also more. However, if asymmetric key mechanism is opted in CC, then one part of key would be saved with CSP, which is a constant threat for the users.

This architecture presents hybrid two tier security engine henceforth termed as HT2SE, it is an agent based framework which uses both types of encryption i.e. symmetric and asymmetric in combination, before sending data to CSP. This mechanism has two layers, first layer makes use of symmetric key algorithm i.e. Blowfish to encrypt data, this key would only be known to the user. Output of the first layer would be processed by second layer, which would again encrypt it with asymmetric key ECC, for this layer ECC private key will be with user and corresponding public key will be with CSP.

Figure 15 provides high level view of HT2SE architecture where first layer makes use of symmetric key algorithm BF and second layer makes use of asymmetric key algorithm ECC.

Whenever a user wants to keep his/her data on the cloud, the user will need to get encryption keys from the standard authorities. Every user will receive a set of two keys as shown in equation below:

$$Key_i = \left\{ BF_i, \left\{ ECC_{prti}, ECC_{pubi} \right\} \right\}$$

Figure 15.

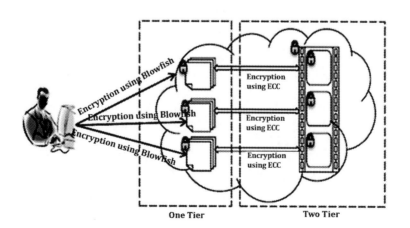

567

Here BF_i refers to symmetric key of ith user, this key is known and used by user only. ECC_{prti} refers to asymmetric private key of ith user, this key is known and used by user only. ECC_{pubi} refers to asymmetric public key of ith user, this key is known and kept with the CSP.

In the same way, a CSP will also acquire the above set of keys for it, to be used at its end. Now whenever user has to save his/her data on cloud, it will first encrypt it with its BF_i, ciphertext obtained after encryption is again encrypted using ECC_{prti} before sending it to CSP. ECC_{pubi} of the user is available with the CSP, however even if CSP wishes to decrypt data for some reason, it can only decrypt data to one level only, because first level symmetric key of the user is unknown to the CSP. This way threat of security decreases and data security threats due to multi-tenancy in cloud may be resolved.

Figure 16 provides detailed architecture of proposed HT2SE framework and illustrates working of crypto and CSP agents, which are responsible for encryption / decryption at user and cloud service provider's end respectively:

After user registration, whenever data is received from the cloud user for storage on cloud database, CA gets activated. It first applies Blowfish algorithm for converting original data into cipher form in level 1 and then it applies ECC private key to encrypt cipher text obtained from level 1 to encrypt it for the second time. It then sends this data for travel in the network and its subsequent storage in cloud database. When data reaches cloud data center, CSPA gets activated, it fetches user ECC public key stored in Server key log and decrypts data to level1 and then saves it in cloud data center data base. Whenever data is required by a particular user, CSPA fetches requested data, encrypts it for the second time using its own ECC private key and sends it on the network. This way data is always double protected while travelling in the network and both encryption keys can't be hacked as they are distributed. Further, CSPA encrypts its Server key log file using its own BF symmetric key which is kept with this agent only. This is an additional safety measure, however since CSP is an agent, it is also vulnerable to attack possible for other software components. But even compromising CSP can't solve purpose of the hacker since data placed in data center data base is still encrypted by BF keys of various users which are unknown to CSP. This way security of user data placed in cloud data centre is enhanced to a high level.

The algorithms of Crypto agent and Cloud Service Provider Agent are presented in Table 2 and 3.

CONCLUSION

This chapter exemplifies the concept of cloud in the era of academia and industry. it express the various applications of cloud computing which can be application in different areas. Apart from it, this chapter lights on the various issues like technological, business, performance and other miscellaneous issues

Figure 16.

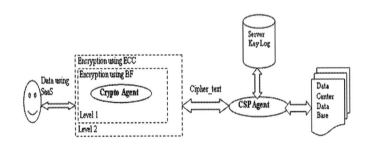

Table 2.

Crypto Agent (CA)
Input: Ordinary Data from User/ Cipher Text from DC;   Set of user keys $Key_i = \left\{ BF_i, \left\{ ECC_{prti}, ECC_{pubi} \right\} \right\}$;   *Output:* Cipher Text/ Ordinary Data

CA ()
 {
 If (incoming_data == ordinary data)
 {
 CA applies BF_i (Plain_text);
 CA applies ECC_{pubi} (cipher_text$_1$);
 Forward cipher_text$_2$ to CSPA();
 }
 Else
 {
 Decrypt cipher_text$_2$ with $ECC_{pub-csp}$;
 Decrypt cipher_text$_1$ with BF_i of user;
 }
 }

Table 3.

Cloud Service Provider Agent()
Input: Cipher Text   *Output:* Store Data into DC Database; Fetch Data from DC Database;

CSPA ()
 {
 Receive <cipher_text, ECC_{pubi} >;
 Store <cipher_text> in database;
 Update server_key_loag_file;
 If(user_demands_data)
 {
 CSPA checks authenticity;
 If (successful)
 {
 Apply ECC_{pubi} for decyption;
 CSPA apply $C_{prt-csp}$;
 Convert data into cipher form;
 Forwards cipher text to CA();
 }
 Else
 Send message<unsuccessful> to CA ;
 }
 }

prevailing in cloud environment. Further it illustrates the concept of mobile agents and their benefits of adoption of them in different technologies. It also explains the incorporation of mobile agents in cloud computing. This chapter explains that how agents can ensure scalability in cloud computing environments. Scalability is one of the main feature if cloud which can be employing mobile agents. Algorithm for implementing the agents involved is also provided. The second part of this chapter focused on security issue of cloud. Data security is one of the most debated and important issue in Cloud computing. Although cloud service providers claim of providing high level of security but still there are increasing number of incidents of security breaches in cloud environments. For increasing trust of user in cloud, there is dire need of robust security mechanism. However, cloud service providers are still using traditional symmetric key algorithms for data security and not providing much transparency on the security algorithms being deployed. This work presents a hybrid two tier security engine which combines symmetric and asymmetric key algorithms, further the algorithms deployed have already proved their excellence for lesser time and better speed of encryption. Future work aims to focus on providing security solutions for other levels of cloud computing.

REFERENCES

Aljawarneh, S., Aldwairi, M., & Yassein, M. B. (2017). Anomaly-based intrusion detection system through feature selection analysis and building hybrid efficient model. *Journal of Computational Science*. doi:10.1016/j.jocs.2017.03.006

Aljawarneh, S., Yassein, M.B., & Talafha, W.A. (2017). A multithreaded programming approach for multimedia big data: encryption system. *Multimed Tools Appl*. doi:10.100711042-017-4873-9

Aljawarneh, S. A., Alawneh, A., & Jaradat, R. (2017). Cloud security engineering: Early stages of SDLC. *Future Generation Computer Systems*, *74*, 385–392. doi:10.1016/j.future.2016.10.005

Aljawarneh, S. A., Moftah, R. A., & Maatuk, A. M. (2016). Investigations of automatic methods for detecting the polymorphic worms signatures. *Future Generation Computer Systems*, *60*, 67–77. doi:10.1016/j.future.2016.01.020

Aljawarneh, S. A., Vangipuram, R., Puligadda, V. K., & Vinjamuri, J. (2017). G-SPAMINE: An approach to discover temporal association patterns and trends in internet of things. *Future Generation Computer Systems*, *74*, 430–443. doi:10.1016/j.future.2017.01.013

Armbrust, M., Fox, A., Griffith, R., Joseph, A., Katz, R., Konwinski, A., . . . Stoica, M. (2009). Above the Clouds: A Berkeley View Of Cloud Computing. UC Berkeley Reliable Adaptive Distributed Systems Laboratory, 1-23.

Armbrust, M., Fox, A., Griffith, R., Joseph, A. D., Katz, R. H., & Konwinski, A. (2010). A View of Cloud Computing. ACM Communication, 53(4), 50–58.

Banerjee, C. (2012). Framework ON Service Based Resource Selection In Cloud Computing. *International Journal of Information Processing and Management*, *3*(1), 17–25. doi:10.4156/ijipm.vol3.issue1.2

Chen, K., Shen, M., & Zheng, W. (2005). Resources Allocation Schemas For Web Information Monitoring. *Tsinghua Science and Technology*, *10*(3), 309–315. doi:10.1016/S1007-0214(05)70074-2

Chen, M., Mao, S., & Liu, Y. (2014). Big Data: A Survey. *Mobile Networks and Applications*, *9*(2), 171–209. doi:10.100711036-013-0489-0

Danny, B. (1998). Mobile Objects And Mobile Agents: The Future Of Distributed Computing. *12th European Conference on Object-Oriented Programming*, *1445*, 1-12.

Doelitzscher, F., Reich, C., Knahi, M., Passfall, A., & Clarke, N. (2012). An Agent Based Business Aware Incident Detection System For Cloud Environments. *Journal of Cloud Computing: Advances Systems and Applications, 1*(9), 239-246.

Flavio, L., & Roberto, D. P. (2011). Secure Virtualization For Cloud Computing. *Journal of Network and Computer Applications, 41*(1), 45–52.

Foster, I., Yong, Z., Raicu, I., & Lu, S. (2008). Cloud Computing And Grid Computing 360-Degree Compared. *Workshop on Grid Computing Environments*, 1-10. 10.1109/GCE.2008.4738445

Funmilade, F., Rami, B., & Georgios, T. (2012). A Dynamic Data Driven Simulation Approach For Preventing Service Level Agreement Violations In Cloud Federation. *International Conference on Computational Science Procedia of Computer Science*, 1167-1176.

Gebai, M., Giraldeau, F., & Dagenais, M. R. (2014). Fine Grained Preemption Analysis for Latency Investigation Across Virtual Machines. *Journal of Cloud Computing: Advances System and Applications, 3*(23), 1–15.

Gonzalez, N., Miers, C., Redigolo, F., Carvalho, T., Naslund, M., & Pourzandi, M. (2012). A Quantitative Analysis Of Current Security Concerns And Solutions For Cloud Computing. *Journal of Cloud Computing: Advances, System and Applications*, 1-11.

Goyal, O., Pandey, A., & Sahai Waters, B. (2006). Attribute-Based Encryption For Fine-Grained Access Control Of Encrypted Data. *ACM Conference Computer Communication Security*, 89–98. 10.1145/1180405.1180418

Hossein, R., Elankovan, S., Zulkarnain, M. A., & Abdullah, M. Z. (2013). Encryption As A Service As A Solution For Cryptography In Cloud. *International Conference on Electrical Engineering and Informatics indexed in Science Direct*, 1202-1210.

Huiqi, X., Shumin, G., & Keke, C. (2014). Building Confidential And Efficient Query Services In The Cloud With Rasp Data Perturbation. *IEEE Transactions on Knowledge and Data Engineering, 26*(2), 322–335. doi:10.1109/TKDE.2012.251

Jungwoo, R., Syed, R., William, A., & John, K. (2013). Cloud Security Auditing: Challenges And Emerging Approaches. *IEEE Security and Privacy*, 1–13.

Kalpana, G., Kumar, P. V., Aljawarneh, S., & Krishnaiah, R. V. (2017). Shifted Adaption Homomorphism Encryption for Mobile and Cloud Learning. *Computers & Electrical Engineering*. doi:10.1016/j.compeleceng.2017.05.022

Kumarswamy. (2009). Cloud Security And Privacy: An Enterprise Perspective On Risks And Compliances. Academic Press.

Lamb, C. C., & Heileman, G. L. (2012). Content Centric Information Protection In Cloud Computing. *International Journal of Cloud Computing and Services Science, 2*(1), 28–39.

Li, Chinneck, Wodside, & Litoiu. (2009). Fast Scalable Optimization To Configure Service System Having Cost And Quality Of Service Constraints. *IEEE International Conference on Autonomic System Barcelona*, 159-168 10.1145/1555228.1555268

Loke, S. W (1999). A Technical Report On: Mobile Agent Technology For Enterprise Distributed Applications: An Overview And An Architectural Perspective. *CRC for Distributed Systems Technology*, 1-45.

Matos, M., Sousa, A., Pereira, J., & Oliveira, P. (2009). Clon: Overlay Network For Clouds. *Third Workshop on Dependable Distributed Data Management*. 10.1145/1518691.1518696

Moharana, S. S., Ramesh, R. D., & Powar, D. (2013). Analysis Of Load Balancers In Cloud Computing. *Computing in Science & Engineering*, 2(2), 101–108.

Morikawa, T., & Ikebe, M. (2011). Proposal And Evaluation Of A Dynamic Resource Allocation Method Based On The Load Of Vms On Iaas. *4th IFIP International Conference on New Technologies, Mobility and Security, 5*(6), 1–6.

Orellana, L., Silva, D., & Castineira, F. (2010). Privacy For Google Docs: Implementing A Transparent Encryption Layer Cloud Views. *International Conference on Cloud Computing*, 41-48.

Philipp, H., Rolf, W., Joachim, S., & Thomas, B. (2013). Virtual Fort Knox: Federative Secure And Cloud Based Platform For Manufacturing. *46th Conference on Manufacturing System indexed in Science Direct*, 527-532.

Qian, W., Cong, W., Kui, R., Wenjing, L., & Jin, L. (2011). Enabling Public Auditability And Data Dynamics For Storage Security In Cloud Computing. *IEEE Transactions on Parallel and Distributed Systems*, 22(5), 847–859. doi:10.1109/TPDS.2010.183

Quan, Z., Chunming, T., Xianghan, Z., & Chunming, R. (2015). A Secure User Authentication Protocol For Sensor Network In Data Capturing. *Journal of Cloud Computing: Advances System and Applications*, 4(6), 1–12.

Ryoo, J., Rizvi, S., Aiken, W., & Kissell, J. (2013). Cloud Security Auditing: Challenges And Emerging Approaches. *IEEE Security and Privacy*, 1–13.

Safiriyu, E., Olatunde, A., Ayodeji, O., Adeniran, O., Clement, O., & Lawrence, K. (2011). A User Identity Management Protocol For Cloud Computing Paradigm. *Int J Commun Network Syst Sci, 1*(4), 152–163.

Sapuntzakis, C., Brumley, D., Chandra, R., Zeldovich, N., Chow, J., Lam, M., & Rosenblum, M. (2008). Virtual Appliances For Deploying And Maintaining Software. *17th USENIX Conference on System Administration*, 181–194.

Singh, A., Juneja, D., & Malhotra, M. (2015). A Novel Agent Based Autonomous Service Composition Framework for Cost Optimization of Resource Provisioning in Cloud Computing. In JKSU-CIS. Elsevier.

Singh, A., & Malhotra, M. (2012). Analysis For Exploring Scope Of Mobile Agents In Cloud Computing. *International Journal of Advancements in Technology*, 3(3), 172–183.

Singh, A., & Malhotra, M. (2015). Analysis Of Security Issues At Different Levels In Cloud Computing Paradigm: A Review. *Journal of Computer Networks and Applications*, 2(2).

Singh, A., & Malhotra, M. (2015). Evaluation of a Secure Agent based optimized Resource Scheduling Framework in Cloud Environment. IJCAR, 188-198.

Singh, A., & Malhotra, M. (2016). Hybrid Two Tier Framework for Improved Security in Cloud Environment. India-Com, 1601-1606.

Singh, A., & Malhotra, M. (n.d.). A Novel Agent Based Framework for Cost Optimization in Cloud Computing Environment. *International Journal of Cloud Applications*, 53–61.

Villalpando, L. E. B., April, A., & Abran, A. (2014). Performance Analysis Model For Big Data Applications In Cloud Computing. *Journal of Cloud Computing*, *4*, 3–19.

Wang, B., Li, B., & Li, H. (2013). Panda: Public Auditing For Shared Data With Efficient User Revocation In The Cloud. *IEEE Transaction*, 1-14. Retrieved from http://www.thinkgrid.com/docs/computing-whitepaper.pdf

Wiese, L. (2014). Clustering Based Fragmentation And Data Replication For Flexible Query Answering In Distributed Databases. *Journal of Cloud Computing*, *2*, 3–18.

Yang, H., & Tate, M. (2009). Where Are We At Cloud Computing? A Descriptive Literature Survey. Association for Information System, 807-819.

Yang, K., & Jia, X. (2013). An Efficient And Secure Dynamic Auditing Protocol For Data Storage In Cloud Computing. *IEEE Transactions on Parallel and Distributed Systems*, *24*(9), 1717–1726. doi:10.1109/TPDS.2012.278

Yassa, M. M., Hassan, H. A., & Omara, F. A. (2012). New Federated Collaborative Network Organization Model (FCNOM). *International Journal of Cloud Computing and Services Science*, *1*(1), 1–10.

Yuefa, D., Bo, W., Yaqiang, G., Quan, Z., & Chaojing, T. (2009). Data Security Model For Cloud Computing. *International Workshop on Information Security and Application New York*, 141-144.

Zhang, C., & Sterck, H. D. (2009). Cloudwf A Computational Workflow System For Cloud Based For Hadoop. *Lecture Notes in Computer Science*, *5391*, 393–404. doi:10.1007/978-3-642-10665-1_36

Zhang, Q., & Cheng, L. (2010). Cloud Computing: State-Of-The-Art And Research Challenge. *Raouf Boutaba J Internet Serv Appl*, 7-18.

Zhen, C., Fuye, II., Junwei, C., Xin, J., & Shuo, C. (2013). Cloud Computing-Based Forensic Analysis For Collaborative Network Security Management System. *Tsinghua Science and Technology*, *18*(1), 40–50. doi:10.1109/TST.2013.6449406

Zissis, D., & Lekkas, D. (2012). Addressing Cloud Computing Security Issues. *Future Generation Computer Systems*, *28*(3), 583–592. doi:10.1016/j.future.2010.12.006

This research was previously published in Critical Research on Scalability and Security Issues in Virtual Cloud Environments edited by Shadi Aljawarneh and Manisha Malhotra, pages 19-47, copyright year 2018 by Information Science Reference (an imprint of IGI Global).

Chapter 29
Runtime Reusable Weaving Model for Cloud Services Using Aspect–Oriented Programming:
The Security–Related Aspect

Anas M.R. Alsobeh
Yarmouk University, Jordan

Aws Abed Al Raheem Magableh
Yarmouk University, Jordan

Emad M. AlSukhni
Yarmouk University, Jordan

ABSTRACT

Cloud computing technology has opened an avenue to meet the critical need to securely share distributed resources and web services, and especially those that belong to clients who have sensitive data and applications. However, implementing crosscutting concerns for cloud-based applications is a challenge. This challenge stems from the nature of distributed Web-based technology architecture and infrastructure. One of the key concerns is security logic, which is scattered and tangled across all the cloud service layers. In addition, maintenance and modification of the security aspect is a difficult task. Therefore, cloud services need to be extended by enriching them with features to support adaptation so that these services can become better structured and less complex. Aspect-oriented programming is the right technical solution for this problem as it enables the required separation when implementing security features without the need to change the core code of the server or client in the cloud. Therefore, this article proposes a Runtime Reusable Weaving Model for weaving security-related crosscutting concerns through layers of cloud computing architecture. The proposed model does not require access to the source code of a cloud service and this can make it easier for the client to reuse the needed security-related crosscutting concerns. The proposed model is implemented using aspect orientation techniques to integrate cloud security solutions at the software-as-a-service layer.

DOI: 10.4018/978-1-5225-8176-5.ch029

1. INTRODUCTION

Cloud Computing environment is accessed via the internet, which enables end-users to access a range of distributed resources and web services over a network. It can give several clients access to secure shared data at the same time by tokenizing the data during transmission or when it is processed (Zhang, Cheng & Boutaba, 2010; Asma, Chaurasia & Mokhtar, 2012). Cloud vendors (providers) provide a certain level of security for client data; however, clients of cloud services may also need to implement their own security features for peace of mind. When clients add their own security features, this obviously increases the complexity of each application logic in the cloud computing environment as well as that of the physical distributed system itself. There are several security aspects that are in place/time that attempt to ensure the security of cloud services (Look, 2011; The Apache Software Foundation, 2016; Apache Axis, 2016), but access to the base code of the services being protected is required and these aspects are usually controlled by the cloud services vendor (e.g., Amazon Web Service (AWS), Microsoft Azure, etc.)

Cloud computing offers a variety of ways to manage how data flows across a plethora of applications on the web. Cloud computing is relatively new and the range of cloud services is still growing but there is already a wide range of tools available that support the development and deployment of web applications. However, these tools have some serious drawbacks, particularly with respect to ensuring the security aspect of client applications. They are almost completely static and thus do not support the dynamic adaptation of cloud services (Powell, Stembridge and Yuan, 2012). This is unfortunate to say the least as the cloud computing environment is very dynamic. However, due to the quality of the existing support tools, it cannot easily take on new features and it is difficult to reuse some applications or crosscutting concerns already on the cloud logic for different purposes. Cloud computing has to deal with a number of security aspects related to encryption, authentication, denial-of-services attacks, access control and privacy threats (Alani, 2014). The ways in which these are dealt with are usually defined and set when developing or deploying a cloud application and this means that they cannot be altered when the application is running in the cloud. Additionally, cloud services are tightly coupled to cloud applications logic. For instance, when data security involves encrypting the data there is also a need for suitable and well-defined security aspects to be in place for safe and effective data sharing. Ensuring that this is the case, is made more complicated by the highly complex nature of the cloud.

Aspect-oriented software development (AOSD) and aspect-oriented programming languages (AOPL) have been developed to handle such limitations. They can capture new crosscutting concerns and new changes that relate to security. In fact, AOP weaving, as it is commonly known, is a relatively easy way to separate and the scattered or tangled crosscutting concerns logic between modules of the core cloud service with constituting a new cloud service layer. This research aims to propose an approach to enhance the security of applications in the cloud environment. It proposes the utilization of Reusable Service Layer (RSL) to improve the implementation of security-related crosscutting concerns in cloud services and proposes a way in which these concerns can be integrated into the cloud environment at runtime. The proposed approach provides an adequate amount of cloud service metadata (i.e., context information) so that the requisite information can be obtained for effective implementation of security aspects. This is based-on employ AOP to decouple and isolate the security characteristics from the core cloud service.

This research introduces an aspect-oriented cloud reusable security service (ACRSS) model, which can be used for several security scenarios in distributed cloud applications. The main objective of ACRSS lies in the fact that it enables developers to design and implement cloud services that can adapt to the addition of any new security aspects automatically and dynamically. The version of ACRSS library discussed in this paper is based on AOP and is designed to intercept the cloud application at specific execution points that match relevant primitive cloud abstractions. It encapsulates security logic into a separate aspect that can be managed by a dynamic mechanism whereby the entire application could self-reconfigure according to the cloud's aspect.

The remainder of the paper is organized as follows. Section 2 illustrates the problem by describing a motivational example. Section 3 discusses the background to highlight how this study contributes to the topic of maintaining application security in the cloud. Section 4 discusses related works. Section 5 explains the architecture and metadata of our model. Section 5 also discusses the designed model and its implementation. Finally, Section 6 summarizes the work and provides a conclusion and some suggestions for future work.

2. MOTIVATIONAL EXAMPLE

To secure the data of customers and to handle multiple concurrent clients, both the client and provider may execute services related to a single process on different threads, which makes it very difficult to follow shared context information dynamically. Moreover, directly implementing this kind of concern in a cloud application could make the code scatter and tangle.

To secure customer data in cloud applications, data is often encrypted over method calls. If encryption/decryption occurs at both the initiation point and the response or invoked point, this results in scattering and tangling into otherwise cohesive modules. Thus, the encryption/decryption (E /D) process is a common security-related crosscutting concern. Cloud encrypts (E) when the client initiates a data request and decrypts (D) when the client receives the corresponding information. Cloud represents an execution region between the instant (Er) when the client initiates the request and the instant (Dr) when the client receives the corresponding response, as illustrated in Figure 1.

Throughout this paper, we assume that data privacy is primarily dealt with at the SaaS level of the cloud computing architecture. In addition, we assume that a cloud application might be running on

Figure 1. Example of client receiving a response to a data request

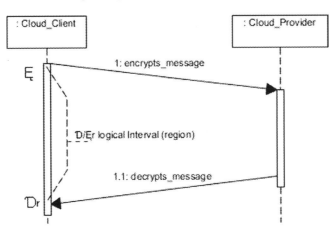

multiple distributed threads on shared resources, making the context even harder to follow during execution. It is noteworthy that current AOP techniques do not fully support pointcut designators to inject security-related crosscutting concerns into high-level cloud abstractions. As our proposed approach uses AOP, it can be easily implemented and new functionalities can be added with ease to remove or change the behaviour of cloud-related services. This is because the emerging aspect orientation paradigm is designed to address crosscutting concerns such as security, resource allocation, scheduling, logging and a lot more. To realize and employ an AOP approach in cloud computing, the cloud service needs to be extended by enriching it with AOP-compliant semantics including advices, pointcuts and joinpoints so that the original cloud service behaviour can be amended. Importantly, this approach will enable developers to add security aspects without touching the core cloud code.

3. BACKGROUND

This section provides an overview of the background topics that are needed to understand and to get a better picture of the contribution of AOP and cloud computing to the aim of this research study.

3.1. Aspect-Oriented Programming

Aspect-oriented programming (AOP) is one of the most promising methods that developers can use to produce encapsulated objects that do not have any unnecessary additional functionality. This type of programming enables the developer to divide crosscutting concerns (i.e., an activity also known as the separation of concerns (SoCs)) into single logics, i.e., aspects. These aspects are the modular units of crosscutting concerns. In addition, as mentioned above, new behaviour can be added to a cloud application without the need to alter or interfere with the base source code. There are three key components in AOP: joinpoints, pointcuts and advices. Joinpoints are specific points that occur during the execution of a program, pointcuts to denote a set of joinpoints, while advices are codes that only run when specific joinpoint are met (Razzaq et al.,2014; Lee& Hur, 2012).

AOP has emerged due to the need to find a better way to implement SoCs. This type of programming is targeted at improving the efficacy of software engineering principles in order to achieve for instance loose coupling between the various logics of software solutions (Lohmann, Hofer, Schröder-Preikschat & Spinczyk, 2011). It is also an improvement on object-oriented programming (OOP). While OOP was groundbreaking at the time for including encapsulation, inheritance and polymorphism in the software development process whereby a hierarchy of objects could be created to model a common set of behaviours, it was not designed to deal with common behaviours that cut across unrelated objects (Bernardi & Di Lucca, 2005).

The benefit of using AOP to address crosscutting concerns can be seen if we consider a classical example, that of implementing the logging functionality, handling exceptions, required security logic are often scattered across object hierarchies and has nothing to do with the core functions of the object's metadata (Hmida, Tomaz & Monfort, 2005). This is known as crosscutting code and the need to deal with this type of code was the motivation for the development of AOP.

Instead of embedding crosscutting concerns in classes, AOP can be used to place the crosscutting concern into a separate module or aspect and then the logic can be applied when and where required. It is able to apply the crosscutting concern by defining some joinpoints in the object model and then placing the crosscutting code into the defined joinpoint by using a pointcut. This is a simple process compared to OOP, where adding functionality to an application involves the programmer manually adding the security concern into all the appropriate objects. Moreover, the AOP aspects can be merged into core classes by using weaving which further eases the process. Thus, objects can focus on their core tasks without being affected by the amendments to these concerns. Figure 2 illustrates how the AOP weaving process can work in cloud computing with respect to the issue of security.

Security-related crosscutting concerns for cloud services can be efficiently handled by the AOP weaving process. The crosscutting concerns must get the necessary information on the context before, after or around the call or execution of a cloud application. The actual technical implementation of a cloud application is hidden in a lot of different layers in the cloud; however, by the location for the new behaviour that needs to be incorporated into the service can be identified by referring just to the client application. The AOP weaver merges the code in core cloud application classes with the new logic in AOPL. There are a lot of tools for implementing AOP and they are available in a range of programming languages. However, it should be noted that these tools are language or platform dependent, so, for instance, AspectJ (Kastner, Apel and Batory, 2005) only extends Java and Jasco, while Net (Verpecht, Vanderperren, Suvee and Jonckers, 2003) only extends C#. Nevertheless, the AOP weaver processes the aspects and the core classes in the relevant languages to generate the specified security behaviour. Since security-related crosscutting concerns such as authentication or encryption are scattered and tangled throughout the various cloud layers, using the AOP weaver makes it easier to implement a function across the various requisite parts of a cloud application. Figure 3 shows how the implementing security-related crosscutting concerns in cloud application without aspect (A) or with aspect (B).

Figure 2. Weaving different security-related crosscutting concerns in a cloud computing environment

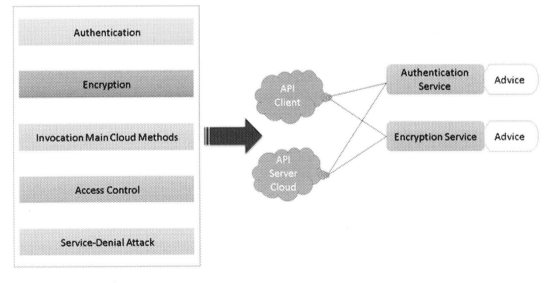

Figure 3. Security-related crosscutting concerns over a cloud application

3.2. The Cloud Computing Environment

The client application accesses the cloud via a special interface to gain access to services residing in the cloud. The cloud computing environment consists of high-level customized services that reside in layers of the cloud architecture and it is via these layers that application developers can offer their services through the cloud's application programming interface (API) to a client and server as shown in Figure 4 (Jadeja & Modi, 2012). There are several APIs that developers can use, but Axis Apache is one of the most useful and common used. The main services currently available over the cloud are software as a service (SaaS), platform as a service (PaaS) and infrastructure as a service (IaaS) (Zhang, Cheng and Boutaba, 2010). SaaS allows clients to use cloud provider applications that are run on a cloud infrastructure, (2) PaaS gives users all the tools they require to create, check and deploy applications to the cloud and (3) IaaS delivers a computing infrastructure as a completely outsourced service thereby reducing the need for in-house resources and infrastructure.

Apache Axis, which is an open-source API created and updated by the Apache Software Foundation, can be used to create interoperable, distributed computing applications. Apache Axis stands for Apache eXtensible Interaction System and it was submitted to W3C (The World Wide Web Consortium) as a

Figure 4. Hierarchical organization of cloud services layers with a reusable service layer

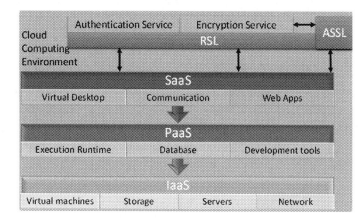

second-generation simple object access protocol (SOAP) engine, succeeding the earlier Apache SOAP project. The SOAP is a lightweight protocol that can be used to exchange structured information in a decentralized yet distributed environment (Rao, Kumar, Sunder & Chandrasekaran, 2013). Apache Axis is XML-based, can be implemented in Java and, C++, has a SOAP server and also has several utilities and APIs (Rao, Kumar, Sunder & Chandrasekaran, 2013). The Apache Axis framework has an envelope for defining a service and how to deal with it, some encoding rules to describe application-defined data types and a method for representing remote calls and responses (Apache Axis, 2016). Axis and Sun's implementation are the only two SOAP-based APIs currently available. Cloud applications that need to utilize or add web services can use the Apache Axis API standard library (i.e., *org.apache.axis*) to add a new web service (Axis, 2016).The library contains a set of operations that can be extended to add or adapt cloud computing behaviours.

4. RELATED WORK

To reduce the complexity of application development and the possibility of developing well-structured cloud applications, developers should be aware of the implementation details of the cloud layers so that they can add new features (e.g, security-related crosscutting concerns) effectively. Some researchers have investigated AOP (Kiczales et al., 1997; Kiczales et al., 2001; Masuhara & Kiczales, 2003) as a separate field and numerous research studies have been conducted on the general issue of cloud computing (Krutz& Vines, 2010; Xiao& Xiao, 2013; Catteddu, 2010). However, less focus has been paid by researchers to investigating the possibility of using AOP to separate the cloud-related crosscutting concerns. In this section, a brief overview of some related works on AOP and security in the context of cloud services is provided. In (Mdhaffar et al., 2011; Shahin et al., 2014), the topic of AOP in cloud computing is covered in general terms, rather than the security-related crosscutting concern specifically. The aim of the proposition in (Mdhaffar, Halima, Juhnke, Jmaiel & Freisleben, 2011) is to utilize AOP to monitor the quality of service parameters in the SaaS layer without modifying the cloud service implementation. Similarly, this approach does not require access to the source code of a service and it can be installed by the client. The researchers in (Mdhaffar, Halima, Juhnke, Jmaiel & Freisleben, 2011) also used Apache Axis in their approach. Another indirectly related work is that of (Rao, Kumar, Sunder & Chandrasekaran, 2013), which analysed the performance of AOP in monitoring the quality of a cloud service. The proposed approach, called Aspect-oriented Programming for Cloud Service Monitoring (AOP4CSM), was demonstrated to be efficient by comparing the results of monitoring obtained with and without AOP.

In (Ashraf et al., 2014), the researchers stated that some SaaS application can have a huge number of customizations that have complicated relationships, which increases complexity and reduces understandability. Thus, modelling such customizations, validating each tenant's customization and adapting SaaS applications on the fly based on each tenant's requirements become very complex tasks. To address these challenges, the researchers proposed an approach that depends on an aspect-oriented that makes use of the orthogonal variability model and met graphs. In (Roshan et al., 2006), the researchers discussed their proposed approach of granularity of control, how authentication is accommodated, the problems of covert channels, how improved modularity and maintainability are achieved, the issue of trusted subjects and how to appropriately handle security failures. They proposed to forced security by intercepting system calls rather than application calls. For example, they worked on intercepting file reads and writes rather than defining a read or write pointcut that intercepted application methods related to file access. The dame goes for the other security related activities such as authentication and trusted subjected, Figure 5 illustrates how they intercepted the file read and write to ensure security (Roshan et al., 2006).

Some other related research is (Pasquier et al., 2004), the approach proposed focused on how looking at the data flow will help in ensuring security at cloud. It represents and constrains the flow of information within an application. Authors focus also on the aspects of the model relating to a single application rather than a distributed, multi-application environment. AOP was used to enforce the model by inserting the desired security policy around the selected methods. The proposed model called FlowR IFC. Additionally, (Toledo & Tanter, 2013), proposed a secure and modular access to be controlled with aspects, they came up with ModAC, ModAC has some main objectives that were achieved including (1) The base language must be completely oblivious to access control, (2) Untrusted aspects must not inhibit protected aspects, but are otherwise free to advise any join points and (3) Trusted aspects should be able to advise any join point. In (Viren and Frank, 2003), they considered security as a crosscutting concern, they proposed Aspect-Oriented Security Framework (AOSF), the framework is flexible and intended to integrate seamlessly. The current implementation of their proposition works with the C language. The central feature of this framework is the ability to encode security solutions as separate entities called aspects. The aspects are essentially recipes in a template form that provide generic instructions for performing code transformations to achieve a particular security objective.

4.1. ACRSS Architectural Design and Context

In cloud computing architecture, there is no clear separation of the concerns related to a cloud's core logic and those related to its non-functional logic, as shown in Figure 4. Non-functional logic includes security concerns, which are the focus of this paper. Figure 4 shows the architectural design of the aspect-oriented cloud reusable security service model or ACRSS for short. The model has a number of advantages in relation to managing the complexity of cloud computing applications. However, most importantly, it can break down crosscutting concerns into separate logics. The main concern of each logic is to provide a service, such as encryption, for its particular cloud domain.

Practically web cloud service is considered as a closed black box, that makes it very difficult to maintain or reuse an application in a cloud as and when required. Therefore, one of the aims of our proposed model is to enable developers to weave the security-related crosscutting concerns into the original cloud service on a more abstract level. This should allow changes to be made to the cloud service's behaviour more easily and give clients in the cloud the ability to add a new behaviour to a service or modify an existing one as desired without having to re-deploy or re-implement the entire application. The proposed

Figure 5. Sample of granularity of control approach

```
pointcut read(Object o): target(o) &&
(call(* inputstream.read*(..)) || call(* Reader.read*(..)) ||
...;
pointcut write(Object o): target(o) &&
(call(* outputstream.write*(..)) || call(* Writer.write*(..)))
...;
```

approach essentially intercepts the instant when the client initiates the service and adds the security-related logic without changing the core code of the actual cloud. To do this we created a reusable layer that can be used to add a new web service into the cloud, as shown in Figure 4.

Web services are key blocks that are used to build the cloud layer (Zhang, Cheng & Boutaba, 2010). However, it is difficult to identify common core cloud services in a cloud application for this building process. Nevertheless, despite this challenge, the AOP technique is eminently suitable for extending and changing cloud behaviour to achieve secondary objectives. When amending cloud services, developers need to find all the variations across the entire cloud context application. A difficulty arises in trying to do this because the metadata in a cloud is unlike that in AspectJ because the former is linked with dynamic generated elements. Hence cloud metadata is not like the advice contexts in AspectJ. In AspectJ, the context consists of single programming concepts such as constructors, fields and exceptions. In contrast, in ACRSS the contexts are any sequence of service initiation, response or invoke events in the cloud as seen by an entire communication process from a cloud client's and server's perspective. In ACRSS, the RSL provides information on the cloud-related context by using a web service framework.

We can illustrate why ACRSS is so useful by looking how secure access to a health data system (HDS) can be ensured. Such a system contains highly sensitive patient data (electronic medical records), such as personal identifying information (PII), that needs to be shared and accessed by the appropriate medical staff and organizations. However, there needs to be a robust way to prevent unauthorized entities from gaining access either directly or indirectly to this type of data. Hence, it needs to be encrypted in some way to ensure its security is maintained and that only a matched client or entity can access it. A web services manages PII over a wide range of shared data sources. The cloud provider may have an encryption pattern, but it is not that unusual for the client to want to add to or change this pattern. If a traditional approach is employed to do this, the developer has to identify all the encoding methods and then comprehensively modify the encryption pattern in the client and/or the server. This is a convoluted process that involves changing, resetting, reconfiguring and redeploying the cloud services. The advantage of our proposed model is that the developer can create an aspect called 'encryption' and select points where the advice for this aspect needs to be implanted and interwoven into the original cloud service. This advice can be injected before, after or around the initiation and response abstractions. Hence, crucially, there is absolutely no need to make changes to the core cloud services. In essence, the behaviour of the original cloud service can be changed by means of interactions with the relevant aspects (which in the context of our paper relate to security aspects).

In our model, the application-level security service layer (ASSL) as shown in Figure 4, is used to define a set of joinpoints that then enable the dynamic implementation of the logics of any security aspects. The ASSL contains a set of high level abstract pointcuts and joinpoints. Moreover, some aspects can be newly designed as independent abstracts. Thus, the cloud application developer can design each security-related crosscutting concern (e.g. encryption) as an independent aspect. For the application presented in this paper, we need to extend an abstract pointcut in the ASSL for the encryption process. This will enable the developer to dynamically inject the encryption aspect with its corresponding joinpoints, as shown in Figure 6. The way in which we implemented this in the ACRSS layers is described in the next section.

Figure 6. Example of the execution of the cloud security aspect in ACRSS

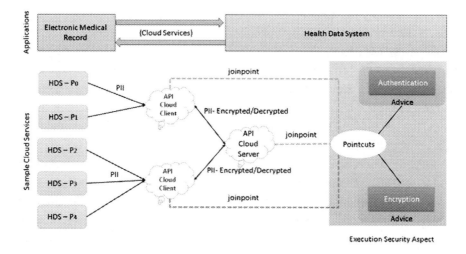

5. ACRSS MODEL AND IMPLEMENTATION

5.1. ACRSS Model

This sub-section first discusses the design of the ACRSS model illustrated in Figure 7 and then how it is implemented to achieve the aim of this study. It covers the abstract aspects as well as some fundamental concepts. Figure 7 illustrates the cloud-related joinpoint events that allow reusable service aspects (e.g., security aspects) to be injected dynamically into a cloud application at runtime. The pink boxes represent

Figure 7. Joinpoints and base cloud aspects in the ACRSS model

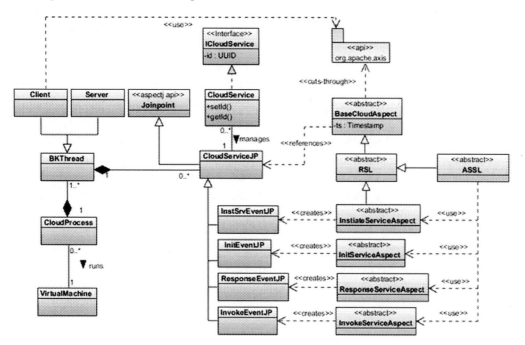

class implementations and the yellow ones denote service aspect behaviours. As mentioned, ACRSS allows developers to not only intercept client and server abstractions at the joinpoint, but also to collect metadata on the cloud context at important instants based on sequencing primitive cloud methods (i.e., instantiate, initiate, response and invoke).

The BKThread is a key class that contains several executed parts of a cloud application on different cloud components. However, implementing some of the advice processes for instantiating, initiating, responding and invoking in a separate logic allows the injection of these advices at the required time-points. Moreover, the advices can be handled on separate execution threads.

The AspectJ pointcut designators and joinpoint context are limited to AOP language constructs and do not handle application-level run time web-cloud abstractions. Each cloud-based service has an instantiated instant, one initiation and one response, but no more than that. The CloudService class contains the data exchanges between clients and servers over the cloud. An instance of CloudServiceJP finds the instantiation, initialization, receiving and/or invoking state(s) of the service being provided. The cloud event joinpoints are service event joinpoints relate to when an abstract is instantiated, initiated, received or invoked. In short, CloudServiceJP represents logical interval where/when advices can be executed before, after or around the context of the cloud service. It consists of a set of joinpoints for the sequence of events that occurs in a cloud. These joinpoints are InstEventJP, InitiEventJP, ResponseEventJP and InvokeEventJP. After all the instants have been processed, ACRSS specifies an execution interval. In other words, it executes the advice that is relevant to each joinpoint, and the aspects contain the recorded timestamp and required service-related context information to deal with the security service-related metadata such as type of service, message, identifier, sender, receiver and the allocation of shared resources for the security context.

ACRSS uses BaseCloudAspect, RSL and ASSL, which are basic abstract aspects that find cloud events to identify the correct service metadata and which inject the required observational logic into the intervals where the events in the cloud may occur. BaseCloudAspect defines pointcuts that can obtain the cloud service-related context metadata dynamically, as shown in Figure 7. This aspect is designed to intercept the relevant core abstraction in the cloud at the joinpoint that relates to a execution event. In addition, it can record timestamps to inject the appropriate security-related crosscutting concern in a certain execution interval. It also matches cloud and joinpoint events to find individual events and deal with them from a high-level cloud perspective. It is specifically designed for instantiate, initiate, response and invoke operations and is based on standard API specifications (Axis, 2016, Sept.).

ReusableServiceLayerAspect (RSL) is a derived abstract aspect that extends BaseCloudAspect by using pointcut abstractions that are relevant to a particular cloud service. The advices in RSL can access the joinpoints of BaseCloudAspect to get cloud service-related metadata such as the service ID, service timestamp and client addresses. This aspect allows developers to implement their own cloud-related service aspects at the application level. They can also use it to define high-level cloud pointcuts and to inject advice into joinpoints by customizing the corresponding abstract ACRSS service aspects.

Application-Level Security Service Layer Aspect (ASSL) is a simple abstract dynamic security-related aspect that is derived from the perspective of the client using the cloud. In other words, it exemplifies the concepts of reusability for service-related concerns using ACRSS. This aspect can be used to inject advices before, after or around a simple initiate-response-invoke joinpoint model. Hence, in the context of this study, aspects derived from the ASSL can represent common security-related crosscutting concerns in applications that have cloud requirements such as encryption and authentication. This enables developers to adapt the model to meet the security requirements of their particular cloud applications by extending the template methods as discussed in the next sub section.

5.2. Implementation of ACRSS

As previously mentioned, cloud-related crosscutting concerns consist of many distributed components in the cloud. Figures 8 to 11 describe the implementation of the proposed ACRSS model as an extension of AspectJ. Using this model, developers can create common security-related crosscutting concerns in a

Figure 8. Part of the code for the implementation of the base cloud aspect

```
public abstract aspect BaseCloudAspect {
        private pointcut InstSrv(): call(Service+.new(..)); // instantiate service

        public pointcut init(): call(* org.apache.axis.AxisEngine+.init(..));
        public pointcut response(): execution(* org.apache.axis.client.Stub+.extractAttachments(..));

        protected InstSrvEventJP instJp =null;
        protected InitEventJP initJp = null;
        protected ResponseEventJP rspJp = null;
        protected InvokeEventJP invokeJp = null;

        public pointcut invoke(): execution(* org.apache.axis.handlers.soap.SOAPService+.invoke(..));

        // Joinpoints for collecting different Cloud-related context information at execution time
        Service around() : InstSrv(){
                Service service = proceed();
                InstSrvEventJP serviceJP = new InstSrvEventJP(service);
                ...
                InstSrvJoinpoint(serviceJP);
                return service;
        }

        after() : init(){
                ...
                InitJoinpoint(initJp);
        }

        int around() : response(){
                ...
                ResponseJoinpoint(rspJp);
        return proceed();
}

        void around() : invoke(){
                ...
        proceed();
                ...
                InvokeJoinpoint(invokeJp);
}

        //service
        public void InstSrvJoinpoint(InstSrvEventJP instJp){
                //pull Service-Related context information at the instant of service instantiation
                ...
        }

        // client
        public void InitJoinpoint(InitEventJP initJp){
                //pull Client-Related context information at the instant of requesting
                ...
        }

        public void ResponseJoinpoint(ResponseEventJP respJp){
                //pull Client-Related context information at the instant of responding
                ...
        }

        //server
        public void InvokeJoinpoint(InvokeEventJP invokeJp){
                //pull Server-Related context information at the instant of requesting/responding
                ...
        }
...
```

loosely coupled way. ACRSS is implemented by AspectJ framework. It contains a set of reusable aspects and a set of reusable advices that can be placed dynamically into the appropriate part of the program during the instantiating, initiating, responding and invoking processes. These advices can be placed into three different joinpoints, JP1, JP2 and JP3, as shown in Figure 8. The first joinpoint, JP1, is the logical interval that occurs between the instant of instantiating the service and that of initializing said service. The second one, JP2, is the logical interval between the points in time when the client initiates a request (for a service) and when the server receives said request. JP1 and JP2 represent the region, i.e., interval, which is extended from the instant of instantiation to the response instant. Lastly, JP3 is a web service joinpoint that represents the logical interval between the time when the server invokes the received service and the time at which the client receives the response (required service), as shown in Figure 8. These three joinpoints in AspectJ are high-level joinpoints on the client side that can be used by developers to inject cloud service-related aspects dynamically. ACRSS can deal with multiple clients with using their internet addresses (IPs) to identify each of them separately. It also uses request references (service identifiers) to identify concurrent requests on the same client. Therefore, cloud service-related context metadata needs to be gathered and associated correctly with the relevant client. In ACRSS, BaseCloudAspect extracts the client addresses and service messages that match the cloud service-related context arguments, i.e., the cloud joinpoint objects. It should be noted that the ACRSS components are completely independent from the original client and server code, as shown in Figure 8. The tracing of cloud application behaviours is a crosscutting concern, so this needs to be implemented as an aspect so that the necessary monitoring logic can be injected. As mentioned earlier, this approach can be used to extract cloud-related metadata at the right time and then bring it together in a high-level cloud context.

In Figure 9, the ASSL is a RSL aspect that finds the common security-related context metadata in cloud applications for a client. RSL has been designed to find the states/events of a cloud service on BaseCloudAspect. At instantiation state, it crosscuts the initialization of service and introduces cloud context metadata before starting the service. The advices in RSL can access the joinpoints to obtain service-related context metadata and create pointcuts that crosscut BaseCloudAspect. There are four key pointcuts: (1) InstServicethat cuts through the BaseCloudAspect instantiation related to the pointcut(instSrvJoinpoint), (2) InitClientthat cuts through the BaseCloudAspect initiation related to the pointcut(InitJoinpoint), (3) ResponseClientthat cuts through the BaseCloudAspect response related to the pointcut (ResponseJoinpoint) and (4) InvokeWSthat cuts through BaseCloudAspect invoke related to the pointcut(InvokeJoinpoint). ASSL is a reusable security service-related aspect that can be employed to provide some extended high-level pointcuts, namely, CloudServiceStart, CloudServiceResponse and CloudServiceInvoke that cut through the state of the service to establish a security-related service on the client side and that marks services as start, response or invoke, respectively.

The context of a cloud service is maintained in terms of its own current state and its associated join-point event. ACRSS implements four aspects: InstiateServiceAspect, InitServiceAspect, ResponseServiceAspect and InvokeServiceAspect. These aspects identify states of the cloud service and define a set of common security crosscutting concern metadata as a single object, i.e., a joinpoint object, which directly implements an aspect. The actual service behaviour changes in accordance with the state of the advice. Figure 10 shows the part of the code for the instantiation state of the service, i.e., instantiation aspect, to create instantiation joinpoint and inject security-related crosscutting concerns when the service has been instantiated. In addition, ACRSS provides more abstract tracking aspects of initiated, responded and invoked states. It captures quite naturally the essential elements of these four individual aspects. It is important to note how the advices in those aspects follow the template and method patterns, which

Figure 9. Part of the code for the implementation of the ASSL aspect

```
public abstract aspect ASSL extends RSL {

        public pointcut CloudServiceStart(InitEventJP _initJp, Timestamp _timeout):
            execution(* SecServiceAspect.BeginService(CloudServiceJP, Timestamp)) && args(_initJp, _timeout);
        public pointcut CloudServiceResponse(ResponseEventJP _responseJp):
            execution(* SecServiceAspect.ResponseService(..)) && args(_responseJp);
        public pointcut CloudServiceInvoke(InvokeEventJP _invokeJp):
            execution(* SecServiceAspect.InvokeService(..)) && args(_invokeJp);
        private CloudService currentCloudService = null;
        void around(InitEventJP _initJp, Timestamp _time) : CloudServiceStart(_initJp,_time){
            InitEventJP initRequestJp = new  InitEventJP();
            initRequestJp.setServiceJp(_initJp);
            if (_initJp!= null && _initJp.getService() == null){
                if(currentCloudService == null)
                    currentCloudService = new CloudService();
                _initJp.setService(currentCloudService);
            }else{currentCloudService = _initJp.getService();}
            if(_initJp.getService()!= null)
                initRequestJp.setServiceJp(_initJp.getServiceJp());
            Begin(initRequestJp, Timestamp.getCurrentTime());
            proceed(_initJp, _time);
        }
        void around(ResponseEventJP _receiveJp) : CloudServiceResponse(_receiveJp){
            ...
            proceed(_receiveJp);
        }
        void around(InvokeEventJP _invokeJp) : CloudServiceInvoke(_invokeJp){
            ...
            proceed(_invokeJp);
        }
        protected void Begin(CloudServiceJP _cloudServiceJp, Timestamp _timeout){
        }

        protected void End(CloudServiceJP _cloudServiceJp){
        }

        protected void Invoke(CloudServiceJP _cloudServiceJp){
        }
}
```

allows developers to quickly adapt them to the specific needs of their cloud applications by using the begin, end and invoke method, as shown in Figure 10. Figure 11 shows some of the code for a reusable security aspect, EncryptionAspect, which is an example of a common security-related crosscutting concern in HDS. It is derived from the ASSL and overrides the begin and end methods to define an encryption service. In other words, after initiating the service, it injects the advice that encrypts the service between the client and server with an appropriate symmetric-security key level that matches the shared key level. It can handle the key requests from the client and server processes. The client can send a key request to the server. Then the server authenticates the client, creates a shared key and encapsulates it in response service and returns it to the client.

Nutshell, in ACRSS, the injecting mechanism allows developers to place service-related advices at defined joinpoints and to gather relevant context metadata without modifying the source code of API. The client only must deploy in the ACRSS library with the cloud application. Developers can use it directly to weave security behaviours in both the client and the server side while also launching traditional injecting code. It ensures that advice codes are executed at defined joinpoints dynamically. The injection process does not require access to the core code; rather, it is applied to the executable, built-in Apache Axis files (.jar files). The weaving process only needs access to the source code of ACRSS, which is completely independent of the server code, to extend abstract aspects and pointcuts.

Figure 10. Part of the code for the implementation of the instantiate service aspect

```
public abstract aspect InstiateServiceAspect extends RSL{

    public static Service srv = null;
    public static Process process =null;

    public pointcut InstiateService(InstSrvEventJP _instEventJp) :
        execution(* ServiceInitiatorAspect.Instantiate(..)) && args(_instEventJp);
    private pointcut ConfigureService(ICloudService _service) :
        execution(void ICloudService.setService(..)) && target(_service);
    before(ICloudService _service):ConfigureService(_service){
      Class<?> className = thisJoinPointStaticPart.getSignature().getDeclaringType();
    }
    after(ICloudService _service):ConfigureService(_service){
        _service.setService(_service);
    }
    void around(InstSrvEventJP _instJp) : InstiateService(_instJp){
        if(_instJp.getService() == null)
            _instJp.setService(new CloudService());
        Instantiate(_instJp);
        proceed(_instJp);
    }
    public void Instantiate(InstSrvEventJP _instJp){

    }
    public Object invokeSrv(String _methodName, Class<?> _class){
        try{
            Method method = _class.getMethod(_methodName, null);
            return method.invoke(null, null);
            }catch(Exception e){
        return null;
        }
    }
}
```

6. CONCLUSION AND FUTURE WORK

In this work cloud computing security is integrated into the cloud in a flexible manner through a novel approach to secure the cloud computing environment. The proposed model, called ACRSS, is an aspect-oriented approach that addresses cloud service-related crosscutting concerns; mainly security-related crosscutting concerns. The main aim of creating the ACRSS is to make it possible for developers to deal with the service-related aspects of the cloud's behaviour as separately as possible. The capability of ACRSS in terms of separating the service-related crosscutting concern logic from the core cloud logic is achieved by extracting the relevant service-related context metadata. Therefore, our model is a non-invasive approach that does not require direct access to or modifications of the core application code of the client. Moreover, ACRSS defines interaction points dynamically.

At the time of writing, we have finished the development of our first prototype as a proof-of-concepts. ACRSS has been used to implement a simple HDS to get a basic understanding of the model. The results were promising but could be improved. We have not discussed the experiment and evaluation in this paper because it would be more relevant to do so in paper that reports on our future work. In a forthcoming paper, we intend to demonstrate through an experiment that we can integrate ACRSS into a self-healing architecture for cloud computing. Then ACRSS will be able to cooperate with other security tools in the infrastructure and platform layers of cloud architecture.

Figure 11. Part of the code for the implementation of the (reusable) encryption aspect

```
public aspect EncryptionAspect extends ASSL{
        byte[] wrappedKey;
        Key unwrappedKey;
        SecretKey passwordKey;
        PBEParameterSpec paramSpec;
        Key sharedKey;
        Cipher cipher;
        PBEKeySpec keySpec;
        @Override
        protected void Begin(CloudServiceJP _cloudServiceJp, Timestamp _timeout){
            KeyGenerator newKey = null;
            try {
                newKey = KeyGenerator.getInstance(_cloudServiceJp.getService().getKey());
            } catch (NoSuchAlgorithmException e) {
                e.printStackTrace();
            }
            sharedKey = newKey.generateKey();
            String password = "pass";
            byte[] arg = "yu1234".getBytes();
            paramSpec = new PBEParameterSpec(arg, 20); // Parameter based encryption
            keySpec = new PBEKeySpec(password.toCharArray());
            _cloudServiceJp.setKey(sharedKey);
            Encrypt(_cloudServiceJp.getService(),sharedKey);
        }

        @Override
        protected void End(CloudServiceJP _cloudServiceJp){

        }
        public byte[] Encrypt(CloudService serv, Key _sharedKey) {
            try {
                SecretKeyFactory kf = SecretKeyFactory.getInstance("987654321");
                return encrypted;
            } catch (Exception e) {
                e.printStackTrace();
                return null;
            }
        }

}
```

REFERENCES

Alani, M. M. (2014). Securing the Cloud: Threats, Attacks and Mitigation Techniques. *Journal of Advanced Computer Science &. Technology*, *3*(2), 202.

Wikipedia. (n.d.). Apache Axis. Retrieved August 2016 from https://en.wikipedia.org/wiki/Apache_Axis

Asma, A., Chaurasia, M. A., & Mokhtar, H. (2012). Cloud Computing Security Issues. *International Journal of Application or Innovation in Engineering & Management*, *1*(2), 141–147.

AxisT. M. (2016, August.). Retrieved from http://axis.apache.org/axis/java/index.html

Bernardi, M. L., & Di Lucca, G. A. (2005). Improving Design Patterns Modularity Using Aspect Orientation. *STEP*, *2005*, 209.

Catteddu, D. (2010). Cloud Computing: benefits, risks and recommendations for information security. In Web application security (p. 17). Springer Berlin Heidelberg. doi:10.1007/978-3-642-16120-9_9

Hmida, M. M. B., Tomaz, R. F., & Monfort, V. (2005, August). Applying AOP concepts to increase web services flexibility. In *Proceedings of the International Conference on Next Generation Web Services Practices NWeSP '05* (p. 6). IEEE.

Jadeja, Y., & Modi, K. (2012, March). Cloud computing-concepts, architecture and challenges. In *Proceedings of the 2012 International Conference on Computing, Electronics and Electrical Technologies (ICCEET)* (pp. 877-880). IEEE. 10.1109/ICCEET.2012.6203873

Kastner, C., Apel, S., & Batory, D. (2007, September). A case study implementing features using AspectJ. In *Proceedings of the 11th International Software Product Line Conference SPLC '07* (pp. 223-232). IEEE. 10.1109/SPLINE.2007.12

Kiczales, G., Hilsdale, E., Hugunin, J., Kersten, M., Palm, J., & Griswold, W. G. (2001, June). An overview of AspectJ. In *Proceedings of the European Conference on Object-Oriented Programming* (pp. 327-354). Springer Berlin Heidelberg.

Kiczales, G., Lamping, J., Mendhekar, A., Maeda, C., Lopes, C., Loingtier, J. M., & Irwin, J. (1997). Aspect-oriented programming. In *ECOOP'97—Object-oriented programming* (pp. 220-242).

Krutz, R. L., & Vines, R. D. (2010). *Cloud security: A comprehensive guide to secure cloud computing.* Wiley Publishing.

Lee, J., Kang, S., & Hur, S. J. (2012, February). Web-based development framework for customizing Java-based business logic of SaaS application. In *Proceedings of the 2012 14th International Conference on Advanced Communication Technology (ICACT)* (pp. 1310-1313). IEEE.

Lohmann, D., Hofer, W., Schröder-Preikschat, W., & Spinczyk, O. (2011, March). Aspect-aware operating system development. In *Proceedings of the tenth international conference on Aspect-oriented software development* (pp. 69-80). ACM. 10.1145/1960275.1960285

Look, A. (2011). *Expressive scoping and pointcut mechanisms for aspect-oriented web service composition.* Vorgelegt Diplomarbeit von Alexander Look, Technische Universitaet Darmstadt.

Masuhara, H., & Kiczales, G. (2003, July). Modeling crosscutting in aspect-oriented mechanisms. In *European Conference on Object-Oriented Programming* (pp. 2-28). Springer Berlin Heidelberg.

Mdhaffar, A., Halima, R. B., Juhnke, E., Jmaiel, M., & Freisleben, B. (2011, August). AOP4CSM: an aspect-oriented programming approach for cloud service monitoring. In *Proceedings of the 2011 IEEE 11th International Conference on Computer and Information Technology (CIT)* (pp. 363-370). IEEE. 10.1109/CIT.2011.67

Pasquier, T. F. M., Bacon, J., & Shand, B. (2014, April). FlowR: aspect oriented programming for information flow control in ruby. In *Proceedings of the 13th international conference on Modularity* (pp. 37-48). ACM. 10.1145/2577080.2577090

Ramachandran, R., Pearce, D. J., & Welch, I. (2006). AspectJ for multilevel security. Bonn, Germany, March, 20, 13-17.

Rao, T. N., Kumar, A., Sunder, S. S., & Chandrasekaran, K. (2013). Performance Analysis of Aspect Oriented Programming for Cloud Service Monitoring.

Razzaq Malik, K., Umar Chaudhry, M., Munwar Iqbal, M., Saleem, Y., & Farhan, M. (2014). Data Security and Privacy in Cloud Computing: Threat Level Indications. *Science International, 26*(5).

Shah, V., & Hill, F. (2003, April). An aspect-oriented security framework. In DARPA Information Survivability Conference and Exposition. In *Proceedings of the DARPA Information Survivability Conference and Exposition* (Vol. 2, pp. 143–145).

Shahin, A. A., Samir, A., & Khamis, A. (2014). An Aspect-Oriented Approach for SaaS Application Customization. arXiv:1409.1656

Shahin, A. A., Samir, A., & Khamis, A. (2014). An Aspect-Oriented Approach for SaaS Application Customization. arXiv:1409.1656

The Apache Software Foundation. (2016, August).Retrieved from http://www.apache.org/dyn/closer.lua/Cloudstack/releases/4.9.0/apache-Cloudstack-4.9.0-src.tar.bz2

Toledo, R., & Tanter, É. (2013, March). Secure and modular access control with aspects. In *Proceedings of the 12th annual international conference on Aspect-oriented software development* (pp. 157-170). ACM. 10.1145/2451436.2451456

Verspecht, D., Vanderperren, W., Suvée, D., & Jonckers, V. (2003). JasCo .NET: Unraveling Crosscutting Concerns in .NET Web Services. *Vrije Universiteit Brussel.*

Xiao, Z., & Xiao, Y. (2013). Security and privacy in cloud computing. *IEEE Communications Surveys and Tutorials, 15*(2), 843–859. doi:10.1109/SURV.2012.060912.00182

Yu, H., Powell, N., Stembridge, D., & Yuan, X. (2012, March). Cloud computing and security challenges. In *Proceedings of the 50th Annual Southeast Regional Conference* (pp. 298-302). ACM. 10.1145/2184512.2184581

Zhang, Q., Cheng, L., & Boutaba, R. (2010). Cloud computing: State-of-the-art and research challenges. *Journal of Internet Services and Applications, 1*(1), 7–18. doi:10.100713174-010-0007-6

This research was previously published in the International Journal of Web Services Research (IJWSR), 15(1); edited by Liang-Jie Zhang, pages 71-88, copyright year 2018 by IGI Publishing (an imprint of IGI Global).

Chapter 30
Security in Ad Hoc Network and Computing Paradigms

Poonam Saini
PEC University of Technology, India

Awadhesh Kumar Singh
National Institute of Technology Kurukshetra, India

ABSTRACT

Resource sharing is the most attractive feature of distributed computing. Information is also a kind of resource. The portable computing devices and wireless networks are playing a dominant role in enhancing the information sharing and thus in the advent of many new variants of distributed computing viz. ubiquitous, grid, cloud, pervasive and mobile. However, the open and distributed nature of Mobile Ad Hoc Networks (MANETs), Vehicular Ad Hoc Networks (VANETs) and cloud computing systems, pose a threat to information that may be coupled from one user (or program) to another. The chapter illustrates the general characteristics of ad hoc networks and computing models that make obligatory to design secure protocols in such environments. Further, we present a generic classification of various threats and attacks. In the end, we describe the security in MANETs, VANETs and cloud computing. The chapter concludes with a description of tools that are popularly used to analyze and access the performance of various security protocols.

INTRODUCTION

The ad hoc network is a collection of wireless mobile nodes that dynamically self-organize in arbitrary and transient network topologies (Macker & Corsen, 1998; Weiser, 1999; Prasant, 2005). The nodes[1] can thus be internetworked in areas without a pre-existing communication infrastructure or when the use of such infrastructure requires wireless extension. The ad hoc networks and computing models have the following typical features (Chlamtac, Conti & Liu, 2003; Basagni, Conti, Giordano & Stojmenovic, 2003; Macker & Corson, 2003; Corson, Maker & Cernicione 1999):

DOI: 10.4018/978-1-5225-8176-5.ch030

- **Continually Changing Topology and Membership:** Nodes continuously move in and out of the radio range of other nodes in the network, thereby, frequently reconfiguring the membership information to update the nodes.
- **Unreliable Wireless Links:** Due to high mobility and dynamic nature of ad hoc protocols, the links between nodes in such networks are inconsistent. Therefore, the susceptibility to active/passive link attacks increase.
- **Lack of Security Features and Poor Scalability of Security Mechanisms:** The security features implemented in statically configured protocols are not sufficient to take care of the requirements of an ad hoc environment. Moreover, with the growth of scalable networks, the security mechanism must be scalable too. Also, the physical protection of mobile hosts is generally poor.
- **Aggregation of Data on Cloud:** Clouds have the capability to aggregate private and sensitive information about users in diverse data centers. Hence, the isolation and protection of customer data is an important concern.
- **Browser Security Failures:** As the cloud users and administrators rely heavily on Web browsers, the browser security failures can lead to cloud security breaches.
- **Transparency:** Customers need confidence and transparency about the performance of the cloud system and its management strategy.

Because of features listed above, ad hoc networks and computing paradigms are more vulnerable to security attacks as compared to traditional networks. Hence, security and privacy becomes necessary to safeguard the leakage of information in such hostile environment.

SECURITY ATTACKS: A BACKGROUND

There are many types of security attacks in an ad hoc and computing environment (Karpijoki, 2000; Lundberg, 2000; Hubaux, Buttyan & Capkun, 2001; Buttyan & Hubaux, 2002; Deng, Li & Agrawal, 2002; Ilyas, 2003). Primarily, the attacks can be categorized as following:

1. **Internal vs. External:** Internal attacks initiated by the authorized nodes into the network. The network itself may contain compromised or arbitrary behaving nodes. On the other hand, external attacks are initiated by the adversaries, initially not a part of network, to cause delay in network services, congestion and disrupt other network related operations.
2. **Passive vs. Active:** Passive attacks include eavesdropping on or monitoring packets exchanged within an ad hoc network whereas active attacks involve some modifications of the data steam or the creation of a false stream.
3. **Malicious vs. Rational:** Usually, a malicious attacker aims to harm the users or network. Hence, a malicious attacker may employ any means of forging without considering loss and consequences involved. On the other hand, a rational attacker looks for personal benefit and hence is more predictable.
4. **Local vs. Extended:** Though, an attacker may control several entities, it can be limited in scope and hence its affect remains local. An extended attacker controls several entities that are scattered across the network, thus extending the scope. This distinction is especially important in privacy-violating and wormhole attacks that will be described shortly.

Besides, the primary category of attacks, an ad hoc network may suffer from the following generic attacks (Gong, 1993; Stajano & Anderson, 1999; Zhou & Hass, 1999; Hu, Perrig & Johnson, 2002; Michiardi & Molva, 2003):

1. **Wormhole Attack:** In the attack, an adversary receives data packet at one end in the network and tunnel the packets to other end in the network. Further, the packets are replayed into the network and the tunnel between two adversaries is known as a wormhole. The communication can be established through a single long-range wireless link or a wired link between the two adversaries. Hence, it is simple for the adversary to make the tunneled packet arrive faster than other packets transmitted over a normal multi-hop route. A compromised node in the ad hoc network collides with external attacker to create a shortcut in the network. By creating such shortcut, they could trick the source node to win in the route discovery process and later launch the interception.

2. **Black Hole:** Initially, the attacker attempts to attract the nodes to transmit the packet through itself. It can be achieved by sending the malicious route reply with fresh route and low hop count continuously to the nodes. Afterwards, as soon as the packet is forwarded through the malicious node, the packet is dropped. The main purpose of the attack is to increase the congestion in network. Here, the malicious node does not forward any packet instead drops them all. As a result, the packets forwarded by the nodes do not reach their intended destination and the congestion in the network escalates due to retransmissions.

3. **Gray Hole:** The gray hole attack is an extension of black hole attack. Here, a malicious node may forward all packets to a subset of nodes, however, drop packets coming from or destined to a specific set of nodes. In this type of attack, a node may behave arbitrary for a certain period of time and behave normal for rest of communication. Therefore, the gray hole attack is difficult to manage as compared to black hole. The malicious node drops the packet selectively which can be of two type:
    a. Drop the UDP packet while successfully transmitting TCP packets.
    b. Drop the packet based on probabilistic distribution.

4. **Impersonate:** In this type of attack, the attacker assumes identity and privileges of an authorized node, either to make use of network resources that may not be available to it under normal circumstances, or to disrupt the normal functioning of the network. The attack is performed by active attackers that can be either an internal node or external. Also, it is a form of multilayer attack where an attacker can exploit the vulnerabilities on either network layer, application layer or transport layer. This attack can be performed in two ways:
    a. **False Attribute Possession:** An attacker captures some attribute of a legitimate user. Later, using the same attributes, the attacker presents itself as a legitimate user. For example, in a VANET environment, a normal vehicle may claim that it is a police or fire protector to acquire the traffic free path.
    b. **Sybil:** An attacker may use different identities at the same time (Douceur, 2002).

5. **Session Hijacking:** The authentication process is performed at the start of the session. Hence, it becomes easy to hijack the session after the connection between nodes is established. Further, the attacker takes control of session between nodes and poses threat to safety-critical communication among nodes.

6. **Repudiation:** The main threat in repudiation is denial or attempt to denial of a service by any node involved in the communication. It is different from the impersonate attack. In this attack, two or

more entities may have common identity. Hence, it becomes difficult to identify the nodes which can be repudiated further (Choi & Jung, 2009).

7. **Eavesdropping:** It is an attack on confidentiality which belongs to network layer and is passive in nature. The main goal of the attack is to get access to confidential or private data.

8. **Denial of Service:** DoS attacks are most prominent attack in this category. The attacker prevents the legitimate user to use the service from the node under attack. DoS attacks can be performed in many ways.

    a.   **Jamming:** The attacker senses the physical channel and retrieves information about the frequency at which the receiver receives signal. Afterwards, the attacker transmits its signal in that channel in order to amplify traffic on the route.

    b.   **SYN Flooding:** A large number of *SYN* request is sent to the victim node by spoofing the sender address. Further, the victim node sends an acknowledgement *SYN-ACK* to the spoofed address; however, it does not receive any *ACK* packet in return. Therefore, a legitimate request can easily be discarded.

    c.   **Distributed DoS Attack:** Multiple attackers attack the victim node and prevents legitimate user from accessing the service.

Figure 1 represents a classification of commonly observed threats and attacks (Isaac, Zeadally & Camara, 2010).

SECURITY IN MOBILE AD HOC NETWORKS

A mobile ad hoc network (MANET) is a collection of mobile hosts (MHs) that operate without any fixed infrastructure and utilize multi-hop relaying. Due to mobility of nodes and insufficient fixed infrastructure, a MANET relies on peer node communication (Freebersyser & Leiner, 2001, Michiardi,

Figure 1. Threats and attacks in ad hoc networks

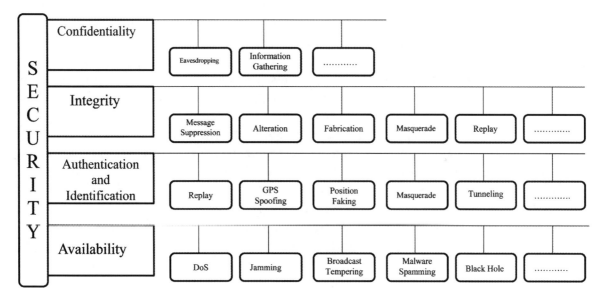

& Molva, 2004). The nodes have capability to reconfigure themselves and create a temporary and ad hoc topology. However, if a MANET joins an external network in order to access internet, it may come across various threats and challenges (Wu, Chen, Wu & Cardei, 2006). A misbehaving or arbitrary node on the network may induce an *active* or *passive* attack in the network to retrieve critical information. Various vulnerabilities that exist in MANETs are as follows (Hubaux, Buttyan & Capkun, 2001; Yang, Luo, Ye, Lu & Zhang, 2004; Zhang & Lee, 2005):

- **Insecure Perimeter:** There are no defined perimeters in MANETs and the nodes are free to join, leave and move in and out of the network. In case of wired network, the adversaries ought to have physical access to the network medium, or pass through firewall and gateway before executing any malicious behavior. However, in MANET, adversaries need not gain the physical access to enter into the network. In fact, once the adversary is in the radio range of an MH, it can communicate with it and thus join the network automatically. As a consequence, MANET does not provide secure boundary or perimeter in order to protect itself from potentially unsafe network accesses. Therefore, insecure perimeter makes the mobile ad hoc network more susceptible to different attacks (peer nodes or communication links). The attacks mainly include passive eavesdropping, active interfering, and leakage of secret information, data tampering, message replay, message contamination, and denial of service.

- **Compromised Nodes in the Internal Network:** There are some adversary in the network that aims to take control over another node which, afterwards, termed as a compromised node. Further, the compromised node is used to execute malicious actions. This vulnerability can be viewed as the threat that is initiated by the compromised node inside the network. Since MHs are autonomous units that can join or leave the network any time, it is more difficult for the nodes to execute safely due to diversity in the behavior of nodes. Moreover, the target attack node is changed frequently, by the adversary, in a large scale and dynamic network. Hence, the threats from compromised nodes inside the network are far more serious than the attacks from outside the network. Such attacks are much harder to detect because they come from the compromised nodes, which behave well before they are compromised. An example of such threat is Byzantine (arbitrary) failures. A Byzantine failure is a category of failures where a subset of processes may fail *i.e.*, nodes may send fake messages, nodes may not send any message, or nodes try to disrupt the computation. The arbitrary node may seemingly behave well. Thus, Byzantine failure is very harmful to the mobile ad hoc network.

- **Insufficient Centralized Facility:** In mobile ad hoc networks, there can be no oracle *i.e.*, a centralized entity that can monitor the traffic in a highly dynamic and large scale ad hoc network. In ad hoc networks, benign failures, such as path breakages, transmission impairments and packet dropping happen frequently. Hence, it becomes difficult to detect malicious failures, especially, when an adversary frequently changes its attack pattern and attack target. Also, it obstructs the trust management for the nodes in the ad hoc network. Furthermore, the lack of centralized management facility causes an adversary to execute attacks.

- **Limited Power Backup:** In mobile ad hoc networks, the restricted battery power causes several problems. The attack caused by an adversary, due to limited power supply, turns into Denial-of-Service (DoS) attack. Here, the adversary knows that the target node is battery-restricted. Therefore, the adversary either continuously sends additional packets to be routed to a node or it

Figure 2. Security Architecture in MANET

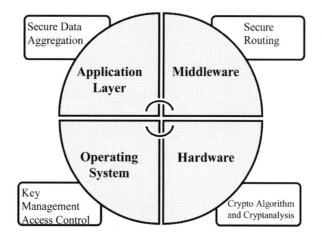

can engage a node in some compute-intensive task. In this way, the battery power of the attacked node is exhausted faster and thus the node is out of service to all the benign service requests.

- **Scalability:** Unlike the traditional wired network, the scale of the mobile ad hoc network keeps on changing. As a consequence, the protocols and services such as routing and key management should be compatible to the continuously changing scale of the ad hoc network ranging in thousands of nodes. Hence, the services need to be scaled up and down efficiently.
- **Routing Attacks:** Security in underlying routing protocols is a major concern in MANETs. The authors in (B. Kumar, 1993; Royer, 2003; Beraldi & Baldoni, 2003) define two broad categories of routing attacks, namely, *routing disruption attack* and *resource consumption attack*. In routing disruption attack, the main goal is to interrupt the routing process of a subset of nodes by means of introducing wrong routes on the network. In the attack, the extent of the attack depends upon number of attacking nodes in a network and the attacking probability P. Here, the intention of attacker is to make the process of identifying the attacker more difficult with the use of probabilistic attack and not dropping all packets (Royer & Toh, 1999). In case of resource consumption attacks, an attacker introduces a set of non-cooperative nodes that inject false packets in order to increase payload on the network, thereby, consuming a major portion of network bandwidth.

Security Architecture in MANETs

The section describes the security architecture in MANETs as shown in Figure 2. The detailed description of major components is as follows:

- **Secure Data Aggregation:** Aggregation reduces the amount of network traffic. The two main security challenges in secure data aggregation are *confidentiality* and *integrity of data* (Yang, Wang, Zhu & Cao, 2006). Here, traditional encryption is used to provide end-to-end confidentiality. Further, in a secure data aggregation state, the aggregator needs to decrypt the encrypted data in order to perform aggregation. This leads to depiction of the plaintext at the aggregator end, thereby, making the data vulnerable to attacks from an adversary. Similarly, an aggregator can inject false data into the aggregate and make the base station accept false data.

Figure 3. Security Layers in MANETs

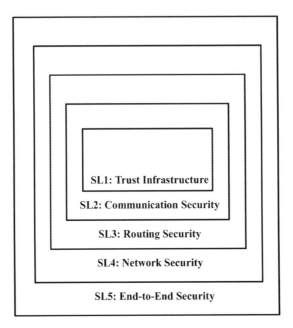

- **Secure Routing:** Secure routing plays an important role in MANETs security as there is no fixed infrastructure. Due to dynamic nature of MANET environment, the traditional routing protocols are unsuitable. Hence, routing protocols are focused and designed towards *on-demand* or interchangeably *reactive* mechanism, where, dynamic routes are created on the basis of demand and need of end-users (Perkins & Royer, 1998). In the existing literature, the popular routing protocols are DSR (Johnson, Maltz & Broch, 2001) and AODV (Perkins, Belding-Royer & Das, 2003) which are based on reactive approach.
- **Key Management and Access Control:** The generic network security implementation of keys involves a trusted authority. However, due to lack of infrastructure in ad-hoc networks, it is not feasible to have a fixed trusted authority. It is a major component at operating system level which defines roles and rules for resource management as well as secure communication.
- **Crypto Algorithms and Cryptanalysis:** Security at any level can be achieved by cryptographic algorithms. There is an encryption and decryption process using keys that aims to provide security to information. Security in MANETs can be summarized in a five-layer hierarchy as shown in Figure 3 (Yu, Zhang, Song & Chen, 2004):

The layers designed for the security issues perform the following function:

- SL1 defines the trust relationship among the nodes.
- SL2 applies various security mechanisms while transmitting data packets among nodes.
- SL3 refers to routing related security mechanisms.
- SL4 defines security measures used by network layer protocols.
- SL5 refers to application specific security measures like SSH, SSL.

Security Mechanisms in MANETs

Security mechanisms designed for mobile ad-hoc networks aims to provide security services and may prevent any of the following attacks (Taugchi, 1999; Nishiyama & Fumio, 2003; R.B. Machado; A. Boukerche; Sobral, Juca & Notare, 2005; Zhang, Lee & Huang, 2003).

1. **Link Level Security:** In a mobile environment, links are susceptible to attacks where an intruder can intercept the data packets. The commonly used perimeter protections such as firewalls are not sufficient to overcome link attacks.
2. **Routing Security:** The routing of data packets within an ad hoc network is more vulnerable to attacks as each MH also acts as router. Thus, an attacker can pretend itself to be an integral component of network and may route packets to erroneous paths. It may result in Denial of service (DoS) attack easily. Therefore, in order to achieve secure routing, IP traffic should be protected from attackers.
3. **Key Management:** In general, the network security implementation of keys involves a trusted authority. However, in an infrastructure less network, it is not feasible to have a fixed trusted authority. The conventional approaches such as authentication, access control, encryption, and digital signature act as primary mean to counter various attacks. Further, intrusion detection system (IDS) and other defence mechanisms like enforce cooperation also improve security by lowering the self-centred behaviour of nodes.
4. **Network layer Security:** Network layer security mechanisms can be classified on the basis of the number of attacks being identified. There are two major categories: (i) Point Detection and (ii) Intrusion Detection Systems (IDSs) (refer Figure 4)

Point detection algorithms can detect a single category of network layer attacks while IDSs may detect a wide range of attacks (Madhavi, 2008). The recent advancement in network layer security is the development of neural network algorithms (Ahmad, Abdullah & Alghamdi, 2009), which are used for intrusion detection. The architecture of system is shown in Figure 5.

The IDS mechanism initially extracts MAC layer features followed by data collection and intrusion detection using an engine. Finally, intrusion response is applied. Afterwards, each node creates a map that exhibits its security status. Subsequently, the node distributes the map to the neighbouring nodes. In the end, a global map is generated after a node has received all maps from its neighbours. It helps to know the security status of routes in a MANET and to continue routing accordingly.

Figure 4. Network Layer Security Mechanisms

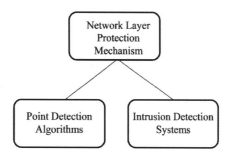

Figure 5. Schematic view of IDS Architecture

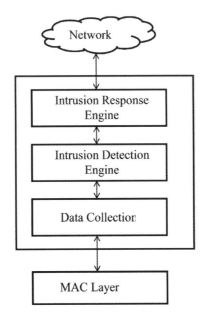

Secure Routing in MANETs

The section describes various existing solution to secure routing in MANETs.

- **SRP:** Secure Routing Protocol (SRP) (Panagiotis Papadimitratos, & Haas, 2006) is based on Destination Source Routing protocol (DSR). The execution of SRP requires the existence of a Security association (SA) between source node, which initiates a route query, and the destination node. The SA is used to establish a shared secret key between two nodes. In the protocol, a SRP header is appended to basic routing protocol packet. Further, in order to identify an outdated request at the destination node, the source node sends a route request with a query sequence number *QSEQ* and a random query identifier *QID* that is used to identify a specific request. The intermediate nodes broadcast the request query to their neighbours only after updating their routing tables.

- **Ariadne:** Ariadne is another secure routing protocol (Hu, Perrig & Johnson, 2002) based on the Dynamic Source Routing protocol (DSR) (Johnson & Maltaz, 1996). It is an on demand routing protocol which attempts to track the routes only when it is required and thus it is dynamic in nature. The protocol employs the concept of Message Authentication Code (MAC) and shared keys for authentication and time stamp to follow packet lifetime. It consists of two phases, *Route discovery* and *Route maintenance*. In route discovery phase, source node attempt to establish route by flooding route request packets *RREQ* containing source IP address and destination IP address. On the other hand, route maintenance is carried whenever a link loss is observed in a particular route to the destination. If a packet is forwarded through a specific route, each intermediate node forwards that packet to the next node on the route and then next node acknowledges the packet being received. However, in case, a broken link is found on the destination path, the intermediate node sends a route error message *RERR* to the source node.

- **ARAN:** The Authenticate Routing for Ad-hoc Network (ARAN) is a secure routing protocol for MANETs (B. Hahill, 2002). ARAN utilizes cryptographic methods like authentication, message integrity, and non-repudiation in order to achieve security goals. It also uses asymmetric cryptography where a trusted third party is assumed. There are three distinct operational stages as follows:
  ○ Preliminary certification process: It is the first stage that requires existence of a trusted certificate authority (CA).
  ○ Route Discovery: It is the second operational stage that provides end-to-end authentication. This also ensures that the intended destination was indeed reachable.
  ○ The third operation stage of ARAN protocol is optional and ensures that the shortest path is discovered.
    ARAN uses public key cryptography and a central certification authority server for overall node authentication in route discovery. It avoids attack like spoofing via timestamp, replay, however, denial-of-service is possible with compromised nodes.
- **SAR:** Security Aware Routing (SAR) uses a trust-based framework (Yi, Naldurg & Kravets, 2001). Each node in the network is assigned a trust level. Hence, the attacks can be analyzed and security of SAR can be evaluated based on trust level and message integrity. The authors define trust and message integrity as under:
  ○ **Trust Level:** It is a binding between the identity of the user and the associated trust level. To follow the trust-based hierarchy, cryptographic techniques like encryption, public key certificates, shared secrets, etc. can be employed.
  ○ **Message integrity:** The compromised nodes can utilize the information communicated between nodes and read the packets in order to launch attacks. This results in corruption of information, confidentiality breach and denial of network services.
- **SAODV:** Secure Ad-hoc On-demand Distance Vector (SAODV) is an extension to the AODV protocol (Guerrero, 2001). The protocol utilizes digital signatures and hash chains to secure AODV packets. Further, in order to facilitate the transmission of additional information needed for the implementation of security mechanisms, SAODV extends the standard AODV message format. The SAODV extensions consist of the following fields:
  ○ Hash function field to identify the one way hash function that is being used.
  ○ Max hop count is a counter to specify maximum number of nodes a packet is allowed to traverse.
  ○ Sequence numbers to prevent the possible replay attacks.
- **SPAAR**: Secure Position-aided Ad hoc Routing (SPAAR) is designed to provide a very high level of security; however, sometimes it is achieved at the cost of performance (Yasinsac & Carter, 2002). Further, along with other parameters, the protocol requires that each device must own a GPS locator to determine its position, although, the nodes may use a so-called "locator-proxy", in case, complete security is not required. In SPAAR, packets are accepted only between 1-hop neighbours. This avoids "invisible node-attack". The basic transmission procedure is similar to ARAN. A group neighbourhood key is used for encryption in order to ensure one-hop communication only. Since all nodes have information about their locations due to inbuilt GPS locator, the RREQs is forwarded by a node only if it is close to the destination node.
- **SEAD:** Secure Efficient Distance Vector Routing protocol (SEAD) is a proactive secure routing protocol based on DSDV-SQ-protocol (Hu, Johnson & Perring, 2002). It relies on one-way hash chain for security unlike AODV that uses asymmetric encryption. The algorithm assumes that

there exists an authenticated and secure way to deliver the initial key K_N. This can be achieved by delivering the key in advance or by using public key encryption and signatures for key delivery. The basic idea of SEAD is to authenticate the sequence number and metric of a routing table using hash chains elements.

- **S-DSDV:** Secure Destination-Sequenced Distance-Vector (S-DSDV) is a secure routing protocol where a non-faulty node can successfully detect a malicious routing update (Wan, Kranakis & Oorschot, 2002). There can be sequence number deception or any distance fraud provided no two nodes are involved in any agreement process. SDSDV requires cryptographic mechanisms for entity and message authentication.

SECURITY IN VEHICULAR AD HOC NETWORKS

The VANETs incorporate general ad hoc network security features and faces attacks such as eavesdropping, traffic analysis and brute force attacks. The unique nature of VANET also raises new security issues such as location detection, illegal tracking and jamming. In an article "Threat of Intelligent Collisions" (Blum & Eskandarian, 2004), the authors raised an important question, *"A wireless network of intelligent vehicles can make a highway travel safer and faster. But can hackers use the system to cause accidents"*? Therefore, the security and safety becomes crucial in VANETs as it affects the life of people. The generic cryptographic approaches used for VANET security include public key scheme to distribute one time symmetric session keys for message encryption, certificate schemes for authentication and randomizing traffic patterns against traffic analysis (Wasef and Shen, 2009; Isaac, Zeadally & Camara, 2010). Potential security measures could include a method of assuring that the packet/data was generated from a trusted source (neighbor vehicle, sensors, etc.), as well as a method of assuring that the packet/data was not tampered after it was generated. Any application that involves a financial transaction (such as tolling) requires the capability to perform a secure transaction.

Characteristics of VANET

In a VANET environment, there are two types of communications, *Roadside to Vehicle Communication* (RVC) and *Inter Vehicle Communication* (IVC). Various types of hardware units that are required to effectively implement VANET includes On-Board Units (OBUs), mounted on vehicles and Road Side Units (RSUs), placed on road side for communication with plying vehicles. VANET is an application of MANET, however, it has its own distinct characteristics which can be summarized as under (Blum, Eskaindarian & Hoffman, 2004; Jiang & Delgrossi, 2008; Moustafa H, Zhang, 2009; Olariu & Weigle, 2009; Sultan, Doori, Bayatti & Zedan, 2013):

- **High Mobility:** The nodes in VANETs usually are moving at high speed. Thus, it is harder to predict a node's position and difficult to protect the node privacy. Further, high mobility causes frequent disconnection that makes the communication highly unreliable. Nevertheless, the mobility patterns of vehicles on the same road exhibit strong correlation. However, each vehicle would have a frequently changing set of neighbors, a subset of which have never communicated before and are unlikely to -communicate again. The short-lived nature of interactions or communications in a VANET limits the efficacy of reputation-based schemes. Additionally, as two vehicles may only be within communication range for a very short period (*e.g.*, few seconds), one cannot rely on protocols that require significant communication between the sender and receiver.

- **Low Tolerance for Errors:** Some applications can afford security protocols that rely on probabilistic schemes. However, in VANETs' safety (mission-critical) related applications, even a small probability of error would be unacceptable. The margin of error of a security protocol in VANETs based on deterministic or probabilistic scheme is infinitesimally small. Additionally, for many applications, security mechanism must focus on prevention of attacks, rather than detection and recovery. In MANETs it may suffice to detect an attack and alert the user, leaving recovery and clean-up to the humans. However, in many safety-related VANETs applications, detection will be inadequate, as by the time the driver can react, the warning may be too late. Therefore, the prevention of attacks comes in the first place, which requires extensive foresight into the types of attacks likely to occur.

- **Key Distribution:** Key distribution is often a fundamental building block for security protocols. In VANETs, key distribution faces several significant challenges. The government may impose standards, however, it would require significant changes to the current infrastructure for vehicle registration, and thus is unlikely to implement in near future. However, without a system for key distribution, applications like traffic congestion detection may be vulnerable to spoofing and sybil attacks. A potential approach for secure key distribution would be to empower the Motor Vehicles licensing authority to take the role of a Certificate Authority (CA) and to certify each vehicle's public key.

- **Co-Operation:** Successful deployment of VANETs would require cooperation amongst vehicle manufacturers, consumers, and the government, and reconciling their frequently conflicting interests would be challenging. For instance, law-enforcement agencies might quickly adopt a system in which speed-limit signs broadcast the mandated speed and vehicles are automatically reported any violations. Understandably, consumers might reject such invasive monitoring, giving vehicle manufacturers little incentive to include such a feature. On the other hand, consumers might appreciate an application that provides an early warning of a police speed trap. Manufacturers might be keen to meet this demand, but law-enforcement is unlikely to do so.

- **Rapidly Changing Network Topology and Unbounded Network Size:** Due to swift node mobility and random speed of vehicles, the position of node changes frequently. As a result of this, network topology in VANETs tends to change frequently. Further, VANET can be implemented for one city, several cities or for countries. This means that network size in VANET is geographically unbounded.

- **Frequent Exchange of Information:** The ad hoc nature of VANET motivates the nodes to gather information from the other vehicles and road side units. Hence, the information exchange among node becomes frequent.

- **Time Critical:** The information in VANET must be delivered to the nodes within specified time limit so that a decision can be made by the node to perform an action accordingly.

Privacy vs. Security in VANETs

Similar to other IP-based networks *e.g.*, Internet, MANETs, etc., it is essential to bind each driver or vehicle to a single identity to prevent Sybil or other spoofing attacks (Hussain, Kim & Ho, 2012). Further, in order to prevent attacks on VANETs, authentication is the main requirement that may provide important forensic evidence and allows to use external mechanisms such as traditional law enforcement. However, the drivers or other vehicle users also want to preserve their privacy and are unlikely to adopt such systems where anonymity is discarded. Therefore, privacy compliant security policies are needed that requires codifying legal, societal and practical considerations. Moreover, nowadays, most vehicle manufacturers operate in multinational markets, thereby, generating a need to adopt only those security solutions that may circumvent stringent privacy laws as well as meet legal obligations, if any. Further, authentication schemes must consider societal expectations of privacy against practical considerations. Also, the vehicles are not fully anonymous as each vehicle has a license plate that uniquely identifies the vehicle and its owner. Hence, in this way, drivers have already shared a portion of their privacy while driving. Therefore, we must design security policies based on existing compromises instead of approaching the driver for more parameters.

Security Requirements in VANETs

As the applications of VANETs are diverse, their communications and/or system level security requirements could be unlike. Potential security measures should include a way of assuring that the packet/data was generated by a trusted source, as well as a way of assuring that it was not tampered with or altered after it was generated. It is obvious that any malicious user behavior, such as an alteration and replay attack of the disseminated messages, could be disastrous to other users. A security system needs to be capable of establishing the liability of drivers, while preserving their privacy to maximum possible extent. Considering the aforementioned attacks and suggestion made in other works, VANET security should satisfy the following requirements (Golle, Greene & Staddon, 2004; Raya & Hubaux, 2007; J. Choi & Jung, 2009; Hartenstein & Laberteaux, 2009):

- **Authentication:** This is the most important requirement in preventing most of the aforementioned attacks in VANETs. Vehicle responses to events should be based on legitimate messages (i.e., generated by legitimate users). Therefore, On Board Units (OBUs), Road Side Units (RSUs) and senders of the messages needs to be authenticated.
- **Verification of Data Consistency:** The legality of messages also comprises their consistency with similar ones (those generated in close space and time), as the sender can be legal but the message contains false data. This requirement also known as "plausibility".
- **Message Integrity:** Message alteration is very common and crucial attacks in VANETs. We need to maintain the integrity of the message to prevent the alteration attacks.
- **Availability:** Some attacks, like DoS by jamming, bring the VANETs down even though the considered communication channel is robust. Thus, the availability should be provided by some other means.
- **Non-Repudiation:** Drivers causing accidents should be reliably identified to prove his/her liability. Based on this principle, a sender will not be able to refuse the transmission of a message (it may be key for investigation in determining the correct sequence and content of messages exchanged before the accident).
- **Privacy:** Generally, people are increasingly cautious of being monitored or tracked. Hence, the privacy of drivers or vehicle owners against unauthorized observers should be protected.

- **Traceability and Revocation:** An OBU or RSU that has violated the VANET must be traceable. Further, the authority can disable such misbehaving units and revoke them in time to prevent future problems.
- **Real-Time Constraints:** At the high speeds in typical VANETs, strict time constraints should be respected. It ultimately imposes computation and communication wise efficient schemes.

Security Architecture in VANETs

The section describes general security architecture in VANETs as shown in figure 6. In a secure VANET structure, each device has identification authority and an associated certificate. At the start of communication, the device is registered with the user's account where the user information is maintained along with the provider ID. Further, whenever a user enters a service area, on board payment device can be used. Afterwards, the authorization request message is encrypted using provider's public key and thus hiding the identity of device as well as requested services from attackers. The service provider issues a pseudonym and other identities to users that are essential to obtain the services. Alternate way is to issue temporary credentials for the time a user is using any service. This may incorporate essential security attributes in VANET applications including vehicle to vehicle (V2V) communications (Plossl, Nowey & Mletzko, 2006.). For example, certificate, IP address, MAC address etc. can all be issued on temporary basis and should be refreshed periodically.

Figure 6. Security Architecture in VANETs

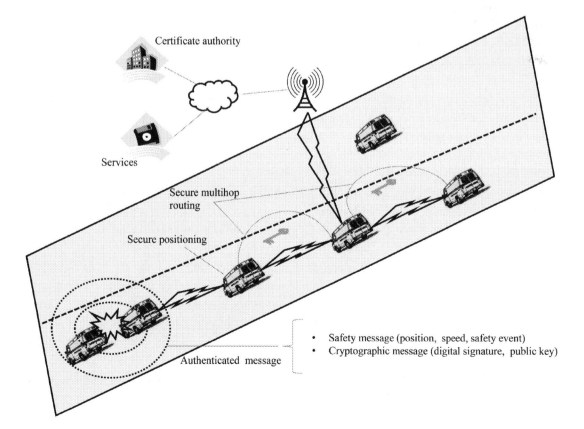

Existing Security Mechanisms in VANETs

The VANET security requires vehicular units to exchange safety related messages in order to keep the vehicles aware of road conditions and unsafe situations. Such messages are categorized in *periodic* and *event driven safety*. Further, since encryption and decryption incur time overhead at both ends, the necessity of securing the message is an issue. Secondly, a false message or an intentional delay may lead to unsafe situation like vehicle collision. Hence, a tradeoff is essential between speed and security (Mohan Li, 2014). Following is summary of existing protocols used to enforce security in VANETs:

- **TPM:** Trusted Platform Module (TPM) is a trust framework. It implements a hybrid method that takes advantage of both, asymmetric and symmetric cryptographic schemes for safe messaging (Chowdhury, Tornatore, Sarkar, Mukherjee, Wagan, Mughal & Hasbullah, 2010). In addition, the protocol describes trust grouping strategies developed for vehicles in vicinity. The protocol has four major components in the proposed framework: (i) message dispatcher (ii) TPM (iii) group entity, and (iv) group communication. Together, these components form the desired trusted group. The TPM module includes cryptographic methods (asymmetric and symmetric encryption), random number generation and hash function. It accepts messages from the message dispatcher. Thereafter, an encrypted message is returned with required security strength. There are other entities that form a group with an elected group leader, generally, Road Side Unit (RSU) and group members that are vehicular units in the vicinity. The leader is responsible to generate one time secret session key and distribute it among the members using asymmetric scheme. Hence, the framework assists the vehicles in the network to form trusted groups that use symmetric scheme for message security while preserving the security strength of asymmetric schemes.

- **PPDT:** Privacy Preserving Defense Technique (PPDT) is an identity based security system for VANET that resolves the conflict between privacy and tractability (Sun, Zhang, Zhang, & Fang, 2010). The system employs a pseudonym based scheme to preserve user privacy and threshold signature based scheme to enable tractability for the purpose of law enforcements. The privacy preserving defense scheme is an integral part of the structure that controls the authentication threshold. Hence, authentication beyond the defined threshold is considered as a transgression which may result in revocation of the user credentials. In addition, the scheme employs a dynamic accumulator for the authentication threshold. Further, it is used to restrict other communicating users beyond the threshold. This feature is beneficial especially to service providers as they can achieve better efficiency of their services.

- **APLM:** Asymmetric Profit Loss Markov (APLM) model computes the integrity level of various security schemes for VANET content delivery (Azogu, Ferreira, & Hong Liu, 2012). The model is based on black box technique to evaluate and document the profit and loss of data delivery. Here, profit is defined as the successful detection of data corruption whereas loss as the reception of corrupted data. The model uses Markov chains to analyze a system's ability to adjust itself with given profit and loss data. The authors claim that the model is asymmetric in a sense that a system generally experience more loss than profits. The model generates heuristics of measurement that can be applied to optimize the integrity schemes for VANET in order to ensure better content delivery. Further, cost performance tradeoff has been described with the help of simulation results. However, the effectiveness of integrity metrics has net been validated.

- **PBS:** Position Based Security (PBS) mechanism provides security to sensitive information related to position of vehicles in VANET (Gongjun, Bista, Rawat & Shaner, 2011). It is a novel position detection scheme to prevent position based attacks. The need to design such scheme erupted from the general requirement to form the topology for applications like the alert system for congestion. Such applications may utilize the available position detection devices such as radio transceiver and cameras. It presents a vehicle model that uses four types of sources of observations, (i) *data from an eye device data*, (ii) *data from an ear device*, (iii) *data from opposite direction of vehicle's eye device* and (iv) *data from opposite direction of vehicle's ear device*. In position detection scheme, a vehicle periodically broadcast its positional information and receives such information from its neighbors. Further, upon the reception of positional information from a nearby vehicle, receiver vehicle verifies the accuracy of information with its own eye device and ear device data. It is possible only if the line of sight is not blocked. Otherwise, receiver vehicle request the eye device and ear device data from sender's vehicle to confirm its own position and speed information. Another method to achieve position security is to exchange blacklists of faulty nodes among vehicles in vicinity in ad hoc manner.
- **DM:** Defensive mechanism (DM) is an essential accompaniment to the passive encryption methods (Prabhakar, Singh, & Mahadevan, 2013). The main perception to evaluate a defensive mechanism is *reliability*, *defensive probabilities* and *security*. Reliability ensures integrity of message and truthfulness of the source. The defensive probability is computed based on the optimality of the deployment of traffic control for both static and dynamic traffic conditions. Lastly, security takes into consideration the density of traffic rates for rural and urban areas. The defensive mechanism works on game theoretic approaches and is comprised of three stages.
  - The first stage employs heuristics based on ant colony optimization to identify known and unknown opponents.
  - In the second stage, Nash Equilibrium is used to select the model for a given security problem.
  - The third stage enables the defensive mechanism to evolve over traffic traces through the game theoretic model from the first stage.
- **DM for DoS**: The Denial of Service (DoS) attack (specifically jamming-style DoS) can be avoided by security mechanisms used in VANETs (Azogu, Ferreira, Larcom, & Hong Liu, 2013). The authors presented a new class of anti-jamming defensive mechanisms termed hideaway strategy. The effectiveness of this new mechanism has been investigated and compared with traditional channel surfing called retreat strategy. The authors implement a simulation package integrating VANET modules (OBUs and RSUs) and attack/defense modules along with traffic simulation. The results confirm that the hideaway strategy achieves steady efficiency over traditional anti jamming schemes.

SECURITY IN CLOUD COMPUTING

The increase in demand for cloud computing has increased the security and privacy concern. The service layer architecture of cloud computing consists of Software as a service (SaaS), Platform as a service (PaaS) and Infrastructure as a service (IaaS). It is also known as SPI model in which Software as a Service (SaaS) is a software distribution model in which applications are hosted by a vendor or service provider and made available to customers over a network. Platform as a Service (PaaS) is a paradigm for delivering operating systems and associated services. Infrastructure as a Service (IaaS) involves outsourcing the equipment used to support operations, including storage, hardware, servers and networking components (Buyya, Vecchiola & Selvi, 2013; Saurabh, 2014). Further, depending upon the access allowed to the users, cloud systems can be deployed in four forms *viz.* private, public, community and hybrid (Buyya, Broberg & Goscinki, 2011; Jayaswal, Kallakurchi, Houde & Shah, 2014). Figure 7 represents a schematic view of cloud services and cloud delivery model.

- **Private Cloud:** This model is implemented solely for an organization and is exclusively used by their employees at organizational level and is managed and controlled by the organization or third party. The cloud infrastructure in this model is installed on premise or off premise. In this deployment model, management and maintenance are easier, security is very high and organization has strict control over the infrastructure and accessibility.
- **Public Cloud:** This model is implemented for general users. It is managed and controlled by an organization providing cloud services. The users can be charged for the time duration they use the services. Public clouds are more vulnerable to security threats than private cloud models because all the application and data remains available to all users making it more prone to attacks. The services on public cloud are provided by proper authentication.
- **Community Cloud:** This cloud model is implemented jointly by many organizations with shared concerns *viz.* security requirements, mission, and policy considerations. The cloud may be managed by one or more involved organizations or may be managed by third party. The infrastructure may exist on premise to one of the involved organization or it may exist off premise to all organizations.
- **Hybrid Cloud:** This model is an amalgamation of two or more clouds (private, community, public or hybrid). The participating clouds are bound together by some standard protocols. It enables the involved organization to serve its needs in their own private cloud and if some critical needs (cloud bursting for load-balancing) occur they can avail public cloud services.

Figure 7. Schematic view of cloud services and cloud delivery model

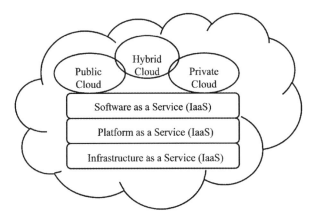

Characteristics of Cloud Computing

Cloud computing must have some characteristics in order to meet expected user requirements and to provide quality services. According to NIST (Mell & Grance, 2011), there are five essential characteristics of a cloud computing environment.

1. **On-Demand Self-Service:** A consumer can access different services *viz.* computing capabilities, storage services, software services etc. as needed automatically without service provider's intervention.
2. **Broad Network Access:** The internet works as a backbone of cloud computing in order to avail cloud computing services. The services are available over the network and are also accessible through standard protocols using web enabled devices *viz.* computers, laptops, mobile phones etc.
3. **Resource Pooling:** The resources are pooled at a single physical location or at different physical location taking into consideration the optimality conditions like security, performance, and customer demand. The resources allocated to users are processing, software, storage, virtual machines and network bandwidth. Though, the cloud mediates for resource location independence at lower level (*e.g.*, server, core), it is not meant for higher level (*e.g.*, data centre, city, country).
4. **Rapid Elasticity:** The most attractive feature of cloud computing is its elasticity. The resources appear to users as unlimited and are also accessible at any time. The resources can be provisioned without service provider intervention and can be quickly scale in and scale out according to the user needs in a secure way to deliver high quality services.
5. **Measured Service:** A metering capability is deployed in cloud system in order to charge users for the services being avail. The users may achieve different quality of service for resources at different level of abstraction to the services (*e.g.*, SaaS, PaaS and IaaS).

Security Concerns in Cloud Computing

Major security concerns in cloud computing occur when an individual is not clear about "*why their personal information is requested or how it will be used or passed on to other parties*". Therefore, cloud security is an important factor in the adoption of cloud services by an end-user. Following is the table of major (though not limited to) security concerns (Krutz & Vines, 2010; Dawoud, Takouna & Meinel, 2010; Jasti, Shah, Nagaraj & Pendse, 2010; Garfinkel & Rosenblum, 2005):

Security Architecture in Cloud

The exceptional feature of a Cloud-computing platform is comprehensive virtualization. It leads to flexible system construction and makes operation at different levels easier. In Fujitsu's Cloud services platform (Okuhara; Shiozaki & Suzuki, 2010) known as *Trusted-Service Platform*, the network, operating-system, and data layers attributes to logical separation of computing environments through advanced virtualization technology. The logical separation (virtualization) achieves the same level of security as physical separation of computing environments (Figure 8). The proposed architecture ensures sufficient reliability, especially in the virtual server layer. Further, the source-code reviews of the virtualization software may be conducted in the model.

Table 1. Major security concerns in Cloud Computing

1. Physical security is lost due to sharing of computing resources with third-party user. Hence, there is no knowledge or control on the execution of resources.
2. Legal issues associated with the violation of law on a provider part. Hence, data may be seized by a foreign government if actual services have been hired from them.
3. Incompatibility in the storage services and structures provided by different cloud vendors. Hence, if a user decides to migrate from one cloud to another, it is a concern. For example, Microsoft cloud is incompatible with Google cloud.
4. Control on cryptographic mechanisms like encryption/decryption keys. Hence, a customer may need them to ensure complete security of their data.
5. To ensure the integrity of the data while its transfer/migration, storage, and retrieval. Hence, a standard should be defined and maintained for the same.
6. To provide all data logs to security managers and regulators in case of Payment Card Industry Data Security Standard (PCI DSS). Hence, such functionaries should to be reliable to avoid transaction fraud.
7. To ensure end-users with the latest updates in the improvisation of the application in order to retain a customer's belief.
8. To comply with government regulatory where there is restriction on the duration and type of citizen data storage. For example, banking regulators require that customer's financial data should remain in their home country.
9. To cope up with dynamic and flowing nature of virtual machines that further complicates the consistency of security.
10. Customers may be able to sue cloud service providers, in case, their privacy rights are violated and the cloud service providers may face damage to their reputation.

Figure 8. Security architecture in cloud computing

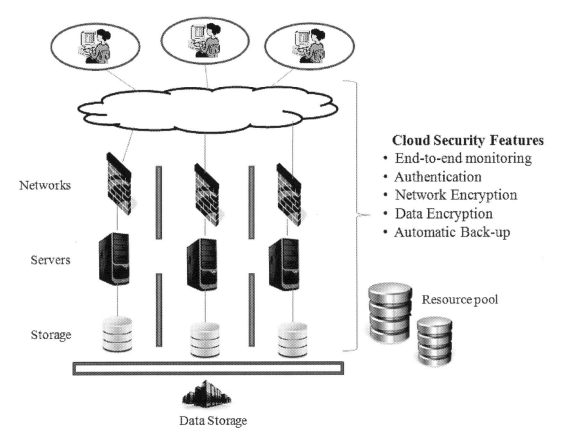

Furthermore, the sender encrypts the message digest with its private key resulting into digital signature. Lastly, SHA (Secure Hash Algorithm) is used as a key for message encryption and decryption. The protocol ensures authentication, data security and verifiability. Also, by using Tri-Mechanism approach, data breach, data loss, shared technology issues threats can be controlled.

- **PDP:** Provable Data Possession model is used for data checking (Giuseppe, 2011). A client can verify that the server contains original data being stored on distrusted server without retrieving it. The authors presented correctness proofs by sampling random sets from server which in turn reduces the input output cost. The client maintains a database to verify the proof. Also, this is a public verification scheme which can be used for auditing purpose. Here, RSA homomorphic tag has been used for auditing. However, the public verification algorithm does not use a secret key. PDP model is lightweight and supports large databases. The simulation results exhibit that the performance of PDP is delimited by disk I/O and not by cryptographic computation.

- **CloudProof:** Enabling Cloud storage using CloudProof is a secure storage system, especially, designed for the cloud (Popa & Raluca Ada, 2011). In CloudProof, a client can detect violation of integrity, write-serializability, and may validate the occurrence of such violations to a third party user. The system ensures security via Service Level Agreements (SLAs) wherein clients pay for a desired level of security and may be given compensation in the event of cloud misbehavior. Furthermore, CloudProof is suitable only for large enterprises. It uses cryptographic tools to allow customers to detect and prove cloud misbehavior. CloudProof adds reasonable overhead to the base cloud service.

- **Trusted Cloud Computing Using TCP:** The paper describes the need of security in cloud environment (Shen & Tong, 2010). The proposed model assumes a trusted environment by merging both, *trusted computing platform* and *cloud computing system* with trusted platform module. The trusted computing mechanism is the base of the trusted computing and ensures to establish a secure environment. As the network computing is the main computing, a trusted computing model is being developed to the network computing. Therefore, the trusted computing mechanisms can be extended to cloud computing services by combining TCP into cloud computing system. The model consists of the following components:
  - Authentication of cloud computing environment with TCP.
  - Role based access control model in cloud computing environment.
  - Data security in cloud based on TCP environment.
  - Traces of the user's behavior.
    The integration of TCP with cloud computing module leads to better authentication, communication security and data protection.

- **Trust Matrix for Risk analysis:** The authors introduced a risk analysis approach in order to analyze security risks in the cloud computing environment endowed by the service providers (Sangroya, Kumar, Dhok & Varma, 2010). Risk assessment has been done using trust matrix. The trust matrix is fabricated using two important trust variables, *Data cost and Provider's history*. Further, in order to correlate with trust variables, Data location and Regulatory compliance parameters have also been used. These variables have been used in common area where related statistics about service providers has been specified. The relationship has been represented using trust matrix with Low Risk/High Trust Zone, High Risk/Low Trust Zone area. The corresponding

X-axis, Y-axis, and Z-axis represent the data cost, service provider's history and data location. Also, a risk defensive approach called *Trust Action* has been used for risk impact assessment. Thus, the proposed trust based approach has been used for measuring trust and analyzing data security risks for future transactions by service providers.

SECURITY ANALYSIS TOOLS

In general, distributed networks are vulnerable as the attackers may analyze/influence network traffic or the communicating parties are compromised by attackers. For this reason, cryptographic protocols form an essential ingredient of current network communications. The security protocols in MANET/ VANET use cryptographic primitives to ensure secure communications over insecure networks. These protocols need to be designed correctly, and their analysis is complex. The security protocols at each layer of the network architecture have some cryptographic algorithms with defined parameters. Many security protocols developed over time have shown some breaches in providing optimal security after being published or even used. Therefore, it becomes an important aspect in the development of a security protocol that its performance is extensively analyzed before any practical deployment. Some of the tools developed for the purpose are:

- **Scyther:** The Scyther tool is used for security protocol verification (Cremers & Cas J.F., 2008). Security Protocol Description Language (SPDL) is used to write protocols in Scythe. Verification of protocols with an unbounded number of sessions and nonces[2] can be done. The tool characterizes protocols, thereby, yielding a finite representation of all possible protocol behaviors. Many security frameworks for MANET have been analyzed with Scyther. The graphical user interface of the tool makes it user friendly to verify and understand a protocol. All possible claims can be easily verified. An attack graph is generated whenever there is a successful attack against the mentioned claim. The tool can be used to find problems that arise from the way the protocol is constructed. It can also be used to generate all the possible trace patterns. The verification here can be done using a bounded or an unbounded number of sessions.
- **ProVerif:** ProVerif is a software tool for automated reasoning about the security properties found in cryptographic protocols (Blanchet & Bruno, et. al., 2010). An unbounded number of sessions and messages are used to verify the working of a protocol. The tool has properties like action reconstruction and generation of execution trace, in case, an attack is successful for the mentioned claim. It can easily handle different cryptographic primitives, including shared and public-key cryptography (encryption and signatures), hash functions, and Diffie-Hellman key agreements that are specified either as rewrite rules or as equations. An unbounded verification for a class of protocols is performed by using an abstraction of fresh nonce generation.
- **AVISPA**: The Automated Validation of Internet Security Protocols and Applications (AVISPA) is a collection of separately maintained tools that provide the framework for verification of security protocols (Armando & Alessandro, et. al., 2005). The validation portion of AVISPA consists of the tools, namely, Constraint Logic-Attack Searcher (CL-AtSe), On-the-Fly Model Cheker (OFMC), and SAT-based Model-Checker (SATMC), for performing model checking.

- ○ **CL-Atse:** (Version: 2.2-5) It applies constraint solving with simplification heuristics and redundancy elimination techniques (Turuani & Mathieu, 2006).

- ○ **OFMC:** (Version of 2006/02/13) It employs symbolic techniques to perform protocol falsification as well as bounded analysis. It explores the state space in a demand-driven way. A number of optimizations are implemented by OFMC, including constraint reduction that can be viewed as a form of partial order reduction. Using these optimizations the verification problem is solved optimally (Basin; David; Sebastian & Vigano, 2003).

- ○ **Sat-MC:** (Version: 2.1, 3 April 2006) It uses Boolean satisfiability to build a propositional formula encoding all the possible traces (of bounded length) on the protocol (Armando, Alessandro & Luca, 2005). A SAT solver is then used to solve the reduced set. In general, some parameters can be modified and, in particular, one can choose the SAT solver in the configuration file of Sat-MC.

- ○ **TA4SP:** (Version of Avispa 1.1) Tree Automata based on Automatic Approximations for the Analysis of Security Protocols. It approximates the intruder knowledge by using regular tree languages and rewriting to produce under and over approximations (Boichut, Yohan, 2004).

- • **SPEAR:** Security Protocol Engineering and Analysis Resource (Bekmann; Goede & Hutchison, 1997). It is a protocol engineering tool which focuses on production and verification of security protocols, with the specific aims of secure and efficient design outcomes and support for the `production' process. It provides a complete design environment to the developers for the correct designing of the security protocols. The design environment helps the protocol developers in a way that the security can be analyzed later in an efficient way. SPEAR supports protocol specification via a graphical user interface in the style of message sequence charts (MSCs). For protocol specification and cryptographic logics, SPEAR allows a user to design a security protocol in such a way that there is enough specification for the automatic generation of code that implements the protocol. By integrating various aspects of cryptographic logics into development process, logical analysis is automatically incorporated into this design process. The combination of formal protocol specification and cryptographic logics provides users a mechanism that automates the most important aspects of the design process and offers a powerful and flexible test-bed for security protocol design.

- • **CASPER/FDR:** The tool translates protocol specifications into the process algebra CSP (Communicating Sequential Process) and the CSP model checker FDR (*Failures Divergences Refinement*) (Lowe & Gavin, 1998). It can be used either to find attacks upon protocols, or to show that no such attack exists, subject to the assumptions of the Dolev-Yao Model (Dolev & Yao, 1983) (*i.e.*, that the intruder may overhear or intercept messages, decrypt and encrypt messages with keys that he knows, and fake messages, but not perform any crypto logical attacks).

Table 2. Outline the summary of security tools with special characteristics

Name of Tool	Designed for	Special Characteristics
Scyther	MANETs/VANETs	*To verify the security protocol without any limitation on number of sessions to be carried out.*
ProVerif	MANETs/VANETs	*To perform automatic reasoning of various cryptographic characteristics in a protocol.*
Avispa	MANETs/VANETs	*To perform automatic verification by means of a subset of specific-task related tool.*
Spear	MANET	*To design security protocols via graphical user interface.*
Casper/FDR	MANET	*To translate protocol for failure divergence refinement to inform if an attack exists or not.*

CHAPTER SUMMARY

The wireless networks (VANETs, MANETs, FANETs) and flexible computing paradigms are highly susceptible to security threats and attacks. The chapter presented a brief study of prominent security attacks and summarizes the need to design secure protocols. Further, security in MANET, VANET and Cloud computing has been discussed in detail. Finally, a brief account of security tools has been presented.

REFERENCES

Ahmad, I., Abdullah, B., & Alghamdi, A. (2009). Application of Artificial Neural Network in Detection of probing attacks. In *IEEE Symposium on Industrial Electronics and Applications* (pp 557-562). 10.1109/ISIEA.2009.5356382

Armando & Alessandro. (2005). The AVISPA tool for the automated validation of internet security protocols and applications. In *Computer Aided Verification.* Springer Berlin Heidelberg.

Armando, Alessandro, & Luca. (2005). An optimized intruder model for SAT-based model-checking of security protocols. In *Electronic Notes in Theoretical Computer Science* (pp. 91-108). Academic Press.

Azogu, I. K., Ferreira, M.T., Larcom, J.A., & Liu, H. (2013). A new anti-jamming strategy for VANET metrics directed security defense. In IEEE Globecom Workshops (vol. 913, pp. 1344-1349). IEEE.

Azogu, I. K., Ferreira, M. T., & Liu, H. (2012). A security metric for VANET content delivery. In *Proceedings of IEEE conference on Global Communications* (vol. 37, pp. 991-996). 10.1109/GLOCOM.2012.6503242

Basin, D., & Vigano, S. (2003). *An on-the-fly model-checker for security protocol analysis.* Springer Berlin Heidelberg.

Bekmann, Goede, & Hutchison. (1997). SPEAR: Security protocol engineering and analysis resources. In *DIMACS Workshop on Design and Formal Verification of Security Protocols.*

Belding-Royer, E. (2003). Routing approaches in mobile ad hoc networks. In S. Basagni, M. Conti, S. Giordano, & I. Stojmenovic (Eds.), *Ad Hoc Networking.* New York: IEEE Press Wiley.

Belding-Royer, E., & Toh, C.-K. (1999). A review of current routing protocols for ad-hoc mobile wireless networks. IEEE Personal Communications Magazine, 46–55.

Beraldi, R., & Baldoni, R. (2003). Unicast routing techniques for mobile ad hoc networks. In M. Ilyas (Ed.), *Handbook of Ad Hoc Networks.* New York: CRC Press.

Blanchet, B. (2010). *Proverif: Cryptographic protocol verifier in the formal model.* Retrieved from http:// prosecco. gforge. inria. fr/personal/bblanche/proverif

Blum, J., & Eskandarian, A. (2004). The Threat of Intelligent Collisions. IT Professional Journal, 6(1), 24-29. doi:10.1109/MITP.2004.1265539

Blum, J. J., Eskaindarian, A., & Hoffman, L. J. (2004). Challenges of Inter vehicle Ad Hoc Network-s. *IEEE Transactions on Intelligent Transportation Systems*, 5(4), 347–351. doi:10.1109/TITS.2004.838218

Boichut & Yohan. (2004). Improvements on the Genet and Klay technique to automatically verify security protocols. In *Proceedings of AVIS (vol. 4)*. Academic Press.

Buttyan, L., & Hubaux, J. P. (2002). Report on a working session on security in wireless ad hoc networks. *Mobile Computing and Communications Review*, 6(4).

Buyya, R., Broberg, J., & Goscinski, A. (2011). *Cloud Computing- Principles and Paradigms*. Wiley. doi:10.1002/9780470940105

Buyya, R., Vecchiola, C., & Selvi, S. T. (2013). *Matering Cloud Computing*. McGraw Hill.

Carter, S., & Yasinsac, A. (2002). Secure position aided ad hoc routing protocol. In *Proceedings of the IASTED International Conference on Communications and Computer Networks*.

Chen, S., & Nahrstedt, K. (1998). An overview of quality-of-service routing for the next generation high-speed networks: problems and solutions. In *IEEE Network*. IEEE.

Chiasserini, C. F., & Rao, R. R. (1999). Pulsed battery discharge in communication devices. In *Proceedings of Fifth Annual ACM/IEEE International Conference on Mobile Computing and Networking* (pp. 88–95). 10.1145/313451.313488

Chlamtac, I., Petrioli, C., & Redi, J. (1999). Energy-conserving access protocols for identification networks. *IEEE/ACM Transactions on Networking*, 7(1), 51–59. doi:10.1109/90.759318

Choi, J., & Jung, S. (2009). A security framework with strong non-repudiation and privacy in VANETs. In CCNC.

Chowdhury, P., Tornatore, M., Sarkar, S., Mukherjee, B., Wagan, A. A., Mughal, B. M., & Hasbullah, H. (2010). VANET Security Framework for Trusted Grouping Using TPM Hardware. In *Proceedings of International Conference on Communication Software and Networks* (vol. 2628, pp. 309-312).

Corson, S., Maker, J. P., & Cernicione, J. H. (1999). Internet-based mobile ad hoc networking. *IEEE Internet Computing*, 3(4), 63–70. doi:10.1109/4236.780962

Cremers, C. J. F. (2008). The Scyther Tool: Verification, falsification, and analysis of security protocols. In *Computer Aided Verification*. Springer Berlin Heidelberg.

Dawoud, W., Takouna, I., & Meinel, C. (2010). Infrastructure as a service security: Challenges and solutions. In *7th IEEE International Conference on Informatics and Systems*, (pp 1-8).

Deng, H., Li, W., & Agrawal, D. P. (2002). Routing security in wireless ad hoc networks. *IEEE Communications Magazine*, 40(10), 70–75. doi:10.1109/MCOM.2002.1039859

Dolev & Yao. (1983). On the security of public key protocols. IEEE TIT, 29(2), 198-208.

Douceur, J. (2002). The Sybil Attack. In *First International Workshop on Peer-to-Peer Systems* (pp. 251-260). 10.1007/3-540-45748-8_24

Freebersyser, J. A., & Leiner, B. A. (2001). DoD perspective on mobile ad hoc networks. In C. Perkins (Ed.), *Ad Hoc Networking* (pp. 29–51). Addison Wesley.

Garfinkel, T., & Rosenblum, M. (2005). When virtual is harder than real: Security challenges in virtual machine based computing environments. In *Proceedings of the 10th conference on Hot Topics in Operating Systems*, (vol. 10, pp 227-229)

Giuseppe, A. (2011). Remote data checking using provable data possession. *ACM Transactions on Information and System Security*, *14*(1), 1–12. doi:10.1145/1952982.1952994

Golle, P., Greene, D., & Staddon, J. (2004). Detecting and correcting malicious data in Vanets. In *Proceedings of the first ACM workshop on Vehicular ad hoc networks*. ACM Press. 10.1145/1023875.1023881

Gong, L. (1993). Increasing availability and security of an authentication service. *IEEE Journal on Selected Areas in Communications*, *11*(5), 657–662. doi:10.1109/49.223866

Gongjun, Y., Bista, B. B., Rawat, D. B., & Shaner, E. F. (2011). General Active Position Detectors Protect VANET Security. In *International Conference on Broadband and Wireless Computing, Communication and Applications* (vol. 2628, pp. 11-17).

Guerrero, Z. M. (2001). *Secure Ad hoc On-Demand Distance Vector (SAODV) Routing*. Retrieved from http://www.cs.ucsb.edu/~ebelding/txt/saodv.txt

Gupta, A., & Chourey, V. (2014). Cloud computing: Security threats & control strategy using tri-mechanism. In *Proceedings of IEEE International Conference on Control, Instrumentation, Communication and Computational Technologies*. 10.1109/ICCICCT.2014.6992976

Hahill, B., ... (2002). A Secure Protocol for Ad Hoc Networks. In OEEE CNP.

Hartenstein, H. & Laberteaux, K. (2009). *VANET Vehicular Applications and Inter-Networking Technologies*. Academic Press.

Hiroyuki, N., & Fumio, M. (2003). Design and implementation of security system based on immune system. In *Software Security - Theories and Systems Lecture Notes in Computer Science, Hot Topics No. 2609* (pp. 234–248). Springer-Verlag.

Hu, Y., Johnson, D., & Perring, A. (2002). SEAD: Secure Efficient Distance Vector Routing for Mobile Wireless Ad Hoc Networks. In IEEE WMCSA. IEEE.

Hu, Y. C., Perrig, A., & Johnson, D. B. (2002). *Wormhole detection in wireless ad hoc networks*. Technical Report TR01-384, Rice University, Department of Computer Science.

Hu, Y. C., Perrig, A., & Johnson, D. B. Ariadne: a secure on demand routing protocol for ad hoc networks. In *Proceedings of the Eighth ACM International Conference on Mobile Computing and Networking*. 10.1145/570645.570648

Hubaux, J. P., Buttyan, L., & Capkun, S. (2001). The Quest for Security in Mobile Ad Hoc Networks. In *Proceedings of the 2nd ACM International Symposium on Mobile ad hoc Networking & Computing* (pp. 146-155). 10.1145/501416.501437

Hussain, R., Kim, S., & Oh, H. (2012). Privacy-Aware VANET Security: Putting Data-Centric Misbehavior and Sybil Attack Detection Schemes into Practice. *Lecture Notes in Computer Science, 7690,* 296–311. doi:10.1007/978-3-642-35416-8_21

Ilyas, M. (2003). *Handbook of Ad Hoc Networks.* New York: CRC Press.

Isaac, J. T., Zeadally, S., & Camara, J. S. (2010). Security attacks and solutions for vehicular ad hoc networks. *IET Communications, 4*(7), 894–903. doi:10.1049/iet-com.2009.0191

Jasti, A., Shah, P., Nagaraj, R., & Pendse, R. (2010). Security in multi-tenancy cloud. In *IEEE International Carnahan Conference on Security Technology* (pp 35-41).

Jayaswal, K., Kallakuchi, J., Houde, D., & Shah, D. (2014). *Cloud Computing Black Book.* Dreamtech.

Jiang, D., & Delgrossi, L. (2008). IEEE 802.11p: towards an international standard for wireless access in vehicular environments. In Vehicular technology conference (pp. 2036–2040).

Johnson, D. B., & Maltaz, D. A. (1996). Dynamic Source Routing. In T. Imielinski & H. Korth (Eds.), *Ad Hoc Wireless Networks, Mobile Computing* (pp. 153–181). Kluwer Academic Publishers.

Johnson, D. B., & Maltz, D. A. (1996). Dynamic source routing in ad-hoc wireless networks. Mobile Computing.

Johnson, D. B., Maltz, D. A., & Broch, J. (2001). SR: the dynamic source routing protocol for multihop wireless ad hoc networks. In Ad hoc Networking book (pp. 139-172). Academic Press.

Karpijoki, V. (2000). *Security in Ad Hoc Networks.* Academic Press.

Krutz, R. L., & Vines, R. D. (2010). *Cloud Security (A Comprehensive Guide to Secure Cloud Computing).* Wiley.

Kumar, B. (1993). Integration of security in network routing protocols. SIGSAC Reviews, 2(11), 18–25. doi:10.1145/153949.153953

Li, M. (2014). *Security in VANETS.* Retrieved from http://www.cse.wustl.edu/~jain/cse57114/ftp/vanet_security/index.html

Lowe & Gavin. (1998). Casper: A compiler for the analysis of security protocols. Journal of Computer Security, 6(1), 53-84.

Lundberg, J. (2000). *Routing Security in Ad Hoc Networks.* Academic Press.

Machado, R. B., Boukerche, A., Sobral, J. B. M., & Juca, K. R. L. & and Notare, M.S.M.A. (2005). A hybrid artificial immune and mobile agent intrusion detection based model for computer network operations. In *Proceedings of the 19th IEEE International Parallel and Distributed Processing Symposium.* 10.1109/IPDPS.2005.33

Macker, J. P., & Corson, S. (2003). Mobile ad hoc networks (MANET): routing technology for dynamic, wireless networking. In S. Basagni, M. Conti, S. Giordano, & I. Stojmenovic (Eds.), *IEEE Ad Hoc Networking.* New York: Wiley.

Madhavi, S. (2008). An intrusion detection system in mobile ad hoc networks. In *2nd International Conference on Information Security and Assurance.*

Mauve, M., Widmer, J., & Hartenstein, H. (2001). A survey on position-based routing in mobile ad hoc networks. *IEEE Network, 15*(6), 30–39. doi:10.1109/65.967595

Mell, P., & Grance, T. (2011). The NIST definition of Cloud Computing. NIST Special publication 800-145.

Michiardi, P., & Molva, R. (2003). Ad hoc networks security. In S. Basagni, M. Conti, S. Giordano, & I. Stojmenovic (Eds.), *Ad Hoc Networking.* IEEE.

Michiardi, P. & Molva, R. (2004). Ad Hoc Network Security. In *IEEE Mobile Ad Hoc Networking.*

Moustafa, H., & Zhang, Y. (2009). *Vehicular networks: techniques, standards, and applications.* CRC Press. doi:10.1201/9781420085723

Okuhara, M.; Shiozaki, T. & Suzuki, T. (2010). Security architectures for Cloud Computing. *FUJITSU Science Technology Journal, 46*(4), 397-402.

Olariu, S., & Weigle, M. C. (2009). *Vehicular networks: from theory to practice.* Chapman & Hall/CRC. doi:10.1201/9781420085891

Papadimitratos, P., & Haas, Z. J. (2006). Secure data communication in mobile ad hoc networks. *IEEE Journal on Selected Areas in Communications, 24*(2), 343–356. doi:10.1109/JSAC.2005.861392

Perkins, C., Royer, E. B., & Das, S. (2003). *Ad hoc On-Demand Distance Vector (AODV) Routing.* doi:10.17487/rfc3561

Perkins, C. E., & Bhagwat, P. (1994). Highly dynamic destination sequenced distance-vector routing (DSDV) for mobile computers. *Computer Communication Review, 24*(4), 234–244. doi:10.1145/190809.190336

Plossl, K., Nowey, T., & Mletzko, C. (2006). Towards a security architecture for vehicular ad hoc networks. In *First International Conference on Availability, Reliability and Security.* 10.1109/ARES.2006.136

Popa, R. A. (2011). Enabling Security in Cloud Storage SLAs with CloudProof. In *USENIX Annual Technical Conference* (vol. 242).

Prabhakar, M., Singh, J. N., & Mahadevan, G. (2013). Defensive mechanism for VANET security in game theoretic approach using heuristic based ant colony optimization. In *Proceedings of International Conference on Computer Communication and Informatics* (vol. 46, pp. 1-7). 10.1109/ICCCI.2013.6466118

Raya, M., & Hubaux, J. (2007). Securing Vehicular Ad Hoc Networks. Journal of Computer Security, 15(1), 39-68.

Sangroya, A., Kumar, S., Dhok, J., & Varma, V. (2010). Towards Analyzing Data Security Risks in Cloud Computing Environments. In *International Conference on Information Systems, Technology and Management* (pp. 255-265). 10.1007/978-3-642-12035-0_25

Saurabh, K. (2014). *Cloud Computing- Unleashing Next Gen Infrastructure to Application.* Wiley.

Shen, Z., & Tong, Q. (2010). The Security of Cloud Computing System enabled by Trusted Computing Technology. In *2nd International Conference on Signal Processing Systems*. 10.1109/ICSPS.2010.5555234

Sosinky, B. (2011). *Cloud Computing- Bible*. Wiley.

Stajano, F., & Anderson, R. (1999). The resurrecting duckling: security issues for ad-hoc wireless networks. In *Proceedings of the 7th International Workshop on Security Protocols*.

Sun, J., Zhang, C., Zhang, Y., & Fang, Y. (2010). An Identity-Based Security System for User Privacy in Vehicular Ad Hoc Networks. *IEEE Transactions on Parallel and Distributed Systems, 21*(9), 1227–1239. doi:10.1109/TPDS.2010.14

Taugchi, A. (1999). The study and implementation for tracing intruder by mobile agent and intrusion detection using marks. In *Symposium on cryptography and information security*.

Turuani & Mathieu. (2006). The CL-Atse protocol analyser. In Term Rewriting and Applications, Springer Berlin Heidelberg.

Wan, T., Kranakis, E., & Oorschot, P. C. (2002). *Securing the Destination Sequenced Distance Vector Routing Protocol (S-DSDV)*. Retrieved from http://www.scs.carleton.ca/~canccom/Publications/tao-sdsdv.pdf

Wasef, A., & Shen, X. (2009). AAC: message authentication acceleration protocol for vehicular ad hoc networks. In *Proceedings of the 28th IEEE conference on Global telecommunications* (pp. 4476-4481).

Wu, B., Chen, J., Wu, J., & Cardei, M. (2006). A Survey on Attacks and Countermeasures in Mobile Ad Hoc Networks. In *Wireless/Mobile Network Security*. Springer.

Yang, H., Luo, H., Ye, F., Lu, S., & Zhang, L. (2004). Security in Mobile Ad Hoc Networks: Challenges and Solutions. IEEE Wireless Communications, 11(1), 38-47.

Yang, Y., Wang, X., Zhu, S., & Cao, G. (2006). A Secure Hop-by Hop Data Aggregation Protocol for Sensor Networks. In *Proceedings of 7th ACM International Symposium on Mobile Ad-hoc.*

Yasinsac, A., & Carter, S. (2002). *Secure Position Aided Ad hoc Routing*. Retrieved from http://www.cs.fsu.edu/~yasinsac/Papers/CY02.pdf

Yi, S., Naldurg, P., & Kravets, R. (2001). Security-Aware Ad hoc Routing for Wireless Networks. UIUCDCS-R-2001-2241.

Yu, Zhang, Song, & Chen. (2004). *A Security Architecture for Mobile Ad Hoc Networks*. Academic Press.

Zhang, Y., & Lee, W. (2005). Security in Mobile Ad-Hoc Networks. In *Ad Hoc Networks Technologies and Protocols*. Springer.

Zhang, Y., Lee, W., & Huang, Y. (2003). Intrusion detection techniques for mobile wireless networks. Wireless Networks and Applications, 9(5), 545-556.

Zhou, L., & Hass, Z. J. (1999). Securing Ad Hoc Networks. IEEE Networks.

ADDITIONAL READING

Gupta, B. B., Joshi, R. C., & Misra, M. (2009). Defending against Distributed Denial of Service Attacks: Issues and Challenges. In Information Security Journal: A Global Perspective, (vol. 18, no. 5, pp. 224-247).

Lin, X., & Li, X. (2013). Achieving efficient cooperative message authentication in vehicular ad hoc networks. *IEEE Transactions on Vehicular Technology, 62*(7), 3339–3348. doi:10.1109/TVT.2013.2257188

Pathan, A.-S. K. (2011). *Security of Self-Organizing Networks MANET, WSN, WMN, VANET.* CRC Press, Taylor and Francis.

Pearson, S., & Yee, G. (Eds.). (2013). *Privacy and Security for Cloud Computing.* Springer. doi:10.1007/978-1-4471-4189-1

Raya; Maxim & Jean-Pierre Hubaux. (2007). Securing vehicular ad hoc networks. *In Journal of Computer Security*, (vol. 15, no. 1, pp. 39-68).

Singh, K., Saini, P., Rani, S., & Singh, A. K. (2015). Authentication and Privacy Preserving Message Transfer Scheme for Vehicular Ad hoc Networks (VANETs). *In International Workshop on Future Information Security, Privacy and Forensics for Complex Systems in conjunction with 12th ACM International Conference in Computing Frontiers, Ischia, Italy*, (pp. 58-64). 10.1145/2742854.2745718

KEY TERMS AND DEFINITIONS

Ad Hoc Network: A network of mobile nodes with temporary connection established for a specific purpose *e.g.*, transferring file from one node to another node.

Secure Routing: A way to handle errors and malicious activities that may cause routing stability issues in the design of routing protocols.

Intrusion Detection: A mechanism to monitor network and system related activities for any malicious behavior and policy violation.

Authentication: A way to confirm the truth of any attribute associated with any data or information that has been claimed as true by an entity.

Message Authentication Code (MAC): A small piece of information used to authenticate a message and provide integrity and authenticity of that message.

Non-Repudiation: An assurance that a node cannot deny its authenticity of signing or sending any message that they have originated.

ENDNOTES

[1]   The terms 'node', 'user', 'process' and 'vehicle' have been used interchangeably in our illustration.

[2]   Nonce is an arbitrary number used only once in a cryptographic communication to prevent attacks *e.g.*, replay.

This research was previously published in the Handbook of Research on Modern Cryptographic Solutions for Computer and Cyber Security edited by Brij Gupta, Dharma P. Agrawal, and Shingo Yamaguchi, pages 96-125, copyright year 2016 by Information Science Reference (an imprint of IGI Global).

Chapter 31
A Proactive Approach to Intrusion Detection in Cloud Software as a Service

Baldev Singh
Lyallpur Khalsa College, India

Surya Narayan Panda
Chitkara University Rajpura, India

ABSTRACT

Cloud computing environment is very much malicious intrusion prone hence cloud security is very vital. Existing network security mechanisms face new challenges in the cloud such as DDOS attacks, virtual machine intrusion attacks and malicious user activities. This chapter includes brief introduction about cloud computing, concept of virtualization, cloud security, various DDOS attacks, tools to run these attacks & various techniques to detect these attacks, review of threshold methods used for detection of DDOS attacks & abnormal network behavior and proposed dynamic threshold based algorithmic approach. Although various cloud security measures are prevailing to avoid virtual machine attacks and malicious user activities but these are not foolproof. Hence, new security methods are required to increase users' level of trust in clouds. By scrubbing traffic at major Internet points and backbone connection, a defense line is created for mitigation of DDOS attacks. Dynamic threshold algorithm based approach is proposed as a proactive approach to detect DDOS attacks for achieving secure cloud environment.

INTRODUCTION TO CLOUD COMPUTING

Technology of cloud computing provides a way of using computing and storage resources by using Internet and remote servers. It presents a new way of using remote resources. The usage of computing resources is charged on usage basis where a user contracts services from a service provider by paying according to what it uses. Cloud computing makes it happen to use the applications without particular installation on personal computers, it is only by accessing and using the services by way of Internet. Cloud computing is an enabled service that may be used for various benefits to its like ease of deploying computer and information technology resources for fresh business, a lesser amount of system operating and maintenance costs and lessening of deployment time in any setup.

DOI: 10.4018/978-1-5225-8176-5.ch031

The National Institute of Standard and Technology (NIST) defines Cloud Computing as the model for enabling convenient, on-demand network access to a shared pool of configurable computing resources (e.g., Networks, servers, storage, applications, and services) that can be rapidly provisioned and released with minimal management effort or service provider interaction (Mell & Grance, 2009). Cloud Computing is one of the fastest growing service models on the Internet. Various large scale IT service providers, like Amazon and IBM, share their data centers, by using virtualization concepts, for the public usage of their computational resources. By using cloud computing, the users of cloud can minimize many startup financial overheads as well as obtain an increase in the availability and scalability for their cloud-hosted applications. In addition, cloud users can avail on-demand service with the ease of Pay-As-You-Go subscription.

VIRTUALIZATION

Virtualization is one of the crucial component being used in cloud computing. It becomes a key element to provide a set of dynamically scalable resources such as storage, software, processing power and other computing resources as services to users which could be accessed over the Internet on demand. A user needs only a browser and an Internet connection to use these resources. Virtual machines (VMs) are created within a virtualization layer (Jin et al, 2011). A cloud is built up of numerous host machines these physical machines then run multiple virtual machines, which is what are presented to the end-users.

Virtual machines are only limited in the way that their specifications cannot exceed that of their host machine. A virtual machine is a software implementation of a computing environment in which an operating system (OS) or program can be installed and run. The virtual machine typically emulates a physical computing environment, but requests for CPU, memory, hard disk, network and other hardware resources from the host machine that are managed by a virtualization layer which translates these requests to the underlying physical hardware. Researchers get the ability to test applications, their deployments and upgrades more efficiently by using VMs. They don't need to have multiple OS and installation configurations.

CLOUD SECURITY

Security is one of important issues prevailing in the cloud environment. Cyber attacks against large internet ventures keep on rising and they directly affect the cloud users. Cloud customers (organizations) are questioning the security of moving their computational assets toward the cloud. These improper operations are generally conducted for a number of reasons. Financial gain can also be a motivation to steal valuable information from sensitive organizations such as those in the banking sector. Cyber surveillance operations typically conducted to gather information about financial or industrial adversaries are some of the new trends over the internet. Existing network security mechanisms face new challenges in the cloud such as DDOS attacks (Bhuyan, Kashyap, Bhattacharyya & Kalita, 2013), virtual machine intrusion attacks and malicious user activities. Hence, new security methods (Tao, Hui, Feng & Cheng, 2012), (Subashini & Kavitha,2011) are required to increase users' level of trust in clouds. Presently, cloud service providers implement data encryption for the data centers, virtual firewalls and access control lists.

DDOS ATTACK

A DDOS attack is a malicious attempt to make the resources (a server or a network resource) unavailable to the users usually by blocking or interrupting the services of a host machine to the Internet. DDOS attack took place by using many computers and many Internet connections often distributed globally. Figure 1 shows a simple DDOS attack scenario (Bhadauria, Chaki & Sanyal, 2011), (Weiler, 2002) in which multiple attacking computers are sending streams of malicious packets to victim machine.

DDOS attacks attempt to perform the following malicious operations:

- Control legitimate network traffic by flooding the network with malicious traffic.
- Deny access to a service by way of disrupting communication between legitimate sender and receiver,
- Block the access of a particular service or an individual.

DDOS attacks lead to disruption of services in cloud and is considered as one of the important intrusions in cloud computing. Intrusion detection and prevention systems taxonomy attacks are classified as outside attacks and inside attacks (Vasanthi & Chandrasekar, 2011), (Specht & Lee, 2004). The attacks that come from external origins are called outsider attacks. Insider attacks, involve unauthorized internal users attempting to gain and misuse non-authorized access privileges. Intrusion detection is the mechanism of monitoring computers or networks for unauthorized entry, activity or file modification (Whitman & Mattord, 2011). Attacks may be treated as incidents. Although many incidents are malicious in nature, many others are not; for example, a person might mistype the address of a computer and accidentally attempt to connect to a different system without authorization.

There is an established underground cyber criminal economy which works to achieve their private individual goals best known for their keen interest in spying or for competitive monetary gains, motives that are possible by the use of disruptive technologies like DDOS attack. Thus making the science of DDOS attacks ever evolving and growing in current context in such a manner that a continuous monitoring with sophisticated watchdog capabilities is required as these attacks continues to create online outrages, customer inconvenience and reputation damages across all industries and geographies. The best known victims of recent moves of these DDOS attacks (Udhayan & Anitha, 2009), (Chuiyi,Yizhi, Yuan, Shuoshan & Qin, 2011) and those who have been successfully being able to mitigate such attacks can never get a sound sleep as it is apparent from current incidences of this attack globally.

Figure 1. Distributed Denial-of-Service Attack Scenario

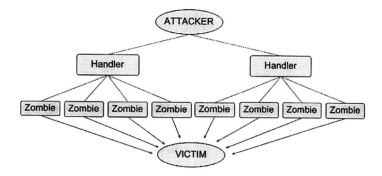

VARIOUS DDOS ATTACKS

DDOS attack results to disruption of services in cloud and is considered as one of the important intrusions in cloud computing (Simon, Rubin, Smith & Trajkovic,2000), (Gupta, Joshi & Misra, 2009). The DDOS attacks ((Mirkovic, 2013) can be classified as under:

- **Bandwidth Attacks:** The common reason of bandwidth attacks is the aspiration to create a severe problem to someone else's infrastructure by way of generating a traffic overload. Bandwidth attacks does vary. These Attacks are anticipated to overflow and consume available resources of the victim (for example: network bandwidth). Some examples of Bandwidth chocking in context of DDOS attacks are TCP SYN Flood, UDP Flood and ICMP Flood (Ning & Han, 2012),(Beardmore, 2013).
- **Protocol Attacks:** Protocol Attacks exploit a specific feature or implementation bug of some protocol installed at the victim for the purpose of consuming maximum amount of its resources to take benefit of protocol intrinsic design. All these attacks require a lot of attackers (zombies) and are mitigated by changing the protocol features. Some examples of popular protocol attacks are as under:
  ◦ Smurf Attack
  ◦ UDP Attack
  ◦ ICMP Attack
  ◦ SYN attack
  ◦ Attack using DNS systems.
  ◦ CGI request attack
  ◦ Attack using spoofed address in ping
  ◦ Authentication server attack etc.
- **Software Vulnerability Attacks:** Software Vulnerability Attacks allows an attacker to exploit a software program design flaw that may be a Land attack, Ping of Death or Fragmentation etc. Vulnerability in software means a weakness which permits an attacker to lessen a system's information assurance. Software vulnerabilities can be into design, implementation and configuration of the software. Vulnerability comprises of three elements that are: system susceptibility, attacker access to the flaw, and capability of attacker to make use of the flaw. To make use of vulnerability, an attacker must have at least one applicable tool or technique that set up the connection to a system flaw. Software vulnerability is also considered as the attack surface. Software vulnerability control is must in computer and network security because of the following reasons:
  ◦ Virus programs are major organs to make the system vulnerable. These programs make use of vulnerabilities in software (operating system and application software) to gain unauthorized access, spread and then harm the system. Intruders also make use of vulnerabilities in software (operating system and application software) to gain unauthorized access of the system, attack other systems, and harm the system. There exists some software that are itself hostile and do damage.
  ◦ Without software vulnerabilities, it is very difficult that viruses would exist and may gain any unauthorized access to the resources and do any harm. Following are some primary tools used for unauthorized access:
    ▪ Network sniffing.

- Trojan horse programs
- Password cracking and
- Man in the middle attacks.

- **SYN Flood Attack: A** SYN flood attack is a form of DOS attack which occurs when a host sends a flood of TCP/SYN packets, frequently with a fake sender address to target's system in an attempt to consume a huge amount of server resources to make the system unresponsive to legitimate traffic (Chuiyi,Yizhi, Yuan, Shuoshan & Qin, 2011). Each of these packets in TCP connection is handled like a connection request by sending a SYN (*synchronize*) message to the server, causing the server to spawn a half-open connection, by sending back a TCP/SYN-ACK packet (known as acknowledgement), and also waiting for a packet in response from the sender address (as a response to the ACK Packet). However, the responses never come because the sender address is fake. Due to these half-open connections, network congestion occurs that saturate the number of available connections that the server is able to make to legitimate requests of the clients.

- **Smurf Attack:** A Smurf attack is a distributed denial-of-service attack in which a system is flooded with spoofed ping messages. These flooded spoofed ping messages create high computer network traffic on the victim's network, which repeatedly make it unresponsive. In this type of attack, ICMP echo request (ping) packets addressed to an IP broadcast address that creates a large number of responses ((CERT, 2000). Hence each host on the subnet replies to the same ping request and the huge responses can consume all available network bandwidth, particularly if data is appended to the ping request. Large number of pings and the resulting echoes can make the network unresponsive for legitimate traffic and prevent legitimate traffic from being transmitted during the attack.

- **ICMP Flood:** An ICMP Flood is like the other flooding attack that sends peculiarly large number of ICMP packets (Udhayan & Anitha 2009). This flood of packets can overwhelm a target server that attempts to process every incoming ICMP request, and can be the cause of denial-of-service condition for the target server. This attack is accomplished by broadcasting a lot of ICMP packets, usually the ping packets. The main aim to send large amount of data to the target server is to slow down it so much and get disconnected due to timeouts. Mainly, Ping flood attacks causes the saturation of a network by sending a continuous series of ICMP echo requests over a high-bandwidth connection to a target system on a lower bandwidth connection.

- **Ping of Death:** A ping of death is a denial of service attack that sends a malformed or otherwise malicious ping to a computer. Normally a ping is of 32 bytes in size. This type of attack is caused by an attacker intentionally sending an IP packet larger than the 65,536 bytes allowed by the IP protocol. When such a packet is sent to a system with a vulnerable TCP/IP stack, it will cause the system to crash. Most modern day firewalls are capable of filtering such oversized packets. Now a different type of ping attack are prevailing like ping flooding that simply floods the victim with so much ping traffic that normal traffic fails to reach the system.

- **LAND Attack:** A LAND (Local Area Network Denial) attack is a kind of denial of service attack that consists of sending a special poison (spoofed packet) to a computer, causing it to lock up. A LAND attack consists of a stream of SYN attack with IP spoofing that occurs when an attacker sends spoofed SYN packets containing the IP address of the victim as both the destination and the source IP address. Therefore the receiving system responds by sending the SYN-ACK packet to itself, creating an empty connection that lasts until the idle timeout value is reached. Figure 2

Figure 2. Local Area Network Denial attack

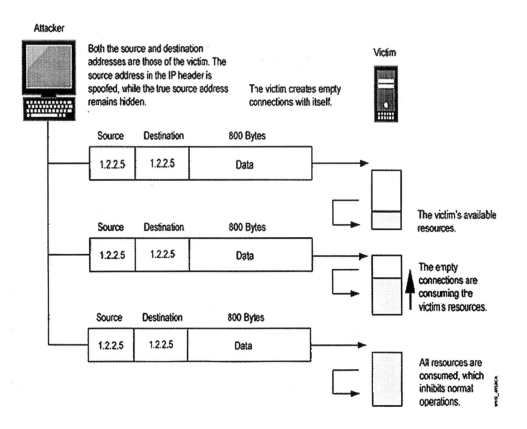

shows local area network denial of service attack. If the system is flooded with such empty connections, it can overwhelm the system that may result a denial of service.

- **Teardrop:** Teardrop attack is an Operating System specific denial-of-service (DOS) attacks these attacks exploit the reassembly of fragmented IP packets. The Teardrop, though, is an old attack that relies on poor TCP/IP implementation that is still around. This kind of attack involves sending fragmented packets to a target machine. Since the machine receiving such packets cannot reassemble them due to a bug in TCP/IP fragmentation reassembly, the packets overlap one another, crashing the target network device. In an IP header, one of the fields is the "fragment offset" field, specifying the starting position, or offset, of the data enclosed in a fragmented packet relative to the data in the original packet. In case the sum of the offset and size of one fragmented packet varies from that of the next fragmented packet, the packets overlap. If this occurs, a system vulnerable to teardrop attacks is unable to reassemble the packets and results in a denial-of-service.

TOOLS FOR RUNNING DISTRIBUTED DENIAL OF SERVICE ATTACK

This section describes the distributed denial of service attack tools that are used by an attacker. These tools facilitate an attacker to coordinate and execute the attack. These kinds of tools overwhelmed the Internet in February 2000. Various distributed tools like Trinoo, TFN, Stacheldraht, Shaft, and TFN2K have become technically more advanced and that is why these are more difficult to detect (Simon et al. 2009). These are briefed below:

- **Trinoo:** Trinoo ia set of computer programs used to conduct a DDOS attack. Trinoo is well-known for permitting attackers to leave a message in a folder known as cry_baby. The file is self replicating and is modified on a regular basis as long as port 80 is active. A compromised host is used by the attacker to compile a list of machines that can be compromised. Most of this course of action is performed automatically from the compromised host, It uses TCP is used for communication between the attacker and the control master program. Master program then communicates with the attack daemons using UDP packets. Trinoo's attack daemons implement UDP Flood attacks against the target victim (Faizal, Zaki, Shahrin, Robiah & Rahayu, 2010).
- **Tribe Flood Network (TFN):** Tribe Flood Network (TFN) program causes a DDOS attack. It is a distributed denial of service tool that allows an attacker to use several hosts at once to flood a target. Tribe Flood Network supports four different types of floods. These are: ICMP Echo flood, UDP Flood, SYN Flood, and Smurf attack. With this tool, client and server use ICMP echo reply packets to communicate with each other. The attacker uses the TFN client to control the remote servers and initiate the denial of service attack. The spoofed source IP address and source ports can be randomized to make the attack more widespread victim (Faizal, Zaki, Shahrin, Robiah & Rahayu, 2010).
- **Stacheldraht:** Stacheldraht acts as a distributed denial of service attack and is based on the TFN attack. Stacheldraht uses an encrypted TCP connection for communication between the attacker and master control program. TCP and ICMP are used for setting up communication between the master control program and attack daemons and there exists an automatic update technique for the attack daemons. Stacheldraht tool supports four different types of floods. These are: ICMP, UDP Flood, SYN Flood, and Smurf attack.
- **Shaft:** Shaft is used in distributed denial of service (DDOS) attacks. Shaft combines well-known denial of service attacks like TCP SYN flood, smurf, and UDP flood with a distributed and coordinated approach to create a powerful program. These programs further act to slow the network communications to a crushing state. Shaft attack tool includes a handler and an agent. Here the attacker is required to install the Shaft handler and agent manually. The attacker controls the handlers through Transmission Control Protocol (TCP) port 20432 that can control many agent hosts. The handler uses User Data Protocol (UDP) port 18753, to communicate with the agents, and the agents responds by using UDP port 20433. These agents perform DDOS attacks using UDP flood attacks, TCP SYN flood attacks and Internet Control Message Protocol (ICMP) flood attacks against one or more target systems. The agent transmits a large number of UDP packets to the target system for flooding purpose.
- **TFN2K:** TFN2K uses masters to exploit the resources of a number of agents in order to coordinate an attack against one or more designated targets. The TFN2K distributed denial of service tool consists of a client/server architecture. In this mechanism, the client is used to connect to master servers, which can then perform specific attacks victim machines. ICMP, UDP and TCP packets are used by this tool. Various commands are sent from the client to the master server within the data fields of ICMP, UDP, and TCP packets including commands to flood a target machine or set of target machines within a specified address range. The master server parses all UDP, TCP, and ICMP echo reply packets for encrypted commands. These flood attacks cause the target machine

to slow down because of the processing required to handle the incoming packets, leaving little or no network bandwidth.

- **Trinity v3:** Trinity is a distributed denial-of-service attack tool that intruders can use to instigate an enormous IP flood against a victim's targeted system, much the way its predecessors TFN and Trin00 do. This tool causes various floods such as TCP fragment floods, TCP established floods, TCP RST packet floods, and TCP random flag packet floods to leave little or no network bandwidth.
- **Knight:** Knight is a very lightweight yet powerful IRC based attack tool. It provides SYN attacks, UDP Flood attacks, and an urgent pointer flooder. It is designed to run on Windows operating systems and has features such as an automatic updater via http or ftp, a checksum generator and more. It uses Trojan horse program called Back Orifice for installation in the target host. The protocols used by Knight are TCP, UDP.
- **LOIC:** LOIC is another powerful anonymous IRC based attacking tol. It operates in three methods of attack: TCP, UDP and HTTP. LOIC uses TCP, UDP, and HTTP.

The Table 1 shows a brief statistics of various attacks.

SCRUBBING CENTER

Understanding the component of a scrubbing center is important here. It is however essentially a combination of software and hardware based algorithms recipes that analyze the incoming envelop of packets and check the integrity of the outgoing envelop of data passing through multiple subnets reaching a particular set of IP addresses. By scrubbing traffic at major Internet points and backbone connection, a

Table 1. DDOS attack statistics

Year	Attack Description
2014	114 percent increase in average peak bandwidth of DDOS attacks in Q1 vs. Q4 2013. The Media and Entertainment industry was the target of the majority of malicious attacks. (Morton, 2014)
2013	DDOS attack on stock exchange websites in London.
2012	DDOS Attack on Canadian Political Party Elections and on US and UK Government Sites
2011	DDOS attack on Sony.
2010	DDOS—December 3-5, 2010 on PayPal.
2009	DDOS flooding attacks on South Korea and the United States in July 2009 against government news media and financial websites.
2008	DDOS Attack on BBC, Amazon.com and eBuy.
2007	Estonia Cyber Attack
2006	Target US Banks for financial gain.
2004	Attack on SCO Group website to make it inaccessible to valid users.
2003	Attack on SCO and Microsoft.
2002	DDOS flooding attack thru Domain Name System (DNS) service.
2001	DNS servers attack as reflectors. DOS attack on Irish Government's Department of Finance server. The target was Register.com
2000	One of the first major DDOS flooding on Yahoo

(CSA, 2014), (Tripathi, Gupta, Mishra & Veluru, 2013)

defense line is created for mitigation of DDOS attacks. In fact they take advantage of bandwidth density and traffic routing options with globally distributed options. They choose more to change direction of traffic and swallow the volume of data rather than just block or filter the data packet as the difference between the good and malicious packet is difficult to assess. Hence, they are able to mitigate the flood of UDP (20) or any other type of traffic artifact creating DDOS attacks.

All cloud service providers cannot afford to build their own scrubbing centers as they need to focus on their core business rather than technological issues of maintaining and defending themselves and moreover, even all cloud service providers can hire third party scrubbing solutions. Not all cloud service providers can maintain following components/processes with high quality and ensure high availability of services for themselves and their customers.

- Detection and Monitoring Centers.
- Threat correlation services.
- Threat alert system.
- Threat identification service with false positives recognition.
- Threat rate of change.
- Threat severity analysis.
- Threat heuristics at every layer.

Hence, when a centralized data cleansing stations are deployed having all possible capabilities as mentioned above where traffic is scrutinized and mischievous traffic (DDOS, known susceptibilities and exploits) are moved or absorbed, there is normally an assumption that a volumetric attack bandwidth consumption can be overcome by adding more and more bandwidth, and swallow all data traffic thereby continuing the services, but it can happen for how much and how long is a question.

NEED OF SCRUBBING CENTERS FOR INTRUSION DETECTION

Scrubbing centers (Ted, 2013) having sophisticated processes that are often used in large enterprises, such as ISP and Cloud Service and Infrastructure Providers, and they often prefer to off-ramp traffic movement to an out of path integrated data cleansing location end-points. When under attack adversary, the whole traffic is redirected (typically using DNS or BGP) to the cleaning/scrubbing focal point where an attack mitigation system mitigates the attacks and passes clean data traffic back to the network for distribution system. The scrubbing center must be adequately equipped to sustain both low and high volumetric floods at the network and application layers, with RFC Compliance checks, with the known vulnerabilities and zero day anomalies addressed. These centers must be able to utilize a multiple diverse range of global network carriers, including Asian, American and European carriers to be really successful in building a defense line stretching beyond single set boundaries. Then, there are multiple ways in which workload management with respect to consolidation of the computing power and storage is done. Moreover, effectively partitioning of the computing capacity of the data centers into multiple tiers, which would improve the nodes utilization and responsiveness for parallel workload is a challenge more so, when there is a mix of solicited and unsolicited traffics of workload is coming into the data center, then the difficulty of realization of parallelism to monitor all ends of the data center effectively remains an issue, leading into a difficult condition in harnessing the heuristics of the scheduling algorithms in running the jobs of data center infected by malicious traffic until fully-meshed with redundancy for 100% availability is incorporated into the defense solution work to our advantage. Since, the target of the any DDOS attackers is normally to block or oversubscribe a resources in such a way that it leads to degraded service performance time, long response time matching the demand of processing the incoming workload remains a constant headache. Many methods have been evolved over a considerable time now and all these methods or technologies that claim to safeguard us from DDOS attacks also consider the various possible correlations that might be working to advantage of the attackers. The most common forces behind DDOS attacks are shown in the Figure 3 (Specht & Lee, 2004):

The following sections takes us to the point where we can now discuss the possible factors that must be observed, monitored and reported for synthesis of such attacks. However, it must be done by using multinational group of professionals with localized understanding of technical environment, cultures and practices to provide consultation and support in multiple languages to the customers so that DDOS attacks are thwarted with involvement of all the stakeholders of the network having protection scope which includes ICMP floods (Udhayan & Anitha, 2009), UDP floods, SYN floods, application level floods, CC attacks (Chuiyi, Yizhi, Yuan, Shuoshan & Qin, 2011), (CERT, 2000), reflective attack (Wang, Schulzrinne & Henning, 2004), degradation of service attacks and last but not least unintentional DDOS outrage.

REVIEW OF TECHNIQUES USED FOR DETECTION OF ATTACKS AND ABNORMAL BEHAVIOR IN CLOUD

There are various studies that have explained the concept of solutions available for providing security with mitigation algorithms for cloud network, The Intrusion detection system (IDS) (Vasanthi & Chandrasekar, 2011), (Patel et. Al, 2012) are first to be debated and implemented as it is known fact the cloud based networks and services are prone to suffer from malicious attacks because of their inherent characteristics of being accessible globally any time and also due to the frequent changes in topology and development of Internet of things as well as because of landscape nature of Internet. Of particular concern, it is the denial of service attacks that makes the service unavailable to its intended cloud users.

Figure 3. Common Forces behind DDOS Attacks

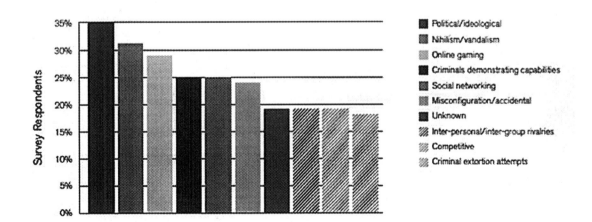

As per our systematic review of related works in the field of intrusion/malicious attack detection (Jagadeeshraj, George & Thenmozhi, 2013), There are many techniques which can be used to detect intruders or malicious behavior in the cloud network are reviewed. These techniques have their own negatives and positives To comprehend this field of IDS we must look at what each technique holds in its favour and what trade-offs it must make to achieve its goals particularly to make out the abnormal behavior which seems to be DDOS attack.

Faizal et al. has used the threshold based intrusion detection system. Two techniques can be used in selecting the appropriate threshold that differentiates between the malign network traffic and abnormal network traffic. These techniques are based on the static threshold value and dynamic threshold value. Dynamic threshold based technique is more complex than the technique based on static threshold. Dynamic threshold value is based on training or priori knowledge of the network activity, after that the threshold is selected (Faizal, Zaki, Shahrind, Robiah & Rahayu, 2010). According to Faizal et al, it is time consuming process to generate priori knowledge required for generating the dynamic threshold. Their study is based on Fast attack detection mechanism. Shahrin et al. has proposed a framework of fast attack detection. The framework is based on the fast attack detection from two perspectives which are Attack Perspective and the Victim Perspective. Faizal et al. use the framework of fast attack detection at the earliest as they are more hazardous for the network. Their technique is based on the victim perspective of fast attack detection. According to Faizal et. al., fast attack can be defined as attacks that make connections within few seconds and it uses the huge volume of packet. According to Faizal et. al., the work for fast attack detection is mainly based on distributed denial of service attack. The selection of right feature selection is important for detection of attack. The features may also include some extraneous features that are to be treated as spurious features and inadvertently increase the computational issues which include memory space, time and CPU cycle and hence may cause decrease of accuracy of attack detection. The features used by (Faizal, Zaki, Shahrind, Robiah & Rahayu, 2010). in the detection of fast attack includes Timestamp (time to send the packet), Duration of connection, IP address of host, Connection protocol, Status flog of connection, Source and destination services and number of connections in Attack-Victim connection. The research work of Faizal et al. is based on static threshold to detect attacks mainly fast attack and has considered not other main protocols like UDP and ICMP for intrusion detection.

The profile based network based network IDS proposed by (Gupta, Kumar & Abraham, 2013) is based on dynamic threshold. They have proposed the concept of privileged domain in which each virtual machine is in privileged domain. In this architecture, each virtual machine in the cloud network is filtered on their IP address based in the privileged domain. The attacks are detected on the basis of profile of each virtual machine (VM) in the cloud network. VM profile is beneficial to detect attacks as traffic of VM is not detected for each attack, only those attacks are detected which are frequent in nature. Although (Gupta, Kumar & Abraham, 2013) claimed the dynamic threshold profiling but no factor analysis for signature design is used and the proposed rank based detection is irrelevant.

Among researchers that proposed static threshold based intrusion detection system are Kim et al. (2004), Gates and Damon (2005), Leckie et al (2002) and Faizal et al (2009). Network IDS technique proposed by (Abdollah, Masud, Shahrin & Robiah, 2009) has used the concept of static threshold although dynamic threshold is better solution. The threshold is used to differentiate between normal traffic and abnormal traffic in the network. This threshold value is acquired by using observation and experimental technique and the verified by using statistical process control approach (Abdollah et al, 2009).

The research work of L. Jun-Ho et.al. has presented in the (Ho et.al, 2011) is based on intrusion detection at multiple levels. As above research work has proposed intrusion detection on basis of fast attacks and slow attacks, the later is based on security implementation at multiple levels. (Ho et.al, 2011) proposed different anomaly levels in cloud environment that are authentication, authorization and accounting (AAA). They also proposed three security levels for effective intrusion detection system that are High, Medium and Low. In case of High level of security requirement, they has suggested that- the patterns of all the known attacks are to be considered and the requisite rules for higher level security are to be implemented. They were of the opinion that when the user access the cloud environment first time, the multi level intrusion detection system (IDS) must judge the anomaly level of the user. For judgment of anomaly level, (Ho et.al, 2011) suggested various parameters like vulnerable ports attack, IP address coverage of user, attack success possibilities, attack occurrence possibilities etc. They suggested risk points for different security groups. If the risk points are greater than six, the anomaly level is of High level, risk points between 3-5 (both inclusive), the anomaly level is of medium level and for risk points 0-2, the anomaly level is of low level and accordingly IDS is required to be imposed.

A VMM based IDS has proposed by Hai Jin et al., which is based on virtual machine monitoring. This virtual machine monitor (VMM) in cloud computing environment has the concept of customizable defense system known as VMFence which is used to monitor network flow and file integrity and suggested a network defense and protection of file integrity in the cloud environment. They have implemented VMFence on Xen (open source VM platform) for intrusion detection and prevention system in cloud computing environment (Jin, Xiang & Zou, 2011). This system monitors the attack patterns coming through all VMs that are connected to the privileged machine.

TRESHHOLD ANALYSIS

As per our systematic review of related works in the field of intrusion/malicious attack detection (Jagadeeshraj, George& Thenmozhi, 2013), there are many techniques which can be used to detect intruders or malicious behavior in the cloud network. Each of these techniques/frameworks holds their own merits and demerits. In fact, there are three major techniques which are: misuse detection, anomaly detection and specific detection like DDOS attack. However, to understand this field we must look at what each technique holds in its favour and what trade-offs it must make to achieve its goals in case of using some threshold technique for identification of abnormal behavior which seems to be DDOS at first glance.

RESEARCH GAPS

Various research gaps are identified in the review literature. These are as under:

- It is complex to detect the DDOS attacks as well as all other such kinds of attacks of every virtual machine (VM).
- Dynamic systems like cloud or adversity causing systems cannot work on such single threshold and detection decision making may be faulty.
- It cannot work on such multi-range threshold systems as the range may be discrete or continuous and may be changing with time.

- Difficult to calculate accurately as ranges may change with pattern which is difficult to realize.
- Threshold may go wrong due to erratic behavior of matrices used.
- Statistically cannot handle extreme high and low values that may lead to wrong calculations.

RESEARCH PROBLEM

Various studies have explained the concept of various solutions available for providing security and solutions in cloud network. DDOS attacks detection approaches, which are based on either anomaly based or signature based, are not robust and reliable. The cloud based networks and services are prone to suffer from malicious behavior because of their inherent characteristics of being accessible globally and due to the frequent changes in topology & development of Internet of things as well as because of landscape nature of Internet. Of particular concern, it is denial of service attacks that makes the service unavailable to its intended cloud users.

Although considerable effort has been made to understand, detect and prevent these attacks, since it is a continuously evolving as technology, new ways are found by anti development sources to compromise the Cloud based Systems, therefore methods that are based on single, multi range thresholds for detection, require constant upgradation as well refinement in terms of the algorithms for accuracy and robustness.

The threshold based algorithms for detection of DDOS attack must always numerically stable as well as must not depend on predefined thresholds.

The current intrusion detection systems mentioned in the review literature, overlooks certain aspects of calculating the threshold for identification of subspace set of abnormal behavior with the whole pattern of VM profile and this is based only frequency calculation happening in particular set of time line, which is not capable of further mathematical treatment or insight and it is more useful in qualitative cases, however, it makes more sense, if relative frequency based threshold could have been used which would have also considered the total outcome of normal and abnormal events in the VM profile. It would be more accurate to consider those methods that would fine in extreme cases when values are either too large or too small or the dataset is skewed due to particular pattern of events. Therefore, we propose variance based mechanism to overcome the demerits of existing solutions, calculate the thresholds more accurately and to achieve our objective of research. Our goal is to propose *a proactive approach to detect DDOS attacks for achieving secure cloud environment.*

In our research work we intend to analyze methods that can deal with

skewed datasets (the ratio of data-row of normal behaviour (benign traffic) to abnormal behaviour (malignant traffic) rows in the profiling session of virtual machines) (trace files or profile files) for detection of DDOS attacks, since the thresholds cannot be static in nature (the statistical behaviour) in any way in cloud environment for parameters that are critical to analyse for identification of DDOS Attacks. The signature based and anomaly based DDOS mechanism is proposed which encompasses the use of dynamic and multi threshold based algorithmic approach.

Secure communication and data transmission in any distributed computing is required. Cloud computing is a shared facility and is accessed remotely, it is vulnerable to various attacks like host and network based attacks and therefore requires immediate attention. Hence there is need of secure cloud network. There is ample scope of the proposed solution in the cloud computing environment as network attacks are glaring day by day. Our research will focus on early detection of network attacks, robust and minimum complex system.

Table 2. Review of Threshold methods used for detection of DDOS attacks and abnormal behavior

Method	Merits	Demerits	Research Papers Referred
Static Threshold	Absolute threshold values easy to implement for intrusion detection. Low computational complexity	• Taken only minimum features for threshold detection. • Static Threshold. • Not applied on UDP and ICMP protocols for ID. • Fix value range is never close to real systems that changing every day, this method is not able to consider differential or cumulative threshold for giving response to adversity in real time.	Faizal, Zaki, Shahrin, Robiah & Rahayu, 2010
Dynamic Threshold	This method considers the dynamic values for detection of intrusion. This method is not having much difficulty in measurement e.g. method based on average, mode, frequency are easy to implement.	• No factor analysis for signature design. • Rank based detection irrelevant. • How signature are designed-Not clear. • Reactive, not proactive • Partial profile of VMs • Only no. of packets considered; No other parameters like bandwidth of cpu, n/w etc. • Threshhold may go wrong due to erratic behaviour of metrices used. • Statistically cannot handle extreme high and low values that may lead to wrong calculations. • May calculate wrong threshold, thereby increase the false alarm rate especially distributed change point detection.(DFA or deviation from Average)	Kumar, Ajith & Abraham, 2013
Single Threshold value based method to identify the fast attacks	Easy and Simple to implement. Clear cut demarcation of normal and abnormal behavior events. Fast attack framework with a minimum set of feature selection. Identify a fast attack at the early stage.	• Single Threshold. • Static Threshold. • Dynamic systems like cloud or adversity causing systems cannot work on such single threshold and detection decision making may be faulty. • Selecting inaccurate threshold value will cause an excessive false alarm especially if the value is too low or too high.	Faial M. A., et. al., 2009
Multilevel intrusion detection system and log management in cloud computing environment	Efficient resource utilization. Economical.	• Enormous log entries so not cost effective; • Lots of rules for Ranking of risks and file monitoring modules require high consideration for absolute solution but reduction in resources will be a question. • Each VM in one security group (H/M/L). Migration of VM from one security group to another is only judgment basis.	L. Jun-Ho et.al., 2011
VMM based IPS in cloud computing	It can monitor n/w packets and file integrity in real time. Functional for a virtualization based Cloud computing, particularly for multi core CPU	• Extra computationally complex as it monitors the attack patterns coming thru all VMs that are connected to the privileged machine. • Due to this heavy workload on privileged machine, the n/w will chock and packet drop rate increases.	Jin, Xiang & Zou, 2011.

PROPOSED METHOD

For the best evaluation of proposed algorithms we shall formulate an experimental framework. This proposed experimental framework will use the Cloud simulator for experimentation purpose. Various aspects to be considered in the proposed method are discussed below:

- **Create Broker:** Once the cloud simulation setup is done, first thing is to create broker (user base). It submits tasks to the data center. A broker is responsible for mediating between users and service providers depending on users' quality of service (QoS) requirements and it also deploys service tasks across clouds. The broker may be become malicious and may cause security concerns in terms of submitting malicious workload leading to DDOS.
- **Create Datacenter:** A data center (Meng, Iyengar, Arun, Rouvellou, Liu, Lee, Palanisamy & Tang, 2012), which is home to the computation power and storage, is central to cloud computing

and contains thousands of devices. Datacenter models the core infrastructure level services (hardware, software) offered by resource providers in a cloud computing environment.

The algorithm for identifying the various thresholds for each component of the cloud network is maintained by the health monitoring system, which is centralized watchdog for the network in question. The HMS maintains daily average of each parameter which represents the performance of the network and other aspects related to the degradation of the network performance, if there are too many VM migrations or too much workload deliveries and throughput is changing in erratic manner, there is huge variation which is calculated continuously by HMS using proposed algorithms.

The above method can be used for calculating the number of VM Migrations (Thresholds per day) for identification of DDOS attack (Beardmore, 2013). Migration of virtual machines improves performance, manageability and fault tolerance of systems but it may also be sign of some issue relating to DDOS attacks as unnecessary migration may occur. VM migration policy helps balance system load, which may be under threat due to adversity.

Although considerable efforts have been made to understand, detect and prevent these attacks, yet because of continuous evolving nature of cloud we have to remain on our toes and try to find out means and tools which can eliminate this malicious threat. Since it is a continuously evolving as technology, new ways are found by anti-development sources to compromise the cloud based systems, therefore methods that are based on single, multi range thresholds for detection need constant upgradation as well refinement in terms of the algorithms accuracy and robustness for identification of DDOS attacks. The threshold based algorithms for detection of DDOS attack must always numerically stable as well as must not depend on predefined thresholds.

The current DDOS attacks detection systems mentioned in the previous works (Vasanthi & Chandrasekar, 2011) overlook certain aspects of calculating the threshold for identification of subspace set of abnormal behavior with the whole pattern of VM profile and this is based on frequency calculation happening in particular set of time line, which is not capable of further mathematical treatment or insight and it is more useful in qualitative cases, however, it makes more sense, if relative frequency based threshold could have been used which would have also considered the total outcome of normal and abnormal events in the VM profile. It would be more accurate to consider those methods that would fine in extreme cases when values are either too large or too small or the dataset is skewed due to particular pattern of events.

Therefore, we propose variance based methods that can be used to overcome the demerits of existing solutions, calculate the thresholds more accurately and to achieve our objective of research. Hence, In pursuance of this research work it must be persuaded by all the stake holders to analyze methods that can deal with large skewed datasets ((benign traffic) to abnormal behaviour (malignant traffic) for detection of DDOS attacks, since the thresholds cannot be static in nature in any way in cloud environment for parameters that are critical to analyze for identification of DDOS Attacks.

CONCLUSION

From the systematic review of all the studies done in the context of the DDOS attack we can expect that there will be increase in the frequency of the DDOS attacks due to multifold increase in the online activities and wireless Internet of things. It is also apparent that the very idea of building defending lines of action against such act of destruction depends on computations coming out of the stream of the traffic at different ends of the network of networks. We have also understood that both the internal and external anatomy of the data center matters and also how to structure architecturally to measure the volume of traffic is the main critical point. If somehow the intruders are able to launch a slow attack it must be detectable or if it is a sudden flood of packets then one must be able to mitigate the flood to have clean traffic. This is not possible unless there is continuous monitoring which includes the mapping of threats cope with the understanding correlations of all the factors contributing to the adversary. Therefore, the thresholds of finding inflection points where the traffic changes to malicious is essential to successful running of data centers in cloud in thwarting the DDOS attacks.

REFERENCES

Abdollah, Masud, Shahrin, Robiah, & Siti Rahayu. (2009). Threshold verification using Statistical Approach for Fast Attack Detection. *Intl. Journal of Computer Science and Information Security*, 2(1), 1–8.

Advisory, C. E. R. T. (2010). *SYN Flooding and IP Spoofing Attacks*. CERT® Coordination Center Software Engineering Institute, Carnegie Mellon. Retrieved from http://www.cert.org/advisories/CA-1996-21.html

Beardmore, K. (2013). *The Truth about DDoS Attacks: Part 1*. Retrieved from TheCarbon60 Blog: http://www.carbon60.com/the-truth-about-DDOS-attacks-part-1/

Bhadauria, R. C. R., Chaki, N., & Sanyal, S. (2011). *A survey on security issues in cloud computing*. Retrieved December 5, 2014 from http://arxiv.org/abs/1109.5388

Chuiyi, X., Yizhi, Z., Yuan, B., Shuoshan, L., & Qin, X. (2011). *A Distributed Intrusion Detection System against flooding Denial of Services attacks*. 13th International Conference on, Advanced Communication Technology (ICACT).

Cloud Security Alliance. (2010). *Top Threats to Cloud Computing*. Retrieved from http://www.cloud-securityalliance.org/topthreats/csathreats.v1.0.pdf

DDOS Attacks. (n.d.). Retrieved from http://www.DDOSattacks.biz/DDOS-101/glossary/scrubbing-center/

Ding & Yeung. (2002). *User Profiling for Intrusion Detection Using Dynamic and Static Behavioral Models*. Springer Berlin Heidelberg.

Faizal, M.A., Zaki, M.M., Shahrin, S., Robiah, Y., & Rahayu, S.S. (2010). Statistical Approach for Validating Static Threshold in Fast Attack Detection. *Journal of Advanced Manufacturing*.

Gupta, Joshi, & Misra (2000). Defending against Distributed Denial of Service Attacks: Issues and Challenges. *Information Security Journal: A Global Perspective, 18*(5), 224-247.

Gupta, S., Kumar, P., & Abraham, A. (2013). A Profile Based Network Intrusion Detection and Prevention System for Securing Cloud Environment. *International Journal of Distributed Sensor Networks*, *2013*, 364575. doi:10.1155/2013/364575

Institute, I. S. (2015). *DDOS Attack Categorization, University of Southern California. DDOS Bechmarks*. Retrieved December 11, 2014 from http://www.isi.edu/~mirkovic/bench

Jagadeeshraj, V.S., Lijoy, C. G., & Thenmozhi, S. (2013). Attaining Pre-Eminent Cloud Security Using Intrusion Detection Systems. *International Journal of Emerging Technology and Advanced Engineering, 3*(2), 214-219.

Jin, H., Xiang, G., Zou, D., Wu, S., Zhao, F., Li, M., & Zheng, W. (2011). A VMM-based intrusion prevention system in cloud computing environment. *The Journal of Supercomputing, 66*(3), 1133–1151. doi:10.100711227-011-0608-2

Jun-Ho, Min-Woo, Jung-Ho, & Tai-Myoung. (2011). Multi-level intrusion detection system and log management in cloud computing. In *Proceedings of the13th International Conf.* Academic Press.

Mell & Grance. (2009). *The NIST Definition of Cloud Computing version 15.* National Institutes of Standards and Technology (NIST), Information Technology Laboratory -Intrusion Detection. Retrieved December 5,2014 from http://en.wikipedia.org/wiki/Intrusion_detection_system

Meng, S., Iyengar, A. K., Rouvellou, I.M., Liu, Lee, Palanisamy, B., & Tang. (2012). Reliable State Monitoring in Cloud Datacenters. In *Proceedings of IEEE 5th International Conference on Cloud Computing* (CLOUD). IEEE.

Monowar,, H., Bhuyan, H. J., Kashyap, D. K., Bhattacharyya, & Kalita. (2013). Detecting Distributed Denial of Service Attacks: Methods, Tools and Future Directions. *The Computer Journal.*

Ning, S., & Han, Q. (2012). Design and implementation of DDOS attack and defense testbed. *International Conference on Wavelet Active Media Technology and Information Processing (ICWAMTIP),* 2012, 220-223. 10.1109/ICWAMTIP.2012.6413478

Patel, A., Taghavi, M., & Bakhtiyari, K. (2012). An intrusion detection and prevention system in cloud computing: A systematic review. *Journal of Network and Computer Applications.* doi:10.1016/j.jnca.2012.08.007

Simon, Rubin, Smith, & Trajkovic. (2000). *Distributed Denial of Service Attacks.* Retrieved from http://www2.ensc.sfu.ca/~ljilja/papers/smc00_edited.pdf

Specht, S. M., & Lee, R. B. (2004). Distributed Denial of Service: Taxonomies of Attacks, Tools, and Countermeasures. *In Proceedings of the International Workshop on Security in Parallel and Distributed Systems.* San Francisco, CA: Academic Press.

Subashini, S., & Kavitha, V. (2011). A survey on security issues in service delivery models of cloud computing. *Journal of Network and Computer Applications, 34*(1), 1–11. doi:10.1016/j.jnca.2010.07.006

Tripathi, S., Gupta, B., Almomani, A., Mishra, A., & Veluru, S. (2013). Hadoop Based Defense Solution to Handle Distributed Denial of Service (DDOS) Attacks. *Journal of Information Security, 4*(03), 150–164. doi:10.4236/jis.2013.43018

Udhayan, J.; Anitha, R. 2009). *Demystifying and Rate Limiting ICMP hosted DoS/DDOS Flooding Attacks with Attack Productivity Analysis.* Advance Computing Conference IACC 2009.

Vasanthi, S., & Chandrasekar, S. (2011). A study on network intrusion detection and prevention system current status and challenging issues. *3rd International Conference on Advances in Recent Technologies in Communication and Computing (ARTCom 2011).* 10.1049/ic.2011.0075

Wang, B-T., & Schulzrinne, H. (2004). An IP traceback mechanism for reflective DoS attacks. *Canadian Conference on Electrical and Computer Engineering* (vol. 2, pp. 901-904). Academic Press.

Weiler. (2002). Honeypots for Distributed Denial of Service Attacks. In *Proceedings of Eleventh IEEE International Workshops on Enabling Technologies: Infrastructure for Collaborative Enterprises*. IEEE.

Xia, Du, Cao, & Chen. (2012). *An Algorithm of Detecting and Defending CC Attack in Real Time*. International Conference on Industrial Control and Electronics Engineering (ICICEE).

KEY TERMS AND DEFINITIONS

Cloud Computing: Cloud Computing defined as a model for enabling convenient, on-demand network access to a shared pool of configurable computing resources that can be rapidly provisioned and released with minimal management effort or service provider interaction.

Cloud Computing Security: Cloud computing security is defined as a set of control-based technologies and policies that ensure the protection of data applications, information, and infrastructure used in cloud computing.

DDOS Attack: DDOS attack is a malicious attempt to make the resources of a server/network unavailable to the users usually by blocking or interrupting the services of a host machine to the Internet.

Intrusion Detection System: Intrusion Detection System is a security technology that monitors a network for any suspicious activity or policy violations and produces a report to the concerned authority.

Virtualization: Virtualization is a key element of cloud computing that provides a set of dynamically scalable resources such as storage, software, processing power and other computing resources as services to users which could be accessed over the Internet on demand.

Virtual Machine: A virtual machine emulates a physical computing environment but requests for CPU, memory, hard disk, network and other hardware resources from the underlying host machine.

Vulnerability: Vulnerability can be defined as an intrinsic weakness or absence of a protection that could be exploited by an attacker.

This research was previously published in Achieving Enterprise Agility through Innovative Software Development edited by Amitoj Singh, pages 287-305, copyright year 2015 by Information Science Reference (an imprint of IGI Global).

Chapter 32
Cryptography in Big Data Security

Navin Jambhekar
S. S. S. K. R. Innani Mahavidyalaya Karanja, India

Chitra Dhawale
P. R. Pote College of Engineering and Management, India

ABSTRACT

Information security is a prime goal for every individual and organization. The travelling from client to cloud server can be prone to security issues. The big data storages are available through cloud computing system to facilitate mobile client. The information security can be provided to mobile client and cloud technology with the help of integrated parallel and distributed encryption and decryption mechanism. The traditional technologies include the plaintext stored across cloud and can be prone to security issues. The solution provided by applying the encrypted data upload and encrypted search. The clouds can work in collaboration; therefore, the encryption can also be done in collaboration. Some part of encryption handle by client and other part handled by cloud system. This chapter presents the security scenario of different security algorithms and the concept of mobile and cloud computing. This chapter precisely defines the security features of existing cloud and big data system and provides the new framework that helps to improve the data security over cloud computing and big data security system.

1. INTRODUCTION

1.1 Background

Nowadays due to recent technological development, the amount of data generated by internet, social networking sites, sensor networks, healthcare applications, Banking Sector and many other companies, is drastically increasing day by day. All the enormous measure of data produced from various sources in multiple formats with very high speed (Bagheri & Jahanshahi, 2015) is referred as big data. The term big data (Bosch et al, 2014; Chan, 2009) is defined as "a new generation of technologies and architectures,

DOI: 10.4018/978-1-5225-8176-5.ch032

designed to economically separate value from very large volumes of a wide variety of data, by enabling high-velocity capture, discovery and analysis".

From this definition, we can say that big data are reflected by 3V's, which are, volume, velocity and variety. A common theme of big data is that the data are diverse, i.e., they may contain text, audio, image, or video etc. This big data is stored on cloud and to attain the big data security over cloud computing, the mono encryption technique is not adequate. Because of the voluminous architecture of cloud computing system, the traditional data security systems are not adequate to provide the complete security solution.

During mobile communication, the encryption and decryption facilities are harder to implement. Clouds can work in collaboration, even if they have their own security features. Therefore, without modifying the sequence of the encryption process, the parallel and distributed encryption facilities will be available at every cloud during surfing from cloud to cloud. Every cloud manages the essential resources and allocation can be done on every request of the resource while user moves from one cloud to another. The major issues when dealing with the cloud computing system is the network and resource availability. If the resources are not allocated during cloud computing, the encryption and decryption cannot feasible and can be difficult to pursue. The cloud collaborative encryption is a technique where, various clouds can work concurrently with distributed processing facilities. Here, the security can be enhanced by implementing the homomorphic encryption.

2. BASICS OF CRYPTOGRAPHY

Data communication plays a vital role for every individual or organization all over the world. Every organization completely relies on the day-to-day data processed by their systems. Massive amount of data transferred from one location to another, contains the confidential information and must be protected from the various potential attacks occurring during network communication. Recent advances in the information technology offered new business, personal, social, educational, research opportunities to everyone.

Cryptography is the science of "Secret Writing" that helps the trusted secure communication over the non-trusted communication channel. Encryption is a technique through with the confidential data can be secure by applying the specific encryption algorithm with a combination of a key. Decryption is a technique that reverts, or extracts the original data only using the valid key used for encryption.

Encryption is used in two ways such as; one-way encryption and two-way encryption. One-way encryption is used to encrypt the unique key used for encryption and decryption to enhance the security of the key itself. This encryption key is only used for encryption and decryption of valuable information. The key itself is not required to decrypt and is worthless. Two-way encryption technique is used to encrypt the valuable information flows over the communication channel and need to protect from the potential network attacks. This encrypted information is then decrypted to get the original information. Encryption is done with the help of single and multiple keys i.e. symmetric key and asymmetric key. The symmetric key encryption is a technique where the same key is used for encryption and decryption of the original message. In case of asymmetric key, different keys are used to encrypt and decrypt the original message. Figure 1 depicts the basic encryption and decryption mechanism.

The decryption is a reverse procedure of encryption that extracts the original message processed by the cipher technique and the encryption key. For this, a key plays a very important role in decryption. Decryption process takes the cipher text and the right key and performing those operations are more mathematical until the plaintext is recovered.

Figure 1. Encryption and Decryption Mechanism

Cryptography is nothing but a framework that protects the digital documents even if adversary may present at the communication channel. One cryptographic algorithm can be identified as useful by comparing its ability to protect the data against attacks, its speed, throughput, key transmission method, resources used, power consumption and the algorithm structure.

2.1 Classification of Cryptographic Algorithms

The classification of the cryptographic algorithms based on the way it uses the key agreement and exchange routines are

2.1.1 Secret Key Cryptography (SKC)

Secret Key cryptography also known as symmetric; is possible with the help of stream ciphers or block ciphers. The stream cipher uses bit or byte of information at a time and uses feedback mechanism. Therefore, the key is constantly changing.

In case of Block cipher, the secret message is divided into equal size block and the same key is used to encrypt all blocks.

2.1.2 Public Key Cryptography (PKC)

The asymmetric key cryptographic algorithm such as Public Key cryptography (PKC) was invented in 1976 by Diffie and Hellman. Here, the security has been provided during the data communication between receiver and sender without a common key agreement.

In PKC, the sender encrypts the secret message with the help of receiver's private key, known to everyone. The receiver then decrypts the secret message with the help of its private key. Here, both public and private keys are different. One algorithm is used for encryption and decryption. Here, one of the two keys must be kept secret and no one can decrypt the message without the private key. The RSA algorithm is one of the PKC algorithms.

Figure 2. Typical Secret Key Cryptography Process

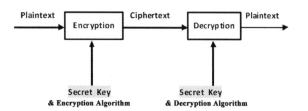

Figure 3. Typical Public Key Cryptography Process

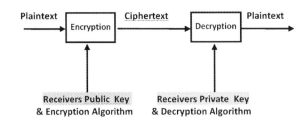

3. DATA COMMUNICATION NETWORKS

Data refers to the raw facts collected from various sources. The valuable information can be discovered from the collected data. Data communication is the transfer of valuable information between two or more different points by means of optical and electrical transmission system. This system is called as Data Communication Network. Data communication enables different organizations or individual to work remotely and controls the working from its source.

The fundamental use of a data communications system is to exchange the data between the parties engaged in the communication. The entities required for the data communication are the source, encoder, transmission system, decoder and destination.

The source device who transmits the data can be client computer and the destination becomes the server. Modem plays a role of encoder and decoder that converts digital data from a computer into a form suitable for transmission over the electrical/wired transmission network. The data transmitted from client computer to the switching office by means of wired or wireless lines. The Inter Exchange Channel IXC plays a role to transmit the data between the switching offices. The destination computer collects the data decoded by the modem. If the server is the destination computer, the Front End Processor FEP controls the communication traffic.

4. MOBILE COMPUTING

Mobile computing gives the power to the employees to work efficiently in the remote places. Personnel can work together where they are not in a same place and can get the benefits of mobile computing feature. Mobile computing is not the essential factor for everyone, but increases use of smart phones,

Figure 4. The common Data Communication System

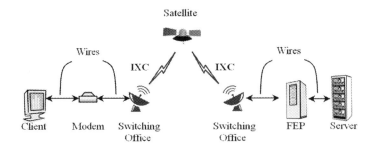

Personal Digital Assistant-PDA makes the mobile computing a crucial factor. Mobile computing is a great invention, but the information security of mobile communication is the biggest issue for everyone. Mobile computing is a distributed wireless computing technology that enables desktop computer users to work outside anywhere from office or home. Mobile computing enabled devices use wireless communication feature makes them accessible and present online on any remote place anywhere anytime. Mobile computing supports two advantageous entities such as mobility and computing. However, it is facing the challenges such as wireless communication bandwidth and information security.

4.1 Mobile Computing Security

Mobile networks are open to everyone and introduce various security risks. To resists from different attacks on the data transmission and the mobile computing enabled device attacks, the security protocols are strong enough that rescue the system from different attacks. Secure data transmission over the insecure network can be achieved by encryption and can be implemented by software and hardware itself. Mobile computing environment can use static and dynamic servers i.e. cloud servers to store the data. Both client and server can maintain the security of this data. If the client encrypts the data, then the increased size data overload the network communication. At the other end, if the data is encrypted at server side, it will resolve the security problem. However, during the decryption or searching, the security is required. This security key must be transmitted to the client for decryption. Information security fails due to the intrusion or unauthorized gain of the security key during transmission. A mobile communication network cannot provide the information security therefore, the parties engaged in the data communication handle the security mechanism with the help of security system such as cryptography.

4.2 Security Threats

Security plays a critical role for both the parties engaged in the sensitive data communication over the insecure communication channel. Information or network security attacks are classified as Passive and Active attacks are discussed below.

4.2.1 Passive Attacks

The motivation behind the passive attacks is to monitoring the services and communication of two parties engaged in the communication.

Two types of passive attacks are classified such as release of message contents and traffic analysis is depicted using Figure 5. The release of message contents is a type of attack that analyzes and read the

Figure 5. Traffic Analysis and Release of Message Contents

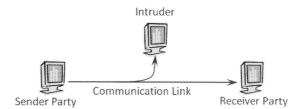

message delivered between senders to receiver. Under the traffic analysis, the data transmission patterns are studied and trying to extract the original hidden data. The types of attacks are difficult to detect, because they do not reflect the presence of an intruder on the unauthorized gain of control on network traffic.

4.2.2 Active Attacks

The attacker directly involved in the attack by making his impression on the network communication. This attack includes the modification of data, hacking of resources and false replay of messages, delaying and denial of the services.

- **Masking:** Intruder gets the unauthorized access by getting the authorized permission to access the confidential information. Figure 6 depicts the masking by an intruder.
- **Hacking Resources:** Hackers get the unauthorized access of resources of both parties engaged in confidential data transmission. The resources may be a computer, network or memory device. The hacking of resources is depicted using Figure 7.
- **Unauthorized Capturing of Information:** Data flows from one party to another get access in an unauthorized way silently without giving knowledge to the original owners is depicted using Figure 7.
- **Unauthorized Modifications of Information:** Blocking the original service, accessing of information, modifying the original message and resend it is depicted using Figure 8.
- **Service Denial or Repudiation:** The traffic of the sender is completely stopped by regulating the communication resources and giving the false messages by blocking the services which is depicted using Figure 9.

Figure 6. Masking

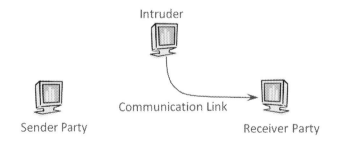

Figure 7. Hacking Resources & Unauthorized Capture of Information

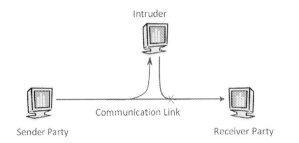

4.3 Life Cycle of Attacks on Mobile Computing

The prime goal of adversaries is to find the weak positions to attack. The weakest part of the mobile computing is the wireless network. Planning is carried out by hackers to enter into the system, spread over, collecting data and access by wireless network.

The phases of Mobile network attack life cycle are discussed below and are depicted using Figure 10.

- **Scouting:** Adversary collecting network and mobile computing system information to set the attacks.
- **Loading:** Adversary assembles and ready to put the executable object on the target system.
- **Deploy:** Adversary deploy the executable tools or software to the target system.
- **Execute:** The deployed executables get run on the target system to collect the data.

Figure 8. Modification of Message

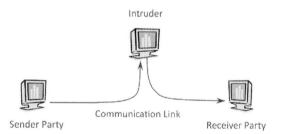

Figure 9. Service Denial

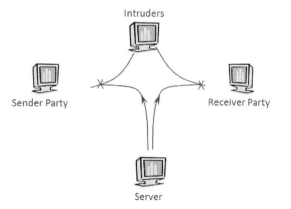

Figure 10. Attack Life Cycle on Mobile Computing

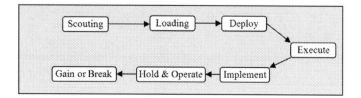

- **Implement:** Adversary implements the remote access software to gain the control of the target system and bind to their servers.
- **Hold & Operate:** Adversary fully grab the target system and operate by their own way without making any acknowledgement or impression on the normal execution of the target system.
- **Gain or Break:** Adversary gets the confidential information by mailing to itself or destroy the confidential information from the target system.

To break the life cycle attack on mobile computing, the precautions should be taken at the host system and the network side information security management. Different phases of this attack life cycle can be controlled. Communication network is open to everyone, but the mobile computing device must be protected by the external firewall against the Scouting.

The external firewall can protect the mobile computing system from the adversaries to deploy the malicious tools. If the external firewall fails to protect, then the mobile computing operating system restricting to install unwanted tools and software without the permission of the user. The Operating system can play a role to protect the system by restricting the actions of unwanted software to hold the system resources and work with them. The internal firewall has an important feature that prohibits the use of network prior permission of the user. The network connection terminates only if the mail program tries to send mail without entering a password key using physically

5. CLOUD COMPUTING

Mobile computing becomes valuable because of the cloud computing by offering network and resources on demand. The resources are available on the shared pool independently. The facilities provided by the cloud computing system are the network, virtual information storages, collaborating servers, utilities and application of cloud without any efforts.

5.1 Cloud Computing Framework

Cloud computing provides various services and resources with and without demand. Figure 11 shows the data storage and cloud computing scenario. The facilities provided by various clouds are-

- **On-Demand Self Service:** Various services required for user can be available as on-demand while user connected to any cloud.
- **Heterogeneous Platforms:** Even with the heterogeneous platforms used by the user, network access can be provided by the cloud computing system.
- **Resource Sharing:** Every cloud has the resource scheduling facility to the incoming online users from other cloud. A resource bank is maintained by each cloud and allocation of resources can be done on first come and first serve basis. The cloud resources can be acts as virtual resources even if they are physical. The resources provided by the cloud systems are the virtual storages, processors and network bandwidth.

Figure 11. Big Data Security

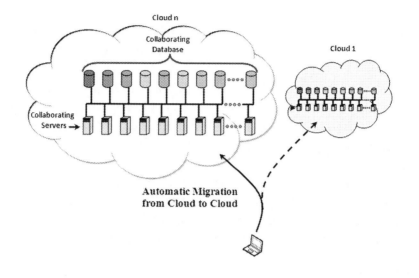

5.2 Cloud Collaboration

Collaboration of multiple clouds provides the uninterrupted services to the users connected during mobile communication.

Clouds are classified depending on the requirements by various types of users, such as:

5.2.1 Private Cloud

It is sometimes known as the intranet cloud system, limited to the campus area users with its own limited and predefined facilities provided as on-demand only.

5.2.2 Community Cloud

Multiple private clouds system are interconnected with each other to form a backbone network cloud and shared by multiple organizations within their own cloud. Each cloud connected to community cloud has its own limitations and policies.

5.2.3 Public Cloud

The public cloud is open freely to every individual user and other cloud members. All the resources of public cloud can be accessible openly without any restrictions. But the resource sharing is scheduled here by the public cloud. The public cloud sometimes owned by private or public organization. The services of public cloud can be accessible as on-demand.

- **Hybrid Cloud:** Heterogeneous technologies used by different clouds are available in collaboration. They provide different services to the users relocating from one cloud to another. The services are provided as on-demand to the users.

6. BIG DATA

Big data technology's promising features relatively acquire more importance than the cloud computing. Cloud computing changes the traditional non-virtual world to virtual by providing smart computing and data storage.

Big data is storage with massive dataset having universe of dissimilar information and facilitates to store in multiple locations. Massive amount of information is recorded on every second all over the world and disseminated. For this, massive amount of data storages should be required. The difficulties arise when, the data structure contains monolithic structure and difficult to maintain, organize, analyze, store and retrieve.

The world is moved towards the digital era. The hard-coded paper document becomes digital and paper less. The digital libraries take the place of paper and books libraries. The paperless digital libraries are more attractive due to non-requirement of physical space in a building. Due to their virtual use, any remote user can access any digital content without any limitations.

6.1 Big Data Security Challenge

A massive data stored digitally on various servers is the big data and it can be easily available through the use of cloud computing system. The smaller data can be easily secured before and during the communication and in the storage. Figure 12 shows the security of big data. Some issues arise while handling the big data such as hardware offload, security problems, data acquisition, processing workloads, operating and resource management, data analysis, data mining, cataloging, indexing, searching and dissemination. The text data is easier to process but, if the data is in the images, audio and video form then, the manipulation is difficult due to large size. The processing big data in terabytes or petabytes recorded by any organization is very harder by supercomputer or cluster machines.

6.2 Encrypted Storage

Cloud storages are frequently used by every individual or organization to save their secret information. The data stored by the clients are in the form of plain confidential information or the secured encrypted data. The data can be secured by the client computer prior sending to cloud or cloud server can secure the incoming data or both are engaged in the security implementation.

Figure 12. Big data security platform

6.3 Encrypted Workload

The amount of data which is being secured during encryption is the workload known as payload. If larger data comes for encryption then, the workload becomes heavier for the cloud system. Client and servers works in collaboration to implement the security to the data. If client encrypts the data, then server becomes offloaded to work on other work. But the network traffic issues arise here to transfer the secured data from client to cloud server, because the data size increases after providing security. For various security issues, it is more beneficial to secure the data at its local place by client. It can solve security issues such as key maintenance, encryption, decryption and data transfer.

6.4 Decryption

If client machines are engaged in the data encryption and decryption, the cloud servers can only store the encrypted data. Cloud can perform the work to handle the secured data, storage and transfer.

6.5 Failure and Recovery

Any Database Management System (DBMS) itself is a complete software package that uses the ACID properties for the complete successful transaction processing such as Atomicity, Consistency, Isolation, and Durability. The log based recovery system is available for the failure recovery.

In big data cloud computing, the transaction failure recovery can be enforced by the log based recovery system with the enforcement of ACID properties.

The big data security is not singly controlled by the single security framework; rather it can be controlled by the integrated encryption system and collaborating encryption system. Here, the client security mechanism must be work with the collaborating cloud servers to handle the security of big data.

7. EXISTING BIG DATA SECURITY FRAMEWORK

Recently, the following security challenges arises for big data

7.1 Secure Parallel and Distributed Processing

The client's big data is divided into equal number of pats and processed in distributed and parallel way. As the data is separately used for encryption and collected, the security at each level from machine to machine must be enforced.

7.2 Secured Data Storage and Retrieval

However, the size of big data storages increases tremendously from cloud to cloud, availability and scalability is a major issue during the maintenance of massive data.

7.3 Source Input Validation

Massive data comes to the cloud storage from variety of clients. Here, it is not possible to ensure the data coming from trusted sources or not. It must be required to ensure the validation of the incoming data to store over the cloud.

7.4 Active Monitoring

The active monitoring of the big data is a major challenge for every cloud. As the data is massive, several extra cloud servers are required to monitor the security threats of the incoming real time data flow incoming from other cloud servers and storages.

7.5 Privacy Preserving

Different cloud servers are required to store the massive amount of big data. The transaction log plays a vital role to keep track the privacy leakage of the big data. The major issue which must be handle by the cloud servers is to keep track the access of confidential information and its storage form other clouds.

7.6 Secure Communication

The data secure prior communication from client to cloud server preserves the insecure data communication and restricts the security flaws of communication.

7.7 Access Control

No access other valid sources must be restricted to preserve the security of the data. The access to the original source by identifying its authentication restricts the malicious users. This can be possible by maintaining the metadata about the user and their access. Other resources are restricted to access the secured data from cloud storages. The access must be granted to the original and valid sources by identifying their authentication and restrict the unwanted users. This can be possible by using the secured front end processors before cloud and maintain the metadata for the big data its users and their access.

8. BIG DATA SECURITY

The security is harder for the bigger data stored on the cloud. Weaker security is a bottleneck for the big data and the cloud computing. The following section explores the big data platform.

8.1 Big Data Platform

Not all the data is useful and scientists do the work to refine the useful data across the big data store on cloud storages. The specialized architecture is essential for the Big Data that can handle the storage, move and integrate massive data with greater accuracy and speed. The only solution is to convert the unstructured Big Data to a structured form using complex structured database management system. Figure 13 shows the essential Big Data security platform.

Number of large storages is required to keep the massive huge data. As the huge clients' increases, big number of storages is required. Due to massive data, a single store point is not adequate; therefore, parallel storages must in collaboration to perform the big data storage.

8.1.2 Communication and Distribution

Massive data is moving from server to server and client to servers need huge amount of communication and distribution capacity with the requirement of agility and speed.

8.1.3 Structuring of Unstructured Data

The structure data is valuable and unstructured data must be omitted that occupy large storage space. The incoming unstructured data must be transformed into structured form and this work requires processing, large hardware and networking cost.

8.1.4 Metadata Management

The metadata becomes bigger for the voluminous data stored over the cloud storage. The unstructured data cannot provide the right metadata. The structured data and its metadata is useful in searching the right information.

8.2 Big Data Processing

The data processing cost for the big data is heavier. The required cost of storage, hardware, software and networking is bigger to process the voluminous data.

- **Sharing:** Data sharing across cloud to cloud, servers to servers and client to servers is a time-consuming job. The security trouble arises during the data sharing. The data security and confidentiality is a prime goal of every individual, organization and the big data cloud also.

Figure 13.

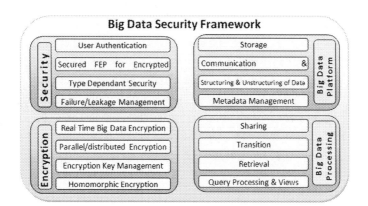

- **Transition:** The conversion of unstructured data into structured form solves the ordering, indexing and recognizing issues.
- **Retrieval:** The complex query processing architecture is essential to retrieve the useful part of data across the massive data storage. The well-structured and well-organized data preserves the cloud resources and easy for searching. As client increases, the communication, sharing and retrieval speed declines.
- **Query Processing and Views:** The fruitful views are produced for the clients by using the complex query processing for the huge data. The collaborating function and distributed query processing for multiple clouds and its multiple servers and storages helps to gain the valuable information across the massive data.

Security:

- **User/Administrator Authentication:** The metadata for the guest, registered users and administrators is required for their authentication. The security is provided by the Front End Processor machine on every single door of every cloud.
- **Secured Front End Processors for encrypted search:** The encrypted search plays a vital role to provide the security in the big data security system. The front-end processor with its secured software and hardware support plays a great role in the big data security.
- **Type Dependent Security:** Different type of digital data comes to the cloud require different security. The cryptographic algorithms are used to secure the text data while images, audio and video security are handle by the different steganographic techniques.
- **Failure/Leakage Management:** The log based recovery is essential in maintaining the failure of transaction over cloud. The big data leakage can be maintained efficiently by the Two-Phase-Locking protocol.
- **Encryption:** The basic to big security can be available through the different encryption techniques such as AES, TDES to secure the big data.
- **Real Time Big Data Encryption:** The local encryption known as offline encryption is feasible for the small data stored in client machine. However, the huge data moves from client to cloud must be secured by real time encryption. This can be possible by capture the incoming data from client to cloud and encrypt it before store.
- **Parallel/Distributed Encryption:** If cloud handles the security task of huge data, it can be effectively handled by the parallel and distributed encryption technique. The collaboration encryption can be effectively handled by multiple servers across different clouds.
- **Encryption Key Management:** The trusted third party plays an important role to handle the encryption key. The digital certification technique is useful if servers handle the encryption part. But, if client performs the encryption work at its source, the key need not be maintained at server.
- **Homomorphic Encryption:** One of the emerging techniques in the information security is the homomorphic encryption, which merge several parts of encrypted data and can supports the encrypted search. The data encrypted by different parties are merged into a single place by collaborating encryption and search can be possible. The encrypted query is available to search the encrypted data stored on the cloud storage.

9. LIMITATIONS AND CHALLENGES TO BIG DATA SECURITY

Till now companies were using ordinary security measures to secure their data; however, with the increased use of web-based, mobile and cloud-based applications, sensitive data has become accessible from different platforms. These platforms are highly vulnerable to hacking, especially if they are low-cost or free.

Nowadays, organizations are collecting and processing massive amounts of information. The more data is stored, the more vital it is to ensure its security. A lack of data security can lead to great financial losses and reputational damage for a company. As far as Big Data is concerned, losses due to poor IT security can exceed even the worst expectations.

Almost all data security issues are caused by the lack of effective measures provided by antivirus software and firewalls. These systems were developed to protect the limited scope of information stored on the hard disk, but Big Data goes beyond hard disks and isolated systems.

9.1 Big Data Security Challenges

- Unethical IT specialists practicing information mining can gather personal data without asking users for permission or notifying them.
- Access control encryption and connections security can become dated and inaccessible to the IT specialists who rely on it.
- Recommended detailed audits are not routinely performed on Big Data due to the huge amount of information involved.
- Most distributed systems' computations have only a single level of protection, which is not recommended.
- Non-relational databases (NoSQL) are actively evolving, making it difficult for security solutions to keep up with demand.
- Automated data transfer requires additional security measures, which are often not available.
- When a system receives a large amount of information, it should be validated to remain trustworthy and accurate; this practice doesn't always occur, however.
- Due to the size of Big Data, its origins are not consistently monitored and tracked.

9.2 Need for Big Data Security Be Improved?

Cloud computing experts believe that the most reasonable way to improve the security of Big Data is through the continual expansion of the antivirus industry. A multitude of antivirus vendors, offering a variety of solutions, provides a better defense against Big Data security threats. Refreshingly, the antivirus industry is often touted for its openness. Antivirus software providers freely exchange information about current Big Data security threats, and industry leaders often work together to cope with new malicious software attacks, providing maximum gains in Big Data security.

Here are some additional recommendations to strengthen Big Data security:

- Focus on application security, rather than device security.
- Isolate devices and servers containing critical data.
- Introduce real-time security information and event management.
- Provide reactive and proactive protection.

10. FUTURE RECOMMENDATION

Companies using big data should allocate top most to the security of cloud-based systems. Intel Security has recently published the McAfee Labs' Threat Predictions Report that contains their expectations for the near-future of data security. Of particular concern in this report is the supposition that legitimate cloud file hosting services such as Dropbox, Box, and Stream Nation, are at risk of being used as control servers in upcoming cyber espionage campaigns. If targeted, these popular cloud services could enable the malware to transfer commands without raising suspicion.

11. SUMMARY

The mobile computing with the security threats and the type of security attacks with their life cycle has been discussed in this chapter. The collaborating network and encryption technique discussed in this chapter facilitates the network users to keep their information and database safe. The mobile computing environment requires the rapid encryption and decryption system that keep the sensitive information safe. In this chapter, the preliminary analysis has been conducted on the fundamental issues such as data communication, mobile computing, information security, attacks and their types. The most tedious part of the security for cloud big data is the practical implementation of security mechanism. The present cryptosystem and its single algorithm are not suitable to provide the full security. The encrypted data stored across various cloud data servers cannot search by the traditional encryption techniques. This chapter presents the real-time encryption system scenario for the flowing data over the cloud. Major technology changes occurred in a few years where formal encryption techniques are not suitable to fulfill the security requirements. In this chapter, the concept of parallel and distributed encryption technique is introduced to overcome the confidentiality and data security issues.

REFERENCES

Ahmed, S. T., & Loguinov, D. (2014). On the performance of MapReduce: A stochastic approach. In *Proceedings of IEEE International Conference on Big Data (Big Data)* (pp. 49-54). 10.1109/Big-Data.2014.7004212

Alguliyev, R., & Imamverdiyev, Y. (2014). Big Data: Big Promises for Information Security. In *Proceedings of IEEE 8th International Conference on Application of Information and Communication Technologies (AICT)* (pp. 1-4). 10.1109/ICAICT.2014.7035946

Bagheri, R. & Jahanshahi, M. (2015). Scheduling Workflow Applications on the Heterogeneous Cloud Resources. *Indian Journal of Science and Technology,* 8(12), doi:10.17485/ijst/2015/v8i12/57984

Bosch, C., Peter, A., Leenders, B., Lim, H. W., Tang, Q., Wang, H., ... Jonker, W. (2014). Distributed Searchable Symmetric Encryption. In *Proceedings of Twelfth Annual International Conference on Privacy, Security and Trust (PST)* (pp. 330-337). 10.1109/PST.2014.6890956

Chan, A. C.-F. (2009). Symmetric-Key Homomorphic Encryption for Encrypted Data Processing. In *Proceedings of IEEE International Conference on Communications ICC '09.* 10.1109/ICC.2009.5199505

Chen, X.-W., & Lin, X. (2014). Big Data Deep Learning: Challenges and Perspectives. *IEEE Access*, *2*, 214–225.

Dev, D., & Baishnab, K. L. (2014). A Review and Research Towards Mobile Cloud Computing. *Proceedings of 2nd IEEE International Conference on Mobile Cloud Computing, Services and Engineering (MobileCloud)* (pp. 252-255). 10.1109/MobileCloud.2014.41

Dong, X., Li, R., He, H., Zhou, W., Xue, Z., & Wu, H. (2015). Secure sensitive data sharing on a big data platform. *Tsinghua Science and Technology*, *20*(1), 72–80. doi:10.1109/TST.2015.7040516

Hu, H., Wen, Y., Chua, T.-S., & Li, X. (2014). Toward Scalable Systems for Big Data Analytics: A Technology Tutorial. *IEEE Access*, *2*, 652–687. doi:10.1109/ACCESS.2014.2332453

Hwang, Y. H., Seo, J. W., & Kim, I. J. (2014). Encrypted Keyword Search Mechanism Based on Bitmap Index for Personal Storage Services. In *Proceedings of IEEE 13th International Conference on Trust, Security and Privacy in Computing and Communications (TrustCom)* (pp. 140-147). 10.1109/TrustCom.2014.22

Jasmine, R.M. & Nishibha, G.M. (2015). Public Cloud Secure Group Sharing and Accessing in Cloud Computing. *Indian Journal of Science and Technology*, *8*(15). doi:10.17485/ijst/2015/v8i15/75177

Jeuk, S., Szefer, J., & Zhou, S. (2014). Towards Cloud, Service and Tenant Classification for Cloud Computing. In *Proceedings of 14th IEEE/ACM International Symposium on Cluster, Cloud and Grid Computing (CCGrid)* (pp. 792-801). 10.1109/CCGrid.2014.71

Ji, C., Li, Y., Qiu, W., Awada, U., & Li, K. (2012). Big Data Processing in Cloud Computing Environments. In *Proceedings of the 12th International Symposium on Pervasive Systems. Algorithms and Networks (ISPAN)* (pp. 17-23).

Kalpana, V. & Meena, V. (2015). Study on Data Storage Correctness Methods in Mobile Cloud Computing. *Indian Journal of Science and Technology*. doi:10.17485/ijst/2015/v8i6/70094

Kirubakaramoorthi, R., Arivazhagan, D. & Helen, D. (2015). Analysis of Cloud Computing Technology. *Indian Journal of Science and Technology*, *8*(21). doi:10.17485/ijst/2015/v8i21/79144

Lee, J.-Y. (2015). A Study on the Use of Secure Data in Cloud Storage for Collaboration. *Indian Journal of Science and Technology*, *8*(S5), Doi no:. doi:10.17485/ijst/2015/v8iS5/61462

Marchal, S., Jiang, X., State, R., & Engel, T. (2014). A Big Data Architecture for Large Scale Security Monitoring. In *Proceedings of IEEE International Congress on Big Data (Big Data Congress)* (Vol. 2, pp. 56-63). 10.1109/BigData.Congress.2014.18

Matturdi, B., Xianwei, Z., Shuai, L., & Fuhong, L. (2014). Big Data security and privacy: A review. *China Communications*, *11*(14), 135–145. doi:10.1109/CC.2014.7085614

Murthy, P. K. (2014). Top ten challenges in Big Data security and privacy. In *Proceedings of IEEE International Test Conference (ITC)*. 10.1109/TEST.2014.7035307

Pal, A.S. & Pattnaik, B.P. (2013). Classification of Virtualization Environment for Cloud Computing. *Indian Journal of Science and Technology*, *6*(1). doi:10.17485/ijst/2013/v6i1/30572

Parthiban, P. & Selvakumar, S. (2016). Big Data Architecture for Capturing, Storing, Analyzing and Visualizing of Web Server Logs. *Indian Journal of Science and Technology, 9*(4). Doi:10.17485/ijst/2016/v9i4/84173

Rajathi, A. & Saravanan, N. (2013). A Survey on Secure Storage in Cloud Computing. *Indian Journal of Science and Technology, 6*(4). doi:10.17485/ijst/2013/v6i4/31871

Ranjan, R. (2014). Streaming Big Data Processing in Datacenter Clouds. *IEEE Cloud Computing, 1*(1), 78–83. doi:10.1109/MCC.2014.22

Ren, D.-Q., & Wei, Z. (2013). A Failure Recovery Solution for Transplanting High-Performance Data-Intensive Algorithms from the Cluster to the Cloud. In *Proceedings of IEEE International Conference on High Performance Computing and Communications & IEEE 10th International Conference on Embedded and Ubiquitous Computing (HPCC & EUC)* (pp. 1463-1468). 10.1109/HPCC.and.EUC.2013.207

Shyamala, K. & Sunitha Rani, T. (2015). An Analysis on Efficient Resource Allocation Mechanisms in Cloud Computing. *Indian Journal of Science and Technology, 8*(9). doi:10.17485/ijst/2015/v8i9/50180

Singh, J. (2014). Real time BIG data analytic: Security concern and challenges with Machine Learning algorithm. In *Proceedings of Conference on IT in Business, Industry and Government (CSIBIG)*. 10.1109/CSIBIG.2014.7056985

Stallings, W. (2011). *Cryptography and Network Security: Principles and Practice* (5th ed.). Pearson Education.

Tan, Z., Nagar, U. T., He, X., Nanda, P., Liu, R. P., Wang, S., & Hu, J. (2014). Enhancing Big Data Security with Collaborative Intrusion Detection. *IEEE Cloud Computing, 1*(3), 27–33. doi:10.1109/MCC.2014.53

Xiang, G., Yu, B., & Zhu, P. (2012). A algorithm of fully homomorphic encryption. In *Proceedings of 9th International Conference on Fuzzy Systems and Knowledge Discovery (FSKD)* (pp. 2030-2033).

Xu, L., Jiang, C., Wang, J., Yuan, J., & Ren, Y. (2014). Information Security in Big Data: Privacy and Data Mining. *IEEE Access, 2*, 1149–1176. doi:10.1109/ACCESS.2014.2362522

Zhao, F., Li, C., & Liu, C. F. (2014). A cloud computing security solution based on fully homomorphic encryption. In *Proceedings of 16th International Conference on Advanced Communication Technology (ICACT)* (pp. 485-488). 10.1109/ICACT.2014.6779008

This research was previously published in HCI Challenges and Privacy Preservation in Big Data Security edited by Daphne Lopez and M.A. Saleem Durai, pages 71-94, copyright year 2018 by Information Science Reference (an imprint of IGI Global).

Chapter 33

Glorified Secure Search Schema Over Encrypted Secure Cloud Storage With a Hierarchical Clustering Computation

Shweta Annasaheb Shinde
VIT University, India

Prabu Sevugan
VIT University, India

ABSTRACT

This chapter improves the SE scheme to grasp these contest difficulties. In the development, prototypical, hierarchical clustering technique is intended to lead additional search semantics with a supplementary feature of making the scheme to deal with the claim for reckless cipher text search in big-scale surroundings, such situations where there is a huge amount of data. Least relevance of threshold is considered for clustering the cloud document with hierarchical approach, and it divides the clusters into sub-clusters until the last cluster is reached. This method may affect the linear computational complexity versus the exponential growth of group of documents. To authenticate the validity for search, minimum hash sub tree is also implemented. This chapter focuses on fetching of cloud data of a subcontracted encrypted information deprived of loss of idea and of security and privacy by transmission attribute key to the information. In the next level, the typical is improved with a multilevel conviction privacy preserving scheme.

INTRODUCTION

Individuals are profited with cloud computing as cloud computing reduces it work and make computing and storage simplified. (Liang, Cai, Huang, Shen & Peng, 2012), (Mahmoud & Shen, 2012), (Shen, Liang, Shen, Lin & Lou, 2012). Data can be stored remotely in the cloud server as data outsourcing and accessed publicly. This embodies a mountable, constant and low-cost method for public access of data as per the high productivity and mount ability of cloud servers, and so it is favored.

DOI: 10.4018/978-1-5225-8176-5.ch033

Sensitive privacy information is of concern. Data should be encrypted before sending to the cloud servers (Jung, Mao, Li, Tang, Gong & Zhang, 2013), (Yang, Li, Liu & M, 2014). The data encryption comes with it the difficulty of searching the data on the cloud servers. (Cao, Wang, Li, Ren & Lou, 2014) Encryption comes with it many of other security apprehensions. Secure Sockets Layer is used by Google search to encrypt the connection be the authors the google server and search user.

Nevertheless, if the user clicks from the authors site of search result, to another the authors site will identify the search terms the user has used.

On dealing with the above matters, the searchable form of encryption (e.g., (Song, Wagner & Perrig, 2000), (Li, Xu, Kang, Yow & Xu, 2014), (Li, Lui, Dai, Luan & Shen, 2014)) has been established as a basic method to allow searching over encrypted data of cloud, which profits the procedures. At first the owner of data will produce quite a few keywords rendering to the outsourced data. Cloud server will be used to store this encrypted keywords. When the outsourced data needs to be accessed, it can choice approximately appropriate keywords and direct the cipher text of the designated keywords to the cloud server. The cloud server then usages the cipher text to contest the outsourced keywords which are encrypted, and finally will yields the matching consequences to the user who search. To attain the like search effectiveness and accuracy over data which is encrypted as like plaintext search of keyword, a widespread form of research has been advanced in literature. Wang et al.(2014) recommended a ranked keyword search system which deliberates the scores of relevance's of keywords. Inappropriately, because of using order-preserving encryption (OPE)(Boldyreva, Chenette, Lee & Oneill, 2009) to attain the property of ranking, the planned arrangement cannot attain unlikability of trapdoor.

Later, Sun et al.(Sun, Wang, Cao, Li, Lou, Hou & Li, 2013)suggested a multi-keyword text search arrangement which deliberates the scores of relevance's of the keywords and exploits a multidimensional tree method to realize the authors organized query of search. (J. Yu, P. Lu, Y. Zhu, G. Xue, & M. Li, 2013) suggested a multi-keyword top-k retrieval organization which practices fully homomorphic encryption to encrypt the index/trapdoor and assurances high security. Cao et al. (2014) suggested a multi-keyword ranked search (MRSE), which put on machine of coordinate as the matching of keyword rule, i.e., it will return the data with the maximum matching of keywords. Even though many of the functionalities of search have been advanced in former literature on the way to exact and the authors organized searchable encryption, it is still problematic for searchable encryption to attain the similar user involvement as that of the plaintext search, like Google search. This mostly attributes to subsequent two issues. At first, query with user favorites is popular in the search of plaintext (Liang, Cai, Huang, Shen, & Peng, 2012), (Mahmoud & Shen, 2012). It allows tailored search and can more precisely represent requirements of users, but has not been methodically studied and maintained in the encrypted domain of data. At second, to further improve the user's experience on searching, a significant and vital function is to allow the multi-keyword search with the comprehensive logic operations, i.e., the "AND", "OR" and "NO" operations of keywords. This is vital for search users to trim the space of searching and rapidly classify the anticipated data.

Cao et al. advise the coordinate matching search scheme (MRSE) which can be the authors as a searchable encryption system with "OR" operation (Shen, Liang, Shen, Lin, & Luo, 2014) recommended a conjunctive keyword search scheme which can be observed as a searchable encryption scheme with "AND" operation with the refunded documents matching all keywords. Though, most current suggestions can only allow search with single logic operation, somewhat than the mixture of numerous logic operations on keywords, which encourages the work.

Here, the authors discourse above two issues by emerging two Fine-grained Multi-Keyword Search (FMS) arrangements over encrypted data of cloud. Our unique donations can be abridged in three characteristics as tracks:

- The authors familiarize the relevance scores of relevance's and the preference factors of keywords for searchable encryption. The scores of relevance's of keywords can allow more detailed refunded consequences, and the factors of preferences of keywords signify the standing of keywords in the search for keyword set quantified by search of users and consistently the authors search at personalized level to cater to precise preferences of users. Thus, additional advances the search of functionalities and experience of user.
- The authors understand the "AND", "OR" and "NO" processes in the multi-keyword search for searchable encryption. Associated with arrangements in the proposed arrangement can accomplish more all-inclusive functionality and the authors query complexity of query.
- The authors employment the classified sub-dictionaries technique to improve the effectiveness of the above two arrangements. Extensive experimentations establish that the enhanced arrangements can attain better effectiveness in terms of building of index, trapdoor generating and query in the judgement with arrangements in.

Hardware restriction of mobile devices is overcome by Mobile cloud computing (Dinh, Lee, Niyato, & Wang, 2013; Li, Dai, Tian, & Yang, 2009) by discovering the accessible and virtualized storage of cloud and computing resources, and consequently can deliver much more significant and mountable services of mobile to user. In the technology of mobile cloud computing, mobile operators characteristically are outsourcing their information to cloud servers which are external, e.g., iCloud, to adore a steady, low-cost and climbable way for storage of data and access. Though, as outsourced data has sensitive private information, such as personal photos, emails., which would lead to severe confidentiality and privacy violations (W. Sun, 2013), if without efficient protections. It is therefore essential to encrypt the sensitive data before outsourcing them to the cloud. The data encryption, the authors would result in salient problems when other users need to access interested data with search, due to the problems of search over encrypted data. This fundamental issue in mobile cloud computing consequently inspires an extensive body of investigation in the recent years on the examination of searchable encryption performance to attain the authors ll-organized thorough over outsourced encrypted data (Wang, Lou, & Hou, 2014; Yang, Liu, & Yang, 2014)

An assortment of research the whole thing have freshly been established about multi-keyword search over the data which is encrypted. Cash et al. (Jarecki,Jutla,Krawczyk,Ro^{3}u, & Steiner, 2013) offer a symmetric searchable encryption organization which attains high effectiveness for big databases with uncertain on security guarantees. Cao et al. (Cao, Wang, Li, Ren, & Lou, 2014)suggest a multi-keyword search structure supportive consequence ranking by approving k-nearest neighbors (kNN)technique (Wong, Cheung,Kao, & Mamoulis,2009). Naveed et al. (2014) proposition an active searchable encryption system complete blind storage to obscure admittance pattern of the user for search. In demand to encounter the practical search necessities, search concluded data which is encrypted should provision the subsequent three functions. First, the encryption systems which are searchable should provision multi-keyword search, and deliver the same experience for user as thorough in search for Google with different keywords; search for single-keyword is far from acceptable by only recurring very incomplete and imprecise results for results. Second, to rapidly classify most applicable results, the user for search would characteristically favor cloud servers to category the refunded search consequences in a relevance-based command (Pang, Shen, & Krishnan, 2010) ranked by the order of relevance of the request for search documents. In accumulation, display the search based on rank to users can also eradicate the needless traffic of network by only distributing back the utmost results which are relevant from to search users from cloud. Third, as for the effectiveness of search, then the quantity of the documents which are imperfect in a database could be tremendously large, encryption which is searchable constructions should be organized in the authors-mannered to quickly response to the requirements for search with interruptions and they are smallest. In modification to the proposed prosperities, frequently of the usual proposals, the authors, nose dive to proposal satisfactory intuitions near the construction of full performed encryption which is searchable. As an application near the subject, the authors proposition and the authors-organized multi-keyword ranked search (EMRS) preparation over encrypted cloud data for mobile through blind storage. Our important charities can be abridged as surveys:

- The authors explain a relevance for score in encryption which is searchable to accomplish multi-keyword ranked search finished the cloud data for mobile which is encrypted. In gathering to that, the authors proposition and the authors organized index to advance the efficiency for search.
- By adapting the blind storage scheme in the Meurthe authors resolve the trapdoor unlikability problematic and obscure admittance pattern of the user for search from the cloud server.
- The authors give systematic analysis of security to prove that the EMRS can spread a high security level counting documents for confidentiality and index, privacy with trapdoor, trapdoor unlikability, and covering admission pattern of the search user. Moreover, the authors implement extensive experiments, which show that the EMRS can achieve enhanced efficiency in the terms of functionality and search effectiveness compared with prevailing proposals.

Cloud computing is known as a substitute to outdated information technology and has been progressively familiar as the greatest significant revolving point in the expansion of information technology owing to its inherent sharing of resource and low maintenance characters. Cloud computing is a computing model, where the information which is shared, resources and software are supplied to devices and computers based on requirement. This allows the end user to admittance the resources for cloud computing anytime from required platform such as mobiles, or desktops which is the mobile computing platform.

Clouds are huge pools of easily practical and available resources which are virtualized. The data and the applications which are software essential by the workers are not stored on their self-computers; in its place, they are the authors on servers which are remote which are the control of users. It is a model which is pay-per-use in that the structure benefactor by resources of service level agreements(SLAs) which (Vaquero, Rodero-Merino, Caceres, & Lindner, 2009). As cloud computing becomes prevalent, more and more sensitive information's are being centralized into the cloud. Such as emails, photo albums, personal health records, financial transactions, tax documents and government documents etc.

The detail that owners of data and cloud server are no extended in the similar trusted domain may place the data at risk outsourced unencrypted. The cloud server escape information of data to illegal enables or can be hacked. To deliver privacy for data, data which is sensitive needs to be encrypted first of outsourcing to the profitable public cloud (Kamara & Lauter, 2010). The unimportant explanation of transferring all the information and decrypting in the vicinity is clearly unreasonable, due to the gigantic amount of band width rate in level of cloud scale systems.

Discovering preserving privacy and real search over encrypted date of cloud is of supreme position seeing the possibly great amount of on claim users of data & enormous quantity of outsourced document of data in the cloud, this problem is predominantly challenging as it is tremendously difficult to meet also the necessities of presentation, system usability and scalability encryption makes operative utilization of data a very stimulating task given that there could be a big quantity of outsourced information files. Also in the cloud computing owners of data may portion their outsourced information with numerous users who might want to only recover certain exact files of data. They are engrossed in during a conference. One of the utmost prevalent imposts to do so is whole keyword search method licenses users to intelligently recuperate files of interest. Need for information retrieval is the most commonly occurring commission in cloud to the user to from server. Usually, cloud servers complete relevance result ranking in instruction to make the exploration as earlier. Such ranked search scheme allows users of data to find the most applicable info quickly, instead of returning undistinguishable results. Ranked search can stylishly remove unnecessary traffic for the network by distribution back only the greatest data for relevance which is highly wanted in the "Pay-As-You-Use" paradigm for cloud.

For confidentiality shield, such process of ranking, the authors, must not escape any keyword connected data. On the other side, to recuperate the result for accuracy of search as the authors as to recover the searching for user experience, it is also necessary for such ranking system to support multiple keywords search, as single keyword search often yields far too coarse results. As a common practice indicated by today's the authors search engines (e.g., Google search), data users may tend to provide a set of keywords instead of only one as the indicator of their search interest to retrieve the most relevant data. And each keyword in the search request can help narrow down the search result further. "Coordinate matching" (Witten,Moffat & Bell,1999), i.e., as numerous matches as conceivable, is a the authors-organized similarity amount among such multi-keyword meaning to improve the relevance of result, and has been extensively used in the plaintext data retrieval (IR) community. Though, how to put on it in the encrypted cloud data search scheme remains a very stimulating assignment because of distinguishing privacy and security problems, counting numerous strict supplies like the privacy of data, the privacy of index, privacy of keyword, and many more.

Cloud computing is known as a substitute to old-style data technology and has been progressively familiar as the greatest important rotating point in the expansion of information technology due to its inherent sharing of resource and maintenance of low characters. Cloud computing is also an internet based computing model, where the information is shared, resources and software are on condition that on other devices and computers on demand upon demand. This allows the end user to admission the cloud computing possessions anytime any platform such as a mobile computing platform, cell phone Clouds are big puddles of effortlessly serviceable and available resources which are virtualized. The information and the applications of software compulsory by the workforces are not deposited on their own processers; instead they are deposited on remote servers which will be under the control of other users. it is a pay-per- use model in which the organization earner by resources of service level agreements customized (SLAs) (Vaquero, Rodero-Merino, Caceres, & Lindner, 2009)

Security in Cloud

There are a portion of interests to tolerant Cloud Computing, there are also some significant walls to receipt (Seung Hwan, Gelogo & Park, 2012). One of the greatest major fences to acceptance is the security, surveyed by matters concerning acquiescence, privacy and matters which are authorized. Since Cloud

Computing characterizes a comparatively new figuring model, there is an enormous deal of ambiguity about how security at every level (network, host, application, data levels, etc.) can be attained and in what way security of application is stimulated to Cloud Computing. That indecision has dependably controlled information managers to state that security is their number one apprehension with Cloud Computing. Security anxieties recount to hazard areas such as outside data storage, dependence on the internet which is public, absence of control, integration and multitenancy with security is internal. Associated to conservative technologies, cloud has many exact topographies, such as its countless gauge and the detail that resources going to cloud providers are completely disseminated, heterogeneous and totally virtualized. Conservative security machineries such as Identity authentication, and authorization are no longer enough for clouds in their current form. For of the cloud facilities replicas working, the working replicas, and practices cast-off to allow services for cloud. Cloud computing may present-day dissimilar dangers to suggestion than old-style IT resolutions. Unfortunately, participating safety into these explanations is frequently supposed as making them more inflexible.

Search in Encrypted Cloud Data

As Cloud Computing turn into extensive, more delicate data are being transported into cloud, such as individual health records, emails, confidential videos and images, data for business finance, documents for government, etc. As per this i.e., storage their information into the cloud, the data owners can be reassured from the problem of information storing space and preservation so to like the on- demand high brilliance storage for data service (Reddy, 2013). Though, the reality that information suppliers and cloud servers are not in the alike reliable area may put the subcontracted information at danger. By way of the cloud server can no extended be completely reliable in such an environment for cloud since of a variety of reasons, they are: the cloud server may leakage data to illegal things or it may be slashed. It tracks that delicate information characteristically can be encrypted before outsourcing for data confidentiality and fighting undesirable admissions. Though, encryption for data makes data utilization effectiveness and efficiency a very challenging task given that there could be a large amount of outsourced data files. Furthermore, in Cloud Computing, data owners/provider may share their outsourced data with many users. The individual users shall wish to only recover certain exact files of data they are absorbed in through a given conference. One among the most recognized customs is to specifically recover files complete keyword-based search as a substitute of regaining all the files which are encrypted like before which is totally unreasoning in cloud computing circumstances (Khan, Wang, Kulsoom & Ullah, 2013) Like this keyword-based search technique allows users to meaningfully regain files of awareness and has approximately valuable in search of plaintext situations, such as Google search. Miserably, encryption for information limits user's capability to perform search for keyword and subsequently makes the out-of-date plain text search methods not appropriate for Cloud Computing.

Lately, the cloud computing pattern (Mell & T. Grance, 2011) is transforming the establishments in method of effective their information mainly in the method they accumulation, admittance and process information (Paillier,1999). As a developing calculating pattern, for cloud computing, it interests many establishments to correlated potential for cloud in relations of flexibility, cost-efficiency and rid of managerial overhead. Cloud will originate valuable and delicate data about the real data matters by detecting the variable data admission designs even if is an information is encrypted (Capitani, Vimercati, Foresti, & Samarati, 2012; Williams, Sion, & Carbunar, 2008). Most often, governments characteristic their computational procedures in accrual to their data to the cloud. The advantage of cloud is that the privacy and security matters in the cloud which circumvents the productions to use those plunders. The information can be encrypted earlier subcontracting to cloud when information is highly delicate. When information is encrypted, regardless of the fundamental encryption system, it is very interesting to accomplishment any information mining responsibilities ever decrypting the information (Samanthula, Elmehdwi, & Jiang, 2014).

Cloud computing is extended fantasized dream of computing as usefulness, from cloud customs can at all store their information into cloud so to like on-demand in height excellence claims and facilities from a public lake of configuring computing possessions (Vaquero, Lodero-Merino, Caceres, & Lindner, 2009). Its countless elasticity and financial investments are inspiring both persons and initiatives to outsource their local composite information organization scheme into cloud. To shield information confidentiality and battle the authors come y*admissions in the cloud and outside, delicate information, e.g., electronic mail, private healthiness histories, snap scrapbooks, tax papers, economic communications supposed to be encrypted by information proprietors before subcontracting to the profitable public cloud (Kamara & Lauter, 2010) This takes away the old-style information use service basis on plaintext keyword searches. The unimportance of transferring all the information and decrypting nearby is obviously unreasonable, due to the enormous quantity of bandwidth price in cloud gage schemes. Furthermore, aside from removing the local storing organization, storage information into serves for cloud no drive except they can effortlessly have examined and used. Therefore, discovering preserving privacy and real service for search done encrypted data for cloud is of supreme position. Seeing the possibly big amount of on-demand information operators and enormous quantity of subcontracted information forms in cloud, this problem is predominantly stimulating as it is tremendously problematic to encounter also the necessities of presentation, scheme scalability and usability. To encounter the real information recovery essential, the big amount of forms request the server for cloud to achieve consequence relevance ranking, in its place of recurring undistinguishable consequences. Ranked search scheme allows information operators to discovery the greatest applicable data rapidly, somewhat than categorization finished every competition in the gratified group (Singhal, 2001). Search based on rank can gracefully eradicate pointless traffic for network by distribution posterior only the most applicable information, which is extremely necessary in "pay-as-you use" cloud model. For protection, of privacy such ranking process, though, should not escape any keyword associated data. Respective, to recover the effect for accurateness of search to recover the experience for user for going through, it is important for system for ranking to provision many searches based on keywords, as sole search for keyword frequently produces far too uneven consequences. As a mutual repetition designated by todays search for the trains (e.g. Search for Google), data administrators may grade to convey a standard of watchwords in its place of just exceptional as the pointer of their enthusiasm of hunt to recoup the most relevant data. What's more, exclusively watchword seek request is brilliant to help thin discouraged the outcome for pursuit extra. "Arrange coordinating" (Witten, Moffat, & Bell,1999), i.e., as various rivalries as likely, is an efficient correlation sum among such multi-watchword intending to enhance the outcome pertinence, and broadly utilized as a part of the plaintext data recovery (IR) people group. Be that as it may, how to apply it in the scrambled cloud information seek framework remains an extremely difficult assignment in view of characteristic security and protection snags, including different strict prerequisites like the information security, the list protection, the catchphrase security, and numerous others. In the writing, searchable encryption (Song, Wagner, & Perrig, 2000; Golle, Staddon, & Waters, 2004) is a useful strategy that regards scrambled information as reports and permits a client to safely seek through a solitary catchphrase and recover archives of intrigue. In any case, coordinate use of these ways to deal with the protected extensive scale cloud information usage framework would not be fundamentally reasonable, as they are created as crypto primitives and can't suit such high administration level prerequisites like framework ease of use, client look in understanding, and simple data revelation. Some current plans have been proposed to bolster Boolean watchword look (Golle, Staddon, 2004; Shen, Shi, & Waters, 2009) as an endeavor to enhance the hunt adaptability, they are as yet not sufficient to give clients adequate outcome positioning usefulness. Our initial work (Wang, Cao, Li, Ren, & Lou, 2010) has known about this issue, and given the authors for the safe positioned seek over scrambled information issue yet just for inquiries comprising of a solitary watchword. The most effective method to outline a proficient scrambled information seek system that backings multi-catchphrase semantics without security ruptures remains a testing open issue. In this chapter, surprisingly, the authors characterize and take care of the issue of multi-watchword positioned look over encoded cloud information (MRSE) while safeguarding strict framework savvy security in the distributed computing worldview. Among different multikey word semantics, the authors pick the proficient comparability measure of "facilitate coordinating", i.e., whatever number matches as would be prudent, to catch the pertinence of information reports to the pursuit question. The authors utilize "internal item comparability" i.e., the quantity of question watchwords showing up in a record, to quantitatively assess such similitude measure of that archive to the pursuit inquiry. Amid the file development, each record is related with a double vector as a subindex where each piece speaks to whether comparing catchphrase is contained in the report. The pursuit is likewise depicted as a parallel vector where each piece implies whether comparing watchword shows up in this hunt ask for, so the comparability could be precisely measured by the inward result of the question vector with the information vector. Be that as it may, straightforwardly outsourcing the information vector or the question vector will damage the file protection or the pursuit security. To meet the test of supporting such multi-catchphrase semantic without protection breaks, the authors propose an essential thought for the MRSE utilizing secure internal item calculation, which is adjusted from a safe k-closest neighbor (kNN) procedure and afterward give two fundamentally enhanced MRSE plots in a he authors ordered way to accomplish different stringent protection necessities in two danger models with expanded assault abilities. Our commitments are abridged as takes after:

1. For the first occasion when, the authors investigate the issue of multi keyword positioned seek over encoded cloud information, and build up an arrangement of strict protection necessities for such a safe cloud information usage framework.
2. The authors propose two MRSE plans considering the similitude measure of "organize coordinating" while at the same time meeting distinctive protection prerequisites in two diverse danger models.
3. Thorough examination exploring protection and effectiveness assurances of the proposed plans is given, and investigations on this present reality dataset additionally demonstrate the proposed conspires undoubtedly present low overhead on calculation and correspondence.

Distributed computing has been considered as another model of big business IT foundation, which can compose enormous asset of registering, stockpiling and applications, and the authors clients to appreciate omnipresent, helpful and on-request arrange access to a mutual pool of configurable processing assets with extraordinary effectiveness and negligible monetary overhead. Pulled in by these engaging components, both people and undertakings are roused to outsource their information to the cloud, rather than buying programming and equipment to deal with the information themselves. Regardless of the different favourable circumstances of cloud administrations, outsourcing touchy data, (for example, messages, individual the authors being records, organization back information, government reports, and so forth) to remote servers brings protection concerns. The cloud specialist organizations (CSPs) that keep the information for clients may get to clients' delicate data without approval. A general way to deal with ensuring the information secrecy is to encode the information before outsourcing. Notwithstanding, this will bring about an immense cost as far as information ease of use. For instance, the current systems on watchword based data recovery, which are generally utilized on the plaintext information, can't be specifically connected on the scrambled information. Downloading every one of the information from the cloud and unscramble locally is clearly unrealistic. Keeping in mind the end goal to address the above issue, scientists have planned some universally useful arrangements with completely homomorphic encryption (Gentry, 2009) or unmindful RAMs (Goldreich & Ostrovsky,1996). Nonetheless, these techniques are not common sense because of their high computational overhead for both the cloud separate and client. More down to earth extraordinary reason arrangements, for example, searchable encryption (SE) plans have made commitments as far as effectiveness, usefulness and security. Searchable encryption plans for the customer to store the encoded information to the cloud and execute catchphrase seek over cipher text area. Up until this point, plentiful works have been proposed under various risk models to accomplish different hunt usefulness. For example, single catchphrase inquiry, closeness look, multi-watchword Boolean pursuit, positioned seek, multi-catchphrase positioned look, and so forth. Among them, multikey word positioned look accomplishes increasingly consideration for its pragmatic relevance. As of late, some dynamic plans have been proposed to bolster embedding and erasing operations on record accumulation. These are critical fills in as it is profoundly conceivable that the information proprietors need to refresh their information on the cloud server. Be that as it may, few of the dynamic plans bolster productive multikey word positioned look.

Distributed computing is one method for processing. Here the figuring assets are shared by numerous clients. The advantages of cloud can be stretched out from individual clients to associations. The information stockpiling in cloud is one among them. The virtualization of equipment and programming assets in cloud invalidates the money related venture for owning the information stockroom and its upkeep. Many cloud stages like Google Drive, iCloud, SkyDrive, Amazon S3, Dropbox and Microsoft Azure give stockpiling administrations.

Security and protection concerns have been the major challenges in distributed computing. The equipment and programming security instruments like firewalls and so forth have been utilized by cloud supplier. These arrangements are not adequate to secure information in cloud from unapproved clients because of low level of straightforwardness (Cloud Security Alliance, 2009). Since the cloud client and the cloud supplier are in the diverse put stock in area, the outsourced information might be presented to the vulnerabilities (Cloud Security Alliance, 2009; Ren, Wang, & Wang, 2012; Brinkman, 2007). In this manner, before putting away the important information in cloud, the information should be encoded (Kamara & Lauter, 2010). Information encryption guarantees the information classification and trustworthiness. To save the information protection the authors must outline a searchable calculation that takes a shot at scrambled information (Wong,Cheung, Kao, & Mamoulis, 2009). Numerous specialists have been adding to seeking on scrambled information. The hunt systems might be single catchphrase look or multi watchword seek (C. Wang, N. Cao, J. Li, K. Ren, & W. Lou, 2010). In gigantic database, the inquiry may bring about many reports to be coordinated with watchwords. This causes trouble for a cloud client to experience all archives and have generally applicable reports. Look in view of positioning is another arrangement, wherein the reports are positioned in view of their pertinence to the watchwords (Singhal, 2001). Practical searchable encryption systems help the cloud clients particularly in pay-as-you utilize show. The analysts consolidated the rank of archives with numerous watchword pursuit to think of proficient financially suitable searchable encryption strategies. In searchable encryption, related writing, calculation time what's more, calculation overhead is the two most as often as possible utilized parameters by the specialists in the space for dissecting the execution of their plans. Calculation time (moreover called "running time") is the period required to play out a computational procedure for instance looking a watchword, creating trapdoor and so forth. Calculation overhead is identified with CPU usage regarding asset distribution measured in time. In this examination work, the authors dissect the security issues in distributed storage and propose the authors for the same. Our commitment can be compressed as takes after:

1. Interestingly, the authors characterize the issue of secure positioned watchword seek over scrambled cloud information, and give such as the authors convention, which satisfies the protected positioned look usefulness with no pertinence score data spillage against watchword protection.
2. Exhaustive security examination demonstrated that our deviated based positioned searchable encryption plot utilizing CRSA and B-tree to be sure appreciates "as-solid as possible". security ensure contrasted with past searchable symmetric encryption (SSE) plans.
3. Broad exploratory outcomes exhibit the adequacy and productivity of the proposed arrangement.

Distributed computing has changed the way businesses approach IT, the authors them to end up noticeably more nimble, present new plans of action, offer more administrations, and trim down IT costs. Distributed computing innovations can be executed in a wide assortment of designs, under different administration and arrangement models, and can exist together with numerous advancements and programming outline strategies. The distributed computing foundation keeps on acknowledging unstable development. The authors, for security experts, the cloud displays a tremendous quandary: How would you grasp the advantages of the cloud while keeping up security controls over your associations' advantages? It turns into an issue of adjust to decide if the expanded dangers are genuinely justified regardless of the nimbleness and monetary advantages. Keeping up control over the information is foremost to cloud achievement. 10 years prior, undertaking information regularly lived in the association's physical framework, all alone servers in the association's server farm, where one could isolate touchy data in individual physical servers. Today, by virtualization and the cloud, information might be under the association's intelligent control, yet physically put away in foundation possessed and oversaw by an alternate element. This move in charge is the main reason new methodologies and systems are required to guarantee associations can keep up information security. At the point when an outside party claims, controls, and oversees foundation and computational assets, how might you be guaranteed that business or administrative information stays private and secure, and that your association is shielded from harming information breaks? This makes cloud information security fundamental. Distributed computing the significance of Cloud Computing is expanding also, it is accepting a developing thought in the logical also, mechanical groups. The NIST (National Institute of Standards and Technology) proposed the accompanying meaning of distributed computing:

Distributed computing is a demonstrate for the authors ring advantageous, on-request arrange get to a common pool of configurable processing assets (e.g., systems, servers, stockpiling, applications, and administrations) that can be quickly provisioned and discharged with negligible administration exertion or specialist co-op communication. This cloud show advances accessibility (Mell & Grance, 2012).

The cloud enhances joint effort, nimbleness, versatility, accessibility, capacity to adjust to varieties as indicated by request, speed up advancement work, and gives potential to cost diminishment through enhanced and effective processing. Distributed computing consolidates various processing thoughts what's more, advances, for example, Service Oriented Architecture (SOA), The authors 2.0, virtualization and different advances with dependence on the Internet, supporting regular business applications online through the authors programs to fulfil the processing needs of clients, while their product and information are kept up on the servers.

Cloud Delivery Models are:

- **Private Cloud:** Cloud framework is provisioned for use by a solitary association that involves different inhabitants. Private mists might be worked on-or off-premises and are behind the organization firewall.
- **Public Cloud:** A cloud specialist co-op offers administrations to different organizations, scholastic foundations, government offices, and different associations with get to by means of the Internet.
- **Hybrid Cloud:** Hybrid mists join two cloud conveyance models that stay novel as elements, yet they are bound together by innovation that the authors information and application transportability. Cloud blasting is a case of one way undertaking that utilize cross breed mists to adjust loads amid pinnacle request periods.
- **Community Cloud:** Cloud foundation is provisioned for the selective utilization of a group of client associations with shared figuring prerequisites for example, security, strategy, and consistence.

The Service layers for these conveyance models are:

- **Infrastructure as an Administration (IaaS):** Cloud framework is the accumulation of equipment and programming that the authors the fundamental qualities of the cloud. IaaS permits clients to self-arrangement these assets to run stages and applications.
- **Platform as an Administration (PaaS):** PaaS the author clients to adjust legacy applications to a cloud situation or create cloud-mindful applications utilizing programming dialects, administrations, libraries, and other designer devices. Programming as an administration (SaaS) – Users can run applications by means of numerous gadgets on cloud foundation.

SECURITY IN CLOUD

Although there is a considerable measure of advantages to receiving Distributed computing, there are additionally some extensive hindrances to acknowledgment (Seung Hwan, Gelogo & Park. 2012). A standout amongst the most significant obstructions to selection is the security, trailed by issues in regards to consistence, protection and approved matters. Since Cloud Processing speaks to a moderately new registering model, there is an enormous arrangement of vulnerability about how security by any stretch of the imagination levels (arrange, have, application, information levels, and so forth.) can been accomplished and how application security is moved to Cloud Figuring. That vulnerability has reliably driven data administrators to express that security is their number one worry with Cloud Computing. Security concerns identify with hazard territories, for example, outside information stockpiling, reliance on general society the authors, absence of control, multitenancy what's more, incorporation with inside security. Contrasted with traditional advances, cloud has numerous elements, for example, its extraordinary scale and the reality that assets having a place with cloud suppliers are totally disseminated, heterogeneous and totally virtualized. Regular security components, for example, character, validation, and approval are no sufficiently longer for mists in their present shape. Considering the cloud benefit models utilized, the operational models, and the philosophies used to the authors cloud administrations, cloud registering may exhibit distinctive dangers to an affiliation than customary IT arrangements. Unfortunately, incorporating security into these arrangements is regularly seen as making them more inflexible.

The distributed computing research group, especially the Cloud Security Alliance, has perceived security issues in cloud. In its Top Threats to Cloud Processing Report (Ver.1.0) (Top Threats to Cloud Computing Report (Ver.1.0),2010), it recorded seven top dangers to distributed computing:

1.   Mishandle and terrible utilization of distributed computing.
2.   Uncertain application programming interfaces.
3.   Pernicious insiders.
4.   Shared innovation vulnerabilities.
5.   Information misfortune or spillages.
6.   Record, administration and movement capturing.
7.   Obscure hazard profile.

ENCRYPTED CLOUD DATA

By doing as such i.e., putting away their information into the cloud, the information proprietors/suppliers can be eased from the authors right of information storage room and support to appreciate the on-request high fabulousness information stockpiling administration (Reddy, 2013). Notwithstanding, reality that information suppliers and cloud server are not in the comparative trusted space may put the outsourced information at hazard, as the cloud server may no longer be completely confided in such a cloud situation considering several reasons, they are: the cloud server may spill data substance to unapproved elements or it might be hacked. It takes after that delicate information ordinarily ought to be scrambled preceding outsourcing for information security and battling undesirable gets to. Information encryption makes information usage adequacy and proficiency an extremely difficult assignment given that there could be a lot of outsourced information records. Moreover, in Cloud Computing, information proprietors/supplier may impart their outsourced information to a substantial number of clients. The individual clients may be earning to just recover certain exact information records they are occupied with all through a given session. A standout amongst the most acknowledged routes is to specifically recover documents through catchphrase based hunt as an option of recovering all the scrambled documents back which is totally outlandish in distributed computing situations (Khan & Wang, 2010).

BACKGROUND

Firstly, they use the "Dormant Semantic Analysis" to uncover relationship amongst terms and reports. The inert semantic examination exploits certain higher-arrange structure in the relationship of terms with archives ("semantic structure") and receives a diminished measurement vector space to speak to words and reports. In this manner, the relationship be the authors terms is naturally caught. Furthermore, their plan utilizes secure "k-closest neighbour (k-NN)" to accomplish secure hunt usefulness. The proposed plan could return the correct coordinating records, as the authors as the documents including the terms inactive semantically related to the question watchword. At long last, the exploratory result exhibits that their strategy is superior to the first MRSE conspire (Song & Wagner, 2000). Their procedures have various pivotal focal points. They are provably secure: they give provable mystery to encryption, as in the untrusted server can't learn anything about the plain content when just given the cipher text; they give inquiry disengagement to quests, implying that the untrusted server can't learn much else about the plaintext than the query output; they give controlled seeking, so that the untrusted server can't hunt down a subjective word without the client's approval; they likewise bolster concealed inquiries, so that the client may approach the untrusted server to hunt down a mystery word without uncovering the word to the serve (Sun, Wang, Cao, Li, Lou, Hou, & Li, 2013). They propose a tree-based list structure and different versatile techniques for multi-dimensional (MD) calculation so that the handy hunt proficiency is greatly improved than that of direct inquiry. To further improve the inquiry protection, they propose two secure file plans to meet the stringent protection prerequisites under solid danger models, i.e., known cipher text display and known foundation demonstrate. What's more, they devise a plan upon the proposed file tree structure to the authors genuineness check over the returned indexed lists. At long last, the authors show the viability and productivity of the proposed plots through broad trial assessment. (Yu, Lu, Zhu, Xue, & Li, 2013) Distributed computing has developing as a promising example for information outsourcing and astounding information administrations. Worries of touchy data on cloud conceivably causes security issues. Information encryption ensures information security to some degree, yet at the cost of traded off proficiency. Searchable symmetric encryption (SSE) permits recovery of encoded information over cloud. In this chapter, the concentration is on tending to information security issues utilizing SSE. Interestingly, the authors define the security issue from the part of comparability significance and plan vigor. They watch that server-side positioning considering request saving encryption (OPE) spills information security. To take out the spillage, the authors propose a two-round searchable encryption (TRSE) conspire that backings beat k multikey word recovery. (Wong, D, Cheung, Kao, & Mamoulis, 2009) In This chapter they talk about the general issue of secure calculation on an encoded database and propose a SCONEDB (Secure Computation ON an Encrypted Database) show, which catches the execution and security necessities. As a contextual analysis, the authors concentrate on the issue of k-closest neighbour (kNN) calculation on an encoded database. The authors build up another lopsided scalar-item protecting encryption (ASPE) that jelly a unique kind of scalar item. They utilize APSE to develop two secure plans that bolster kNN calculation on scrambled information; each of these plans is appeared to oppose down to earth assaults of an alternate foundation learning level, at an alternate overhead cost. Broad execution studies are done to assess the overhead and the proficiency of the plans (Zhang & Zhang, 2011). Since Boneh et al. proposed the thought and development of Public Key Encryption with Keyword Search (PEKS) conspire, numerous updates and expansions have been given. Conjunctive watchword inquiry is one of these expansions. A large portion of these built plans cannot understand conjunctive with subset catchphrases look work. Subset watchwords look implies that the beneficiary could inquiry the subset catchphrases of all the catchphrases implanted in the cipher text. The authors ponder the issue of conjunctive with subset watchwords seek work, talk about the disadvantages about the existed plans, and after that give out a more effective development of Public Key Encryption with Conjunctive-Subset Keywords Search (PECSK) conspire. A correlation with different plans about effectiveness will be displayed. They additionally list the security prerequisites of their plan, then give out the security investigation (Song, Wagner, & Perrig, 2000).

MAIN FOCUS OF THE AUTHORS

Issues, Controversies, Problems

Data Owner

The information proprietor subcontracts her information to the cloud for suitable and consistent data admission to the equivalent search operators. To defend the information confidentiality, the information proprietor encrypts the unique information over symmetric encryption. To recover the exploration effectiveness, the data owner makes approximately keywords for each subcontracted document. The equivalent index is then formed giving to the keywords and a secret key. Afterward, the data owner directs the encrypted brochures and the equivalent directories to the cloud, and directs the symmetric key and secret key to exploration workers.

Cloud Server

The cloud server is an in-the authors entity which supplies the encrypted brochures and equivalent indexes that are established from the information proprietor, and delivers information admittance and exploration facilities to exploration users. When an exploration operator directs a keyword access to the cloud server, it resolves re-emergence a group of equivalent brochures founded on firm processes.

Search User

A search operator enquiries the subcontracted brochures from the cloud server with subsequent three steps. First, the exploration operator accepts together the symmetric key and the secret key from the information proprietor. Second, as per the exploration keywords, the exploration operator usages the secret key to make hatch and directs it to cloud server. Last, he obtains the corresponding text collection from the cloud server and is decrypting them with the symmetric key.

RSA Algorithm

RSA is the process shaped by the modern computers to decrypt and encrypt messages. It is an asymmetric cryptographic technique. Asymmetric resources that there are two different keys. This is public key cryptography, since one of them can be prearranged to everyone. The other key must be private. In conclusion, the factors of an integer are rigid (the factoring problem). A worker of RSA kinds and then issues the produce of two big prime figures, with a supplementary rate, as public key of theirs. The factors which are prime remain secret. Anybody can use the public key to encrypt a communication, but with presently published approaches, if the public key is large, only somebody with information of the prime factors can practicably decode the communication. It is used by modern computers to encrypt and decrypt communications. It is an asymmetric cryptographic procedure. Asymmetric means that there are two different keys. This is public key cryptography, since one of them can be given to all. The other key must be kept private.

Hierarchical Clustering

It produces hierarchy of clusters.

Two approaches:

1. **Agglomerative:**

Being a bottom-up approach. Individually opinion starts in its individual cluster. And couple of clusters combine as one changes up the hierarchy.

2. **Divisive:**

It is top-down approach. Explanations starts in one cluster, and splits are achieved recursively as one transfers up the hierarchy.

SOLUTIONS AND RECOMMENDATIONS

Symmetric Key Algorithm

1. Symmetric encryption practices the similar key to mutually decrypt and encrypt
2. DES is used as symmetric key algorithm
3. They are fast and their complexity is low so they can be easily implemented
4. Secret key should be configured in all hosts

Asymmetric Key Algorithm

1. Asymmetric key uses one key to decrypt and one key to encrypt
2. RSA is one of the asymmetric key algorithm
3. It is slow then symmetric key algorithm
4. No need of configuring secret keys in all hosts

Knn Algorithm

1. Partitional clustering
2. Partitions independent of each other
3. Sensitive to cluster center initialization

4. Poor convergence speed and bad overall clustering can happen due to poor initialization
5. Works only for around shapes
6. Doesn't work well for non-convex shapes

Hierarchical Clustering Algorithm

1. Hierarchical clustering
2. Visualize using a tree structure
3. Can give different partitioning
4. Doesn't need specification of number of clusters
5. It can be slow
6. Two types agglomerative and divisive

FUTURE RESEARCH DIRECTIONS

The authors propose to additionally spread the application to deliberate the extensibility of the set of file and the multi-user environments of cloud. This way, some initial consequences on the extensibility and the multiuser cloud environments. Another stimulating theme is to progress the highly ascendable searchable encryption to allow the authors organized exploration on large practical databases.

CONCLUSION

Fine-grained multikey word search (FMS) method was studied over encrypted data from cloud and delivered two FMS schemes. The FMS I constitute both the preference factors and relevance scores of keywords to improve more accurate search and improved users' knowledge, correspondingly. The FMS II attains safe and the authors organized search with functionality, i.e., "AND", "OR" and "NO" operations of keywords. Additionally, the authors have projected the improved methods supporting classified sub-dictionaries (FMSCS) to advance efficiency. The authors have used hierarchical clustering computation for the same.

REFERENCES

Abdalla, M., Bellare, M., Catalano, D., Kiltz, E., Kohno, T., Lange, T., ... Shi, H. (2008). Searchable encryption revisited: Consistency properties, relation to anonymous ibe, and extensions. *Journal of Cryptology, 21*(3), 350–391. doi:10.100700145-007-9006-6

Alliance, C. S. (2009). *Security Guidance for Critical Areas of Focus in Cloud Computing*. Retrieved from http://www.cloudsecurityalliance.org

Ballard, L., Kamara, S., & Monrose, F. (2005). Achieving efficient conjunctive keyword searches over encrypted data. *Proc. of ICICS*. 10.1007/11602897_35

Bellare, M., Boldyreva, A., & Neill, A. O. (2007). Deterministic and efficiently searchable encryption. *Proc. of CRYPTO.*

Boldyreva, A., Chenette, N., Lee, Y., & Oneill, A. (2009). Order-preserving symmetric encryption. In *Advances in Cryptology-EUROCRYPT* (pp. 224–241). Springer.

Boneh, Kushilevitz, Ostrovsky, & W. E. S. III. (2007). Public key encryption that allows pir queries. *Proc. of CRYPTO.*

Boneh, D., Crescenzo, G. D., Ostrovsky, R., & Persiano, G. (2004). Public key encryption with keyword search. *Proc. of EUROCRYPT.*

Boneh, D., & Waters, B. (2007). Conjunctive, subset, and range queries on encrypted data. *Proc. of TCC*, 535–554.

Brinkman, R. (2007). *Searching in encrypted data.* PhD thesis.

Brinkman. (2007). *Searching in encrypted data.* PhD thesis.

Cao, N., Wang, C., Li, M., Ren, K., & Lou, W. (2014). Privacy-preserving multikeyword ranked search over encrypted cloud data. *IEEE Transactions on Parallel and Distributed Systems, 25*(1), 222–233. doi:10.1109/TPDS.2013.45

Cao, N., Wang, C., Li, M., Ren, K., & Lou, W. (2014). Privacy-preserving multikeyword ranked search over encrypted cloud data. *IEEE Transactions on Parallel and Distributed Systems, 25*(1), 222–233. doi:10.1109/TPDS.2013.45

Cao, Wang, & Li, Ren, & Lou. (2014). Privacy-preserving multikeyword ranked search over encrypted cloud data. *IEEE Transactions on Parallel and Distributed Systems, 25*(1), 222–233.

Cash, J., & Jutla, K., Ro3u, & Steiner. (2013). Highly-scalable searchable symmetric encryption with support for Boolean queries. *Proc. CRYPTO*, 353-373.

Chang, Y.-C., & Mitzenmacher, M. (2005). Privacy preserving keyword searches on remote encrypted data. *Proc. of ACNS.* 10.1007/11496137_30

Curtmola, R., Garay, J. A., Kamara, S., & Ostrovsky, R. (2006). Searchable symmetric encryption: improved definitions and efficient constructions. *Proc. of ACM CCS.* 10.1145/1180405.1180417

De Capitani di Vimercati, S., Foresti, S., & Samarati, P. (2012). Managing and accessing data in the cloud: Privacy risks and approaches. CRiSIS, 1 –9.

Dinh, Lee, Niyato, & Wang. (2013). A survey of mobile cloud computing: Architecture, applications, and approaches. *Wireless Commun. Mobile Comput., 13*(18).

Gentry, C. (2009). *A fully homomorphic encryption scheme* (Ph.D. dissertation). Stanford University.

Goh, E.-J. (2003). *Secure indexes.* Retrieved from http://eprint.iacr.org/2003/216

Goldreich, O., & Ostrovsky, R. (1996). Software protection and simulation on oblivious rams. *Journal of the Association for Computing Machinery, 43*(3), 431–473. doi:10.1145/233551.233553

Golle, P., Staddon, J., & Waters, B. (2004). Secure conjunctive keyword search over encrypted data. *Proc. of ACNS*, 31–45. 10.1007/978-3-540-24852-1_3

Hwan, Gelogo, & Park. (2012). Next Generation Cloud Computing Issues and Solutions. *International Journal of Control and Automation, 5*.

Hwang, Y., & Lee, P. (2007). *Public key encryption with conjunctive keyword search and its extension to a multi-user system*. Pairing. doi:10.1007/978-3-540-73489-5_2

Jung, T., Mao, X., Li, X., Tang, S.-J., Gong, W., & Zhang, L. (2013). Privacy preserving data aggregation without secure channel: multivariate polynomial evaluation. *Proceedings of INFOCOM*, 2634–2642. 10.1109/INFCOM.2013.6567071

Kamara & Lauter. (2010). Cryptographic cloud storage. In *RLCPS*. Springer.

Kamara, S., & Lauter, K. (2010). Cryptographic cloud storage. In RLCPS. Springer. doi:10.1007/978-3-642-14992-4_13

Kamara, S., & Lauter, K. (2010). Cryptographic cloud storage. In RLCPS. Springer. doi:10.1007/978-3-642-14992-4_13

Katz, J., Sahai, A., & Waters, B. (2008). *Predicate encryption supporting disjunctions, polynomial equations, and inner products. Proc. of EUROCRYPT*. doi:10.1007/978-3-540-78967-3_9

Khan, Wang, Kulsoom, & Ullah. (2013). Searching Encrypted Data on Cloud. *International Journal of Computer Science Issues, 10*(6).

Khan, Wang, Kulsoom, & Ullah. (2013). Searching Encrypted Data on Cloud. *International Journal of Computer Science Issues, 10*(6).

Lewko, A., Okamoto, T., Sahai, A., Takashima, K., & Waters, B. (2010). Fully secure functional encryption: Attribute-based encryption and (hierarchical) inner product encryption. *Proc. of EUROCRYPT*. 10.1007/978-3-642-13190-5_4

Li, H., Dai, Y., Tian, L., & Yang, H. (2009). Identity-based authentication for cloud computing. In Cloud Computing. Berlin, Germany: Springer-Verlag. doi:10.1007/978-3-642-10665-1_14

Li, H., Liu, D., Dai, Y., Luan, T. H., & Shen, X. (2014). Enabling efficient multi-keyword ranked search over encrypted cloud data through blind storage. *IEEE Transactions on Emerging Topics in Computing*. doi:10.1109/TETC.2014.2371239

Li, J., Wang, Q., Wang, C., Cao, N., Ren, K., & Lou, W. (2010). Fuzzy keyword search over encrypted data in cloud computing. Proc. of IEEE INFOCOM'10 Mini-Conference. doi:10.1109/INFCOM.2010.5462196

Li, R., Xu, Z., Kang, W., Yow, K. C., & Xu, C.-Z. (2014). Efficient multikeyword ranked query over encrypted data in cloud computing. *Future Generation Computer Systems, 30*, 179–190. doi:10.1016/j.future.2013.06.029

Liang, Cai, Huang, Shen, & Peng. (2012). An SMDP-based service model for interdomain resource allocation in mobile cloud networks. *IEEE Trans. Veh. Technol., 61*(5).

Liang, H., Cai, L. X., Huang, D., Shen, X., & Peng, D. (2012). An smdpbased service model for interdomain resource allocation in mobile cloud networks. *IEEE Transactions on Vehicular Technology, 61*(5), 2222–2232. doi:10.1109/TVT.2012.2194748

Mahmoud & Shen. (2012). A cloud-based scheme for protecting source-location privacy against hotspot-locating attack in wireless sensor networks. *IEEE Trans. Parallel Distrib. Syst., 23*(10).

Mahmoud, M. M., & Shen, X. (2012). A cloud-based scheme for protecting source-location privacy against hotspot-locating attack in wireless sensor networks. *IEEE Transactions on Parallel and Distributed Systems, 23*(10), 1805–1818. doi:10.1109/TPDS.2011.302

Mell & Grance. (2011). The nist definition of cloud computing (draft). *NIST Special Publication, 800*, 145.

Naveed, Prabhakaran, & Gunter. (2014). Dynamic searchable encryption via blind storage. *Proceedings - IEEE Symposium on Security and Privacy*, 639–654.

Paillier, P. (1999). Public key cryptosystems based on composite degree residuosity classes. Eurocrypt, 223–238. doi:10.1007/3-540-48910-X_16

Pang, Shen, & Krishnan. (n.d.). Privacy-preserving similarity-based text retrieval. ACM Transactions on Internet Technology, 10(1), 4.

Reddy. (2013). Techniques for Efficient Keyword Search in Cloud Computing. *International Journal of Computer Science and Information Technologies, 4*(1).

Ren, K., Wang, C., & Wang, Q. (2012). Security Challenges for the Public Cloud. *IEEE Internet Computing, 16*(1), 69–73. doi:10.1109/MIC.2012.14

Samanthula, B. K., Elmehdwi, Y., & Jiang, W. (2014). *k-nearest neighbor classification over semantically secure encrypted relational data.* eprint arXiv:1403.5001

Shen, E., Shi, E., & Waters, B. (2009). Predicate privacy in encryption systems. *Proc. of TCC.*

Shen, Q., Liang, X., Shen, X., Lin, X., & Luo, H. (2014). Exploiting geodistributed clouds for e-health monitoring system with minimum service delay and privacy preservation. *IEEE Journal of Biomedical and Health Informatics, 18*(2), 430–439. doi:10.1109/JBHI.2013.2292829 PMID:24608048

Shen, Liang, Shen, Lin, & Luo. (2014). Exploiting geodistributed clouds for a e-health monitoring system with minimum service delay and privacy preservation. *IEEE J. Biomed. Health Inform., 18*(2).

Singhal, A. (2001). Modern information retrieval: A brief overview. *A Quarterly Bulletin of the Computer Society of the IEEE Technical Committee on Data Engineering, 24*(4), 35–43.

Singhal, A. (2001). Modern information retrieval: A brief overview. *A Quarterly Bulletin of the Computer Society of the IEEE Technical Committee on Data Engineering, 24*(4), 35–43.

Singhal, A. (2001). Modern information retrieval: A brief overview. *A Quarterly Bulletin of the Computer Society of the IEEE Technical Committee on Data Engineering, 24*(4), 35–43.

Song, D., Wagner, D., & Perrig, A. (2000). Practical techniques for searches on encrypted data. *Proc. of S&P.*

Song, D. X., Wagner, D., & Perrig, A. (2000). Practical techniques for searches on encrypted data. In *Proceedings of S&P*. IEEE.

Song, D. X., Wagner, D., & Perrig, A. (2000). Practical techniques for searches on encrypted data. *Proceedings of S&P*, 44–55.

Stefanov, Papamanthou, & Shi. (2014). Practical dynamic searchable encryption with small leakage. *Proc. NDSS*. doi:10.1109/TPDS.2013.282

Sun, Wang, Cao, Li, Lou, Hou, & Li. (2013). Verifiable privacy-preserving multi-keyword text search in the cloud supporting similarity-based ranking. *IEEE Transactions on Parallel and Distributed Systems*. Doi:10.1109/TPDS.2013.282

Sun, W. (2013). Privacy-preserving multi-keyword text search in the cloud supporting similarity-based ranking. Proc. 8th ACM SIGSAC Symp.Inf., Comput. Commun. Secur., 71-82.

Sun, Wang, Cao, Li, Lou, Hou, & Li. (2013). Verifiable privacy-preserving multi-keyword text search in the cloud supporting similarity-based ranking. *IEEE Transactions on Parallel and Distributed Systems*. Doi:10.1109/TPDS.2013.282

Vaquero, L. M., Rodero-Merino, L., Caceres, J., & Lindner, M. (2009). A break in the clouds: Towards a cloud definition. *ACM SIGCOMM Comput. Commun. Rev.*, *39*(1), 50–55. doi:10.1145/1496091.1496100

Vaquero, L. M., Rodero-Merino, L., Caceres, J., & Lindner, M. (2009). A break in the clouds: Towards a cloud definition. *ACM SIGCOMM Comput. Commun. Rev.*, *39*(1), 50–55. doi:10.1145/1496091.1496100

Vaquero, L. M., Rodero-Merino, L., Caceres, J., & Lindner, M. (2009). A break in the clouds: Towards a cloud definition. *ACM SIGCOMM Comput. Commun. Rev.*, *39*(1), 50–55. doi:10.1145/1496091.1496100

Wang, C. (2010). Secure Ranked Keyword Search Over Encrypted Cloud Data. *Proc. ICDCS '10*. 10.1109/ICDCS.2010.34

Wang, C., Cao, N., Li, J., Ren, K., & Lou, W. (2010). Secure ranked keyword search over encrypted cloud data. In *Proceedings of ICDCS*. IEEE. 10.1109/ICDCS.2010.34

Wang, C., Cao, N., Li, J., Ren, K., & Lou, W. (2010). Secure ranked keyword search over encrypted cloud data. *Proc. of ICDCS'10*. 10.1109/ICDCS.2010.34

Wang, Yu, Lou, & Hou. (2014). Privacy-preserving multi-keyword fuzzy search over encrypted data in the cloud. *Proceedings - IEEE INFOCOM*.

Williams, P., Sion, R., & Carbunar, B. (2008). Building castles out of mud: practical access pattern privacy and correctness on untrusted storage. ACM CCS, 139–148. doi:10.1145/1455770.1455790

Witten, Moffat, & Bell. (1999). *Managing Gigabytes: Compressing and indexing documents and images*. Morgan Kaufmann Publishing.

Witten, Moffat, & Bell. (1999). *Managing gigabytes: Compressing and indexing documents and images*. Morgan Kaufmann Publishing.

Wong, W. K., Cheung, D. W., Kao, B., & Mamoulis, N. (2010). Secure kNN computation on encrypted databases. Proc. ACM SIGMOD Int. Conf. Manage. Data, 139-152.

Wong, W. K., Cheung, D. W., Kao, B., & Mamoulis, N. (2009). Secure knn computation on encrypted databases. *Proc. of SIGMOD*. 10.1145/1559845.1559862

Wong, W. K., Cheung, D. W.-l., Kao, B., & Mamoulis, N. (2009). Secure knn computation on encrypted databases. *Proceedings of SIGMOD International Conference on Management of Data*, 139–152. 10.1145/1559845.1559862

Yang, L., Liu, & Yang. (2014). Secure dynamic searchable symmetric encryption with constant document update cost. *Proc.GLOBECOM*.

Yang, Li, Liu, Yang, & M. (2014). Secure dynamic searchable symmetric encryption with constant document update cost. In *Proceedings of GLOBCOM*. IEEE.

Yu, J., Lu, P., Zhu, Y., Xue, G., & Li, M. (2013). Towards secure multikeyword top-k retrieval over encrypted cloud data. *IEEE Transactions on Dependable and Secure Computing*, *10*(4), 239–250. doi:10.1109/TDSC.2013.9

Yu, J., Lu, P., Zhu, Y., Xue, G., & Li, M. (2013). Towards secure multikeyword top-k retrieval over encrypted cloud data. *IEEE Transactions on Dependable and Secure Computing*, *10*(4), 239–250. doi:10.1109/TDSC.2013.9

Zhang, B., & Zhang, F. (2011). An efficient public key encryption with conjunctive-subset keywords search. *Journal of Network and Computer Applications*, *34*(1), 262–267. doi:10.1016/j.jnca.2010.07.007

KEY TERMS AND DEFINITIONS

Big Data: Large data sets that are analyzed computationally.

Cipher-Text: Encrypted form of text.

Cloud Computing: Provides shared computing resources.

Clusters: Unit of allocable hard disk space.

Encryption: Process of converting information into code.

Hierarchical Clustering: Which builds a hierarchy of clusters.

Minimum Hash Sub-Tree: Root is having the minimum value in the subtree.

Symmetric Scheme: Algorithm used for cryptography.

This research was previously published in Big Data Analytics for Satellite Image Processing and Remote Sensing edited by P. Swarnalatha and Prabu Sevugan, pages 72-98, copyright year 2018 by Engineering Science Reference (an imprint of IGI Global).

Chapter 34
Classification of File Data Based on Confidentiality in Cloud Computing Using K-NN Classifier

Munwar Ali Zardari
Universiti Teknologi Petronas, Malaysia

Low Tang Jung
Universiti Teknologi Petronas, Malaysia

ABSTRACT

Cloud computing is a new paradigm model that offers different services to its customers. The increasing number of users for cloud services i.e. software, platform or infrastructure is one of the major reasons for security threats for customers' data. Some major security issues are highlighted in data storage service in the literature. Data of thousands of users are stored on a single centralized place where the possibility of data threat is high. There are many techniques discussed in the literature to keep data secure in the cloud, such as data encryption, private cloud and multiple clouds concepts. Data encryption is used to encrypt the data or change the format of the data into the unreadable format that unauthorized users could not understand even if they succeed to get access of the data. Data encryption is very expensive technique, it takes time to encrypt and decrypt the data. Deciding the security approach for data security without understanding the security needs of the data is a technically not a valid approach. It is a basic requirement that one should understand the security level of data before applying data encryption security approach. To discover the data security level of the data, the authors used machine learning approach in the cloud. In this paper, a data classification approach is proposed for the cloud and is implemented in a virtual machine named as Master Virtual Machine (Vmm). Other Vms are the slave virtual machines which will receive from Vmm the classified information for further processing in cloud. In this study the authors used three (3) virtual machines, one master Vmm and two slaves Vms. The master Vmm is responsible for finding the classes of the data based on its confidentiality level. The data is classified into two classes, confidential (sensitive) and non-confidential (non-sensitive/public) data using K-NN

DOI: 10.4018/978-1-5225-8176-5.ch034

algorithm. After classification phase, the security phase (encryption phase) shall encrypt only the confidential (sensitive) data. The confidentiality based data classification is using K-NN in cloud virtual environment as the method to encrypt efficiently the only confidential data. The proposed approach is efficient and memory space friendly and these are the major findings of this work.

INTRODUCTION

Cloud Computing is an internet based distributed virtual environment. All computational operations are performed on cloud through the Internet (Rawat 2012). It consists of a set of resources and services offered through the internet. Cloud computing is also called Internet computing because they both have same symbolic icon. Applications, Operating systems, data, processing capacity, and storage all exist on the Web, ready to be shared among the users (Sadiku et al., 2014). Cloud computing is basically a collection of different e-resources available twenty four hours and accessible from anywhere through browser software. Many companies are getting benefits from cloud computing due to its pay-as-you-go cost model and elasticity of resources, where users pay for only those services that they used (Prakash, 2013), and cloud provides customizable services to users. Compared to the traditional models which provide in-house infrastructure, cloud provides low cost services with high availability (Li et al., 2010). In cloud model the user is exempted from hardware and software maintenance cost.

The National Institute of Science and Technology (NIST) defines the cloud computing in a more appropriate way:

A model for enabling convenient, on-demand network access to a shared pool of configurable computing resources (networks, servers, storage, applications and other services) that can be rapidly provisioned and released with minimal management effort or service provider interaction. (AlZain et al., 2012)

The cloud computing can be defined in a simpler way: "A distributed virtual environment that provides virtualization based IT-as-Services by rent". That is it is often better to get the required resources on the rent rather than purchasing one's own resources. The main purpose for users to avail the cloud services is to avoid IT infrastructure purchasing and maintenance cost to get data accommodatable storage space for their large amount of data in the cloud. Beside all cloud services such as Software-as-a-Service (SaaS), Platform-as-a-Service (PaaS) and Infrastructure-as-a-Service (IaaS) (Jansen et al., 2011), cloud also provides storage service as a sub-service of IaaS service model. In storage as a service, the distributed database servers are available on rent to store users' data. These services are available for all kinds of users without any business discriminations.

Cloud computing is facing a number of challenging threats due to its virtualized multi-tenant nature (Purushothaman & Abburu, 2012). Data security is always the main challenging threat to the quality of services in cloud and may suppress the users' interest to adopt cloud services for their enterprise benefits (Ransome et al., 2010). All integrated and communicated environment business decisions and operations depend on the quality of the data and information risk management (Yanjun & Wen-Chen, 2009), good quality data is required for better decisions (Lam & Chun, 2008).

In cloud environment, all kinds of data are stored on servers, and these services are distributed over the world. User does not have any idea where physically their data are stored. The loss of control on the data is the main concern of the users. Cloud servers store data in traditional methods. The first method is to encrypt the received data and store in the cloud servers. The second method is to store the data in cloud servers without data encryption. These data storage methods are subject to data confidentiality issue. It is known that data are often not of the same type and have different properties and characteristics. In a cloud environment, a consumer's data are stored on remote servers not physically known to the consumer causing high chances of data confidentiality leakages. When the data are transferred to cloud, they passed through some security mechanism, such as data encryption (without understanding the features of data) or directly being stored on servers without encryption. Data have different kinds of sensitivity levels. So, it would be non-technical to just send data into a cloud without understanding its security requirements. The traditional methods are no more appropriate for new distributed environment. When the nature of business changed, the security measures must be reconsidered and prepare for new challenges. This research focuses on the confidentiality threat in the cloud environment and also to address the confidentiality level of the data. We have proposed a data classification model for the cloud environment to classify data according to their sensitivity level.

RELATED WORK

Concerning the importance of data security in cloud computing, the European Network and Information Security Agency (ENISA) published a report titled "Cloud Computing: Benefits, risks and recommendations for information security" in Nov-2009. In the report, ENISA identified and discussed different cloud risks and their effects on the cloud customers (Catteddu et al., 2009). A crypto co-processor was suggested in (Ram et al., 2010) to solve the data security threats in cloud. The crypto co-processor is a tool which provides security-as-a-service on demand controlled by a third party. Crypto co-processor allows the users to select the data encryption technique to encrypt the data and divide the data into different fixed chunks. This is to make hacker not knowing the starting and ending points of the data. But the limitation with this tool is that the end user may not be technically savvy enough to select powerful technique for data encryption.

The single cloud providing a central storage place for all consumers' data is easier to hack, whereas multi-storage system is more secure than single storage. IBM proposed a new concept of inner-cloud in 2010 where it defines the inner-cloud as: "the clouds of a cloud". The inner-cloud storage model is more reliable and trustworthy as compared to a single cloud storage model (Cachin et al., 2010). In the inner-cloud model, the hash function and digital signature are hybridised to provide data authentication and integrity security techniques in cloud. Whereas the data security key is divided and shared on multiple clouds; but this process of sharing of keys leads to an issue when one cloud is not available due to some technical reasons. The integrated Data Protection as a Service (DPaaS) model is also used for data security (Song et al., 2012). DPaaS integrates information flow checking, encryption, and application installation in cloud computing to avoid the implementation of the FDE and FHME techniques which are not affordable by small and medium enterprises and the cloud service providers. The public cloud has security challenges and data outsourcing is still a big challenge. In data outsourcing, the users are not sure about the location, data transaction accuracy and security of the stored data.

Recently, Security as a Service model is proposed in (Hassan Takabi, James B.D. Joshi, 2010). These authors focused on IaaS service of cloud. According to them, IaaS is a service model on which users have complete control on the virtualised systems. Due to the complete control of tenants, they can install malicious software on their virtual machines to create new attacks. These attacks may cause the leakage of data. As mentioned in (Varadharajan et al., 2014) there are significantly more security challenges in IaaS compared to SaaS and PaaS. Different tenants use one centralized distributed system (cloud) and everyone has different security requirements, and same security policies may not fit all tenant. A Network Virtualization model is proposed to meet different security requirements of different tenants with the underlying physical network, enabling multi-tenant datacenters to automatically address a large and diverse set of tenant's requirements (Chen et al., 2014). The network virtualization is implemented through a collaborative network security prototype system used in a multi-tenant data center. Authors demonstrated vCNSMS with a centralized collaborative scheme and deep packet inspection with an open source UTM system. A security level based protection policy is proposed for simplifying the security rule management for vCNSMS. Different security levels have different packet inspection schemes and are enforced with different security plugins. A smart packet verdict scheme is also integrated into vCNSMS for intelligence flow processing to protect from possible network attacks inside a data center network (Chen et al., 2014). Another study conducted by Junbeom Hur about the data security challenges in distributed data in distributed environment (Hur, 2013). The data access policy in distributed system is another challenging issue. A novel CP-ABE scheme is proposed in (Hur, 2013) for data sharing by exploring different characteristics of distributed system. CP-ABE scheme achieve two main achievements i.e. the key escrow problem could be solved by escrow-free key issuing protocol, which is constructed using the secure two-party computation between the key generation center and the data-storing center, and fine-grained user revocation per each attribute could be done by proxy encryption which takes advantage of the selective attribute group key distribution on top of the ABE (Hur, 2013).

Most of the above discussed techniques work on data encryption for data security. However to encrypt complete data is very expensive in the context of time and memory. It would be better to separate the confidential (sensitive) data from the non-confidential (public) data and then encrypt only the sensitive data.

Classification of objects is an important area of research and of practical applications in a variety of fields, including pattern recognition and artificial intelligence, statistics, cognitive psychology, vision analysis and medicine (Keller et al., 1985). There are numerous machine learning techniques been developed and investigated for classification processing. However, in many pattern recognition problems, the classification of an input pattern is based on the data where the respective sample size of each class is small. Moreover, the sample may possibly not be representative of the actual probability distribution, even if it is known (Keller & Gray, 1985). In such cases, there are many techniques work on similarity and distance in feature space. For instance, clustering and discriminate analysis (Richard et al., 1973). In many areas, the K-Nearest Neighbour (K-NN) algorithm is used for classification of instances. K-NN is the simplest data classification technique with low complexity. This decision rule provides a simple non-parametric procedure for assigning a class label to the input pattern based on the class labels represented by the k-nearest neighbour of the vector. K-NN classification is more suitable for those problem domains characterized by data that is only partially exposed to the system prior to employment (Dasarathy, 1980).

Literature review leads us to identify an important gap that: "How to classify the data based on its security requirements in cloud virtual environment. Every data has different security level and must be secured based on its security level". To outsource the data on to cloud without understanding the security level of the data is not a technically sound approach and has many drawbacks.

PROPOSED MODEL

Machine learning techniques are widely used in pattern recognition, image processing, data clustering and data segmentation. Our proposed model uses K-NN data classification algorithm to identify which data need security and which data do not need security. The security level of data depends on the degree of importance of the data. Each data has different level of security. The K-NN algorithm is applied only on the file schema (file attributes) level because the security level of the data or file can be determined by the file schema, file metadata, file owner, and file name. In this proposed model, we used the K-NN machine learning technique in the cloud computing environment to solve the data confidentiality problem. Many algorithms are used in text classification but K-NN is extensively discussed in the literature due to its simple implementation, high efficiency (Shi et al., 2011), better accuracy (Bijalwan et al., 2014) and easily to understand.

To understand the confidential and non-confidential data in a file, the K-NN classifier is used in a designed simulation environment. The value of K is maintained to one (1) for better accuracy. After finding the confidential and non-confidential data, the confidential data is further transferred to the RSA encryption algorithm for data encryption to protect confidential data from unauthorized users. Therefore, the public data is directly stored without encryption. Most of the clouds implement data encryption techniques to protect data. But it is technically a better approach to decide the security for the data based on the security level of the data instead imposing the encryption on complete dataset or just sending complete data to the cloud server without any proper security. The two common data storage methods practiced by clouds are 1) encrypt complete data and then store in cloud 2) store data without encryption. The first method is secure method but expensive because encrypting all data is illogical. In this method public and private data all are treated similarly. The data security level of public data is different from the confidential data. So before data encryption the cloud must know which data need to be encrypted and which data do not. The second method is unsecure but cheap. The classification technique in cloud will easily decide the security requirements of the data. In this way data can be saved from over-security and under-security situations and to save time and memory resources. In this research, data are into two different classes: class1 (non-confidential data) and class2 (confidential data). Figure 1 in the Appendix shows the detailed steps to solve the data confidentiality issue in cloud computing.

Data Classification

The classification of data in the context of confidentiality is the classification of data based on its sensitivity level and the impact to the organization that data be disclosed only to authorized users. The data classification helps determine what baseline security requirements/controls are appropriate for safeguarding the data.

In this research, the data are classified into two classes i.e. confidential and public (non-confidential). However the number of classes may change depending on the requirements of the data owner. Some example are given here, Michigan Technological University published a report titled "Data Classification and Handling Policy" in which they categorized data based on security into confidential data, internal/privacy data, and public data (M. T. University, 2011). Another report published by University of Texas Health Science Centre at San Antonio (UTHSCSA) titled "Protection by Data Classification Security Standard", in which data are classified as public, internal, confidential, and confidential/high risk (UTH-SCSA, 2006). The California State University published a document titled "Information Security Data

Classification Standards". This document describes the three classes of data regarding the data security placed on the particular types of information assets. These three classes are confidential, internal use, and general (C. S. University, 2011). In this research we treat all data as confidential except public data because all these data need to be secure at different stages of data processing.

In this research, the confidential (sensitive) data are defined as data that can contain very important information of individuals or organizations. The unauthenticated access to confidential data will have catastrophic effect on the owner. Such information might include:

- **Personal data:** Includes personal identifiable information such as social security number, national identification number, passport number, credit card number, driver's license number, medical records, and health insurance policy ID number but not limited;
- **Financial Records:** Includes financial account number, transaction information;
- **Business Material:** Such a document or data that is unique or specific intellectual property;
- **Legal Data:** Includes potential attorney-privileged material;
- **Medical/Health Data:** Includes sample code number, address, date of admission, medical record number, date of discharge, health plan beneficiary number;
- **Government Data:** Includes government intellectual documents, government agency documents, government future plan information.

The non-confidential (non-sensitive/public) data are defined as data and files that are not critical to business needs or operations. This data that are deliberately been released to the public for their consumption, such as press announcements, marketing material or introductory information of any organization.

K-NN Algorithm for Data Classification

The K-Nearest Neighbour (K-NN) is a supervised machine learning technique which is widely used for classification, pattern recognition, prediction and estimation. K-NN is one the instance-based learners, where a set of training data is stored for the classification of new unclassified datasets (Larose, 2005). It is the simplest iterative technique to classify unclassified datasets into user specified classes. This algorithm used by several researchers across different disciplines, most notably Lloyd (1957, 1982), Forgey (1965), Friedman and Rubin (1967), and McQueen (1967) (Lloyd, 1982).

The KNN Classifier is a classifier that works well on basic recognition problems. Using a relatively large value of K may include some not so similar pixels. On the other hand, using a small value of K may exclude some potential candidate pixels. In both cases the classification accuracy will decrease (Khan et al., 2002). The computational complexity of K-NN depends on the size of the training dataset. If the training dataset is large the computing complexity of K-NN is high (Suguna & Thanushkodi, 2010). The two main steps of K-NN which distinguish it from others are distance/similarity measure and majority voting. The algorithm must compute the distance/similarity and sort all of the training data distance/similarity at each prediction. Another issue in K-NN is the approach to combining the class labels. The K-N uses the simplest method to take a majority vote, but this can be a problem if the nearest neighbours vary widely in their distance and the closer neighbours more reliably indicate the class of the object (Wu et al., 2007).

The K-NN algorithm has a set of n labeled samples; n is the number of data items in the dataset. This dataset is called training dataset to train K-NN for further prediction. This can be represented as:

$$D = \{d_1, d_2, d_3, ..., d_n\}$$

where D is the set of total samples and $d_1, d_2, d_3, ..., d_n$ are different samples in dataset. The D must be assigned n labels. The set of n labelled samples can be represented as:

$$D = \{d_1, d_2, d_3, ..., d_n, \mid c_1, c_2, c_3, ..., c_n\}$$

where, $c_1, c_2, c_3, ..., c_n$ are classes of the training dataset. For simulation, we assigned one class to all training dataset elements. We only trained K-NN with confidential attributes and except these attributes all others are considered as non-confidential attributes.

How the K-NN Algorithm Works

Step 1: Determine the set of n labelled samples:

$$D = \{d_1, d_2, d_3, ..., d_m \mid c_1, c_2, c_3, ..., c_n\}$$

Step 2: Set the value of K (for this simulation we chose k=1 because we have single class training dataset).
Step 3: Calculate the distance between the test dataset and training dataset using Euclidean distance:
   Step 3.1:   Store each distance between each parameter into an arraylist:

ArrayList ← Distance

Step 4: Sort the arraylist and determine the K-nearest neighbours based on the value of K (step 2).
Step 5: Find the class of most closet neighbours based on majority voting.
Step 6: Label test data with class.

Confidentiality Based Data Classification in Cloud

The CloudSim simulator was used for simulation purpose. Figure 2 in the Appendix shows the proposed simulation environment for cloud service providers to solve data sensitivity/confidentiality issue in the cloud. At the bottom, CloudSim engine was used to run the simulation. The Xen Virtual Machine Monitor (VMM) was used to create, manage and allocate VMs to cloudlets (cloud tasks).

In Vm creation phase, it is created from scratch with abstract configuration. Every Vm is assigned a specific "ID" which distinguishes it from other virtual machines, and Vm ID is used to manage, process and maintain the phases of virtual machine. In Vm configuration phase, Vm needs to initialize RAM memory, hard drive image, input and output size of user application or user request. Vm also configured with Machine Instructions per Second (MIPS) that will decides how many instructions Vm executes in one second. After proper configuration, the Vm is ready to be initialized to user application (or user request). A Vm is a virtual instance that requires scheduling for the allocation of computing resources on physical host (Shiraz et al., 2012). The Vm is scheduled with workload or spaceshare scheduler. A Vm enters in to the running state when physical CPU is scheduled for its execution. Vm can be suspended or paused from its current host and migrated to another host. In configuration phase, the Vm must be assigned value for the following attributes before execution:

- Machine Instructions Per Second (MIPS)
- Image Size
- Size of RAM
- Bandwidth
- Virtual Machine Monitor (VMM)

The unclassified data are received from the user and the classification process will start based on the user requirements in cloud. After determining the classes of the data, the confidential class data is encrypted and non-confidential data is directly processed in the cloud. The number of cloud resources used for the simulation is given in Table 1 in the Appendix. In our research, we chose 2 different data centres to store confidential and public data separately on single host. One broker is used to hold cloud attributes and two virtual machines are used, one for confidential data and other for public data. One VMM is used to manage and create VMs. We used three cloudlets in our research where one cloudlet hold confidential data and other cloudlets hold public data and third cloudlet holds the original mixed data.

Cloud Service Properties and Description

Before simulation, it is important to set the properties of all three service models Software-as-a-Service (SaaS), Platform-as-a-Service (PaaS) and Infrastructure-as-a-Service (IaaS). Table 2 in the Appendix shows the properties of the SaaS modeller which was deployed on a VM in CloudSim. In the SaaS modeler each cloudlet has a specific identification for the VM. Here "ID" represents a specific cloudlet, and length is the size of the cloudlet. The size of the input and output file is given in Bytes.

- **Length:** The length or size (in MI) of this cloudlet is to be executed in a data centre.
- **Input File Size:** The file size (in Bytes) of the current cloudlet BEFORE being submitted to a data centre.
- **Output File Size:** This is the file size (in Bytes) of the current cloudlet AFTER execution.

Table 3 in the Appendix shows the properties of PaaS for the application deployment which contains VM properties. It shows the processing power of the physical computing node which is assigned at the virtual machine level, VM image size (in MB), amount of bandwidth, and the number of cores in which the MIPS' power is shared at the VM level to run the cloudlet. The VMs are managed by VMM.

- **Machine Instructions Per Second (MIPS):** This is the processing power assigned to the VM to execute the instructions according to the specified MIPS.
- **Image Size:** The Image Size (in MB) is the VM image size that represents a virtual hard disk file that is used as a template for creating a VM.
- **Pes Number:** The Pes number is the number of processors used at the VM level.

It is also important to use better and stronger infrastructure resources in cloud for better computation and response time. The available resources at data centre level put a limit on the SaaS modeller requirement, i.e., resources allocated at the VM level can't exceed IaaS limit. Table 4 in the Appendix shows the IaaS properties and their values, where "DC ID" is the data centre identity which is assigned to the VM.

CONFIDENTIALITY BASED DATA CLASSIFICATION IN CLOUD

In this section we discuss the data classification process in cloud environment. The implementation of data classification in cloud is called Confidentiality based Classification–as-a-Service (C2aaS). Before applying any security policy on data, the proposed system recognizes the security requirements of the data to avoid over security and under security issues. The proposed system will decide which data in file are confidential and which data are non-confidential (public) based on the class label of the file schema (file attributes/columns names). After categorizing the file schema into confidential and non-confidential classes, the data of confidential attributes is labeled as confidential and data of non-confidential attributes is labeled as non-confidential. The security requirement of the data is measured based on the class of the data.

The data classification service is deployed in cloud at virtual machine level. For classification service, virtual machine (Vm) is categorized into two levels i.e. top level and bottom level. Top level contains a single Vm and bottom level contains "2" Vms. We integrated K-NN classification approach into a Vm which is in top level. This Vm is named as Master Vm in shorts Vmm. The Vmm directly interacts with users' file/data or application. When there is any user request for cloud storage, the cloud system shall prompt the user whether the user needs to classify the data based on the confidentially. The Vmm is followed by many other virtual machines called Slave virtual machines (Vm_s). The Vm_s are managed at the bottom level as shown in Figure 3 in the Appendix. Vmm is the main gate to interact with user/broker and distributes workload among the slave virtual machines. The number of slave virtual machines could be "n" but in our experiment, we used one Vmm for data classification and two Vms machines for further processing.

After the classification phase, Vmm calls slaves virtual machines when Vmm needs to process the data into the cloud servers. The Vmm performs two operations i.e. data classification and data encryption. After data classification Vmm applies RSA encryption technique on only confidential/sensitive data predicted by K-NN; whereas the public data is directly sent to one Vm_s and stored on server without any encryption.

C2aaS only classify data based on the confidentiality level of data because based on our findings the security of data must be decided according to the security need of data. Each and every data is different and has different features (Cachin, et al., 2010). If the values of data are different the security level must be different (Cachin, et al., 2010). Vmm is responsible to classify data into confidential and non-confidential classes. Vmm uses K-NN classifier to predict the class of the data of a test file dataset. K-NN uses Euclidean distance to measure the distance between training and test objects. Two data security modules are integrated with Vm_m. These modules are Data Classifier and RSA Encryption as shown in Figure 4 in the Appendix.

Figure 4 is a general internal view of cloud infrastructure which is divided into four different layers. The layer 1 is called user application layer, where user's applications are specified for cloud resources, layer 2 is called master virtual machine layer where Vm_m is installed and integrated with data classification and encryption. Layer 3 defines the "n" number of slave Vm_s which are connected to layer 2 and layer 4. Layer 3 is assigned computation tasks by layer 2. In other words, layer 3 works under the order of layer 2. The VMM is important for both layer 2 and 3 to monitor all virtual machines in layer 2 and layer 3. The layer 4 is the datacenter layer where it contains number of data storage servers. In cloud, the number of datacenters is not fixed; number of servers depends on the strength of service provider. The second layer contains File/Data (FD) classifier (K-NN). The FD classifier is implemented on the top of data encryption module.

RESULTS AND DISCUSSION

In this section, we discuss the results taken after the implementation K-NN and RSA algorithms to improve and manage the confidentiality level of data in a cloud environment. In the situation when you have small number of test and training dataset, the K-NN algorithm performs with better results. The other classification algorithms like decision tree, rule based algorithms work with the detailed attribute values whereas the Naive Bayes algorithm work on the number of occurrences of a word in document. These algorithms do not fit in our problem domain when we are working with file attributes instead of file attributes values (data). File attributes do not repeat in the file i.e. the attribute "employee name" or "employee salary" is single time in a file, so, finding frequency of a word in such scenario may cause the misclassification of attributes or may not work with single occurrence of a word. From the definitions of file attributes, it is clear that every file attribute occurs at once in file. The duplicate file attributes may be considered as human typing error. To avoid such ambiguities we need to preprocess the data to remove duplication and delimiters.

During data simulation, we observed that RSA algorithm is very slow and time consuming algorithm. It took huge amount of time to encrypt a small chunk of the data as shown in following results. The encrypted data size also increased more than original data size. The two main limitation of RSA algorithm which was observed during implementation in cloud environment are:

- High calculation complexity to convert original text into encrypted text;
- It increases the size of data more than its original size.

The data selected for this study is the individual/personal/employee records. This data was taken from UCI repository (SGI n.d.), which contains different types of datasets mostly used by the research community. The value of K can be N (K=N), but here the K=1 is used to get accurate classification result.

The data of a file is classified into two classes "sensitive" and "non-sensitive" by considering the file attributes standard rules. The K-NN is applied on the file attributes to find which attributes are confidential and which attributes are non-confidential. The selection of confidential and non-confidential data is based on the label of their attributes for individual/personal/employee record which are listed in Table 5 in the Appendix. These rules are taken from reports published by world data quality managing organization and universities (UTHSCSA 2006) (C. S. University, 2011).

After identifying confidential and non-confidential attributes in file, the data of file is divided into two parts according to its attributes class. The data of confidential attributes are separated from data of non-confidential attributes. The non-confidential attributes are labeled as non-confidential and denoted with "Class1" and the data of confidential attributes are labeled as confidential and denoted with "Class2". Now we have two sets of data based on classified two sets of file attributes. These data sets with their attributes are shown in following equations.

Confidential data of confidential attributes/parameters:

$$Confidential\_paramters\left\{p_1, p_2, p_3, ..., p_n\right\}$$
$$= \left[\begin{array}{l}\left\{p_1\left(d_1, d_2, d_3, ..., d_m\right)\right\}, \left\{p_2\left(d_1, d_2, d_3, ..., d_m\right)\right\}, \\ \left\{p_3\left(d_1, d_2, d_3, ..., d_m\right)\right\}, ..., \left\{p_n\left(d_1, d_2, d_3, ..., d_m\right)\right\}\end{array}\right]$$

This equation can be summarized as:

$$Confidential\_paramters\left\{p_1, p_2, p_3, ..., p_n\right\}$$
$$= \left[\left\{p_n\left(d_{n1}, d_{n2}, d_{n3}, ..., d_{nm}\right)\right\}\right]$$

Non-confidential data of non-confidential attributes/parameters:

$$Non-onfidential\_paramters\left\{p_1, p_2, p_3, ..., p_n\right\}$$
$$= \left[\begin{array}{l}\left\{p_1\left(d_1, d_2, d_3, ..., d_m\right)\right\}, \left\{p_2\left(d_1, d_2, d_3, ..., d_m\right)\right\}, \\ \left\{p_3\left(d_1, d_2, d_3, ..., d_m\right)\right\}, ..., \left\{p_n\left(d_1, d_2, d_3, ..., d_m\right)\right\}\end{array}\right]$$

This equation can be summarized as:

$$Non-Confidential\_paramters\left\{p_1, p_2, p_3, ..., p_n\right\}$$
$$= \left[\left\{p_n\left(d_1, d_2, d_3, ..., d_n\right)\right\}\right]$$

where, n is total number of confidential or non-confidential attributes. Each ith parameter has m number of values.

Table 6 in the Appendix shows the details of the file before and after classification. The total size of the file was 512KB and total records in file were 5094. Table 6 shows that total 7 attributes out of 15 file attributes are confidential and remaining attributes are non-confidential. Based on these attributes we split the data accordingly. The size of confidential data is 160KB and the size of non-confidential data is 352KB. The classification time taken by the K-NN classifier to classify 5094 records (512KB) was 1075ms as shown in Table 6. After classification, the data of both classes are assigned to different cloudlets as new tasks for VMs as shown below:

$$\left(cloudlet\_ID = 0\right) \leftarrow class1\_data$$

$$\left(cloudlet\_ID = 1\right) \leftarrow class2\_data$$

The cloudlet is a task assigned to the virtual machines. Here, cloudlet having ID=0 is assigned non-confidential data and cloudlet with ID=1 is assigned confidential data. The slave Vm_s are assigned individual cloudlet for further process. Before assigning the cloudlet to the VM, make sure that VM has enough capacity to handle a particular cloudlet of particular size. This task of VM management is done by virtual machine monitor. The slave Vm_s processed the data to the selected data centres with information of user id and broker id. To avoid data confidentiality risk, the data of confidential attributes are encrypted to make it secure while the public data do not need encryption due to its non-security level.

The total simulation time taken by both cloudlets is shown in Table 7 in the Appendix. The cloudlet with ID=0 represents the Class1 data and cloudlet ID=1 represents the Class2 data. In Table 7 the label "status" is the simulation status which means that the simulation was performed successfully. For this simulation each class data was assigned to a different VM and each VM was assigned different data-centers. The non-confidential data was stored on different server and confidential (in encrypted form) was stored on other server. In this way the Information Retrieval (IR) from the cloud will be easy for the users. If user needs one part of the data he/she will only access the required part of the data instead of complete dataset as we published in more details in our previous paper (Zardari et al. 2013).

Evaluation of Data Classification

The process of evaluation is to assess the proposed algorithm in context of accuracy, F1-score. These measures include recognition rate (accuracy), sensitivity (recall), specificity, precision and F1-Score. To measure accuracy of an algorithm is not enough to measure the how good or accurate algorithm is; with accuracy we need to find precision, recall and F1-Score for better evaluation of the algorithm.

There are four terms used in the calculation of precision, recall and accuracy. These terms are described as below:

- True Positive (TP) refers to the positive tuples that were correctly labeled by the classifier;
- True Negative (TN) are negative tuples that were correctly labeled by the classifier;
- False Positive (FP) are the negative tuples that were incorrectly labeled as positive;
- False Negative (FN) are the positive tuples that were mislabeled as negative.

Table 8 in the Appendix shows the values of above described measures and the total correctly classified instances in percentage called accuracy. These measures show that the dataset is classified in two classes with good results.

Encryption of Class2 (Sensitive Data)

After the classification, the confidential data (class2) was encrypted using the RSA algorithm to make it secure. The simulation time and the size of overall data were increased as compared with the original size of data and total simulation time taken by both cloudlets as mentioned in Table 9 in the Appendix. Table 9 shows the time taken by K-NN to classify the data, the time taken by RSA to encrypt data, total simulation time and total size of data. After encryption the size of data and the simulation time is increased due to the data encryption process. Class1 data took the same time during simulation but the simulation time of class2 data changed after the encryption. After encryption, the size of the data increased up to 50166.86KB. The total time taken by the RSA to encrypt 160KB was 2796237 ms. The total time of the simulation with classification and encryption time is 7953112 ms. The total simulation time was calculated using Equation (1):

$$TST = \left(CT + ET + TC_i\right) \tag{1}$$

where, TST is the total simulation time, CT is the classification time, ET is the encryption time and TC_i is the time that was taken by both cloudlets after classification and encryption. Here $i = 1, 2$.

CONCLUSION

In this paper, we have proposed a confidentiality based data classification model for cloud computing which classifies data based on its confidential level. The confidential level of data is determined based on file attributes. The focus of this study was to classify the file data based on its security needs i.e. what kind of data need to be secure and what kind of data need to be public. The basic contribution of this model is the selection of confidential level data using machine learning technique (data classification). For data classification, the K-NN classifier is used to classify the data based on the security demand of the data. Based on data security requirements, the data of a file is classified in to two classes, confidential and non-confidential data. The confidential data required more security and therefore are encrypted using the RSA algorithm, whereas the non-confidential data is public data and are directly stored on to the cloud servers. The proposed model has been implemented in a designed simulation environment using a CloudSim simulator. This proposed model is the model to be used in cloud computing with a data classification technique to improve the security of data stored in cloud servers/data centres.

In future, the number of users can be increased to observe the performance of master virtual machine. A separate study can be conducted on confidential data sets' parameter of different organizations and the working efficiency of k-NN can be increased in cloud virtual environment.

ACKNOWLEDGMENT

I am using this opportunity to express my gratitude to Universiti Teknologi PETRONAS for supporting me to finish this work. I am also thankful to my supervisor Dr. Low Tang Jung for their aspiring guidance, invaluably constructive criticism and friendly advice during the project work.

It is a courtesy to acknowledge the reviewers in the revised paper for their constructive and helpful comments.

REFERENCES

AlZain, M., Pardede, E., Soh, B., & Jams, T. (2012). Cloud Computing Security: From Single to Multi-clouds. *Proceedings of the 2012 45th Hawaii International Conference on System Sciences* (pp. 5490–5499). IEEE.

Bijalwan, V., Kumar, V., Kumari, P., & Pascual, J. (2014). KNN based Machine Learning Approach for Text and Document Mining. *International Journal of Database Theory and Application, 7*(1), 61–70. doi:10.14257/ijdta.2014.7.1.06

Cachin, C., & Haas, R. (2010). *Dependable Storage in the Intercloud* (pp. 1–6). IBM.

Catteddu, D., & Hogben, G. (2009). Cloud Computing: Benefits, Risks and Recommendations for Information security. *Europe*.

Chen, Z., Dong, W., Li, H., Zhang, P., Chen, X., & Cao, J. (2014). Collaborative Network Security in Multi-Tenant Data Center for Cloud Computing. *Tsinghua Science and Technology, 19*(1), 82–94. doi:10.1109/TST.2014.6733211

Dasarathy, & B. V. (1980). Nosing Around the Neighborhood : A New System Structure and Classification Rule for Recognition in Partially Exposed Environment. *IEEE Transaction on Pattern Analysis and Machine Intelligence,* 1(1), 369–371.

Hassan, T., James, B. D. J., & Gail-Joon, A. H. N. (2010). Security and Privacy Challenges in Cloud Computing Environment. *IEEE Security and Privacy, 8*(6), 24–31. doi:10.1109/MSP.2010.186

Hur, J. (2013). Improving Security and Efficiency in Attribute-Based Data Sharing. *IEEE Transactions on Knowledge and Data Engineering, 25*(10), 2271–2282. doi:10.1109/TKDE.2011.78

Jansen, W. & Grance, T. (2011). *Guidelines on Security and Privacy in Public Cloud Computing.* National Institute of Standards and Technology, U.S. Department of Commerce, 800-144, 1–70.

Keller, J.M. & Gray, M.R. (1985). A Fuzzy K-Nearest Neighbor Algorithm. *IEEE Transactions on Systems and Cybernetics,* 1(4), 580–585.

Lam, I. B., & Chun, W. (2008). Facing the Challenges of RFID Data Management. *International Journal of Information Systems and Supply Chain Management, 1*(4), 1–19. doi:10.4018/jisscm.2008100101

Larose, & D.T. (2005). Discovering Knowledge in Data and Introduction to Data Mining (1st ed.). Canada: Wiley & Sons.

Li, A., Yang, X., Kandula, S., & Zhang, M. (2011). CloudCmp : Comparing Public Cloud Providers. *Proceedings of the 10th ACM SIGCOMM Conference on Internet measurement IMC '10* (pp. 1–14).

Lloyd, & S., 1982. Least Squares Quantization in PCM. *IEEE Transactions on Information Theory,* 28(2), 129–137.

Maleq khan, Q.D. & W.P. (2002). K-Nearest Neighbor Classification on Spatial Data. *Advances in Knowledge Discovery and Data Mining Lecture Notes in Computer Science,* 2336, 517–528.

Prakash, K. (2013). A Survey On Security and Privacy in Cloud Computing. *International Journal of Engineering Research & Technology*, *2*(2), 1–9.

Purushothaman, D. & Abburu, S. (2012). An Approach for Data Storage Security in Cloud Computing. *International journal of computer science*, *9*(2), 100–105.

Ram, C. P., & Sreenivaasan, G. (2010). Security as a Service (SasS): Securing User data by Coprocessor and Distributing the Data. Proceedings of the *Trendz in Information Sciences & Computing (TISC2010)* (pp. 152–155). IEEE. doi:10.1109/TISC.2010.5714628

Ransome, J. W. R.,s & James F. (2010). *Cloud Computing: Implementation, Management, and Security*. CRC Press, Taylor & Francis Group.

Rawat, P. S. (2012). Quality of Service Evaluation of SaaS Modeler (Cloudlet) Running on Virtual Cloud Computing Environment using CloudSim. *International Journal of Computers and Applications*, *53*(13), 35–38. doi:10.5120/8484-2424

Richard, D., & Heart, P. (1973). *Pattern Classification and Scene Analysis*. New York: Wiley.

Sadiku, M. N. O., Musa, S. M., & Momoh, O. D. (2014). Cloud Computing: Opportunities and Challenges. *IEEE Potentials*, *33*(1), 34–36. doi:10.1109/MPOT.2013.2279684

SGI, SGI - MLC++ Datasets from UCI. UCI. (n. d.).

Shi, K., Li, L., Liu, H., He, J., Zhang, N., & Song, W. (2011). An Improved KNN Text Classification Algorithm Based on Density. *Proceedings of the 2011 IEEE International Conference on Cloud Computing and Intelligence Systems* (Vol. 1, pp. 113–117). 10.1109/CCIS.2011.6045043

Shiraz, M., Abolfazli, S., Sanaei, Z., & Gani, A. (2012). A Study on Virtual Machine Deployment for Application Outsourcing in mobile Cloud Computing. *The Journal of Supercomputing*, *63*(3), 946–964. doi:10.100711227-012-0846-y

Song, D., Shi, E., Fischer, I., & Shankar, U. (2012). Cloud Data Protection for the Masses. IEEE Computer Society. *Computer*, *45*(1), 39–45. doi:10.1109/MC.2012.1

Suguna, N. & Thanushkodi, K. (2010). An Improved k-Nearest Neighbor Classification Using Genetic Algorithm. *International journal of Computer Science*, *7*(4), 7–10.

University, C. S. (2011). *Information Security Data Classification Standards, University, M.T. (2011)*. Data Classification and Handling Policy.

UTHSCSA. (2006). Protection by Data Classification Scope Purpose. Retrieved from http://ims.uthscsa.edu/

Varadharajan, V., & Tupakula, U. (2014). Security as a Service Model for Cloud Environment. *IEEE eTransactions on Network and Service Management*, *11*(1), 60–75. doi:10.1109/TNSM.2014.041614.120394

Wu, & X. et al. (2007). Top 10 Algorithms in Data Mining. *Knowledge and Information Systems*, *14*(1), 1–37.

Yanjun, Z., & Wen-Chen, H. (2009). Trust-Based Information Risk Management in a Supply Chain Network. *International Journal of Information Systems and Supply Chain Management, 2*(3), 19–34. doi:10.4018/jisscm.2009070102

Zardari, M. A., Jung, L. T., & Zakaria, M. N. B. (2013). Hybrid Multi-Cloud Data Security (HMCDS) Model and Data Classification. *Proceedings of the 2013 International Conference on Advanced Computer Science Applications and Technologies* (pp. 166–171). IEEE. 10.1109/ACSAT.2013.40

This research was previously published in the International Journal of Business Analytics (IJBAN), 3(2); edited by John Wang, pages 61-78, copyright year 2016 by IGI Publishing (an imprint of IGI Global).

APPENDIX

Table 1. Cloud items and quantity

Items	Quantity
Data Centre	2
Host	1
Broker	1
VM	3
VMM	1
Cloudlet	3

Table 2. SaaS properties

Cloudlet ID	Length (MI)	Input File Size (Bytes)	Output File Size (Bytes)
0	4000	158	158
1	3000	139	139

Table 3. PaaS properties for virtualisation management

VM ID	MIPS	Image Size (MB)	Bandwidth (Mbps)	Pes No.	VMM
0	100	10000	1000	1	Xen
1	100	10000	1000	1	Xen

Table 4. IaaS properties for Cloud simulation

DC ID	RAM (Mb)	Storage (MB)	Data Architecture	OS	Bandwidth ((Mbps)
0	2048	10000000	X86	Linux	10000
1	2048	10000000	X86	Linux	10000

Table 5. List of employee/personal attributes collected from different reports to train K-NN

S. No	File Attributes
1	salary
2	Address
3	Phone number
4	Email address
5	Payment history
6	Mother's maiden name
7	Race
8	Ethnicity
9	Parents' and other family members information
10	Birthplace
11	Gender
12	Marital status
13	Physical description

Table 6. Data classification results

Before Classification		After Classification						
		Class1 (Non-Confidential)			Class2 (Confidential)			K-NN Time (ms)
Total Size of File (KB)	Total Records in File	Attributes	Size (KB)	Records	Attributes	Size (KB)	Records	
512	5094	8	352	3450	7	160	1644	1075

Table 7. Cloud simulation results

Cloudlet ID	VM ID	Datacentre ID	Status	Start Time	Finish Time	Total Time	Total Time (Taken by Both Cloudlets)
0	0	1	SUCCESS	0 ms	3400 ms	3400 ms	5040 ms
1	1	2	SUCCESS	0 ms	1640 ms	1640 ms	

Table 8. Performance measure of algorithm

Class	TP Rate	FP Rate	Precision	Recall	F1-Score	Accuracy
Public	0.843	0.325	0.843	0.843	0.843	78%
confidential	0.675	0.157	0.675	0.675	0.675	
Average	0.788	0.27	0.788	0.788	0.788	

Table 9. Total simulation time

Classification Time	Time Taken by RSA	Simulation Time	Total Time (Both Cloudlets)	Total Size of Data (KB)
1075ms	2796237 ms	5155800 ms	7953112 ms	50166.86

Figure 1. Proposed model for data confidentiality

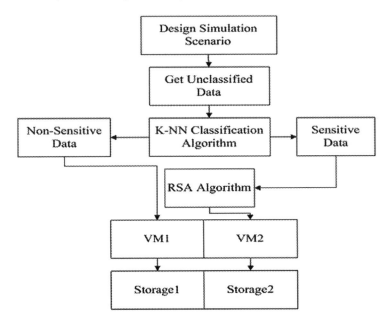

Figure 2. Cloud simulation environment

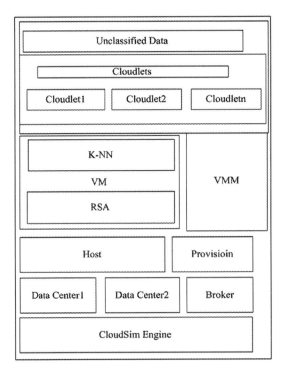

Figure 3. Master and slave VMs

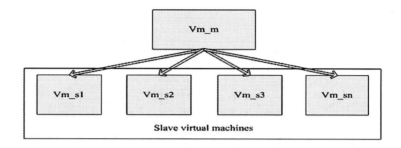

Figure 4. General cloud scenario with Vm_m and Vm_s

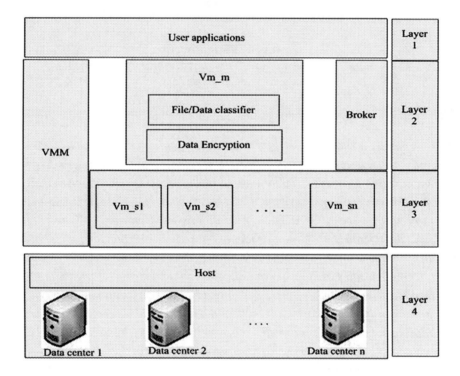

Chapter 35
Access Control Framework for Cloud Computing

Kashif Munir
King Fahd University of Petroleum and Minerals, Saudi Arabia

Lawan A. Mohammed
King Fahd University of Petroleum and Minerals, Saudi Arabia

ABSTRACT

Access control is generally a rule or procedure that allows, denies, restricts or limit access to system's resources. It may, as well, monitor and record all attempts made to access a system. Access Control may also identify users attempting to access unauthorized resources. It is a mechanism which is very much important for protection in computer security. Various access control models are in use, including the most common Mandatory Access Control (MAC), Discretionary Access Control (DAC) and Role Based Access Control (RBAC). All these models are known as identity based access control models. In all these access control models, user (subjects) and resources (objects) are identified by unique names. Identification may be done directly or through roles assigned to the subjects. These access control methods are effective in unchangeable distributed system, where there are only a set of Users with a known set of services. For this reason, we propose a framework which is well suited to many situations in cloud computing where users or applications can be clearly separated according to their job functions. In this chapter, we proposes a role based access control framework with various features including security of sensitive data, authorization policy and secure data from hackers. Our proposed role based access control algorithm provides tailored and fine level of user access control services without adding complexity, and supports access privileges updates dynamically when a user's role is added or updated.

INTRODUCTION

Cloud computing describes a new delivery model for IT services based on the Internet, and it typically involves over-the-Internet provision of dynamically scalable and often virtualized resources. It is a by-product and consequence of the ease-of-access to remote computing sites provided by the Internet. This

DOI: 10.4018/978-1-5225-8176-5.ch035

frequently takes the form of web-based tools or applications that users can access and use through a web browser as if it is a program installed locally on their own computer (Armbrust et. al, 2009).

In the "cloud", all data processing tasks are handled by a large number of distributed computers, end-users get access to the computer and storage systems through network on their demand. Enterprise Data Center is responsible for handling customer' task which is from customer' computer, so that it can provide data services for all kinds of users who use variety of different devices through just one data center and allow anyone who has the right Internet links to get access to the cloud applications (Arnold, 2008).

Aside from the huge marketing efforts, cloud security has been criticized for its unknown privacy and security protection. There could be benefits from a security perspective since most customers utilizing cloud may not have the expertise to safeguarding their information assets using traditional IT approaches, and using cloud services could mitigate this problem. On the other side, companies hosting the cloud services have in general full control over the services they provide. They could control and monitor data essentially at will. It has been noted by the research community that confidentiality and auditability are one of the top 10 obstacles to the growth of cloud computing (Armbrust et. al, 2009(b)).

As the goal of Cloud Computing is to share resources among the cloud service consumers, cloud partners, and cloud vendors in the cloud value chain. There has been a growing trend to use the cloud for large-scale data storage. However, the multi-tenant nature of the cloud is vulnerable to data leaks, threats, and malicious attacks. Therefore, it is important for enterprises to have strong access control policies in place to maintain the privacy and confidentiality of data in the cloud. The cloud computing platform is highly dynamic and diverse. Current access control techniques, like firewalls and VLAN, are not exactly well-suited to meet the challenges of cloud computing environment. They were originally designed to support IT systems in an enterprise environment. In addition, any weak access control mechanisms in the cloud can lead to major data breaches.

For instance, a few years back a massive data breach took place on the server of Utah Department Technology Services (DTS) as reported in *InformationWeek* (http://www.darkreading.com/risk-management/utahs-medicaid-data-breach-worse-than-expected/d/d-id/1103823). A hacker group from Eastern Europe succeeded in accessing the servers of DTS, compromising 181,604 Medicaid recipients and the Social Security numbers of 25,096 individual clients. The reason behind this massive breach is believed to be a configuration issue at the authentication level when DTS moved its claims to a new server. The hacker took advantage of this busy situation and managed to infiltrate the system, which contained sensitive user information like client names, addresses, birth dates, SSNs, physicians' names, national provider identifiers, addresses, tax identification numbers, and procedure codes designed for billing purposes. The Utah Department of Technology Services had proper access controls, policies, and procedures in place to secure sensitive data. However, in this particular case, a configuration error occurred while entering the password into the system. The hacker got access to the password of the system administrator, and as a result accessed the personal information of thousands of users. The biggest lesson from this incident is that even if the data is encrypted, a flaw in authentication system could render a system vulnerable. Enterprises should be sure to limit access to control policies, enforcing privileges and permissions for secure management of sensitive user data in the cloud. In another cloud computing survey conducted by *PC Connection* (PCConnection, 2013), it was mentioned that in 2011, 174 million records were compromised, costing organizations an average of $5.5 million—or $194 per compromised record.

According to the *Ponemon Institute* (Ponemon, 2013) Research Report of 2013 findings, organizations have improved their security practices around cloud use when compared to 2010 responses. However, only about half of respondents had positive perceptions about how their organizations are adopting cloud security best practices and creating confidence in cloud services used within their organization. In summary, the research showed that:

- While the use of SaaS and IaaS services has increased and security practices have improved since 2010, only half of organizations (51 percent for SaaS and 49 percent for IaaS) are evaluating these services in terms of security prior to deployment. And only about half are confident in the security of those services (53 percent confident in SaaS and 50 percent confident in IaaS).
- Fifty percent of respondents say they are confident they know all cloud computing services in use in their organization. While just at half, this is an improvement over the 2010 response of 45 percent.
- Only 50 percent of the respondents say they are engaging their security team (always or most of the time) in determining the use of cloud services. This is a slight decrease from 2010 (which was 51 percent).

To manage cloud security in today's world, you need a solution that helps you address threats to your data and infrastructure, as well as the major challenges of cloud computing. These include:

- Changing attackers and threats—Attacks aren't coming just from isolated hackers now. More and more, organized crime is driving well-resourced, sophisticated, targeted attacks for financial gain.
- Evolving architecture technologies—with the growth of virtualization and rise in cloud adoption, perimeters and their controls within the data center are in flux, and data is no longer easily constrained or physically isolated and protected.
- Consumerization of IT—As mobile devices and technologies continue to become more common, employees want to use personally owned devices to access enterprise applications, data, and cloud services.

As the popularity of cloud computing increases, more and more organizations want to migrate their data and applications to cloud computing. As a result the main concern for all cloud service providers is to provide security to their information and to their data. For that the identity of all the users must be known to the cloud provider administrator. To solve the security problem of cloud computing, one should first solve the user access. By implementing role based access control (RBAC) cost and complexity of security can be reduced (Rao & Vijay, 2009). With RBAC, the administrators grant permissions to the roles that he created according to job functions performed in an organization, and then assign users to the roles on the basis of their specific job responsibilities. To access the cloud computing resources user first have to register themselves into one or more classes and get credentials to identify themselves (R.S. Sandhu, et.al, 1996). In a cloud numbers of systems are implementing RBAC. Each system has its own user accounts or system accounts with credentials. As the environment grows, number of accounts will also increase which leads to the increase of credentials. And all this is managed by system administrator.

For these reasons, security in cloud computing is still ongoing issue. This chapter intends to focus on the access control aspect of cloud security, and provide a RBAC framework to protect data in cloud. First we will look at the history of access control models, then we propose a framework for RBAC for cloud computing.

HISTORY OF ACCESS CONTROL MODELS

In present day, people rely less and less on personal face-to-face contact as they need to use computer and telecommunication technology to access information both at home, office, shops etc. Therefore this signifies the importance of protecting information from unauthorized access. The aspect of protecting information by authenticating users to ensure authorized access is commonly known as the *Access Control System* (ACS).

In the 1970s, under the sponsorship of the US Department of Defence, work on developing models for secure information systems where carried out. Bell and La Padula published a paper that modeled computer security after military secrecy methods (Bell, 1973) and Biba published another based on integrity (Biba, 1977). One of the constrains of Bell La Padula model is that it was developed in the context of military secure systems and assumed the existence of a method of classifying the security levels of users and information. The concept of "mandatory access control" is not appropriate for commercial information systems as there is no application of security classifications to data and security clearance accorded to employees in commercial organizations.

There has been further research but these are largely deviations based on the above two models, like the Clark-Wilson model (Clark, 1987). In 1983, the US Government introduce the Trusted System Evaluation Criteria (TSEC) to provide computer manufacturers with a set of guidelines and an evaluation system for the development of trusted computer systems, (known as the Orange Book). This prompted commercial and government organizations to turn to TSEC as a guideline for the development of secure information systems. The European Community produced a set of criteria called the ITSEC. It is common for manufacturers to build the criteria spelt out into their new commercial product. The drawback of TSEC and ITSEC is that their specifications are limited to the use of mathematical concepts to achieve the objective of maintaining secrecy and integrity, by introducing concepts like mandatory and discretionary access controls. There are no specifications for the development of access devices and it is largely left to technologist.

Currently there are several types of access devices. Generally, they are fall into one of the following categories:

1. Verification of something known, like password, PIN. This category is known as *codeword*. Details are provided in the next subsection.
2. Verification of something possessed, like smart card. This is refers to as *token*. Token has some drawbacks, as there are many cases of forgery of tokens, people have also been known to be complacent in their handling of the token.
3. Verification of some unique features of our body. This is known as *biometric*. One of the limitation of this method is that it is very expensive to implement, moreover, it is also not common therefore cannot fit into our daily life style.

CODEWORDS

Identification is an essential part of securing information processing systems and networks. Source identification can be achieved by the use of either secret key or public key cryptosystems (to be discussed later). In general, it is the process of obtaining assurance that the identity of some participant in a networking scenario is as claimed. For example, when a user seeks the services of a computer, the computer needs to make sure that the user is not forging a false identity. The classical solution to this is through the use of *passwords*. The National Computer Security Centre defines the probability of guessing a particular password as:

$$P = \frac{LXR}{S}$$

where, L is the password lifetime (The maximum amount of time it can be used before it must be changed). R is the guess rate (the number of guesses per unit time that it is possible to make). S is the password space (the total number of unique passwords that can be used). S is defined in turn as $S = A^M$, where A is the number of characters in the alphabet (the set of characters that may be used in a password), and M is the password length.

If we assume that most people restrict their passwords to upper and lowercase letters, numbers, and punctuation. A takes a value of about 92. Now, let us assume that a password lifetime is up to one year, and that a password can be tried at a rate of 1,000 per second (a reasonable value on many of today's architectures).

As we lower our estimate of A (for example, it would probably be more realistic to assume only letters and numbers, for a value of 62) or increase our estimate of R (to account for faster processors), these probabilities only gets worse. Manipulating our equation also gives us a procedure for determining the minimum acceptable password length for a given system:

1. Establish an acceptable password lifetime L (a typical value might be one month).
2. Establish an acceptable probability P (the probability might be no more than 1 in 1,000,000).
3. Solve for the size of the password space S, using the equation derived from the previous one:

$$S = \frac{LXR}{P}$$

Determine the length of the password, M, from the equation:

$$M = \frac{logS}{\log A}$$

Using this procedure with L equals to 1 month, R equals to 1,000 guesses/second, A equals to 92, and P equals to 1 in 1,000,000, we end up with M equals to 7.85, which rounds up to 8. Thus the minimum acceptable password length to insure no better than 1 in 1,000,000 chance of guessing the password is eight characters. There are other means for securing codewords one of the most effective is known one-way function.

Cryptographic Algorithms

Cryptography is the method of converting data from a human readable form to a modified form, and then back to its original readable form, to make unauthorized access difficult. Cryptography is needed to make electronic transactions as trustworthy and legally binding as physical communication.

Different access control mechanisms with high level of security have been developed. So one may like to know the role of encryption techniques in such system. One of its use is, of course, its standard application – the protection of data transmitted across conventional links. Generally, cryptography is used in the following ways:

- Ensure data privacy, by encrypting data
- Ensures data integrity, by recognizing if data has been manipulated in an unauthorized way
- Ensures data uniqueness by checking that data is "original", and not a "copy" of the "original". The sender attaches a unique identifier to the "original" data. This unique identifier is then checked by the receiver of the data.

The original data may be in a human-readable form, such as a text file, or it may be in a computer-readable form, such as a database, spreadsheet or graphics file. The original data is called unencrypted data or plain text. The modified data is called encrypted data or cipher text. The process of converting the unencrypted data is called encryption. The process of converting encrypted data to unencrypted data is called decryption. Cryptography can be classified as either conventional or asymmetric, depending on the type of keys used.

In order to convert the data, you need to have an encryption algorithm and a key. If the same key is used for both encryption and decryption that key is called a secret key and the algorithm is called a symmetric algorithm. Symmetric algorithms include DES, Triple DES, Rijndael, RC2, RC4, IDEA, Blowfish, CAST, Red Pike and a host of others.

If different keys are used for encryption and decryption, the algorithm is called an asymmetric algorithm. Some of these algorithms include RSA, DSA and Diffie-Hellman as well as El Gamal and various forms of Elliptic Curve Cryptography (ECC). Asymmetric algorithms involve extremely complex mathematics typically involving the factoring of large prime numbers. Asymmetric algorithms are typically stronger than a short key length symmetric algorithm but because of their complexity they are used in signing a message or a certificate. They not ordinarily used for data transmission encryption.

RELATED WORK

For providing secure and reliable cloud computing one should first secure the cloud resources from unauthorized access. Now a day's many cloud computing platforms implementing role based access control. Still lots of researches are going on to secure RBAC in cloud. Georgia institute of Technology introduced a middleware security platform CASA which provides security with user bio information or location information (Covington. et.al, 2000). For context-information modeling SOCAM proposes OWL, which consists of several components (Gu et.al, 2004). (Komlenovic et. al, 2011) proposes distributed access for role based access control. Their approach uses directed graph, access matrix. If there is limit on number of users and permission than access matrix is an optimal choice and if it is variable then directed graph.

(Ching-Ching & Kamalendu, 2008) proposes distributed authorization caching technique which helps to improve performance, scalability of an authorization system . (Ei Ei & Thin, 2011) combines RBAC and Attribute based access control system and proposes a new framework ARBAC which supports both mandatory and discretionary needs.

ROLE BASED ACCESS CONTROL (RBAC)

Role Based Access Control (RBAC) is a method that offers a satisfactory level of safety & security for organizational resources & data because of rules & policies put into effect for the user in the form of login & password. However, the description is not limited to the organization resources but gives security and protection for users' personal information and actions.

There are two main user attributes i.e. presence & location (Takabi & Joshi, 2010). Presence is linked with the real -time communication systems such as: Instant Message and (IM) and Voice over IP (VoIP), where it gives the required explanation about users category all through the communication and even after that also, tells the status as idle or active, online or offline and for specific tasks it is done in the form of writing documents or email.

The current application Role Based Access Control RBAC offers Authentication, Authorization and Auditing for users using the cloud computing as follows:

- **Authentication:** Cloud computing authentication includes validating the identity of users or systems. For example, facility to service authentication engages in certifying the access demand to the information which served by another service.
- **Authorization:** After the authentication process, the system will put security rules to bring legitimate users.
- **Auditing:** Auditing is a process that involves reviewing & examining the records of authorization & authentication to check over organizations compliance with set security standards & policies in order to evade system breaches.

According to (Mather, et,al, 1996) RBAC will go through five stages as follow:

- **Provisioning and deprovisioning:** User will be authorized to access to the information based on the organization & role. This process is long as every user is to be provided with an identity. Nevertheless, cloud management uses techniques such as identity Management as a Service (IDaaS).
- **Authentication and Authorization:** A significant authentication and authorization infrastructure will be requisite to make a custom authentication and authorization representation that fulfills the business goals.
- **Self-Service:** Facilitating self-service in the identity management will improvise the identity management systems. Users can reset their information like password and uphold their data from any location.
- **Password Management:** Single Sign on (SSO) support system is to access cloud-base services. Password management comprises of how the password will be stored in the cloud database.

- **Compliance and Audit:** Here, the access will be scrutinized & tracked to monitor the security breaches in the system. This process also assists to audit the fulfillment to diverse access control policies, periodic auditing and reporting.

PROPOSED FRAMEWORK

In this chapter, we propose a *Role-Based Access Control* (RBAC) model suitable for cloud computing environment. RBAC model is defined in terms of three model components-Core RBAC, Hierarchical RBAC and Constraint RBAC Core RBAC includes sets of six basic data elements called users (U), roles(R), objects (0), operations (Ops), permissions (P) and sessions (Sessions). The basic concept of RBAC is that users are assigned to roles rather than users. Through a set of maps, this model makes the role and a group of related operations manage each other, the user belongs to roles has the right to execute corresponding actions which are associated to these roles (Blaze et al, 1998).

Role-Based Access Control, introduced by Ferraiolo and Kuhn, has become the predominant model for advanced access control because it reduces the complexity and cost of security administration in large networked applications (Kong and Li, 2007). With RBAC, system administrators create roles according to the job functions performed in an organization, grant permissions to those roles, and then assign users to the roles on the basis of their specific job responsibilities and qualifications (Sandhu et al., 1996). Role based access control (RBAC) introduces the concept of "role" between the users and the operations of objects.

The researcher's framework attempts to solve the above-mentioned problems. The proposed architecture is shown in Figure 1. The following terminologies were used in our model:

- *AC*: Access Control
- *UC*: Usage Control
- *PPN*: Privacy Policy Negotiation

The following are the access control elements used in our model:

A. *Data administrator:* In a cloud, various services like the data services, applications services, and VM services can be created by the cloud users and stored in the storage allocations in the.
B. *Data users:* Cloud users can access their services and data post receipt of the data owner's permission.
C. *Cloud Service Providers (CSP):* Users can operate the cloud, its components and services according to the rules defined by cloud service providers.

Administrator: The administrator has all the rights to authorize the user and give him/her access rights according to policy. The administrator also keeps one's information confidential from unauthorized users. All the groups are controlled by the administrator. It is only with his approval that users and groups can be added or deleted.

D. *Group:* Every group has its own group owner who will control access, and assign privacy privileges to the users. If any user tries to access sensitive data, he/she has to take permission from the group owner first. The group owner will first check the user's credentials and if that user has the rights

Figure 1. Proposed framework

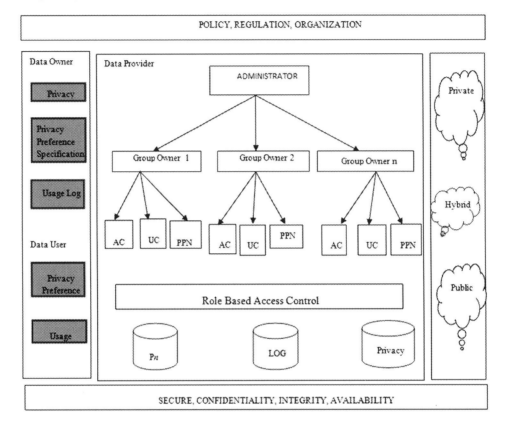

to access the resource concerned. It is only after that verification that the group owner will send a key to the user's email id. Only with that key, will the user access sensitive resources. One user can be placed within several groups. There can be two possible cases with this framework.

Scenario # 1

If a user is present in a number of groups and the access rights that are given to him/her are different. In this case, we will take the optimistic approach. High priority will be given to less restriction. For example, if a user is present in group 1 as well as in group 4, and if within group 1, he is assigned FULL ACCESS while in group 4, he gets READ ONLY rights, then, he will be eligible for FULL ACCESS. If the access rights are for sensitive data, then, that user will have to consult his group owner first and only after that can he access that resource.

The algorithm for scenario 1 is given as Algorithm 1.

The algorithm first checks, the number of groups in which the user is present. That count is stored in variable C. For loop, this count is stored in an array named list [length(C)]. D is a variable that is used to store the access rights of a user. If the user is present in one group only, then, the designated access rights will be given. If the user is present in number of group then access rights will be decided according to less restriction.

Algorithm 1.

```
 [Initialize]. Set A: = 1, B: = Number of User's Group, access: = 'No Access',
list
    [Length (C)]:= Groups of Users, D.
If B = 0, then access: = 'User's Access' and Exit.
If B = 1, then access: = 'User's Access in Group' and Exit.
Repeat Steps 5 to 10 while A ≤ B:
D: = list [A].getUserAccessInGroup.
If D = 'Full Access', then access: = 'Full Access' and Exit.
If D = 'Read/Write', then access: = 'Read/Write'.
If D = 'Read' and access ≠ 'Read/Write', then access: = 'Read'.
If D = 'NO Access' and access ≠ 'Read/Write' and access ≠ 'Read', then access:=
    'No Access'.
Set A: = A+1.
[End of Step 4 Loop]
Exit.
```

Scenario # 2

How will shareable resources be handled in this framework? For instance, if one user has access rights to read that resource and another user has access rights to write on that resource at same time, the researcher suggests synchronization. If one user is accessing some resource then other user will have to wait to access same resource.

The algorithm for Scenario #2 is given as Algorithm 2.

In the entry section, user i first raises a flag indicating a desire to access the resource. Then the turn is set to j to allow the other user to access the resource, if user j so desires. While the loop is a busy loop (notice the semicolon at the end), which makes user i wait for as long as user j has his turn, and accessing the resource user i lowers the flag[i] in the exit section, allowing user j to continue if he has been waiting.

Algorithm 2.

```
do{
flag[i]=TRUE;
turn=j;
while(flag[j]&&turn==j);
flag[i] = FALSE;
remainder section
} while (TRUE);
```

Framework Features

The proposed framework helps to secure the system more efficiently with the following features.

- Security of Sensitive information: The proposed framework helps to secure information that is private or sensitive to the user. When a user wants to access the sensitive information first, an email is sent to the group owner, who then, checks the user's credentials to see if he has access rights to use the data or not. If he does have the requisite right, then, an email with security key will be sent to the user, and using this, the user can access that sensitive information.
- Security from hackers: Sometimes a user leaves his account open and anyone can access that account. If a hacker wants to access any private information then, the group owner gets intimated that private data is being misused leading to him blocking the access to that data.
- Addition of user or group dynamically: This framework helps to add or update users and groups, dynamically. For example, if a user is no longer working in an organization, a user's access rights will be changed and then, this framework will update these changes dynamically.

SECURITY POLICIES

The need to prove that data and files are authentic is always important, but that requirement is particularly compelling when organizations must show compliance with laws and regulations. This includes situations related to:

- *Regulated industries*, where companies need to document, for example, how they comply with Health Insurance Portability and Accountability Act or HIPAA rules for protecting personally identifiable health information, SEC 17a-4 requirements for retaining data on securities transactions, and 21 CFR Part 11 requirements for protecting records required by the FDA.
- *Financial information*, used for SEC reporting and compliance with Sarbanes-Oxley (SOX) and other investor protection regulations.
- *Documents with legal and contractual implications*, whose admissibility as evidence needs to be protected.
- *Intellectual property*, such as engineering and patent documents, trade secrets and business plans, whose date and provenance might need to be proved in court.
- *Records management applications*, where documents and files might need to be retrieved and validated after years or even decades.

CONCLUSION

In conclusion, today's business environment is very attracted by cloud computing paradigm because of providing services in a very effective way. On top of commodity hardware there is a virtualization layer which is drive force and helps cloud providers to respond promptly to cloud user requests.

Instead of all these advantages of cloud computing, there is still a question mark on its usage. Security and privacy are main challenges from storage and processing of sensitive data due to multi-tenancy feature of cloud computing. For the efficient use of cloud computing providing proper security is very important. Cloud computing security begins with implementing Identity and Access Management to ensure Authentication, Authorization and Auditing.

Cloud computing is so named because the information being accessed is found in the "clouds", and does not require a user to be in a specific place to gain access to it. cloud computing structure allows access to information as long as an electronic device has access to the web.

In this chapter, we present the RBAC framework that protects the sensitive information in the cloud, specifies the privacy policies for the private cloud; and protects the data from hackers. Two scenarios have been presented. Scenario 1 deals with what if is present in a number of groups and the access rights that are given to him/her are different whereas scenario 2 deals with shareable resources be handled in this framework. Algorithm has been presented to support the scenarios.

REFERENCES

Armbrust, M., Armando, F., Rean, G., Anthony, D. J., Katz, R. H., Konwinski, A., et al. (2009b). Above the Clouds: A Berkeley View of Cloud Computing. *Tech. Report UCB/EECS-2009-28.*

Armbrust. M., Fox A., Griffith, R., Joseph, A. D., Katz, R., Konwinski, A., Lee, G., Patterson, D., Rabkin, A., Stoica, I., & Zaharia, M. (2009a). *Above the Clouds: A View of Cloud Computing* [EB/OL]. UC Berkeley. Retrieved from https://www.eecs.berkeley.edu/Pubs/TechRpts/2009/EECS-2009-28.pdf.

Arnold, S. (2008, July-August). *Cloud computing and the issue of privacy. KM World.* Retrieved from http://www.kmworld.com

Bell, D., & LaPadula, J. (1973). Secure Computer System: Mathematical foundation and model, Mitre Corp, MTR 2547, 2.

Biba, R. R. (1977). Integrity Considerations for Secure Computer Systems: Unified exposition and multics interpretation. *Mitre Corp., MTR 3153.*

Blaze, M., Feigen, B., & Keromytis, J. (1998). A.D. keynote: trust management for public-key infrastructures. In: Christianaon, B., Crispo, B., Willian, S., et al. (Eds.) Security Protocols International Workshop. Berlin: Springer-Verglag.

Ching – Ching. L, Kamalendu. B. (2008). Distributed Authorization Cache. Proceedings of Security & Management, pp. 381-386.

Clark, D., & Wilson, D. (1987). A Comparison of Commercial and Military Computer Security Policies", *IEEE Symposium on security and privacy.* 10.1109/SP.1987.10001

Overcoming the Security Challenges of the Cloud: Best Practices for Keeping Your Data and Your Organization Safe. (2013, May 13). *PC Connection.* Retrieved from http://www.pcconnection.com/~/media/PDFs/Brands/C/Cisco/Survey/25240_PCC_CloudSurvey.pdf

Covington, M. J., Moyer, M. J., & Ahamad, M. (2000, October). Generalized role-based access control for securing future application. NISSC, pp. 40–51.

Ei Ei, M., Thinn, T. N. (2011). The privacy-aware access control system using attribute-and role-based access control in private cloud. *IEEE International conference on Broadband Network and Multimedia Technology, pp. 447-451.*

Gu, T., Pung, H. K., & Zhang, D. Q. (2004). *A Middleware for Building Context-Aware Mobile Services. Proceedings of IEEE Vehicular Technology Conference, VTC.*

Kong, G., & Li, J. (2007). Research on RBAC-based separation of duty constraints. *Journal of Information and Computing Science*, 20, 235–24.

Marko, K., Mahesh, T., & Toutik, Z. (2011). An Empirical Assessment of Approaches to Distributed Enforcement in Role Based Access Control. *Proceedings of ACM conference on Data & Application Security & Privacy, pp. 1-29.*

Mather, T., Kumarasuwamy, S., & Latif, S. (2009). Cloud Security and Privacy. O'Rielly.

Maxwell, J. C. (3 Ed.). (2009). A Treatise on Electricity and Magnetism, 2. Oxford: Clarendon, 1892.

Ponemon (2013, December 21). Security of Cloud Computing Users Study. Retrieved from http://www.ca.com/kr/~/media/Files/IndustryAnalystReports/2012-security-of-cloud-computer-users-final1.pdf

Rao, M., & Vijay, S. (2009). Cloud Computing and the Lessons from the Past. The 18th IEEE international Workshops on Enabling Technologies: Infrastructures for Collaborative Enterprises, pp. 57-62, 2009.

Sandhu, R. S., Coyne, E. I., Feinstein, H. L., & Youman, C. E. (1996, February). Role based access control models. *IEEE Computer*, 29(2), 38–47. doi:10.1109/2.485845

Sandhu, R. S., Coyne, E. J., Feinstein, H. L., & Youman, C. E. (1996, February). Role based access control models. *IEEE Computer*, 29(2), 38–47. doi:10.1109/2.485845

Takabi, H., Joshi, J. B. D. (2010, November). Security and privacy challenges in cloud computing environment. *IEEE Journal on Security and Privacy, 8(6), pp. 24-31.*

KEY TERMS AND DEFINITIONS

Algorithm: A self-contained step-by-step set of operations to be performed.

Authentication: The act of confirming the truth of an attribute of a single piece of data (datum) or entity.

Confidentiality: A set of rules or a promise that limits access or places restrictions on certain types of information.

Framework: An abstraction in which software providing generic functionality can be selectively changed by additional user-written code, thus providing application-specific software.

Role-Based Access Control: An approach to restricting system access to authorized users.

Security Policy: A definition of what it means to *be secure* for a system, organization or other entity.

Security: The degree of resistance to, or protection from, harm. It applies to any vulnerable and valuable asset, such as a person, dwelling, community, nation, or organization.

This research was previously published in the Handbook of Research on Security Considerations in Cloud Computing edited by Kashif Munir, Mubarak S. Al-Mutairi, and Lawan A. Mohammed, pages 314-325, copyright year 2015 by Information Science Reference (an imprint of IGI Global).

Chapter 36
Cloud Computing Data Storage Security Based on Different Encryption Schemes

Hicham Hamidine
University of Bridgeport, USA

Ausif Mahmood
University of Bridgeport, USA

ABSTRACT

Cloud Computing (CC) became one of the prominent solutions that organizations do consider to minimize and lean their information technology infrastructure cost by fully utilizing their resources. However, with all the benefits that CC promises, there are many security issues that discourage clients from making the necessary decision to easily embrace the cloud. To encourage the use of CC, clients need to be able to strategically plan their future investments without the uncertainties of security issues that come with hosting their data in the cloud. This chapter will discuss different mitigation techniques and the common proposed security algorithm schemes for data storage encryption based on classical "symmetric and asymmetric" and with an emphasis on fully homomorphic encryption schemes.

INTRODUCTION

Globalization has forced organizations to accomplish a lot with far less technical, personnel and budget resources. Therefore, when the cloud model was introduced and started to mature it became an obvious choice to many corporations regardless of size. This new model promises that clients can have as many hardware, and software resources as they wish and when it's most needed, which made scalability an issue of the past and at a much less cost. Today, most of the cloud services are in the nature of Infrastructure as a Service (IaaS), Platform as a Service (PaaS), and Software as a Service (SaaS). These services revolutionized the way information technology decision makers assess projects and their related risks versus return on investments. However, the looming security risks and issues an organization may face

DOI: 10.4018/978-1-5225-8176-5.ch036

still are the biggest obstacles that refrain clients from fully harnessing the benefits of the cloud; especially for those whom their data security is an essential component of their daily business.

Many solutions have been identified to achieve security in the cloud and protect data either by using access control, data storage encryption, or a combination of the two. This paper presents a comprehensive survey of different encryption schemes used or are proposed to protect data in the cloud including the algorithm(s) the scheme uses to achieve the sought after level of confidentiality, integrity, and authenticity.

Storing and accessing data in the cloud has its own challenges that compounded the classical issues of security. Today, an organization may choose to host its sensitive data in the cloud to harness the benefits of cloud computing and compete in the respective domain of business it relies on for day to day operations. However, when the data is sensitive its stewards need to implement the most rigorous security scheme that not only should provide them with the appropriate access level but makes sure that no data is compromised or leaked. The classical scenarios of security schemes may still be used. However, there is a limitation that comes with them. For instance, if the data need to only be accessed by the internal staff then a symmetric encryption scheme may be used and the key management is less of a concern but a key management control must be in place. On the other hand, if the data must be accessible to internal and external users, then an asymmetric scheme will be more preferable. In both scenarios, the cloud provider need to gain access to the key to perform usable functionalities against the encrypted data. This exposure of the key may not be acceptable due to the fact that the CP itself may be curious to know the nature of the sensitive data stored on its premises. To accommodate clients' security requirements, researchers are turning to the mathematical characteristics of fully homomorphic algorithms which enables search to be performed against encrypted data without the need of decrypting it.

In the rest of this paper we will examine different secure proposed solutions for accessing and transferring data in the cloud using different schemes that are based on the classical symmetric or asymmetric algorithms. Then, state the new solutions that are based on fully homomorphic schemes. These schemes are trying to solve the same problem which is securing data while enabling arbitrary calculation to be performed against it, except introducing asymptotically better performance in time and space. Finally, analyze these solutions in the paper conclusion based on the need of cloud computing in a multi-tenant environment and secure delegation computation.

Literature Review

Dent (2006) Cryptography is the branch of information security which covers the study of algorithms, protocols that secure data, and addresses several security properties mostly what's known as CIA. One of cryptography's goal is masking the plaintext to an unreadable format using a key to create a cipher text. Diffie and Hellman (1976) stated that classical cryptography systems are based on the NP-hardness of a mathematical problems, such as factoring two large primes or discrete logarithm. Authors also mentioned that these problems are said to be trapdoor functions because it is easy to compute the function one way, but extremely taxing to compute the reverse without some special information, known as the trapdoor. Diffie and Hellman (1976) classified cryptography schemes into two main categories: symmetric and asymmetric. Symmetric cryptography, uses one secret key for both encryption and decryption. Asymmetric cryptography "or public key cryptography" uses two different keys known as public and a private key, either of which can be used for encryption or decryption. The most widely used public key system is RSA, which relies on the factorization of two large prime numbers. In addition to the classical cryptosystems, scientists are researching homomorphic cryptography schemes to ensure privacy of data in

Figure 1. Cryptography diagram
Source: Khan, Hussain, & Imran, 2013

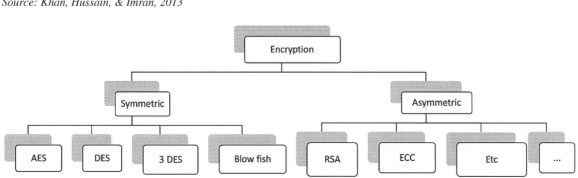

communication, storage or in use by processes with mechanisms similar to conventional cryptography, but with added capabilities of computing over encrypted data. Homomorphism is a property by which a problem in one algebraic system can be converted to a problem in another algebraic system, be solved and the solution later can also be translated back effectively. Thus, homomorphism makes secure delegation of computation to a third party possible. Many conventional encryption schemes possess either multiplicative or additive homomorphic property and are currently in use for respective applications. However, on based on Gupta, and Sharma, (2013) a scheme that contains a special functions that form an arbitrary encryption system and capable of performing any arbitrary computation over encrypted data only became feasible in 2009 due to Gentry's work.

Chapter 1: Data Storage Security Based on Symmetric Encryption Schemes

Sharma, Chugh, and Kumar (2013), proposed a solution to the data storage security issues in the cloud. This solution relies on DES to construct the security component which is one of many components proposed to achieve secure working system in the cloud. For users, the system proposed a scheme for data support which includes block update, delete, and appended operations. For administrators, the system guarantees dependability and storage correctness by relying on DES and erasure-correcting code in the file distribution preparation to provide redundancy parity vector. Moreover, it uses homomorphic token with distributed verification of erasure coded data to achieve the integration of storage correctness insurance and data error localization. The scheme consists of seven components that are:

1. **Client Authentication Component:** Client initiates communication with the server by sending the query to the cloud server as a request. The server then sends the corresponding file back to the client as a response. However, before sending the response to the client the server initiates the authorization step and either finalize the response or mark as an intruder.
2. **System Component:**
   a. **User:** Either individual or an organization and rely on the cloud for data computation.
   b. **Cloud Service Provider (CSP):** It's the central entity of the cloud and whom has significant resources and expertise in building and managing distributed cloud storage servers, owns and operates live Cloud Computing systems.

Figure 2. Client authentication
Source: Sharma et al., 2013

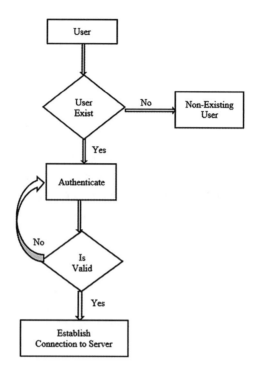

c. **Third Party Auditor (TPA):** Optional but who has expertise and capabilities that users may not have, is trusted to assess and expose risk of cloud storage services on behalf of the users upon request.

3. **Cloud Data Storage Component:** This component refers to the actual process of data storing, retrieving, and interaction with the cloud servers via CSP.

4. **Cloud Authentication Server Component:** Cloud Authentication Server (CAS) functions are as any authentication server (AS) but with a few additional behaviors added to the typical client-authentication protocol such as behaving as a ticketing authority, and controlling permissions on the application network:

a. Sending of the client authentication information to the masquerading router.

b. Updating of client lists, causing a reduction in authentication time or even the removal of the client as a valid client depending upon the request.

5. **Unauthorized Data Modification and Corruption Component:** Responsible of effectively detecting any unauthorized data modification and corruption including tracing to find which server the data error lies in.

6. **Data Security Component:** Responsible for storing and retrieving secure data using DES and therefore enabling security in the system.

7. **Adversary Component:** Any adversary source which are classified to two types with different levels of capabilities:

a. **Weak Adversary:** The adversary is interested in corrupting the user's data files stored on individual servers.

b. **Strong Adversary:** Worst case scenario, in which assumed that the adversary can compromise all the storage servers to the level that they all are conspiring together to hide a data loss or corruption incident.

In the Security Model proposed in Nafi, Shekha, Hoque, and Hashem (2012) which deals with the security system of the entire cloud environment, the encryption key for a particular file system of a particular user is only known to the main system server. The communication from the main system server to the storage server is fully encrypted and therefore there is no need for channel security. Moreover, the model is proposing a hardware encryption to make databases fully secure from attackers and unauthorized users. Kawser et al, proposed the use of these security algorithms: RSA algorithm for secure communication, AES for secure file encryption, and MD5 hashing for cover the tables from user. Moreover, there is an enforcement of using a onetime password for authentication. This model of authentication is cumbersome as users get a onetime pass for the future every time they log in to the system.

The algorithm for generating the hash table which is used for inserting a file in the database table of the storage server is described below:

Step 1: Select a seed for generating the hash table which is equal to the block size of the table. Block size means with how many positions of files will be taken from a series of execution

Step 2: Compute the position where to insert a file. Position = N2 mod S. Where N represents the no. of file and S represents the seed value.

Step 3: A - If Position is empty, then insert the file in that Position. B - Else, increment the Position and set Offset. Repeat step 3.

The analysis of the simulation results of this model showed that the proposed solution works smoothly and ensures higher security than the current running models in the cloud computing environment.

Figure 3. Working architecture of system
Source: Sharma et al., 2013

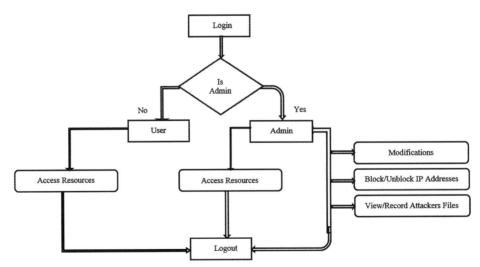

Figure 4. Proposed security model/ structure
Source: Nafi et al., 2012

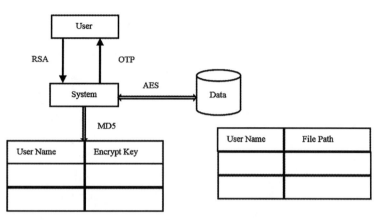

Chapter 2: Data Storage Security Based on Asymmetric Encryption Schemes

In Tirthani, and Ganesan (2014), the authors proposed a solution for designing cloud architectures that ensures secure movement of data at the client and server ends. The solution is based on the notion of the non-breakability of Elliptic Curve Cryptography for data encryption and Diffie Hellman key exchange mechanism which uses a combination of linear and elliptical cryptography methods to establish connections.

1. **Connection Establishment:** The connection is secured using the HTTPS and SSL protocols to enable users to create an account.
2. Account Creation
3. Authentication
4. Data Exchange

In Tirthani, and Ganesan (2014), authors proposed architecture, the key generation takes place at two levels, Elliptic Curve Cryptography (ECC) and Diffie Hellman. In ECC, The public key is a point on the curve which get generated by multiplying the private key with the generator point of the used function here the private key is a random number. One of the ECC algorithm properties is its ability to get a new point on the curve given by computing the product of two points. The general equation of an elliptic curve is given as: $y^2 = x^3 + ax + b$

Key generation step in Tirthani, and Ganesan (2014) is responsible for producing both public and private key and can be achieved as follows:

1. Choose a number d where $d \in \{1, n-1\}$
2. **Public Key:** $Q = d * P$, where P is a point on curve.
3. **Private Key:** d

Figure 5. Account creation process

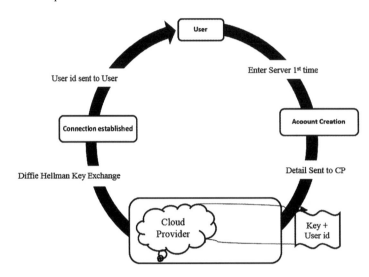

Figure 6. Account authentication process

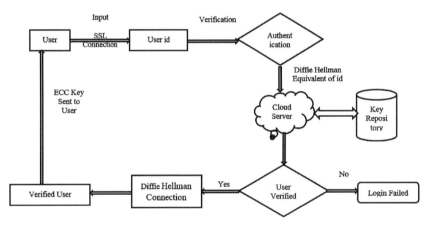

For encrypting user's message m which has point M on the curve E. the algorithm randomly select a value $K \in [1, n-1]$ which will result in two cipher texts C_1 and C_2. Where: $C_1 = K * P$ and $C_2 = M + (K * P)$. To decryption m we simply compute: $m = C_2 - d * B$.

Data Storage Security in the Cloud Using RSA

In Yellamma, Narasimham, and Sreenivas (2013), authors proposed a security scheme for providing data storage and security in cloud using the widely used public key cryptosystem RSA. In the proposed solution by Yellamma et al. (2013)'s Cloud environment, Pubic-Key is known to all, whereas Private-Key is known only to the original data owner. This architecture implies that encryption is done by the cloud service provider and decryption is done by the cloud user. However, this implementation is identical to the current RSA regardless of the environment.

Figure 7. Data processing view of client

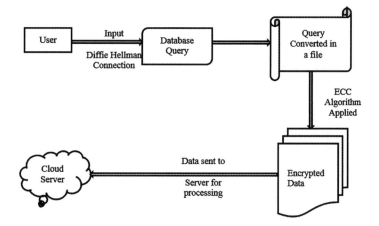

RSA Based Storage Security (RSASS)

In Venkatesh, Sumalatha, and SelvaKumar (2012) scheme RSA based storage security (RSASS) which uses public auditing of the remote data by improving existing RSA based signature generation which support large and different size of files and provide better security in storing the file data. There are three entities involved to carry out the overall process flow in the system.

The client stores data in the remote cloud server and continuously monitors it using the third party auditor (TPA) which is a monitoring tool that analysis the integrity of the stored file in the server using

Figure 8. Data processing view of server

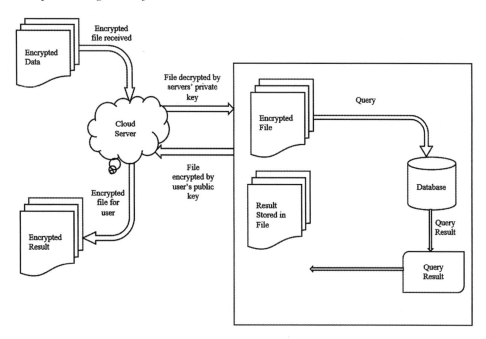

Figure 9. RSASS data flow architecture

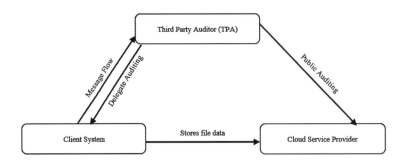

the RSA based signature generation algorithm and report. Based on the analysis results of the TPA, the user is notified if there is any sign of misbehavior on the data files. These analysis are done using RSA algorithm and are described as follows:

1. **Methodology:** In the RSASS, data is continuously monitored using RSA based signature algorithm by having the user challenging the server using the provable data possession (PDP) model which is a challenge and response protocol.
2. **Setup Phase:**
   a. Client generates a file $F = \{m_1, m_2, ..., m_n\}$, which is a finite ordered collection of n blocks.
   b. Generates public key 'rpk' and secrete key 'rsk' using the key generation of RSA algorithm.
   c. Five step process illustrated in Figure 10.
      i. Client generates the signature (tag) for each file block using the secret key rsk and hash algorithm as $T_i = (H(m_i).g^{m_i})^{rsk}$
      ii. A signature set $\phi = \{T_i\}$ is generated which is the collection of signature of file blocks.
      iii. A Merkle Hash Tree (MHT) is constructed for each file block using hash algorithm.
      iv. The root R of the MHT is signed using the secret key as $sig_{rsk}(H(R)) = H(R)^{rsk}$.
      v. The generated client advertise $\{F, \Phi, sig_{rsk}(H(R))\}$ to the server and deletes Φ and $sig_{rsk}(H(R))$ from its local storage. The client delivers the public key to the third party auditor (TPA) to monitor the remote files.
3. **Integrity Phase:**
   a. Selecting a subset of file blocks as $I = \{s_1, s_2, ..., s_c\}$ of set $[1, n]$ such that $s_1 \leq s_2 \leq ... \leq s_c$ and random coefficient $a_i = f_k(s_i)$ for $i \in I$ and k is the security parameter.
   b. Client sends the challenge $\{i, a_i\}$ to the server.
   c. The server generates the proof based upon the challenge it receives. Proof P contains $\{T, M, \{H(m_i), \Omega_i\} \, s_1 \leq i \leq s_c, \, sig_{rsk}(H(R))\}$ where
      i. Tag Blocks: $T = \Pi \, T_i^{a_i} mod \, N \, \left(for \, i = s_1 to \, s_c \right)$
      ii. Data Blocks: $M = \Sigma a_i m_i mod \, N \left(for \, i = s_1 to \, s_c \right)$

Figure 10. Preprocessing of file blocks

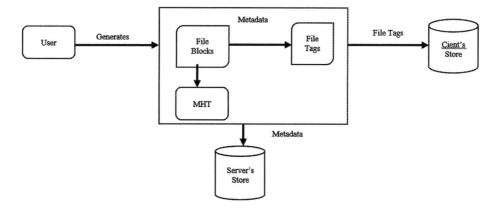

ii.   Auxiliary Authenticate Information: $\{\Omega_i\}$ $s_1 \leq i \leq s_c$

d.   The server sends the generated Proof P to the client as a response.

e.   Validates proof by generating the root R using $\{\Omega_i, H(m_i)\}$ $s_1 \leq i \leq s_c$ and authenticates by checking its secret key rsk.

f.   Send final response based on verification process flow.

RSASS Scheme Algorithms

The Proposed RSASS system generates the signature using RSA algorithm which supports large and different size of files and provides much security in storing the file data. This system ensures the possession of the file stored in the remote server using frequent integrity checking. This system is applicable to large public databases such as digital libraries, astronomy, medical archives, etc. In future, this RSASS system will be incorporated in a dynamic real time application to have much more effective data storage security in cloud computing.

Figure 11. Merkle hash tree (8 blocks)

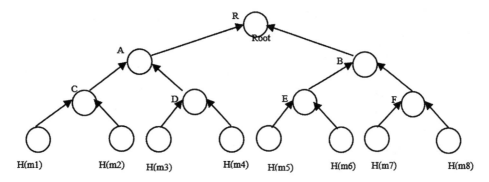

Figure 12. Integrity checking process flow

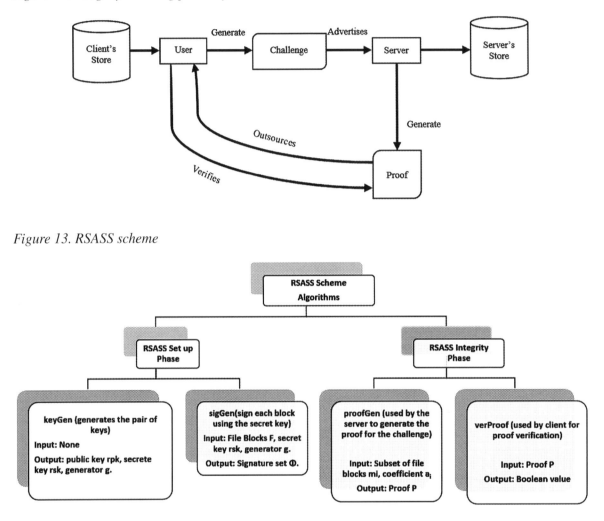

Figure 13. RSASS scheme

Secure Cloud Storage Framework (SCSF)

In Xiao, Zeng, and Hoon (2014) authors proposed a scheme to securely store and access data via internet. The authors designed a secure cloud storage framework (SCSF) that relies on ECC based PKI for certificate procedure instead of RSA to reduce computation cost and overhead due to that fact that ECC 160 bit key size provides equal security level complexity as RSA 1024 bit key size. This framework promised to enable users to store and access data through an unsecure channel in a secure manner ensuring the security and privacy of the data in the cloud. This scheme works by encrypting data on the client promises before uploading it to the cloud and decrypting it on the client promises after downloading it from the cloud. Moreover, the authors provided a way to share data with more than one authenticated user by encrypting it with the owner's private key and therefore have it available for download and decrypting with the owners public key in the certificate.

SCSF consists of two parts for every user's data:

- Private where users can store sensitive data, and
- Public where users can share data with multiple authenticated users.

There are four steps that users must follow to successfully gain access to the system:

- First, user must authenticate to the CA.
- Second, user authenticates to the Cloud interface.
- Third, for private data part user first need to encrypt the data at its side with the help of the PKI Enabled Application (PEA) before uploading it to the private data part of the cloud. Then downloads and decrypts the data with his session key when needs to operate on it.
- Finally, for shared data part user can share data with other authenticated users by first encrypting it using their session key then encrypts the session key with the private key of the key pair provided by CA.

Second, uploads the concatenation data to the shared data part of the cloud. SCSF Scheme utilizes symmetric encryption algorithm to encrypt data with different session keys. However, for shared data, the scheme encrypt the session key using ECC public key algorithm with their private key and decrypt with public key. Finally, all CA and cloud interface operations are managed through PEA.

PKI Certificate Management Procedure consist of five steps:

1. User sends request message to CA.
2. CA verifies user's identity and sends request message to user.
3. User authenticates to CA.
4. CA sends to acknowledgement message to user.
5. Certificate Issuance.

Chapter 3: Data Storage Security Using "Fully" Homomorphic Encryption Scheme

Homomorphic Encryption Cryptosystems

Fully Homomorphic cryptosystems can be used to securely search clients' encrypted data on the CP premises without the need to share the private key with the Cloud Provider and therefore eliminating the concern of non-secure or curious cloud providers.

Additive Homomorphic Encryption

An additively homomorphic scheme is one with a cipher text operation that results in the sum of the plaintexts. That is: $Encrypt\left(m1\right).Encrypt\left(m2\right) = Encrypt\left(m1 + m2\right)$ where the decryption of both sides yields the sum of the plaintexts.

Figure 14. Secured cloud storage framework (SCSF)

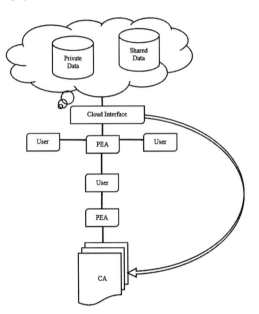

Table 1. Notations

Symbol	Definition
h(.)	One way hash function
ID_{USER}	Identity of the user
ID_{CA}	Identity of the CA
E	An elliptic curve defined on F_p with prime order n
P	A point on elliptic curve E with order n
(s_1, V_1)	Private/public key pair of user, where $V_1 = s_1 P$
(s_2, V_2)	Private/public key pair of CA, where $V_2 = s_2 P$
p, n	Two large prime numbers
M	Requested Message M
‖	Concatenate
K	ECDH Session Key
H′	Hash digest H′ of received M. H′ = h (M)

$$Decrypt\ \left(Encrypt\ \left(m1\right).Encrypt\ \left(m2\right)\right)\ =\ Decrypt\ \left(Encrypt\ \left(m1\ +\ m2\right)\right)\ =\ m1\ +\ m2$$

Example: Additively homomorphic Paillier by Coron, Mandal, Naccache, and Tibouchi (2011)

$$c_1\ =\ g^{m_1} r^N mod\ N^2,\ and\ c_2 = g^{m_2} s^N mod\ N^2,\ Then\ c_1 \cdot c_2 =\ g^{m_1 + m_2} \cdot \left(rs\right)^N mod\ N^2$$

Figure 15. SCSF PKI certificate management procedure

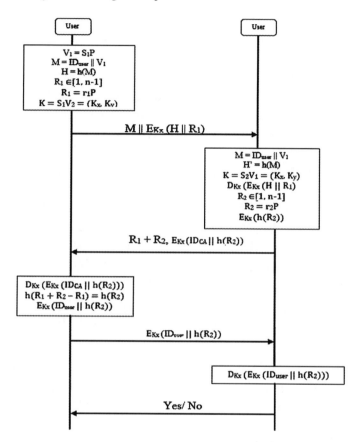

Multiplicative Homomorphic Encryption

A multiplicatively homomorphic scheme is one that has an operation on two cipher texts that results in the product of the plaintexts. That is: $Encrypt\ (m_1).Encrypt\ (m_2)\ =\ Encrypt\ (m_1.\ m_2)$ where the decryption of both sides yields the product of the plaintexts.

$$Decrypt\ (Encrypt\ (m_1).Encrypt\ (m_2))\ =\ Decrypt\ \left(Encrypt\ (m_1.\ m_2)\right)\ =\ m_1.\ m_2$$

Example: Multiplicatively Homomorphic of RSA by Coron et al. (2011)

$$c_1 =\ m_1^e mod\ N,\ and\ c_2 =\ m_2^e mod\ N,\ Then\ (c_1.c_2)\ =\ (m_1.m_2)^e\ mod\ N$$

Half Homomorphic Encryption

Half, partial, or somewhat homomorphic is an encryption scheme that allows a limited number of operations due to the growth of the error rate that prevents the proper decryption of the message to its original form. Therefore, an additive homomorphic scheme is a scheme that allows an unlimited number of additions with the plaintext message such as Pailler and Goldwasser-Micalli cryptosystems. Similarly, a multiplicative homomorphic scheme is a scheme that allows an unlimited number of multiplications with the plaintext message such as RSA and El Gamal cryptosystems.

Full Homomorphic Encryption

A Full Homomorphic Encryption (FHE) is a scheme that allows an unlimited number of operations (addition, and multiplication) on the plaintext message without the risk of preventing the decryption of the cipher text due to error growth such as Craig Gentry's. In another word, authors of Tebaa, El Hajji, and El Ghazi (2012) describe it as it is a scheme that allows unlimited number of addition and multiplication operations. Algebraically, it's the mapping ∂ between two groups (G, $\Diamond$) and (H, *) such that:

$$\partial \left(X \Diamond Y \right) = \partial \left(X \right) * \partial \left(Y \right) \text{ for } X, \ YG \text{ and } \partial \left(X \right), \ \partial \left(Y \right) H.$$

With Gentry's work and discovery that a feasible fully homomorphic scheme is possible, many subsequent proposals have been introduced that made improvements to the original proposal including new protocols from Gentry himself.

Gentry's Homomorphic Scheme

During Gentry's PhD dissertation research he was able come up with an alternative approach to the fully homomorphic encryption scheme by constructing it first from a somewhat homomorphic, then refreshing the cipher message periodically instead of relying on the structure of the encryption scheme. However, Gentry (2009) author's proposed scheme uses a key that grows substantially in length as the number of operations grow. This scheme uses of hard problems on ideal lattices and must allow an unlimited number of addition and multiplication operations on the ciphertext. However, the exponential error growth prevents the scheme from executing unlimited number of additions and multiplications on the message after a threshold number of operations that makes it difficult to decrypt the message to its original form. In particular, suppose that there is an "error" associated with each ciphertext, that ciphertext's output by Encrypt$_e$ have a small error, but have larger error that increases with the depth of the circuit being evaluated after receiving the ciphertext output of Evaluate$_e$, and that eventually results in a decryption error when applying Decrypt$_e$ to the ciphertext. Aguilar, Bettaieb, Gaborit, and Herranz (2011) stated that this is due to the fact that in lattice based schemes, the number of homomorphic operations that can be performed had a direct impact on the ciphertext size. These facts is what pushed researchers including Gentry himself to either rethink Gentry's initial scheme and produce techniques to refresh the ciphertext or move from algorithms that are based on the hardness of lattices to ones over integers. In Gentry (2009), author constructed a FHE scheme based on ideal lattices with three main steps starting from initial construction using ideal lattices, bootstrapping, then squashing technique to permit bootstrapping. All schemes that were introduced based on ideal lattices the ciphertext takes the form of a $C = V + X$, where V is an ideal lattice and X is an error vector that encodes a plaintext m. Moreover, the ciphertext vectors are intercepted as coefficient vectors of elements in a polynomial ring $Z_{[x]} / f(x)$ where ciphertext are added and multiplied using ring operations. Compared to previous work especially Boneh-Goh-Nissim, Gentry (2009) work is an improvement as it allows greater depth for multiplication. Yet, the scheme is only homomorphic for a threshold number of addition and multiplication operations as the errors vector grows beyond the level that allows the ciphertext to be correctly decrypted to its original plaintext. To overcome this issue, refreshing the ciphertext technique was introduced. This technique enables the algorithm to obtain a new ciphertext with a shorter error vector and therefore, making it bootstrappable. Finally, Gentry (2009) stated that the scheme's security is based on the natural decisional version of the closest vector of ideal lattices for ideal in a fixed ring and therefore makes it semantically secure.

DGHV Scheme

Dijk, Gentry, Halevi, and Vaikuntanathan (2010) stated that DGHV scheme that was introduced in 2009 included many of Gentry's constructions but didn't require the use of ideal lattices. In Jian, Danjie, Sicong, and Xiaofeng (2012) proposal, the authors show that the component which uses the ideal lattices can be replaced by a simpler one that uses integers instead for the somewhat homomorphic scheme introduced in Gentry (2009) and keeps similar properties with regards to homomorphic operations and efficiency.

van Dijk, Gentry, Halevi, and Vaikuntanathan (2010) authors stated in Def 3.7 that to overcome the limitation imposed on the scheme due to the growth of noise, Gentry introduces two techniques: Bootstrapping: encryption of the secret-key bits. And Squashing: a method for reducing the decryption complexity at the expense of making an additional and fairly strong assumption, namely the sparse subset sum assumption. These techniques are used to truly make the scheme fully homomorphic with unlimited number of additions and multiplications on the ciphertext. Finally, the Jian et al. (2012) scheme can be converted from a symmetric as described above to asymmetric by introducing "The public key consists of many "encryptions of zero", namely integers $x_i = q_i p + 2r_i$ where q_i, r_i are chosen from the same prescribed intervals as above. Then to encrypt a bit m, the ciphertext is essentially set as m plus a subset sum of the x_i's.

Gentry (2010) scheme implies that ciphertext is: $c = pq + m$ where c is the ciphertext, m is the plaintext, p is the key, and q is a random number. This encryption function is homomorphic with respect to addition, subtraction, and multiplication.

1. **KeyGen:** produces a P-bit odd integer p.
2. **Encrypt$_\varepsilon$** (p,m) where m $\in \{0,1\}$ and m' is a n-bit random number where

$m' = m \ mod \ 2$. $C \leftarrow m' + pq$, where q is a random Q-bit number.

3. **Decrypt$_\blacklozenge$** $(p,c) = c \ mod \ p \ where \ p \in \left(-p \ / \ 2, \ p \ / \ 2\right)$
4. **Homomorphic Operations:**

Figure 16. DGHV

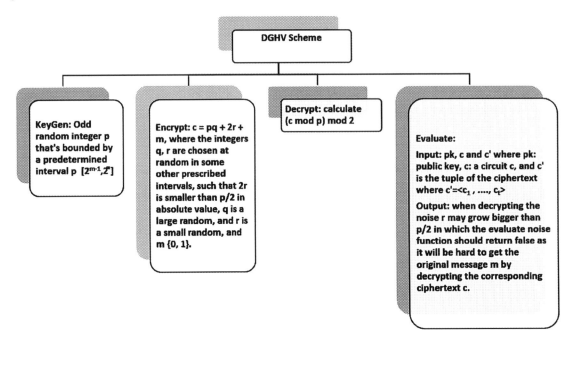

1. $Add_\varepsilon\left(c_1, c_2\right) \quad = \quad c_1 + c_2$
2. $Sub_\varepsilon\left(c_1, c_2\right) \quad = \quad c_1 - c_2$
3. $Mult_\varepsilon\left(c_1, c_2\right) \quad = \quad c_1 * c_2$

$Evaluate_\varepsilon\left(f, c_1, ..., c_t\right)$ which expresses the boolean function f as a circuit C with XOR and AND gates.

Coron et al (2011) introduced an improvement to Dijk et al. (2010) DGHV scheme by showing how to reduce the somewhat homomorphic public key from its original complexity of $O\left(\lambda^{10}log\lambda^{10}loglog\lambda^{10}\right)$ to $O\left(\lambda^{7}log\lambda^{7}loglog\lambda^{7}\right)$ by storing only a smaller subset of the public key. In addition, authors describe how to implement a fully homomorphic DGHV scheme under new variant, using some of the optimizations from Gentry, and Halevi (2011) and proved that the scheme still semantically secure and of same asymptotic performance as of Gentry-Halevi implementation in Gentry, and Halevi (2011). However, with the work of Chunsheng (2012) which showed the possibility of a heuristic attack using lattice reduction algorithm on fully homomorphic encryption schemes constructed over the integers, there is a concern that an attacker in case of not carefully choosing the parameter may derive the plaintext from a ciphertext and the public key without need to the secret key. Moreover, Chunsheng (2012) author showed that an attack can be avoided by setting parameter $\gamma=\lambda^6$ but with the concern that performance will be greatly hindered. Finally, they provided an improvement to the scheme while keeping it semantically secure by replacing the secret key from large integer to a matrix.

Coron, Lepoint, and Tibouchi (2012) extended the DGHV scheme to support encrypting and homomorphically processing a vector of plaintext bits as a single ciphertext. Yet, keeping the variants semantically secure under the Error-Free Approximate-GCD problem. In addition, Coron et al. (2012) proposed scheme homomorphically evaluates a full AES circuit with close efficiency as Graig et al "Homomorphic evaluation of AES Circuit" paper. However, for encrypting multiple bits into a single ciphertext, the authors rely on the Chinese Remainder Theorem to obtain:

$$C = q \cdot \prod_{i=0}^{l-1} p_i + CRT_{p0,\dots,pl-1}\left(2r_0 + m_0, \dots, 2r_{l-1} + m_{l-1}\right)$$

and produce the correct plaintext bit vector

$$m_i = \left[c \bmod p_i\right]_2 \; for \; all \; 0 \leq i \leq l^{CRT^{(a0,\dots,al-1)}_{p0,\dots,pl-1}}$$

Finally, authors proved the proposed scheme semantic security by proving that ciphertext is independently randomized modulo each pf the p_i's by first proving that the batch DGHV scheme is semantically secure under new assumptions, then showed that these assumptions are applied by the Error-Free Approximate-GCD. In the same context and by using the Chinese Remainder Theorem (CRT), the authors of Kim, Lee, Yun, and Cheon (2012) paper revisited Rivest, Adleman, and Dertouzos old proposal from 1978 that is based on the CRT and is a ring homomorphic. In Kim et al. (2012), authors presented a secure modification of their proposal by showing that the proposed scheme is fully homomorphic and secure against the chosen plaintext attacks under approximate GCD and the sparse subset sum assumptions when the message space is restricted to the Z_2^k. This scheme can be seen as a generalization of the DGHV scheme with larger plaintext with support for SIMD operations. Yet, its overhead is reduced to $O\left(\lambda^5 log\lambda^5 loglog\lambda^5\right)$ compared with DGHV's $O\left(\lambda^8 log\lambda^8 loglog\lambda^8\right)$ for the security parameter λ. Moreover, this scheme can have an $O\left(\lambda\right)$ if restricted to a depth of $O\left(log \; \lambda\right)$.

In Jian et al. (2012), authors proposed a practical and simple fully homomorphic encryption scheme called SDC which only used elementary modular arithmetic based on Gentry's cryptosystem but more secure and feasible when it comes to the aspect of ciphertext retrieval. This paper compared SDC algorithm to those proposed by Gentry (2009) and Dijk et al. (2010) where the retrieval algorithm of DGHV needs to transfer the private key P to server and retrieval algorithm for Gentry (2009) have to submit the constant number q to server. In addition, the authors claim that SDC is much secure as it doesn't provide the private key P and merely share random number q with the server and therefore no opportunity to leak out any valuable information during the application of ciphertext retrieval. Moreover, due to its nature of utilizing elementary modular arithmetic its performance evaluation proved that SDC is practical but I'll argue what the authors claim that its security analysis proved its validity as the same need that their statement used for labeling Gentry's retrieval algorithm as unsecure is also needed by SDC to compute R.

SDC Scheme

SDC Scheme of Jian et al. (2012), which is derived from Gentry's cryptosystem defined as followed as supports the following homomorphic operations:

- **Homomorphic Operations:**

$$c_1 = m_1 + p + r_1 {}^* p {}^* q$$

$$c_2 = m_2 + p + r_2 {}^* p {}^* q$$

○ **Additive Property:**

$$c_3 = c_1 + c_2 = \left(m_1 + m_2 \right) + \left(r_1 + r_2 \right) {}^* p {}^* q + 2p$$

$$m_3 = c_3 \bmod p = m_1 + m_2$$

○ **Multiplicative Property:**

$$c_4 = c_1 {}^* c_2 = m_1 {}^* m_2 + \left(m_1 + m_2 + p \right) p + r_1 \left(p + m_2 + r_2 \right) pq + r_2 \left(p + m_1 \right) pq$$

$$m_4 = c_4 \bmod p = m_1 {}^* m_2$$

Figure 17. SDC scheme

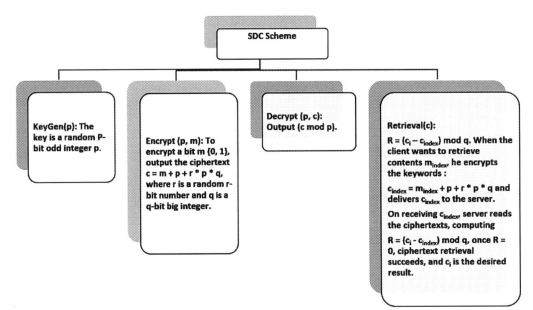

Single Instruction Multiple Data (SIMD)

In Smart, and Vercauteren (2011), authors presented a variant of Gentry's fully homomorphic public key encryption scheme with support to SIMD operations. The paper showed how to select parameters to enable SIMD operations while keeping the practicality of the key generation technique addressed by Gentry and Halevi where they used an efficient key generation procedure based on Fast Fourier Transform (FFT) and a simpler decryption circuit. This is achieved by obtaining a somewhat homomorphic scheme supporting both SIMD operations and operations on large finite fields of characteristic two. Then, converting the SHE to a FHE scheme by recrypting all data elements separately. The bootstrapping process requires a "dirty" ciphertext to be publicly reencrypted into a "cleaner" ciphertext. Based on Smart, and Vercauteren (2011), this implies that the SHE scheme must implement its own decryption circuit homomorphically to a certain threshold depth. Gentry and Halevi (2011), presented an optimized version of Smart and Vercauteren variant by introducing efficiency in the Key Generation procedure based on the FFT and simpler decryption circuit. These changes allowed the implementation of the FHE including the ciphertext cleaning operation.

Yet, Smart and Vercauteren scheme can support SIMD operations on non-trivial finite fields of characters two instead of operations on a single bit under certain conditions when it comes to choosing the parameters, the proposed parameters in these schemes do not allow SIMD operations to be realized. The method used to generate keys efficiently precludes the use of parameters that support SIMD. The goal is to allow any FHE scheme to embed a number of small plaintext within large ciphertexts independently and therefore enabling more efficient use of both space and computational resources. This paper, investigate SIMD operations in FHE schemes and show that by adapting the parameter settings from Gentry, and Halevi (2011) and Smart, and Vercauteren (2010) we can realize the benefits SIMD operations yet, continue to support the efficiency improvement from Gentry and Halevi (2011) work. Moreover, authors' show how we can benefit from FHE scheme with enabled SIMD operations to perform AES encryption homomorphically and searching an encrypted database on a remote server. Finally, the main contribution of this paper is a recryption procedure that makes use of the SIMD operations to improve the overall computational cost of the scheme by reducing the cost of recryption which was described in Chapter 5 and stated how to use SIMD operations to recrypt the r bits embedded copies of F2 in parallel.

- Recrypt Ciphertext Algorithm without SIMD

$C' \leftarrow 0$

$For \ i_1 \ from \ 0 \ to \ n - 1 \ do$

$\quad For \ i_2 \ from \ 0 \ to \ l - 1 \ do$

$\quad\quad C'i_1,i_2 \leftarrow BitRecrypt\left(\left[C.V \ i_1, i_2\right] d \ , \ pk\right)$

$\quad\quad\quad C' \leftarrow C' \oplus C'i_1, i_2 \odot (Tn, l \ (0, \ldots, 0, \overset{\Psi}{i1}, \ 0, \ldots, 0)) \ | \ \alpha$

$Return \ \left(C'\right)$

- Recrypt Ciphertext Algorithm with SIMD: Parallel recryption

$C' \leftarrow 0$

$\quad For\ i_1\ from\ 0\ to\ n - 1\ do$

$\quad Sum \leftarrow 0$

$\quad A \leftarrow 0,\ where\ A \in Ms\ x\ \left(p + 1\right)\ \left(Z / dZ\right)$

$\qquad For\ i_2\ from\ 0\ to\ l - 1\ do$

$\qquad\quad Ci_1, i_2 \leftarrow C\ .\ V\ i_1, i_2 \left(mod\ d\right)$

$\qquad\qquad For\ j\ from\ 0\ to\ s\ do$

$\qquad\qquad\quad y \leftarrow Ci_1, i_2\ .\ x_j\ \left(mod\ d\right)$

$\qquad\qquad\qquad For\ k\ from\ 0\ to\ s - 1\ do$

$\qquad\qquad\qquad\quad If\ y\ is\ odd\ then$

$\qquad\qquad\qquad\qquad Sum \leftarrow sum\ \overset{\oplus}{\ } e_j, k, i_2$

$\qquad\qquad\qquad\qquad b \leftarrow compute\_bits\left(y\right)$

$\qquad\qquad\qquad\qquad For\ u\ from\ 0\ to\ p\ do$

$\qquad\qquad\qquad\qquad A_{j,u} \leftarrow A_{j,u} \oplus \left(b_u\ .\ e_j, k, i_2\right)$

$\qquad\qquad\qquad\qquad y \leftarrow y\ .\ R\left(mod\ d\right)$

$\qquad\qquad\quad a \leftarrow school\_book\_add\left(A\right)$

$\qquad\qquad\quad C'' \leftarrow sum \oplus a_0$

$\qquad\qquad\quad C' \leftarrow C'\ C''\ i_1 \overset{i}{\odot}(T_{n,l}(0,\ldots,0, \Psi 1,\ 0,\ldots,0))\ |_{\alpha}$

$\qquad Return\ \left(C'\right)$

FHE-LWE

Brakerski, and Vaikuntanathan (2010) presented a FHE scheme based on learning with error (LWE) assumption which uses lattices and its security is based on the worst case hardness of the shorth vector problem. Yet the scheme deviates from Gentry's squashing technique and showed that SHE can be based on LWE by using a new re-linearilization technique. This scheme has a very short ciphertext and therefore it was used to construct an asymptatically efficient LWE based on using private information retrieval protocol for the public key model with a complexity of:

$$K.PolyLog\Big(K\Big) \ + \ Log\big|DB\big|$$

bits per single bits query. Where K is a security parameter.

- **Encryption:** $\Big(a, b \ = \ <a, b> \ + \ 2e \ + \ m\Big)$
- **Decryption:** $\Big(b \ - \ <a, s> \ mod \ q\Big) \ mod \ 2$

Instead of using squashing which is a method for reducing the decryption complexity at the expense of making an additional and fairly strong assumptions namely the sparse subset sum assumption this paper used as dimension modulus reduction which will transform a cyphertext with parameters(n, log q) into a cyphertext of the same message m but with parameters (k, log p) which are much smaller. This achievement enabled the LWE scheme to become a bootstrappable and the combination of all mentioned techniques in the paper resulted in a very short cyphertext of $\Big(k+1\Big)log \ p \ = \ O\Big(k \ log \ k\Big)$ bits. Moreover, the paper analyses the PIR protocol in the public key model and therefore ignoring the public key when calculating the communication complexity which yields to $LogN. \ PolyLogLogN$ compared to Gentry's $O\Big(Log^3 N\Big)$ bit communication.

Xiao, Bastani, and Yen

In Xiao, Bastani, and Yen (2012) authors developed a non-circuit based symmetric key homomorphic encryption scheme with security that is equivalent to the large integer factorization problem and can withstand an attack up to ($m \ ln \ poly\Big(\lambda\Big)$) chosen plaintexts for any predetermined m where λ is the security parameter. The scheme analysis showed that its multiplication, encryption, and decryption are linear in mλ, and that its performance is much faster compared to Gentry's original homomorphic scheme. However, to achieve efficiency the scheme downgrades the security requirements especially the encryption algorithm which encrypts plaintexts over Z_N into the matrix ring $M_4\Big(Z_N\Big)$ by applying a similarity transformation by the key $K \in M_4\Big(Z_N\Big)$ to a diagonal matrix with two entries equal to the plaintext where m is the product of $2m$ prime numbers and is of size nm bits. m is any predetermined constant that is polynomial in the security parameter λ. And the decryption is performed by applying the inverse similarity transformation. This scheme implemented a diferent aproach to construct homomorphic encryption algorithms with plaintexts over a finite domain such as finite field and therefore eliminating the circuit based computation overhead. However, authors claimed that all previous schemes that were constructed using non-circuit based either have been attached or luck securit evidence. Thus, homomorphic encryption scheme of Xiao et al. (2012) can be used in applications where semantic security is not required and one-wayness security is sufficient. A further consideration in Xiao et al. (2012) is practical multiple-user data-centric applications. To allow multiple users to retrieve data from a server all users need to have the same key. In Xiao et al. (2012) the master encryption key is transformed into different user keys to develop a protocol to support correct and secure communication between the users and the server using different user keys. The data in the data center are encrypted using homomorphic encryption with a master key. Different keys are assigned to different users which are actually transformations of master key k. This proposed multi-user system can withstand an adversary with up to m ln $poly(\lambda)$ plaintext ciphertext pairs.

Design Concept of Xiao et al. (2012) were based on Rabin's encryption algorithm which is a multiplicative homomorphic encryption then generalizing the ciphertext domain from Z_N to ring of matrices over Z_N. Given a plaintext x, the encryption algorithm is $E(x) = x^2 mod\ N,\ where\ N = f = pq.$

To a new transformation:

$$E_1(x) = \begin{pmatrix} x & 0 \\ 0 & r \end{pmatrix} mod\ N$$

where x is the eigenvalue of the vector $V_{1,0} = (1,0)^t$. However, an adversary can reverse x gevin the ciphertext by solving the linear equation $E_1(x)\overrightarrow{v_{1,0}} = x\overrightarrow{v_{1,0}}$. Therefore, the encryption algorithm applied a randomly selected similarity transform k to $\begin{pmatrix} x & 0 \\ 0 & r \end{pmatrix}$ which becomes:

$$E_2(x,k) = k^{-1} \begin{pmatrix} x & 0 \\ 0 & r \end{pmatrix} k\ mod\ N$$

where k is a randomly selected 2 x 2 invertible matrix. With this similarity transformation that transforms the eigenvector of x from $V_{1,0}$ to $k^{-1}V_{1,0}$, and since the adversary has no knowledge of the value of the key k it can't know the transformed eigenvector and therfore can't establish the linear equation system to optain the plaintext. Yet, E_2 is not resistant to the chosen plaintext attack and therefore the scheme associated the eigenvalue x with two eigenvectors V_1 and V_2 instead of only one eigenvector V. To maintain the homomorphic addition and multiplication of the scheme all plaintext must use one eigenvector V_1 but randomly choose V_2 with property distribution D.

Kipnis and Hibshoosh

FSERF is a fully homomorphic symetric key encryption and randomization function presented in Kipnis, and Hibshoosh (2012) and it's a set of methods for practical randomization of data over commutative ring, and symetric key encryption of random mod N data over ring Z_N. These methods provide security to the multivariate input of the coefficients of a polynomial function. Beacuse the scheme is based on non deterministic linear transformations, the authors show that FSERF scheme only requires a randon plaintext to be secure and therfore enable the algorithm to run on any untrusted cloud while keeping the data secure. This means that the scheme security semantics is based on contraining the plaintext to have random large numbers in Z_N. Moreover, the paper showed how to take advantage of the scheme methods to provide enhanced protection against certain attacks such as enhancing security of Ong, Schnorr, and Shamir (OSS) public key signature agaist Pollard attack, and protection for AES key agaist side channel attacks. Finally, FSERF methods provide fault detection and verification of computed data integrity.

FSERF methods are imviariant under encryption or randomization where each of the two isomorphic methods the authors defined a domain for secure encryption and another one for randomization. The schemes defined two isomorphic methodes, Matrix Operation for Randomization or Encryption (MORE), and Polynomial Operation for Randomization or Encryption (PORE).

Zhou and Wornell

In Zhou, and Wornell (2014), the authors showed that a more efficient FHE is practical when only supporting those encryption computation needed by the target application. This scheme was developed based on the constrain that it's for signal processing applications and operates directly on integer vectors that supports three operations. The approch was different from the main stream previousely proposed papers about FHE, where the authors concentrated on efficiency not by introducing a new technique that will make the encryption, decryption, or the evaluation algorithms have a smaller complexity but rather by examining the need of the applications and the tasks each needs to perform.

In Zhou, and Wornell (2014) mentioned proposal above, the sever has the processing algorithm which can't be leaked to the users. Therefore, the server computes $f(x)$ and returns the result to the user. All computation take place in the encrypted domain. This scheme is an extension of a pereviously proposed scheme by operating on integer vectors instead of binary vectors. Moreover, it support three operations on the encrypted data: Addition, Multiplication, and Weighted Inner products.

CONCLUSION

In this paper, we have surveyed cloud data storage security based on the classical symmetric / asymmetric cryptography and the newly discovered fully homomorphic schemes starting with Gentry's work. We have presented samples of the latest papers with related work showing their solution to ensure data

Figure 18. FSERF scheme

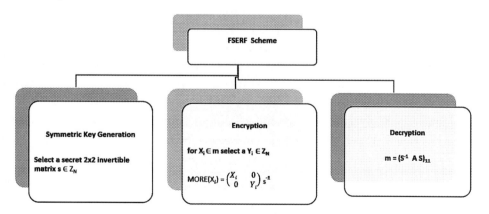

Figure 19. Traditional proposals vs. proposed solution

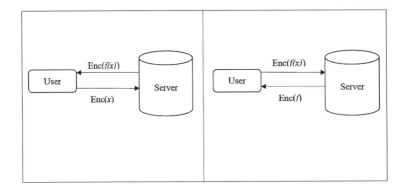

security in the cloud by relying on old and most used classical security algorithms and those that are based on either Half or Fully homomorphic schemes. Both Chapter one and two solutions are very feasible and implementable as they are built on schemes that most organizations are already using and familiar with and have a fair decryption performance that can be tolerated even when dealing with big data, especially when the solution is implemented using symmetric algorithm. In Chapter three, however, we presented a newly discovered solutions based on Gentry's work in 2009 which allowed encrypted data to be operated against without the need of decrypting it first. This solutions are based on what's known as fully homomorphic encryption schemes and are based on either Lattices as of Gentry's, Approximate GCD as of DGHV, Learning with Error as in paper by van Dijk et al. (2010), or Ring Learning with Error as BGV. Even though, these are a very powerful solutions that have proven security complexities as equal or close to the classical ones due to their mathematical nature of how they were constructed, their implementation is far from being ideal for real business applications or against big data due to the complexity of their algorithms that requires intensive computational resources such as: refreshing and squashing with Gentry's initial work and size of the used keys or the error growth for others. Since Gentry's proposal for a FHE scheme, many new proposals have tried to reduce his initial work complexity including Gentry himself. The reduction was based on introducing new techniques such as ciphertext combining or packing which combines multiple ciphertext into a single one like Smart and Vercauteren's that was based on the Chinese Remainder Theorem (CRT). Or based on lattices, encrypt and process based on a binary vector instead of a single bit, based on ring learning with error, applying a technique to support SIMD operations by encrypting multiple bits within the same ciphertext and perform the same operation on them. Using SIMD made the FHE scheme faster and reduces the ciphertext space. Gentry's initial scheme complexity bound for the approximate shortest vector problem (SVP) in lattices and ideal lattices bounded distance decoding problem (BDD). In Dijk et al. (2010) paper, the scheme's semantic security is based on the hardness of the approximate greatest common divisor problem as well as the hardness of the sparse subset sum problem (SSSP) for the squashed scheme. For the FHE LWE scheme presented in van Dijk et al. (2010) paper, the security is based on the $LWE_{n,q,e}$ with the note of the bigger the noise e, the more secure the scheme becomes however it must be within a predefined constraint. This scheme also accomplish a poly-logarithmic overhead for wide enough arithmetic circuits on $Z_p for\ p\ =\ poly(\lambda)$. For the asymptotic time complexity when it comes to computation, constructing a scheme over integers rather than lattices prove to be faster. For Kim et al. (2012), which is a generalization of the DGHV scheme but with larger plaintext space. In Gupta, and

Table 2. Comparison of key and ciphertext sizes (in bits)

Scheme	Secret key size	Ciphertext size	Public key size
LWE (Brakerski, and Vaikuntanathan(2011))	$n\ log\ q$	$(n\ +\ 1)\ log\ q$	$O\left(n^2 log^2 q\right)$
LWE/RLWE (Brakerski, Gentry, and Vaikuntanathan(2011))	$2d\ log\ q$	$2d\ log\ q$	$2dn\ log\ q$

Based on van Dijk et al. (2010)

Sharma (2013), the authors presented a solution based on the hardness of factorization of large integers and support operation based on matrices. This scheme has a constant plaintext expansion and better time space.

Finally, both symmetric and asymmetric classical cryptography schemes provide semantic security with asymptotically linear time and space complexities. In contrast, FHE schemes have an asymptotic complexity that is far greater in time and space "at least as of now" than its classical ones and uses larger security keys that makes the computation complexity also greater. However, FHE schemes provide the ability to query encrypted data without the need of sharing any keys and protects against security leaks or curious servers and therefore have far more security semantics especially when computation is done on the cloud or in a multi-tenant environment.

REFERENCES

Aguilar, M. C., Bettaieb, S., Gaborit, P., & Herranz, J. (2011). *Improving Additive and Multiplicative Homomorphic Encryption Schemes based on Worst-Case Hardness Assumption.* Cryptology ePrint Archive Report 2011/607.

Brakerski, Z., Gentry, G., & Vaikuntanathan, V. (2011). *Fully homomorphic encryption without boot-strapping.* Cryptology ePrint Archive, Report 2011/277.

Brakerski, Z., & Vaikuntanathan, V. (2011). *Efficient Fully Homomorphic Encryption from (Standard) LWE.* Electronic Colloquium on Computational Complexity, Report No. 109 (2011).

Chunsheng, G. (2012). *Attack on fully homomorphic encryption over the integers.* Cryptology ePrint Archive Report 2012/157.

Coron, J., S., Lepoint, T., & Tibouchi, M. (2012). *Batch fully homomorphic encryption over the integers.* Cryptology ePrint Archive Report 2013/036.

Coron, J. S., Mandal, A., Naccache, D., & Tibouchi, M. (2011). Fully homomorphic encryption over the integers with shorter public-keys. *Advances in Cryptology - Proc. CRYPTO 2011*, (LNCS), (vol. 6841). Springer. 10.1007/978-3-642-22792-9_28

Dent, W., A. (2006). *Fundamental problems in provable security and cryptography.* Royal Society. Cryptology ePrint Archive Report 2006/278.

Diffie, W., & Hellman, M. E. (1976). New Directions in Cryptography. *IEEE Transactions on Information Theory, 22*(6), 644–654. doi:10.1109/TIT.1976.1055638

Dijk, M. V., Gentry, C., Halevi, S., & Vaikuntanathan, V. (2010). Fully homomorphic encryption over the integers. *LNCS, 6110,* 24–43.

Gentry, G. (2009). *A Fully Homomorphic Encryption Scheme* (PhD thesis). Stanford University. Retrieved from https://crypto.stanford.edu/craig/craig-thesis.pdf

Gentry, G. (2009). *Fully homomorphic encryption using ideal lattices.* ACM. doi:10.1145/1536414.1536440

Gentry, G. (2010). Computing arbitrary functions of encrypted data. *Communications of the ACM, 53*(3), 97–105. doi:10.1145/1666420.1666444

Gentry, G., & Halevi, S. (2011). Implementing Gentry's fully homomorphic encryption scheme. EURO-CRYPT 2011, (LNCS). Springer. doi:10.1007/978-3-642-20465-4_9

Gupta, C. P., & Sharma, I. (2013). *Fully Homomorphic Encryption Scheme with Symmetric Keys.* University College of Engineering, Rajasthan Technical University. Retrieved from http://arxiv.org/abs/1310.2452

Jian, L., Danjie, S., Sicong, C., & Xiaofeng, L. (2012). A Simple Fully Homomorphic Encryption Scheme Available in Cloud Computing. *Proceedings of IEEE CCIS2012.*

Khan, M., Hussain, S., & Imran, M. (2013). Performance Evaluation of Symmetric Cryptography Algorithms: A Survey. *ITEE Journal of Information Technology & Electrical Engineering, 2*(2).

Kim, J., Lee, M., S., Yun, A., & Cheon, J., H. (2012). *CRT-based fully homomorphic encryption over the integers.* Cryptology ePrint Archive Report 2013/057.

Kipnis, A., & Hibshoosh, E. (2012). *Efficient Methods for Practical Fully-Homomorphic Symmetric-key Encryption, Randomization, and Verification.* Cryptology ePrint Archive, Report 2012/637.

Landau, S. (n.d.). *Standing the Test of Time: The Data Encryption Standard.* Academic Press.

Nafi, K. W., Shekha, K. T., Hoque, S. A., & Hashem, M. M. A. (2012). A Newer User Authentication, File encryption and Distributed Server Based Cloud Computing security architecture. *International Journal of Advanced Computer Science and Applications, 3.*

Sharma, S., Chugh, A., & Kumar, A. (2013). Enhancing Data Security in Cloud Storage. *International Journal of Advanced Research in Computer and Communication Engineering, 2*(5).

Smart, N. P., & Vercauteren, F. (2010). Fully homomorphic encryption with relatively small key and ciphertext sizes. Public Key Cryptography – PKC 2010. doi:10.1007/978-3-642-13013-7_25

Smart, N., P., & Vercauteren, F. (2011). *Fully homomorphic SIMD operations.* IACR Cryptology ePrint Archive, Report 2011/133.

Tebaa, M., El Hajji, S., & El Ghazi, A. (2012). Homomorphic Encryption Applied to the Cloud Computing Security. *Proceedings of the World Congress on Engineering.*

Tirthani, N., & Ganesan, R. (2014). *Data Security in Cloud Architecture Based on Diffie Hellman and Elliptical Curve Cryptography.* School of computing Sciences and Engineering, M. tech. – Computer Science, VIT, Chennai Campus.

Venkatesh, M., & Sumalatha, M. (2012). *Improving Public Auditability, Data Possession in Data Storage Security for Cloud Computing.* ICRTIT.

Xiao, C. Y., Zeng, G. L., & Hoon, J. L. (2014). *An Efficient and Secured Data Storage Scheme in Cloud Computing Using ECC-based PKI.* ICACT.

Xiao, L., Bastani, O., & Yen, I. L. (2012). *An efficient homographic encryption protocol for multiuser systems, 2012.* Cryptology ePrint Archive Report 2012/193.

Yellamma, P., Narasimham, C., & Sreenivas, V. (2013). Data Security in the Cloud Using RSA. *IEEE - 31661.* ICCCNT.

Zhou, H., & Wornell, G. (2014). *Efficient Homomorphic Encryption on Integer Vectors and Its Applications.* Dept. Electrical Engineering and Computer Science, Massachusetts Institute of Technology. Retrieved from http://www.mit.edu/~hongchao/papers/Conference/ITA2014_HomomorphicEncryption.pdf

This research was previously published in the Handbook of Research on End-to-End Cloud Computing Architecture Design edited by Jianwen "Wendy" Chen, Yan Zhang, and Ron Gottschalk, pages 189-221, copyright year 2017 by Information Science Reference (an imprint of IGI Global).

APPENDIX

RSA Algorithm (Tebaa et al. (2012))

Key Generation Algorithm

1.   Randomly and secretly choose two large primes: p, q.
2.   Compute $n = p.q$.
3.   Compute $\phi(n) = (p-1)(q-1)$.
4.   Select Random Integer e where e $\in]1,n[$ and $gcd(e, \phi) = 1$.
5.   Compute d such as $e.d \equiv 1 \ mod \ \phi(n)$ and $d \in]1,\phi(n)[$.
6.   Public Key: (e, n)   and   Private Key: (d, n)

Encryption Process

1.   Suppose entity A needs to send message m to entity B where $m \in]0,n[$.
2.   Entity A will encrypt m using B's public Key:
$c = m^e mod \ n$, then sends encrypted text $c \in]0,n[$ to entity B.

Decryption Process

1.   Entity B decrypts the received encrypted message to obtain the plaintext message:

$$m = c^d mod \ n$$

Paillier Algorithm (Tebaa et al. (2012))

Key Generation Algorithm

1.   Randomly and secretly choose two large primes:
$p, q \ where \ gcd\left(pq, \ (p-1)(q-1)\right) = 1$
2.   Compute $n = p.q \ and \lambda = lcm\left(p-1, \ q-1\right)$
3.   Select Random Integer g where $g \in Z^*_{n^2}$
4.   Must satisfy: $\mu = \left(L\left(g^\lambda mod \ n^2\right)\right)^{-1} mod \ n$, where function L is:

$$L(\mathrm{u}) = \frac{(u-1)}{n}$$

5.   Public Key: $(n, \ g)$
6.   Private Key: $(\lambda, \ \mu)$

Encryption Process

1.   Suppose entity A needs to send message m to entity B where $m \in]0, n[$
2.   Select random r where $r \in Z_n^*$. Then compute:

$c = g^m . r^n mod\ n^2$, then sends encrypted text c to entity B.

Decryption Process

1.   Entity B decrypts the received encrypted message $c \in Z_{n}^{*\,2}$ to obtain the plaintext message: $m = L\left(c^\lambda mod\ n^2\right) . \mu\ mod\ n$

Data Encryption Standard (Landau)

The Data Encryption Standard (DES) is a symmetric- key block cipher published as FIPS-46 in the Federal Register in January 1977 by the National Institute of Standards and Technology (NIST). At the encryption site, DES takes a 64-bit plaintext and creates a 64-bit ciphertext, at the encryption site, it takes a 64-bit ciphertext and creates a 64-bit plaintext, and same 56 bit cipher key is used for both encryption and decryption. The encryption process is made of two permutations (P-boxes), which we call initial and final permutation, and sixteen Feistel rounds. Each round uses a different 48-bit round key generated from the cipher key according to a predefined algorithm as shown in Figure 20.

The function f is made up of four Chapters: 1. Expansion P-box, 2. A whitener (that adds key), 3. A group of S-boxes, 4. A straight P-box.

Diffie Hellman (Tirthani & Ganesan, 2014)

Diffie Hellman key exchange mechanism is one of the traditional protocols used to obtain a public key.

Input: Consider G as an abelian group where $g \in G$ and m is a prime multiplicative order.

Output: A secret $s \in G$ which will be shared by both the sides.

Steps:

- Sender generates random $d_A \in \{2..., m-1\}$ and compute $e_A = g^d_A$.
- Sender sends e_A to receiver.
- Receiver generates a random $d_B \in \{2..., m-1\}$ and computes $e_B = g^d_B$.
- Receiver sends e_B to receiver.
- Sender calculates $s = \left(e_B\right)^d A = g^d A^d B$
- Receiver calculates $s = \left(e_A\right)^d B = g^d A^d B$

Figure 20. DES

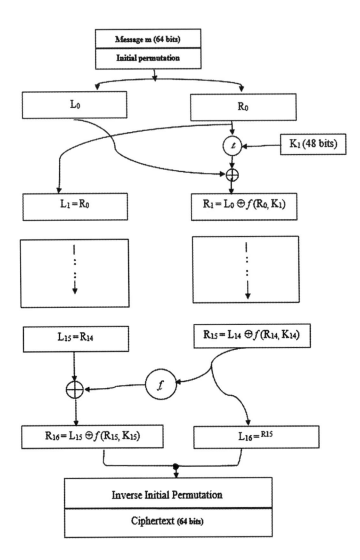

Elliptic Curve Cryptography (ECC) (Tirthani & Ganesan, 2014)

Implementing Group Operations

1.   Main operations - point addition and point multiplication
2.   Adding two points that lie on an Elliptic Curve - results in a third point on the curve
3.   Point multiplication is repeated addition
4.   If P is a known point on the curve (aka Base point; part of domain parameters) and it is multiplied by a scalar k,
$Q = k * P$ is the operation of adding P (k times)

5.   Q is the resulting public key and k is the private key in the public-private key pair

Adding Two Points on the Curve

1.   P and Q are added to obtain $P+Q$ which is a reflection of R along the X axis

2.   A tangent at P is extended to cut the curve at a point; its reflection is 2P

3.   Adding P and 2P gives 3P

4.   These operations can be performed as many times as desired to obtain $Q = k*P$

Chapter 37

Healthcare SaaS Based on a Data Model With Built-In Security and Privacy

Ruchika Asija
Indira Gandhi National Open University, India

Rajarathnam Nallusamy
Embnology Solution Private Limited, India

ABSTRACT

Cloud computing is a major technology enabler for providing efficient services at affordable costs by reducing the costs of traditional software and hardware licensing models. As it continues to evolve, it is widely being adopted by healthcare organisations. But hosting healthcare solutions on cloud is challenging in terms of security and privacy of health data. To address these challenges and to provide security and privacy to health data on the cloud, the authors present a Software-as-a-Service (SaaS) application with a data model with built-in security and privacy. This data model enhances security and privacy of the data by attaching security levels in the data itself expressed in the form of XML instead of relying entirely on application level access controls. They also present the performance evaluation of their application using this data model with different scaling indicators. To further investigate the adoption of IT and cloud computing in Indian healthcare industry they have done a survey of some major hospitals in India.

1. INTRODUCTION

A methodical, continuous and systematic adoption of innovative solutions is required in healthcare sector for giving cost- effective, efficient, organized and high quality services. Traditionally, in healthcare, the primary focus has been on digitisation of health records and automation of back office systems, billing and reimbursements making the healthcare industry a slow adopter of technology. But these days, technology has taken roots in human lives making it more intrinsic. Our expectations on communications, data, content, and applications have increased in a way such that an immediate and global access to

DOI: 10.4018/978-1-5225-8176-5.ch037

information has become a de-facto requirement in today's world. With the enactment of HITECH Act (Health Information Technology for Economic and Clinical Health Act) in 2009 (HITECH, 2009), by the end of 2010, most of the doctors in United States were using electronic medical records. The PPACA (Patient Protection and Affordable Care Act) enacted in March 2010, elevated the goals of high quality and affordable health insurance, expansion of public and private insurance coverage and reduced the costs of healthcare for individuals and the government. While choosing the best option to store and backup electronic protected health information (ePHI) as represented by the Act, many healthcare providers are looking at cloud storage. The proliferation of cloud computing has allowed many organisations to extend their environments, utilize flexible resources, and empower their users. It can improve the delivery of healthcare services and can also benefit healthcare research. With the adoption of cloud computing, large IT investments can be converted to a series of smaller operating expenses. Cloud architecture could potentially be superior to traditional electronic health record (EHR) designs in terms of economy, efficiency and utility (Eugene J Schweitzer, 2011). According to a survey of cloud computing adoption in healthcare provider organizations, HIMSS Analytics found that 83% of IT executives are using cloud services today, with SaaS based applications being the most popular (HIMSS Analytics, 2014). Considering the proliferation of cloud computing in various domains, we propose to leverage it to create an application that can foster and support the healthcare system. The accelerating migration of healthcare to cloud can help in supporting increased sharing and accessibility of health data. But it also raises the concerns over the security and privacy of healthcare data. The challenging task of providing a solution which can protect the security and privacy of health data along with efficient performance by using a data model with built in secuirty is addressed in this paper.

The rest of the paper is organized as follows: The need and importance of cloud computing in healthcare is discussed in Section 2. Some of the frameworks and models which have been implemented in cloud are briefly outlined in Section 3. The concerns and challenges in providing security and privacy to healthcare data are presented in Section 4. To deal with such concerns and security and privacy challenges, the application "Healthcare SaaS" is presented in Section 5 implemented in cloud and its architecture is described in Section 6. Implementation and performance evaluation with all scaling indicators for our application "Healthcare SaaS" on cloud are discussed in Section 7. The advantages of the application using the data model (Asija et al., 2014) is discussed in Section 8. In order to understand the level of adoption and implementation of IT in healthcare and the move towards cloud, we have done a survey in three major hospitals of India which is discussed in Section 9 and the conclusions and future work are presented in Section 10.

2. CLOUD COMPUTING CONCEPTS

As defined by National Institute of Standards and Technology (NIST) (Cloud Survey, 2011), Cloud Computing is a model for enabling on-demand and convenient access to shared pool of computing resources that can be configured, provisioned, and released rapidly with minimum effort or cloud provider interaction. Five essential characteristics of cloud computing identified by NIST are: broad network access, on-demand self-service, resource pooling, measured service and rapid elasticity or expansion. *Broad network access* defines the capabilities available over the network and accessed through standard mechanisms and used by heterogeneous thick or thin client platforms, for example, tablets, laptops and mobile phones. *Resource pooling* incorporates a multi-tenant model with dynamically assigned physical and virtual resources to serve multiple consumers as per their demands. Capabilities elastically provisioned and released to scale rapidly outward and inward commensurating with demand are included in *rapid elasticity*. *Measured service* is characterised by leveraging a metering capability at abstract level for different services such as storage, processing, bandwidth and active user accounts to automatically control and to optimise the resource use. Resource usage is monitored, controlled and reported to provide complete transparency between the provider and consumer of the utilized services. *Cloud Computing* encompasses several variations of service models (i.e. IaaS, PaaS and SaaS) and deployment models (i.e. private, public, hybrid and community clouds). *SaaS (Software-as-a-Service)* provides complete applications to a cloud's end user. It is accessed through a web portal and service oriented architectures based on web service technologies. *PaaS (Platform-as-a-Service)* comprises the environment for developing and provisioning cloud applications. This layer is particularly used by developers seeking to develop and run a cloud application for a particular platform. *IaaS (Infrastructure-as-a-Service)* combines services on the infrastructure layer and used to access essential IT resources. These essential IT resources include services linked to computing resources, data storage resources and the communications channel. While service models delineate the specific capabilities of cloud solutions, deployment models describe where, how and by whom the cloud's physical servers are managed. With a *Private cloud*, users have immediate access to IT resources that are running on internal systems and / or in a data center. *Public cloud*, as the name suggests is a deployment model under which resources are made generally available to everyone. A *Hybrid cloud* combines one or more private clouds. Hybrid clouds potentially provide the best of both public and private cloud. EMR (Electronic Medical Record), HIS (Health Information System), PACS (Picture Archiving and Communication System) are creating a critical need for more data storage. Cloud computing blends a vast network of servers. Instead of downloading any medical software on each computer, a central set of centrally managed servers are accessed by the whole network. This results in lower costs while freeing data storage capacity. All of these efforts combine together to allow hospitals to better utilise their resources and focus on their core mission which is patient care.

2.1. Related Work

Storing data in the cloud computing Operating System (OS) is not new, but processing and accessing medical data with secure system using Cloud Computing is a source of concern these days for healthcare organizations. There are various healthcare models and frameworks available which are using a cloud-based system in an attempt to improve healthcare service. One such model was proposed that automates the process of collecting patient's data via a network of sensors connected to legacy medical devices, and deliver this information to the medical center's "cloud" for storage, processing and distribution (Rolim et al., 2010). Fan et al. (Fan et al., 2012) proposed a cloud based system which presented the analysis of phyiological signal data and the early warning mechanism for diseases. The collection of signals is done through body sensors. A mobile application is developed for ambulatory electrocardiographic monitoring that helps medical personnel to guide diagnose procedures efficiently using their smartphone and manage the daily activities connecting different zones (Saldarraiga et al., 2013). Mobile devices' usage extends point-of-care medical services beyond the clinic or hospital, providing obvious benefits to providers and patients. However, accessing medical data on unsecured medical devices runs the risk of data theft or loss and of regulatory non-compliance. HCX (Health Cloud eXchange) is a private cloud-based distributed web interactive system that provides data sharing service allowing dynamic discovery of various healthcare records and related services (Mohammed et al., 2010). TCLOUD (Deng et al., 2011) proposed a home healthcare system using cloud computing. In TCLOUD system, patients, medical personnel and doctors are connected to get different services like drug therapy management, sleep and light management and physical activity management of patients. It uses STRIDE (Howard et al., 2006) and LIDDUN (Deng et al., 2011) methods for security and privacy threat modeling. A security system was developed which was meant not only to monitor and give notifications but also to record data and to track intruders. They used re-encryption formula to control the user access to the medical data (Louk et al., 2014). Doukas et al. (Doukas et al., 2010) have developed @HealthCloud, a healthcare information management system, for mobile devices utilizing cloud computing and Android operating system. The functionality of the application lies in providing medical experts and patients, with a mobile user interface for managing healthcare information. Despite many benefits associated with these healthcare applications, a major issue regarding security and privacy of health data in cloud still needs to be addressed. Many of the leading software companies have invested heavily in the cloud such as Microsoft's Health Vault, Amazon Web Services (AWS) and Oracle's Exalogic Elastic Cloud, promising an explosion in the storage of personal healthcare information online. But the main challenge lies in lack of trust in data security and privacy by users, organisational inertia, loss of governance and uncertain provider's compliance. Dai Yuefa et al. (Dai Yuefa et al., 2009) proposed a data security model built on three level defense structure in cloud computing. The first layer is responsible for user authentication, second layer is used for user's data encryption to protect the privacy of users and third layer is responsible for recovery of user data. One more data security model for cloud computing was presented which implemented a software to select the suitable and the highest security encryption algorithm (Mohamed E.M. et al., 2012). A cloud architecture (Chander Kant et al., 2013) was proposed which consist of a cryptographic application installed on client side and allows for encryption and decryption operation on data. To achieve scalability and data confidentiality of access control, Shucheng Yu et al. (Shucheng Yu et al., 2010) have combined the techniques of attribute-based encryption (ABE), proxy re-encryption and lazy re-encryption. All the models discussed here are using encryption as a security method in one way or the other way. But to provide a more fine-grained and enhanced security in cloud computing, this paper provides an approach of assigning security levels to each user and each data element. Assigning security levels to each user and data and then encrypting the portions of the data according to the security levels ensures enhanced security of health care data.

2.2. Security and Privacy Challenges

The emergence of healthcare with cloud computing has introduced a number of specific security and privacy threats. A report from the Cloud Security Alliance, *The notorious nine: Cloud computing top threats in 2013* (CSA, 2013), identifies nine major security concerns associated with the use of the cloud which include - data breaches, data loss, account hijacking, insecure APIs, denial of service, malicious insiders, abuse of cloud services, insufficient due diligence and shared technology issues:

- Cloud Computing is easily accessible to most of the customers. If the provider fails to separate the resources, it could lead to various security risks. For example, if a customer requests to delete some data stored in cloud, it does not result in full deletion of the data. This data may not be available but is still stored on the disk. Due to the multiple tenant environment nature of the cloud, these hardware resources can be reused by other customers such as a third party and could have access to another customer's "deleted" data. This poses a higher risk to the cloud customer than with dedicated hardware;

- Managing encryption keys is one of the challenges in cloud environment. The main challenge is that if data is encrypted before being uploaded on cloud and the remote device is not having the decryption key, then the resulting data will be in encrypted form and will be useless;

- The use of cloud computing is distributed widely across multiple jurisdictions, each jurisdication having different laws for data security, privacy, usage and intellectual property (Kuner, 2010), (Ward, 2010). For example, the US Health Insurance Portability and Accountability Act (HIPAA) restricts companies from disclosing personal health data to non-affiliated third parties, and the Providing Appropriate Tools Required to Intercept and Obstruct Terrorism (PATRIOT) Act (PATRIOT, 2011) gives the U.S government the right to demand data if it declares conditions as being an emergency or necessary to homeland security. Similarly, the Canadian Personal Information Protection and Electronic Documents Act (PIPEDA) (PIPEDA) limits the powers of organisations to collect, use, or disclose personal information in the course of commercial activities.

However, a provider may move the user's information from jurisdiction to jurisdiction without notice to a user. Data in the cloud may have more than one legal location at the same time, with different legal consequences. Failure of mechanisms of separate storage, memory and routing generates privacy risk that harms the reputation of different tenants for the shared infrastructure.

- In healthcare, even partial disclosure of patient's health data is undesirable. For example, if any patient goes for an HIV test, then his identity is considered at risk. It shows that a fine-grained access control is required to provide confidentiality and integrity of data.

3. HEALTHCARE SaaS BUILT ON A SECURE DATA MODEL

Security and data privacy issues are of vital importance in the adoption of any IT-based healthcare solution. Recognizing the need for enhancing the security and privacy in healthcare, we developed a data model (Asija et al., 2014) which offers a granular access control in healthcare XML documents. By introducing security levels for each element inside an XML schema thereby within the XML data itself, as well as assigning security levels to each and every user accessing the data ensures full security of health records. Continuing further with our work, we have developed an application "Healthcare SaaS" as shown in Figure 1 which is designed using the datamodel (Asija et al., 2014) as described above.

According to our datamodel, there are different categories of users, like, Patient, Doctor, Nurse, and Pharmacist. We assign these users and data with different security levels (see Tables 1, 2, and 3).

The stakeholders involved in the application include patients, healthcare professionals and security administrator. Whenever a request comes from a user for fetching / insertion / updation of data, the access rights to the data by the user is assessed based on the mapping $SL(data) \leq SL(User)$. Only upon satisfying this condition and the mapping algorithm (Asija et al., 2014), access rights are granted to the user for the data:

Figure 1. Application

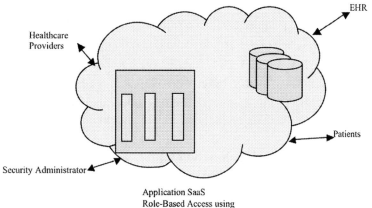

Table 1. Users with security levels

User	Security Level (SL)
Patient/Doctor	3
Nurse	2
Radiologist	1
Pharmacist/Physiotherapist	0

Table 2. Data with security levels

Data	Security Level (SL)
Name, ContactNumber, PID, Gender, Prescription, Age	0
X-Ray Reports, X-RayImags, EId, BldGr, DOB	1
Address, dateOfVisiting, Sample Collection, Injection, Diagnosis, dateOfTreatment	2
AnySpeclAllergies, TestRcmd	3

Table 3. Users accessing data according to their security level

User	Data Access
Patient/Doctor	Name, ContactNumber, PID, Gender, Prescription, X-Ray Reports, X-RayImags, EId, BldGr, Age, DOB, Address, dateOfVisiting, SampleCollection, Injection, Diagnosis, dateOfTreatment, AnySpecialAllergies, TestRcmd
Nurse	Name, ContactNumber, PID, Gender, Prescription, X-Ray Reports, X-RayImgs, EId, BldGr, Age, DOB, Address, dateOfVisiting, SampleCollection, Injection, Diagnosis, dateOfTreatment
Radiologist	Name, ContactNumber, PID, Gender, Prescription, X-Ray Reports, X-RayImags, EId, BldGr, Age, DOB
Pharmacist/Physiotherapist	Name, ContactNumber, PID, Gender, Prescription, Age

Definition: A security level SL is defined as SL(entity)=value, where entity $\in$ {user, data}and value specifies the security level, where, $0 \leq$ value $\leq$ max.

Example: In an XML schema, SL(Radiologist)=1, defines a security level of value=1 for user Radiologist and data with security levels 0 and 1 are: SL(Name, ContactNumber, PID, Gender, Prescription) and SL(X-Ray Reports, X-RayImags, EId, BldGr, Age, DOB).

Definition: Two entities are defined as matching, when SL(data) $\leq$ SL(user).

Example: In the above example, Radiologist having SL=1, can access the data upto security level SL=1, i.e. 0 and 1, as:

SL(Name, ContactNumber, PID, Gender, Prescription), SL(X $-$ Ray Reports, X $-$ RayImags, EId, BldGr, Age, DOB) $\leq$ SL(Radiologist)

Therefore, a Radiologist with SL $= 1$ can access all the data available upto security level 1.

The advantage of this approach is that the mapping of security levels can be assigned to the metadata also ensuring full security to the healthcare data without depending on any external security and privacy technique. Implementing this application in cloud without using any external security and privacy technique will ensure an efficient and secured healthcare system.

3.1. Architecture

For providing a granular access control in healthcare records, ensuring full security and privacy of health data and providing a quick access to computing and large storage facilities we propose an architecture shown in Figure 2 of our above mentioned application "Healthcare SaaS" hosted in cloud which can improve the operational efficiency of healthcare services. It consists of web application providing health web services and a database, residing inside a cloud that maintains the information about each patient's Electronic Health Records (EHRs).

Figure 2. Operational architecture

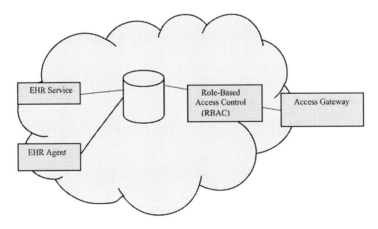

Major components of Healthcare SaaS are:

- **EHR Agent:** Locates all pieces of a patient's EHR. It uses a patient identification number to identify the EHR of a patient. An EHR Agent maps each identification number to a particular data in the database that stores it and maintains it;
- **EHR Service:** This service provides read-write-update operations in EHR as requested by the user. It identifies the appropriate user authorized to access a particular portion of data using RBAC (Role-Based Access Control) mechanism;
- **Access Gateway:** This service provides the communication channel to the internal IT services used by the healthcare provider. This web service translates the requests and notifications from the formats used by the application to those native formats used by the healthcare providers and patients.

The whole process is implemented in a cloud based environment which involves computational tasks and database lookups to either fetch, insert or update related data. While implementing our architecture, we considered a database solution based on open source "exist-db" XML database on a cluster of Linux cloud instances. We are using MySQL cloud instances for storing username and passwords. Consider one example: a patient requests an EHR service of fetching his personal details. The request passes through the front-end to the data repository at the back end. EHR Agent then identifies the Patient ID and fetches the requested data from the data store hosted in cloud. The fetched data is then shared with the patient using Access Gateway.

4. PERFORMANCE EVALUATION OF WEB APPLICATION IN CLOUD

Performance is a web application's ability to execute an acceptable level within a given time span (Microsoft Developer Network). Web applications with few users executing in real time (for example, healthcare applications) struggle more than normal web applications with equal number of users. On the other hand, scalability of a web application is its capability to handle growing demands with increasing number of requests without incurring major design changes. Scalability and performance often go together as an application is said to be scalable and performing well if it handles more requests without decreasing the response time. We have tried to maintain a balance between scalability and response time giving a good performance for the application. If a web application is capable of handling twice as many users and performance remains the same, it is said that the web application is scalable, since no changes were necessary to handle a large amount of users. Thus, scalability of a web application depends on the amount of changes needed to support increasing demand. There is a series of criteria for evaluation of factors affecting the performance of a web application in cloud.

Different web applications may perform in different manner but their scaling factors are common. In order to scale the application in dynamic manner, these scaling indicators are used to monitor and track the performance of the web applications. Typical scaling indicators for a web application at the web server include:

- Number of concurrent users;
- Number of active connections;

Figure 3. Graphical results showing throughput

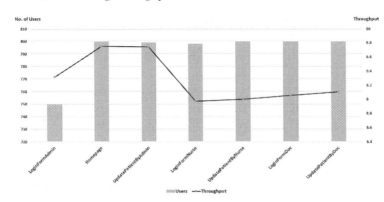

- Number of requests per second;
- Average response time per request.

To scale a web application, a scaling indicator is selected, samples are collected and statistics is calculated periodically. Based on the statistics, the scaling rules can be defined to scale up or down the amount of web application instances (see Table 4). Performance and scalability are two quality-of-service (QoS) considerations. Other QoS attributes which can be helpful to evaluate performance metrics of a web application include *Availability and Response time*. Availability (Quality Attributes) measures the

Table 4. Survey for IT adoption in three major hospitals in India

Survey Questions	H1	H2	H3
Whether Hospital application is LAN based or WAN based (Web Application) or cloud based?			
LAN		✓	✓
WAN	✓		
CLOUD			
Who developed the application?			
In-house			
3rd Party	✓	✓	✓
Where is the data centre?			
In-house			
3rd Party	✓	✓	✓
What database is used?			
Oracle	✓		
SQL		✓	✓
Who maintains the application and database?			
In-house			
3rd Party	✓	✓	✓
What are the security measures?			
Firewall	✓	✓	✓
Access Control	✓	✓	✓
Other (ISO 9001 Compliant)		✓	
What are the information security and privacy laws and regulations the hospital adheres to?			
HL7 (including all medical standards)	✓	✓	✓
IT Act	✓	✓	✓
Personal Data Protection Act	✓	✓	✓
How the data are captured and stored (Diagnosis By Doctor)?			
Scan	✓		
Form Entry		✓	
Automated			✓
How the data are captured and stored (Prescription)?			
Scan			
Form Entry	✓	✓	✓
Automated			
Any future plan on application hosting, Data storage, security and privacy?			
Already on cloud	✓	✓	
Using EHRs	✓	✓	✓
Future plan- Mobility Platform			data recovery strategy

752

readiness for service provision of a cloud application. The availability is a ratio of the uptime of an application to the aggregate of the up and down time. In our implementation we deploy the Healthcare SaaS developed in Java on Linux Nitrous.io (www.Nitrous.io) Cloud. The following services on Nitrous.io are leveraged for this deployment: Nitrous.io exist-db database, virtual machine, Nitrous.io SQL database, Jetty as a web server on Nitrous.io. At user-end, we simulate large number of users ≈ 5500 concurrent users using Jmeter (Apache JMeter, 2014) to evaluate the scalability of our application hosted on cloud.

Apache JMeter is a Java application designed to load test server software (such as web application). Simulating a heavy load on a server and network, it is used to test its strength and performance under different load conditions. It is having a Test Plan that consist of test components that determine the simulation of load test. One of the component of test plan is Thread Group, that has three properties:

- Number of users or threads that JMeter attempt to simulate. Here, we are simulating with 800 users per web page, such that ≈ 5500 concurrent users are simulated;
- Ramp-up period (in seconds) is the time duration that JMeter distribute the start of the threads over. We have set it to 10 seconds such that each thread will start (10/800 = 0.0125) seconds per web page after the previous thread was begun;
- Loop Count is the number of times to execute the test. We have set it to 1.

For ≈ 5500 concurrent users, ≈ 9 requests per second for each web page evaluates to total throughput of 61.8 /second as shown in Figure 5. Figure 3 shows the graphical presentation of throughput calculated. Figure 4 shows the response time for each request in milliseconds.

Figure 6 shows the test results of all web pages in one table. Status of requests is indicated by a triangle with a checkmark in it which means "success". It also shows the sample time which the server took to fully serve the request and the latency. To further support logon users, load balancing (Load Balancing) can be used which increases the capacity and reliability of web application. Load balancing improves the overall performance by distributing the traffic across a number of servers thus decreasing the burden on servers.

Figure 4. Response time graph

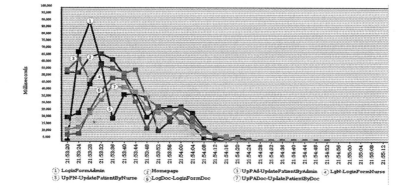

Figure 5. Summary report

Label	# Samples	Average	Min	Max	Std. Dev.	Error %	Throughput	KB/sec	Avg. Bytes
LoginForm...	750	12939	214	77601	17554.71	0.00%	9.3/sec	10.82	1189.0
Homepage	800	4722	79	68240	8631.38	0.00%	9.8/sec	14.32	1503.9
UpPAd-Upd...	799	4753	81	68319	8665.70	0.00%	9.7/sec	26.37	2771.9
LgN-LoginF...	798	3298	77	62421	5909.04	0.00%	9.0/sec	10.42	1188.9
UpPN-Upd...	800	3191	87	55090	5906.27	0.00%	9.0/sec	17.51	1992.0
LogDoc-Lo...	800	2825	76	68378	5771.14	0.00%	9.1/sec	10.53	1190.9
UpPADoc-U...	800	2588	87	40450	5092.27	0.00%	9.1/sec	16.13	1814.0
TOTAL	5547	4830	76	77601	9630.61	0.00%	61.8/sec	100.69	1668.6

Figure 6. Results for testing the application in cloud

	Start Time	Thread Name	Label	Sample Time(ms)	Status	Bytes	Latency
1	19:07:12.675	Thread Group 1-1	LoginFormA...	214		1189	214
2	19:07:12.690	Thread Group 1-2	LoginFormA...	281		1188	281
3	19:07:12.743	Thread Group 1-6	LoginFormA...	231		1190	231
4	19:07:12.731	Thread Group 1-5	LoginFormA...	245		1190	245
5	19:07:12.893	Thread Group 1-1	Homepage	92		1504	92
6	19:07:12.703	Thread Group 1-3	LoginFormA...	342		1188	342
7	19:07:12.714	Thread Group 1-4	LoginFormA...	333		1189	333
8	19:07:12.756	Thread Group 1-7	LoginFormA...	333		1189	333
9	19:07:12.820	Thread Group 1-12	LoginFormA...	270		1190	270
10	19:07:12.769	Thread Group 1-8	LoginFormA...	322		1189	322
11	19:07:12.834	Thread Group 1-13	LoginFormA...	259		1188	259
12	19:07:12.846	Thread Group 1-14	LoginFormA...	249		1190	249
13	19:07:12.783	Thread Group 1-9	LoginFormA...	336		1189	336
14	19:07:12.797	Thread Group 1-10	LoginFormA...	355		1189	355
15	19:07:12.807	Thread Group 1-11	LoginFormA...	353		1188	353
16	19:07:12.984	Thread Group 1-2	Homepage	180		1505	179
17	19:07:12.991	Thread Group 1-1	UpPAd-Upda...	179		2771	176
18	19:07:12.984	Thread Group 1-6	Homepage	189		1503	188
19	19:07:12.885	Thread Group 1-17	LoginFormA...	290		1188	290
20	19:07:12.984	Thread Group 1-5	Homepage	194		1504	194
21	19:07:12.860	Thread Group 1-15	LoginFormA...	340		1189	340
22	19:07:13.057	Thread Group 1-3	Homepage	260		1504	260
23	19:07:13.057	Thread Group 1-4	Homepage	260		1503	260
24	19:07:13.177	Thread Group 1-10	Homepage	140		1503	140
25	19:07:13.129	Thread Group 1-9	Homepage	189		1503	189

5. ADVANTAGES OF HEALTHCARE SAAS USING THE PROPOSED MODEL

- In the proposed model, security levels are defined XML schema, outside the XML document. Therefore, security level is applied to all the elements in all documents that are associated with that schema;

- The security that our model is providing is not only restricted to 'data at rest'. If the health data about a patient from one hospital is required to be exchanged with another hospital, then the health data exchange should provide the capability to securely move the electronic data to the other hospital. This secure interchange of health data needs a uniformity in defining security levels which can be achieved by conforming to the same XML schema;

- To strengthen the security provided by our model another layer of security namely, encryption can be used. Encryption consists of encrypting different portions of the same document according to different encryption keys and selectively distributing these keys to various users;

- The proposed model can be applied to any operation - Read, Write (Add / Delete, Update);

- The definition of security levels inside the XML schema makes it more flexible and portable. According to the security policies of any country or any hospital, the model can be applied by only changing the security levels inside the XML schema without changing the hard-code ensuring full security.

6. ADOPTION OF CLOUD COMPUTING IN INDIAN HEALTHCARE

Excellence in patient care is top priority in the healthcare industry across the globe. According to a report by Frost and Sullivan (Frost & Sullivan Research, 2013), India's healthcare information technology market is expected to hit $1.45 billion in 2018, more than three times the $38.13 million reached in 2012. Increased adoption of telemedicine, HIS, electronic health records, mHealth and web-based services have made digital patient data expand, demanding the deployment of robust IT infrastructure in Indian healthcare organisations. The Indian Vision 2020 document (Cloud Revolution, 2012) by the Planning commission acknowledges that "A powerful set of analytic forces is accelarating the speed of social change throughout the world". Technology, organization, information, education and productive skills therefore play a critical role in governing future development. Cloud is one such technological change that is continuing to grow in popularity across the globe. India no longer lags behind in adopting advanced technologies in almost all sectors. Cloud computing has reached a soaring height in the global market with well managed clouds that offer constant web hosting services in India and across the globe. Services to citizens such as banking, insurance, healthcare, education and governance are increasingly moving to the cloud, mainly because it is cost effective and has potentially infinite storage capacities and ensures mobility. In hospitals, cloud based approach helps to better manage the massive capital IT investments needed to support EMR implementations. Hospitals and physicians are starting to see cloud-based medical records and medical image archiving services coming online. The Micro Health Centre Cloud (Bhattacharya et al., 2012) aims upon harnessing cloud technology through a Health Cloud for providing specialist medical care to remote areas, to aid in disease surveillance by tracking disease patterns and risk factors, disaster management and a means of providing efficient collection, storage and analysis of patient data. In cloud-based physician collaboration solutions such as remote video conference, physicians visits are extended to a mobile environment for rural telehealth and disaster response is becoming more real with wireless broadband and smartphone adoption. One such effort in India is ASHA (Accredited Social Health Activist) which is a key component of the National Rural Health Mission and plays an important role in reaching primary health to rural areas (National Health Mission, ASHA). ASHA is an inevitable component in bringing health services to the grass root level by creating awareness on health and mobilizing the community towards local health planning. Earlier, the health workers of ASHA used to carry registers for tracking the health record of women in their public health centre area. But now they carry a tablet PC. Under a pilot project "E-ASHA" of UNICEF and the Rajasthan state Health department, the ASHA Sahyoginis are the first ones in the country to go hi-tech. For the better healthcare of mothers and their children, Indian government is working to make around six lakh 'ASHA' workers digitally competent and socially connected. Using this "Digital India" programme with a better connectivity, ASHA workers would be taught to keep track of mother and new born childand making them aware of nutritional food intake and preventing against various diseases like anemia. Larger hospitals in the cities are moving towards increased technology adoption. There is a healthy conversation emerging for EMRs, HIS, PACS, PRM and Chronic Disease Management using cloud based services.

6.1. Case Study

In order to assess the inroads IT has made in Indian healthcare industry and the level of adoption of cloud computing, a survey was done on three major hospitals. The hospitals are named here as H1, H2, H3. The head and assistant manager of the IT departments were interviewed. The survey also captures how security concerns are addressed and regulatory compliances are achieved by the hospitals to ensure safe and qualitative healthcare as shown in Table 1. In the survey we found that hospitals realize the potential of IT to improve the quality of care and are committed to clinical applications. Hospitals use different kinds of IT applications including administrative systems for billing, storing and viewing images. Out of the survey done for three hospitals we found that the information regarding the tests done in Lab like blood tests, urine tests are stored using EHRs, but the prescriptions by the doctors are still manually done. The CPOE (Computerized Physician Order Entry) system is still not popular in the hospitals in India. The survey questions also included the security and privacy policies followed by the hospitals. It was found that all hospitals are taking measures like firewall, access controls and adhere to the rules and regulations for the protection of health data and have outsourced the data centers to third party. Health Information System (HIS) application is developed by third parties for these hospitals. Two of the hospitals have already hosted their application in cloud. Outsourcing the development of HIS and the ownership of data centers in the hands of some third party may create certain security and privacy risks to patient data while hosted on cloud. In this scenario, we feel that the data and metadata should be secured within itself without depending on any outside measures. Our solution attaches security levels within the data itself and access rights are granted to a particular user for a portion of the data depending upon the user's security level. This enhances the security and privacy of health data leading to safe, secure and improved healthcare.

7. CONCLUSION AND FUTURE WORKS

Cloud-based solutions are highly scalable, accessible and flexible and can deliver integrated clinical and commercial systems for healthcare service providers. Cloud computing ensures that providers have rapid and quick access to uniform workflows and custom-built reports across the organizations and the globe. Focusing on the role of cloud in enabling better services for healthcare, we have presented a healthcare application that uses EHRs with all read / write capabilities having a granular role-based access control mechanism achieved by assigning security levels to all the data elements and the users. We have done performance evaluation of our application while hosting it on to the cloud. The performance evaluation takes care of all scaling indicators like number of concurrent users, number of active connections, number of requests per second and average response time per request. To assess the levels of IT adoption and cloud implementations by hospitals in India, we carried out a small survey in three major hospitals in India and found that Indian healthcare is accelerating towards cloud based approach in order to reduce massive capital IT investments and provide access of right information to right person at right time thus increasing the operational efficiency of the system. The future work will include encrypting the selected portions of the healthcare data according to their sensitivity as defined by the data model (Asija et al., 2014) in Healthcare SaaS so as to provide enhanced security and privacy of healthcare data providing an efficient healthcare.

REFERENCES

Abdelkader, H.S., & El-Etriby, S. (2012). Enhanced Data Security Model for Cloud Computing. *Proceedings of the 8th IEEE International Conference on Informatics and Systems (INFOS)*, Cairo.

HIMSS Analytics. (2014). 2014 HIMSS Analytics. Retrieved from www.himssanalytics.org/research/AssetDetail.apsx?pubid=82160

Apache JMeter. (n. d.). Retrieved from jmeter.apache.org/usrmanual/intro.html

Asija, R., & Nallusamy, R. (2014). Data Model to Enhance the Security and Privacy of Healthcare Data. *Proceedings of the Global Humanitarian Technology Conference - South Asia Satellite GHTC-SAS* (pp. 237–244). 10.1109/GHTC-SAS.2014.6967590

Bhattacharya, J., Ghosh, R., & Nanda, A. (2012). Micro Health Centre (μHC) Cloud enabled Healthcare Infrastructure. *Journal of Health Informatics In Developing Countries*.

Casavola, A., Famularo, D., & Franze, G. (2002). A feedback min-max MPC algorithm for LPV systems subject to bounded rates of change of parameters. *IEEE Transactions on Automatic Control, 47*(7), 1147–1153. doi:10.1109/TAC.2002.800662

ChanderKant and Yogesh Sharma (2013, May). Enhanced Security Architecture for Cloud Data Security. *International Journal of Advanced Research in Computer Science and Software Engineering*, 3(5).

CSA. (2013). The Notorious Nine Cloud Computing Top Threats in 2013. Retrieved from https://downloads.cloudsecurityalliance.org/initiatives/top_threats/The_Notorious_Nine_

Deng, M., Petkovi'c, M., Nalin, M., & Baroni, I. (2011). A home healthcare system in the cloud âŁ" addressing security and privacy challenges. *Proceedings of the IEEE International Conference on Cloud Computing (CLOUD)* (pp. 549–556). 10.1109/CLOUD.2011.108

Deng, M., Wuyts, K., Scandariato, R., Preneel, B., & Joosen, W. (2011). A privacy threat analysis framework: Supporting the elicitation and fulfillment of privacy requirements. *IRequirements Engineering, 16*(1), 3–32. doi:10.100700766-010-0115-7

Doukas, C., Pliakas, T., & Maglogiannis, I. (2010). Mobile Healthcare Information Management utilizing Cloud Computing and Android OS. *Proceedings of the Engineering in Medicine and Biology Society (EMBC), Annual International Conference of the IEEE*, Argentina. 10.1109/IEMBS.2010.5628061

Fan, X., He, C., Cai, Y., & Li, Y. (2012). HCloud: A novel application oriented cloud platform for preventive healthcare. *Proceedings of the IEEE 4th International Conference on cloud computing technology and science*. 10.1109/CloudCom.2012.6427482

Frost & Sullivan Research Service. (2013). Healthcare Information Technology Market in India. Retrieved from http://www.frost.com/prod/servlet/report-brochure.pag?id=P41F-01-00-00-00

HITECH. (2009). Health Information Technology for Economic and Clinical Health Act. Retrieved from en.wikipedia.org/wiki/Health_Information_Technology_for_Economic_and_Clinical_Health_Act

Howard, M., & Lipner, S. (2006). *The Security Development Lifecycle*. Redmond, WA, USA: Microsoft Press.

Kuner, C. (2010). 'Data Protection Law And International Jurisdiction On The Internet (part 1)', Cloud_Computing_Top_Threats_in_2013.pdf. *International Journal Of Law And Information Technology*, *18*(2), 176–193. doi:10.1093/ijlit/eaq002

Load Balancing. (n. d.). Wikipedia.com. Retrieved from en.wikipedia.org/wiki/Load_balancing_computing

Louk, M., Lim, H., & Lee, H. (2014). Security System for Healthcare Data in Cloud Computing. *International Journal Of Security And Its Applications*, *8*(3), 241–248. doi:10.14257/ijsia.2014.8.3.25

Mell, P., & Grance, T. (2011). Cloud Survey. In *The NIST definition of Cloud Computing*. Retrieved from csrc.nist.gov/publications/nistpubs/800-145/SP800-145.pdf

Microsoft Developer Network. (n. d.). Design Guidelines For Application Performance. Retrieved from msdn.microsoft.com/en-us/library/ff647801.aspx

Microsoft.com. (n. d.). Quality Attributes. Retrieved from msdn.microsoft.com/en-us/library/ee658094.aspx

Mohammed, S., Servos, D., & Fiaadhi, J. (2010). HCX: A distributed OSGI based web interaction system for sharing health records in the cloud. *Proceedings of the IEEE/WIC/ACM International Conference On Web Intelligence And Intelligent Agent Technology*. 10.1109/WI-IAT.2010.26

National Health Mission, Government Of India. (n. d.). About Accredited Social Health Activist (ASHA). Retrieved from http://nrhm.gov.in/communitisation/asha/about-asha.html

Nitrous Cloud. (n. d.). Retrieved from www.nitrous.io

Patient Protection and Affordable Care Act. (n. d.). Wikipedia. Retrieved from en.wikipedia.org/wiki/Patient_Protection_and_Affordable_Care_Act

PATRIOT. (2011), 'Uniting and Strengthening America By Providing Appropriate Tools Required To Intercept And Obstruct Terrorism (USA PATRIOT) Act Of 2001', Financial Crimes Enforcement Network, US Department of Treasury FinCEN. Retrieved from http://www.fincen.gov/statutes_regs/patriot/index.html

PIPEDA. Justice Laws Website. (n. d.). Personal Protection and Electronic Document Act. Retrieved from http://laws-lois.justice.gc.ca/eng/acts/p-8.6/

Revolution, C. (2012). *Indian Cloud Revolution*. Confederation Of Indian Industry; kpmg.de/docs/Indian-Cloud-Revolution.pdf

Rolim, C. O., Koch, F. L., Westphall, C. B., Werner, J., Fracaloss, A., & Salvador, G. S. (2010). A cloud computing solution for patient's data collection in healthcare institutions. *Proceedings of the Second International Conference On eHealth, Telemedicine and Social Medicine* 10.1109/eTELEMED.2010.19

Saldarraiga, A. J., Perez, J. J., Restrepo, J., & Bustamante, J. (2013). *A mobile application for ambulatory electrocardiographic monitoring in clinical and domestic environments.* Health Care Exchanges PAHCE. doi:10.1109/PAHCE.2013.6568306

Schweitzer, E.J. (2011). Reconciliation Of The Cloud Computing Model With Us Federal Electronic Health Record Regulations. *Journal Of The American Medical Informatics Association.* Retrieved from group.bmj.com

Ward, B. T., & Sipior, J. C. (2010). The Internet Jurisdiction Risk of Cloud Computing. Information Systems Management, 27(4), 334–339. DOI: doi:10.1080/10580530.2010.514248

Yu, S., Wang, C., Ren, K., & Lou, W. (2010). Achieving Secure, Scalable and Fine-grained Data Access Control in Cloud Computing. *Proceedings - IEEE INFOCOM.*

Yuefa, D., Bo, W., Yaqiang, G., Quan, Z., & Chaojing, T. (2009). Data Security Model for Cloud Computing. *Proceedings of the 2009 International Workshop on Information Security and Applications (IWISA 2009).*

This research was previously published in the International Journal of Cloud Applications and Computing (IJCAC), 6(3); edited by B. B. Gupta and Dharma P. Agrawal, pages 1-14, copyright year 2016 by IGI Publishing (an imprint of IGI Global).

Chapter 38
Security Model for Mobile Cloud Database as a Service (DBaaS)

Kashif Munir
University of Hafr Al-Batin, Saudi Arabia

ABSTRACT

There's a big change happening in the world of databases. The industry is buzzing about Database-as-a-Service (DBaaS), a cloud offering that allows companies to rent access to these managed digital data warehouses. Database-as-a-service (DBaaS) is a cloud computing service model that provides users with some form of access to a database without the need for setting up physical hardware, installing software or configuring for performance. Since consumers host data on the Mobile Cloud, DBaaS providers should be able to guarantee data owners that their data would be protected from all potential security threats. Protecting application data for large-scale web and mobile apps can be complex; especially with distributed and NoSQL databases. Data centers are no longer confined to the enterprise perimeter. More and more enterprises take their data to the Mobile Cloud, but forget to adjust their security management practices when doing so. Unauthorized access to data resources, misuse of data stored on third party platform, data confidentiality, integrity and availability are some of the major security challenges that ail this nascent Cloud service model, which hinders the wide-scale adoption of DBaaS. In this chapter, I propose a security model for Mobile Cloud Database as a Service (DBaaS). A user can change his/ her password, whenever demanded. Furthermore, security analysis realizes the feasibility of the proposed model for DBaaS and achieves efficiency. This will help Cloud community to get an insight into state-of-the-art progress in terms of secure strategies, their deficiencies and possible future directions.

INTRODUCTION

DBaaS provides professional databases that can get running and ready in a matter of minutes without a lot of training or personnel. A service provider chooses most of the options, offering the "best" configuration for most needs.

While individual systems can become unique "snowflake" servers, DBaaS tends to avoid that by simplifying and normalizing the customization, management, and upkeep for administrators. Overall,

DOI: 10.4018/978-1-5225-8176-5.ch038

Figure 1. Cloud DBaaS (Krishna & Roger, 2012)

the service makes it easier to solve problems, correct mistakes, and transfer data from one system to the next. They can scale as large as necessary, fit the needs of the customers, and offer better availability and security than most in-house operations.

DBaaS is also accessible to a larger audience because, like other "as a service" cloud innovations, it is largely defined, configured, and driven by code—not commands typed into a terminal. So, instead of requiring database specialists, developers themselves can easily create and manage database-backed apps on cloud-based development platforms.

DBaaS is already responsible for much of the growth in some key technologies, particularly open-source databases like MySQL. In other words, traditional database deployment is somewhat stagnant, and most new deployments are DBaaS.The demand is so high that some tech giants started offering a managed "as a service" version of their own (Baron S, 2015).

DBaaS provides automated services where consumers can request database-oriented functionalities from a dedicated service hosted on Cloud. The model is end user driven and provides self-service provisioning. It is based on architectural and operational approach (Oracle, 2011), which provides new and distinctive ways of using and managing database services. There are many other database services which are available today but DBaaS differs from those traditional databases because its architecture has two major attributes (Oracle, 2011), Service-orientated as database facilities are available in the form of service. Customer self-service interaction model as organizations are allowed to use, configure and deploy the Cloud database services themselves without any IT support and without purchasing any hardware for specified purpose. These are the three main phases in the overall DBaaS architecture as depicted in Figure 1.

1. Consumers request the database deployment via Cloud.
2. Consumers adjust the capacity as demand changes.
3. Consumers can retire from the app when not needed.

Luca et al. (2012) advised against using any intermediary component for accessing the database on behalf of the clients, since it becomes a single point of failure. Security and availability of DBaaS services are bounded by this trusted intermediary proxy server.

Cong et al. (2013) proposed a similar approach which puts forth an idea of using third party auditors. This approach is suitable for preserving data integrity when data is outsourced to the DBaaS providers and users get access on-demand high quality services without facing maintenance burden of local data storage.

Nithiavathy (2013) proposed integrity auditing mechanism that utilizes distributed erasure-coded data for employing redundancy and homomorphic token. This techinque allows third party auditors and users to audit their logs and events at Cloud storage using light weight communication protocol at less computation cost.

Qingji et al. (2012) investigated the issues of query integrity and a solution was proposed. The solution allows users to verify executed queries in Cloud database server along with the additional support of flexible join and aggregate queries. Similarly, the solution proposed by Maciej et al. (2013) covers data key management, data encryption and data integrity which ensure high data security and access efficiency.

Cryptonite is a secure data repository solution proposed by Alok et al. (2012) which addresses availability requirements as well. It runs within Microsoft Azure and provides service APIs compatible with existing Cloud storage services.

DATABASE-AS-A-SERVICE (DBAAS) IN MOBILE CLOUD

Database-as-a-Service (DBaaS) is a service that is managed by a cloud operator (public or private) that supports applications, without the application team assuming responsibility for traditional database administration functions. With a DBaaS, the application developers should not need to be database experts, nor should they have to hire a database administrator (DBA) to maintain the database (Qingji et al., 2012). True DBaaS will be achieved when application developers can simply call a database service and it works without even having to consider the database. This would mean that the database would seamlessly scale and it would be maintained, upgraded, backed-up and handle server failure, all without impacting the developer. Database as a service (DBaaS) is a prime example of a service that's both exciting and full of difficult security issues.

Cloud providers want to offer the DBaaS service described above. In order to provide a complete DBaaS solution across large numbers of customers, the cloud providers need a high-degree of automation. Unction's that have a regular time-based interval, like backups, can be scheduled and batched. Many other functions, such as elastic scale-out can be automated based on certain business rules. For example, providing a certain quality of service (QoS) according to the service level agreement (SLA) might require limiting databases to a certain number of connections or a peak level of CPU utilization, or some other criteria. When this criterion is exceeded, the DBaaS might automatically add a new database instance to share the load. The cloud provider also needs the ability to automate the creation and configuration of database instances (Maciej et al., 2013). Much of the database administration process can be automated in this fashion, but in order to achieve this level of automation, the database management system underlying the DBaaS must expose these functions via an application programming interface.

Cloud operators must have to work on hundreds, thousands or even tens of thousands of databases at the same time. This requires automation. In order to automate these functions in a flexible manner, the DBaaS solution must provide an API to the cloud operator (Hacigumus et al., 2012) The ultimate goal of a DBaaS is that the customer doesn't have to think about the database. Today, cloud users don't have to think about server instances, storage and networking, they just work. Virtualization enables clouds to provide these services to customers while automating much of the traditional pain of buying, installing, configuring and managing these capabilities. Now database virtualization is doing the same thing for the cloud database and it is being provided as Database as a Service (DBaaS). The DBaaS can substantially reduce operational costs and perform well. It's important as well as simple thing that the goal of DBaaS is to make things easier. Cloud Control Database as a Service (DBaaS) provides:

- A shared, consolidated platform on which to provision database services.
- A self-service model for provisioning those resources.

- Elasticity to scale out and scale back database resources.
- Chargeback based on database usage.

The aggressive consolidation of information technology (IT) infrastructure and deployment of Database as a Service (DBaaS) on public or private clouds is a strategy that many enterprises are pursuing to accomplish these objectives. Both initiatives have substantial implications when designing and implementing architectures for high availability and data protection. Database consolidation and DBaaS also drive standardization of I.T. infrastructure and processes. Standardization is essential for reducing cost and operational complexity. Databases deployed in the Bronze tier include development and test databases and databases supporting smaller work group and departmental applications that are often the first candidates for database consolidation and for deployment as Database as a Service (DBaaS).

SECURITY CHALLENGES TO DATABASE-AS-A-SERVICE (DBAAS)

There has been a growing concern that DBMSs and RDBMSs are not *cloud-friendly*. This is because, unlike other technology components for cloud service such as the webservers and application servers, which can easily scale from a few machines to hundreds or even thousands of machines, DBMSs cannot be scaled very easily. There are three challenges that drive the design of Relational Cloud: efficient multi-tenancy to minimize the hardware footprint required for a given (or predicted) workload, elastic scale-out to handle growing workloads, and database privacy. In fact, past DBMS technology fails to provide adequate tools and guidance if an existing database deployment needs to scale-out from a few machines to a large number of machines (Mohammed & Eric, 2011). Cloud computing and the notion of large-scale data-centers will become a pervasive technology in the coming years. There are some technology hurdles that we confront in deploying applications on cloud computing infrastructures: DBMS scalability and DBMS security. In this paper, we will focus on the problem of making DBMS technology cloud friendly. In fact, we will argue that the success of cloud computing is critically contingent on making DBMSs scalable, elastic, available, secure and autonomic, which is in addition to the other well-known properties of database management technologies like high-level functionality, consistency, performance, and reliability.

In Table 1 security challenges of DBaaS infrastructure along with their consequences and causes has been highlighted (Kashif, 2015).

PROPOSED SECURITY MODEL

Major concerns and issues in DBaaS have been discussed in the previous sections with emphasis on security challenges. It has been observed that, despite quality research on secure data outsourcing and data services for almost a decade, existing approaches on database encryption, authentication, digital signatures (Merkle, 1989), contractual agreements etc. have not gained much success in operations. To date, there is minimal work done in the field of security and privacy of DBaaS as compared to traditional data storage. Different approaches for securing DBaaS are discussed under this section with assorted categories of confidentiality, privacy, integrity and availability.

Table 1. Cloud DBaaS security challenges

No.	Security Challenge	Description
1	Availability	• Temporary and permanent unavailability cause service breakdown • DOS Attacks, natural disasters, equipment failure
2	Access Control Issues	• Physical, personnel and logical control missing on organization's internal and DBaaS Provider's employees • Increase development and analysis cost is incurred when user management and granular access control is implemented
3	Integrity Check	• Need to avoid modification of configuration, access and data files • Require accuracy and integrity of data
4	Auditing and Monitoring	• Configuration requirements change continuously • Important for avoiding failures, backup maintenance, configuration of auto fail-over mechanisms • Require stark network and physical device, expertise and relevant resources
5	Data Sanitization	• Recovery of data by malicious sources if not properly discarded
6	Data Confidentiality	• Unencrypted data in memory, disk or in network may cause data breaches • Co-located application data is vulnerable to software bugs and errors in the Cloud • External organizations might also generate attacks
7	Data Replication and Consistency Management	Replications between multiple servers cause management as well as consistency issues
8	Network Security	• Data flowing over the network (internet) is prone to hazardous circumstances and network performance issues. • Possible network failure reasons are: misconfiguration, lack of resource isolations, poor or untested business continuity, disaster recovery plan, network traffic modification
9	Data Locality	• Compliance and data-security privacy laws prohibit movement of sensitive data among countries • Issues faced when no one takes responsibility of data in location independent data storage
10	Data Provenance	• Complexity and time sensitiveness in provenance metadata • Intensive computations involved in getting required history • Fast algorithms, auto logs are needed
11	Insider Threats	• Employees can tap into sensitive and confidential data • Strict supply chain management and assessment is required
12	Outside Malicious Attackers	• Malicious attacks by hackers • Difficulty in synchronizing data between users and reporting corruption • Absence of authentication, authorization and accounting controls • Poor key management for encryption and decryption

State-of-the-art approaches mainly address generally adopted methods for their proposed models. Those methods are: Encryption based data security, which means hiding data content from service providers. Private information retrieval, which allows user to retrieve an item from the data server without revealing the content of that item. Information distribution, which is based on dispersing information instead of encrypting the data.

The model shown in Figure 2 used Four-layer system structure, in which each floor performs its own duty to ensure that the data security of cloud layers.

The first layer: responsible for user authentication, it is one time password authentication. User Interface Layer used to access the service via internet. This allows users to easily utilize scalable and elastic database services available on Cloud infrastructure. The second layer: is used to access software services and storage space on the Cloud. As stated previously, consumers do not need to have hardware resources to avail these services.

Figure 2. Secure model for cloud DBaaS (Kashif, 2015)

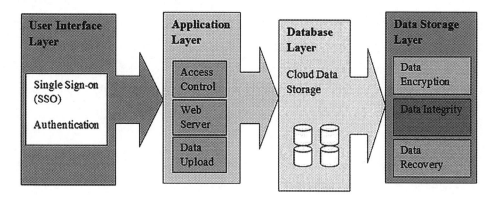

for user's data upload, access control. Third layer provides efficient and reliable service of managing database residing in the Cloud. It allows reuse of the query statements residing in the storage, thus saving time for querying and loading data. Fourth layer is data storage layer where Data is encrypted and decrypted at storage and retrieval stages, respectively. Data integrity and data recovery is also provided at this layer.

Storage virtualization (Moeller, 2013) is a part of data storage layer, which forms a pool of resources using multiple network storage devices. A central console is responsible for the management of the resources. Taking backups, archiving and recovering data are now more feasible and less time-consuming because of these available features. Condition monitoring Error detects significant changes that cause errors in storing and managing data. Storage layer also provides data management services, such as traffic analysis, compression, virtualization, security, and replication etc., through the use of tools, policies and processes. This layer also provides database upgrades when some major changes are made in the database structure or between different releases. Our solution has three phases; Registration, Login, and Authentication.

Registration Phase

In the registration phase, user needs to register at the server by providing appropriate identification details. The server process user's data and issue a smartcard to the user. The procedure is as follows: Let *f* be a one-way has function, and p be a very large prime such that $p = 2q + 1$ where q is also a large prime, also let δ be a primitive element of *GF (p)*, which are all known public parameters. A random number $\eta \in [1, \ p \ - \ 1]$, with $gcd \ (\eta, \ p \ -1) \ = \ 1$, is selected by the system as its private key which is used to compute the public key $\lambda = \delta^{\eta} mod \ p$.

Now, due to the property of $gcd \ (\eta, \ p \ -1) \ = \ 1$, the public key λ is also a primitive element of *GF(p)*. Assuming that a new user U_i submits his identity *IDi* to the system for registration, the system computes an image of the ID_i^* as (ID_i^*) and the signature (χ_i, γ_i) of ID_i^* as

$$\gamma_i = \ (ID_i^* - \alpha_i \chi_i) \eta^{-1} - \ 1 \, mod \, p - 1$$

Where $\chi_i = \delta^{\alpha i} mod \ p$, and α_i is randomly selected from $\begin{bmatrix} 1, & p & - & 1 \end{bmatrix}$. We note here that due to ElGamal attack, our scheme is designed to signed the image of user identity ID_i^*, rather than directly signing the original user ID_i. Further, α_i should be used repeatedly to avoid uncovering the system's secret key η as a result of users collusion. It is clear here that γ_i is U_i secret key generated from the system's secret key. Further, this can be a sort of shared secret between the system and the user.

Login Phase

At this phase, if user i wants to login, he inserts the smart card to the input device. Then send (ID_i, χ_i) to the device. Then the smart card will perform the following computations:

1. Selects an odd random number $v \in \begin{bmatrix} 1, & p & - & 1 \end{bmatrix} \ni gcd \left(v, \ p \ - \ 1 \right) = 1$, and then computes $\beta \ = \lambda^v mod \ p$, where λ is the public key of the system/server.
2. Computes another value: $Z = \beta^{vi} \bmod \rho$ and sends Z to the server or system.

Authentication Phase

After receiving the authentication message Z, the remote server authenticates the login as follows:

1. Use Z and the image of U_i identity (i.e. ID_i^*) to verify that

$$\delta^{ID_i^*} = \chi_i^{ID_i^*} Z^{v-1} \bmod \rho$$

2. If the above condition holds, then the remote system generates a random number ρ and then sends the following to the smart card. Otherwise the request is rejected:

$$\{F(ID_i^* \oplus \rho)\}\chi_i \ or \ \{F(ID_i^* \oplus \rho)\}\kappa$$

Where κ is a predetermined secret key shared between the server and the card. Similarly, the function F is an agreed secret function.

3. User i uses its secret key γ_i or the shared key κ to decrypt the message and recover ρ, i.e:

$$[\{F(ID_i^* \oplus \rho)\}]^{-1} = (ID_i \oplus \rho)$$

and compute:

$$K = \{F(\rho)\}\lambda \ or \ K = \{F(\rho)\}\kappa$$

4. The smart card finally forwards K to the remote server. The system verifies whether $F^{-1}(K) = \rho$. If yes, the authentication process is completed. Otherwise, the request is rejected.

SECURITY ANALYSIS

To show the strength of our scheme, let's assume an intruder I knows Z, β, ρ, and $Z = \beta^{\gamma i} \bmod \rho$. Now trying to solve yi from the information is always equivalent to computing the discrete logarithm problem over *GF(ρ)*, thus U_i's secret key γ_i will never be revealed to the public. Again, suppose an intruder impersonates U_i by developing v and V. Since $Z = \lambda^{\nu \gamma i} \bmod \rho$ and by knowing Z, υ, and V, the intruder can derive as $Z = Z^{v-1 \upsilon} \bmod \rho$ without knowing γ_i. However, trying to compute v from β is equivalent to computing the discrete logarithm, again this attack is infeasible. Moreover, suppose ID_i is compromised, this information is not enough to derive either γ_i, or χ_i since the values where derived using ID_i^* not just ID_i.

During authentication phase, the agreed secret function F and shared secret key k are used to protect the system against any guessing attack. Moreover, for additional security, multiple shared secret keys can be used, so that whenever an encrypted message is to be sent to the system or the user, a different secret key will be used. This will ensure that even exhausted search key by an intruder will not reveal the keys, since for any guessed value for one key, there is very likely to be a corresponding value of another key such that the message will appear correlated. Additionally, the system has an option to use public key system by using γ_i to encrypt any message for U_i.

CONCLUSION

We have described the design of, a software security model for Mobile Cloud DBaaS environment. Data is possibly the most important asset a business has. Businesses today are trying hard to deal with the explosion of data and leverage it to their advantage. Database as a Service (DBaaS) is an increasingly popular Cloud service model, with attractive features like scalability, pay-as-you-go model and cost reduction that make it a perfect fit for most organizations. However, no extensive research work has been done which meticulously covers each and every aspect of DBaaS. Data storage security in Cloud is a domain which is full of challenges and is of paramount importance as customers do not want to lose their data at any cost. It is also a major hurdle in the way of adopting Cloud platform for storage services. Unfortunately, this area is still in its infancy and many research problems are yet to be identified. There is a need for effective strategies, proper measurements and methodologies to control this problem by having mature practices in the form of secure architectures to make DBaaS platform more secure, and ultimately, widely-adopted. In this chapter, I have presented a security model for cloud DBaaS environments. I have described its components, discussed existing solutions and identified possible approaches to deal with different security issues related to the DBaaS. Although many challenges remain in moving this idea from vision to implementation, the benefits of such an environment should serve to motivate the Mobile Cloud Computing research that can meet those challenges. These challenges are in addition to making the systems fault-tolerant and highly available.

FUTURE DIRECTIONS

Various techniques have been proposed for securing relational data model. However, these techniques need improvement in order to make them efficient and effective for DBaaS environment. Majority of such available solutions are based on traditional cryptographic techniques where the general idea is based on the outsourcing of encrypted data by owner only. Publishers do not manage and encrypt data; rather encryption is performed by the owner before outsourcing. Since publishers do not receive keys for decrypting the data; therefore, it is recommended to devise such techniques which allow publishers to perform queries on the encrypted data.

Thus, after conducting a thorough study on DBaaS, it can be inferred that all the practical and widely adopted approaches for providing security in relational databases can also be adopted for Cloud DBaaS model (database outsourcing) after transforming them accordingly. Moreover, all extant solutions for mitigating security challenges have room to be improved and evaluated according to a benchmark for making them more mature, practical and reliable in order to provide secure Cloud database services.

REFERENCES

Alok, K., Yogesh, S., & Viktor, P. (2012). Cryptonite: A Secure and Performant Data. *5th IEEE International Conference on.* IEEE.

Baron, S. (2015). *Why DBaaS Will Be The Next Big Thing In Database Management.* Retrieved from http://readwrite.com/2015/09/18/dbaas-trend-cloud-database-service

Cong, W., Sherman, S. M. C., Qian, W., Kui, R., & Wenjing, L. (2013). Privacy Preserving Public Auditing for Secure Cloud Storage. *IEEE Transactions on Computers, 62*(2), 362–375. doi:10.1109/TC.2011.245

Moeller. (2013). *Executive's guide to IT Governance: Improving Systems Processes with Service Management.* John Wiley & Sons.

Hacigumus, H., Iyer, B., Li, C., & Mehrotra, S. (2004). Efficient Execution of Aggregation Queries over Encrypted Relational Databases. In *Proc. of the 9th International Conference on Database Systems for Advanced Applications (DASFAA'04).*

Krishna, K., & Roger, L. (2012). *Database as a Service (DBaaS) using Enterprise Manager 12c.* Oracle Open World.

Luca, F., Michele, C., & Mirco, M. (2012). Lecture Notes in Computer Science: Vol. 7672. *Supporting security and consistency for Cloud database.* Cyberspace Safety and Security.

Maciej, B., Gracjan, J., Michał, J., Stanisław, J., Tomasz, J., & Norbert, M. … Sławomir, Z. (2013). National Data Storage 2: Secure Storage Cloud with Efficient and Easy Data Access. Academic Press.

Merkle, R. C. (1989). A Certified Digital Signature, Advances in Cryptology - CRYPTO '89. *9th Annual International Cryptology Conference Proceedings, 435,* 218–238.

Mohammed, A., & Eric, P. (2011). Using Multi Shares for Ensuring Privacy in Database-as-a-Service. *Proceedings of 44th Hawaii International Conference on System Sciences.*

Munir. (2015). Security Model for Cloud Database as a Service (DBaaS). *IEEE Proceedings of the International Conference on Cloud Computing Technologies and Applications.*

Nithiavathy, R. (2013). Data Integrity and Data Dynamics with Secure Storage Service in Cloud. *Proceedings of the 2013 International Conference on Pattern Recognition, Informatics and Mobile Engineering.* IEEE. 10.1109/ICPRIME.2013.6496459

Oracle Corporation. (2011). *Database as a Service: Reference Architecture – An Overview.* Author.

Qingji, Z., Shouhuai, X., & Giuseppe, A. (2012). Efficient Query Integrity for Outsourced Dynamic Databases. CCSW'12, Raleigh, NC.

This research was previously published in Security Management in Mobile Cloud Computing edited by Kashif Munir, pages 169-180, copyright year 2017 by Information Science Reference (an imprint of IGI Global).

Chapter 39

Securely Communicating With an Optimal Cloud for Intelligently Enhancing a Cloud's Elasticity

S. Kirthica
Anna University, India

Rajeswari Sridhar
Anna University, India

ABSTRACT

One of the principle features on which cloud environments operate is the scaling up and down of resources based on users' needs, called elasticity. This feature is limited to the cloud's physical resources. This article proposes to enhance the elasticity of a cloud in an intelligent manner by communicating with an optimal external cloud (EC) and borrowing additional resources from it when the cloud runs out of resources. This inter-cloud communication is secured by a model whose structure is similar to the Kerberos protocol. To choose the optimal EC for a particular request of a user, a list of parameters, collectively termed as RePVoCRaD, are enumerated. Once chosen, trust is established with the chosen EC and inter-cloud communication begins. While existing works deal with third parties to establish or secure inter-cloud communication, this work is novel in that there is absence of third parties in the entire process, thereby reducing security threats and additional costs involved. Evaluating this work based on turnaround time and transaction success rate, in a real-time cloud environment, it is seen that the cloud's elasticity is so enhanced that it successfully accommodates its users' additional demands by the fastest means possible.

1. INTRODUCTION

Cloud computing, a fast-growing technology, allows the cloud users to enjoy all the computing components as a service on-demand, instantly and dynamically. Cloud providers attract users by creating an illusion of availability of unlimited resources at one's disposal using a feature called *Elasticity*. This is

DOI: 10.4018/978-1-5225-8176-5.ch039

carried out by instant on-demand provision (scaling up) and withdrawal (scaling down) of resources. Thus, elasticity is agile and also ensures low operating cost (Armbrust et al., 2010; Dustin oWens, 2010; Varia, 2011). However, it works within the available resources of a cloud. If the demand of cloud users exceeds this limit, then the cloud will be unable to satisfy the user's needs (Chiu, 2010). Such a situation calls for interoperating with other clouds (Rochwerger et al., 2011).

Interoperability is the ability of one cloud to use another cloud, which is ready to accept a transaction with the requesting cloud thus presenting to the user an increased volume of resources (Bernstein & Vij, 2011; Grozev & Buyya, 2014). In our work, the requesting cloud is considered to be a private cloud of an organization and is termed as internal private cloud (IPC). On the other hand, the cloud (private, public or hybrid) which is ready to accept the transaction with the IPC is considered as external cloud (EC).

Within the IPC, elasticity is provided by effectively distributing its resources among its users using any of the following: Self Adaptive Particle Swarm Optimization (SAPSO) algorithm (Jeyarani, Naga-veni, & Vasanth Ram, 2011), Queue Based Q-Learning algorithm (Meera & Swamynathan, 2015) or live migration of resources allocated to the users (Kirthica & Sridhar, 2015a). In our work, the scope of elasticity is intelligently enhanced further by borrowing resources from an EC. The EC is considered *optimal* when it satisfies a particular request of a user in terms of resources in a prompt manner. Such an optimal EC is identified using a set of parameters collectively termed as *RePVoCRaD*. The EC so identified may be open to different types of users including individuals, professionals, organizations and malicious users. Hence, interoperating with such an EC causes an indirect security threat. Therefore, in order to securely interoperate with the EC, we have proposed a modified version of the Trusted Federa-tion model (Bernstein & Vij, 2011). An additional level of security is also provided to prevent intentional or unintentional usage of the obtained resource by other users of the EC (Kirthica & Sridhar, 2015b).

This solution to achieve a secure inter-cloud communication for enhancing elasticity is novel with the following highlights:

1. Communication is not with a random EC but with the optimal EC at the time a user's request is raised.
2. Resource is provided from multiple clouds (IPC and ECs) to accommodate demand of a single user.
3. There is no use of third parties or external components throughout the process.

Third parties or external components with their inherent security related weaknesses such as getting corrupted, being imitated and being eavesdropped, result in an increased area for compromise. Further-more, additional costs are incurred to purchase, hire, setup and maintain these components. In our work, as there are no third parties involved these security threats and additional costs are avoided. Moreover, the intricate process of identifying the optimal EC, establishing inter-cloud communication and provid-ing security does not involve the user, thereby providing convenience to him.

The rest of the paper is organized as follows. Section 2 briefs the existing works in cloud interopera-tion. Section 3 deals with the flow of activities involved in extending elasticity by communicating with ECs. The detailed design of the proposed work is discussed in Sections 4, 5 and 6. The implementation and evaluation details of our work are provided in Section 7. Section 8 concludes the paper by giving the overall contribution of our work and possible future works in the area.

2. RELATED WORKS

Many solutions have been proposed to provide interoperation between clouds for which an EC has to be chosen. Analytical Hierarchical Process (Garg, Versteeg, & Buyya, 2013) chooses the best cloud service based on certain attributes proposed by the Cloud Service Measurement Index Consortium (CSMIC - Carnegie Mellon University [CMU], 2014). Instead of choosing between cloud services, our work proposes to choose the best among several available cloud environments for interoperation.

Two approaches (Parameswaran & Chaddha, 2009) are suggested for interoperation: Unified Cloud Interface / Cloud Broker approach and Enterprise Cloud Orchestration Platform / Orchestration Layer approach. In the former approach, an external agent acts as a bridge between the users and the individual clouds, whereas, in the latter, an orchestration layer routes client's requests considering only the clouds registered in it. Hence, this layer may not be able to provide the user with the best cloud which could satisfy one's specification as it does not consider those clouds that are not registered in it. Also, both these approaches deal with an unreliable third party which poses an additional security threat.

Yet another work that involves unreliable third parties is InterCloud (Buyya, Ranjan, & Calheiros, 2010), where similar utilities of a federation of several clouds are grouped as a single resource by Cloud Coordinators. A two-level brokering mechanism (Client's Broker and Cloud Exchange), along with these coordinators, satisfies the user's requests. Here, the performance is very low due to utility abstraction from all the clouds participating in the federation.

For interoperation to be effective, security in both intra-cloud and inter-cloud environments is essential. Specific security characteristics within a cloud environment are assured by a Trusted Third Party and trust is established using a security mesh (Zissis & Lekkas, 2012). Trust is also established between Cloud Consumer and Cloud Provider using trust relationship tables (Li & Ping, 2009). In our work, this consumer-provider relationship is applied to IPC and EC and the part played by the trusted third party is handled by their administrators.

In the Trusted Federation model (Bernstein & Vij, 2011), an Intercloud Exchange hosting an XMPP server enables inter-cloud communication. A trust provider service, the Intercloud Root, establishes secure communication. This federation model is adapted in our work by interpreting it as the traditional Kerberos (Neuman & Ts'o, 1994) protocol (three-headed structure (Rogers & SAS Institute Inc., 2013)) and modifying it to overcome its existing disadvantages which are as follows:

1. Clouds are considered to be available in clusters i.e. multiple cloud providers co-exist under one Intercloud Exchange.
2. There is reliance on a third party to establish trust.
3. Additional systems like Intercloud Root, Intercloud Exchange and XMPP server, effecting inter-cloud communication, act as an overhead.

One of the major security-related myths in any cloud environment is that traditional cryptographic primitives cannot be utilized to protect data correctness (Ren, Wang, & Wang, 2012). Our work contradicts this statement by using a traditional encryption algorithm along with other security measures in appropriate places. The traditional Digital Signature Standard (Boneh, 2011) is also used such that integrity is not compromised. Intrusion detection is another research challenge in the area of cloud security which is handled by an effective Temporal Constraint based on feature selection algorithm and a hybrid decision tree (Kannan et al., 2015).

In the following sections, we present an approach for an IPC to interoperate in a secure manner with any of the available ECs, also overcoming the drawbacks identified in the existing works, thereby satisfying the user's demand and hence retaining him.

3. PRELIMINARIES

Problem Definition. When the IPC runs short of resources due to increased usage by its users, it cannot satisfy its user's demands. As the denial of resources by IPC causes high inconvenience to the user, in our work, the IPC, instead of denying the request, accommodates it by seeking the help of one or more ECs securely to satisfy the user's demand, thus enhancing the concept of elasticity by interoperating with ECs. We term this *Enhancement of Elasticity by Secure Inter-cloud Communication* which is represented by the following proposition:

$$A \rightarrow B \wedge \neg A \rightarrow C$$

where, A, B and C respectively refer to the availability of resources in IPC, satisfying of user's request by IPC and satisfying of user's request by EC. The non-reliance on any third parties for this inter-cloud communication is proposed in this work.

Case Scenario. A sample scenario can be visualized in a department of an education institute where an IPC is set up to serve the requirements of the staff and students of the department. When such an IPC is, at any point of time, unable to satisfy its user's request for want of resources, instead of denying the request, our work enables the IPC to communicate with clouds set up in other departments in the institute or with public clouds (if necessary), considered as ECs to the IPC, to satisfy the request and hence avoid its denial.

Work Flow. Figure 1 gives a bird's eye view of the flow we have proposed to implement an intelligent algorithm for enhancement of elasticity by secure inter-cloud communication.

The first task of the IPC on receiving an unsupportable request is to choose the best-suited EC to outsource the resources and which can positively satisfy the user's request. To accomplish this, certain parameters are used to select one among the many available ECs. The procedure to choose the best EC is discussed in detail in Section 4. On identifying the right EC, the administrator of the IPC sends a request to the chosen EC for a *volume* of the size requested by the user. To the EC, the administrator of the IPC is yet another user to whom its resources are to be allocated. Now, it is assumed that unused resources are always available in at least one of the ECs when the IPC is in need. Hence, all the requests of IPC are always satisfied by any of the ECs. This inter-cloud communication, beginning with requesting of resources to acquiring it, follows a new modified version of the trusted federation model (Bernstein & Vij, 2011) to communicate with EC in a secure manner. Based on an existing work on inter-cloud security (Kirthica & Sridhar, 2015b), another level of security is provided to prevent unauthorized access by other users of IPC and EC. This flow clearly shows that no third party is used in the process.

It is to be noted here that the volume allocated by the EC to the IPC is used to satisfy only the additional demand of the user of the IPC and not his entire demand. The initial resource provided by IPC is still in use by the user and unable to satisfy a request for an additional resource by itself, the IPC uses the EC's resource to do it. Hence, the user has an illusion that the additional resource is provided by the IPC, thus avoiding the need for an additional layer (orchestration layer (Parameswaran & Chaddha,

Figure 1. Flow of events in enhancement of elasticity by secure inter-cloud communication

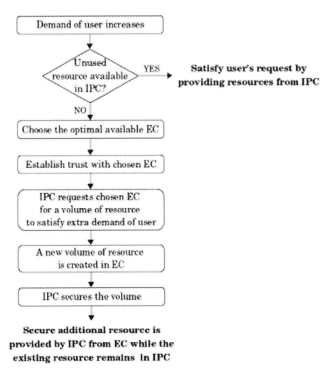

2009)). So, the user's resources do not migrate from IPC to EC and the IPC remains the cloud provider for the user. As this intricate resource-provisioning process is not made known to the user, he enjoys the cloud-provided resources hassle-free. Table 1 gives the notations used in our work.

4. CHOOSE THE OPTIMAL EXTERNAL CLOUD

When an IPC is unable to satisfy R_U with its own resources, there is a need to acquire resources from an EC, in which case the IPC has to identify EC_o from EC_A. Algorithm 1 describes the process of choosing EC_o from EC_A.

After analyzing the parameters discussed (Garg et al., 2013; CSMIC - CMU, 2014), we have coined *RePVoCRaD* to choose EC_o. It is an acronym formed from each parameter required to choose EC_o: *re*-sponse time (t_r), *p*rocessing time (t_p), time to get *v*olume running (t_v), free ***CPU*** cores (f_{cpu}), free ***RAM*** space (f_{ram}) and free ***disk*** space (f_{disk}). These parameters forming RePVoCRAD are grouped under the following two components:

Weighted time, t_W, which is inversely proportional to performance and

Weighted free resources, f_W, which is proportional to availability.

In general, the weighted total of any quantity, to which 'n' entities contribute, is calculated as follows:

$$weighted\,total = \sum_{i=1}^{n} w_i \times a_i \tag{1}$$

774

Table 1. Table of Notations

Notation	Definition
EC_A	list of all available ECs
EC_o	the optimal EC among the available ECs
R_U	request for resource by a user
V_{EC_o}	volume created in EC_o to satisfy R_U
t_w	weighted time
f_w	weighted free resources
t_r	response time
t_p	processing time
t_v	time to get volume running
f_{cpu}	free CPU cores
f_{ram}	free RAM space
f_{disk}	free disk space
$RegEx$	regular expression
S_{RegEx}	string matching $RegEx$

where, a_i is the ith entity contributing to the weighted total and w_i is the weight assigned to it.

Algorithm 1. Choose the Optimal EC among the available ECs

$\underline{ChooseOptimalEC(R_U)}$

Input: R_U

Output: EC_o

1: *flag ← true*;
2: **foreach** $EC_i \in EC_A$ **do**
3: $t_w(EC_i) \leftarrow w_1 \times t_r(EC_i) + w_2 \times t_p(EC_i)$;
4: $f_W(EC_i) \leftarrow \text{w} \times (f_{cpu}(EC_i) + f_{ram}(EC_i) + f_{disk}(EC_i))$;
5: **if** $t_v(EC_i) = \varphi$ **then**
6: *flag ← false*;
7: **end if**
8: **end for**
9: **if** *flag = true* **then**
10: **foreach** $EC_i \in EC_A$ **do**
11: $t_w(EC_i) \leftarrow t_w(EC_i) + w_3 \times t_v(EC_i)$;
12: **end for**
13: **end if**
14: Sort EC_A based on $t_w(EC_i)$ in ascending order and then on $f_W(EC_i)$ in descending order, where $EC_i \in EC_A$;
15: **foreach** $EC_i \in EC_A$ **do**
16: **if** $R_U <$ free resources in EC_i

17: $EC_o \leftarrow EC_i$;
18: **return** EC_o;
19: **end if**
20: **end for**

4.1. t_w Calculation

t_w of an EC is calculated by giving weights to each of the following parameters:

t_r, the time taken to receive an acknowledgement from an EC for the request sent by IPC,

t_p, the time taken for performing a set of operations in an EC and

t_v, the time taken for V_{EC_o} to come to "running" state. This parameter will become available for an EC only if the EC had earlier satisfied another request of any of the IPC's users. Naturally, this parameter may not be available for all of EC_A until each EC has successfully responded to some request. Hence, for EC_A to be compared in an equal footing, this parameter may not be helpful if it is not available for even a single EC.

The highest weight is given to t_v because this factor contributes to the time taken for V_{EC_o} to be created. t_p is given the next highest weight as this factor contributes to the time taken to satisfy the prerequisites for creating V_{EC_o}. The least weight is given to t_r since this factor will be required only once to get an acknowledgement from the EC to access it. Using equation 1, if t_v is available for EC_A, t_w for each available EC is calculated as:

$$t_W = w_1 \times t_r + w_2 \times t_p + w_3 \times t_v \tag{2}$$

where, w_1, w_2 and w_3 respectively are the weights allotted to t_r, t_p and t_v, such that $w_3 > w_2 > w_1$. On the other hand, if t_v is not available for any of EC_A, t_w for each available EC is calculated as:

$$t_W = w_1 \times t_r + w_2 \times t_p \tag{3}$$

4.2. f_w Calculation

The parameters, f_{cpu}, f_{ram} and f_{disk}, obtained by considering the resources which are not in use by users of an EC account for f_W. f_W of an EC is calculated by giving equal weights to all these parameters since all the resources are equally important to satisfy R_U. Thus, applying equation 1, f_W for each available EC is calculated as:

$$f_W = w_4 \times f_{cpu} + w_5 \times f_{ram} + w_6 \times f_{disk} \tag{4}$$

where, w_4, w_5 and w_6 respectively are the weights allotted to f_{cpu}, f_{ram} and f_{disk}, such that $w_4 = w_5 = w_6$ (= w say). Hence, equation 4 can be written as:

$$f_W = w \times (f_{cpu} + f_{ram} + f_{disk}) \tag{5}$$

4.3. EC_o Selection

EC_A is ordered such that $t_w(EC_i) < t_w(EC_{i+1}) \vee (t_w(EC_i) = t_w(EC_{i+1}) \wedge f_w(EC_i) \geq f_w(EC_{i+1}))$, where i ranges from 1 through $|EC_A|$. Then, each EC_i is checked to see if it has sufficient resources to satisfy R_U. If enough resources are available, that EC_i is chosen as EC_o. Otherwise, the check iteratively goes to the next EC until EC_o is found. The EC_o so found is the one best-suited to meet this R_U at that instant of time.

5. ACQUIRE RESOURCES FROM EXTERNAL CLOUD

For enhancement of elasticity, the IPC borrows resources from ECs. To do so safely, the IPC must essentially secure its users from possible security threats posed by this inter-cloud communication. With the borrowing of resources from any EC becoming inevitable, securing the connection is necessitated. For this, we propose a model whose structure is similar to the traditional Kerberos (Neuman & Ts'o, 1994) protocol applying the following modifications to the trusted federation model (Bernstein & Vij, 2011). The *Cloud Administrators* in our model take the place of the Intercloud Roots (Bernstein & Vij, 2011) and trust is established between the IPC and EC, as a result of which the IPC becomes a user of the EC. The advantages of our model over the trusted federation model (Bernstein & Vij, 2011) are as follows:

1. Clouds are not maintained by or grouped under third parties i.e. no master-slave mechanism.
2. Available cloud components are utilized to establish and secure communications.
3. Direct communication is established between IPC and other ECs without interference by external systems (third parties).
4. Additional systems like Intercloud Root, Intercloud Exchange and XMPP server are eliminated, thus reducing the additional costs.

The process involved in acquiring resources from EC_o is discussed in algorithm 2. It clearly shows that the various steps involved to satisfy R_U are performed intelligently by IPC, thus enabling the user to continue his connection without being involved in the process.

Algorithm 2. Acquire resources from the optimal EC among the available ECs

AcquireResourcesFromEC(R_U)

Input: R_U

Output: V_{EC_o} attached to available resource of user who requested for R_U

1: $EC_o \leftarrow$ *ChooseOptimalEC(R_U)*;
2: **if** first time to contact EC_o **then**
3: Agree *RegEx* with EC_o using Digital Signature Standard;
4: **else**
5: Acquire *RegEx* agreed with EC_o;
6: **end if**
7: Generate S_{RegEx};
8: Send S_{RegEx} to EC_o;
9: **if** EC_o validates S_{RegEx} **then**

10: Acquire passphrase from EC_o;

11: Send passphrase to EC_o;

12: **if** EC_o validates passphrase **then**

13: $V_{EC_o} \leftarrow CreateVolumeInEC(EC_o)$;

14: Attach V_{EC_o} to already available resource of user;

15: **return**;

16: **end if**

17: **end if**

Once EC_o is chosen, it is essential that trust should be established with it. If EC_o has been chosen for the first time for communication, in order to establish trust with it, a *RegEx* is designed and is securely agreed upon between the administrators of IPC and EC_o using the Digital Signature Standard (Boneh, 2011). If IPC has contacted the chosen EC_o previously to satisfy any of its user's requests, then it would have already established trust with that EC_o, in which case the already agreed *RegEx* can be utilized for this transaction.

Figure 2 shows the process of acquiring resource from an EC. When the IPC is in need of V_{EC_o} to satisfy R_U, it generates S_{RegEx} and sends it to the administrator of EC_o to gain its trust. The administrator validates S_{RegEx} and sends IPC the passphrase to access EC_o. This passphrase is sent to EC_o.

Algorithm 3, discussing the creation of V_{EC_o}, shows that EC_o, on successfully validating the passphrase sent by IPC, gives necessary credentials to the IPC to create V_{EC_o} in it. V_{EC_o}, of the size requested by the user, is then created in EC_o with a key. This key provides a second level of security for accessibility as it will be made available to the user for whom V_{EC_o} is created, thereby only the user who has the key can access V_{EC_o}. Hence, V_{EC_o} will not be accessible by any other users of either IPC or EC_o. Once V_{EC_o} is created, a timer is started (t_0). This timer is stopped (t_r) when V_{EC_o} is ready to be used by the user of IPC

Figure 2. Process of acquiring resources from EC_o

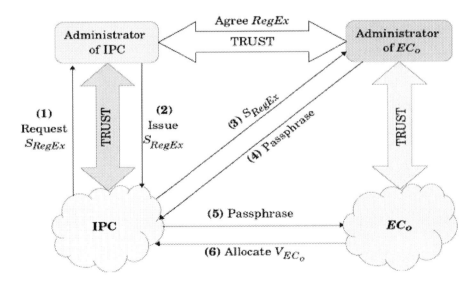

who requested for R_U. The time recorded by the timer is the parameter, t_v, which can be used during subsequent requests to choose EC_o. Thus, no external components other than the communicating clouds have been used to securely acquire resources from EC.

Algorithm 3. Create volume in EC

CreateVolumeInEC(EC_o)

Input: EC_o

Output: V_{EC_o}

1: Create a key K;
2: Create V_{EC_o} with K in EC_o;
3: $t_0 \leftarrow t_{curr}$; (Current time is set)
4: Wait for V_{EC_o} to run;
5: $t_r \leftarrow t_{curr}$;
6: $t_v(EC_o) \leftarrow t_r - t_0$;
7: **return** V_{EC_o};

In a real-time scenario, there may be several requests by a user, some of which can be accommodated by IPC if it has the necessary resources. Those requests that cannot be handled by IPC require resources from any of EC_A. For every such request, there is a new search for EC_o, where the EC which satisfied the previous request may be unable or ineligible to meet the current R_U, in which case the IPC chooses any other EC from the pool of EC_A satisfying the requirements. Thus, resources may be provided to the user from multiple clouds (IPC and several ECs) while he enjoys the services uninvolved in the complexities of the tasks.

6. SECURE THE VOLUME CREATED IN EXTERNAL CLOUD

In addition to the above security provision using our model, a third level of security is provided for V_{EC_o} by transparently encrypting and storing data in it, thereby securing it from threats that may arise from any user of EC_o (Kirthica & Sridhar, 2015b). This encryption process used by the IPC is visible to none other than the IPC. Thus, no other user will be able to access the data stored in V_{EC_o} leased out to IPC, regardless of the security principles in EC_o which may be unknown or unreliable, or even if the key with which V_{EC_o} is created is compromised, thereby providing a stronger third level of security. This also disproves the general perception that traditional cryptographic algorithms will not work in cloud environments (Ren et al., 2012), since any traditional encryption algorithm can be used in this process.

7. IMPLEMENTATION AND RESULT

7.1. Cloud Setup

To demonstrate our work, the open source computer software for building real-time cloud computing environments, Eucalyptus (Nurmi et al., 2009), OpenStack (Sefraoui, Aissaoui, & Eleuldj, 2012) and OpenNebula (Milojičić, Llorente, & Montero, 2011) are used. The Eucalyptus, OpenStack and Open-Nebula clouds are respectively created using Eucalyptus Faststart v3.4.2 in Cloud-in-a-box configuration, DevStack Juno on Ubuntu 14.04 and OpenNebula 4.6 on Ubuntu 14.04, each in a single machine having either of the following two configurations:

Configuration 1: Intel (R) Core™ i7-3770 processor with RAM Capacity of 3.48 GB and Disk Capacity of 200 GB

Configuration 2: Six-core Intel Xeon E5-2630 processor with RAM Capacity of 96 GB and Disk Capacity of 300 GB

One of the clouds so set up is considered as IPC and the rest as ECs. The details of the cloud setup are tabulated in Table 2.

7.2. Evaluation Parameters

Enhancement of elasticity by secure inter-cloud communication is evaluated using the following parameters:

- *Transaction Success Rate*, the percentage of successful transactions and
- *Turnaround time*, the time difference between the initial time a request is raised for additional resource and the time at which the resource is made available to the user.

7.3. Results and Justification

The proposed work is evaluated by scaling the size of EC_A from 0 to 5. It is intended to be extended for $|EC_A| > 5$, the behavior of which is to be investigated as future direction of this work. When $|EC_A| = 0$, the IPC satisfies R_U with its own resources leading to an intra-cloud scenario and the rest of the cases

Table 2. Cloud setup

Cloud Label	Software used to setup Cloud Environment	Configuration of the Machine in which Cloud is setup
IPC	Eucalyptus	Configuration 2
EC1	OpenStack	Configuration 2
EC2	OpenNebula	Configuration 1
EC3	Eucalyptus	Configuration 1
EC4	OpenStack	Configuration 1
EC5	Eucalyptus	Configuration 2

are inter-cloud scenarios. For obtaining results for each of $0 \leq |EC_A| \leq 5$, 100 random R_U are raised in the IPC at random instants of time.

t_W for an EC is calculated by giving the weights, 1, 2 and 5 respectively to each of its parameters (in seconds), t_r, t_p and t_v, on a scale of 5 (1 being the least and 5 being the highest). To calculate f_W for an EC, a weight of 1 is given for each of f_{cpu}, f_{ram} (in MB) and f_{disk} (in GB), thus giving equal weight to all the three parameters.

7.3.1. Transaction Success Rate

Ideally, the transaction success rate should be 100%. From Figure 3, in an intra-cloud environment ($|EC_A| = 0$), the transaction success rate is seen to be 23.23% which is the least in the figure. As $|EC_A|$ with which the IPC interacts, increases, we expect the transaction success rate to increase. A good trend is observed up to $|EC_A| = 5$ in the figure, with a slight variation at $|EC_A| = 4$.

7.3.2. Turnaround Time

To measure the effectiveness of the proposed work on interoperating with ECs, the metric, turnaround time, is used which includes the time taken for all of the following components, if R_U is satisfied by EC_o:

- Choosing EC_o for interoperation, by obtaining RePVoCRaD parameters for every available EC,
- Establishing trust with EC_o,
- Acquiring V_{EC_o} using our model and
- Allocating V_{EC_o} to the user.

The turnaround time when R_U is satisfied by EC_o is proportional to the time taken to choose EC_o, as all other components contributing to it remain a constant. The time taken to choose EC_o is in turn proportional to $|EC_A|$ as all the parameters forming RePVoCRaD except t_v have to be obtained for each

Figure 3. Transaction success rate

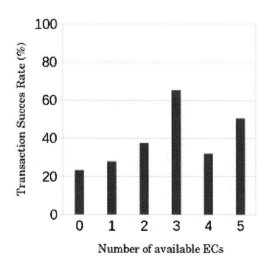

of EC_A at the time R_U is raised. If R_U is satisfied by the IPC itself, then the turnaround time is expected to be constant since it includes only the time taken for providing resources from IPC.

Figure 4 gives the turnaround time obtained for each satisfied R_U in all the scenarios i.e. $0 \leq |EC_A| \leq 5$. The figure uses a color coding to represent the cloud satisfying each R_U. As expected, it is found that the turnaround time when R_U is satisfied by IPC is low and constant and the time for satisfying R_U by any EC_i ($1 \leq i \leq 5$) is high due to the above discussed components.

Evaluating our work in a real-time cloud environment with a setup as discussed earlier in this section, the average turnaround time obtained in different scenarios ($0 \leq |EC_A| \leq 5$) are tabulated in Table 3. The result obtained is inclusive of the traffic consideration in the network in which the different clouds (IPC and ECs) are setup. The table shows the real-world picture of having a lower turnaround time when obtaining resources from within a single cloud than when obtaining resources from several clouds (IPC and ECs) simultaneously. The increase in the time, though to be expected, is worthwhile as waiting for R_U to be satisfied would be better than having R_U denied. It is to be noted that the average turnaround time is significantly low, even though the setup is only of low-end machines. Hence, it is quite obvious that with high-end machines which is a standard for setting up clouds in most of the leading cloud providers (Google, Amazon, etc), there will be a considerable reduction in the turnaround time.

On an average, the turnaround time obtained for R_U satisfied with resources of IPC is *0.428684* seconds. The average turnaround time for R_U satisfied by any EC_i ($1 \leq i \leq 5$) in each scenario i.e. $1 \leq |EC_A| \leq 5$, is given in Table 4. A steady increase is noticed in the turnaround time with increase in $|EC_A|$, thereby justifying the previously discussed proportionality.

Figure 4. Turnaround time obtained for requests that are satisfied in the following scenarios: (a) $|EC_A|$ = 0, (b) $|EC_A|$ = 1, (c) $|EC_A|$ = 2, (d) $|EC_A|$ = 3, (e) $|EC_A|$ = 4, and (f) $|EC_A|$ = 5

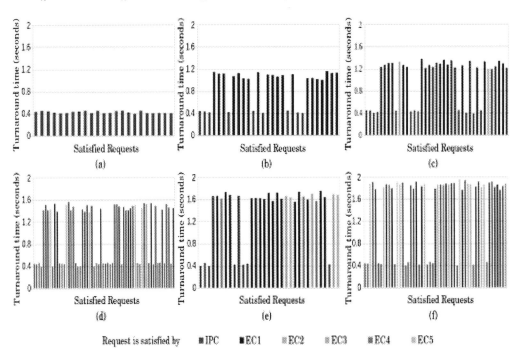

Table 3. Average turnaround time

Environment fulfilling R_U	Number of available ECs	Average Turnaround time (seconds)
intra-cloud	0	0.426977
inter-cloud	1	0.880709
	2	1.01565
	3	1.00292
	4	1.39423
	5	1.48339

Table 4. Average turnaround time obtained for EC_A to satisfy R_U

Number of available ECs	Average Turnaround time (seconds)
1	1.08705
2	1.27666
3	1.47008
4	1.65671
5	1.86272

The non-use of any third party to establish this secure inter-cloud communication is novel. As the interoperation environment is limited to the components of IPC and EC_A, the advantage of reduced security threats is thereby obvious. Also, with no additional costs due to absence of third parties, higher security provided due to direct communication between the interacting clouds, and better performance guaranteed by higher configured systems as heavy advantages, the increase in the average turnaround time as shown in Table 3 is essentially considerable. The only trade-off is that the IPC, along with its own activities, does that of the third parties, resulting in the turnaround time of inter-cloud environment to be higher than that of intra-cloud environment.

8. CONCLUSION AND FUTURE WORK

Enhancement of elasticity by secure inter-cloud communication provides an intelligent solution for an IPC to interoperate with an EC after choosing the optimal EC among the many available ECs using our proposed *RePVoCRaD* parameters. When a secure IPC initiates communication with an EC, several security threats arise, for which an algorithm whose structure is similar to the traditional Kerberos algorithm is proposed in order to establish a secure connection with the optimal EC without relying on any third party - trusted or not. The additional demands of a single user are fulfilled by multiple clouds (IPC and ECs) simultaneously and the user enjoys uninterrupted service without being involved in the process. Security provided in the communication is triple-fold: connection between IPC and EC is secured, resources are acquired from EC using a key (without use of third parties), and data is by encrypted and stored in the obtained resource. The absence of third party to achieve secure inter-cloud communication is an added advantage due to reduced security threats and no additional costs involved. The evaluation parameters used - transaction success rate and turnaround time - demonstrate the efficiency of the proposed inter-cloud communication.

The ECs used are those whose descriptions are provided by the administrator of IPC. Hence, our work performs only a static search for ECs. This offers a possible area of future work on dynamic search for ECs. Also, the efficiency of the proposed work can be improved by running the process of choosing the optimal EC at regular intervals in the background so that whenever a need to use an EC arises, the EC chosen by the background process can be accessed, resulting in reduced turnaround time.

To the best of our knowledge, this proposed work is the only known implemented solution for inter-cloud communication in a *real-time* setup, although there exists quite a lot of research in this area. The lack of similar work in a real-time setup makes it impossible to present the results obtained herein on a comparative scale. As real-time evaluation is more comprehensive of the exact behavior of a system than a simulated environment, this work proves to be more reliable than existing works. Though the setup used is a small environment, this work is intended to be expanded in future.

ACKNOWLEDGMENT

We immensely thank DST-INSPIRE Fellowship programme for providing research fellowship while carrying out this work. We are also grateful to Krupa Sivakumaran, T. Hema and S. Monica for their valuable insights and comments on improving the presentation of the work.

REFERENCES

Armbrust, M., Fox, A., Griffith, R., Joseph, A. D., Katz, R., Konwinski, A., ... Zaharia, M. (2010). A view of cloud computing. *Communications of the ACM*, *53*(4), 50–58. doi:10.1145/1721654.1721672

Bernstein, D., & Vij, D. (2011). Intercloud exchanges and roots topology and trust blueprint. In *11th International Conference on Internet Computing* (pp. 135–141).

Boneh, D. (2011). Digital signature standard. In *Encyclopedia of cryptography and security* (pp. 347–347). Springer.

Buyya, R., Ranjan, R., & Calheiros, R. N. (2010). Intercloud: Utility-oriented federation of cloud computing environments for scaling of application services. In Algorithms and architectures for parallel processing (pp. 13–31). Springer.

Chiu, D. (2010). Elasticity in the cloud. *ACM Crossroads*, *16*(3), 3–4. doi:10.1145/1734160.1734162

CSMIC - Carnegie Mellon University. (2014). *Service measurement index framework version 2.1*. Retrieved Dec 21, 2016, from http://csmic.org/downloads/SMI_Overview_ TwoPointOne.pdf/

Garg, S. K., Versteeg, S., & Buyya, R. (2013). A framework for ranking of cloud computing services. *Future Generation Computer Systems*, *29*(4), 1012–1023. doi:10.1016/j.future.2012.06.006

Grozev, N., & Buyya, R. (2014). Inter-cloud architectures and application brokering: Taxonomy and survey. *Software, Practice & Experience*, *44*(3), 369–390. doi:10.1002pe.2168

Jeyarani, R., Nagaveni, N., & Vasanth Ram, R. (2011). Self adaptive particle swarm optimization for efficient virtual machine provisioning in cloud. *International Journal of Intelligent Information Technologies*, *7*(2), 25–44. doi:10.4018/jiit.2011040102

Kannan, A., Venkatesan, K. G., Stagkopoulou, A., Li, S., Krishnan, S., & Rahman, A. (2015). A novel cloud intrusion detection system using feature selection and classification. *International Journal of Intelligent Information Technologies*, *11*(4). doi:10.4018/IJIIT.2015100101

Kirthica, S., & Sridhar, R. (2015a). Provisioning rapid elasticity by light-weight live resource migration. *International Journal of Modern Trends in Engineering and Research*, *2*(7), 99–106.

Kirthica, S., & Sridhar, R. (2015b). Solution for traversal vulnerability and an encryption-based security solution for an inter-cloud environment. In *Computational intelligence in data mining-volume 2* (pp. 283–291). Springer. doi:10.1007/978-81-322-2208-8_26

Li, W., & Ping, L. (2009). Trust model to enhance security and interoperability of cloud environment. In *Cloud computing* (pp. 69–79). Springer. doi:10.1007/978-3-642-10665-1_7

Meera, A., & Swamynathan, S. (2015). Queue based Q-learning for efficient resource provisioning in cloud data centers. *International Journal of Intelligent Information Technologies*, *11*(4), 37–54. doi:10.4018/IJIIT.2015100103

Milojičić, D., Llorente, I. M., & Montero, R. S. (2011). OpenNebula: A cloud management tool. *IEEE Internet Computing*, *15*(2), 11–14. doi:10.1109/MIC.2011.44

Neuman, B. C., & Ts'o, T. (1994). Kerberos: An authentication service for computer networks. *IEEE Communications Magazine*, *32*(9), 33–38. doi:10.1109/35.312841

Nurmi, D., Wolski, R., Grzegorczyk, C., Obertelli, G., Soman, S., Youseff, L., & Zagorodnov, D. (2009). The eucalyptus open-source cloud-computing system. In *9th IEEE/ACM International Symposium on Cluster Computing and the Grid (CCGRID)* (pp. 124–131).

Owens, D. (2010). Securing elasticity in the cloud. *Communications of the ACM*, *53*(6), 46–51.

Parameswaran, A., & Chaddha, A. (2009). Cloud interoperability and standardization. *SETlabs briefings*, *7*(7), 19–26.

Ren, K., Wang, C., & Wang, Q. (2012). Security challenges for the public cloud. *IEEE Internet Computing*, *16*(1), 69–73. doi:10.1109/MIC.2012.14

Rochwerger, B., Breitgand, D., Epstein, A., Hadas, D., Loy, I., Nagin, K., Tordsson, J., Ragusa, C., Villari, M., Clayman, S., Levy, E., Maraschini, A., Massonet, P., Muñoz, H., & Tofetti, G. (2011). RESERVOIR - When one cloud is not enough. *IEEE computer*, *44*(3), 44–51.

Rogers, S. J. (2013). Kerberos and SAS® 9.4: A Three-Headed Solution for Authentication. *SAS Institute Inc.* Retrieved Dec 23, 2016, from http://support.sas.com/resources/papers/ proceedings13/476-2013.pdf

Sefraoui, O., Aissaoui, M., & Eleuldj, M. (2012). OpenStack: Toward an open-source solution for cloud computing. *International Journal of Computers and Applications*, *55*(3), 38–42. doi:10.5120/8738-2991

Varia, J. (2011). *Architecting for the Cloud: Best Practices. Amazon Web Services.* Retrieved Dec 23, 2016, from https://media.amazonwebservices.com/AWS_Cloud_Best_Practices.pdf

Zissis, D., & Lekkas, D. (2012). Addressing cloud computing security issues. *Future Generation Computer Systems*, *28*(3), 583–592. doi:10.1016/j.future.2010.12.006

This research was previously published in the International Journal of Intelligent Information Technologies (IJIIT), 14(2); edited by Vijayan Sugumaran, pages 43-58, copyright year 2018 by IGI Publishing (an imprint of IGI Global).

Chapter 40
Semantic++ Electronic Commerce Architecture and Models in Cloud

Guigang Zhang
Chinese Academy of Sciences, China & Tsinghua University, China

Chao Li
Tsinghua University, China

Yong Zhang
Tsinghua University, China

Chunxiao Xing
Tsinghua University, China

Sixin Xue
Tsinghua University, China & Renmin University, China

Yuenan Liu
Renmin University, China

ABSTRACT

Electronic commerce is playing a more and more important role in today's commercial activities. In this chapter, the authors propose a kind of new electronic commerce architecture in the cloud and give two kinds of new electronic commerce models. This chapter opens the discussion of why we need to design a new architecture in the cloud environment. Firstly, the authors have a discussion about the semantic++ computing. After the discussion, they give the architecture that can satisfy the requirements in the cloud. This architecture mainly includes five technologies, which are the massive EC data storage technology in the cloud, the massive EC data processing technology in the cloud, the EC security management technology in the cloud, OLAP technology for EC in the cloud, and active EC technology in the cloud. Then, the authors propose two kinds of semantic++ electronic commerce models based on big data. These two models are the new electronic commerce models. The first model is semantic++ electronic commerce Q/A (Questions/Answers) model and another is the active semantic++ electronic commerce model. These two models are all based on big data. Finally, the authors conclude this chapter and give future work.

DOI: 10.4018/978-1-5225-8176-5.ch040

INTRODUCTION

With the rapid development of electronic commerce, the traditional technologies can't satisfy the applications' requirements again. We need to transplant the traditional EC into the cloud environment. And so, we need to construct a kind of new electronic commerce architecture in the cloud environment. This kind of new architecture needs to satisfy massive data's storage, data computing and data's security in cloud so on.

Nowadays, people would like to use the electronic commerce software comfortably. And so some new electronic commerce models will to be appeared, especially in the big data era. In this background, we propose two new electronic commerce models. The first model is a kind of semantic++ electronic commerce Q/A model and another is the active semantic++ electronic commerce model based on big data. More and more people would like to ask questions about the electronic commerce in the internet. For example, which kind of dried milk is the cheapest in the Ebay? And they hope to get a good answer from lots of answers come from the public or electronic commerce web sites in the world. The crowd-sourcing is a typical application of Q/A system. Some companies or enterprises publish their projects through the internet, and lots of public and experts can attend the research for these projects. And then, these companies and enterprises can select some good results from millions of answers. At the same time, lots of consumers want to find products from the electronic commerce web sites according to their requirements, too.

In order to complete these internet applications in the EC (electronic commerce) area, we propose a semantic++ EC Q/A model. From this semantic++ EC Q/A system model, questions publishers can publish their questions through this system, and lots of publics can answer their questions. This system can execute some semantic++ computing through the big data platform and get some semantic knowledge extraction, knowledge analysis, semantic++ results sort and so on.

The semantic++ EC Q/A system model is a kind of passive EC model, EC consumers need to get EC information themselves. With the development of economics, lots of consumers are very busy and they hope to get some EC information automatically. The rule technology is the most important technology to realize this model. In order to realize the active semantic EC model, we will use the rule processing technology to complete this model in this paper. All EC consumers can set their rules in the EC web sites according to their conditions. And when their conditions have been satisfied in some times, the rules that have set will be trigged. And so, the results will be sent to the consumers through emails, telephones and other ways so on.

BACKGROUND

In order to understand the semantic++ electronic commerce architecture and models in cloud better, some related area with our paper will be introduced, which are electronic commerce models, cloud computing, big data, security, semantic computing and rule processing so on.

Electronic commerce is becoming more and more important in the 21St. lots of traditional trade activities have been migrated into the internet. Electronic commerce is playing a more and more important role all over the world. According to the report of electronic commerce research and development (Ali-research, 2011), the e-commerce transactions accounted for a total GDP of China in 2011 is 12.1%. And it will arrive at the 20% in the next five years. Now, more and more users have become the participants of electronic commerce. They buy and sell products from the EC web sites. The electronic commerce mainly undergoes three stages. The first stage is from the 1990 year to 2000 year. In this stage, the electronic commerce concept begins to be formed. The most important form is that the companies publish their commerce information in their web pages, the buyers or sellers can find the commerce information from these web pages, and they can complete their commerce trade offline. The second stage is from the 2001 year to 2010 year. In this stage, the electronic commerce has a very big development. Lots of electronic commerce web sites occur. The national trade and international trade have gotten a very big development. Lots of traditional companies have developed their electronic commerce, too. The main electronic business models (He, 2003) have B2B, B2C, B2G and C2C. The most important electronic commerce web sites have Ebay, Alibaba and Taobao etc. In the ten years, the EC has become the most important commerce activity. The third stage is from the 2011 year to now. In this stage, the electronic commerce has entered into a new era. We can name it the new electronic commerce era. The traditional electronic commerce has little intelligence. It only need help the sellers and buyers can complete their trades online or offline. However the new electronic commerce has more intelligence. It not only needs to help all buyers and sellers to complete their trades, but also can help the buyers and sellers can analyze their markets. At the same time, all the sellers and buyers want to have more interactivities each other and wish exchange more information each other.

In the new electronic commerce stage, the cloud computing will play an important role. Lots of cloud technologies will be applied in the EC. The mainly technologies include the cloud storage technology, the big data processing technology, the intelligence computing technology in the cloud, how to ensure the electronic commerce security in the cloud and so on.

In order to storage big data for all kinds of electronic commerce applications, lots of cloud databases and distributed file systems occur. As we know, in the traditional electronic commerce, the data only include the structured data, and all these structured data will be stored into the relational databases such as the Oracle, My SQL, DB2 and SQL Server so on. However, in the new electronic commerce stage, lots of structured data, semi-structured data and non-structured data should be stored all together. In order to store all these non-structured data, lots of distributed file systems occur. The most important distributed file systems are Google' GFS (Sanjay, 2003), Hadoop's HDFS (Ghoting, 2009), KFS (EDITORIAL, 2010), Taobao FS (Taobao, 2010) and Hystack (Doug, 2010). All these distributed file system can run on top of millions of machines and they can manage all files automatically. In addition, lots of semi-structured data need to be storage, too. And so, lots of cloud databases have been developed, too. The most important cloud databases have the Google's BigTable (Fay, 2006) Hadoop's HBase (Jianling, 2010), HyperTable (HypertableInc, 2012), Facebook's Cassandra (Avinash, 2010) and Amazon's SimpleDB (Amazon, 2009) so on. For example, the Google uses the BigTable to storage the index information of all web pages files in the internet. All these cloud databases uses the key/value mechanism.

In order to process massive data in the cloud environment, lots of new technologies occur, too. Google MapReduce is the most important massive data processing framework for Google's all kinds of applications. Each Google search will use the MapReduce to process massive data. Based on the Google MapReduce, the Hadoop MapReduce emerges. It is the open source version of Google MapReduce. However, the MapReduce (Biswanath, 2009) (Lin, 2010) (Kovoor, 2010) (De, 2009) still cannot process some applications well with the loop conditions. And so, lots of others big data processing frameworks emerge such as the Haloop and Twister. The Haloop (Bu, 2010) and Twister (Jaliya, 2010) are the iterative MapReduce. They can satisfy these applications with loop conditions well. Although these massive data processing frameworks can process data quickly, they have little computing abilities. Unlike the relational databases, they can't execute complete computing such as complex queries, complex join and some other complex computing. In order to improve the computing ability, lots of technologies attempt to combine the databases and these frameworks together. The HadoopDB(Abouzeid,2009) is the most famous product which hopes to combine the MapReduce and the Parallel relational database together. Later, the Hadoop++(Dittrich,2010) emerges, too. It adds a Trojan index and Trojan join based on the Hadoop. And it can improve the processing efficiency in some degree and it can complete some complex computing, too.

The traditional EC does not consider the intelligent analysis a lot, especially the real time intelligent analysis. The intelligent analysis technologies mainly include the semantic computing technologies. The semantic computing can help the buyers and sellers to get some semantic OLAP results and help them to improve their decision efficiency. The most important semantic applications in the EC have the semantic rules processing technologies and semantic queries. The semantic rules allow the EC users to set all kinds of semantic rules based on the EC products, and if the conditions are satisfied, these rule engines will make some intelligent decision for the users. In addition, in order to process the big data rapidly, we need to construct some semantic indexes based on the original data. With the semantic indexes, some EC applications can satisfy the real time requirements.

Security(Junsheng,2005) is the most important part in the EC. The security of EC is the PKI(Joo-Kwan,2010) (Christopher,2011) security model. The PKI security technologies include the symmetric encryption, asymmetric encryption, digital digest, digital signature, digital envelope, SSL security protocol and SET security protocol so on. If we transplant the traditional EC into the cloud environment, we need consider not only the traditional EC security technologies, but also we need consider the cloud data security technologies, too. Some trust computing technologies and homomorphism encryption technology need to be applied.

In order to let the electronic commerce applications more suitable for the people in the future, more and more semantic computing technologies will be applied into the EC. As we know, the traditional semantic computing technology has the Ontology, knowledge base technology, tag techniques and the rule base technology. It will construct some relationship among the concepts. Phillip C-Y Sheu defined semantic+ computing based on the semantic computing(Qi Wang,2010)(S. Ikeda,2010)(Shu Wang,2010)(W. Ying,2010). Semantic+ computing = semantic computing + natural-like human interface. The natural-like human interface likes a bridge between the human's ideas and computers. The SemanticObjectsTM(Phillip,2007)(P.C-Y,2007)(P.C-Y Sheu,2007)(P. C-Y Sheu,2009) is a good human interface in the semantic+ computing(Jennifer Kim,2013)(Ke Hao,2011)(Min Gyo Chung,2011)The semantic+ computing can construct a bridge between the human and computers. However it cannot process some complex semantics, still. With the development of big data, we propose semantic++ computing. It can be expressed as: semantic++ computing = semantic computing + natural-like human interface +big data. Because of the big data, lots of complex semantics can be processed. For example, what is the relationship between the haze weather and regional coal combustion? The traditional semantic computing and semantic+ computing can't solve this problem well, because this complex application needs big data computing.

In order to realize the active electronic commerce applications, the rule processing technologies is very important. Lots of active systems(Morgenstern M,1983) (Dayal U,1989)come from the databases' trigger tools at first such as R(Astrahan M,1976), HiPAC(Chakravarthy S,1989), Starburst(Lohman G.

Figure 1. Semantic+ computing

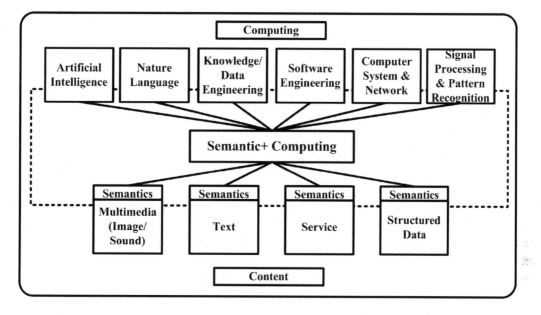

M,1991) and POSTGRES(Stonebraker M,1986). Later, most of active systems are worked base on the rule engines(Widom J,1990)(Buchman A,1992)(Gatziu S,1992)(Hanson E,1992)(Fahl G,1993)(Ceri S,1992). The most important rule processing algorithms have RETE (Forgy,1982), TREAT(Miranker,1987), LEAPS and RETE2(ProductionInc, 2012) so on.

SEMANTIC++ COMPUTING

Semantic++ computing is a kind of computing based on the human's ideas. It is based on the semantic+ computing. In this section we will take a simple introduction for semantic+ computing and semantic++ computing.

Semantic+ Computing

Professor Phillip C-Y Sheu(UCIrvine) first propose the definition of semantic+ computing, Figure 1 shows the basic model of semantic+ computing)(P.C-Y,2007)(P.C-Y Sheu,2007)(P. C-Y Sheu,2009).

Figure 1 shows the semantic+ computing. The semantic+ computing combine the artificial intelligence, nature language processing, knowledge engineering, data engineering, software engineering, computer system, computer network, signal processing and pattern recognition into a completed system. And it will consider their interaction each other. It will exact all kinds of the semantics from the multimedia, text, service and structured data so on.

The most important is that the semantic+ computing will utilize the nature processing technologies to construct an interface which close to the human-like thinks. It is the most differences between the semantic computing and semantic+ computing.

Semantic++ Computing

Although the semantic+ computing have more semantics than the traditional semantic computing, however, it cannot satisfy some more complex semantic applications, still. With the development of cloud computing and big data, more complex semantics can be computed. And more complex semantics can be applied into all kinds of applications.

Semantic++ Computing is a kind of advanced computing based on the human's ideas. It can process very complex semantics such as "what is the hottest topic in the Twitter in USA?", "What do the Beijing people like to buy in the Taobao web site?" and "How to judge the relationships between the Haze and the car ownership" so on. Just like the description in the front, the semantic++ computing have more semantics than the traditional semantic computing. We can summarize the semantic++ computing into a formula: Semantic++ Computing=Semantic Computing + Human-Machine Interface close to the human thinking+ Big Data. Figure 2 shows the basic mechanism of the semantic++ computing.

Firstly, the user such as the consumer will form an idea. For example the consumer would like to buy a book "The world is flat" from all kinds of EC web sites, and he/she want to select a cheapest.

Secondly, we need to develop a human-machine interface. This interface is close to the human thinks. And so, the people can let their thinks to be easily understood by the computers.

Thirdly, some algorithms will be executed based on the semantic models and electronic commerce big data. These semantic models and big data will be executed and get a good results to the consumer.

Finally, the consumer can get a cheapest book "The world is flat" through the semantic++ computing.

THE NEW ELECTRONIC COMMERCE ARCHITECTURE IN THE CLOUD

Figure 3 shows the new electronic commerce architecture in the cloud. From Figure 3, we can see that this architecture includes the following several aspects.

1. **Operation Systems:** In the electronic commerce web sites, there are millions of machines. Some of them maybe run on top of the Linux operation system, some of them maybe run on top of the

Figure 2. An example of semantic++ computing

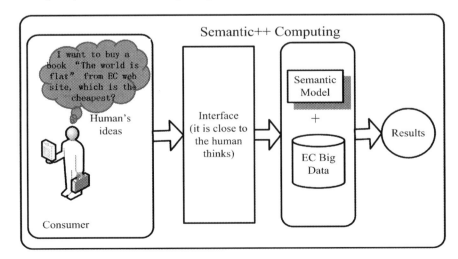

Windows operation system and some of them run on top of the Unix operation system. Sure of course, in order to integrate all machines and improve their computing and storage capabilities, we can use the virtualization tools such as the OpenStack or VMWare to let all these different physical machines and different operation systems become a entirety all together and eliminate all these heterogeneity.

2. **Semantic Cloud File System:** It is a kind of distributed file system based on the Hadoop distributed file system. It runs on top of millions of common machines. All these non-structured electronic commerce files will be stored into the semantic cloud file system directly. Compared with the HDFS, the semantic cloud file system will have more semantics and it will improve the processing efficiency, too. We will have detail introduction in later section.

3. **HUABASE:** It is a kind of distributed database. It runs on top of the semantic cloud file system. HUABASE is a kind of column-based database. It adapts the new storage model and it can improve the performance a lot in some key technologies optimization. HUABASE(Chun, 2011) is not only good at processing OLTP applications, but also especially is good at processing OLAP applications. It can help companies to make good decisions after the analysis for massive data. Figure 4 shows the HUABASE database.

In our architecture, firstly, the HUABASE database is used to store massive non-structured files' (photos, pictures, texts, videos) indexes. And we will construct the semantic index based on these semantic indexes' records. In addition, HUABASE database is used to store the analysis data, too. From Figure 4, we can see that all kinds of data resources such as the Oracle, Db2 and Sybase can be merged into using the HUABASE ETL. After the ETL processing, all these data can be stored into the HUABASE database. And HUABASE database can help users to analyze all kinds of business intelligent applications and to help they make decisions, too.

4. **Rule Engine:** Rule engine is the most important part for the active electronic commerce applications. The existing rule engines can't process massive rules well. Especially, the existing rule engines have little semantics, they can't let the users set the rules themselves, and so all these rules are the passive rules. Our rule engine uses the semantic rules. And it will help the traditional electronic commerce companies to develop the active electronic commerce applications. For example, the users set many semantic rules through the electronic commerce web sites, and if the conditions have been satisfied, the semantic rules will be executed and send information to the users proactively.

5. **Semantic MapReduce:** As we know, the Google MapReduce and Hadoop MapReduce are used to process big data computing. However, these MapReduce programming models have little capabilities in processing complex computing such as the complex queries, especially some complex Join computing. Semantic MapReduce is used to process massive non-structured data stored in the semantic cloud file system and massive semi-structured data stored in the HUABASE database. Owning to we have constructed the relevant semantic indexes based on the semantic cloud file system and HUABASE database. And so we design a kind of new big data processing framework semantic MapReude. Owning to the support of semantics, we can execute some intelligent and complex computing than the Google MapReduce and Hadoop MapReduce.

6. **Electronic Commerce Requirements:** In order to process all kinds of computing includes the intelligent computing, we will extract lots of electronic commerce requirements. These requirements mainly include OLAP, OLTP, semantic electronic commerce, active electronic commerce, real time

Figure 3. The new electronic commerce architecture in the cloud

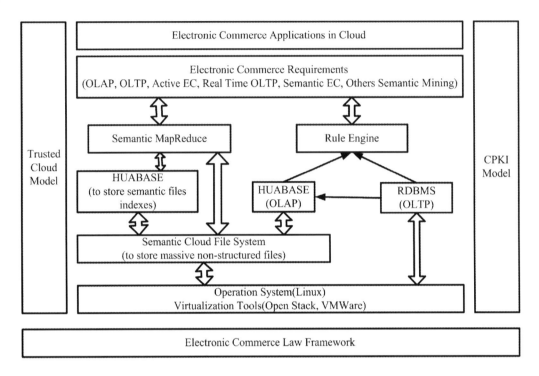

OLAP, real time OLTP and some others semantic mining applications for electronic commerce applications.

7. **Electronic Commerce Applications in the Cloud:** With the development of electronic commerce, cloud computing and IoT, lots of new applications occur. The most important applications include massive EC transaction data mining and processing system, electronic commerce society community analysis system, active electronic commerce system based on the semantic rules and electronic commerce products recommend system based on some semantic data mining and semantic rules.

8. **CPKI Model:** As we know, the security is the most important in the electronic applications. The traditional electronic commerce uses the PKI security model to ensure the electronic security. However, with the changes of electronic commerce environment, especially the cloud environment,

Figure 4. HUABASE database

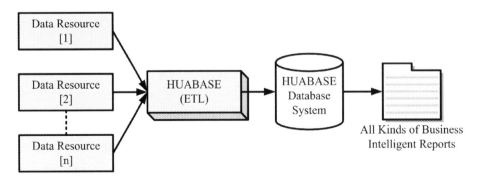

lots of new security technologies should be added into the PKI security model. And so, we design a new electronic commerce model in the environment, we name it CPKI security model. CPKI security model is based on the traditional security model PKI. We will make a detail introduction in the later section.

9. **Trusted Cloud Model:** Trusted computing is very important in the electronic commerce. If we move the traditional electronic commerce into the cloud environment, we should use a kind of new trusted computing model.

10. **Electronic Commerce Law Framework:** In the former, we discuss the security solution using the CPKI security model and trusted cloud model. These solutions are used to ensure the electronic commerce security from the technologies perspective. In fact, except the technologies, the electronic commerce laws are very important to ensure the transaction security. Since the appearance of electronic commerce, lots of electronic commerce laws have published. The most famous electronic laws has "The United Nations Commissionon International Trade Law Model Law on Electronic Commerce", which is published in the 1991. In china, the first electronic commerce law is the "Electronic Signature Law", which is published in the 2004. Except these special laws for the electronic commerce, lots of other traditional laws add some electronic commerce contents based on the original laws. For example, the contract law adds the signature, electronic contract and electronic time into the law framework for the new contract law.

DATA STORAGE FOR EC APPLICATION

In order to store all these EC application data, we should classify the data at first. The data can been classify into structured data, semi-structured data and non-structured data.

In the EC, the structured data will be stored into the RDBMS (relational database management system). Most of these data is the transaction data such as the user information, products information and all kinds of transaction information. These data should be processed for many OLTP requirements. These data can be operated by SQL sentence.

With the development of EC, lots of interactive data occur. The EC web sites will provide many non-structured data such as the products' picture and video data. For example, the cloths seller should submit many cloths photos into the web site. In addition, buyers can interactive in the EC web site. They can commit the products; even they can send some pictures and videos into the EC web sites. All these text data, picture data and videos data are the non-structured data. They can't be stored into the RDBMS. In addition, with the development of data, the data scale in the EC web site will arrive at the PB-scale, or even EB-scale. In order to store these data, we should use the cloud file system. The cloud file system is a kind of distributed file system like the GFS, HDFS and KFS so on. Sure of course, in order to improve the processing efficiency, we will construct a semantic index based on these non-structured data.

We can use the semantic file system to store all these non-structured data such as the text and picture files. However, we should store some useful metadata information for these files, too. The metadata information can be stored into the key/value format. The key is the key is the title of non-structured data. And the value is the simple text description. All kinds of key/value data are the semi-structured data. These data are the index information for massive non-structured data. We use the HUABASE to store these semi-structured data.

RULE ENGINE FOR EC APPLICATION

Rule engine is used to monitor all data stored in the RDBMS or HUABASE. Most of the pub/sub systems use the rule engines. In the EC, especially some active EC applications, the rule engines will play a very important role in the future. The most important rule processing tools have JBoss and Drools(JBoss,2009). And the most important rule processing algorithms have the Rete(Forgy,1982), Rete2(ProductionInc, 2012) and TREAT(Miranker,1987) so on. In order to support the active electronic commerce, we design a kind of active rule engine. Figure 5 shows the active electronic commerce application based on the semantic rule engine.

In the active electronic commerce applications, user can set all kinds of semantic rules through the active EC web pages. The biggest difference between the traditional EC and active EC is that use can set rules themselves in the active EC. After users have set all kinds of semantic rules, these rules will be formed into the semantic rule language. The semantic rule engine tool (that is the semantic rule language compiler tool) will execute the rules after the data come from the RDBMS(such as the My SQL, Oracle and DB2 so on) or HUABASE have satisfied the conditions of these rules.

The semantic rule language is the following format:

```
IF Condition 1AND Condition 2 AND……. AND Condition c
Then Active
[Example 1] a semantic rule for active EC application
IF product.Name=="Iphone 5" AND product. Price is less than RMB5000
THEN send the information to my cell phone.
```

The example 1 shows a simple semantic rule set by user himself/herself. From this example, we can see that the active electronic commerce can let the users interact with the EC web sites. They can set all kinds of rules according to their requirements.

Figure 5. Active electronic commerce application based on the semantic rule engine

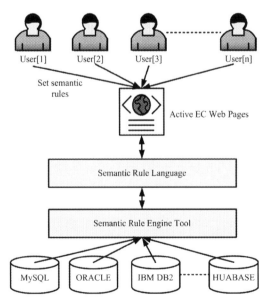

Sure of course, with the increasing of semantic rules, the optimization of semantic rules will become very important. In order to improve the processing speed, we design a kind of optimization strategy for it. It can be described as the follows.

- Merge all these semantic rules into a very big semantic rules network. Millions of users will set billions of semantic rules. Firstly, we should merge all these rules into a very big semantic rules network.
- Optimize this semantic rule network according to the graph theory. After getting this network, this network is still very raw. We should use the graph theory to optimize this network. For example, we will delete the repeat nodes in the rule network.
- Get an optimized semantic rule network. After step 2, we will get an optimized rule network.
- Submit this optimized semantic rule network into the semantic rule engine. The semantic rule engine will return the rules processing results to the users if their conditions have been satisfied with these rules which they have set before in the active electronic commerce web sites.

SEMANTIC CLOUD FILE SYSTEM

Semantic cloud file system is based on the Hadoop distributed file system. It includes a metadata cluster and a data storage cluster. The biggest differences between the semantic cloud file system and HDFS have two aspects. The first is that the semantic cloud file system has a metadata cluster, that is to say, we have several metadata nodes, however the HDFS has only one metadata node. The second is that the semantic cloud file system has more semantics(Phillip,2007) (Deng,2006) than the HDFS. Figure 6 shows the architecture of semantic cloud file system.

Figure 6. Architecture of semantic cloud file system

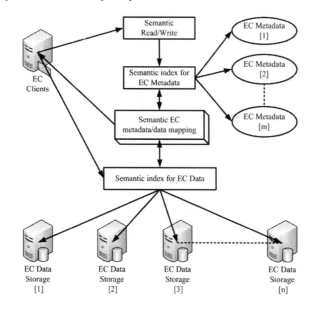

The work flow of semantic cloud file system includes the write operation and read operation. The read/write workflow can be described as the follows.

1.   The read workflow of semantic cloud file system:

Step 1: The electronic commerce client sends the read commands to the semantic read module.

Step 2: The semantic read module will query the semantic index for electronic commerce metadata

Step 3: After finding the metadata's location, then go to the semantic electronic commerce metadata/data mapping. And this mapping will return the data storage locations for these queries.

Step 4: After finding the data storage node location, we should go to the semantic index for electronic commerce data, and find the physical storage locations for these data which need to be read.

Step 5: The semantic electronic commerce metadata/data mapping should tell the electronic commerce clients the locations of data, and the EC clients can read the data which they need.

2.   The write workflow of semantic cloud file system

Step 1: The electronic commerce client sends the write commands to the semantic write module.

Step 2: The semantic write module will query the semantic index storage locations for electronic commerce metadata.

Step 3: After finding the metadata's locations, then write the metadata in these locations.

Step 4: After completing the writing operations for the metadata, then go to the semantic electronic commerce metadata/data mapping. And this mapping will return the data storage locations for these data which need to be written.

Step 5: After finding the data storage node location, we should go to the semantic index for electronic commerce data, and find the physical storage locations for these data which need to be written.

Step 6: The semantic electronic commerce metadata/data mapping should tell the electronic commerce clients the writing locations for all data and the EC clients can write the data which they need to write.

SEMANTIC MAPREDUCE

Semantic MapReduce is a kind of new programming model for massive electronic commerce data with semantic indexes. All these electronic commerce data are stored in the relational databases, HUABASE database and semantic cloud file system. Semantic MapReduce only executes computing for these data stored in the semantic cloud file system or HUABASE database. The semantic MapReduce includes five parts:

1.   Read data from the semantic cloud file system. It is the first step, semantic MapReduce should get the jobs' data from the file system. Generally speaking, the split size of semantic cloud file system is the same with the HDFS, which is the 64M size.

2.   Execute the map operations. In this step, all map tasks will be executed according to the requirements of jobs.

3. Execute the semantic shuffle operations. The semantic shuffle operations are the most important part in the semantic MapReduce. The semantic shuffle strategy can see the algorithm 1.

4. Execute the reduce operations. In this step, all reduce tasks will be executed according to the requirements of jobs after getting the middle data come from the map tasks.

5. Write the final data into the semantic cloud file system. When a job has been completed, the reduce will product the computing results for the job. And these final results come from these reduce computing will be stored into the semantic cloud file system at last.

[Algorithm 1] Semantic Shuffle Strategy Algorithm

Input: Map tasks, map tasks' stations, workload of every machine, data's locations.
Output: Optimized semantic shuffle strategy.
1. Start.
2. For (i=0; i<jobs.length; i++){
3. Find a job job[i];
4. For (j=0;j<maptasks.length; j++) {
5. Find all the map tasks of a job job[i][j];
6. Find every task's station; // the stations have four kinds of types. First is 'OK', second is timeout, the third is breakdown and the forth is the physical breakdown.
7. If job[i][j].stations=="OK"
8. Then go on;
9. If job[i][j].stations=="timeout"
10. Then find a new data storage node that stored the same data according to the semantic index and if there are several storage nodes satisfy the condition, then select a data storage node which workload is the smallest.
11. If job[i][j].stations=="Logical breakdown"
12. {
13. If the machines' workload is very small, then restart this machine;
14. Then select a new data storage node that stored the same data according to the semantic index and if there are several storage nodes satisfy the condition, then select a data storage node which workload is the smallest.
15. }
16. If job[i][j].stations=="physical breakdown";
17. Then select a new machine that stored the same data according to the semantic index and if there are several storage nodes satisfy the condition, then select a data storage node which workload is the smallest.
18. }
19. }
20. End.

CPKI MODEL

CPKI model is a new security model based on the traditional electronic commerce model PKI security model. Figure 7 shows the architecture of CPKI model.

Compared with the traditional electronic commerce security model PKI model, we add three parts based on the PKI. The first is the data consistency maintenance. In the cloud environment, all data stored in the semantic cloud file system will have more than one replica. That is to say, an electronic commerce order maybe has several replicas. For example, the GFS and HDFS' default replicas factor is 3. That is to say that every data stored in the GFS and HDFS will have 3 times same data in the cloud. Although the cloud computing technology gives the electronic commerce applications a lot, however the data maintenance, especially to those electronic orders will bring very big challenge which is how to keep the consistency of massive electronic orders. And so, in the CPKI model, we should have a module to maintain the data consistency. The second is that we add an electronic orders maintenance module in the CPKI model. In the traditional electronic commerce security model PKI, we don't consider the loss of electronic orders. In the PKI, we only consider the transmission security of electronic orders. In order to manage these electronic orders (contracts) efficiently, we use the electronic orders maintenance module to ensure the security of electronic orders not only in the transmission or its numbers. The third is that we add some cloud security infrastructure for the CPKI. Compared with the traditional electronic commerce environment, the cloud environment needs some new security infrastructure to ensure the transaction security.

Figure 7. Architecture of CPKI model

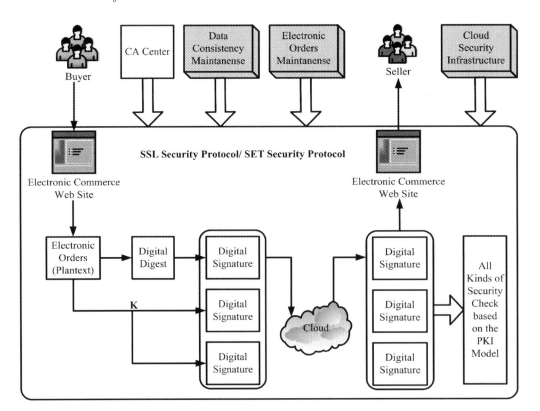

TRUSTED CLOUD MODEL

In order to ensure the security of electronic commerce, the traditional trusted computing model attempt to ensure the security of E-commerce's participants, all kinds of electronic commerce servers, all kinds of electronic commerce softwares and all kinds of electronic commerce security protocols so on.

However, in the cloud environment, we not only need to ensure the trust for all elements in the traditional electronic commerce, but also we need to ensure the trust for some special requirements in the cloud. The new requirements include: trusted performance indemnification, trusted encryption algorithm, trusted decryption algorithm and trusted privacy protection for electronic commerce data in the cloud. Figure 8 shows the trusted cloud model in the cloud.

In the traditional electronic commerce applications, we needn't to process massive non-structured data. And the traditional databases such as the Oracle and DB2 can satisfy these transaction data's processing speed well. However, after the electronic commerce applications have been migrated into the cloud, lots of non-structured and semi-structured data need to be processed. It will face a very big challenge for the computing performance. So, we should use some trusted algorithm to ensure the electronic commerce applications' executing speed, especially to those real time applications.

The traditional encryption algorithms and decryption algorithms are not suit for the encryption and decryption in the cloud. Some efficient homomorphism encryption algorithms and homomorphism decryption algorithms will be designed to execute the encryption and decryption in the cloud.

All commerce data stored in the cloud is very important to every company. How the let these data's privacy can be protected is very important, too. And so, in the trusted cloud model, we consider the privacy protection, too.

Figure 8. Trusted cloud model

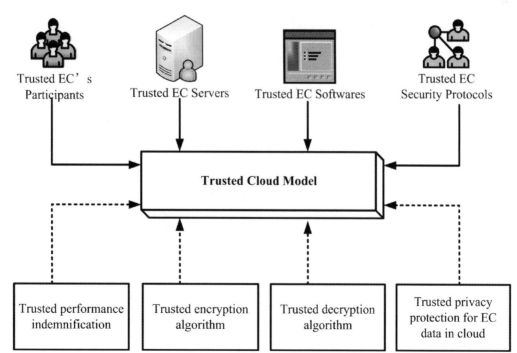

CASE STUDY OF ACTIVE ELECTRONIC COMMERCE APPLICATION IN THE CLOUD

There are lots of different kinds of electronic commerce applications in the cloud such as the product recommend system based on the massive data mining for the users' reviews, volume of business transactions analysis for electronic commerce and sellers and buyers behaviors mining so on. In this section, we make an introduction about the active electronic commerce application. Figure 9 shows the framework of active electronic commerce.

1. Users set semantic rules in the active electronic commerce web site:
    Rule 1: If the product.name =="shirt" AND the product.price<$50
    THEN send the information to Guigang Zhang.
    Rule 2: If the product.name =="tea" AND the product.Date>2012.6.1
    THEN send the information to Guigang Zhang.
    Rule 3: If the product.name =="shirt" AND the product.price<$56
    THEN send the information to Chao Li.

Figure 9. Framework of active electronic commerce

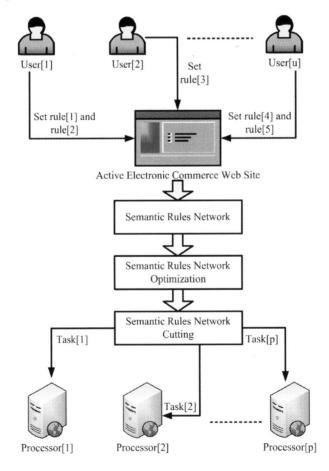

Rule 4: If the product.name =="shirt" AND the product.price<$58
THEN send the information to Sixin Xue.
Rule 5: If the product.name =="tea" AND the product.price<$10
THEN send the information to Sixin Xue.

2. All these semantic rules merge into a semantic rules network

The rule 1, rule 2, rule 3, rule 4 and the rule 5 will form a semantic rules network. Sure of course, this semantic rule network is very raw, it has not any optimization.

3. Optimize the semantic rules network

After the step 2, we can optimize the original semantic rules network, and get the optimization results.

4. Cutting the semantic rules network

From Figure 7, we can see that there p processors to execute these computing. And so, we need to cut this semantic rules network into p parts. The basic principle is that we should ensure the workload is relevant balance for every processor.

5. Assigning the computing tasks to every processors

After the cutting for the semantic rule network, we can assign tasks to every processor.

SEMANTIC++ ELECTRONIC COMMERCE MODELS

In this section, we will introduce two semantic++ commerce models, which are the semantic++ electronic commerce Q/A model and active semantic++ electronic commerce model. These two kinds of electronic commerce models will become the EC web sites' trend in the future. They will provide more convenient electronic commerce services for consumers over around the world.

Semantic++ Electronic Commerce Q/A Model

Figure 10 shows the framework of the semantic++ Q/A model.

The question provider will propose their questions, and these questions will be decomposed into some semantic++ requirements.

And these semantic++ requirements will be considered as the input for semantic++ computing.

After the questions have been proposed, lots of answer providers will provide their answers to these questions. And these answers will be considered as the input for semantic++ computing, too.

The answer providers' data, the answers and the question providers' data will be stored into the big data warehouse. And these big data will be considered as the input of semantic++ computing, too.

After executing these semantic++ computing based on the big data, this semantic++ Q/A system can find a best answer for the user.

Figure 10. Semantic++ Q/A model

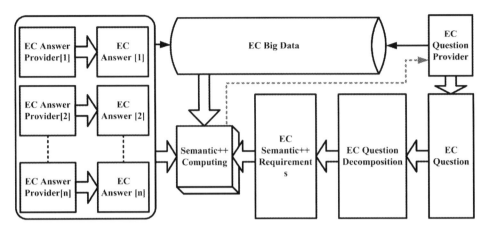

Active Semantic++ Electronic Commerce Model

Figure 11 shows the active semantic++ electronic commerce model.

From Figure 11, we can see that the active electronic commerce model involve six parts, which are active semantic++ electronic commerce system (rule processing engine), buyers, sellers, banks/financial enterprises, logistics and CA.

1.   Active semantic++ electronic commerce system (rule processing engine)

It is the electronic commerce web site, and a rule processing engine is embedded in this web site. People can set all kinds of semantic++ rules in this web site.

Figure 11. Active semantic++ electronic commerce model

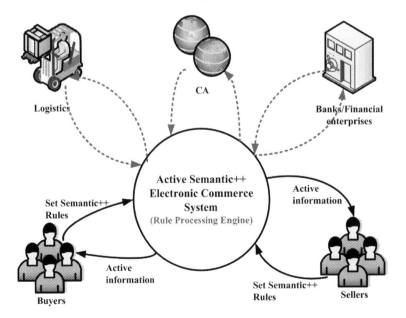

2.   Buyers

Buyers can set their semantic++ rules in the semantic++ electronic commerce system. If the conditions are satisfied, they will get the purchasing information from the web site automatically.

3.   Sellers

Sellers can set their semantic++ rules in the semantic++ electronic commerce system. If the conditions are satisfied, they will get the sales information from the web site automatically.

4.   Banks/financial enterprises

They will provide the finance services for buyers of sellers.

5.   Logistics

They will provide the logistics services for buyers of sellers.

6.   CA

It will provide the certification services for buyers of sellers.
Figure 12 shows an example of active semantic++ Beijing farm products EC system.

Figure 12. Active semantic++ Beijing agricultural e-commerce trade system

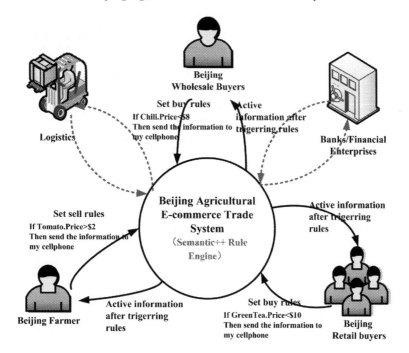

In the Beijing agricultural E-commerce trade system, there is a semantic++ rule engine. It can provide active electronic commerce services for Beijing farmers, Beijing retail buyers, Beijing wholesale buyers, logistics and banks/financial enterprises so on.

For example, the Beijing farmer can set a semantic++ rules as the follows.

IF

Tomato. Price>$2

Then

Notify the information "Hello, the tomato's price is good, please to contact the buyers and sale your tomato" to the farmer's cell phone.

FUTURE RESEARCH DIRECTIONS

With the development of big data, how to utilize the big data technologies into the electronic commerce will become the trend in the future. Figure 13 shows the framework of electronic commerce based on big data.

Figure 13 gives the future research directions of EC. It includes six parts, which are:

Figure 13. Future research directions of EC

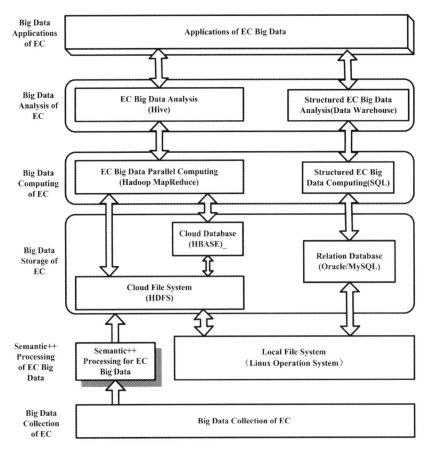

1. Big data collection of electronic commerce.
2. Semantic++ processing of electronic commerce big data.
3. Big data storage of electronic commerce.
4. Big data computing of electronic commerce.
5. Big data analysis of electronic commerce.
6. Big data applications of electronic commerce.

CONCLUSION

In this paper, we propose a kind of new electronic commerce architecture in the cloud and provide two kinds of semantic++ electronic commerce models. At first, we make a discussion about why do we need a new electronic commerce architecture. After the discussion, we give the architecture that can satisfy the requirements in the cloud. Then we make a detail analysis about some key technologies such as the semantic cloud file system, HUABASE database, semantic MapReduce technologies, semantic rule language, and semantic rule engine, CPKI security model in the cloud and some law issues in the cloud. Finally, we introduce two kinds of semantic++ electronic commerce models, which are semantic++ electronic commerce Q/A model and active semantic++ electronic commerce model.

ACKNOWLEDGMENT

This research was supported by the Support Program of the National '12th Five-Year-Plan' of China under Grant No. 2015BAK25B04 and National Basic Research Program of China (973 Program) No.2011CB302302.

REFERENCES

Abouzeid, A., Bajda, K., & Abadi, D. (2009). HadoopDB: An architectural hybrid of MapReduce and DBMS technologes for analytical workloads. In *Proceedings of VLDB2009* (pp. 922-933). VLDB.

Aliresearch, C. (2011). *Across the critical point: 2011 annual net development research report.* Retrieved October 1, 2012, from http://www.aliresearch.com/index.php?m-cms-q-view-id-68642.html

Amazon, C. (2009). *Amazon SimpleDB getting started guide API version.* Retrieved September 2, 2012, from http://docs.amazonwebservices.com/AmazonSimpleDB/latest/GettingStartedGuide/Welcome.html

Astrahan, M. M. (1976). System R: Relational approach to database management. ACM Transactions on Database Systems, 1(2), 97-137.

Avinash, L., & Prashant, M. (2010). Cassandra - A decentralized structured storage system. *ACM SIGOPS Operating Systems Review, 44*(2), 35-40.

Biswanath, P., Herbach, J., & Basu, S. (2009). PLANET: Massively parallel learning of tree ensembles with MapReduce. In Proceeding of Very Large Data Base (pp. 1426-1437). Lyon, France: Academic Press.

Bu, Y.Y., Howe, B., & Balazinska, M. (2010). HaLoop: Efficient iterative data processing on large clusters. In *Proceeding of Very Large Data Base* (pp. 285–296). VLDB.

Buchman, A. P., Branding, H., Kudrass, T., & Zimmermann, J. (1992). REACH: A real-time, active and heterogeneous mediator system. IEEE Data Engineering Bulletin, 15(1-4), 44-47.

Ceri, S., Fraternali, P., Paraboschi, S., & Letizia, T. (1992). Constraint enforcement through production rules: Putting active databases at work. IEEE Data Engineering Bulletin, 15(1-4), 10-14.

Chakravarthy, S. (1989). HiPAC: A research project in active time-constrained database management. Xerox Advanced Information Technology.

Christopher, W., Erlanger, K., & Wasim, A. (2011). PKI and access control in office environments. In *Proceedings of the 2011 Information Security Curriculum Development Conference* (pp. 20-24). Al-Hamdani Kentucky State University.

Chun, Z., & Chunxiao, X. (2011). *Huabase database report*. Retrieved September 2, 2012, from http://www.huabase.cn

Dayal, U., & McCarthy, D. (1989). The architecture of an active database management system. In *Proceedings of ACM SIGMOD Conf.* (pp. 215-224). ACM.

De Kruijf, M., & Sankaralingam, K. (2009). MapReduce for the cell broadband engine architecture. *IBM Journal of Research and Development, 53*(5), 1–12. doi:10.1147/JRD.2009.5429076

Deng, D., & Phillip, C. S. (2006). DPSSEE: A distributed proactive semantic software engineering environment. In Advances in machine learning applications in software engineering (pp. 409-438). Academic Press.

Dittrich, J., Quian'e, J.A., & Jindal, A. (2010). Hadoop++: Making a yellow elephant run like a cheetah (without it even noticing). In *Proceedings of VLDB2010* (pp. 518–529). VLDB.

Doug, B., Sanjeev, K., & Harry, C. L. (2010). *Finding a needle in Haystack: Facebook's photo storage*. Retrieved October 2, 2012, from http://static.usenix.org/event/osdi10/tech/full_papers/Beaver.pdf

EDITORIAL. (2010). Grid computing, high performance and distributed application. *Concurrency and Computation, 22*(11), 1433–1449.

Fahl, G., Risch, T., & Sköld, M. (1993). AMOS - An architecture for active mediators. In *Proceedings of Intl. Workshop on Next Generation Information Technologies and Systems*. NGITS.

Fay, C., Jeffrey, D., & Sanjay, G. (2006). Bigtable: A distributed storage system for structured data. In *Proceedings of OSDI'06: Seventh Symposium on Operating System Design and Implementation* (pp. 205-218). OSDI.

Forgy, C. L. (1982). Rete: A fast algorithm for the many pattern/many object pattern match problem. *Artificial Intelligence, 19*(1), 17–37. doi:10.1016/0004-3702(82)90020-0

Gatziu, S., & Dittrich, K. R. (1992). SAMOS: An active object-oriented database system. *A Quarterly Bulletin of the Computer Society of the IEEE Technical Committee on Data Engineering, 15*(1-4), 23–26.

Ghoting, A., & Pednault, E. (2009). Hadoop-ML: An infrastructure for the rapid implementation of parallel reusable analytics. In A. Culotta (Ed.), *Proc. of the Large-Scale Machine Learning: Parallelism and Massive Datasets Workshop* (pp. 38–48). Vancouver, Canada: MIT Press.

Hanson, E. N. (1992). Rule condition testing and action execution in ariel. In *Proceedings of ACM SIGMOD Conf* (pp. 49-58). ACM.

He, M., Jennings, N. R., & Leung, H.-F. (2003). On agent-mediated electronic commerce. *IEEE Transactions on Knowledge and Data Engineering*, *15*(4), 985–1003. doi:10.1109/TKDE.2003.1209014

Hypertable, C. (2012). *Overview of hypertable*. Retrieved October 2, 2012, from http://hypertable.com/documentation/

Jaliya, E., Hui, L., & Bingjing, Z. (2010). Twister: A runtime for iterative MapReduce. In *Proceedings of the First International Workshop on MapReduce and its Applications* (MAPREDUCE'10) (pp. 110-119). Academic Press.

JBoss C. (2009). *Drools introduction*. Retrieved September 2, 2012, from http://docs.jboss.org/drools/release/5.5.0.Beta1/droolsjbpm-introduction-docs/pdf/droolsjbpm-introduction-docs.pdf

Jianling, S., & Qiang, J. (2010). *Scalable RDF store based on HBase and MapReduce: Advanced computer theory and engineering*. ICACTE.

Joo-Kwan, L., & Moon-Seog, J. (2010). Security protocol design for electronic-cash transactions in a mobile-PKI environment. In *Proceedings of the 2010 IEEE/ACIS 9th International Conference on Computer and Information Science* (pp. 887-891). IEEE.

Junsheng, W. (2005). The thinking of securities on electronic commerce. In *Proceedings of the 7th International Conference on Electronic Commerce* (pp. 45–47). Academic Press.

Kim, Ostrowski, Yamaguch, & Sheu, P.C.-Y. (2013). Semantic computing and business intelligence. *Int. J. Semantic Computing*, 87-117.

Hao, Gong, Huo, & Sheu. (2011). Semantic computing and computer science. *Int. J. Semantic Computing*, *5*(1), 95–120.

Chung, Wang, & Sheu. (2011). Video summarisation based on collaborative temporal tags. Online Information Review, 35(4), 653 – 668.

Ikeda, Sheu, & Tsai. (2010). Object relational OLAP. *International Journal of Tools with Artificial Intelligence, 19*(5), 551-595.

Kovoor, G., Singer, J., & Lujan, M. (2010). Building a java map-reduce framework for multi-core architectures. In *Proc. of the HiPEAC* (pp. 87-98). Pisa: HiPEAC Endowment.

Lin, J., & Schatz, M. (2010). Design patterns for efficient graph algorithms in MapReduce. In *Proc. of the KDD* (pp. 78-85). Washington, DC: ACM Press. 10.1145/1830252.1830263

Lohman, G. M., Lindsay, B., Pirahesh, H., & Schiefer, K. B. (1991). Extensions to Starburst: Objects, types, functions and rules. Communications of the ACM, 34(10), 94-109.

Miranker. D. P. (1987). TREAT: A better match algorithm for AI production systems. In *Proceedings of AAAI 87 Conference on Artificial Intelligence* (pp. 42-47). AAAI.

Morgenstern, M. (1983). Active databases as a paradigm for enhanced computing environments. In *Proc. 9th VLDB Conf.* VLDB.

Phillip, C. S., & Kitazawa, A. (2007). From semantic objects to semantic software engineering. *International Journal of Semantic Computing, 1*(1), 11-28.

Production, I. (2012). *Benchmarking CLIPS/R2.* Retrieved September 2, 2012, from http://www.pst.com/rete2.htm

Sanjay, G., Howard, G., & Shun-Tak, L. (2003). The Google file system. In *Proceedings of 19th Symposium on Operating Systems Principles* (pp. 29-43). Lake George, NY: Academic Press.

Sheu, P.C-Y., Kitazawa, A., Ishi, C., Kaneko, K., & Xie, F. (2007). From semantic objects to structured natural language. *Int. J. Semantic Computing, 1*(3), 359-375.

Sheu. (2007). Editorial preface. *Int. J. Semantic Computing, 1*(1), 1-9.

Sheu & Ramamoorthy. (2009). Problems, solutions, and semantic computing. *Int. J. Semantic Computing, 3*(3), 383-394.

Stonebraker, M., & Row, L. (1986). The design of POSTGRES. In *Proceedings of ACM SIGMOD Conf.* Washington, DC: ACM.

Taobao, G. (2010). *TFS introduction.* Retrieved October 2, 2012, from http://www.taobaodba.com/html/tag/fs

Wang, & Sheu. (2010). Synthesis of relational web services. *Int. J. Semantic Computing, 4*(3), 385-417.

Wang, & Sheu. (2010). Applying syntactical information in web search. *Int. J. Semantic Computing, 4*(4), 535-558.

Widom, J., & Finkelstein. S.J. (1990). Set-oriented production rules in relational database system. In *Proceedings of ACM SIGMOD Conf* (pp. 259-270). Academic Press.

Ying, Li, & Sheu. (2008). A GA-based approach to optimizing combinatorial queries in SCDL. *Int. J. Semantic Computing, 2*(2), 273-289.

KEY TERMS AND DEFINITIONS

Active Electronic Commerce: People can receive information automatically. For example, when the consumers set the semantic++ rules in a EC web site, when the conditions have been satisfied, the EC web site can send the triggered information to users automatically.

Cloud Database: All kind of distributed database systems such as the Hadoop HBase and Google BigTable so on.

Cloud File System: All kind of distributed file systems such as the Hadoop Distributed file system (HDFS) and Google File System (GFS) so on.

HUABASE Database: It is a kind of distributed database. It runs on top of the semantic cloud file system. HUABASE is a kind of column-based database. It adapts the new storage model and it can improve the performance a lot in some key technologies optimization. HUABASE is not only good at processing OLTP applications, but also especially is good at processing OLAP applications. It can help companies to make good decisions after the analysis for massive data. It developed by Tsinghua University. http://www.huabase.cn/

Semantic Computing: It is based on the traditional computing such as the Ontology, Tag and others traditional computing technologies.

Semantic+ Computing: The semantic+ computing combines the artificial intelligence, nature language processing, knowledge engineering, data engineering, software engineering, computer system, computer network, signal processing and pattern recognition into a completed system. And it will consider their interaction each other. It will exact all kinds of the semantics from the multimedia, text, service and structured data so on. The most important is that the semantic+ computing will utilize the nature processing technologies to construct an interface which close to the human-like thinks. It is the most differences between the semantic computing and semantic+ computing. It is proposed by Phillip C-Y Sheu (UCIrvine). It can be summarized as semantic+ computing= semantic computing + Human-Machine Interface close to the human thinking.

Semantic++ Computing: Semantic++ Computing is a kind of advanced computing based on the human's ideas. It can process very complex semantics such as "what is the hottest topic in the Twitter in USA?", "What do the Beijing people like to buy in the Ebay web site?" and "How to judge the relationships between the Haze and the car numbers in a city" so on. Just like the description in the front, the semantic++ computing have more semantics than the traditional semantic computing. We can summarize the semantic++ computing into a formula: Semantic++ Computing=Semantic Computing + Human-Machine Interface close to the human thinking+ Big Data. Figure 2 shows the basic mechanism of the semantic++ computing.

Semantic++ Rule: It is a kind of rule which based on the semantic++ computing. This kind of rule can be set by everyone including the users.

This research was previously published in Strategic E-Commerce Systems and Tools for Competing in the Digital Marketplace edited by Mehdi Khosrow-Pour, D.B.A., pages 1-25, copyright year 2015 by Business Science Reference (an imprint of IGI Global).

Chapter 41
Better Security and Encryption Within Cloud Computing Systems

K. Y. B. Williams
Walden University, USA

Jimmy A. G. Griffin
NETE Solutions, USA

ABSTRACT

Better security and encryption is necessary with regard to all forms of Cloud Computing, Cloud Infrastructure, and Cloud Storage. Areas that are affected the hardest by security breaches include: retail/e-commerce, communications, transportation, and banking. Illustrated within this article are ways that companies such as Walmart, Verizon, Wells-Fargo, and BWM would be affected by a lapse in security and/or a breach in their Cloud Infrastructure. In this article issues that can magnify these breaches and data loss is discussed as it relates to Cloud Structure and Cloud Services based on known vulnerabilities and lack of product testing. This article concludes with why it is necessary to have Public Policies as part of the governing system on Cloud Computing, Cloud Infrastructure, and Cloud Storage

INTRODUCTION

Security has always been an issue with any type of new innovation. Whether securing the information, technology, design details, or schematics of the newly developed innovation (from the public) before initial release to the public, to securing the new innovation, technology, design details, schematics, and/or information once it has been released, to securing the next updates and improvements on existing technology and improvements on the technology, security at each stage of development is necessary and important. With any lapse of security at any of these stages the results can range from financial loss to loss of intellectual property as a whole. It is not surprising that any lapse in security on any of these levels will result in law suits from one company claiming another company had infringed upon their intellectual property, trade secrets, or may have engaged in espionage (corporate and/or cyber) to gain

DOI: 10.4018/978-1-5225-8176-5.ch041

an advantage that they could only have gotten from looking at the existing or new technology from the company and/or from the company's prior innovations, design details, schematics, and/or proprietary information. Therefore, it is imperative that security measures are built into ever level of the process: from design to production, and even after the technology is obsolete.

Once the technology is considered obsolete, it is usually decommissioned, even if the technology has been decommissioned, the need for storage of that information in the form of Data Storage is still needed. An old design can still produce a wealth of information on how to improve on the existing technology, and also on how to think about new forms of innovation based off older designs. Therefore, securing the designs is important, as the designs and design concepts can lead to new ideas and lead to new innovations, and these new innovations can result in new forms of technology based on one concept (resulting in intellectual property). Therefore, security at the storage level is just as important as securing the designs of the developed technology and when transporting the information to/from/and within the data storage facility.

When transporting information from one facility to another, any and all researchers will state that once the amount of data reaches a certain level, it becomes necessary to move large volumes of data via external hard drives as communication networks and file transfer protocols will be slowed based on the sheer volume of data. Although it is possible to send the data via a secured network, the reliability that all the data will be captured and received within a reasonable and suitable timeframe may be a concern for any company that is transmitting any proprietary form of technology. Therefore, encryption of the information when in transit is essential, whether via network transport over a secured system connection or via external hard drive.

Encryption has become the solution for many security issues as it has advantages that allows the user of the system to get around various security issues that can be found within computing systems, and within the products that they are used on a daily basis. However, it is not impossible to get the information once it is encrypted, but it does make it more difficult to get to the actual information once it is encrypted. By using encryption methods, it allows the company, security team, system administration, and user to have a sense of feeling protected and viewing the data as being unreadable and possibly "irretrievable" in an encrypted form. However, encryptions can be broken and the information can be retrieved given enough skill, computing time, and processers.

Therefore, better security and encryption methods is necessary at all stages of development and in the processing, transport, and storage of information within all forms of computing systems especially on-demand systems such as Cloud Systems.

Within this article, a discussion on security, encryption, and how to improve on the current forms of security and encryption is discussed. Within this article, it will be necessary to look at some of the major companies in various markets to illustrate, discuss, and speculate on the effect that an unwanted intrusion would have on the company. The discussion and speculation will focus on: the reputation of the company, customer base, and their system design if their systems were penetrated. For illustrative purposes, the companies that will be used include: Walmart, Verizon, Wells Fargo and BMW. In the illustrations, the view point that will be used is based on the vulnerabilities that exists within the infrastructure of Cloud Systems.

BACKGROUND

Cloud Computing and its infrastructure has many advantages and capabilities that goes beyond the traditional or standard model of IT. Where IT systems administrators once had to constantly provision and configure their servers, system, and user accounts, then re-provision and re-configure a system based on the needs of the user, the advent of Cloud Computing and the design of Cloud Infrastructures and services allows for the dynamic provision and configuration of the system based on the needs of the user and the on-demand nature of the user.

Presumably when one secures a device (phone, computer, car, or home) they expect it to be protected, untouched, safe, and impenetrable. Additionally, when the system is encrypted, users of the system believe that the added layer of security and protection is used to make the system as secure and protected as possible. This is usually true, but all forms of encryption can be broken give enough computing time and processors. Finally, monitoring of the system adds the final layer of protection to a system that leaves the company, security team, system administrator, and user with a feeling that they are totally "safe and secure" and their information is protected from harm; however, this is a fallacy.

With the advances in current technology and internet technologies that have been discovered, improvements on existing technologies, and the increase in capabilities of current technologies, securing technology in the 21st century is becoming more difficult by the day. Many systems that exist exist in a state where the newly configured system is based on physical hardware that required manual intervention and necessary work-orders to get a machine configured to a form that can be used by anyone. This means that Systems Administrators must be able to get the updates, patches, and information even in a secured network. By allowing the computers to reach out to unsecured networks or repositories on the internet it allows for security issues to be announced and used for exploitation. When those security issues are not removed in a timely fashioned, these issues make it possible for intrusions. Therefore, they require intervention from the System Administrator to patch the system, complete the provisioning for the initial system, and re-purpose the hardware from the initial system to bring the system to a known secured state to ensure that nothing within the system or the connections to the system were compromised.

Cloud Systems and Cloud Computing has many areas of concern for companies, as some of the issues that have surfaced in the areas of Cloud Computing resides in the use of products such as OpenStack's Compute, Storage, and Network Infrastructure; Large Volume Encryption; Ceph Storage; Encryption used within High Performance Computing (HPC) systems, and Seagate's Kinetic Open Storage. Encryption and security in Cloud Systems such as the aforementioned systems and other cloud systems have inherent security issues that are compounded by increased advances in technology and improvements on existing technology. With new capabilities being brought online each day and improvements to existing technology, it compounds the security issues over time. Therefore, it is not surprising that patches, fixes, and increases in the number of securities/dependencies cannot be corrected as quickly as the technology is improving. Development of new technologies without removing former security issues leaves many openings and flaws in security systems that have not been corrected and allows for exploitation. When the issues are part of a Cloud System, it allows for exploitation from computers, cell phones, tablets, or any other electronic or handheld device.

MAIN FOCUS OF THE PAPER

Stored, Secured, Protected, Trusted, Monitored, Reassured

Words that describe the users experience (or perceived experiences) when using online systems, accessing on-demand services, working with Cloud Services, and with companies such as Walmart, Wells Fargo, Verizon, and/or BMW. However, if any of these companies are have a lapse in security that results in data loss, an unwanted intrusion, or their security procedures and protocols are completely hacked or their defenses are penetrated by unwanted intruders, it leaves the consumer with concerns about the company, and it then leaves the company's reputation at stake. Then the consumer would question the company and worry about the information that they entrusted to the company, and wonder if that information is still safe and secure, and what repercussion(s) it will have on their lives now and/or in the future.

To illustrate the point, let's explore each of these companies to review how an unwanted intrusion, denial of service, or security incident would affect each of the areas. Each of these companies listed represent one area of the daily activities that normal consumers used in their daily lives based on local and global services. The average consumer can complete 75% of their normal daily transactions and activities by interacting with each of these areas and/or these companies. Additionally, each of these companies hold a large percentage of the market place, and support daily activities of millions of consumers.

- **Walmart:** Local/Global online retailers and neighborhood markets such as Walmart has a large number of customers that rely of the security and storage of their cloud system. Walmart supplies groceries, produce, normal household goodies, and activities in the way of bill payments and banking. However, Walmart Canada has been vulnerable to security lapses via the Walmart.com website as user's information was compromised and resulted in over 60,000 customers information being compromised (Iyer, 2015).
- **Wells-Fargo:** E-commerce in a local and global financial market can be hampered if Wells Fargo experiences any of the issues that were recently perpetrated by hackers into the financial and banking area which resulted in hackers stealing up to $1 Billion (Snider and Whitehouse, 2015). Wells-Fargo represents the area of e-commerce, banking, mortgages, and personal savings.
- **Verizon:** Communications within local areas, global areas, and in storage would hinder and hurt the reputation of Verizon if any of their Cloud Systems were affected by a breach, a leak, or unwanted intrusions that occurred in data storage or personal information. Verizon represents the communications industry, digital streaming, digital storage, and computer processes. Even tough Verizon denies a hack result in the loss of data from their communication system occurred, the service cannot deny that a denial of service did occur with their system (Singh, 2014).
- **BMW:** Hacking the electronic system within personal transportation vehicles such as cars have caused great concern for BMW and other companies as a result of reports of vehicles being hacked and the footage of such exploits being placed on Internet sites with instructions on how to hack various types of cars using the known vulnerabilities. BMW represents the area of personal transportation. However, the auto industry giant did experience a violation that resulted in video showing how two million automobiles were left vulnerable as a result of a security flaw that exists within their automobiles on-board systems (Bigelow, 2015).

Although each of these companies may not have had unwanted intrusions in the way of security issues, some have had issues with lapses in security. If each of those companies have the same system that had the same security flaws that were not patched, addressed after being configured and provisioned, or had issues resulting from Cloud Storage and/or Cloud Services then they would all be vulnerable to attack from different sources.

Ed Anderson, Gartner research vice president stated, "When cloud services are introduced, organizations, have to rethink their operating processes if they want to recognize the benefits of cloud. Whereas cloud services are dynamic, flexible, available on-demand, etc., many organizations do not operate assuming their technology has these attributes." (Anderson, 2015) Cloud services has an allure that attracts many companies. This allure exists in the way of scalability, storage, hardware installation, software compatibility, climate controlling of systems, scheduling, connections, and connection speeds.

At the forefront of anyone's mind when working in a secured environment and cloud deployment should me the following issues that attacks customers to cloud computing: scalability (of the system over time); storage (and data retrievable units); hardware installation (and space limitations of the compute system); software compatibility (and updates to the operating system); climate control (to guard against death of the servers); scheduling (as users must share the new system and demands of the system can and will grow), and connections and connection speeds to and from the servers within a secure environment.

However, these are not the only reasons that companies look to cloud adoption and cloud processes. Cliff Grossner, Ph.D., research director at Infonetis Research/HIS Research, found that enterprises look to cloud adoption for numerous reason, including for improve application performance, quicker access to new technologies, better agility in responding to business needs, and faster application deployment (Anderson, 2015). It is the suggested that before arrival of the new computing system, additional challenges within the system should be explored as similar systems may have the same vulnerabilities that exists and, if the companies are using the same Cloud System then they each of the companies may be vulnerable to the issues that reside in each of the systems. If these issues arise then they could hinder the compute cluster, cloud storage, data processing, and data retrievable while making all the data that is on the system vulnerable to any intrusion. Usually those challenges may not be a priority for others but they have shown to be an issue when an intrusion occurs. Usually, computer architects and system engineers stop to think about issues such as structural design and networking issues, access to the data and the level of security of the data when they are developing a system. However, this type of concern, if not carried across the entire process, can result in security lapses.

When such challenges arise, by having a forward-thinking mindset, and coordinating the efforts of the System Administrator with the efforts of members of a networking department, it is possible to review the variety of vendors and platforms that cater to the different business infrastructures and the companies computing infrastructure. Companies such as Red Hat OS, Cent OS, simpler Linux environments and Ubuntu can become options for a company depending on the system.

However, challenges in the way of the users and the preparing for the new future of their computing system can be an internal issue as well as an external issue. Cliff Grossner also stated, "Enterprises unprepared for cloud adoption find that cloud-based systems make certain assumptions about enterprise operations and employee workflows." (Anderson, 2015) Systems that are created by open-source developers gives rise to many concerns as the aspect of preparation that is needed to get "up and running" in a short period of time is of concern, and these systems make it possible for anyone who desires access to Cloud Systems and Cloud Services to have access to the best possible technologies even if they are working with a limited budget. These open-source technologies allow for Information Technology professionals that possess little or no experience to experts in the field of computing system design and implementation to be productive on the system, but it does not mean that each system has been properly configured, patched, and placed into production.

Many options existed that any member of the IT profession can chose from and this would define the environment and the system. Most systems and companies tend to go with pre-packaged default installations that can meet most of the user's needs and are probably customized based on the area and the anticipated use of the system. However, at times the need may arise for a customized system and this may mean some applications, products, and systems may have to take an a la carte approach of the system in order to satisfy the needs of the company. This may mean building a system with components that are proprietary coupled with open-source material. For instance, coupling the following services and products together for a system: Metal as a Service (MaaS), Juju, VMWare and OpenStack, with schedulers such as Torque or Oracle Grid Engine (SGE), with Apache web servers to handle PHP coding and the HTML environment. With this type of setup, a forward thinking and forward looking company focused on Scale Out Technology, Big Data problems and development of clouds and computing systems would place themselves at risk by each of the components within the list as known vulnerabilities exists within each of the components listed. In the case of Walmart, Wells-Fargo, Verizon, and BWM if the known issues are not addressed, patched, and secured they would be vulnerable to unwanted intrusions.

If one was to select options that are simple and straight forward on their new operating system and in the packages on the system such as MaaS and JuJu then additional vulnerabilities would exist as MaaS allows one to attach, commission, and set up physical servers in record time, however the system administrator should have the wherewithal to secure the system based on the packages and updates to the software. With cloud systems modifying nodes between services can be very dynamical, and one can keep them up to date with little effort, and in due course retire them from use when finished. This is only one of the attractive feature of a cloud system, and it makes it easy to setup the servers on which to deploy any service that needs to scale up and down dynamically while Juju manages the services. However, if the environment is not secure then the system can dynamically scale into areas that would leave data on unsecured environments and allow for data loss as unsecured data could be easily retrieved.

What is needed to ensure that these types of issues are addressed properly on all levels is the development of Public Policies and Public Administration of these policies on a governmental and global scale. The structuring of these policies can be added to the current Data Security and Breach Notification Act of 2015. Because cyber intrusions, data loss, and cyber espionage occurs at an alarming rate in the current Cloud System provisions on how the systems should be designed, built, installed, tested, patched, and secured should be a national and global concern for companies, businesses, and facilitates that work with the public in any capacity. Although these articles look at the various areas of security and encryption and discusses how companies and rivals have penetrated "secure and monitored" systems and the flaws that exists within each of these systems, it is necessary to state the companies should have requirements that have to be met before they place a product onto the market since the customers will be affected the most by a data loss or a data breach to the company's system.

It is generally understood that encryption is necessary with regard to e-commerce, banking, communications, and transportation and it will affect global industrial companies such as Walmart, Wells Fargo, Verizon, and BMW as their services are utilized by millions. However, if they possess services and products that have been deployed to Cloud Systems that have been infiltrated by unwanted intrusions then this can have a lasting and proud effect on the company's reputation and customer base.

SOLUTIONS AND RECOMMENDATIONS

Recommendations and solutions to the issues and flaws that reside within Cloud Computing can range from the initial design of the product or service to the end product that is sold on the market. However, in order to address the issues that reside in the design and the product that is sold on the market, additional effort in the way of research and technology upgrades to sufficiently evaluate, and determine the security exposure and encryption of the system is necessary. If this type of information is not ascertained prior to the product going on the market then the security issues that exists will leave many users of the systems vulnerable to cyber-attacks and to unwanted intrusions.

Every computer and/or computing system that have ever been designed will have flaws in the design, errors as a result of the installation and/or configuration, and vulnerabilities when placed in production. Addressing the issues of each of these areas prior to placing the product on the market would have allowed for better security and safe usage by the user if implemented correctly. In order to provide for a safe experience and better usage of a system, 6 key areas must be considered when trying to address the vulnerabilities that exists within the current state of development of Cloud Computing and Cloud Storage. These areas include: Encryption, Design based on Security, Security during Build and Design, Enhanced Security Standards, Patches, Standard Product Testing, and Product testing prior to the product entering the market.

Exploration of each of these areas lead to suggestions that can result in solutions and recommendations that can be used to understand how to address these issues.

Encryption

Better encryption is needed and this encryption should be impenetrable on all levels. Although current methods of encryption uses a key/value method for authenticating the information, complete encryption within the entire system should be explored as it can hold a means of safeguarding information as it passes through the system, from user to user, and to the outside network. However, this level of encryption will have an effect on processing speed and data access. This process would reduce the concern that information being captured or loss via infiltration would be retrievable or accessible if a system intrusion did occur.

Design Based on Security Standards

It is not impossible to re-design a system based on issues that exist with current system. However, exploration into designing a totally secure system based on the security standards that exists at certain timeframes and computer/computing standards should produce a fairly stable and secure system. This would entail decommissioning existing systems, learning from the errors, issues, and existing vulnerabilities, and then designing and building a system from scratch that removes these vulnerabilities and still allows for processing speed, data access and retrieval, and enhanced security.

Security During Build and Design

Security should be a concern at all stages of the design and build process; however, many companies leave security as a concern at the end of the process or for the customer that purchases the product or the service. One solution or recommendation would be to address the security concerns of the Cloud System at every stage of the process, and then remove those issues in the development (build and design) process as this would reduce the possibility that security issues would exist in the final product.

Enhanced Security Standards

Instead of waiting for the security issues to surface, companies should take a proactive approach to removing the issues that reside in the systems. This means enhancing and developing better security and encryption measures prior to customers requesting this in their systems. This in turn would enhance the reputation of the company and leave many to think of the company as a forward thinking company that is innovative and at the forefront of security and encryption.

Patches

Security on all levels should be explored as it is imperative to have a secure system that is free from vulnerabilities and from intrusions. It is not impossible to produce a system that would reduce the number of security patches, but this would enhance and enable additional research into this area to perform this recommendation.

Standard Product Testing

In addition to the normal product testing, the product should be tested on all levels internal to the company and external that is accessed by the customer. This includes testing by the customer, the user, developer, system administrator, security team, and ethical hackers (among others) that may try to gain access to the system. Prior to production and to placing the system on the market, penetration testing should be included in the testing phase as it allows for the reduction of patches/updates to the system that would be placed on the market. This would allow for determination of flaws prior to selling the product on the market; although all of the flaws will not be captured and resolved, product testing should be a large part of the process of designing a system. This method or area would assist with other areas in terms of patches, enhancing security standards, and connecting systems that are designed based on security.

FUTURE RESEARCH DIRECTIONS

Discussions within the area of Cybersecurity, Cloud Computing, and Cloud Storage have always revolved around ensuring that the users' information, data, and access is secure within their usage of the system and when accessing the system. Recent security lapses, unwanted intrusions, and data loss events that have occurred in the areas of banking, e-commerce, securities, transportation, and retail have led to new discussions concerning security and implementing new forms of computing systems as the current state of security procedures, processes, and levels of encryption is not enough. What is required are means to change the current system and standards and updating the systems to meet an industrial standard of computing, encryption, and product testing is needed and necessary for better connection of processes. However to do this, research must be conducted and questions that pertain to the state of Cloud Security must be answered.

Research within the fields of encryption and security can encompass many different paths based on the background and direction of the research, the background of the researcher, and the type of flaw that the researcher is exploring. Within this article six areas were focused on in terms of possible solutions that can address the issues in Cloud Computing and Cloud Storage: Encryption, Design based on Security Standards, Security during Build and Design, Enhanced Security Standards, Patches, and Standard Product Testing (prior to marketing).

Based on the approach and direction that the researcher takes and the questions that the researcher asks as it relates to the system, any new information in each of these areas can have a profound effect on the way that computer systems can be protected. With a focus on any of these areas, the results of the research and the questions can be used to enhance the current state of computing systems and allow for better product design and development. Within each of the areas simple and clear research questions can be asked and answered with the right approach, research plan, and research direction. However, having the infrastructure to test the results of the research and implement it in a secure environment would allow for better approaches and can lead to protection of the system, and within the systems. Some of the research questions that can be easily asked and answered in each of the areas include:

Encryption

Current encryption requires a method of authenticating the information and decrypting the information at the reception point; however, can encryption throughout all processes of Cloud Computing and data flow within the Cloud Structure and processes still allow for fast processing and data access, and still meet user demands?

Design Based on Security Standards

Using the current standards in network and computing security is it possible to design a completely, secure Cloud Computing service (from scratch) based on the security standards that currently exists? What factors would have to be reconsidered to enable the design of a system based on current security standards?

Security During Build and Design

During the build and design of a Cloud Computing service and system, security is not a major concern until the final product is provided; however, can building on the proper security during the build and design of a system reduce the security concerns once the final product is placed on the market?

Enhanced Security Standards

Security standards change and update as quickly as new innovations in computing systems are made; however, patches and updates are needed to meet the new innovations and to address the flaws in the technology. What measures must be taken to enhance the security standards that currently exist, and what policies should be developed to standardize the development of systems based on security concerns?

Patches

What security standards and good computing practices should be updated and designed to reduce the number of patches implemented each year?

Standard Product Testing

Companies test their product prior to selling the product on the market; however, flaws will still exist within products prior to the system being sold on the market. Even though companies are aware of the flaws, each flaw is not usually addressed prior to placing the product on the market. Research shows that the number of products that have been independently tested and certified reduces the number of flawed products on the market. In terms of research, how much effort would be required to test, verify, and certify that the product that is placed on the market is safe and secure for use (to the level of the current industry security standards)?

The results of any of the six areas proposed within this article can only improve the way that Cloud Computing Services and Cloud Storage can be enhanced in their security and design. Enhancing any of these six areas would not only improve the security of the systems and services that are supposed to protect the information that is stored and used within Cloud Systems, but it would also lead to changes and innovations in Network Infrastructure, Cloud Computing, Cloud Architecture, and Cybersecurity.

CONCLUSION

Cloud Computing and Cloud Storage has progressed within the digital age and have set the standard by which information can be processed, accessed, made available, and used within the current century. The strides that have been made within the computing field have increased as a result of the innovations that the field have made in terms of storage, services on demand, scalability, and networking; and the innovations in these four areas have allowed the cyber field to become an area of major concern. However, security within each of these areas have not converged to a point where the security in each of these areas have allowed the users of the systems to feel safe or secure in terms of their data and information storage. Security within these areas is not impenetrable and the number of flaws within these systems outweigh the benefits of the systems. Current usage of Cloud Computing and Cloud Storage have inherent flaws within the systems as a result of the lag of security that was not developed into the systems. These flaws are well known and have allowed outside users and hackers to infiltrate the Cloud Computing systems based on the flaws and the designs.

Cybersecurity has increased in recent years because of the need for better protection based on the innovations within the computing field and in the design of computer networks and overall networking infrastructure within cloud systems. Although Cybersecurity supposed to be able to protect users and computing systems against the criminal activities or unauthorized access and use of electronic systems, nothing is totally impenetrable when flaws within systems exists. The measures that one can take to achieve total security is limited by the experience, knowledge, creativity, and abilities of the developer and programmer that programmed the system, the system architect that designed the system, and the system administrator that have been charged with securing the system.

Within every system better encryption is needed. In order to improve on the systems it may be necessary to work within an entirely encrypted system. Encryption may be the answer that is needed to assist the developer, programmer, System Architect, Cloud Architect, and System Administrator with the issues that exists within the Cloud Computing system even within the current Cloud System. Working within one's own Cloud with information being passed in an encrypted fashion would seem pointless, but in the current computing landscape, it may be imperative to implement this type of system to safeguard the system from hackers and unwanted intrusions.

REFERENCES

Anderson, E. (2015, December). Managing Cloud Disruption. *CyberTrend, 13*(12), 16-17.

Bigelow, P. (2015). BWM Hack: The Auto Industry Big Cyber-Security Warning Sign. *Autoblog.com*. Retrieved January 1, 2016, from http://www.autoblog.com/2015/02/06/bmw-hack-cyber-security-warning-feature-video/

Iyer, K. (2015). Walmart Canada Hacked, Credit Card Details of 60,000 customers exposed. *Techworm*. Retrieved January 1, 2016, from http://www.techworm.net/2015/07/walmart-canada-hacked-credit-card-details-of-60000-customers-exposed.html

Singh, A. (2014). Verizon Wireless: Hacked or Billing System Down? *Androidorigin*. Retrieved January 1, 2016, from http://www.androidorigin.com/verizon-wireless-hack-billing-system-down

Snider, M., & Whitehouse, K. (2015). Banking Hack Heist Yields Up to $1 Billion. *USA Today*. Retrieved January 1, 2016, from http://www.usatoday.com/story/tech/2015/02/15/hackers-steal-billion-in-banking-breach/23464913/

KEY TERMS AND DEFINITIONS

Cloud Computing: Internet-based computing that uses shared resources, information, processors, and data to meet the demands of users as needed.

Cloud Storage: Physically-based storage that saves digital data in logical pools via shared resources and servers where the physical storage is usually owned and managed by a hosting company.

Encryption: The encoding of messages and information that allows only individuals with the proper authority to read the message or information.

Espionage: The practice of spying, infiltrating, eavesdropping, surveillance, or hacking to obtain political and/or military information, trade secrets, or intellectual property.

Intellectual Property: A work or invention that is the result of creativity, such as a manuscript or a design, to which one has rights and for which one may apply for a patent, copyright, and/or trademark.

Network: A group or system of interconnected people or things.

Security: The state of being free from danger or threat.

This research was previously published in the International Journal of Public Administration in the Digital Age (IJPADA), 5(2); edited by Manuel Pedro Rodríguez Bolívar, pages 1-11, copyright year 2018 by IGI Publishing (an imprint of IGI Global).

Chapter 42
Analyzing Virtualization Vulnerabilities and Design a Secure Cloud Environment to Prevent From XSS Attack

Nitin Nagar
Devi Ahiliya University, India

Ugrasen Suman
Devi Ahiliya University, India

ABSTRACT

Cloud virtualization has created an enormous impact on IT and networking worlds. A cloud environment is built on virtualization technology. Virtualization and its exclusive architecture have numerous features and advantages over non-conventional virtual machines. However, these new uniqueness create new vulnerabilities and attacks on a virtualization based cloud system. Cross Site Scripting (XSS) is among the top cloud vulnerabilities, according to recent studies. This exposure occurs when a user uses the input from a cloud environment application without properly looking into them. This allows an attacker to execute malicious scripts in cloud. The scripts execute harmful actions when a user visits the exploited cloud. Current approaches to mitigate this problem, especially on effective detection of XSS vulnerabilities in the application or prevention of real-time XSS attacks. To address this problem, the survey of different vulnerability attacks on cloud virtualization performed and also presents a concept for the removal of XSS vulnerabilities to secure the cloud environment.

1. INTRODUCTION

Cloud virtualization technology offers a direction to use IT resources among Virtual Machines (VMs) using hardware and software partitioning, emulation, time-sharing, resource sharing and so on. Traditionally, the OS manages the hardware resources, but virtualization technology adds a new layer between the operating system and hardware. A virtualization layer provides infrastructural support to an operating

DOI: 10.4018/978-1-5225-8176-5.ch042

system; therefore, multiple VMs can be created and managed independently. Virtualization layer is often called the hypervisor or Virtual Machine Monitor (VMM). A computer on which a hypervisor installed to control various virtual machines is defined as a host machine and each VM is called a guest machine. Various approaches are used to provide virtualization, such as para-virtualization (PV), full virtualization (FV), and hardware-assisted virtualization (HVM). PV requires changes to the client operating system when PV access to protect the resources and knowledge of the operating system on which the hypervisor is situated (Venkatesha, 2009). This mechanism simplifies the hardware abstraction layer, but provides difficulty between version control of the hypervisor and the PV operating system. FV supports unmodified guest passes through binary translation. VMware hypervisor uses the binary translation direct execution techniques for creating VMs on proprietary base operating system such as Windows (Buyya, 2011).

Several tools and techniques are used to implement cloud based virtualization. There exist commercial and open source solutions such as OpenNebula, Eucalyptus, Nimbus, OpenStack and so on (Nagar, 2012). The commercial solutions are Hyper-V, VMware, ESX, etc. It is observed that the open source solution such as OpenStack provides more flexibility than the other commercial solutions. Nevertheless, open source solutions suffer from a lack of documentation and are more difficult to enforce. The hypervisors, such as Hyper-V, KVM, Xen and VMware vSphere are used with this open source solution (Nagar, 2012). Hypervisor uses different architectures, although it is limited to hardware-assisted virtualization mode. The Windows-based Hyper-V delivers a significantly different architecture than the Linux based hypervisors. Xen and KVM are based on open-source modification of the Linux kernel, whereas VMware uses custom build functions (Nagar, 2012) (Hwang, 2013) (Clark, 2005). Xen hypervisor uses PV of separate management domain; controls the VMs, access to user defined block and network drivers. KVM considered as a core module that employs most of the Linux features. For example, instead of providing the CPU scheduler to VMs, each VM KVM treated as a process and uses the standard Linux scheduler to in order to allocate resources (Cherkasova, 2005). VMs services and cloud service providers offer more powerful and anchor ecosystem of cloud services. User provides their VMs and cloud provider leads them often without the knowledge of the guest operating system. Cloud providers, security-as-a-service based on VM introspection and ensures the best security (Christodorescu, 2009) (Kong, 2010).

Cloud virtualization threats and vulnerabilities are a foremost challenge in the field of research. The rest of the paper is organized as follows. Section 2 includes a virtualization security challenges and the associated issues in a cloud environment. The section 3 states literature reviews with virtualization threats and vulnerabilities. In section 4, we discuss the top most vulnerabilities of cloud virtualization named as XSS (Cross Site Scripting) attack or CSRF (Cross Site Request Forgery). We also discuss the seriousness of XSS attacks, their types and problems in XSS. In Section 5, we proposed work on XSS detection and recovery in the DOM. We also discuss the implementation work to solve the problems, HTML parsing, analyzing modification with Jsoup and performance evaluation of different aspects. In section 6, we state the conclusion and final, references of the paper.

2. VIRTUALIZATION SECURITY CHALLENGES AND ISSUES

The transmission of computing resources in a virtualized environment has unaffected on the majority of the resources through vulnerabilities and threats. For example, if service inherent vulnerabilities and service is moving from a non-virtualized server to a virtualized server, the revision is still as vulnerable to victimization. However, the usage of virtualization can help to reduce impact of such exploitation, but virtualization can provide additional attack vectors and therefore, increases the possibility of successful attacks. With this safety benefit of virtualization, there are following the challenges, risks and problems with virtualization.

2.1. File Sharing Between Hosts and Guests

File is used to share guest OS to access the host file system and modify or change the directories that are available for sharing. If clipboard is shared, and drop by the client and host or APIs are used by drag. The possibility of a significant error in this condition and it can affect the entire infrastructure.

2.2. Up-to-Date Snapshots

Images and snapshots contain proprietary information, such as PII (Personally Identifiable Information) and passwords, similar as physical hard drive. Any unnecessary or additional icons could be causes for security concern. If any crack is stored in the images that it is undetected malware then it could be recharged in the future date and cause destruction.

2.3. Network Storage

The fiber channel and iSCSI are clear-text protocols and they are vulnerable to Man-In-The-Middle (MITM) Attacks. Sniffing tools are used to recognize or trace memory traffic and it also can be helpful for the attackers to re-set up in the environments.

2.4. Hypervisor

Hypervisors can enable VMs to communicate each other, and the communication will not even go into the physical network and ends up acting as a private network for the VMs. This traffic cannot always be seen as it leads by the hypervisor. If the hypervisor is compromised, then all associated VMs will also be affected, and the default configuration to the hypervisor is not secure at all.

2.5. Virtual Machines

VMs are quite moderated and remote computers or portable storage devices easily copied in a cloud environment. The VM security concern is similar as physical server security which includes loss of data, a data center physical security, bypassing the time out and so on. Users do not always follow organization's security policies and any VMs installed security software. Whenever a virtual machine created another operating system, protected agreement is necessary to save, and that has to be added in advance. The additional operating system issues can increase the risk. Inactive VMs or VMs can no longer be used contain important information, such as credentials and configuration information.

2.6. Separation of Duties and Administrator Access

A network administrator manages specific physical network and server administrator deals with the server management. Security personnel usually work with these two areas. In the cloud virtualized environment, servers and network management from a single management console presents new challenges for an effective separation of tasks. By default, many cloud virtualization systems provide total access to all cloud infrastructure activities.

In spite of these issues, virtualization is difficult for software, and it provides more potential software vulnerabilities and attack surface for attackers to target. Virtual disks are usually placed in non-encrypted files on a host, and access to them is having legitimate access. Despite the countless issues mentioned, virtualization is not inherently uncertain, but the way it is used may be of an uncertain nature. Immature security policies and procedures as well as the lack of training may be the biggest concerns and vulnerabilities can run the risk more in cloud environments.

3. LITERATURE REVIEW

The architecture is built to protect the confidentiality of user data for the guest VM by building a virtualization platform based on Xen hypervisor. TPM (Trusted Platform Module) is integrated on the motherboard. Before the booting of the guest, VM user creates encrypted disk image of the root file system. Now, it is preparing to install a boot disk image grub on a hard drive and install a kernel. These two disk images send to the dom0 on the cloud server (Szefer, 2012). The cyber-physical security framework for data centers is proposed to combine the security mechanisms in cyber and physical space.

The framework is based on the time difference between the detection of attacks and the actual attack. It is based on the physical devices such as sensors. It is also possible to encrypt the defense mechanism to clear, and move from included data. The security mechanism is taken in accordance with the demands of the end user and granting to the type of data that are stored onto the host. The proposed logging VM mechanism is to secure logging of auditable file system. Auditing logs are classified in another VM on the same server. The logs will be usable by the separation of VMs to secure different VMs. Hence, the privileged user is denied access to change data by an unprivileged user (Zhao, 2009). Cloud-based VM security concerns such as threats of hypervisor security, data leakage, data protection, data issues with virtualization and virtualization layer attacks are analyzed (Wen, 2011). Security risks are compromising the virtual machine and the hypervisor itself. These threats include VM hope that VM exits in the mobility. In multi-tenancy environment data come from several organizations and users on the same physical location. In such systems, resources will be transparently shared between the VM and different users. Thus, a malicious user tries to control a VM to gain access to other VM or attempt to interfere with the data of the other VM. For this attacker uses the resources such as CPU, memory and network (Jasti, 2010). We can conclude the data storage and virtualization are the most critical attack area and virtualization layer have additional harm influence as compare to other layers from Table 1. The threats on different models in cloud environments, and also specifies the cloud service models are exposed to these threats shown in Table 2. We place more emphasis on threats associated with data storage and remote process request, sharing of resources and the uses of virtualization. The relationship between Cloud VM threats, vulnerabilities and their countermeasures is represented in Table 3.

Table 1. Virtualization vulnerabilities in cloud computing

Vulnerabilities ID	Vulnerabilities	Description	Model (SaaS, PaaS or IaaS)
VID1	Insecure Interface and APIs and Cross-site-scripting (XSS) or Cross-site Scripting Request Forgery (CSRF)	Cloud Service Provider (CSP) offers services that can be accessed via APIs such as SOAP, REST or HTML with XML / JSON. XSS attacks are basically injection attacks – a script is injected into the system – and then either executed on the users, or someplace during the processing on the backend. A cloud security depends on the protection of these interfaces. Some of the most significant problems are weak credentials, insufficient input data validation and authorization checks.. Cloud APIs are still Immature which means that are often updated. A fixed bug can introduce another security problem in whole cloud application.	Saas, PaaS and IaaS
VID2	Resource Allocation limitation	Inaccurate modeling resource usage can cause of over provisioning.	Saas, PaaS and IaaS
VID3	Vulnerabilities related to Data	Information can be shuffled with the information of unknown user, such as attacker or intruder with a weak separation. • Backups can be made via un-trusted third party providers. • Data location, different regions have different laws. • Users usually don't know the exact location of data.	Saas, PaaS and IaaS
VID4	VMs Vulnerabilities	Allocation and resource limitation de-allocation of VMs. • VM migration uncontrollably: VMs can be migrated from one server to another through load balancing, fault tolerance and maintenance of equipment. • Uncontrolled Snapshots: VMs are combined with the flexibility that will result in data loss. • Uncontrolled rollback can also back vulnerabilities: VMs can be backed up to a previous state of recovery, but patches of the prior used disappears. • IP addresses are visible to all in cloud environment: attackers can easily map where the target VM is located.	IaaS
VID5	Hypervisors Vulnerabilities	• Complex hypervisor code. • Flexible hypervisor and VM configuration can exploit the organization's need.	IaaS
VID6	VMs Network Vulnerabilities	Multiple VMs shared the different virtual bridges for communication.	IaaS
VID7	VMs Image Vulnerabilities	• Uncontrolled placement of VM images in the public repository. • VM images are not able to patch.	IaaS

4. CROSS SITE REQUEST FORGERY OR XSS ATTACK

CSRF or XSS attack on the virtualized cloud environment is a type of injection attack in which an attacker or hacker injected malicious scripts in a trusted cloud environment (John, 2011). In particular, XSS provides an attacker new dimension to attack along a cloud application across different cloud models with scripting option. For these types of attacks JavaScript is specified in the rule from the time when a malicious script is working. It offers total access to all the resources in the trusted cloud environment such as cookies, authentication tokens, etc. The targeted attack regions of an interloper are represented in Figure 1. The practical importance of research in XSS attacks and browser securities focuses from the security community in recent years (Kieyzun, 2009) (Louw, 2009) (Jakobsson, 2006). XSS recently is among the top most threat in the OWASP ranking (OWASP, 2014). The hosted application scanning management team at IBM found, 17 percent of the approximately 900 dynamic

Table 2. Virtualization threats in cloud computing

Threats ID	Threats	Description	Model (SaaS, PaaS or IaaS)
TID1	Data Leakage	Data loss happens when data is transmitted, stored, processed and tested and is in the wrong hand.	Saas, PaaS and IaaS
TID2	DoS(Denial of Service) or DDoS(Distributed Denial of Service)	When malicious user will read over entirely the possible privileges and resources. Therefore, the system cannot fulfill any request from other legal users due to resources being unavailable.	Saas, PaaS and IaaS
TID3	VM Escape	It is designed to utilize the hypervisor control of the underlying infrastructure.	IaaS
TID4	VM Hoping	It is executed when a VM is obtained capable of access to another VM. It uses some hypervisor vulnerabilities.	IaaS
TID5	Malicious VM Creation	An attacker could host a VM image contains malicious code as a Trojan horse and stored in the cloud provider repository.	IaaS
TID6	Insecure VM creation	Live migration of VMs exposes the contents of the VM's files on the network. An attacker may be performed the following actions: • An attacker can access data illegally during VM migration • An attacker could be passed VM in the un-trusted host. • Create and migrate multiple VMs cause harmful interference and DoS or DDoS attack.	IaaS
TID7	VM Network Sniffing/ Spoofing	A malicious VM can listen to the virtual network.	IaaS

Table 3. Relationship between cloud VM threats, vulnerabilities and countermeasures

VM Threats	VM Vulnerabilities	Occurrence	Countermeasures
TID1	$VID3_{1,2,3,5}$ $VID4_{1-5}$, $VID5_1$, VID7	The stairs to gather secret information in the same server as attacker VMs co-located. Side channel attacks in a VM environment.	For secure storage user can employ techniques such as FRS (Fragmentation Redundancy Scattering), Homomorphic Encryption, Encryption or Digital Signature.
TID2	VID1, VID2	Attackers can more computing resources ought to bear actual users are not able to obtain additional computing capacity through steals the browser side scripts.	CSP can only offer limited computing resources policy and guarantee the script from attackers.
TID3	$VID5_{1,2}$	An exploit in Hyper-VM virtualization applications that destroy millions of websites.	To secure VMs before launching user can employ the techniques such as HyperSafe, TCCP (Trusted Cloud Computing Platforms), TVDc (Trusted Virtual Data Centers).
TID4	$VID4_1$, $VID5_2$	Security flaws in most VMs monitors	Proper monitoring of VMs and filtering of illegal and legal users from the VM networks.
TID5	$VID7_{1,2}$	An attacker can produce a malicious VM image and publish it in a public depository.	User can use Mirage techniques to work out it.
TID6	$VID4_3$	An attacker against the migration functionality of the latest version of the Xen and VMware virtualization resources.	User can use the process to secure migration, such as PALM (Protection Aegis for Live Migration), TCCP or VNSS (Virtual Network Security Sandbox).
TID7	VID6	VM Spoofing and sniffing in virtual networks	Bridge and router in virtual framework of Xen hypervisor.

Figure 1. The attack on cloud application, server and storage

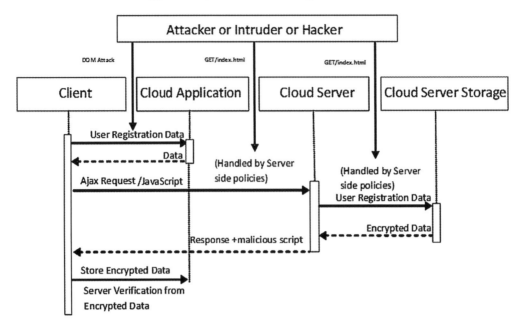

application scans showed vulnerability in XSS. Nevertheless, these data come from companies' robust and mature security systems. A report from White Hat Security Council (WHSC) finds that nearly half of all applications (47.9 percent) are vulnerable to XSS attacks (IBM, 2014). If the targeted end users have an administrator account then it can be exploited cloud application through CSRF or XSS attack. XSS is based on the following subsections.

4.1. Types of XSS

XSS can be classified into three categories such as non-persistent XSS, persistent XSS and DOM-based XSS. Description of XSS categories are discussed in following subsections.

4.1.1. Non-Persistent XSS

Non-persistent XSS is also experienced as a reflected XSS vulnerability. It is the common example of XSS, which injected by attacker to reflect the data of user. A typical non-persistent XSS contains a link with XSS vector.

4.1.2. Persistent XSS

Persistent XSS is also known as stored XSS or cross site scripting. These scripts occur when XSS vectors are stored in database and cloud application is run with unfolded pages by the user. Persistent XSS is more harmful, than the non-persistent XSS because the script is performed automatically when the user uses the cloud application. Orkut was vulnerable to XSS persistent, which ruined the name of the website.

4.1.3. DOM-Based XSS

DOM (Document Object Model) based XSS is a cross-site scripting vulnerability that is part of the HTML and seems to be transmitted in the DOM. In reflection and stored cross-site scripting attacks, users can find out the vulnerability of payload on the response side, but in the DOM-based cross-site scripting is the HTML source code of the response to the attack exactly the same browser and the payload cannot be initiated in the browser. DOM-based XSS is sometimes referred to as "Type 0 XSS". It occurs when the vector results XSS as a result of a DOM modification of a cloud application through a user's browser. On the user side of the HTTP response will not vary, but the script in a malicious manner. It is sited on the user side browser only. DOM based XSS attack occurs when users provided un-desired data in JavaScript using methods such as eval(), document. write() or innerHTML(). The main culprit for this part of the attack is JavaScript code. This is the most advanced and least known type of XSS attack on cloud virtual environment. Most of the time, this vulnerability occurs because the developer does not determine how it works.

In cloud computing, cross-site scripting (XSS) attacks are not similar to other cloud layer attacks. Attacks work as injecting code, usually through client-side scripting such as JavaScript as an output to a cloud application. The cloud environment has numerous injection areas, which include search areas, feedback, forums, and cookies that are vulnerable to cross-site scripting. The purpose of XSS attacks is to gather all cookie data, as cookies are common and regularly used incorrectly to store information such as session IDs and login details. Although client-side scripts cannot directly affect the server-side information, they manipulate in DOM to alter form values or change the build action to send the submitted data to the attacker's browser to gain information (Security-Intelligence, 2012). XSS attacks work, even if the site has an SSL connection and a script is run as a part of the secure site. Browsers cannot distinguish between legal and malicious cloud environment. Phishing email then injected into a display page for giving the attacker to full access of application through URL. This type of attack is known as non-persistent XSS attack. Cloud service providers are focused on reducing the response time of the VM. The proposed solution is not widely applied in existing response time. Thus, in this respect to attained security, we compromise between response time and security.

5. XSS DETECTION AND RECOVERY IN DOM

The existing solutions are implemented as an input filter mechanism to avoid XSS attack. But to deliver user's data as an input is not a good idea since we do not know how that data used by the applications (Bates, 2010). Filtering is the response from the server to the user request which also holds inserted data that is supplied by the user agent in the cloud virtualized environment. Hence the response from the server is filtered in the presence of malicious scripts. The proposed modified cloud applications, we first extract user data inserted from the response and if it is used for malicious scripts then we apply a filter on it. After straining it again payload embedded in the user's response. Our proposed solution uses DOM-based filtering mechanism for the spotting and removal of malicious scripts. This filtering mechanism uses an HTML parser to parse user data provided in DOM after filtering malicious script from the reaction and then result sends to the user's browser. The filter works with a white list based filtering mechanism. In this work, we have also incorporated 'post' method instead of the 'get' method to avoid other attacks (Nagar, Oct-2014). The attack through different malicious scripts is shown in Figure 2.

Figure 2. The attack through malicious script

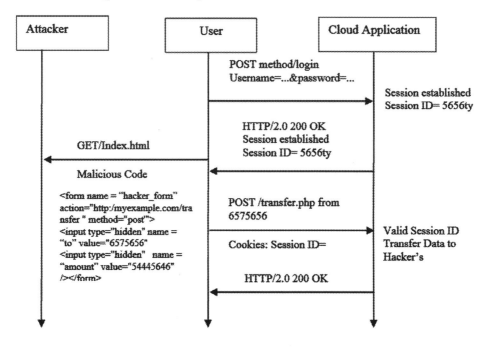

5.1. Implementation

We set up a functional sample where the concepts identified in this paper are placed into practice. The purpose of this section is to monitor the proposed working with filter scripts to control DOM-based XSS attacks. So, we demonstrate the feasibility and effectiveness of the integration models. For functional test on OpenStack, we use several virtual machines with M-pin authentication server and application to perform the analysis (Nagar, 2014).

The OpenStack identity service, known as the keystone which provide services for authentication and management of user accounts and role information in a private cloud computing environment (Report, Jan-2014). It is an important service that transmits the authentication and verification between Open-Stack and cloud services. Authentication mechanism ensures that the only legal user can access the other services such as storage and computing from (Nagar, 2014).

5.1.1. Parsing of HTML

HTML parser is a used to analyze HTML in either a linear or nested manner in the Java library. Primarily, it is used for transformation or extraction. It also content filters, record of visitors, custom tags and it is easily used with Java. HTML parser is fast, robust as well as tested software. There are a number of implementations done in the Java HTML parser. We compare them to upgrade to the bottom of the HTML parsing capabilities, handling of malformed HTML, clean HTML and support for HTML5 features. The comparison between different from HTML parser are represented in Table 4.

Table 4. Comparison of Various HTML Parser of JAVA

Parser	Implementation Language	HTML Update	Clean HTML	HTML Parsing
HTML Cleaner	JAVA	Unknown	Yes	No
Jaunt API	JAVA	Yes	Yes	No
Jericho HTML Parser	JAVA	No	Unknown	Unknown
Jsoup	JAVA	Yes	Yes	Yes
JTidy	JAVA	Yes	Yes	No

5.1.2. Modification of HTML Parsing

We modify the comments handling mechanism of the original Jsoup parser. Since there are many attack comment parsing quirks. We concentrate the Jsoup escapes the every ' (single-quotes), "(double-quotes) and \ with a backslash automatically. For example script>alert ("N") </script> will be filtered as <script>alert (\N\) </script>. So the attacker will not be able to attack on the script. With this we also integrate a hex coding, bypassing using obfuscation and closing tag to build Jsoup more robust.

5.1.3. Deployment of Filter

Java Filter Interface (JFI) is uses for filtering the server response from user (JavaFilter, 2014). For implementation of the filter we created a class named as FailedRequestFilter.java which will implement through Java Interface 'Filter'. In doFilter () method of this class we will chain the response to another class named 'LoginResponse.java' which extends by 'HttpServletResponse Wrapper'. In this call Java program extract user provided contents of the response and calling the filter API. The filtered output from the API is embedded in response and it is sent back to the user. In order to implicitly call the filter for every application request, we need to change in the 'Web.xml'. The updated Web.xml is shown in Figure 3.

5.1.4. Performance Evaluation of Proposed Work With Different Aspects

The M-pin provides two factor authentication server used to design a secure a cloud environment. M-pin authentication server and the cloud filter authentication server worked together. The filter between user and cloud server browser is represented in Figure 4. The equipments used to obtain the measurements are an Intel (R) Pentium (R) Core 2 Duo i3 processor (Virtual Technology enables machine), with 8 GB of RAM, running on Ubuntu 14.04 (LTS). For testing we have created on XSS vulnerable cloud application using JSP and Servlet deployed on Apache Tomcat 8.0 web server. It has enough resources to work. We have tested our filter on around 160 attack vectors from XSS cheat sheet, HTML5 security cheat sheet and other sources (Boganatham, 2009). Out of 160 attack vector some of them are not effective due changes in modern browsers. We have tested on 3 majorly used web browsers.

Figure 3. Changes in xml. Web

```
<?xml version="1.0" encoding="UTF-8"?>
<web-app version="2.5"
    xmlns="http://java.sun.com/xml/ns/javaee"
    xmlns:xsi="http://www.w3.org/2001/XMLSchema-instance"
    xsi:schemaLocation="http://java.sun.com/xml/ns/javaee
    http://java.sun.com/xml/ns/javaee/web-app_2_5.xsd">
  <servlet>
    <servlet-name>CLOUDAPPLICATION</servlet-name>
    <servlet-class>CLOUDAPPLICATION</servlet-class>
  </servlet>

  <servlet-mapping>
    <servlet-name>CLOUDAPPLICATION</servlet-name>
    <url-pattern>/main </url-pattern>
  </servlet-mapping>
  <filter> <filter-name>FailedRequestFilter</filter-name>
   <filter-class>org.apache.catalina.filters.FailedRequestFilter</filter-class>
   <init-param><param-name>Cloud_Test</param-name>
   <param-value>Cloud_Test_Value</param-value> </init-param>
   </filter> <filter-mapping> <filter-name>RequestLoggingFilter</filter-name>
   <url-pattern>/*</url-pattern>
   <servlet-name>CLoudLoginServlet</servlet-name><dispatcher>REQUEST</dispatcher>
  </filter-mapping> <servlet> <servlet-name> myJSP </servlet-name>
<jsp-file> myJSPfile.jsp </jsp-file> </servlet> <servlet-maping> <servlet-name> myJSP </servlet-name>
<url-pattern>/main </url-pattern> </servlet-maping>

</web-app>
```

Figure 4. Filter in between Client and Cloud Server Browser

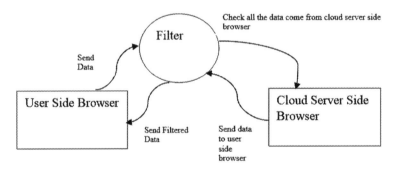

5.1.4.1. Response Time Analysis

The response time analyzed through Firefox 37.0 and Apache Tomcat 8.0 and cloud server deployed on OpenStack. We used firebug extension in Firefox for calculation of response time. For each request of mentioned size, we have performed 20 reloads and the average time is used for analysis. We performed response time with filter and without filter. The response time with filter and response time without filter is represented in Figure 5. Response time with filter and response time without filter and response time without filter is analyzed in Table 5. The response factor is represented in Figure 6. Response factor analysis is shown in Table 6.

Figure 5. Response Time with Filter vs. Response Time without Filter

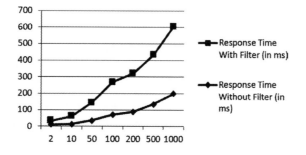

Table 5. Analysis of Response Time with Filter and Response Time without Filter

Size KB	Response Time Without Filter (in ms)	Response Time With Filter (in ms)
2	9.9034	23.0034
10	13.5675	45.9056
50	35.8989	107.9087
100	69.9094	198.8737
200	89.0939	232.2312
500	134.3545	299.2134
1000	198.4657	405.9034

Figure 6. Response factor analysis

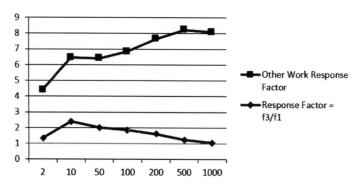

Table 6. Analysis of response factor

Size KB	Response Time Without Filter (in ms) = f1	Response Time With Filter (in ms) = f2	Difference in Response Time (in ms) =f3	Response Factor = f3/f1
2	9.9034	23.0034	13.1000	1.322778
10	13.5675	45.9056	32.3381	2.383497
50	35.8989	107.9087	72.0098	2.005905
100	69.9094	198.8737	128.9643	1.844735
200	89.0939	232.2312	143.1373	1.606589
500	134.3545	299.2134	164.8589	1.227044
1000	198.4657	405.9034	207.4377	1.045207

6. CONCLUSION

Cloud is very fast and growing technology for the last few years. Cloud environment cannot be visualized without virtualization. Virtualization is also very popular and well known technology since last few decades. Cloud virtualization creates a new dimension to organization to think forward apart from traditional approaches because they are less effective and costly. But with these new features, cloud virtualization also faces new security challenges for the organizations. The virtual components and environment cannot be protected by existing security mechanisms. Virtualization creates a different network that is a hybrid between the established physically centered network and the new virtual or logical environment. Additional considerations and protections must be kept in place to ensure a strong security mechanism, planning and preparation as well as training need to be implemented in advance. Our proposed filtering API will filter the cloud server response rather that user input, which will ensure the more insight in attack mitigation. The proposed mechanism employs the API for detection of malicious scripts rather than using a modified browser, which will result in low overhead as discussed in result section, and also it will block attacks vectors targeted to almost all popularly used web browser rather than for one which was used for malicious script detection. The current approach to prevent cloud environment from XSS attack will not ensure that the data will more secure although it gives a new direction and dimensions of security levels in cloud environment.

REFERENCES

Bates, D., Barth, A., & Jackson, C. (2010, April). Regular expressions considered harmful in client-side XSS filters. *Proceedings of the 19th international conference on World wide web* (pp. 91-100). ACM. 10.1145/1772690.1772701

Boganatham, K. K. (2009). *Server side API to secure XSS* [Doctoral dissertation]. National Institute Of Technology Karnataka Surathkal.

Buyya, R., Garg, S. K., & Calheiros, R. N. (2011, December). SLA-oriented resource provisioning for cloud computing: Challenges, architecture, and solutions. *Proceedings of the International Conference on Cloud and Service Computing CSC 2011* (pp. 1-10). IEEE.

Cherkasova, L., & Gardner, R. (2005, April). Measuring CPU Overhead for I/O Processing in the Xen Virtual Machine Monitor. *Proceedings of the USENIX Annual Technical Conference, General Track* (Vol. 50).

Christodorescu, M., Sailer, R., Schales, D. L., Sgandurra, D., & Zamboni, D. (2009, November). Cloud security is not (just) virtualization security: a short paper. *Proceedings of the 2009 ACM workshop on Cloud computing security* (pp. 97-102). ACM. 10.1145/1655008.1655022

Clark, C., Fraser, K., Hand, S., Hansen, J. G., Jul, E., Limpach, C., ... Warfield, A. (2005, May). Live migration of virtual machines. *Proceedings of the 2nd conference on Symposium on Networked Systems Design & Implementation-(Vol 2,* pp. 273-286). USENIX Association.

Hwang, J., Zeng, S., Wu, F. Y., & Wood, T. (2013, May). A component-based performance comparison of four hypervisors. *Proceedings of the International Symposium on Integrated Network Management IM 2013* (pp. 269-276). IEEE.

Input encoding is harmful. (n. d.). Retrieved from http://lukeplant.me.uk/blog/posts/why-escape-on-input-is-a-bad-idea/

Jakobsson, M., & Stamm, S. (2006, May). Invasive browser sniffing and countermeasures. *Proceedings of the 15th international conference on World Wide Web* (pp. 523-532). ACM. 10.1145/1135777.1135854

Jasti, A., Shah, P., Nagaraj, R., & Pendse, R. (2010, October). Security in multi-tenancy cloud. *Proceedings of the 2010 IEEE International Carnahan Conference on Security Technology (ICCST)* (pp. 35-41). IEEE. 10.1109/CCST.2010.5678682

Johns, M. (2011). Code-injection Vulnerabilities in Web Applications—Exemplified at Cross-site Scripting. *It-Information Technology Methoden und innovative Anwendungen der Informatik und Informationstechnik*, *53*(5), 256-260.

Kieyzun, A., Guo, P. J., Jayaraman, K., & Ernst, M. D. (2009, May). Automatic creation of SQL injection and cross-site scripting attacks. *Proceedings of the IEEE 31st International Conference on Software Engineering ICSE 2009* (pp. 199-209). IEEE. 10.1109/ICSE.2009.5070521

Kong, J. (2010, June). A practical approach to improve the data privacy of virtual machines. *Proceedings of the 2010 IEEE 10th International Conference on Computer and Information Technology (CIT)* (pp. 936-941). IEEE. 10.1109/CIT.2010.173

Kumar, K., & Lu, Y. H. (2010). Cloud computing for mobile users: Can offloading computation save energy? *Computer*, *43*(4), 51–56. doi:10.1109/MC.2010.98

Louw, M. T., & Venkatakrishnan, V. N. (2009, May). Blueprint: Robust prevention of cross-site scripting attacks for existing browsers. *Proceedings of the 30th IEEE Symposium on Security and Privacy 2009* (pp. 331-346). IEEE.

Nagar, N., & Suman, U. (2014, June). Architectural Comparison and Implementation of Cloud Tools and Technologies. *International Journal of Future Computer and Communication*, *3*(3), 153-160. 10.7763/IJFCC.2014.V3.287

Nagar, N., & Suman, U. (2014, October). A Secure Cloud Environment through Location Signature and HTML5 WebDB. *Proc. of the 3rd International conference on Advances in Cloud Computing* (pp. 31-36). CSI.

Nagar, N., & Suman, U. (2014, October). Two Factor Authentication using M-pin Server for Secure Cloud Computing Environment. *International Journal of Cloud Applications and Computing*, *4*(4), 42–54. doi:10.4018/ijcac.2014100104

Nance, K., Hay, B., Dodge, R., Wrubel, J., Burd, S., & Seazzu, A. (2009, January). Replicating and sharing computer security laboratory environments. *Proceedings of the 42nd Hawaii International Conference on System Sciences* HICSS '09 (pp. 1-10). IEEE

Oracle. (n. d.). Java response filter. Retrieved from http://docs.oracle.com/javaee/5/tutorial/doc/bnagb.html

OWASP. (n. d.). XSS Prevention Cheat Sheet. Retrieved from https://www.owasp.org/index.php/XSS_(Cross_Site_Scripting)_Prevention_Cheat_Sheet

Robinson, R.M. (2015, January 19). Cross-site attacks pose ongoing threat. Security Inteligence.com. Retrieved from http://securityintelligence.com/cross-site-scripting-attacks-pose-ongoing-threat

Szefer, J., Jamkhedkar, P., Chen, Y. Y., & Lee, R. B. (2012, June). Physical attack protection with human-secure virtualization in data centers. *Proceedings of the 2012 IEEE/IFIP 42nd International Conference on Dependable Systems and Networks Workshops (DSN-W)* (pp. 1-6). IEEE. 10.1109/DSNW.2012.6264664

Venkatesha, S., Sadhu, S., & Kintali, S. (2009). Survey of virtual machine migration techniques. *Memory (Hove, England)*.

VMWare. (n. d.). VMWare Inc. Retrieved from http://www.VMWare.com

Wen, F., & Xiang, L. (2011, December). The study on data security in Cloud Computing based on Virtualization. *Proceedings of the 2011 International Symposium on IT in Medicine and Education (ITME)* (Vol. 2, pp. 257-261). IEEE.

Zhao, S., Chen, K., & Zheng, W. (2009, August). Secure logging for auditable file system using separate virtual machines. *Proceedings of the 2009 IEEE International Symposium on Parallel and Distributed Processing with Applications* (pp. 153-160). IEEE 10.1109/ISPA.2009.32

This research was previously published in the International Journal of Cloud Applications and Computing (IJCAC), 6(1); edited by B. B. Gupta and Dharma P. Agrawal, pages 1-14, copyright year 2016 by IGI Publishing (an imprint of IGI Global).

Chapter 43
Cloud and Cyber Security Through Crypt–Iris–Based Authentication Approach

Sherin Zafar
Jamia Hamdard University, India

ABSTRACT

In today's world, wireless technology utilized by cloud and cyber technology has become an essential part of each and every user. Sensitivity, authentication and validation needs to be looked upon. Traditional technologies using simple encryption and password mechanisms cannot look upon the security constraints of today's cyber world; hence, some better authentication aspects like biometric security utilizing most strong feature like iris are exploited in this chapter to serve as specific secure tool.

INTRODUCTION

Due to the various intrinsic vulnerabilities present in cloud computing, cyber world and various wireless networks, the prime concern for users is the attainment of various secure parameters in form of authentication, integrity of their data present all across, non-repudiation and confidentiality of the various contents spread across the cloud along-with trust management and accessing the control for performing secured peer-to-peer conveyance over a cloud network. Therefore, security, routing and Quality of Service (QOS) are critical issues, that require immediate research attention due to the dynamic, unpredictable nature of most networks and also as they vary from each other greatly from the viewpoint of the area of application. This chapter specifies different attacks, parameters and methods of securing networks, followed by concepts of biometrics, and CIBA (Crypt Iris Based Authentication) approach. This chapter specifies different attacks, parameters and methods of securing networks, followed by concepts of biometrics, and CIBA (Crypt Iris Based Authentication) approach.

DOI: 10.4018/978-1-5225-8176-5.ch043

Security Challenges in Cloud Networks

The conventional cloud networks utilized across the cyber world are dependent upon some of the specific features that include contentment, organization tread and negligible dependency on a permanent architecture. A large number of security restrictions occur in modern day cloud world irrespective of their unique features that include distributed framework, coercive topologies, concerted and undistinguished wireless connectivity, compassed battery power, memory requirements and reckoning power capabilities. Occurrence of attacks from either direction is the major security consideration which is faced by modern day wireless cloud networks indifferent to fixed wired networks therefore each node in such type of networks should accoutre any attack coming from any direction accurately and diffusely. Due to malignant property each node shouldn't trust any node instantaneously. Distributed architecture of any cloud network is preferred over a centralized one due to various security restrictions that lead to various damages due to structure infirmity. A large number of attacks like the black hole, neighbour, worm-hole, denial of service, message betrayal, hastening, jellyfish, byzantine, blackmail etc. which affects cloud security.

Parameters and Methods for Securing a Cloud

Guerin and Orda (1999) have specified authentication, non-repudiation, confidentiality, integrity and availability as some of the most important security goals of MANET which are discussed below:

- **Authentication:** A mobile network before starting communication with a peer node authenticates it to ensure its identity. Not performing authentication can cause unauthorised access, as the attacker can impersonate the node and thus, access sensitive resources and information by interfering with the working of various other nodes of the network.
- **Non-Repudiation:** Non-repudiation is very important for detecting and isolating compromised nodes of various networks, by ensuring message originality of the specified sender and receiver without any denial.
- **Confidentiality:** Maintaining confidentiality is quite important for various military, strategic and sensitive applications, as it ensures non-disclosure of information to unauthorised entities.
- **Availability:** It is also one of the key security goals of MANET, as it ensures that services in a network operate properly by avoiding failures even in case of denial-of-service attack.
- **Integrity:** Integrity specifies accuracy of data. It ensures accurate and correct information to be transmitted across the various nodes of the network. There are many conventional methods for securing a wireless cloud network and a cyber world which are described below.

Key and Trust Management

Basic security supporting element for any system comes from a hybrid of asymmetric and symmetric cryptosystems, referred as key and trust management. Key management includes key exchange and key updating by maintaining authentication, confidentiality, integrity and non repudiation. Trust management leads to building of a trust graph where various nodes (entities) in a mobile network to their respective edges are specified through verifiable credentials. Below are discussed some very important services of key management:

- **Trust Model:** It maintains a trust relationship between various nodes of MANET which depends upon area of application and environment of network.

- **Trusted Third Party (TTP):** It maintains a centralized authority e.g. a key distribution centre or a certification authority which is trustworthy by every node in MANET. A centralized architecture can cause bottleneck and leads to denial-of-service attack.

- **Web of Trust:** A distributed architecture of security is employed, where each node develops its own security parameters, based on some recommendations from other nodes. Since, it is a distributed security scheme it may lead to various attacks and makes difficult to establish trust among various nodes.

- **Localized Trust:** It is a middle way between TTP and Web of Trust. Localized trust is established on a node if any m trusted nodes among one hop neighbour nodes claim within a specified period of time.

- **Cryptosystems:** It makes use of public (symmetric) or Elliptic Curve Cryptography (ECC). Public key cryptography is simpler but slower than other cryptographic measures. Elliptic curve cryptography has better performance when compared to other cryptosystems. It is also not very much exploited method for security enhancements in various networks.

Threshold Cryptography (TC)

Threshold cryptographic systems like Rivest Shamir Adleman (RSA) and ECC are homomorphism in nature as they allow bifurcating cryptographic operations along various multiple nodes of cloud network by comprising subset of n nodes that perform an operation, where n designates a predefined value. The basic idea of a crypt-function h, which is homomorphism in nature, is specified as:

$$Ha (K1+ K2) = Ha (K1)* Ha (K2) \tag{1}$$

where:
a is an input message
K1 and K2 belong to key space = K

Access Control

It governs the way nodes or virtual nodes access data objects. It dictates that only authorized nodes join, form, destroy or leave a group. A number of secure protocols also exist which have their advantages and limitations in securing a cloud network.

CONCEPTS OF BIOMETRIC

A system that involves exclusionary identification lineaments to sustain security in various networks all around is referred as a neoteric biometric mechanism whose procurement is dependent upon image accession and biometric recognition structure. The neoteric secured algorithm of this chapter is directed towards accession of biometric image througheffectual exploitation of bi-orthogonal lazy wavelets to encode the biometric data which is further augmented through various cryptographic attributes providing an effective solution against frequently occurring security breaches in cloud networks. Security, routing and QOS are critical issues, that require immediate research attention due to the dynamic, unpredictable nature of most networks and also as they vary from each other greatly from the viewpoint of the area of application. Security solutions utilized by most of the conventional approaches include simple encryption, username-password authentication scheme on one hand and cryptography that implicates a strong demand for secure and efficient key management mechanism on the other hand. Also, there is a requirement of a proper authentication mechanism that should restrict the access of foreign nodes to the network. Security mechanisms are indispensable for various cloud based networks as they are inherently vulnerable to attacks hence, posing both challenges and opportunities for future research analysis and design. Therefore, this research study focuses on one of the most unique, popular and considered to be the most enhanced security solution for various networks and devices, referred as biometrics. The study of the physical and behavioural characteristics of human beings for the purpose of authentication is referred as biometrics. Commonly exploited biometrics modalities are represented in Figure 1 which can be classified as behavioural or physical. Depending upon the sort of typical behaviour of a user the behavioural modalities make an attempt to identify the user, for e.g. how a person walks, how holds a pen, how presses the key when enter Personal Identification Number (PIN), etc.

Physiological methods on the other hand identify physical traits namely; fingerprint, face, iris, retina, etc., typical to a particular user. Two categories are stated by biometric systems namely identification and verification. "Who you are" is specified by identification system while "Are you the one whom you claim to be" is specified by the verification system. From olden times biometric identification is applied. Thumb impressions, signature, photographs and identity cards are quite important for the verification of the identity of human beings. Automated biometric is the growing area of research of biometric technology. Face, fingerprint, voice, iris, speech, hand geometry, retina, etc., are some of the traits of human beings utilized by a biometric system. For various critical processes reliable personal recognition is

Figure 1. Biometric modalities

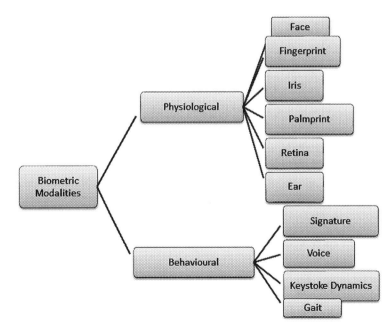

quite important. Systems safeguarded for security and reliability, against criminal attacks are important in modern day world, that's why various public and private organisations have improved the traditional security systems with biometric systems. Main aim of developing a secure biometric system is to establish identity based on who the person is rather than what are the possessions of system or what a person remembers (e.g. ID card or password).

For current scenarios of cloud and cyber security, user authentication is quite critical for preventing various unauthorised users from causing modification of resources of the network. Due to the dynamic nature of such systems there is an extremely high chance of system being captured in a hostile environment therefore, there is frequent and continuous requirement of authentication. Various validation factors namely, knowledge factors, possession factors and biometrics factors are exploited for performing user authentication. Passwords as knowledge factors and tokens as the possession factors are quite easy to be implemented but distinguishing an authenticated user from impostor becomes difficult since, no direct connection exist betwixt user and password or user or token. The technology of biometrics deals with recognition of fingerprints, irises, faces, retina, etc., provides various possible solutions for the authentication problems that exist in various sensitive networks. Processes in a biometric system and iris recognition system are discussed in upcoming sections of this chapter followed by the proposed CIBA approach.

PROCESSES IN A BIOMETRIC SYSTEM

Figure 2 depicts the processes in biometric system independent of the trait being utilized. Data capturing marks the beginning process which acquires the biometric sample. This follows with feature extraction which leads to the creation of biometric signature. The developed biometric signature is compared with a particular or several biometric signatures that are being registered in the knowledge database, together designated as biometric templates. They are collected during the enrolment process which corresponds to an identity that is subject verified. When the acquired biometric signature matches with the template then the identity being claimed is the same identity being stored otherwise it belongs to a different identity.

The comparisons done between the templates determine the basic distinction betwixt the nodes that are exploited for performing biometric recognition namely verification and identification. One to one match is resulted by the verification process where the identity of the person is verified by the biometric system. On presenting a new sample to the system, calculation of the difference between the new sample

Figure 2. Processes in biometric system

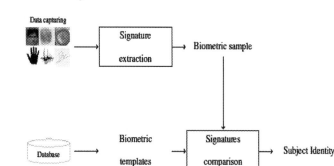

and its corresponding template (which is stored previously in the system) is done and the comparison of the computed difference and predefined threshold takes place. New sample is being accepted if the difference comes out to be smaller otherwise rejection of sample occurs.

Analysis of any biometric system cannot be completed without performing various specificity and sensitivity tests. True acceptance occurs when the accepted new sample and template are being specified from the same subject otherwise the acceptance is referred as false acceptance. False Acceptance Rate (FAR) is the percentage of the false accepts. If the new rejected sample and the corresponding biometric templates are not coming from a same subject the rejection is true rejection otherwise its false rejection. The trade-off between FAR and FRR is depicted in Figure 3. If FAR=FRR equal error rate is obtained. Better performance of the system is indicated by smaller ERR. Selection of ERR to achieve optimal performance is done by setting the acceptance threshold value but it happens rarely as it depends on the application of biometric.

For e.g. during money withdrawal through ATM it's better to risk a few false accepts than to annoy the customers again and again, when the authorized users are rejected by the system. One to one match happens in identification where the new biometric sample is compared with all the existing templates and the template with the minimum difference, greater similarity is being chosen as the ID result. A correct match occurs if the new sample and selected template are coming from the same subject.

IRIS RECOGNITION

Boles and Boashash (1998); Daugman (1994); Ma et al. (2002); Wildes (1997); Wildes et al. (1994); have focussed that biometric identification is becoming quite a popular tool and gaining more acceptance in various sectors. One of the highly accurate and reliable methods to be considered for biometric identification is iris perception due to stability, uniqueness and easy capture ability of strong biometric feature "iris", compared to other biometric identifiers. A biometric template is formulated by utilizing unique and distinguished patterns of human iris for personal identification and for image and signal processing by storing the biometric template in a database for identification purposes. The proposed wavelet based crypt-iris recognition and authentication approach is developed for securing MANET which results in a highly secure environment. Figure 4(a) represents human eye and its various parts and (b) shows the annular component iris. Regulation of the light intensity that can insinuate over the pupil is the function of sphincter and the dilator muscles which they perform by modifying the pupil size. The average

Figure 3. Trade-off between FAR and FRR

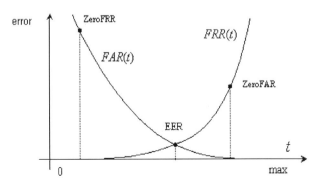

Figure 4. (a) Front view of human eye (b) a view of iris

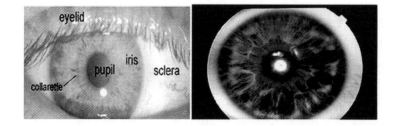

diameter of iris is around 12 mm whereas the size of pupil varies from 10% to 80% of the diameter of iris. Iris perception is considered to be one of the most assured and validating biometric feature as an iris template is developed from 173 by all of 266 relative distinctive predilection. Therefore various iris perception algorithms are procreated by considered to-be an effective, reliable and assured security tool for various cloud networks.

Segmentation is the first step for developing an enhanced biometric system by isolating the iris from an eye image under consideration. Second step, mapping performs matching of each pixel from the isolated iris, from concentric domain resulting in a non-concentric domain. Next step is encoding that performs quantization and mapping of the filter coefficients into a binary bit stream, building a template. Finally matchingis done to reflect the similarity score by various matching algorithms like hamming distance, correlation coefficient, etc. Data Management is very important for testing the designed algorithm on sufficiently large as well as a diverse data set provided by the Chinese Academy of Science, CASIA, West Virginia University and Lions Eye Institute, LEI (standard databases). As specified by Sweldens (1995) an iris perception algorithm not only performs recognition in ideal conditions but is also is easily adaptable and flexible in the non-ideal conditions of various off angle type of images, noise in images, etc. The various steps required for developing a secure iris perception algorithm are described below.

ISOLATION OR SEGMENTATION

Segmentation is termed as the first stage of iris recognition that isolates the actual iris region in a digital eye image. Figure 4(a), depicts the front view of human eye that can be approximated by two circles, one for the iris/sclera and another for the iris/pupil boundary. The upper and lower parts of the iris region are occluded by the eyelids, eyelashes, and specular reflections (referred as noises of iris image) that can occur within the iris region corrupting the iris pattern. Therefore, a technique is required for isolating and excluding the above mentioned artefacts as well as for locating the circular iris region. Image quality of the collected and acquired iris images leads in successful segmentation, which is one of the most critical starting stages of iris recognition system. Compared with LEI database, that contains specular reflections due to imaging under natural light the CASIA iris database doesn't contains specular reflections as it utilizes near infra-red light for illumination. Accurate segmentation is the basic requirement as data can be falsely represented in an iris pattern (persons having darkly pigmented irises results in a very low contrast between the pupil and iris region when imaged under natural light) that will cause corruption of the biometric templates generated hence, resulting in poor recognition rates as specified by Barry and Ritter. Various methods are available in literature for performing the segmentation/isolation of the iris image as discussed below.

Hough Transform

For determining the parameters of various simple geometric objects (lines or circles) a standard computer vision algorithm referred as the Hough transform is applied as described by Kong and Zhang (2001); Ma et al. (2002); Tisse et al. (2002); Wildeset al. (1994). This transform is also employed for deducing the radius and centre coordinates of the parts of eye namely pupil and iris regions. In starting of Hough transform, generation of edge map takes place by calculation of the first derivatives of intensity values in an eye image and then thresh-holding of the result is done. In Hough space votes are casted from the edge map for the parameters (centre coordinates x_c and y_c and the radius r) of circles passing through each edge point, which are able to define any circle according to the equation:

$$x^2_c + y^2_c - r^2 = 0 \tag{1}$$

Kong and Zhang (2001); Wildes et al. (1994) have approximated the parabolic arcs utilizing upper and lower parts of eyelids by making use of parabolic type of Hough transform which is given as:

$$(-(x-h_j)\sin\theta_j + (y-k_j)\cos\theta_j)^2 = a_j((x-h_j)\cos\theta_j + (y-k_j)\sin\theta_j) \tag{2}$$

where:

a_j = curvature control parameter.
h_j, k_j = parameters depicting parabolic peak.
θ_j = rotation angle relative to the x-axis.

To find out edge detection step preceding in nature Wildes et al. (1994) have used a unique method which is depicted in Figure. 5 (a) (b) (c) (d). This method for detecting the eyelids have performed biasing of the derivatives in the direction horizontal in nature and for vertical direction have detected the boundary of iris circular in nature.

The main motivation for performing edge detection is: i) the eyelids are aligned horizontal in fashion ii) the edge map of eyelid will lead to corruption of the iris boundary edge map circular in nature by utilizing the gradient data. For locating the iris boundary only the vertical gradients are taken that will reduce influence of the eyelids for performing circular Hough transform as for successful localisation, not all of the edge pixels defining the circle are required. Hence, making circle localisation more accurate and more efficient as there are less edge points to cast votes in the Hough space.

Figure 5. (a) An eye image (020_2_1 from the CASIA database); (b) corresponding edge map; (c) edge map with only horizontal gradients; (d) edge map with only vertical gradients
http://www.pccegoa.org/pcce/etc/synopsysETCprojects.htm.

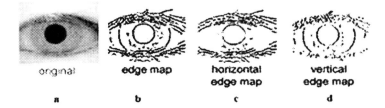

Daugman's Integro-Differential Operator

For locating the iris and pupil regions circular in nature and the arcs of upper and lower portion of eyelids Daugmann made use of the differential integro operator given below:

$$\left| G(r) * \frac{\partial}{\partial r} \cdot_{x_0,y_0,r} \frac{I(x,y)}{2\pi r} ds \right| \tag{3}$$

where:

$I(x, y)$ = location (x, y) in the image's intensity values.

ds = arc circular in nature.

$2\pi r$ = normalizing the integral through it.

$G(r)$ = Gaussian filter used as a smoothing function.

$*$ = convolution operation.

Integral is computed over an arc parabolic in nature rather than using an arc circular in nature by excluding those regions which are detected from the iris image's eyelid. This integro differential can be specified as the variation of the Hough transform but fails due to noise (reflections) that occur in the eye image and works on a scale local in nature.

Contour Models Active in Nature

Ritter (1999) has utilized active contour models for the localising of the pupil in eye images where responses take place by active contour forces internal, external and pre-set in nature through internal deformation until reaching the equilibrium by movement across the image. Contour contains number of vertices where two opposing forces change their position and they are a force that is dependent on the various desired characteristics called as internal force and a force that is dependent on the image referred as an external force. There is a movement of each vertex b/w time t and t+1 given by equation:

$$v_i(t+1) = v_i(t) + F_i(t) + G_i(t) -- \tag{1.4}$$

where:

F_i = force internal in nature.

G_i = force external in nature.

v_i = i^{th} position of vertex.

For global discrete circle expansion of the contour calibration of the internal forces take place for the localisation of the pupil region edge information which is utilized for finding external forces. For accuracy improvement Ritter (1999) has utilized the variance rather than the edge image. DCAC (Discrete Circular Active Contour)creation is done by point location interior to the pupil from an image's variance. DCAC is then moved under influential internal and external forces on equilibrium reaching localization of pupil.

Detection of Eyelash and Noise

For eyelash detection Kong and Zhang (2001) have presented a method. Eyelashes that are isolated are referred as separable eyelashes and those which perform bunching and overlapping in eye image are called multiple eyelashes. Separable eyelashes are detected by One Dimensional (1D) Gabor filters through convolution of an eyelash separable in nature by the smoothing function Gaussian in nature resulting in quite low output value. If resultant point < than a threshold, the point belongs to an eyelash and multiple eyelashes are detected utilising the variance of intensity. If the variance of intensity values in a small window < than a threshold, the eyelash is specified by centre of the window point. A connective criterion is utilized by Kong and Zhang (2001) model connecting each eyelash point to another eyelash point or to an eyelid. During thresh-holding, detection of specular reflections which are alongside eye image takes place due to higher intensity values of these regions compared to any other region of image.

Normalization

Daugman (2002) has described that after segmentation of the iris region successfully next is the transformation of this region, so that it has fixed dimensions to allow comparisons. Due to the pupil dilation, varying levels of illumination and inconsistencies that are dimensional tend to occur between the images of eye. This occurs due to iris stretching due to pupil's dilation resulting to illumination levels. Various other types of inconsistencies like variation in imaging distance, camera's rotation, tilted head, and eye' within the socket's eye tend to occur. Iris regions having same constant dimensions produced by normalization process, so two photographs of the same iris specified with different conditions will have characteristic features at the same spatial location. As the pupil region is not always concentric within the iris region and is usually slightly nasal, care must be taken when trying to normalize the 'doughnut' shaped iris region to have a constant radius. Various methods are available in literature for performing normalization of iris images which are discussed below.

Daugman's Rubber Sheet Model

Sanderson and Erbetta (2000) have illustrated the homogenous rubber sheet model devised by Daugman that remaps each point within the iris region to a pair of polar coordinates (r,θ) as enumerated in Figure 6 where, r's interval [0,1] and θ'sangle $[0,2\pi]$.

Iris region's modelling of remapped iris regions Cartesian coordinates (x,y) to the non-concentric normalized polar coordinates are given as:

$$I(x(r, \theta), y(r, \theta)) \rightarrow I(r, \theta) \tag{5}$$

Also,

$$x(r,\theta) = (1-r)x_p(\theta) + rx_1(\theta) \tag{6}$$

$$y(r,\theta) = (1-r)y_p(\theta) + ry_1(\theta) \tag{7}$$

where:

I(x, y) = image of iris region.

(x, y) = Cartesian coordinates those are original.

(r, θ) = polar coordinates those are correspondingly normalized.

$x_p y_p$ and x_1, y_1 = coordinates of the pupil and iris boundaries along the θ direction.

Pupil dilation and size inconsistencies are taken into account by the rubber sheet model to produce a normalized representation with constant dimensions. Hence, modelling the iris region as a flexible rubber sheet is anchored at the boundary with the reference point specified as the pupil centre.

Image Registration

An image registration technique is employed by Wildes et al. (1994) that geometrically wraps an image $(I_a x, y)$ that is newly acquired, into an alignment of an image $(I_d x, y)$ from a selected database. A mapping function $(u(x,y), v(x,y))$ that transforms the coordinates that are original in the intensity values of the new image which are made to be near to the points that are corresponding in the referenced image. Choosing of the mapped function should be done for minimising the equation below:

$$\int_x \int_y (I_d(x,y) - I_a(x-u, y-v))^2 dxdy \tag{8}$$

Similarity transformation of image's coordinates (x, y) to (x', y') is captured through equation below:

$$\begin{pmatrix} x' \\ y' \end{pmatrix} = \begin{pmatrix} x \\ y \end{pmatrix} - SR\left(\varnothing\right)\begin{pmatrix} x \\ y \end{pmatrix} \tag{9}$$

where:

S = scaling factor.

$R\left(\varnothing\right)$ = matrix representing rotation by $\varnothing$.

Figure 6. Daugman's Rubber Sheet model

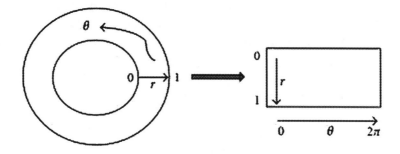

Figure 7. Histogram equalization
https://www.google.co.in/search?q=http://en.wikipedia.org/wiki/Inverse_transform_sampling

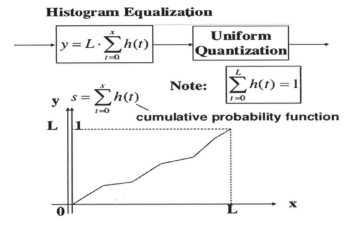

Histogram Equalization

Histogram information reveals that the iris image is under-exposed or over exposed.It finds a map f(x) such that the histogram of the modified (equalized) iris image is flat (uniform).The cumulative probability function (cdf) of a random variable approximates a uniform distribution as shown in Figure 7.Histogram equalization method when compared with other methods of normalization enhances the contrast of iris images by transforming the values in an intensity image so that the histogram's output iris imageapproximately matches the iris image of specified histogram. Histogram equalization method allows better adjustment of the intensities,enhances the global contrast of iris images, in cases where the usable data of the iris image is depicted by close contrast values. When this adjustment is performed intensities are distributed evenly on a histogram which allows lower local contrast areas to acquire a higher contrast. This task is accomplished through effective spreading of areas by frequent intensity values.

Virtual Circles

According to Boles (1998), iris images are firstly scaled to achieve constant diameter by comparing of the two images, one is considered as the reference image. When the two irises achieve the same dimensions, extraction of features from the iris region is done by storing the intensity values along virtual concentric circles with origin at the centre of the pupil. For getting same data point numbers from iris selection of normalization resolution is done by, making the technique essentially similar to Daugman's rubber sheet model. Scaling is performed during match time, and nothing is mentioned regarding how to obtain rotational invariance.

Feature Encoding and Matching

Calderbank et al. (1998); Daubechies and Sweldens (1998); Sweldens (1997); Sweldens (1995); have focussed that for accurate recognition of individuals, extraction of the most discriminating information is extracted from an iris pattern being normalized. Encoding must be done of only the significant features of the iris so that comparisons between templates can be made. For creation of a biometric template most of the iris recognition systems make use of band pass decomposition of the iris image. A corresponding matching metric is required after template is generated in the feature encoding for providing a measure of similarity betwixt two iris templates. The metric should provide intra class comparisons to specify one value ranges when comparing same eye generated templates and inter class comparison to compare another range of values when templates are resulting from different irises, providing distinctively separate values.This decision specifies whether coming of the compared templates if from different or same irises. A number of methods are available in literature for performing feature encoding, which are discussed below.

- **Wavelet Based Encoding:** For decomposing the data in the iris region wavelets are used for making the components appear at quite different specification of resolution. These wavelets can be utilized as they have the advantage over traditional Fourier transform. Fourier transformation method allows matching of the features that occur at same position by localising the feature data which does not provide a compact resolution of the image. Therefore, in wavelet based encoding methods a number of filters are referred as i) bank of wavelets which are applied to the Two Dimensional (2D) iris region, one for each type of resolution of each wavelet. Encoding of the output of applied wavelets provides compact and discriminating representation of the iris pattern.
- **Gabor Filters:** For providing an optimum conjoint representation of a signal in space and spatial frequency, Gabor filters are utilized by modulating a sine/cosine wave through Gaussian function for providing the optimum conjoint localisation and frequency. Perfect localisation in frequency of sine is achieved in localised frequency but not in localised space. Quadrature pairs of Gabor filters provide decomposition of a signal with real part (a cosine modulated by a Gaussian) and an imaginary part (a sine modulated by a Gaussian) which are also referred as even symmetric and odd symmetric components respectively. The frequency of sine/cosine wave of the filter specifies the centre frequency of the filter and the bandwidth is specified by the width of the Gaussian. 2D Gabor filters are utilized by Daugman (2002) for encoding iris data pattern represented over an image domain (x, y) as:

$$f(i, j) = \frac{1}{2\pi\lambda\gamma} \exp\left[-\frac{1}{2}\left(\frac{i'^2}{\lambda^2} + \frac{j'^2}{\gamma^2}\right)\right] \cos(2\pi F_u i') \tag{10}$$

where:

$$i' = i\cos\left(\theta_v\right) + j\sin\left(\theta_v\right)$$

$$j' = -i\sin\left(\theta_v\right) + j\cos\left(\theta_v\right)$$

F_u = frequency of the sinusoidal plane wave.
θ_v = orientation of Gabor filter.

λ and γ = standard deviations of Gaussian envelope along x and y directions respectively referred as scales.

  ○ **Log-Gabor Filters:** As enumerated by Struc et al. (2009), to overcome disadvantages of Gabor filter, log Gabor filter is utilized. Here zero DC component is obtained for any type of bandwidth by utilizing Gabor filter which is Gaussian and logarithmic in nature whose frequency response is given by:

$$G(f) = \exp\left(\frac{-\left(\log\left(\frac{f}{f0}\right)\right)2}{2\left(\log\left(\frac{\sigma}{f0}\right)\right)2}\right) \tag{11}$$

where:

f0 = frequency at center.

σ = filter's bandwidth at zero crossing .

  ○ **1D Wavelet's Zero Crossing:** Boles and Boashash (1998) have utilized one dimensional wavelet for encoding iris data pattern. The mother wavelet is defined as the second derivative of a smoothing function θ(x).

$$\varphi(x) = \frac{d^2\theta(x)}{dx^2} \tag{12}$$

The wavelet transform of a signal f(x) at scale s and position x is given by:

$$Wsf(x) = f * \left(S^2 \frac{d^2\theta(x)}{dx^2}\right)(x) = S^2 \frac{d^2}{dx^2}(f * \theta s)(x) \tag{13}$$

where:

θs = (1/S) θ(x/s).

Wsf(x) = proportional to the second derivative of f(x) smoothed by θs(x).

f * θs(x) = zero crossings of the transform that correspond to points of inflection region.

  ○ **Haar Wavelet:** Lim et al. (2001) utilized Haar wavelet referred as the mother wavelet that computes 87 dimensions based feature vector utilizing filtering multi-dimensional in nature. Each dimension has a real value from -1.0 to +1.0. Sign quantization of feature vector is done so that +ve value is represented by 1 and – ve as 0 resulting in a compact biometric template having only 87 bits. Lim et al. (2001) by comparison showed that the Haar wavelet transformation recognition rate somehow is slightly better by 0.9% when compared with Gabor transformation recognition rate.

◦ **Gaussian Filters Laplacian in Nature:** A system was developed byWildes et al. (1994) that performs decomposition of the iris region through Laplacian Gaussian filters is depicted below:

$$\nabla G = \frac{1}{\tau\sigma 4}\left(1 - \frac{p^2}{2\sigma^2}\right)e^{-p^2/2\sigma^2} \tag{14}$$

where:

σ = It is the standard deviation of the Gaussian function
ρ = It is the radial distance of a point from the centre of the filter.

A number of matching algorithms available in literature are discussed below.

• **Hamming Distance (HD):** Hamming distance gives a measure regarding similar bits in a two bit pattern for concluding whether these patterns are generated from different or from the same type of irises. To compare the bit patterns X and Y, Hamming Distance (HD) is defined as:

$$HD = \frac{1}{N}\sum_{j=1}^{n}Xj\left(XOR\right)Yj \tag{15}$$

where:

The sum of disagreeing bits are sum of the exclusive-OR between X and Y over N.
N= the total number of bits in the bit pattern.

High degrees of freedom are achieved by individual iris region. A bit-pattern that is produced by iris region which is totally independent than that produced by another iris. Two iris codes are produced from the same irises that are highly correlated. When two bits patterns are completely independent, an iris template is generated from different irises, having HD between the two patterns = 0.5. Independence implies that: i) there is 0.5 chance of setting any bit to 1 if two bit patterns are totally random and also vice-versa is true. The two patterns will be derived from the same iris if the bit pattern of half of the bits agree and half disagree leading to HD between them close to 0.0, as they are highly correlated and the bits should agree between the two iris codes. HD was employed by Daugman (2002) as the matching metric, for calculation of the distance only with bits that are generated from the actual iris region.

• **Weighted Euclidean Distance (WED):** WED is utilized for comparing the two templates, especially if the template is composed of integer values. Zhu et al. (2000) discuss how WED provides a measure of similar collection of values between two templates, given by equation below:

$$WED(K) = i = \sum_{i=1}^{N}\frac{((fi - fi^{(k)})^2}{(\delta i^{(k)})^2} \tag{16}$$

where:

fi = ith feature of the unknown iris.

$fi^{(k)}$ = ith feature of iris template k.

$\delta i^{(k)}$ = standard deviation of the ithfeature of iris template ki.

  ◦ **Normalized Correlation (NC):** Wildes et al. (1994) has utilized Normalized Correlation (NC) betwixt the acquired and database representation for goodness of match which is represented as:

$$\sum_{i=1}^{n}\sum_{j=1}^{m}\frac{\left(P1\left[i,j\right]-\mu1\right)\left(P2\left[i,j\right]-\mu2\right)}{nm\sigma1\sigma2} \tag{17}$$

where:

P1 and P2 = two images of size n$_x$ m.

μ1 and σ1 = mean and standard deviation of P1.

μ2 and σ2 = mean and standard deviation of P2.

Normalized correlation is advantageous over standard correlation as it is able to account for local variations in image intensity that corrupts the standard correlation calculation.

THE PROPOSED CRYPT-IRIS BASED AUTHENTICATION APPROACH

The proposed neotric "crypt-iris based authentication approach" has been implemented in MATLAB to provide enhanced security solutions for MANET through biometrics and elliptic curve cryptography. It undergoes the various steps namely: Segmentation (Iris Segmentation/ Disjuncture) by Hough Transformation (refer section 1.5.1), Normalization by Histogram Equalization (refer section 1.5.2), Encoding (Template Formation or Encoding) by Bi-orthogonal Wavelet 3.5(refer section 1.5.3), Matching and Authentication by Hamming Distance and Normalized Correlation (refer section 1.5.4).The basic operations of the proposed neotric "crypt-iris based authentication approach" is specified in Figure 8 and Figure 9.

CONCLUSION

This neoteric study has achieved successful performance parameter results, which is quite effectively depicted in the previous sections. Results achieved by CIBA approach are being summarized below to validate the effectiveness of the developed approach. A flexible simulation environment of the iris perception approach, allows varying of the iris classes as well as images per class, providing effective values for various specificity and sensitivity parameters like TPR, TNR, FPR, FNR, Precision, Accuracy, Recall and F-Measure. Time for Training various iris classes is not very high even with increase in the number of iris classes and images per class.

Figure 8. Basic operations of Neotric crypt-iris based perception and authentication approach

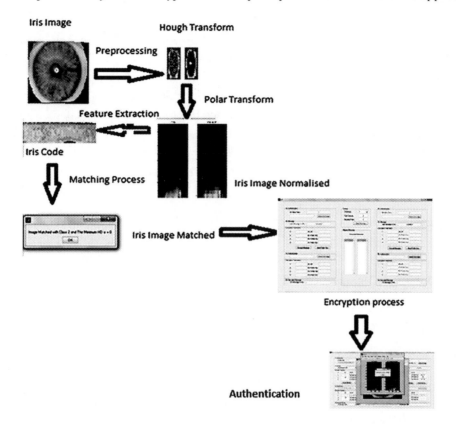

Figure 9. Flowchart of Proposed neoteric crypt-iris based authentication approach

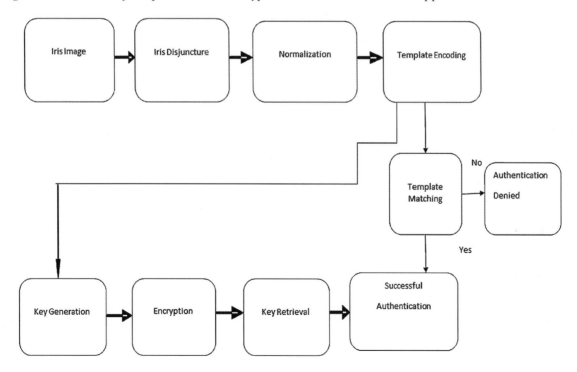

Approximately very accurate values of TPR=nearly 100%, TNR=nearly 100%, FPR=nearly 0%, Accuracy=100%, Recall=100% and F-Measure= Nearly 100% are achieved by the neotric iris perception approach for MANET. When compared with Masek (2003) worked on iris recognition which achieved FNR and FPR (with different classes per samples) as 4.580 and 2.494 on LEI database and 5.181 and 7.599 on CASIA database, the proposed methodology serves as a neoteric approach achieving required values of FNR=0 and FPR=0.012346 (many parameters included in the proposed methodology are not being specified by any of the conventional approaches) leading to enhanced security solution for MANET. Similarly, Abhyankar and Schuckers (2010) achieved values of FNR=0.00 and FPR=3.3 not better than the proposed approach. Also, Panganiban et al. (2011) have achieved accuracy of 94.5 in their developed iris recognition system, when compared with the proposed approach which achieved accuracy of 96.2.

REFERENCES

Abhyankar, A., & Schuckers, S. (2010). Wavelet Based Iris Recognition for Robust Biometric System. *International Journal of Computer Theory and Engineering*, 2(2).

Baek, J., & Zheng, Y. (2003). *Simple and Efficient Threshold Cryptosystem from the Gap Diffie-Hellman Group*. GLOBECOM.

Barry, C., & Ritter, N. (n.d.). Database of 120 Greyscale Eye Images. Perth, Western Australia: Lions Eye Institute.

Boles, W. W., & Boashash, B. (1998). A Human Identification Technique using Images of the Iris and Wavelet Transform. *IEEE Transactions on Signal Processing*, 46(4), 1185–1188. doi:10.1109/78.668573

Calderbank, A.R., Daubechies, I., Sweldens, W., & Yeo, B.L. (1998). Wavelet Transforms that Map Integers to Integers. *Applied and Computation Harmonic Analysis*, (3), 332-369.

Chinese Academy of Sciences Institute of Automation. (2003). *Database of 756 Greyscale Eye Image*. Available from: http://www.sinobiometrics.com

Cho, E.S., Gelogo, Y., & Kim, S.S. (2011). Human Iris Biometric Authentication using Statistical Correlation Coefficient. *Journal of Security Engineering*.

Daubechies, I., & Sweldens, W. (1998). Factoring Wavelet Transforms into Lifting Steps. *The Journal of Fourier Analysis and Applications*, 4(3), 245–267. doi:10.1007/BF02476026

Daugman, J. (1994). *Biometric Personal Identification System Based on Iris Analysis*. United States Patent, 5291560.

Daugman, J. (2002). How Iris Recognition Works. *Proceedings of 2002 International Conference on Image Processing*, 1. 10.1109/ICIP.2002.1037952

Gite, H. R., & Mahender, C. N. (2011). Iris Code Generation and Recognition. *International Journal of Machine Intelligence*, 3(3).

Guerin, R. A., & Orda, A. (1999). QOS Routing in Networks with Inaccurate Information: Theory and Algorithms. *IEEE/ACM Transactions on Networking*, 7(3), 350–364. doi:10.1109/90.779203

Haas, Z., Deng, B., Liang, P., Papadimitratos, & Sajama, S. (2002). Wireless Ad-hoc Networks. Journal of Proakis.

Kejun, L., Deng, J., Varshney, P., & Balakrishnan, K., & Kashyap. (2007). An Acknowledgement Based Approach for the Detection of Routing Misbehaviour in MANET. *IEEE Transactions on Mobile Computing.*

Koh, J., Govindaraju, V., & Chaudhary, V. (2010). *A Robust Iris Localization Method using an Active Contour Model and Hough Transform.* 20th International Conference on Pattern Recognition, ICPR, Istanbul, Turkey.

Kong, W., & Zhang, D. (2001). Accurate Iris Segmentation Based on Novel Reflection and Eyelash Detection Model. *Proceedings of International Symposium on Intelligent Multimedia, Video and Speech Processing.* 10.1109/ISIMP.2001.925384

Lauter, K. (2004). The Advantages of Elliptic Curve Cryptography for Wireless Security. *IEEE Wireless Communications, 11*(1), 62–67. doi:10.1109/MWC.2004.1269719

Lim, S., Lee, K., Byeon, O., & Kim, T. (2001). Efficient Iris Recognition through Improvement of Feature Vector and Classifier. *ETRI Journal, 23*(2).

Liu, J., Yu, F. R., Lung, C. H., & Tang, H. (2007). Optimal Biometric-Based Continuous Authentication in Mobile Ad-hoc Networks. *Third IEEE International Conference on Wireless and Mobile Computing, Networking and Communications,* 76-81. 10.1109/WIMOB.2007.4390870

Llewellyn, L. C., Hopkison, K. M., & Graham, S. R. (2011). Distributed Fault Tolerant Quality of Wireless Networks. *IEEE Transactions on Mobile Computing, 10*(2), 175–190. doi:10.1109/TMC.2010.148

Ma, L., Wang, Y., & Tan, T. (2002). *Iris Recognition using Circular Symmetric Filters.* National Laboratory of Pattern Recognition, Institute of Automation, Chinese Academy of Sciences.

Masek, L. (2003). *Recognition of Human Iris Patterns for Biometric Identification.* University of Western Australia. Retrieved from MATLAB work: http://www.mathworks.com

Namuduri, K., & Pendse, R. (2012). Analytical Estimation of Path Duration in Mobile Ad-hoc Networks. *IEEE Journal Sensors, 12*(6), 1828–1835. doi:10.1109/JSEN.2011.2176927

Panganiban, A., Linsangan, N., & Caluyo, F. (2011). Wavelet-Based Feature Extraction Algorithm for an Iris Recognition System. *Journal of Information Processing Systems, 7*(3), 425–434. doi:10.3745/JIPS.2011.7.3.425

Ritter, N. (1999). Location of the Pupil-Iris Border in Slit-Lamp Images of the Cornea. *Proceedings of the International Conference on Image Analysis and Processing.* 10.1109/ICIAP.1999.797683

Sanderson, S., & Erbetta, J. (2000). Authentication for Secure Environments Based on Iris Scanning Technology. *IEEE Colloquium on Visual Biometrics.* 10.1049/ic:20000468

Sanzgiri, K., Laflamme, D., Dahill, B., Levine, B. N., Shields, C., & Belding-Royer, E. M. (2005). Authenticated Routing for Ad-hoc Network. *IEEE Journal on Selected Areas in Communications, 23*(3), 598–610. doi:10.1109/JSAC.2004.842547

Shanthini, B., & Swamynathan, S. (2009). A Cancelable Biometric-Based Security System for Mobile Ad-hoc Networks. *International Conference on Computer Technology (ICONCT 09)*, 179-184.

Sherin Zafar, M. K., & Soni, M.M.S. (2014b). Sustaining Security: Encircling Wavelet Quartered Extrication Algorithm For Crypt- Biometric Perception. *Data Mining and Intelligent Computing (ICDMIC), International Conference*, 1 – 6. DOI: 10.1109/ICDMIC.2014.6954263

Sherin Zafar, M.K., & Soni. (2014c). Trust based QOS protocol (TBQP) using meta-heuristic genetic algorithm for optimizing and securing MANET. *IEEE Explore*, 173 - 177. Doi:10.1109/ICROIT.2014.6798315

Sherin Zafar, M. K., & Soni, M.M.S. (2015a). A Novel Crypt-Iris Based Authentication Approach. *IEEE Conference INDICON*.

Sherin Zafar, M. K., & Soni, M.M.S. (2015b). An Optimized Genetic Stowed Approach to Potent QOS in MANET. *Procedia Computer Science, 62*, 410-418. doi:10.1016/j.proc.08.434

Sherin Zafar, M. K., & Soni. (2014a). Sustaining Security in MANET: Biometric Stationed Authentication Protocol (BSAP) Inculcating Meta-Heuristic genetic Algorithm. *IJ Modern Education and Computer Science, 9*, 28-35. Doi:10.5815/ijmecs.2014.09.05

Sherin Zafar, M. K., & Soni. (2015c). A Novel Crypt-Biometric Perception Algorithm to Protract Security in MANET. *I.J. Computer Network and Information Security, 6*(12).

Struc, V., Gajsek, R., & Pavasic, N. (2009). Principal Gabor Filters for Face Recognition. *3rd IEEE International Conference on Biometrics: Theory, Applications and Systems*, 1-6.

Sweldens, W. (1995). The Lifting Scheme: A New Philosophy in Bi-Orthogonal Wavelet Constructions. *Wavelet Applications in Signal and Image Processing III, SPIE, 2569*, 68–79. doi:10.1117/12.217619

Sweldens, W. (1997). The Lifting Scheme: A Construction of Second Generation Wavelets. *SIAM Journal on Mathematical Analysis, 29*(2), 511–546. doi:10.1137/S0036141095289051

Tisse, C. L., Martin, L., & Torres, M. (2002). Person Identification Technique using Human Iris Recognition. *International Conference on Vision Interface*.

Wildes, R. (1997). Iris Recognition: An Emerging Biometric Technology. *Proceedings of the IEEE, 85*(9), 1348–1363. doi:10.1109/5.628669

This research was previously published in Detecting and Mitigating Robotic Cyber Security Risks edited by Raghavendra Kumar, Prasant Kumar Pattnaik, and Priyanka Pandey, pages 312-332, copyright year 2017 by Information Science Reference (an imprint of IGI Global).

Chapter 44
Trusted Cloud- and Femtocell-Based Biometric Authentication for Mobile Networks

Debashis De
West Bengal University of Technology, India

Anwesha Mukherjee
West Bengal University of Technology, India

Srimoyee Bhattacherjee
West Bengal University of Technology, India

Payel Gupta
West Bengal University of Technology, India

ABSTRACT

Authentication procedures are conducted in order to control and stop illegitimate access of such valuable data. This chapter discusses the biometric authentication inside the cloud. The authors describe how biometric information of a user can be securely transmitted and then stored inside the user database maintained in the trusted cloud. Femtocell, a recent development in mobile network using which secures biometric data transmission from the mobile device to the cloud, is discussed in this chapter.

INTRODUCTION

Frauds and fraudulent activities are social crimes that are increasing vigorously every day. They are million dollar businesses escalating every year. The PwC global economic crime survey of 2009 suggests that close to 30% of companies worldwide have reported being victims of fraud in the past year (PricewaterhouseCoopers LLP, 2009). The Oxford Dictionary defines fraud as the use of false representations to gain an unjust advantage. It involves people who purposely act in a secret manner to deprive someone from something of value which actually belongs to the victim.

DOI: 10.4018/978-1-5225-8176-5.ch044

Statistics says that in recent years, the development of new technologies has provided new avenues to criminals in which fraud can be committed (Bolton, 2002). With the maximum items of our daily lives gone electronic, the scope of performing such crimes has found a strong platform. Credit / debit card fraud, electronic fraud, identity theft etc. are few of the types of fraud that are encountered regularly. To combat such deceptive activities, it is very important to implement authentication techniques. It is the act of confirming the truth of an attribute of a datum or entity which might involve confirming the identity of a person or some software program. The process of authentication often involves verifying the validity of at least one form of identification which is unique in nature. Biometric authentication is an important authentication method which refers to the identification of humans by their characteristics or traits. In Computer Science, it is used for identification and secured access control. Different aspects of human physiology, chemistry or behavior are used for biometric authentication. Biometrics refers to the use of unique physiological characteristics to identify an individual. It uses human traits like finger prints, tongue impressions, iris and face recognitions (Pugazhenthi, 2013). These are unique to each individual and thus differentiate users. A human physiological or behavioral biometric should possess the following desirable properties (Jain, 1999):

1. **Universality:** Every person should possess the characteristic;
2. **Uniqueness:** No two persons should be the same in terms of the characteristic;
3. **Permanence:** The characteristic should not vary with time;
4. **Collectability:** The characteristic should be measurable quantitatively.

Biometric techniques and cloud computing are combined for the purpose of a secure cloud computation. As cloud is nothing but a remote server, hence, the operations carried out are beyond trusted boundaries and is much more vulnerable to hacking and security breaches (Pugazhenthi, 2013).

As we all know, worldwide adoption of mobile products and cloud computing services is not only continuing, but is accelerating. Biometric security technology seems promising inaddressing the issue of authenticating genuine user that is a fundamental flaw inconventional cryptography. Conventional biometric applications, specifically verification and identification, have been extensively investigated over the past decades,leading to a significant improvement.

BIOMETRIC AUTHENTICATION IN CLOUD ENVIRONMENT

Cloud computing is a promising field in the world of technology. It provides cost effective secure framework and allows software, platforms and infrastructures to be used as a service (Li-qin, 2010). Securing user privacy and data or application from frauds is a task of concern for the cloud service providers. Biometric based authentication is dependent on analyses of human characteristics or traits. It is used for user identification and access control (Wang, 2014). Implementation of biometric based authentication in cloud based storage and at the client end would provide immunity against security attacks (Li-qin, 2010). For enabling biometric authentication in the cloud, the biometric infrastructure including the databases, network connectivity and all the processing required for the authentication must be available to the cloud. Biometric infrastructures are characterized by ease of set up, affordability, scalability and on-demand service provisioning (Armbrust, 2010).

Endorsements of credit cards in cloud environment using biometrics enhance the security of these processes (Ashbourn, 2014). The credit card system used prior to this allows users to perform transactions without the need of authenticating the user to be legitimate or not. The fingerprint of the card owner is used for authentication. The bank stores the fingerprint of the card owner along with the other required information.

As the card is swiped in the credit card machine the card number as well the scanned image of the fingerprint is sent to the vendor system. The card number is forwarded to the cloud database of the bank via the bank server, where the fingerprint image of the card owner is obtained and sent to the server (Ashbourn, 2014). In the vendor system, the holder is asked to give his fingerprint in the scanner which is then sent to the server for comparison. If there is a match, the transaction is continued else it is rejected (Ashbourn, 2014). Thus this system provides efficient authentication of the card owner and prevents the security threats.

A handwritten password can be used for authentication for mobile devices (Sindhu, 2013). Handwritten authentication system verifies the identity of the user in accordance to his biometric characteristics (Sindhu, 2013). An application acts as an interface between user and the cloud. The application collects and encrypts the handwritten password of the user and sends it to the cloud. This mechanism provides two-way authentication as the user is verified by his unique passkey or password as well the way with which the person writes the password i.e. the handwriting. In the cloud side, encrypted handwritten password is decrypted and is then compared with the handwritten password of the user stored previously in the database. If the entry matches the one currently entered by the user he is authenticated successfully and is allowed to access the services.

Thus biometric authentication provides resilience against security threats in the cloud environment and the wide deployment of this strategy would increase the popularity of cloud services to even higher levels.

Mobile Cloud Biometrics

The tremendous growth in the usage of mobile devices as well the rising popularity of the cloud computing gives birth to the mobile cloud computing. Mobile cloud computing allows users to store data and execute complex applications remotely in the resource-rich cloud servers rather than in the resource-limited mobile device itself. Safeguarding user data and applications from outside intruders and threats is a major concern in the field of mobile cloud computing. With the usage of biometric authentication,

Figure 1. Process of credit card endorsements with biometric authentication

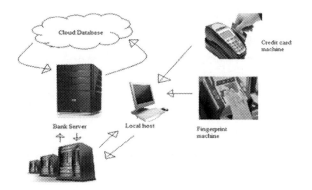

unauthorized access to the user data can be prevented. A very common biometric authentication strategy for mobile devices is the analyses of keystrokes (Omri, 2013). The individuality of typing behavior makes it difficult to forge and thus is a very powerful data for biometric authentication. Moreover behavioral biometrics requires no additional tools for analyses other than the keyboard in contrast to the biometrics like facial features, fingerprints etc (Banerjee, 2012). Thus keystroke analyses are a much attractive option for biometric authentication being cost effective. In the first step for keystroke analyses the characters typed by the users are recognized and the typing pattern is noted. In the second step the words are stored in memory. In the third step the discrete characters are converted into commands and in the third step the actual execution of text takes place followed by a feedback. Keystroke analyses are widely deployed for touch screen mobile devices (Omri, 2013). At the commencement of the enrolment phase the user enters the PIN and the corresponding keystrokes are recorded in a database. During authentication the PIN entered by the user as well the corresponding keystrokes are matched with the samples stored in the database. First the PIN is verified and if it is correct the keystroke features are verified (Banerjee, 2012). Only when both prove to be legitimate the user is provided access to the service provided. Keystroke dynamics find application in recovery of user ids in case users forget their passwords as welling gender detection of users (Banerjee, 2012).

Trusted Cloud

There are various aspects of trust in cloud computing that are essential for the cloud service provider, the cloud consumer, and the other related entities. The trustworthy frameworks in cloud computing are very much important as they form the essential basis for the secure and trustworthy operation of cloud computing. Both the cloud service provider and cloud consumers are benefitted through these frameworks. Cloud providers offer their services to cloud users. Users may be authentic or malicious. Authentic users are interested in doing their job with the service provided by the Cloud Service Provider (CSP). Malicious users always try to make harm to the CSP. The reason may be that the malicious user is a competitor or an attacker. A malicious user may run an application that may take maximum resources. Malicious codes may interfere with other genuine users. So a CSP must evaluate the trustworthiness of a user through the analysis of his behavior. Traditional user identification, authentication is not enough. User behavior trust evaluation gives the CSP to provide its service more reliably to genuine users. The CSP should eliminate malicious user from its domain by evaluating user behavior trust for the sake of its own performance. The details of user behavior trust have been discussed in (Chang, 2012). User behavior trust (UBT) can be subdivided into four categories:

1. **Contract Behavior Sub-Trust (CST):** Contract behavior sub-trust (CST) tells us, whether the user behavior comply with the legal agreement between Cloud Service Provider (CSP) and cloud consumer (CC). Setting up proxy server, or excessive download, all these may not be according to SLA.
2. **Security Behavior Sub-Trust (SST):** Security behavior sub-trust (SST) implies, if the user has the tendency to attack the CSP infrastructure. An attack to the cloud resources or hacking other user's information belongs to this category.
3. **Identity Re-Authentication Sub-Trust (IST):** Identity re-authentication sub-trust (IST) refers to authenticating the user again, second time. The user may use mobile device for using cloud resources and these resources are easy to lose. So, if the device is lost and the CSP identifies some

Box 1.

$$TV_{CSP} = e^{\frac{+}{-}t} * (\frac{VMl}{VMr} + \sum_{i=1}^{n} U_i + \sum_{i=1}^{m} PN + PS) \quad (1)$$

abnormal activity like excessive download, then how to authenticate the user again is the central theme if IST.

4. **Expense Behavior Sub-Trust (EST):** Expense behavior sub-trust (EST) means, whether the user is using the cloud resources optimally. Suppose the user has finished working, and still occupying the resources. This will lead to denial of service to other users. So, the CSP must monitor EST and reward good CCs.

In a cloud computing environment both the cloud service provider (CSP) and cloud Consumer (CC) should be trustworthy. To achieve this, a mobile agent based trustworthy infrastructure is required. A detail description of such a framework is given in (Wang, 2014).

In this model, the cloud broker (CB) maintains the trustworthiness of the cloud environment. CB is a trusted third party. Every CSP has to first register with the CB. CB gives the CSP a dummy job and invokes a mobile agent. The CB evaluates the trustworthiness of the CSP according to the report of the agent. If the CSP is performing good then its trust index is increased, else decreased. There is a threshold value after which the CSP is purged out of the cloud environment by the CB.

The key provider, a subpart of the CB, provides each customer a public private key combination. CC request is first sent to CB and then CB forwards the request. After each service the CC returns gossip message to CB. This message is forwarded to all CCs. This message contains user experience. If the user provides actual experience, the CB gives award to the CC and accordingly the trust index of the CC is increased. If some malicious user provides wrong experience, he is penalized with decreasing trust index. If the trust index goes below of a certain value then the CC is removed from the environment. The CB understands about the wrong or right message by previous experience. The gossip message monitoring is done by another mobile agent of the CB. User experience can be +1 or -1 based on good experience or bad experience.

The trust value (TV) of the CSP may be evaluated as shown in Box 1 (Wang, 2010).

Trust value (TV) of the i_{th} cloud consumer (CC) may be evaluated as shown in Box 2, where:

n = no. of cloud consumer (CC) who have been serviced.

m = tolerance threshold.

U_i = user experience of i_{th} customer.

VMl = No. of virtual machines launched for a job.

VMr = No. of virtual machines required for a job.

Penalty (PN) = punishment given due to malicious behaviour.

Prize (PS) = total no of award given to the of CSP by Cloud Broker for trustworthy behaviour.

Prize points (PPi) = award for trustworthiness to the ith customer, by Cloud Broker.

PNS = PN or PS awarded to CSP by CB.

PC_i = award given to i-th customer by cloud broker.

Box 2.

$$TV_{CC} = e^{\overset{+}{-}t} * (U_i * (PNS) + PC_i) \ (2)$$

If positive trust value comes then it is multiplied with e^{-t} to reduce the trust value with time. If negative trust value comes then it is multiplied with e^{+t} to further reduce the trust value with time. The trust value reduces due to lack of interaction for quite some time. Figure 2 shows the message packets of the cloud consumers.

Here, Message ID is the unique message identifier. Source cloud consumer id is the id of the message sender. Destination cloud consumer id is the id of the customer who receives the message. B stands for broadcasting. S/G field specifies whether the message is a service request or a gossip message. User experience field can have the values +1 or -1 according to user satisfaction. The time stamp field is given to avoid message reply attacks. Figure 3 shows the architecture of mobile agent based trustworthy infrastructure.

Figure 2. Message packets of the cloud consumers

Message ID			
Source Cloud Consumer ID			
Destination Cloud Consumer ID			
B	S/G	User Experience	Time Stamp

Figure 3. Architecture of mobile agent based trustworthy infrastructure

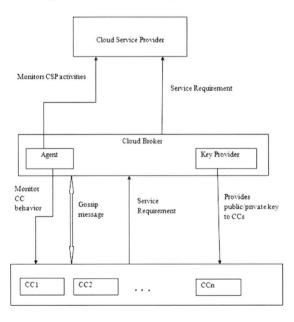

There are few ways in which we can establish trust for Cloud Service Procedures. There are some approaches through which the consumers can decide which of the Cloud Service Providers (CSPs) are trustworthy or dependable. We may classify these approaches as follows (Wang, 2010):

1. **Service Level Agreement (SLA):** SLAs are a way to establish trust on CSPs. SLAs state what exactly the CSP can provide, what are the features, what is the security mechanism applied, which assurances are actually met, all these.In mobile cloud computing environment, the user monitors the SLA violation and can apply for the compensation to the CSP. Unfortunately, SLAs are standardized recently and they are far from implementation. The CSPs take the advantage of this situation. They make the SLAs in such a way that they can deprive the customer from getting compensation.

2. **Audit:** There are manyaudit standards available and different cloud service providers use different audit standards, for example, FISMA, SAS70 II, ISO 27001 etc. This is to assure the cloud consumers about their offered services. For example, the audit SAS 70 II covers the operational performance of the system and relies on specific set of goals. Audit reports are not alone sufficient to alleviate users concern. Moreover, most of the CSPs do not want to share the audit reports. This leads to lack of transparency.

3. **Measuring and Rating:** Recently, a new cloud marketplace named SpotCloud has been launched. It provides a platform where Cloud Consumers can choose among potential providers in terms of location, quality, and cost. This is to support the cloud consumers in identifying dependable CSPs. The CSPs are rated based on questionnaire that is filled by current Cloud Consumers (CCs). There is provision to combine technical measurements with the cloud consumer feedback for comparing and assessing the trustworthiness of the CSPs in the future.

4. **Self-Assessment Questionnaire:** The Cloud Security Alliance (CSA) has provided a questionnaire for ensuring security features of the CSPs, called the CAIQ (Consensus Assessments Initiative Questionnaire). The CAIQ provides ways to assess the capabilities and competencies of the CSPs in terms of different features like information security, governance, compliance, etc. The CAIQ is filled up by the CSPs. CAIQ is basically a set of questions a cloud consumer may wish to ask a cloud service provider. The questions are about the security implementation by the CSPs in their IaaS, PaaS, and SaaS service delivery models. However, the CAIQ evaluation strategy is not standardized yet. The evaluation is necessary for comparing the potential CSPs, through which we can get assurance whether the services offered by the CSPs comply with the industry accepted security standards, regulations, audits or not.

5. **Trust and Reputation Model:** The approaches mentioned in 3.1 to 3.4 are time consuming and cumbersome. Moreover, these trends lack a unified approach where all these criteria can be combined and evaluated to support the customer in selecting the most effective and dependable cloud provider. To assist customers in understanding the differences and selecting the most trustworthy cloud service provider, Trust and Reputation (TR) models represent a promising and essential basis. Trust and Reputation models have some parameters known as QoS+ parameters to support the customers in selecting the most appropriate cloud providers before actually interacting with them. These parameters should be measured and analyzed properly according to their importance.

   ○ **QoS+ parameters for the Trust and Reputation Models:** The following are the standard parameters used in TR models (Ramaswamy, 2011):

     ▪ **Service Level Agreement (SLA):** Service Level Agreements are done between cloud providers (CPs) and cloud consumers (CCs).

- **Compliance or Accreditation or Certification:** Cloud service providers use different audit standards to prove themselves.
- **Portability**: It means the ability to run in different platforms and operating systems. CSPs should provide services to all the platforms.
- **Geographical Location:** CSPs provide information about the Geographical Location of their data centers.
- **Customer Support:** Generally CSPs provide information regarding Customer Support in the SLA.
- **Performance:** Through service monitoring technologies, performance related data regarding cloud providers can be found out. Performance consists of Availability, Elasticity, Latency, Bandwidth,and Reliability.
- **Federated Identity Management:** Through SLA this type of information is found out.
- **Security Measures:** Cloud Consumers are always worried about the security of their data and the CSPs should provide the relevant information. Security measure consists of cryptographic algorithms, key management,physical security support, data security support, and network security.
- **User Feedback:** User feedback, recommendation, publicly available reviews etc. are very important in cloud marketplace. Feedback regarding CSPs can be given as a whole or as the basis of individual criteria.
- **Service Deployment and Delivery Models:** The deployment models (e.g., private, public, and hybrid clouds) and service delivery models (e.g., IaaS, PaaS, SaaS) used by the CSPs are also very important.
  - **Few Promising Trust and Reputation Models:** There are many existing Trust and Reputation (TR) models. Some promising TR models are eBay, RFSN, Beta Reputation, TidalTrust, Buchegger's model, Epinions, CertainTrust, Hang's model, BNTM, Unitec, Abawajy's model, TESM, FIRE, GridEigenTrust, EigenTrust, socialREGRET, and Billhardt's model (Habib, 2012).

Biometric Data Security During Transmission Using Femtocell

Now-a-days energy efficiency is a major challenge in mobile network (Habib, 2010), (Mallik, 2012), (Mukherjee, 2012), (Ashraf, 2010). The increasing awareness of the harmful effects to the ecosystem caused by the CO_2 emission and the depletion of the non-renewable energy sources leads to a growing demand for the development of energy efficient mobile network (Lu, 2012). Besides the obvious environmental benefits, reducing energy consumption makes good business sense. In mobile network the access points and in particular the base stations are the largest energy consumer and thus energy efficiency improvements are primarily focused in this area. The base stations are categorized into four types in accordance to the coverage area. A macrocell base station has coverage of 1-20km where in case of microcell base station the coverage area is less than 1km (Hasan, 2011), (De, 2011). Due to large coverage the transmission power of a macrocell base station is very high although the quality of service specially at indoor and boundary region is poor (Hasan, 2011). To overcome this problem, microcell and picocell comes into the scenario. But the shortcoming of microcell is high maintenance cost and high transmission power. Picocell with coverage of 4-50m gains popularity in areas like large business centers, offices and malls (Hasan, 2011). But as picocells are required to be installed by operators they incur high deployment cost and thus are not quite feasible for small office or home environment (Hasan, 2011). To achieve better quality of service in terms of reduced cost and power consumption as well better coverage, femtocell is introduced for the indoor environment. The biometric data i.e. the keystroke, fingerprint or retina pattern are transmitted from the mobile station (MS) to the server using femtocell under which the MS is registered.

Femtocell is a secure, low power and low cost base station as it is connected to the internet through a security gateway as observed in Figure 4 (Mukherjee, 2014), (Mukherjee, 2014), (De, 2014), (Mukherjee, 2013). Femtocell has a coverage of approximately 10-20m (Mukherjee, 2013). Femtocells are low-power wireless access points that operate in licensed spectrum to connect standard mobile devices to a mobile operator's network using residential DSL or cable broadband connections (De, 2014). They, by virtue of their small size, low cost and high performance, are a potentially industry changing disruptive shift in technology for radio access in cellular network (De, 2014). The femtocell technology is widely accepted as femto BSs can be bought in the market by users and easily installed in a plug-and-play manner (De, 2014). A femtocell can usually support a maximum of 2-5 users in its range. There are currently two kinds of Femtocell Access Point (FAP) available in the market: (1) Home FAP-Can provide services to 3-5 users in its coverage area, and (2) Enterprise FAP-Can provide services to 16-32 users in its coverage area (Mukherjee, 2012). Mobile device and femtocell are connected via Uu interface (Mukherjee, 2014). Femtocell is connected with the core network by the HNB-GW (HNB-Gateway) (Mukherjee, 2014). A security gateway (SeGW) provides a proper security mechanism between the femtocell and HNB-GW over the internet (Mukherjee, 2014). Femtocell connects with the HNB-GW through the Iuh interface (Mukherjee, 2014). The HNB-GW is connected to the core network via Iucs/Iups interface (Mukherjee, 2014). The security gateway allows the core network operator to do mutual authentication with femto access point (FAP).

A security tunnel is established between the security gateway and FAP to protect the information during transmission through the backhaul link which ensures data integrity and confidentiality during transmission. The FAP management system or the femto gateway verifies the location of a FAP check whether it is operating in licensed spectrum. For security purpose the following precautions are taken by the operator, FAP and security gateway (Chen, 2012):

- For authentication, confidentiality and data integrity purpose the adequate cryptographic algorithms are used.
- International Mobile Subscriber Identities of the users registered under a particular femtocell are not revealed even not to the hosting party of the FAP also.
- No modifications to the hosting party controlled information are done by the operator without permission of the hosting party of the FAP.
- Only the operator of the FAP has the ultimate legal authority to operate the corresponding femtocell.
- To prevent the information of the users as well as the operator from the hackers and outside threats any information from an unauthenticated source from the access network is discarded by the FAP.
- The FAP location is reliably transferred to the network and its time base is also synchronized with the core network.
- Any sensitive data such as authentication details, user information, user and control plane data are not accessible in plain text at the FAP for unauthorized access.

- The security gateway is authenticated by the FAP using a security gateway certificate signed by an authority trusted by the operator and the security gateway authenticates the FAP with the help of FAP certificate.
- The security gateway allows the FAP access to the core network only if all required authentications are fulfilled successfully.

Thus whenever the data is passed through the femtocell if any vulnerability is detected the data is discarded. On the other hand due to the presence of security gateway no unauthorized user can access the biometric data during transmission. Thus for each individual user registered under a femtocell, the biometric data security during transmission from the MS to the server is achieved. When a number of users are registered under a femtocell the location of the users can be tracked as well no user can give incorrect location intentionally to misguide others. Using our proposed method DAS three-dimensional movement of a user under the coverage of a base station can be predicted (De, 2011), (Mukherjee, 2012). Similarly if the user is registered under a femtocell then his or her movement can be predicted. He or she cannot give wrong information whenever accessing a social networking site or other websites or calling someone. With the biometric data i.e. retina, finger pattern or keystroke his or her current location is also sent to the cloud from the femtocell through the security gateway and then stored in the user database inside cloud. Hence no unauthorized user can access the cloud as well none can misguide others by providing incorrect location information of him or her.

On the other hand protecting biometric data during transmission hacking can be prevented. Most of the time data hacking takes place during transmission which can be dealt with using femtocell. Thus the transmitted biometric data is received at the server end in secured form as well stored inside the user database maintained in the cloud. To achieve higher security cryptography can be used to generate cipher text and then steganography can be applied to hide the cipher data (Mukherjee, 2012). Maintaining biometric data inside cloud in secured form unauthorized access to the data can be prevented and hence biometric data security inside cloud can be achieved.

Role of Trusted Cloud in Biometric Authentication

Researches and studies show that biometrics is a very efficient approach to control and reduce fraudulent activities going around in our everyday lives encircling the electronic world. The biometrics used for the authentication procedures are stored in the cloud for future references. Therefore, it is of utmost importance that the clouds viz. remote servers, used for storing the biometrics, are trusted ones. If the cloud servers are not trustworthy, it might so happen that the stored biometric data can be forged or can be accessed by unauthorized users which eventually spoil the purpose of the entire arrangement. For securing these biometric authentication data, powerful access prevention techniques are intended. Signcryption is one of such techniques which perform the function of digital signature and encryption

Figure 4. Security gateway between femtocell and cloud

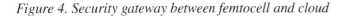

simultaneously that guarantee the confidentiality, integrity and non-repudiation of data. It is used for securing biometric data in the cloud.

Although various types of biometric technologies are there which somehow could uniquely identify the user to some extent, every biometric technology has its own limitations and strengths. Practically, no single biometric technology is expected to meet the required purpose. Hence, various biometrics are collaborated together to get the optimized procedure. These large amounts of data not only are needed to be saved efficiently, but also need to be very secured because these information are the key to successful computation.

Recent Trends and Future Scope

Biometric authentication is a typical security process and is receiving a lot of public attention and it is perhaps the ultimate attempt to prove who you are (Kahate, 2003). It involves the creation of user's sample and its storage in the user database. In real scenario for the authentication the users have to give the sample to the system. The encrypted version of the sample is sent to the server. It is then decrypted and compared with the stored one and the authentication result is given based on comparison and the user gets authenticated (Kahate, 2003). Here we consider the cloud as a storage device where the authentication process is done and the result is sent to the system whether or not the user is authenticated. The process can be used there where high security needed like ATM transaction, money transaction. Though the recent scheme which is used as a authentication process in money transaction is good enough but somehow the system might be hacked by some intruders. Biometric authentication provides security not only in e-cash transaction but also can be used many field where normal security fails to give the protection to the system. The biometric authentication can be categorized into two sub categories namely physiological and behavioral (Kahate, 2003). How the two sub-categories may be used in various field where authentication is needed is shown below:

This section presents how the physiological biometric authentication may be used in various fields like:

1. **Casting Vote:** Voting is the method by which the electorate appoints its representatives in its government. A government is chosen by votes of people so there should be fair vote which help to elect the candidate. Often it is seen that sometimes casting of vote is influenced by unfair means rigging. On that time one gives another's vote and the fair one is deprived from giving fair vote. In this case physiological biometric authentication may be used to organize a fair election.

2. **Use of Fingerprint Sensor in EVM (Electronic Voter Machine):** A fingerprint sensor is an electronic device used to capture a digital image of the fingerprint pattern. The captured image is called a live scan. This live scan is digitally processed to create a biometric template (a collection of extracted features) which is stored and used for matching. This is an overview of some of the more commonly used fingerprint sensor technologies (Maltoni, 2009). This sensor can be used in EVM. At time of voter id card issue every card holder should give the sample of fingerprints to the agent and stored in cloud, at time of giving vote the user give the vote with the help of fingerprint sensor which receive the sample and send it to the respective cloud and matched with the stored one. In this way a fair voting procedure may be possible. Another biometric authentication procedure named retina scan may be used in ATM transaction and how it may be use is shown as follows.

3. **Use of Retina Scan in ATM Transaction:** In retina scanning mechanism the vessels carrying blood supply at the back of human eye which has a unique pattern which help to authenticate an

individual (Kahate, 2003). This retina scan may be used in simple ATM transaction so that no fraud transaction occurs. At the time of opening account the user gives his or her retina pattern with the help of retina scanning device. After that it is stored in the cloud storage where the authentication process will be executed. When the user wants to perform any transaction,he should give the retina pattern to the device which is installed inside ATM machine, and then sample is sent to the cloud via internet and matched with the stored sample. If it matched the user can proceed otherwise the user will be denied access.These are the example of the physiological biometric authentication which may be developed on those fields. There is another biometric authentication named behavioral biometric authentication like keystroke, and how the keystroke mechanism can be used in security purpose is given below.

4. **Behavioral Authentication in Net Banking:** Online banking (or Internet banking or E-banking) allows customers of a financial institution to conduct financial transactions on a secured website operated by the institution, which can be a retail bank,virtual bank, credit union or building society (Maltoni, 2009). In this scheme the security is password based which is not so secure. So to protect the system, keystroke mechanism may be used in net banking. When a user create a net banking profile at that time the keystroke mechanism system records the characteristic like typing speed, strength of keystroke of the user. After creating the profile when the user wants to access the profile then the authentication system match the characteristics of the user with the recorded value. If it matches then the user would be authenticated and gain access to it.

CONCLUSION

Developing trusted cloud models and securing biometric data stored in them is a challenging research issue. During transmission of biometric information from user side to the cloud there is possibility of unauthorized access. To prevent hacking and misuse of biometric data during transmission from mobile device to cloud we have used femtocell. If a mobile device is registered under a femtocell base station then the possibility of hacking is reduced due to the presence of security gateway between femtocell and core network. Due to inbuilt security features femtocell base station serves as a trusted device for accessing the internet. In this chapter we have discussed how femtocell helps to securely transmit biometric data. As not much work has been done in this area, there is always a scope for developing optimized algorithms for maintaining the biometric data security during transmission as well storage inside the cloud.

REFERENCES

Armbrust, M., Fox, A., Griffith, R., Joseph, A. D., Katz, R., Konwinski, A., & ... (2010). A view of cloud computing. *Communications of the ACM*, *53*(4), 50–58. doi:10.1145/1721654.1721672

Ashbourn, J. (2014). Biometrics In the Cloud. In Biometrics in the New World (pp. 37-46). Springer International Publishing.

Ashraf, I. (2010). Improving energy efficiency of femtocell base stations via user activity detection. In *Proceedings of IEEE Wireless Communications and Networking Conference* (pp. 1–5). IEEE. 10.1109/WCNC.2010.5506757

Banerjee, S. P., & Woodard, D. L. (2012). Biometric authentication and identification using keystroke dynamics: A survey. *Journal of Pattern Recognition Research, 7*(1), 116–139. doi:10.13176/11.427

Bolton, R. J., Hand, D. J., Provost, F., Breiman, L., Bolton, R. J., & Hand, D. J. (2002). Statistical fraud detection: A review. *Statistical Science, 17*(3), 235–249. doi:10.1214s/1042727940

Chang, T. Y., Tsai, C.-J., & Lin, J.-H. (2012). A graphical-based password keystroke dynamic authentication system for touch screen handheld mobile devices. *Journal of Systems and Software, 85*(5), 1157–1165. doi:10.1016/j.jss.2011.12.044

Chen, J., & Wong, M. (2012). Security implications and considerations for femtocells. *Journal of Cyber Security and Mobility, 21*(35), 21–36.

De, D., & Mukherjee, A. (2011). *A Cost-Effective Location Management Strategy Based on Movement Pattern of Active Users in a Heterogeneous System.* URSIGA. doi:10.1109/URSIGASS.2011.6050566

De, D., & Mukherjee, A. (2014). Femtocell Based Economic Health Monitoring Scheme using Mobile Cloud Computing. In *Proceedings of International Advance Computing Conference* (pp. 385-390). 10.1109/IAdCC.2014.6779354

Habib, S. M., Hauke, S., Ries, S., & Mühlhäuser, M. (2012). Trust as a facilitator in cloud computing: A survey. *Journal of Cloud Computing, 1*(1), 1–18.

Habib, S. M., Ries, S., & Muhlhauser, M. (2010). Cloud computing landscape and research challenges regarding trust and reputation. In *Proceedings of Seventh International Conference on Autonomic & Trusted Computing* (pp. 410-415). 10.1109/UIC-ATC.2010.48

Hasan, J., Boostanimehr, H., & Bhargava, V. K. (2011). Green Cellular Networks: A Survey, Some research Issues and Challenges. *IEEE Communications Surveys and Tutorials, 13*(4), 524–540. doi:10.1109/SURV.2011.092311.00031

Jain, A. K., Bolle, R., & Pankanti, S. (1999). *Biometrics: Personal identification in networked society.* Springer. doi:10.1007/b117227

Kahate, A. (2003). *Cryptography and Network Security.* Tata McGraw-Hill Education.

Lu, Z. (2012). An energy-efficient power control algorithm in femtocell networks. In *Proceedings of Seventh International Conference on Computer Science & Education* (pp. 395-400). 10.1109/ICCSE.2012.6295100

Mallik, K. G., & De, D. (2012). Energy Efficient Hot Spot Load Balancing in Mobile Cellular Network. In *Proceedings of Third International Conference on Computer and Communication Technology* (pp. 261-266). 10.1109/ICCCT.2012.60

Maltoni, D., Maio, D., Jain, A. K., & Prabhakar, S. (2009). *Handbook of fingerprint recognition.* Springer. doi:10.1007/978-1-84882-254-2

Mukherjee, A., Bhattacherjee, S., Pal, S., & De, D. (2013). Femtocell based green power consumption methods for mobile network. *Computer Networks, 57*(1), 162–178. doi:10.1016/j.comnet.2012.09.007

Mukherjee, A., & De, D. (2012). An Inverse Cell Breathing Based Power Management for Congested Mobile Network. In *Proceedings of Second Annual International Conference on Innovative Techno Management Solutions for Social Sector* (pp. 378-381). Academic Press.

Mukherjee, A., & De, D. (2012). DAS: An Intelligent Three Dimensional Cost Effective Movement Prediction of Active Users in Heterogeneous Mobile Network. *Journal of Computational Intelligence and Electronic Systems, 1*(1), 31–47.

Mukherjee, A., & De, D. (2012). Symmetric Key based Audio Steganography for Mobile Network. *IJEIR, 1*(3), 271–277.

Mukherjee, A., & De, D. (2013). Congestion Detection, Prevention and Avoidance Strategies for an Intelligent, Energy and Spectrum Efficient Green Mobile Network. *Journal of Computational Intelligence and Electronic Systems, 2*(1), 1–19. doi:10.1166/jcies.2013.1044

Mukherjee, A., & De, D. (2014). A Cost-Effective Location Tracking Strategy for Femtocell Based Mobile Network. In *Proceedings of International Conference on Control, Instrumentation, Energy and Communication*. Academic Press.

Mukherjee, A., Gupta, P., & De, D. (2014). Mobile Cloud Computing Based Energy Efficient Offloading Strategies for Femtocell Network. In Applications and Innovations in Mobile Computing (pp. 28-35). doi:10.1109/AIMOC.2014.6785515

Omri, F., Foufou, S., Hamlia, R., & Jarraya, M. (2013). Cloud-based mobile system for biometrics authentication. In *Proceedings of International Conference on ITS Telecommunications* (pp. 325-330). ITS.

PricewaterhouseCoopers LLP. (2009). *2009 Global Economic Crime Survey*. Author.

Pugazhenthi, D., & Vidya, S. B. (2013). Multiple Biometric Security in Cloud Computing. *International Journal of Advanced Research in Computer Science and Software Engineering, 3*(4), 620–624.

Ramaswamy, A., Balasubramanian, A., Vijaykumar, P., & Varalakshmi, P. (2011). A Mobile Agent based Approach of ensuring Trustworthiness in the Cloud. In *Proceedings of IEEE International Conference, Recent Trends in Information Technology* (pp. 678-682). IEEE. 10.1109/ICRTIT.2011.5972467

Rathi, G., Meenakshi, L., Saranya, C., & Sindhu, M. (2013). Credit Card Endorsement using Biometrics in Cloud Computing. *International Journal of Advanced Electrical and Electronics Engineering, 2*(2), 109–114.

Tian, L. Q., Lin, C., & Ni, Y. (2010). Evaluation of user behavior trust in cloud computing. In *Proceedings of IEEE International Conference on Computer Application and System Modeling* (V7-567). IEEE. 10.1109/ICCASM.2010.5620636

Wang, C., Wang, Q., Ren, K., & Lou, W. (2010). Privacy-preserving public auditing for data storage security in cloud computing. In Proceedings of IEEE INFOCOM (pp. 1-9). IEEE. doi:10.1109/INFCOM.2010.5462173

Wang, L., Yan, Y., Hu, Y., & Qian, X. (2014). Speed Measurement and Condition Monitoring of Rotating Machinery Using Electrostatic Sensor Arrays. In *Proceedings of School Research Conference*. Academic Press.

KEY TERMS AND DEFINITIONS

Biometric Authentication: Biometric authentication is defined as a method which is used in computer science to uniquely identify a human being by his or her physiological characteristics and behavior. Physiological characteristics are related to the shape of the body e.g. fingerprint, face recognition, DNA, Palm print, hand geometry, iris recognition, retina etc. Behavioral characteristics are related to the pattern of behavior of a person e.g. typing rhythm, gait, and voice. Each human being has a unique physiological or behavioral characteristic using which he or she can be recognized e.g. voice, face, retina etc. Biometric provides automated methods for identification using unique and measurable physiological or behavioral characteristics such as fingerprint or voice sample etc. These characteristics should not be duplicable, but unfortunately it is possible to create a copy which is acceptable to the biometric system as a true sample. This is where the level of security to be provided. Biometric systems are categorized into two different modes based on their use: (i) Identity verification: It occurs when the user claims to be already enrolled in the system by giving an ID card or login name. In this case the biometric data obtained from the user is compared to the user's data already stored in the database. If the comparison result is true the user gets accessed, (ii) Identification: It occurs when the identity of the user is a priori unknown. In this case the user's biometric data is matched against all the records in the database as the user can be anywhere in the database or he/she actually does not have to be there at all.

Cloud: Cloud refers to an elastic execution environment of resources involving multiple stakeholders and providing a metered service at multiple granularities for a specified level of QoS. Without major technical obstacles cloud platforms allow scalability and global presence. It is also an on demand process when it needs, use it with the help of internet and also pay only for that means as per the nature of uses or services hires. Cloud computing provides basic three services like Infrastructure as a Services (IaaS), Platform as a Services (PaaS) and Software as a Services (SaaS). In IaaS, cloud providers are provided basic storage and compute capabilities as a standardized service over the network as an on demand fashion. IaaS providers supply different resources like virtual machine, servers, storage, firewalls, network etc to perform high performance computing application. In PaaS, cloud providers are encapsulated a layer of software and provided it as a service to build a higher level service. It includes operating system, programming language execution environment, database, and web server etc to provide a clod platform for deploying various applications. In SaaS, cloud providers provide different application software and the software runs on the cloud and cloud users are accessed as a service from the cloud client. Example: salesforce.com, Google application which offers different business application like email, word processing and also different games, communication etc.

Femtocell: The femtocell is a low power and low cost base station which can be deployed inside an indoor building in a plug-and-play manner by the user him or herself. The femtocell is a wireless access point that connects standard mobile devices to a mobile operator's network using residential DSL or cable broadband connection. The functionalities of a femto base station are almost the same as that of a typical macro base station. But the price of femto BS can be significantly lower because: i) a femto BS is expected to serve a small number of users and ii) a relatively low transmission power is enough to cover the service area. Deploying femtocell networks embedded in the macrocell coverage greatly benefits communication quality in variety of manners. Though femtocells are usually deployed in indoor environment to provide in-building coverage enhancements, service can be provided to outdoor users also in vicinity by deploying portable femtocells. A femtocell contains the components: i) Microprocessor, ii) Random access memory, iii) Field Programmable Gate Array (FPGA), iv) RF (Radio Frequency) transmitter, v) RF receiver, and vi) Power amplifier. The microprocessor is used for managing the radio protocol stack and associated baseband processing. The Random access memory is used for handling various data i.e. the collected information related to network traffic, interference condition and user mobility. The FPGA and other circuitry are used for managing the data encryption, hardware authentication and network time protocol. The RF transmitter, RF receiver, power amplifier (PA) and miscellaneous hardware components are used for non-essential functions. The femtocell in idle mode switches off the RF transmitter, RF receiver, miscellaneous hardware and the PA, thus resulting in power saving.

Mobile Cloud Computing: Mobile cloud computing is the combination of mobile computing and cloud computing. It incorporates the cloud computing into the mobile environment. MCC provides a simple and easy infrastructure for mobile applications and services, where both the data storage and the data processing are performed outside the mobile devices and inside the cloud. MCC provides all the cloud services such as Infrastructure as a Service (IaaS), Platform as a Service (PaaS) and Software as a Service (SaaS) which are required for mobile user. MCC provides many applications and services like Mobile commerce, Mobile learning, Mobile healthcare, Mobile gaming etc. Mobile devices can access all the services of the cloud through the internet using MCC. MCC has several advantages for mobile devices like: improving capacity of data storage and processing power, extending battery life, reducing the power consumption of the device, reducing energy consumption of the cloud, improving reliability, scalability, simplicity of integration, on demand service, disaster management etc. Smart phone and tablets are the most useful platform of mobile cloud computing. Smart phones are made by Blakberry, Nokia, Samsung, Google and they use different operating systems like Research in Motion (RIM) BlackBerry operating system, the Windows™ Mobile® operating system, Nokia's Symbian platform, and UNIX variations such as Google Android and Apple iOS to support MCC. Apple iPad and Android tablets made by Samsung, Motorola, and Acer. IBM predicts that by 2015, there will be 1 trillion cloud-ready devices. The 4G technology is the most useful enable technology to improving bandwidth and network latency of Mobile Cloud Computing. HTML5and CSS3 can improve the mobile web applications and allows specification of offline support, which makes local storage possible, helping with connectivity interruptions. Web-4.0 is also used for internet application .Another enabler for cross-platform applications is an embedded hypervisor, which allows a web application to run on any smart phone without concern of the essential architecture. Cloudlet is a device, can be used in MCC for improving the network latency.

Trust: Trust refers to reliability on some person or some system. In computer science, any system is said to be trusted when it behaves the way the user expects it to do. It can be defined as the success rate of any computing system. Mathematically, trust is a probabilistic value which lies between 0 and 1. Trust is a complex concept which has no universally accepted scholarly definition. Evidence from a contemporary, cross-disciplinary collection of scholarly writing suggests that a widely held definition of trust is as follows: "Trust is a psychological state comprising the intention to accept vulnerability based upon positive expectations of the intentions or behaviour of another." Trust is a broader notion than security as it includes subjective criteria and experience. Correspondingly, there exist both hard (security-oriented) and soft trust (i. e. non-security oriented trust) solutions. "Hard" trust involves aspects like authenticity, encryption, and security in transactions. The "soft" trust involves human psychology, brand loyalty, and userfriendliness. Some soft issues are involved in security, nevertheless. When trust is related to cloud computing, it is classified as persistent and dynamic trust to distinguish between social and technological means. Persistent trust referes to trust involving long-term underlying properties or infrastructure and this arises through relatively static social and technological mechanisms. Dynamic trust refers to trust specific to certain states, contexts, or short-term or variable information; this can arise through context-based social and technological mechanisms. Persistent social-based trust in a hardware or software component or system is an expression of confidence in technological-based trust, because it is assurance about implementation and operation of that component or system. In particular, there are links between social-based trust and technological-based trust through the vouching mechanism, because it is important to know who is vouching for something as well as what they are vouching; hence social-based trust should always be considered.

This research was previously published in the Handbook of Research on Securing Cloud-Based Databases with Biometric Applications edited by Ganesh Chandra Deka and Sambit Bakshi, pages 320-336, copyright year 2015 by Information Science Reference (an imprint of IGI Global).

Chapter 45

Modelling of Cloud Computing Enablers Using MICMAC Analysis and TISM

Nitin Chawla
Amity University, India

Deepak Kumar
Amity University, India

ABSTRACT

This article describes how Cloud Computing is not just a buzzword but a shift from IT departments to the outsourcing vendors without impacting business efficiency. Some organizations are moving towards cloud computing but many have resistance to adopting cloud computing due to limitations in knowledge and awareness of the classifying elements, which effect decisions on the acceptance of cloud computing. Therefore, this article has focused on accumulating the elements, which can act as enablers, by reviewing existing literature and studies from both professional and academic viewpoints. All the identified enablers have been structurally modeled to develop the relationship matrix and establish the driving power and dependence power of every element. This is done by employing Total Interpretive Structural Modeling (TISM) and Cross Impact Matrix Multiplication Applied to Classification (MICMAC) analysis.

INTRODUCTION

In this business world, organizations have become competitive and global. The aim of most of the organizations is long-standing endurance and it depends upon organization's ability to enable its business processes and needs by implementing applications with the help of IT at moderate upfront investment and minimum maintenance cost. Now is the time to initiate the deliberation about IT infrastructure and IT application which need to be more dynamic to address the significant infrastructure challenges. Organizations must start cognizant thinking to build or improve IT infrastructure to support flexible and on demand business needs. Flexibility and Agility are the key to tackle the business requirements which are continuously changing or increasing. Cloud computing has given the option to use IT resources

DOI: 10.4018/978-1-5225-8176-5.ch045

either infrastructure or application or both on private cloud or public cloud. From business perspective, self service offerings on SaaS model with pay-as-you-go pricing options are available. Services can be provisioned in very less time with the flexibility to scale up or down along with the prices. From IT perspective, lesser involvement of IT resources in infrastructure management and better service delivery with the improved SLAs are driving factors. Virtualization of IT infrastructure has become the backbone of cloud computing by fulfilling the need of shared usage of large pool of resources.

Internet of Things enabled billions of devices using cloud computing and Smart home is one of the solution where cloud along with IOT is moving along hand in hand. A research provides details of contributions in facilitating the readiness of the concept "Internet of Things" in Smart Homes. In this paper, we have studied roles of cloud computing in supporting Smart Home, scope and components of Smarter Homes' technologies required for Smarter Homes (Sharma, Chawla, & Kumar, 2015).

Internet of Things is getting famous and matured day by day. There might be millions of IOT devices connecting to the Internet via Cloud Computing. Security and QoS shall play a big role while using IOT devices to run the IOT Solutions in smoother way. Mathematical Modelling shows the parameters to be considered for QoS without affecting the performance and security of the solution. The study also proposes the mathematical model for QoS parameters like reliability, communication complexities, latency and aggregation of data for IoT (Mahamure, Railkar, & Mahalle, 2017).

Organizations face difficulties in dealing with complex issues because of availability of ample impacted attributes or criterion and their relationships among each other. The existence of inter relationship between attributes complicates the articulation in an understandable manner. Thus, development of ISM methodology (Sage, 1977), which facilitates in recognizing a structure within a system, took place.

Usage of IT applications and infrastructure is going to increase so that business can run smoothly and that with the right way to manage its data and processes. Advances in Information and Technology has lead the need of cloud computing. Cloud computing is computing paradigm which offers infrastructure or platform or software as a service. Cloud computing backbone is the architecture of need based resource distribution while leveraging multiple technologies such as Virtual Machines. Cloud computing also offers services such has levels of service management, lower downtime and higher uptime window. Cloud computing provides services based on the needs of the organizations for example increased CPUs for faster processing, dedicating RAM to support high transaction volume (Buyyaa, Yeo, Venugopal, Broberg, & Brandic, 2009).

Cloud computing has brought multiple improvements in data center like low utilization of equipment, high energy consumption. A study shows how to establish distributed traffic cloud data center based on SOA (Service-Oriented Architecture) fused with cloud computing along with the application of DENS (Data- center Energy-efficient Network-aware Scheduling) algorithm to realize the full utilization of resources in Cloud Data Center (Zhang, Qi, & Deng, 2017).

Adoption of new technology or concept is always a challenge that's why there are still some reservations to adopt cloud computing. Various strategies and factors have been identified which helps the organizations in adoption of cloud computing. Factors not only cover the technical aspects but also cover other functional and cost related aspects to identify the right Cloud computing environment. Some of the factors are Capital Expenditure required to use an application or infrastructure, lead time to enable the application or its related infrastructure, security related aspects or factors, availability of the application or infrastructure (Nitin & Kumar, 2015).

This paper is divided into multiple sections as follows: Section 2 highlights the review of some of the existing literature to identify the elements that might affect the adoption of cloud computing. Section 3 shows the key enablers that are used for structural modelling by establishing the contextual relationship among the enablers. After which, final reachability matrix has been defined which are used for portioning and then arrive to a MICMAC analysis. Last section presents the conclusion and suggestions for future research.

LITERATURE REVIEW

Cloud computing provides the platform to deploy infrastructure or applications which can be accessed using internet or intranet. The model of Cloud computing is different from the conventional model in which an organization needs to setup the IT infrastructure by procuring servers, hardware, switches, applications licenses etc. Cloud computing offers everything in the form of services and it depends on the needs of IT department of the organization that IT infrastructure is required on cloud or application is required on cloud for example more storage power can be fulfilled by cloud as well as online email as a service is also offered by cloud. Generally, cloud-delivered services have following common attributes in total and are also depicted in Figure 1:

- Clients will need to embrace standards to take advantage of Cloud Services;
- Pay As you go model and low upfront investments give benefits in pricing;
- Higher flexibility to scale up or scale down as per business demands;
- Virtualized servers, network and storage are pooled in a centralized location without impacting the customer's application or usage on sharing basis.

Figure 1. Cloud computing

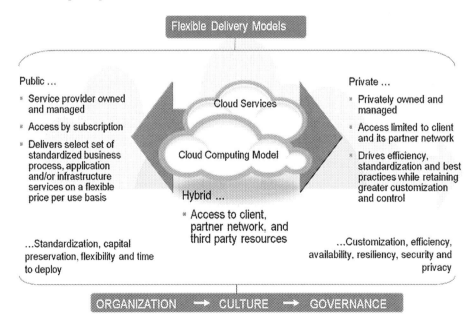

Security is one of the major concerns when somebody think of adopting cloud computing. Some of the security concerns are controlling of encryption/decryption keys, physical security of the server is lost because of usage of shared resources with other organizations, data migration from existing environment to the cloud, ensuring data integrity and data privacy (Kushwah & Saxena, 2013).

Multiple security problems are discussed in cloud computing along with the approach to fight security problems. A study showed that data privacy in the cloud- based systems is the main concern and through comparative analysis security problem cannot be tackled by single security method. Many conventional and recent technologies and strategies are required to protect the cloud-based solutions. There are multiple views in terms of security is concerned such as cloud architecture view, delivery model view, characteristics view, and the stakeholder view. Some solutions are investigated through which the dynamic cloud model can be secured (Liu, 2012; Behl & Behl, 2012).

Senthilnathan mentioned in his study about the retail consumer segment in India and how the whole market is divided into urban and rural markets. This study also talks about shopping behaviour in grocery segment and concluded that shoppers need multiple formats based on multiple geography locations (Senthilnathan, 2016). Cloud Computing can also provide a channel for urban markets as it provides ease and convenience in shopping to the retailers.

Multiple Solutions are getting developed in Cloud Computing and thus providing the feasibility of flexibility, security using resource sharing platform. Distributed Computing is getting replaced by Cloud Computing. Cloud Computing provides the innovative way of delivering infrastructure and applications resources as well as services. A study shows how Medical Information System is deployed using Cloud Computing (Kldiashvili, 2014).

A Study, done by Young-Chan Lee, has presented a framework to choose the cloud computing deployment model suitable for an organization. This decision model is developed using Analytic Hierarchy Process (AHP) and benefit-cost-opportunity-risk (BCOR) analysis. It has four hierarchies: benefits, costs, opportunity and risks). All the hierarchies have some attributes related to its category (Lee, Young-Chan, Hanh, & Nguyen, 2012).

Another study showed key attributes with the advantages and threats of cloud computing influencing the adoption decision. This study has defined the type of attributes affect the adoption of cloud computing. This study not only shows the attributes but also shows the motivation/benefits and concerns/risks related to those attributes. This literature explored the inclination of an enterprise to accept cloud computing services because key drivers for adoption were managed services by third party to adhere better SLAs and usage of advanced technology. Decision of Cloud was based on three theoretical perceptions: Transaction cost theory, resource dependence theory and diffusion of innovation theory (Nuseibeh, 2011).

In the world of millions of applications, infrastructure always plays the crucial part for the deployment. Multiple studies try to optimize the use of infrastructure such as storage such as creation of Data warehouse which helps the organization in generating multiple views but high response time while processing the multiple queries is always an issue. Some of the views are not even materialized due to storage issues (Arun, & Kumar, 2015).

Another study shows the application of Health assistance which will allow the detection of malaise and the management of the driver and the vehicle. This application is offered on cloud as "Health-Assistance as a Service" using Cloud Computing (Benadda, Bouamrane, & Belalem, 2017).

Cloud Computing provides high performance of security and trust. There are service providers who provides Cloud Computing services with better services with assurance of trust about clients' information. A Study shows the statistical method known as Multivariate Normal Distribution is used to select different attributes of different security entities for developing the proposed model. Finally, fuzzy multi objective decision making and Bio-Inspired Bat algorithm are applied to achieve the objective (Sarkar, Banerjee, Badr, & Sangaiah 2017).

The Total Interpretive Structural Modeling (TISM) process is used for finding the relationship among the identified variables or elements that act as enablers and are the source of a problem or an issue. It is a well defined & comprehensive systemic model useful to structure variables that are directly or indirectly linked. A structure was defined to know the relationship of the elements. Lastly the relationship of the elements was represented in the form of diagraph model. All the elements were given the category of driving power or dependence power which helps to identify the complexity of the relationship (Sage, 1977).

Total Interpretive Structural Modeling (TISM) begins with the identification of various attributes, applicable to the issue, and then broadens with the team problem solving technique. After applicable secondary relation is decided, a pairwise comparison of variables is performed to develop structural self-interaction matrix (SSIM). As a subsequent stride, reachability matrix (RM) is arrived based on SSIM to obtain a matrix. Then, using partitioning and diagraph TISM model is derived (Warfield, 1974).

METHODOLOGY

The basic idea to adopt cloud computing is to improve efficiency, cost reduction and increased flexibility. Clientele is the originator of the offering price of the services or products offered by the organizations. Pricing capacity of the customer depends upon the product or services quality. The crucial way to make profits in the organization is by having less operational cost. For the companies, reduction in operational cost is the basic principle and it can have any of the following things to manage:

- Application implementation
- Application maintenance
- Utilization of resources
- Data Security
- Data Privacy
- Software Licensing
- Infrastructure procurement
- Infrastructure life
- Infrastructure maintenance
- Time to market
- Complexity

In this study, identification of key enablers, as mentioned in Table 1, has been performed by going through multiple existing studies and brainstorming session conducted with cloud computing experts. Then, multiple sessions were conducted to recognize the key elements which will act as enablers identified by literature review. The enablers shown in Table 1 were decided for this study. This paper uses TISM and MICMAC Analysis to do modeling to know the interrelationship between the enablers.

Table 1. Identifikation of key enablers

S. No.	Key Enablers
C-1	Upfront Capital Investment for software
C-2	Upfront Capital Investment for infrastructure
C-3	Deployment Model
C-4	Data Security & Privacy
C-5	Data Privacy
C-6	Data Migration
C-7	Deployment/Implementation
C-8	Involvement of Employees
C-9	Process improvement, reduction in cycle time
C-10	Use of advanced technology
C-11	SLA Improvements
C-12	Agility to upscale anytime
C-13	Internet Speed/Latency
C-14	Outages
C-15	Disaster recovery
C-16	Automatic Updates
C-17	Data Ownership

Interpretive Structural Modeling Steps

The different steps involved in TISM modeling are as follows and are also depicted in Figure 2:

Step 1: Literature study and survey contributes the classification of elements relevant to the issue for this study and elements are mentioned in Table 1.

Step 2: Institute a relative relationship between the enablers.

Step 3: Based on the discussion with industry experts, structural self interaction matrix (SSIM) is extended for elements that show pair-wise relations between elements.

Step 4: Initial reachability matrix is shaped based on structural self interaction matrix by substituting 1s and 0s in place of Y and N in the initial reachability matrix. Transitivity concept has been induced to obtain the reachability matrix.

Step 5: Reachability set and antecedent sets are derived for each element and to discover the level of each element partitions are done.

Step 6: Based on the driving power and dependence power, elements are placed on the Conical matrix clusters (Linkages, Dependent, Independent and Autonomous).

Step 7: The preliminary diagraph is obtained. After removing the transitivity, a final diagraph is developed.

Step 8: Diagraph is converted into the TISM model by replacing nodes of the factors with statements.

Figure 2. Flow diagram for preparing TISM model

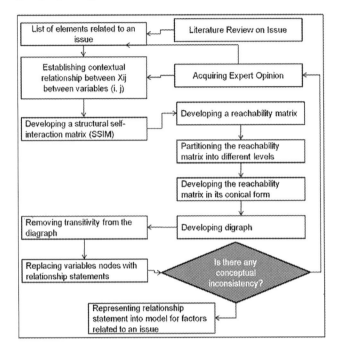

Structural Self-Interaction Matrix (SSIM)

Elements are identified using literature study and integrated approach is required to build a structural relationship among the elements by using various processes like brain storming with industry and academic experts. Nature of contextual relationships among the elements has been achieved.

We are using TISM methodology which guides to create the contextual relationship matrix between the elements. If one element influences another element, then "Y" is marked otherwise "N" is marked as depicted in Table 2.

Table 2. Structural Self-interaction Matrix (SSIM)

Code	Elements	C-17	C-16	C-15	C-14	C-13	C-12	C-11	C-10	C-9	C-8	C-7	C-6	C-5	C-4	C-3	C-2	C-1
C-1	Upfront Capital Investment for software	N	N	N	N	N	N	Y	Y	Y	N	N	N	N	N	N	Y	Y
C-2	Upfront Capital Investment for infrastructure	N	Y	N	N	N	Y	Y	N	Y	Y	N	N	N	Y	N	Y	Y
C-3	Deployment Model	Y	Y	Y	Y	Y	Y	Y	N	Y	Y	Y	Y	Y	Y	Y	Y	Y
C-4	Data Security	N	N	N	N	N	N	Y	Y	Y	N	N	N	N	Y	Y	Y	Y
C-5	Data Privacy	N	N	N	N	N	N	N	Y	Y	N	Y	N	Y	N	Y	N	N
C-6	Data Migration	N	N	N	N	Y	N	Y	Y	Y	N	N	Y	N	N	Y	N	N
C-7	Data Ownership	N	N	N	N	N	N	Y	Y	Y	N	Y	N	Y	N	Y	N	N
C-8	Deployment/Implementation	N	Y	N	N	N	N	Y	Y	Y	Y	N	N	N	Y	Y	Y	N
C-9	Service Model	Y	Y	Y	Y	Y	Y	Y	N	Y	Y	Y	Y	Y	Y	Y	Y	Y
C-10	Process improvement, reduction in cycle time	N	N	N	N	N	N	Y	Y	N	Y	Y	N	Y	Y	N	N	Y
C-11	Use of advanced technology	Y	N	N	N	N	N	Y	N	Y	Y	Y	Y	Y	Y	Y	Y	Y
C-12	SLA Improvements	Y	Y	Y	N	N	Y	N	Y	N	Y	N	N	N	N	Y	Y	N
C-13	Agility to upscale anytime	Y	N	N	N	Y	Y	N	N	Y	N	N	Y	N	N	Y	Y	N
C-14	Internet Speed/Latency	Y	Y	Y	Y	Y	Y	N	N	Y	N	N	Y	N	N	Y	N	N
C-15	Outages	N	N	Y	Y	N	N	N	N	Y	N	N	Y	N	N	Y	N	N
C-16	Disaster recovery	N	Y	Y	Y	N	Y	N	N	Y	N	N	N	N	N	Y	Y	Y
C-17	Automatic Updates	Y	N	Y	Y	N	N	Y	N	Y	N	N	N	N	N	Y	N	N

Development of Reachability Matrix

Reachability matrix from the SSIM is to be developed. The SSIM has been converted into a binary matrix, by substituting Y and N to 1 and 0 and shown in Table 3.

Subsequent step is to redefine few of the cells which are influenced by inference. It can be achieved by inducing the transitivity and final reachability matrix can be defined in Table 4.

Level Partitions

After getting the final reachability matrix, reachability set, antecedent set and intersection set has been found and shown in Tables 5 to 9.

The reachability set consists of the element itself and the other element, which it may help achieve. The antecedent set consists of the element itself and another element, which may help achieving it.

Table 3. Initial reachability Matrix

Code	Elements	C-17	C-16	C-15	C-14	C-13	C-12	C-11	C-10	C-9	C-8	C-7	C-6	C-5	C-4	C-3	C-2	C-1
C-1	Upfront Capital Investment for software	0	0	0	0	0	0	1	1	1	0	0	0	0	0	0	1	1
C-2	Upfront Capital Investment for infrastructure	0	1	0	0	0	1	1	0	1	1	0	0	0	1	0	1	1
C-3	Deployment Model	1	1	1	1	1	1	1	0	0	1	1	1	1	1	1	1	1
C-4	Data Security	0	0	0	0	0	0	1	1	1	0	0	0	0	1	1	1	0
C-5	Data Privacy	0	0	0	0	0	0	0	1	1	0	1	0	1	0	1	0	0
C-6	Data Migration	0	0	0	0	1	0	1	1	1	0	0	1	0	0	1	0	0
C-7	Data Ownership	0	0	0	0	0	0	1	1	1	0	1	0	1	0	1	0	0
C-8	Deployment/Implementation	0	1	0	0	0	0	1	1	1	1	0	0	0	1	1	1	0
C-9	Service Model	1	1	1	1	1	1	1	0	1	1	1	1	1	1	1	1	1
C-10	Process improvement, reduction in cycle time	0	0	0	0	0	0	1	1	0	1	1	0	1	1	0	0	1
C-11	Use of advanced technology	1	0	0	0	0	0	1	0	1	1	1	1	1	1	1	1	1
C-12	SLA Improvements	1	1	1	1	0	1	1	0	1	0	0	0	1	0	1	1	0
C-13	Agility to upscale anytime	1	0	0	0	1	1	0	0	1	0	0	1	0	0	1	1	0
C-14	Internet Speed/Latency	1	1	1	1	1	1	0	0	1	0	0	1	0	0	1	0	0
C-15	Outages	0	0	1	1	0	0	0	0	1	0	0	1	0	0	1	0	0
C-16	Disaster recovery	0	1	1	1	0	1	0	0	1	0	0	0	0	0	1	1	1
C-17	Automatic Updates	1	0	1	1	0	0	1	0	1	0	0	0	0	0	1	0	0
		7	7	7	6	5	7	12	7	15	6	6	7	6	7	14	10	7

Table 4. Final reachability Matrix

Code	Elements	C-17	C-16	C-15	C-14	C-13	C-12	C-11	C-10	C-9	C-8	C-7	C-6	C-5	C-4	C-3	C-2	C-1	Driver Power
C-1	Upfront Capital Investment for software	0	0	0	0	0	0	1	1	1	0	0	0	0	0	0	1	1	5
C-2	Upfront Capital Investment for infrastructure	0	1	0	0	0	1	1	0	1	1	0	0	0	1	0	1	1	8
C-3	Deployment Model	1	1	1	1	1	1	1	0	0	1	1	1	1	1	1	1	1	15
C-4	Data Security	0	0	0	0	0	0	1	1	1	0	0	0	0	1	1	1	0	6
C-5	Data Privacy	0	0	0	0	0	0	0	1	1	0	1	0	1	0	1	0	0	5
C-6	Data Migration	0	0	0	0	1	0	1	1	1	0	0	1	0	0	1	0	0	6
C-7	Data Ownership	0	0	0	0	0	0	1	1	1	0	1	0	1	0	1	0	0	6
C-8	Deployment/Implementation	0	1	0	0	0	0	1	1	1	1	0	0	0	1	1	1	0	8
C-9	Service Model	1	1	1	1	1	1	1	0	1	1	1	1	1	1	1	1	1	16
C-10	Process improvement, reduction in cycle time	0	0	0	0	0	0	1	1	0	1	1	1*	1	1	0	0	1	8
C-11	Use of advanced technology	1	0	0	0	0	0	1	0	1	1	1	1	1	1	1	1	1	11
C-12	SLA Improvements	1	1	1	1	0	1	1	0	1	0	0	0	0	0	1	1	0	9
C-13	Agility to upscale anytime	1	0	0	0	1	1	1*	0	1	0	0	1	0	0	1	1	0	8
C-14	Internet Speed/Latency	1	1	1	1	1	1	1*	0	1	0	0	1	0	0	1	0	0	10
C-15	Outages	0	0	1	1	0	0	0	0	1	0	0	1	0	0	1	0	0	5
C-16	Disaster recovery	0	1	1	1	0	1	0	0	1	0	0	0	0	0	1	1	1	8
C-17	Automatic Updates	1	0	1	1	1*	0	1	0	1	0	0	0	0	0	1	0	0	7

Table 5. Iteration 1 / Level 1

		LEVEL PARTITION - LEVEL1			
Code	Elements	Reachability Set	Antecedent Set	Intersection Set	Level
C-1	Upfront Capital Investment for software	1,2,9,10,11	1,2,3,9,10,11,16	1,2,9,10,11	1
C-2	Upfront Capital Investment for infrastructure	1,2,4,8,9,11,12,16	1,2,3,4,8,9,11,12,13,16	1,2,8,9,11,12,16	
C-3	Deployment Model	1,2,3,4,5,6,7,8,11,12,13,14,15,16,17	2,3,4,5,6,7,8,9,11,12,13,14,15,16,17	2,3,4,5,6,7,8,11,12,13,14,15,16,17	
C-4	Data Security	1,2,3,9,10,11	2,3,4,8,9,10,11	2,3,9,10,11	
C-5	Data Privacy	3,5,7,9,10	3,5,7,9,10,11	3,5,7,9,10	1
C-6	Data Migration	3,6,9,10,11,13	3,6,9,10,11,13,14,15	3,6,9,10,11,13	1
C-7	Data Ownership	3,5,7,9,10,11	3,5,7,9,10,11	3,5,7,9,10,11	1
C-8	Deployment/Implementation	2,3,4,8,9,10,11,16	2,3,8,9,10,11	2,3,8,9,10,11	
C-9	Service Model	1,2,3,4,5,6,7,8,9,11,12,13,14,15,16,17	1,2,4,5,6,7,8,9,11,12,13,14,15,16,17	1,2,4,5,6,7,8,9,11,12,13,14,15,16,17	
C-10	Process improvement, reduction in cycle time	1,4,5,6,7,8,10,11	1,4,5,6,7,8,10	1,4,5,6,8,10	
C-11	Use of advanced technology	1,2,3,4,5,6,7,8,9,11,17	1,2,3,4,6,7,8,9,10,11,12,13,14,17	1,2,3,4,6,7,8,9,11,17	
C-12	SLA Improvements	2,3,9,11,12,13,15,16,17	2,3,9,12,13,14,16	2,3,9,12,16	
C-13	Agility to upscale anytime	2,3,6,9,11,12,13,17	3,6,9,12,13,14,17	3,6,9,12,13,17	
C-14	Internet Speed/Latency	3,6,9,12,13,14,15,16,17	3,9,14,15,16,17	3,9,14,15,16,17	
C-15	Outages	3,6,9,14,15	3,9,12,14,15,16,17	3,9,14,15	
C-16	Disaster recovery	1,2,3,9,12,14,15,16	2,3,8,9,11,14,16	2,3,9,14,16	
C-17	Automatic Updates	3,9,11,13,14,15,17	3,9,12,13,17	3,9,11,13,17	
			0	0	

Table 6. Iteration 2 / Level 2

		LEVEL PARTITION - LEVEL2			
Code	Elements	Reachability Set	Antecedent Set	Intersection Set	Level
C-2	Upfront Capital Investment for infrastructure	2,4,8,9,11,12,16	2,3,4,8,9,11,12,13,16	2,8,9,11,12,16	
C-3	Deployment Model	2,3,4,8,11,12,13,14,15,16,17	2,3,4,8,9,11,12,13,14,15,16,17	2,3,4,8,11,12,13,14,15,16,17	2
C-4	Data Security	2,3,9,10,11	2,3,4,8,9,10,11	2,3,9,10,11	2
C-8	Deployment/Implementation	2,3,4,8,9,10,11,16	2,3,8,9,10,11	2,3,8,9,10,11	
C-9	Service Model	2,3,4,8,9,11,12,13,14,15,16,17	2,4,8,9,11,12,13,14,15,16,17	2,4,8,9,11,12,13,14,15,16,17	
C-10	Process improvement, reduction in cycle time	4,8,10,11	4,8,10	4,8,10	
C-11	Use of advanced technology	2,3,4,8,9,11,17	2,3,4,8,9,10,11,12,13,14,17	2,3,4,8,9,11,17	2
C-12	SLA Improvements	2,3,9,11,12,13,15,16,17	2,3,9,12,13,14,16	2,3,9,12,16	
C-13	Agility to upscale anytime	2,3,9,11,12,13,17	3,9,12,13,14,17	3,9,12,13,17	
C-14	Internet Speed/Latency	3,9,12,13,14,15,16,17	3,9,14,15,16,17	3,9,14,15,16,17	
C-15	Outages	3,9,14,15	3,9,12,14,15,16,17	3,9,14,15	2
C-16	Disaster recovery	2,3,9,12,14,15,16	2,3,8,9,11,14,16	2,3,9,14,16	
C-17	Automatic Updates	3,9,11,13,14,15,17	3,9,12,13,17	3,9,11,13,17	

Table 7. Iteration 3 / Level 3

		LEVEL PARTITION - LEVEL3			
Code	Elements	Reachability Set	Antecedent Set	Intersection Set	Level
C-2	Upfront Capital Investment for infrastructure	2,8,9,12,16	2,8,9,12,13,16	2,8,9,12,16	3
C-8	Deployment/Implementation	2,8,9,10,16	2,8,9,10,11	2,8,9,10,11	
C-9	Service Model	2,8,9,12,13,14,16,17	2,8,9,12,13,14,16,17	2,8,9,12,13,14,16,17	3
C-10	Process improvement, reduction in cycle time	8,10,11	8,10	8,10	
C-12	SLA Improvements	2,9,12,13,16,17	2,9,12,13,14,16	2,9,12,16	
C-13	Agility to upscale anytime	2,9,12,13,17	9,12,13,14,17	9,12,13,17	
C-14	Internet Speed/Latency	9,12,13,14,16,17	9,14,16,17	9,14,16,17	
C-16	Disaster recovery	2,9,12,14,16	2,8,9,14,16	2,9,14,16	
C-17	Automatic Updates	9,13,14,17	9,12,13,17	9,13,17	

Table 8. Iteration 4 / Level 4

		LEVEL PARTITION - LEVEL4			
Code	Elements	Reachability Set	Antecedent Set	Intersection Set	Level
C-8	Deployment/Implementation	8,10,16	8,10,11	8,10,11	
C-10	Process improvement, reduction in cycle time	8,10,11	8,10	8,10	
C-12	SLA Improvements	12,13,16,17	12,13,14,16	12,16	
C-13	Agility to upscale anytime	12,13,17	12,13,14,17	12,13,17	4
C-14	Internet Speed/Latency	12,13,14,16,17	14,16,17	14,16,17	
C-16	Disaster recovery	12,14,16	8,14,16	14,16	
C-17	Automatic Updates	13,14,17	12,13,17	13,17	

Table 9. Iteration 5 / Level 5

		LEVEL PARTITION - LEVEL5			
Code	Elements	Reachability Set	Antecedent Set	Intersection Set	Level
C-8	Deployment/Implementation	8,10,16	8,10,11	8,10,11	
C-10	Process improvement, reduction in cycle time	8,10,11	8,10	8,10	
C-12	SLA Improvements	12,16,17	12,14,16	12,16	
C-14	Internet Speed/Latency	12,14,16,17	14,16,17	14,16,17	
C-16	Disaster recovery	12,14,16	8,14,16	14,16	
C-17	Automatic Updates	14,17	12,17	17	

Thereafter, intersection of these two sets is derived for all elements. One by one the elements having the same reachability set and intersection set are eliminated during consecutive iteration. There are multiple levels defined for the elements and these levels assign in creating the diagraph.

MICMAC Analysis and TISM Diagraph

Cloud Computing adoption enablers are divided into four groups:

- **Autonomous enablers:** These elements have weak driving and weak dependencies power so these are disconnected from the system or have fewer linkages available in the system;
- **Dependent enablers:** These elements have strong dependence but weak driving power;
- **Linkage enablers:** This group have strong driving and strong dependency power. These elements have the direct impact on other elements and are impacted from other elements;
- **Independent enablers:** These elements have strong driving power but weak dependence power. These elements impact other elements but are unaffected by other elements actions.

These enablers are segregated on depending upon their driving power and dependencies as shown in Table 5 and categorized in Figure 3.

Final Reachability matrix, mentioned in Table 4, has been used to create the structural model. This graph is known as directed graph, or diagraph. This diagraph is converted into TISM-based model for the adoption of cloud computing as shown in Figure 4.

Figure 3. Cluster of cloud computing enablers

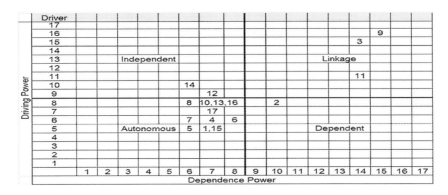

Figure 4. Interpretive structural model of cloud computing adoption enablers

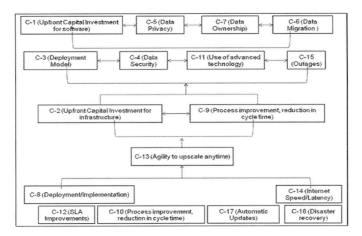

CONCLUSION

The key enablers are essential in adoption of cloud computing for the organizations. There are some important enablers visible in this study and these enablers are put in to an interpretive structure modeling model to explore the relationship among them. Key enablers need to evaluate the successful adoption of cloud computing. The TISM methodology was used to establish the driving power and dependencies of the enablers identified.

TISM proves that all the enablers play an important role in the successful adoption of cloud computing. In this research, some enablers have been used to develop the TISM model, but more enablers can be included to develop the relationship among them using the TISM methodology.

The limitation of this study is that the model developed here is not statistically verified so future study can be conducted to implement this model.

REFERENCES

Arun, B., & Kumar, T. V. V. (2015). Materialized View Selection using Marriage in Honey Bees Optimization. *International Journal of Natural Computing Research*, 5(3), 1–25. doi:10.4018/IJNCR.2015070101

Behl, K., & Behl, A. (2012). An analysis of cloud computing security issues. *IEEE Transactions on Information and Communication Technologies*, 2(2), 109–114.

Benadda, M., Bouamrane, K., & Belalem, G. (2017). How to Manage Persons Taken Malaise at the Steering Wheel Using HAaaS in a Vehicular Cloud Computing Environment. *International Journal of Ambient Computing and Intelligence*, 8(2), 70–87.

Bowers, L. (2011, July). Cloud Computing Efficiency. *Applied Clinical Trials*, 20(7), 45–51.

Buyyaa, R., Yeo, C. S., Venugopal, S., Broberg, J., & Brandic, I. (2009). Cloud computing and emerging IT platforms: Vision, hype, and reality for delivering computing as the 5th utility. Retrieved from www.elsevier.com/locate/fgcs

Chawla, N., Kumar, D., & Strategy, C. C. (2015). Journey to Adoption of cloud. In *Proc. National Conference on Computing, Communication and Information Processing*, Itanagar, India (pp. 112-122).

Dinesh, K.S., Chawla, N., & Kumar, D. (2015). Cloud Computing in Smarter Homes: Enablement of Internet of Things. *Review of Business and Technology Research*, 12(1), 34-39.

Final Version of NIST Cloud Computing Definition Published. (2013, August 25). Retrieved from http://www.nist.gov/itl/csd/cloud-102511.cfm

Forrester Research. (2009). Is Cloud Computing Ready for the Enterprise? Retrieved from http://forrester.com

Katzan, H. (2010). On the Privacy of Cloud Computing. *International Journal of Management & Information Systems*, 14(2), 1–12.

Kldiashvili, E. (2014). Application of the Cloud Computing for the Effective Implementation of the Medical Information System. *International Journal of Natural Computing Research*, 4(3), 52–68. doi:10.4018/ijncr.2014070103

Kushwah, V. S., & Saxena, A. (2013, May). A Security approach for Data Migration in Cloud Computing. *International Journal of Scientific and Research Publications*, 3(5).

Lee, Young-Chan and Hanh, Tang Nguyen, (2012). A Study on Decision Making Factors of Cloud Computing Adoption Using BCOR Approach. *Journal of the Korea society of IT services*, 11(1), 155-171. doi:10.9716/KITS.2012.11.1.155

Liu, W. (2012). *Research on cloud computing security problem and strategy* (pp. 1216–1219). IEEE. doi:10.1109/CECNet.2012.6202020

Mahamure, S., Railkar, P. N., & Mahalle, P. N. (2017). Mathematical Representation of Quality of Service (QoS) Parameters for Internet of Things (IoT). *International Journal of Rough Sets and Data Analysis*, 4(3), 96–107. doi:10.4018/IJRSDA.2017070107

McAfee, A. (2011, November). What every CEO needs to know about the Cloud. Harvard Business Review, 89(11), 124-133

Mell, P., & Grance, T. (2009). The NIST Definition of Cloud Computing. NIST. Retrieved from http:// csrc.nist.gov/publications/nistpubs/800-145/SP800-145.pdf

Nuseibeh, H. (2011). Adoption of Cloud Computing in Organizations (Paper 372). *AMCIS Proceedings*.

Sabahi, F. (May 2011), Virtualization-level security in cloud computing. In Proceedings of the 2011, IEEE 3rd International Conference on Communication Software and Networks (ICCSN), Xi'an, China (pp. 250–254).

Sage, A. P. (1977). *Interpretive structural modeling: Methodology for large scale systems*. New York, NY: McGraw-Hill.

Sarkar, M., Banerjee, S., Badr, Y., & Sangaiah, A. K. (2017). Configuring a Trusted Cloud Service Model for Smart City Exploration Using Hybrid Intelligence. *International Journal of Ambient Computing and Intelligence*, 8(3), 1–21. doi:10.4018/IJACI.2017070101

Sengupta, S., & Kaulgud, V.; Sharma (2011, July 4–9). V.S. Cloud computing security—Trends and research directions. In *Proceedings of the 2011 IEEE World Congress on Services (SERVICES)*, Washington, DC (pp. 524–531). 10.1109/SERVICES.2011.20

Senthilnathan, C. R. (2016). Understanding Retail Consumer Shopping Behaviour Using Rough Set Approach. *International Journal of Rough Sets and Data Analysis*, 3(3), 38–50. doi:10.4018/IJRS-DA.2016070103

Sriram, I., & Khajeh-Hosseini, A. (2010), Research Agenda in Cloud Technologies. In Proceeding of IEEE CLOUD '10, Miami, FL.

Zhang, W., Qi, Q., & Deng, J. (2017). Building Intelligent Transportation Cloud Data Center Based on SOA. *International Journal of Ambient Computing and Intelligence*, 8(2), 1–11. doi:10.4018/ IJACI.2017040101

This research was previously published in the International Journal of Ambient Computing and Intelligence (IJACI), 9(3); edited by Nilanjan Dey, pages 31-43, copyright year 2018 by IGI Publishing (an imprint of IGI Global).

Chapter 46
Byzantine Fault–Tolerant Architecture in Cloud Data Management

Mohammed A. AlZain
Taif University, Saudi Arabia

Alice S. Li
La Trobe University, Australia

Ben Soh
La Trobe University, Australia

Mehedi Masud
Taif University, Saudi Arabia

ABSTRACT

One of the main challenges in cloud computing is to build a healthy and efficient storage for securely managing and preserving data. This means a cloud service provider needs to make sure that its clients' outsourced data are stored securely and, data queries and retrievals are executed correctly and privately. On the other hand, it may also mean businesses are willing to outsource their data to a third party only if they trust their data are not accessible and visible to the service provider and other non-authorized parties. However, one of the major obstacles faced here for ensuring data reliability and security is Byzantine faults. While Byzantine fault tolerance (BFT) has received growing attention from the academic research community, the research done is generally from the distributed computing point of view, and hence finds little practical use in cloud computing. To that end, the focus of this paper is to discuss how these faults can be tolerated with the authors' proposed conceptualization of Byzantine data faults and fault-tolerant architecture in cloud data management.

DOI: 10.4018/978-1-5225-8176-5.ch046

1. INTRODUCTION

One of the main challenges in cloud computing is to build a healthy and efficient storage for securely managing and preserving data. It means a cloud service provider needs to make sure that its clients' outsourced data are stored securely and, data queries and retrievals are executed correctly (in terms of reliability) and privately (in terms of three security attributes: Confidentiality, Integrity and Availability – CIA) (AlZain, Soh et al., 2013; AlZain, Soh et al., 2011; AlZain, Pardede et al. 2012; AlZain, Soh et al., 2013; AlZain, Li et al., 2015). On the other hand, it also means businesses are willing to outsource their data to a third party (cloud service provider) only if they trust their data are not accessible and visible to the service provider and other non-authorized parties (Hore, Mehrotra et al. 2004). However, one of the main obstacles here for ensuring data reliability and security is Byzantine faults. The focus of this paper is to discuss how these faults can be tolerated with our proposed conceptualization of Byzantine data faults and fault-tolerant architecture in cloud computing.

The remainder of this paper is organized as follows. Section 2 presents the background and related work. Section 3 overviews our conceptualization of Byzantine data faults as well as fault tolerant state machines which are the base of our proposed fault-tolerant architecture in cloud data management (in Section 5). Section 4 details three crucial operations in the proposed fault-tolerant architecture. Section 6 gives a qualitative evaluation of the proposed architecture, while Section 7 concludes the paper.

2. BACKGROUND AND RELATED WORK

If something happens to the data or if the data is corrupted by the service provider, the service provider is responsible for data restoration. The service provider should have a mechanism to recover or back-up the data (Agrawal, El Abbadi et al., 2009). There are three issues to be addressed for wide adaptation of the data storage framework in terms of data security: Cryptographic techniques, Private Information Retrieval, and Data Replication Techniques (Agrawal, El Abbadi et al., 2009). These techniques are commonly used for secure data outsourcing.

HAIL (High Availability and Integrity Layer) (Bowers, Juels et al., 2009) is another example of a protocol that controls multiple clouds. HAIL is a distributed cryptographic system that permits a set of servers to ensure that the client's stored data is retrievable and integral. HAIL provides a software layer to address the availability and integrity of the stored data in multi-clouds (Bowers, Juels et al., 2009).

Agrawal et al. (Agrawal, El Abbadi et al., 2009) discuss the issue of information distribution (in terms of data query and retrieval) with the aim of showing that there is an orthogonal approach which is based on information distribution instead of encryption in the area of data and computer security. The need to communicate important or private information from one party to another instigated most of the work on data security. Agrawal et al. (Agrawal, El Abbadi et al., 2009) introduced Shamir's Secret Sharing algorithm (Shamir, 1979) as a solution for the privacy issue.

Data Replication is one of the important approaches for outsourced data security. The data owner divides data and replicates them into different data storage or multi-clouds. RACS (Redundant Array of Cloud Storage) (Abu-Libdeh, Princehouse et al., 2010) for instance, utilizes RAID-like techniques that are normally used by disks and file systems, but for multiple cloud storage. Abu-Libdeh et al. (Abu-Libdeh, Princehouse et al., 2010) assume that to avoid "vender lock-in", distributing a user's data among multiple clouds is a helpful solution. This replication also decreases the cost of switching providers and offers better fault tolerance. Therefore, the storage load will be spread among several providers as a result of the RACS proxy (Abu-Libdeh, Princehouse et al., 2010).

Much research has been dedicated to Byzantine Fault Tolerance (BFT) since its first introduction (Lamport, Shostak et al., 1982), (Pease, Shostak et al., 1980). Although BFT research has received a great deal of attention, it still suffers from the limitations of practical adoption (Kuznetsov and Rodrigues, 2009) and remains peripheral in distributed systems (Vukolic, 2010; Lamport, Shostak et al., 1982). BFT for Web services as well as distributed systems have received more attention. Zhao (Zhao 2007) presented a framework of BFT for Web services which was based on the PBFT protocol (Castro and Liskov 1999) and ran the system with Byzantine faults in a distributed environment. In addition, Merideth et al. (Merideth, Iyengar et al., 2005) discussed a Byzantine fault tolerant middleware for Web services. Furthermore, Li et al. (Li, He et al., 2005) employed replication schemes and the N-Modular Redundancy concept to tolerate Byzantine faults and security attacks in the web services environment. While many recent research studies have often focused on comparing the PBFT (Castro and Liskov, 1999) and improving its performance with the development of Zyzzyva (Kotla, Alvisi et al., 2007) and Aardvark (Clement, Wong et al., 2009), very few studies have addressed the detection of Byzantine failure in a multi-cloud computing environment to ensure the security of stored data within the cloud.

3. CONCEPTUALIZATION OF BYZANTINE DATA FAULTS

In cloud computing, any faults in software or hardware are known as Byzantine faults which usually relate to inappropriate behaviour and intrusion tolerance, as well as arbitrary and crash faults (Vukolic, 2010). Byzantine faults can be caused by malicious attacks or operator errors. Sending inconsistent results from clouds to the clients is considered a Byzantine fault as well (Castro and Liskov, 1999). In the following, we conceptualize fault-tolerant state machines using the Fault-Error-Failure chain (AlZain, Soh et al., 2012). In his paper, we regard faulty cloud data as data that has been corrupted or compromised in terms of CIA.

3.1. Fault-Tolerant State Machines

Lamport et al. (Lamport, Shostak et al., 1982) consider a Byzantine failure to have occurred if a component exhibits arbitrary or malicious behaviour or if there is possible complicity with other faulty components. To build a fault-tolerant state machine (FTSM) in a distributed system, a FTSM can be realized by replicating that state machine and running processors in each replica (Schneider, 1990).

Schneider (Schneider, 1990) argues that if each failure can affect at most one state machine replica, the output for the FTSM could be obtained by matching the output of the state machine replicas of this group. When systems experience a Byzantine problem, FTSM must have at least 2f+1 replicas (f = 1, 2, ...), and the output of the replicas is produced by the majority of these replicas (Schneider 1990). All communications are time-bounded and a time-out mechanism can detect the absence of a message. Each replica state machine uses timeouts to prevent waiting more than the time-bounded to receive a response from a faulty replica state machine. These are the main features of the FTSM (Schneider, 1990; Lamport, Shostak et al., 1982).

Figure 1. BFT-MCDB-Store Algorithm

Algorithm 1: BFT-MCDB-Store
1   **Procedure** BFT-MCDBStore(*D*)
2   **Begin**
3   DP sends *D* // DP sends D to RU.
4   RU ←*D* // D received by *RU*.
5   RU divide *D* into (*n*) shares ($D_1....D_n$)
6   Where $n = 2k - 1$ AND $k < n$
7   IU Generates $q_{(x)}$ for each v_s Where
8    $Shares(v_s, 1) = q(x_1) = ax_1^{k-1} + bx_1^{k-1} ... + v_s$
...
$Shares(v_s, n) = q(x_n) = ax_n^{k-1} + bx_n^{k-1} ... + v_s$
9   DS=[x_1=3, x_2=1, x_3=2, ...] // X_s stored in DS.
10   SU Sends ($D_1....D_n$) into Cs // SU sends *D* to the cloud.
11   Cs.DS ←($D_1....D_n$) // DS stores *D* in the C$_s$.
12   **END**

3.2. Classification of Cloud Data Faults

There are two kinds of cloud data faults: non-latent faults (non-Byzantine faults) and latent faults (Byzantine faults). We discussed the issue of non-Byzantine faults in (AlZain, Soh et al., 2012), while the object of this paper is the latter, Byzantine faults. It is clear the Byzantine faults are considered to be more insidious than non-latent faults in the cloud computing environment. System components can suffer malicious failures in which they make arbitrary outputs. Such failures are known as Byzantine failures. Byzantine failures are difficult to detect before they cause damage to the system because they are hidden and lurking. This detection difficulty can be overcome with fault-tolerant operations discussed in the following section.

4. FAULT-TOLERANT OPERATIONS

The three core operations required in cloud data management with a fault-tolerance approach are: data fault detection mechanism, data storage mechanism, and data retrieval mechanism.

4.1. Cloud Data Fault Detection Mechanism

Here, there are three conditions for implementing data fault detection mechanism in an FTSM: (1) Replica Coordination: All replicas receive and process the same sequence of requests synchronized by the cloud manager (see Section 5); (2) Agreement: all requests should be received by all non-faulty state machine replicas; and (3) Order: All requests that are received by each non-faulty state machine replica will process clients' requests in the same relative order (Lamport, Shostak et al., 1982; Schneider, 1990).

The crucial part of the detection mechanism is the Agreement protocol called Byzantine Agreement protocol that has the following conditions (Lamport, Shostak et al., 1982; Schneider, 1990):

IC1: All non-faulty processors agree on the same value.

IC2: If the transmitter is non-faulty, the value they agree on must be the same value that was sent from the original source.

In our conceptualization of data fault, we regard faulty data as data that has been corrupted or compromised in terms of CIA in cloud data management. Hence, in this paper we rephrase the above two conditions as follows;

IC1: All non-faulty clouds agree on the same data.
IC2: If the sender cloud is non-faulty, the data they agree on must be the same one that was sent from the original source.

4.2. Cloud Data Storing Mechanism

The data storing procedure in the BFT-MCDB design involves data distribution from the data provider to multi-clouds. This is done after executing the polynomial functions on the data using the Shamir's Secret Sharing scheme (Shamir 1979).

Figure 1 shows the BFT-MCDB-Store algorithm. The key idea of the BFT-MCDB-Store algorithm is to first (line 4) receive the data from the client or data provider to be stored in the clouds. Subsequently, the receiver unit inside the cloud manager divides the data into n shares (line 5). Then, (line 7) the interpreter unit inside the cloud manager generates the secret information X (line 8) and random polynomial functions with degree at the same level (line 8) (more information regarding writing shares can be found in (Agrawal, El Abbadi et al., 2009)), one for each cloud to be stored in different clouds. After that, (line 10) the sender unit sends data to the clouds then data storage stores these data in the clouds (line 11).

The following acronyms are used in the algorithms: Data Provider (DP), Receiver Unit (RU), Interpreter Unit (IU), Sender Unit (SU), Data storage (DS), Voter Unit (VU), User (U), Data (D), Clouds (Cs), the secret value wanted to be hidden (vs), and Commit Certificate message (C.C).

4.3. Cloud Data Retrieval Mechanism

The data retrieval process in the BFT-MCDB design starts with rewriting the received query from the user in the cloud manager (n number of queries) based on Shamir's Secret Sharing scheme and then sending these queries, one for each cloud, after constructing the polynomial functions and the order for the secret values. The shares will be returned to the cloud manager in sequence to compute the polynomial function on the retrieved values. Consequently, the sender unit sends the three executed results to the voter unit. As a result, the voter unit applies the Agreement procedure on the output from the sender unit inside the cloud manager to determine whether the results are consistent and if so, sends this to the user in a secure way.

Figure 2 shows the BFT-MCDB-Retrieve algorithm. The purpose of the BFT-MCDB-Retrieve algorithm is to first (line 4) receive from the client the query to be sent to the clouds through the receiver unit in the cloud manager. Consequently, the interpreter unit inside the cloud manager rewrites three queries (one for each cloud) (line 5) to retrieve the result from the clouds. After this, (line 9) the interpreter unit inside the cloud manager computes the secret value of the output from the clouds to send them to the voter. Then, the voter unit applies the Byzantine Agreement protocol (line 12) on the computed result before it is sent to the user. If the retrieved results from 2f+1 clouds are consistent (line 13) then

Figure 2. BFT-MCDB-Retrieve Algorithm

Algorithm 2: BFT-MCDB-Retrieve	
1	**Function** BFT-MCDBRetrieve(*query*)
2	**Begin**
3	U sends *query* // U sends query to RU.
4	RU ←*query* // query received by RU.
5	IU write (*n*) *query* for each C // IU rewrite n queries one for each Cloud.
6	Cs ←*queries* // Cs receives queries.
7	Cs sends *results* // Cs answer queries and sends results to RU.
8	RU ←*results* // RU receives results
9	IU Re-execute $q_{(x)}$ for each v_s // IU translates (re-execute) the retrieved results to know the stored secret value v_s.
10	SU sends executed v_s to VU // SU sends the executed results to the VU for Agreement.
11	VU ←v_s // the secret values v_s received by VU.
12	VU voting results // Byzantine agreement protocol applied on v_s.
13	If (*2f+1 results* are consistent) // If the retrieved results from 2f+1 clouds are consistent.
14	{ then
15	SU ←V_s // SU receives the voted results to be able to send them to the requester.
16	U ←V_s}// }// U receives the voted results.
17	Else If (*f+1 results* are consistent) // If the retrieved results from f+1 clouds are consistent.
18	{ then
19	SU sends *C.C* to Cs // SU sends the commit certificate with its commit messages to all 2f+1 clouds.
20	Cs sends local-commit msg to SU // non-faulty Cs send a local commit message to the cloud manager as proof of a non-faulty cloud.
21	SU ←V_s // SU receives the voted results to be able to be sent to the requester.
22	U ←V_s} }// U receives the voted results.
23	Else // If there are inconsistent responses from the clouds.
24	{ then
25	U← error msg} // error message will be sent to U.
26	**END**

the result will be sent to the user (line 15,16), otherwise (line 17) the sender unit inside the cloud manager sends the commit certificate with its commit messages to all 2f+1 clouds including a list of f+1 consistent clouds with their response messages (line 19). When a cloud n receives a commit message including the commit certificate, cloud n sends a local commit message to the cloud manager as proof of a non-faulty cloud (line 20). When the cloud manager receives the local commit certificate from the non-faulty clouds, the cloud manager considers the request and sends the response to the clients (line 22). If there are inconsistent responses from the clouds (line 23), then an error message will be sent to the user (line 25).

5. PROPOSED FAULT-TOLERANT SYSTEM DESIGN IN CLOUD DATA MANAGEMENT

In fault-tolerant system design, the redundancy concept in FTSM (in Section 3.1) is the central idea, while fault-tolerant operations are essential in driving the redundant parts and in our case the driver is the cloud manager (see Section 4). In this paper, each cloud is deemed a part of the replication and for simplicity we name our proposed design BFT-MCDB (Byzantine Fault Tolerance Multi-Clouds Database).

5.1. Architecture Overview

When systems experience a Byzantine fault, fault-tolerant state machine must have at least $2f+1$ replicas ($f = 1, 2, \ldots$), and the output of the replicas is produced by the majority of these replicas (Schneider, 1990). In our BFT-MCDB design, $2f+1$ clouds communicate with a cloud manager before the client can receive the results from the clouds. The three main components of the BFT-MCDB design are: the clouds side, the BFT communication protocol, and the cloud manager (see Figure 3).

5.1.1. The Clouds' Side

The privacy of the stored data in the clouds is guaranteed by the fact that no single cloud contains any usable data by itself because it contains Shamir's Secret Sharing data which is the changed values of the original data, due to the properties of Shamir's Secret Sharing approach. This will prevent data intrusion by making it impossible for a malicious insider to re-execute revealed data that come from Byzantine clouds.

5.1.2. Communication Protocol

The communication protocol of the BFT-MCDB design is based on the Byzantine Agreement protocol (Lamport, Shostak et al., 1982; Kotla, Alvisi et al., 2007) in that there is one REQUEST message from the client to the cloud manager, one ORDER-REQ message from the cloud manager for each client

Figure 3. BFT-MCDB Overview

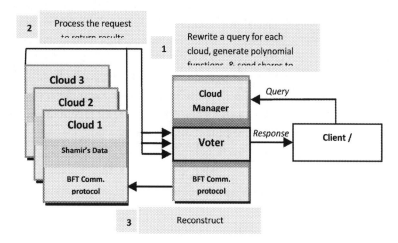

REQUEST which is responsible for handling the client's requests to the clouds, one SPEC-RESPONSE message from the clouds, and a COMMIT message from the cloud manager. The cloud manager receives $2f+1$ REPLY messages from the clouds. Here, clients always receive replies (a COMMIT message) to their requests from the cloud manager which has received replies from all clouds. For operations that do not employ the Shamir's Secret Sharing scheme, the cloud manager has to collect at least $f+1$ REPLY messages with the same content. Once the cloud manager has received $f+1$ identical results from different clouds, it can deliver the accepted result to the client.

5.1.3. Cloud Manager Components

The cloud manager consists of five components: receiver unit, interpreter unit, data source unit, sender unit and voter unit, as shown in Figure 4. The cloud manager is considered the most critical part in the proposed BFT-MCDB design as it is the control centre responsible for crucial fault-tolerant operations mentioned in Section 4: cloud data storing, cloud data retrieval, cloud data fault detection.

In relation to the storing procedure in the BFT-MCDB design, the database provider (client) sends data to the cloud manager to be received by the receiver unit inside the cloud manager. The receiver unit divides the received data into n shares or clusters (in our case, three shares because we are dealing with three clouds) based on Shamir's Secret Sharing scheme. After the receiver unit has divided the data (assuming the data is a numeric value, for example, a worker's salary) into 3 shares to store them in different clouds, the receiver unit sends the shares to the interpreter unit inside the cloud manager. The interpreter unit generates random polynomial functions with degree at the same level, one for each worker's salary in the WORKER table with the actual salary as the constant part of the function. These values will then be stored in different clouds.

In relation to the data retrieval, the requester sends a query to the cloud manager. The receiver unit in the cloud manager then sends the requester's query to the interpreter unit to rewrite three queries, one for each cloud, to retrieve the converted information from the clouds. After the receiver unit has received the results from the clouds, it sends the results to the interpreter unit to re-execute the polynomial functions for each result.

After computing the secret values of the results from the clouds, the sender unit sends the three executed results to the voter unit for majority voting purposes. Consequently, the voter unit applies Byzantine Agreement protocol on the retrieved results from the sender unit inside the cloud manager. In the absence of faults, the voter unit receives matching results from all $2f+1$ clouds. Finally, the sender unit inside the cloud manager receives the voting results from the voter unit and then sends the results to the concerned requester. According to Yin et al. (Yin, Martin et al., 2003), to tolerate Byzantine faults, the minimum replicas required for completion is $2f+1$ replicas = 3 clouds (for $f = 1$ with a replica of $2f+1 = 3$ clouds). For instance, if each cloud contains a copy of the data, the cloud manager needs to perform a voting technique between replies and return the one that has at least $f+1$ majority. The final action after the majority voting has been applied on the retrieved output from the clouds is that the voter unit will send the agreed result to the concerned user or requester.

Figure 4. Cloud Manager Components

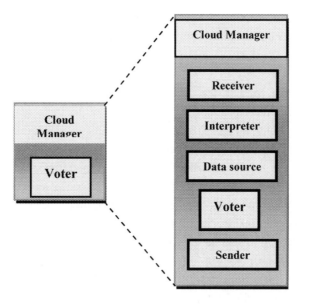

6. QUALITATIVE EVALUATION OF THE PROPOSED BYZANTINE FAULT-TOLERANT ARCHITECTURE IN CLOUD DATA MANAGEMENT

6.1. Protect Data Integrity

One of the most important issues related to cloud security risks is data integrity. The stored data in the cloud may be damaged during transition operations from or to the cloud storage provider. The risk of attacks from both inside and outside the cloud provider exists and should be considered. For example, data integrity was recently compromised in Amazon S3 where users' data became corrupted (Sun). Garfinkel (Garfinkel, 2007) argues that information privacy is not guaranteed in Amazon S3. Data authentication, which assures that the returned data is the same as the stored data, is extremely important. Garfinkel claims that instead of following Amazon's advice that organizations encrypt data before storing them in Amazon S3, organizations should use HMAC (Krawczyk, Bellare et al., 1997) technology or a digital signature to ensure data is not modified by Amazon S3. These technologies protect users from Amazon data modification and from hackers who may have obtained access to their email or stolen their password (Garfinkel, 2007).

However, as explained previously, the proposed BFT-MCDB design uses multi-clouds which is based on state machine replication approach (Schneider, 1990). In addition, the use of Shamir's Secret Sharing approach makes BFT-MCDB robust. For example, the data will be distributed into three different clouds in the proposed BFT-MCDB design. In addition, the secret sharing approach will be applied on the stored data in the multiple clouds. If the Byzantine server or malicious insider wants to know the hidden information inside the cloud, they must retrieve at least two values from three different clouds with their knowledge of the secret information X to be able to know the real value which has been converted and hidden before it is stored in the multi-clouds.

This technique depends on Shamir's Secret Sharing approach with a polynomial functions technique which claims that, if there are 3 shares stored in 3 clouds (n = 3, k = 2), knowledge of the values of 2 shares or more with the secret information X will make the secret able to be constructed, whereas knowledge of the values of less than two shares will make the secret un-constructible even with the knowledge of the secret information X (see section 3.1).

Another benefit of the BFT-MCDB design relating to data integrity in the cloud environment is due to the use of Byzantine Agreement protocol. As mentioned before, our design is based on the state machine replication approach (Schneider, 1990). Replication of clouds in the BFT-MCDB design and the use of Byzantine Agreement protocol have a positive effect in detecting the faulty cloud which increases the level of data integrity. The results provided by the Byzantine cloud will be disregarded after being detected by the voter unit in the cloud manager. In addition, the voting technique facilitates the recovery of erroneous data. For instance, in accordance with the procedure of data retrieval in the BFT-MCDB design, the voter unit simply compares the outcomes from the clouds; if the values are different, the faulty output from the faulty cloud will be identified.

Another advantage of data replication among multi-clouds is that the voter unit inside the cloud manager in the BFT-MCDB design does not have to ask the faulty cloud to resend the results to the voter unit, because the voter can obtain the results from the non-faulty cloud. Thus, the use of Byzantine Agreement protocol in the BFT-MCDB design is helpful in addressing the issue of data integrity due to its ability to detect and identify the faulty cloud, in addition to being able to recover data in the faulty cloud. Therefore, the BFT-MCDB design is superior to a single cloud service in addressing the data integrity problem.

6.2. Protect Data Confidentiality

According to Garfinkel (Garfinkel, 2007), another security risk that may occur with a single cloud provider is a hacked password or data intrusion. For example, if someone gains access to an Amazon account password, they will be able to access all the account's instances and resources. In addition, a stolen password allows the hacker to erase all the information inside the instance of the stolen account, modify it, or even disable its services. Furthermore, there is a possibility that the user's email (Amazon user name) will be hacked. ((Garfinkel, 2003) provides a discussion on the potential risks of E-mail). Since Amazon allows a lost password to be reset by email, the hacker may still be able to log in to the account after receiving the reset password.

However, the BFT-MCDB design, a practical model for building a system with Byzantine fault tolerance in a multi-cloud environment, is different to the single cloud service model. BFT-MCDB replicates the data among three different clouds; therefore, hackers would have to retrieve two out of the three clouds with the knowledge of the secret information X to be able to reconstruct the real value of the data in the cloud. In other words, if the hacker hacks one cloud's password even with the knowledge of the secret information X, they still need to hack the second cloud (in our case) to know the secret.

Another advantage of using the voter unit inside the cloud manager in the BFT-MCDB design is to identify the faulty cloud, depending on its response and determine in which cloud the data intrusion problem has occurred. Hence, replicating data into multi-clouds by using the state machine replication approach (Schneider 1990) may reduce the risk of data intrusion, such as in the BFT-MCDB design.

6.3. Improve Service Availability

Another major concern in cloud services is service availability. Amazon (Amazon, 2006) mentions in its licensing agreement that it is possible that an Amazon user's web service may be terminated for any reason at any time if the user breaks the cloud storage policy. In addition, if damage occurs to any Amazon web service and the service fails, there will be no compensation from the Amazon Company regarding this failure. Companies strive to protect their services from system failure in several ways, such as by making backups or disconnecting any dependent cloud providers to avoid service unavailability to cloud providers (Garfinkel,, 2007). However, the BFT-MCDB is different from single cloud service providers in relation to service availability risk or loss of data. BFT-MCDB distributes the data into different clouds and therefore, it could be argued that the risk of data loss is reduced. If one cloud fails, users can still access their data live in other clouds.

Another benefit of the BFT-MCDB design in relation to service availability is the use of the replication technique. If one of the system's components fails, there is an alternative component instead of the faulty one and the system is still able to conduct its operations by using the alternative component. Hence, using replication techniques in the BFT-MCDB design increases the chance of the cloud services being available.

The use of Byzantine Agreement protocol in the proposed design protects the system if any components fail. The failure of a single cloud will not cause the whole system to fail because it depends on the results of two clouds out of three. In other words, the results from the voter unit to the user are generated after comparing the outputs from two clouds out of three, in our case. Hence, the use of the replication technique with Byzantine Agreement protocol in the BFT-MCDB design may reduce the risk of data loss or service unavailability.

Therefore, in light of the above discussion, our newly proposed BFT-MCDB design has been shown to have a better ability to address the three security dimensions: data integrity, data confidentiality and service availability, than a single cloud service provider. In addition, our newly proposed design offers more security in protecting the user's data from untrusted cloud service providers and from the malicious insider. The Amazon cloud service, for example, asks users to encrypt their data before storing it in their instances, whereas BFT-MCDB takes responsibility for this task.

6.4. Facilitate Cloud Data Fault Detection and Data Recovery

The replication of clouds in the BFT-MCDB design and the use of the voting technique have a positive impact on error detection in Byzantine clouds. The cloud manager can detect a faulty cloud if there are inconsistent replies from clouds. The faulty cloud will be identified and its result will be disregarded after it has been detected by the voter unit in the cloud manager. In addition, the voter helps to recover data which is determined to be erroneous. For example, if the voter indicates that Cloud1 is a faulty cloud, the output result of Cloud2 should not be the same as the output result of Cloud1, after the execution of the polynomial function of both retrieved shares from both clouds by the interpreter unit. This depends on the procedure of data retrieval in the BFT-MCDB design. In other words, the voter unit simply compares the outputs from the clouds with the first received output result; if the values do not match, an error has occurred at some point during the transmission. An error could occur randomly from one of the three clouds and consequently the presence of the voter unit is vitally important to detect errors in clouds.

There are many benefits of data replication among multi-clouds, since the voter does not have to ask the faulty cloud to retransmit the data, rather the voter can obtain the result from a non-faulty cloud. Thus, the use of the voter unit inside the cloud manager in the proposed BFT-MCDB design is helpful in the area of error detection and to identify the faulty cloud, in addition to data recovery in the faulty cloud.

6.5. Improve Cloud Data Reliability

Recall that there is an odd number (2f + 1) of the clouds in our proposed fault-tolerant architecture,

Acceptable results are based on the majority voting procedure, which is undertaken by the voter unit in the cloud manager of the BFT-MCDB design. For example, if f = 1, the replicated system in the clouds will not fail if two of the three clouds do not fail, or if none of the three clouds fails. In other words, the failure of a single cloud will not damage the operation of the whole system. Therefore, the result from the voter unit is more reliable because it is generated after comparing the results from at least two clouds. Hence, the majority voting procedure ensures the reliability of cloud data.

7. CONCLUSION AND FUTURE WORK

It is clear that although the use of cloud computing has increased rapidly, cloud computing security is a major issue in the cloud computing environment. Consumers do not want to lose their private information as a result of malicious insiders in the cloud. In addition, threats to data integrity and data confidentiality leads to many problems for the users of cloud computing. Recently, the loss of service availability caused many problems for a large number of customers. Data security is essential for clients dealing with clouds that may fail due to various Byzantine failures such as failures in software, hardware, or attacks from malicious insiders.

This work aimed to conceptualize Byzantine faults in cloud data management and proposed a Byzantine fault tolerance architecture, named BFT-MCDB, to ensure the robustness of cloud data management in terms of CIA and reliability. The design presented in this paper relies on a novel approach that combines Byzantine Agreement protocol (Lamport, Shostak et al., 1982; Kotla, Alvisi et al., 2007) along with Shamir's Secret Sharing approach (Johnson, 1988) to detect Byzantine fault in the multi-cloud computing environment as well as to ensure the security of data stored within the cloud.

In future work, we plan to compare our design with other multi-cloud models, and propose an improved design. In addition, further analysis of reliability and security issues in the context of the BFT-MCDB design will be undertaken. BFT-MCDB will be deployed and systematically tested in the private cloud computing environment.

REFERENCES

Abu-Libdeh, H., Princehouse, L., & Weatherspoon, H. (2010). RACS: a case for cloud storage diversity. *Proceedings of the 1st ACM symposium on Cloud computing*. ACM. 10.1145/1807128.1807165

Agrawal, D., El Abbadi, A., & ... . (2009). Database Management as a Service: Challenges and Opportunities. *Proceedings of The 2009 25th International Conference on Data Engineering*. IEEE. 10.1109/ICDE.2009.151

AlZain, M. A. (2014). Data security, data management and performance evaluation in a multi-cloud computing model [PhD thesis]. La Trobe University.

AlZain, M. A., Li, A. S., Soh, B., & Pardede, E. (2015). Multi-Cloud Data Management using Shamirs Secret Sharing and Quantum Byzantine Agreement Schemes. *International Journal of Cloud Applications and Computing*, 5(3), 35–52. doi:10.4018/IJCAC.2015070103

AlZain, M. A., Pardede, E., & ... . (2012). Cloud Computing Security: From Single to Multi-clouds. *Proceedings of The 2012 45th Hawaii International Conference on System Science (HICSS)*, Maui, USA. IEEE. 10.1109/HICSS.2012.153

AlZain, M. A., Soh, B., & ... . (2011). MCDB: Using Multi-clouds to Ensure Security in Cloud Computing. *Proceedings of The 2011 Ninth International Conference on Dependable, Autonomic and Secure Computing (DASC)*, Sydney, Australia. IEEE. 10.1109/DASC.2011.133

AlZain, M. A., Soh, B., & ... . (2012). A New Approach Using Redundancy Technique to Improve Security in Cloud Computing. *Proceedings of The 2012 International Conference on Cyber Security, Cyber Warfare and Digital Forensic (CyberSec12)*. Kuala Lumpur, Malaysia (pp. 230-235). IEEE. 10.1109/CyberSec.2012.6246174

AlZain, M. A., Soh, B., & ... . (2013). A Byzantine Fault Tolerance Model for a Multi-cloud Computing. *Proceeding of The 2013 16th International Conference on Computational Science and Engineering CSE*, Sydney, Australia. IEEE. 10.1109/CSE.2013.30

AlZain, M. A., Soh, B., & Pardede, E. (2013). A Survey on Data Security Issues in Cloud Computing: From Single to Multi-Clouds. *Journal of Software*, 8(5), 1068–1078. doi:10.4304/jsw.8.5.1068-1078

Amazon. (2006). Amazon Web Services. Web services licensing agreement.

Bowers, K. D., Juels, A., & ... . (2009). HAIL: A high-availability and integrity layer for cloud storage. *Proceedings of the 16th ACM conference on Computer and communications security*. ACM. 10.1145/1653662.1653686

Castro, M., & Liskov, B. (1999). Practical Byzantine Fault Tolerance. *Proceedings of the 1999 3rd Symposium on Operating Systems Design and Implementation*.

Garfinkel, S. L. (2003). Email-based identification and authentication: An alternative to PKI? *IEEE Security and Privacy*, 1(6), 20–26. doi:10.1109/MSECP.2003.1253564

Garfinkel, S. L. (2007). An evaluation of amazon's grid computing services: EC2, S3, and SQS. Retrieved from http://simson.net/clips/academic/2007.Harvard.S3.pdf

Hore, B., Mehrotra, S., & Tsudik, G. (2004). A privacy-preserving index for range queries. *Proceedings of the Thirtieth international conference on Very large data bases*. VLDB Endowment. 10.1016/B978-012088469-8.50064-4

Johnson, B. W. (1988). *Design & analysis of fault tolerant digital systems*. Addison-Wesley Longman Publishing Co., Inc.

Kotla, R., Alvisi, L., Dahlin, M., Clement, A., & Wong, E. (2007). Zyzzyva: Speculative byzantine fault tolerance. *Operating Systems Review*, 41(6), 45–58. doi:10.1145/1323293.1294267

Krawczyk, H., M. Bellare, et al. (1997). HMAC: Keyed-hashing for message authentication.

Kuznetsov, P., & Rodrigues, R. (2009). BFTW 3: Why? when? where? workshop on the theory and practice of byzantine fault tolerance. *ACM SIGACT News, 40*(4), 82–86. doi:10.1145/1711475.1711494

Lamport, L., Shostak, R., & Pease, M. (1982). The Byzantine generals problem. *ACM Transactions on Programming Languages and Systems, 4*(3), 382–401. doi:10.1145/357172.357176

Li, W., He, J., Ma, O., Yen I.-Y., Bastani, F., & Paul, R. (2005). A framework to support survivable web services. *Proceedings of the 19th International Parallel and Distributed Processing Symposium.* IEEE.

Clement, A., Wong, E. L., Alvisi, L., Dahlin, M., & Marchetti, M. (2009). Making Byzantine fault tolerant systems tolerate Byzantine faults. USENIX Association.

Merideth, M. G., Iyengar, A., Mikalsen, T., Tai, S., Rouvellou, I., & Naramsimhan, P. (2005). Thema: Byzantine-fault-tolerant middleware for web-service applications. *Proceedings of the 24th Symposium on Reliable Distributed Systems (SRDS).* IEEE.

Pease, M., Shostak, R., & Lamport, L. (1980). Reaching agreement in the presence of faults. *Journal of the ACM, 27*(2), 228–234. doi:10.1145/322186.322188

Schneider, F. B. (1990). Implementing fault-tolerant services using the state machine approach: A tutorial. *ACM Computing Surveys, 22*(4), 299–319. doi:10.1145/98163.98167

Shamir, A. (1979). How to share a secret. *Communications of the ACM, 22*(11), 612–613. doi:10.1145/359168.359176

Sun Blog. (n. d.). Silent data corruption. Retrieved from http://blogs.sun.com/gbrunett/entry/amazon_s3_silent_data_corruption

Vukolic, M. (2010). The Byzantine empire in the intercloud. *ACM SIGACT News, 41*(3), 105–111. doi:10.1145/1855118.1855137

Yin, J., Martin, J. P., Venkataramani, A., Alvisi, L., & Dahlin, M. (2003). Separating agreement from execution for byzantine fault tolerant services. *Operating Systems Review, 37*(5), 253–267. doi:10.1145/1165389.945470

Zhao, W. (2007). BFT-WS: A Byzantine fault tolerance framework for web services. *Proceeding of The Eleventh International Conference of EDOC'07.* IEEE. 10.1109/EDOCW.2007.6

This research was previously published in the International Journal of Knowledge Society Research (IJKSR), 7(3); edited by Miltiadis D. Lytras and Linda Daniela, pages 86-98, copyright year 2016 by IGI Publishing (an imprint of IGI Global).

Chapter 47

A Credible Cloud Service Model Based on Behavior Graphs and Tripartite Decision-Making Mechanism

Junfeng Tian
Hebei University, China

He Zhang
Hebei University, China

ABSTRACT

The credibility of cloud service is the key to the success of the application of cloud services. The dual servers of master server and backup server are applied to cloud services, which can improve the availability of cloud services. In the past, the failures between master server and backup server could be detected by heartbeat algorithm. Because of lacking cloud user's evaluation, the authors put forward a credible cloud service model based on behavior Graphs and tripartite decision-making mechanism. By the quantitative of cloud users' behaviors evidences, the construction of behavior Graphs and the judgment of behavior, they select the most credible cloud user. They combine the master server, the backup server and the selected credible cloud user to determine the credibility of cloud service by the tripartite decision-making mechanism. Finally, according to the result of credible judgment, the authors could decide whether it will be switched from the master server to the backup server.

1. INTRODUCTION

With the high-speed development of cloud computing (Udoh and Hsu, 2013), the emerging cloud services, underlying supported by cloud platform, and the use of convenience provided by cloud computing face a variety of new security threats at the same time. The credible cloud service becomes an important object of study for cloud computing (Wang et al., 2015). Chief officer of RSA said that, in the process of enterprise's apply migration to a third party cloud, Credibility is the first thing to consider. Cloud ser-

DOI: 10.4018/978-1-5225-8176-5.ch047

vices can be smoothly promotion depends on the credibility of cloud service (Xu et al., 2012). Formerly, the credibility of cloud service often is stiffly divided into two aspects, respectively, to be studied: (1) Cloud server's credibility: a large number of important sensitive information are stored in the cloud, so it is important of the cloud server's credibility (Srinivisan 2012). A cloud service based on cloudy or cooperation between cloud and cloud is proposed by scholars, that cloudy collaboration (multi-clouds cooperation) (Alzain et al., 2012); Compared with the single server nodes of cloud service, multiple cloud server could be obtained by the information interaction between their respective credible judgment, which effectively reduces the cloud user's security problems (Trostle 2006), in this model, the access to multiple cloud servers' information are delayed and difficult. (2) The credibility of users that enjoy the cloud service: The Distributed Denial of Service attacks (DDoS), the traditional way of security attacks, has become a new threat of cloud services. The malicious users consume resources, makes the cloud service unavailable to other legitimate users. malicious users fake credible users to hide their identity, they didn't give a reliable judgment, which causes an incredibility Cloud Service. One will ensure that the cloud user's identity authenticity and credibility behavior, the technology of identity authentication is mature, but that doesn't prevent the identity authentication failure or malicious cloud users' behavior on the system of legal status, so behavior of analysis and effective control is another research focus on the current cloud computing (Chen et al., 2011). The credibility of the judge in cloud services that is combined with credible cloud user and the cloud servers.

2. THE RELATED WORK

At present, the comprehensive cloud user behavior and cloud server's credibility evaluation research is still rare, but respectively from the aspects of cloud users and cloud server's credible study have been made.

2.1. The Credibility of Cloud User Behavior

Lv Yanxia et al. (2013) proposed a credible evaluation and control of the user behavior analysis based on cloud environment FANP. Zhang kai et al. (2014) for the current role in cloud computing access control's changing over time, the dynamic problems, presented a cloud computing access control model based on user behavior trust. Jiang Ze et al. (2011) used multidimensional decision attribute to measuring the user behaviors' credibility. Elaine et al. (2011) put forward a kind of implicit authentication of user identity based on user behavior method, this method utilized mobile devices to collect user behavior information, simulated user behavior, implicitly authenticated user. Khazzar and Savage (2010) used psychology to study the credibility of the user behavior authentication system, by the user in response to user behavior information of 3 D maze, authenticated the user identity. Accuracy is 88.33%. Almenarez et al. (2004) proposed the PTM (pervasive trust management model base d on D - S theory) model to define the dynamic trust model based on universal between the domain of environment, with the improved evidence theory (d - S theory) method to model, the trust evaluation using probability weighted average method. Brosso et al. (2010) proposed a theory based on user behavior analysis of continuous certification system, in the environmental information to extract a cloud user behavior evidence, the user is divided into different levels of trust, in the process of fuzzification based on related rules to determine the weight of each parameter, through a neural fuzzy logic, we continuously updated database of user behavior, keep the user behavior credible.

2.2. Research for the Credibility of Cloud Service

Al Zain et al. (2012) proposed a cloudy collaboration based on the related architecture and security risk analysis method. In view of the behaviors of cloud services, literature (Xie et al., 2013) based on the theory of membership cloud service behavior trust evaluation model is established, the model doesn't include the effects of user behavior analysis of cloud. Literature (Niyato et al., 2012) multiple cloud service providers' collaboration is presented in this resource pool, mobile applications provide services for the cloud environment, and introduce the best algorithm to control access to achieve maximum profit. Trostle (2006) put forward multiple cloud servers that can use the exchange of information between each other to get their own credibility, increase participants, reduce the security risk for the cloud user. In the Cloud environment, users of DDoS attacks have become a problem which couldn't be ignored, but the traditional defense methods couldn't be directly used in the cloud environment. Literature (Shen et al., 2012), under the complex network environment, we carried out on the server cluster comprehensive monitoring and effective management and focused on mass multi-types server monitoring and warning technology of the data center. Liu and Bi (2012) presented a intrusion detection model, in the model, each cloud server has its own intrusion detection system, each set of cluster servers has an intrusion detection of a dedicated server for management, which is responsible for the alarm messages' passing each other. Liu et al. (2014) put forward a kind of double machine model based on multiple decision-making mechanism, from the perspective of their own comparisons to the server and the status of other party, we combined with the client terminal comparisons on its status, integrated the master and backup servers available, to make the right decision to keep master or switch to backup for service, which ensure the business is available, but the client users withself-interest purpose may not give credible information, the model doesn't consider the credibility of the user. Yang Xiaofen and others in the literature (2012) will make the master server and backup server respectively connected to the client for storage. Real-time database system of dual machine thermal mechanism is proposed to provide data services for the customers together.

Through the above analysis, we get the following deficiencies of credibility evaluation about could service: 1. In the process of evaluation of cloud services credible, no combination of cloud users is not comprehensive. 2. The cloud users' judgement are evaluation factors, but they are not selected. Against the above, this paper will combine the behavior Graphs and tripartite decision-making mechanism, and put forward a credible cloud service model based on behavior Graphs and tripartite decision-making mechanism. According to the characters of cloud service and the application itself, we insert some comparison points in the process of cloud services, In each comparison point, we can use the hardware and software tools to collect user behaviors evidence, usage with index (0, 2) scale weights of AHP method to analyze the user behavior, construct the ideal figure cloud user behavior graph and cloud user behavior graph. By correlating, we choose the most trusted cloud user as a part of judgement for cloud service' credibility. According to their own internal saved state S, we get a conclusion about the credibility of cloud service and the migration of master and backup server.

3. THE RELATED CONCEPTS AND THE LOGICAL FRAMEWORK

3.1. The Relative Concepts

Definition 1: The cloud user behavior(CUB), It is a series of actions or operations of the user who is a subject in the process of using cloud services, such as HTTP requests and responses, click on the page link.

Definition 2: The cloud user behaviors evidence (E_CUB), It is the base value that is direct from the hardware and software (or after a simple calculation) of the quantitative analysis of user behavior in the process of cloud services., such as IP packet transmission delay, IP packet loss rate and the number of page visits.

Definition 3: Comparison Point (OP), It is the key point of getting the information of user behavior in the cloud service process; it has a greater impact on the security of cloud services. In this paper, we select the branch points of cloud services and important pages (user information page, payment page, etc.) as the comparison point.

Definition 4: Ideal cloud user behavior graphs, it is used to describe the ideal user's behaviors in the cloud service. It is a triple, CG=<V, E, N>, V is the set of nodes, V i represents the behaviors of users using cloud services; E is the set of edges; N represents the number of OP in the graphs. "Edge" means the sequence of behavior, V k E i V j shows the relations between nodes and edges in the graphs, k, i and j are integers, and k = j-1.

Definition 5: Cloud user behavior graphs, it is used to describe all cloud users in a cloud service to all behavior.

Definition 6: A single cloud user behavior path, it describes one user's all behaviors in the cloud service.

Definition 7: The Best Behavior Path of Cloud Service (B_BP): It is the most credible BP in the graphs. We select the path that the weighted sum of the value of all nodes on it is the largest as the B_BP in this paper.

Definition 8: The most credible cloud users, these cloud users, their behavior path is consistent with the best path.

Definition 9: Cloud services master server: at the beginning of cloud server, it provides service for cloud user at first, it can give their credible judgment about backup server and cloud users. The 0 is not credible, 1 is credible.

Definition 10: Cloud service backup server: when the master server is in incredible state, the backup server continues to provide services for cloud users of cloud servers, it can give credible judgment about the master server and the cloud user. The 0 is not credible, 1 is credible.

Definition 11; The credible cloud user: it can be selected by the behavior graph, it can give credible judgment about the master server and the backup server. The 0 is not credible, 1 is credible.

Definition 12: Credibility triples: In the tripartite decision-making evaluation mechanism, the master server, the backup server and the credible cloud users hold for judging the cloud service credibility of triple S, < m, b, c >, m is used to represent the credible for master server, b is used to represent the credible for backup server, c is used to represent the credible for cloud users. The 0 is not credible, 1 is credible.

3.2. The Tripartite Decision-Making Mechanism of Credible Cloud Services

In the structure of the Figure 1, Cloud services introduced in TPM + VTPM structure, to measure the credibility of cloud servers. The heartbeat mechanism checks the reliability of the devices. The master server is the main body at the beginning of the cloud services. In cloud services, the mater service and backup server are credible by the heartbeat mechanism. The credibility of cloud service also depends on the cloud user. We will advocate that organic combination for the three parties of cloud user, master server and backup server together to judge the credibility of cloud service. Firstly, we select the credible cloud users, we adopt to construct judgment matrix in AHP index scale method (0.2) (Xu 1999) and the hierarchical structure can be divided into three layers: Cloud user behavior layer (target), behavioral attributes layer(middle) and behavioral evidence layer (measure). We will use the credible choice of cloud users and cloud server through tripartite decision-making mechanism to determine the credibility of cloud services. In the decision mechanism of three parties, one is master server, one is backup server, the last one is cloud user. The three parties have equal status in the credible judgment, Master server and backup server not only rely on themselves to each other's observations to determine the credibility of the state, but also rely on the cloud user observations to further determine the credibility of cloud server. The cloud users' observations is considered as the main case of cloud service status for determining factor which is reasonable, because Cloud service is for cloud users, it could avoid the limitations of bilateral decision-making mechanism.

4. THE CONSTRUCTION OF BEHAVIOR GRAPHS AND THE COGNIZANCE OF CREDIBILITY

4.1. The Screening of Cloud Users

Liking the following Figure 2, After collecting cloud user behavior evidence, we do the data standardization and choose credible user by the establishment of behavior Graphs. Process as shown in the Figure 2 below.

Figure 1. Tripartite Decision-Making Mechanism

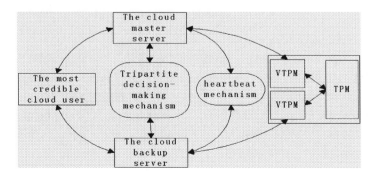

Figure 2. The structure of the most credible cloud users to choose

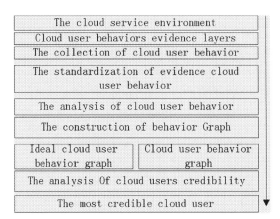

4.1.1. The Behavior Evidence Collection

This model comprehensively studies the behavior of the domestic and the foreign scholars put forward a method of collecting evidence (Liqin 2006) to obtain evidence of the behavior, adopted the following three methods: (1) network traffic monitoring tools, such as Bandwidth, (2) the existing intrusion detection systems, such as Sax2, (3) the Web log files.

4.1.2. The Standardization of E_CUB

The manifestation of the behavioral evidence obtained through the software and hardware tools is diverse. The main types of evidence include: 1) the type of the bigger the better, e.g. data transmission speed, no-failure operation time etc. 2) the type of the smaller the better, e.g. cloud service response time, number of unauthorized access etc. The standardization of E_CUB is convenient for calculating the B_BP in the behavior graphs. Optimal Membership Degree (OMD), the degree of membership of the evidence for the vague concept of "excellent," is introduced to standardize the E_CUB. OMD can be received by the formula (Peizhuang 1983):

1. The type of the bigger the better: $g = \dfrac{e - \max(e)}{\max(e) - \min(e)}$.

2. The type of the smaller the better: $g = \dfrac{\max(e) - e}{\max(e) - \min(e)}$.

The g is the OMD of the behavior evidence, i.e. the standard value of the behavioral evidence; the e is the value of evidence obtained directly or through the simple calculation; the Sup (e) is the upper bound of the value of evidences and the Inf (e) is the lower bound of the value of evidences. The value of g is in [0, 1], and it is the larger the better.

4.1.3. Index (0, 2) Scale Method of AHP Weights Cloud User Behavior Analysis

This article will put forward the improved structure judgment matrix in AHP index (0, 2) scale method to analyse the cloud user's behavior, Specific process is as follows:

1. Establish a hierarchical cloud user behavior hierarchy. Cloud user behavior hierarchy contains three levels, from top to bottom in turn as follows: the cloud user behavior layer (target layer), behavior layer properties (middle layer) and behavior evidence layer (measures layer).
2. Construct a judgment matrix and assignment. we Structure judgment matrix based on recursive class time, matrix elements in the two comparison, with the people most likely to give judgment instead of the original three scales that is very difficult to exactly nine scale (0, 9) give judgment weight. With index (0, 2) scale method, Decision makers, in view of the two comparative importance elements, can get a matrix C:

$$
C = \begin{pmatrix}
a^{c_{11}} & a^{c_{12}} & \cdots & a^{c_{1n}} \\
a^{c_{21}} & a^{c_{22}} & \cdots & a^{c_{2n}} \\
\vdots & \vdots & \ddots & \vdots \\
a^{c_{n1}} & a^{c_{n2}} & \cdots & a^{c_{nn}}
\end{pmatrix}
$$

3. The importance of each element calculation index

$$
\gamma_i = \sum_{j=1}^{n} c_{ij}, (i = 1,2,...n)
$$

4. Get the judgment matrix.

$$
b_{ij} = \gamma_i - \gamma_j \quad B = \begin{pmatrix}
a^{b_{11}} & a^{b_{12}} & \cdots & a^{b_{1n}} \\
a^{b_{21}} & a^{b_{22}} & \cdots & a^{b_{2n}} \\
\vdots & \vdots & \ddots & \vdots \\
a^{b_{n1}} & a^{b_{n2}} & \cdots & a^{b_{nn}}
\end{pmatrix}
$$

5. Use of LLSM (logarithmic least squares method) to calculate parameter vector.

$$
\overline{w} = \left(a^{\left(\sum_{j=1}^{n} b_{1j}\right)/n}, a^{\left(\sum_{j=1}^{n} b_{2j}\right)/n}, ..., a^{\left(\sum_{j=1}^{n} b_{nj}\right)/n} \right)^T
$$

6. Compute the user behavior credibility.

7. Set the properties of the vector for user behavior: $\mathbf{A} = \left(a_1 \cdots a_i \cdots a_n\right)^{\mathrm{T}}$ Weight vector for attributes:

$$\mathbf{W}_A = \left(w_1 \cdots w_i \cdots w_n\right)^{\mathrm{T}}, V_{\mathrm{cub}} = \mathbf{A}^{\mathrm{T}}\mathbf{W}_A = \left(a_1 \cdots a_i \cdots a_n\right)\left(w_1 \cdots w_i \cdots w_n\right)^{\mathrm{T}} = \sum_{i=1}^{n} a_i w_i \quad \text{is}$$

called User Behavior Analysis Value (the Value of User behaviors Analysis, VB).

4.2. The Construction of Behavior Graph

Ideal cloud user's behavior graphics is made of different cloud users within a certain period of time. The process of the construction of the specific as follows:

1. The cloud service is divided into N parts, and then N comparison points (excluding the start node and end node) are established. The E_CUB is collected at each comparison point; the type of E_CUB collected by each comparison point is different, because they have different emphases, some put emphasis on efficiency, some put emphasis on safety and so on. In addition, the comparison point also has a weight, the method of determining the weights is still using the idea of (0.2) AHP described in the fourth section, all the comparison points compare to each other, and ultimately the weight of each relative to the cloud user behavior is determined.
2. There are Si nodes at the i-th comparison point, i.e. The number of the type of behaviors is Si, and Si is less than or equal to the number of users using the cloud service. The values of Si in different comparison point are different.
3. Each node of the i-th comparison point is connected to each node of the (i+1)-th comparison point, then a complete behavior graphs is obtained; it is the Cloud Behavior Graphs (Shown in Figure 3). The behavior graphs built by this way is a complete behavior graphs, and some edges does not have to exist in the actual test, i.e. CG only exists in theory, the actual CG only infinitely close to it. The number of nodes and edges in the UG is less than or equal to those in the CG.

Any one path from the start node to the end node in CG represents the process of user using the cloud service. The node means the value of user behavior analysis, and the value is the larger the better, so the path of the node which the value represented by it is maximum is the Best Behavior Path of Cloud Service (B_BP). B_BP may not actually exist; it is only a standard of user behavior authentication. When a user uses the cloud service, the degree of deviation between the B_BP and his behavior path will be an important basis to determine the trustiness of the user behavior. User Behavior Graphs (UG) is built on the basis of a user multiple use of a cloud service, and its build process is similar to the build process of the CG. The cloud service is divided into N parts, and then N comparison points (excluding the start node and end node) are established. The number and location of the comparison point are consistent with those of the CG. The E_CUB of the observed user is collected at each comparison point, finally the adjacent comparison points are connected to each other, and then the User Behavior Graphs is obtained. The establishment of the best behavior path of a cloud user is also connected the node which the value represented by it is maximum at its comparison point. It also theoretically exists; it may be just happening to the experiment. We get the degree of deviation of user behavior by comparing the best behavior path of a cloud user and the B_BP, and then divide the users into conservative users and radical users, at the same time it is the basis of determining the trust threshold of user behavior. In the actual process of operation and maintenance, the size of behavior graphs will continue to increase with the increase

Figure 3. The cloud behavior graphs

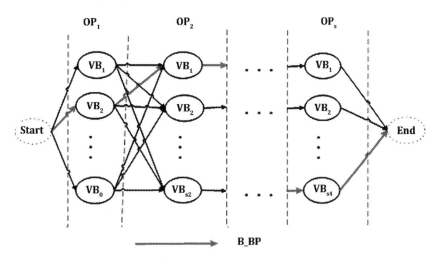

B_BP

in the number of interactions between users and cloud service, but storage resources and computing resources are limited, so we must control the size of the behavior graphs and regularly remove the lapse nodes in the behavior graphs based on the time factor and the node frequency to achieve the dynamic maintenance of the behavior graphs. These are consistent with the stages of user behaviors (the behavior characteristics are not the same in a different period of time).

4.3. The Select of User Behavior Credibility

Ideal cloud user behavior graph and cloud user behavior graph are the foundation of the credible cloud user's selection. The specific steps of selection for credible user are as follows:

Step 1: According to the characteristics of the cloud services, in the recent period of cloud services in the process of selecting N comparison points, Use the cloud user behavior analysis method in section 3 to calculate the weights of each comparison point: W_i *(1≤i≤N)*.

Step 2: We obtain the evidences of cloud user behaviors at each comparison point, and calculate their OMD, and get the value of user behavior analysis V_i *(1≤i≤N)* by CB(0-2)AHP.

Step 3: We calculate the absolute value of the difference between the value of user behavior analysis and the standard value of behavior analysis, it is the value of the node in the B_BP, then the absolute value is multiplied by the weights of the comparison point, finally the result is as the degree of deviation of user behavior of the comparison point $D_i = \left| V_i - V_i^{'} \right| \times w_i$.

(V_i ': standard value of behavior analysis; 1≤i≤N).

Step 4: We accumulatively deemed the comparison point of user behavior deviation, namely

$$D = \sum_{i=1}^{k} D_i$$

(k is that compared to total number of comparison points). The most credible cloud users is the cloud user that's difference is the smallest. A threshold value is set by the cloud service providers, network

Figure 4. Dual system

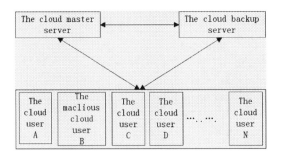

security experts and cloud user at each point, as long as there is a comparison point more than threshold, it rules out, we choose the most credible cloud users, update the cloud service behavior graph and user behavior graph. The certification is divided into two stages: Start model phase and stable model phase. At the start of modeling stage, because of the beginning of cloud users' enjoyment at cloud services, information about the cloud user behavior is not perfect, user behavior graph is not established, the user types are also not clear, so choose the best behavior of cloud service behavior path as a standard authentication of user behavior, the nodes on the path of value is the standard behavior analysis. In stable stage model, multiple cloud service users have held several interactions with cloud server, which formed a comprehensive user behavior graph, and established the optimal path (that path is most concentrated).

4.4. The Cloud Service Credibility of Tripartite Decision-Making Mechanism

The credible cloud users' judgment has higher reference value in the cloud service. Structure as shown in Figure 4, There are malicious users hiding in the cloud users, so we must choose a credible cloud user, and eliminate malicious cloud users. Finally, with the most credible cloud user and the tripartite decision-making judgment rules of credibility of judgment, we make a right judgment. On three sides of the participation in the decision-making evaluation structure entity, judging with triple S< m, b, c > said it to the other two judgments participants credible state, its value is 0 or 1, the value 1 is credible, 0 is no credible, credible definition of our rules between entities is mutual. Each entity assuming it on his own, credible state constant is 1. To describe briefly, M is the judgment credibility of triples in the master server < m.b.c >, B is the judgment credibility of triples in the backup server < m.b.c >, C is the judgment credibility of triples in the cloud user< m.b.c >. There are 4 kinds of circumstances, such as the master server triples: The < 1.1.1 > said that the other two entities are credible, the < 1.1.0 > said that the cloud backup server is credible and the user isn't credible. The < 1.0.1 >said that the cloud backup server isn't credible and the user is credible. The < 1.0.0 > said that two other entities are not credible. The detailed description is given in Table 1.

In order to simplify the model, Credibility is a two-way street, so it can't appear at the same time a triple M = < 1.1.1 > and other triple C = <0.1.1 >. Because M = < 1.1.1 > said that master server considers the cloud user can be credible, C = < 0.1.1> said that cloud users consider that the master server is not credible, this is contradictory. After ruled out all kinds of contradictory combinations, in Table 2 we make a list of all possible combinations of triples, and the relevant meaning explanation is given.

The rules of credibility evaluation: Rule 1, The triple exchange rule: Provisions of a cycle time is t. master server, backup server and cloud user save an internal data structure S, S = < M.B.C >. After

Table 1. Each entity reliable judgment

The entity	S	Explain
Master sever S	<1.1.1>	Backup server and cloud user are credible .
	<1.1.0>	Backup server is credible , cloud user is not credible.
	<1.0.1>	Backup server is not credible , cloud user is credible.
	<1.0.0>	Backup server and cloud user are not credible.
Backup server S	<1.1.1>	Master server and cloud user are credible.
	<1.1.0>	Master serve is credible, cloud user is not credible.
	<0.1.1>	Master serve is not credible, cloud user is credible.
	<0.1.0>	Master server and cloud user are not credible.
The credible user	<1.1.1>	Master server and backup server are credible
	<1.0.1>	Master server is credible, backup server is not credible.
	<0.1.1>	Master server is not credible, backup server is credible.
	<0.0.1>	Master server and backup server are not credible.

system initialization, the entity S is set to $<<0.0.0>.<0.0.0>.<0.0.0>>$. Within the time period t, according to relevant data, we judge the other side of the corresponding state of credibility and generate a triple M, B, C, update to the respective S, and send it to the other two entities involved in credibility judgment. If a particular entity, within the time period t, is not received other entities' credibility of the judge state of triples, S corresponding item will be set$<0.0.0>$. In Table 3 cases each entity and triples the content of the entire cloud service system.

Different cloud service credible states can convert to each other, but in the process of transformation to follow rule 2.

Rule 2: credibility of switching rules:

1. When the master server saved S for $<<1.1.0><1.1.1><0.0.0>>$ or $<<1.0.0><0.0.0><0.0.0>>$, namely above the state of the E3 and E8, The master server doesn't provide cloud services.
2. When the backup server saved S for $<<1.1.0><1.1.1><0.1.1>>$ or $<<0.0.0><0.1.1><0.1.1>>$, namely above the state of the E3 and E7, the backup server will take over the cloud services.
3. When the master server saved S for $<<1.1.0><1.1.0><0.0.0>>$and the backup server saved S for $<<1.1.0><1.1.0><0.0.0>>$, the above state E4, the master server and the backup server consider that cloud users couldn't be credible at that time, they don't provide cloud service.

If there is a battle for providing cloud services to cloud users, the model is unreasonable problem. According to rules 2 switching of the master server and the backup servers, backup server only saved S for $<<1.1.0><1.1.1><0.1.1>>$ or $<<0.0.0><0.1.1><0.1.1>>$, it tries to provide cloud services to users of cloud, at this moment, the master server for a triple S $<<1.0.0><1.1.1><$

Table 2. Judgment possible combinations between entity and its explanation

The entity	S	Explain
Master sever S	<1.1.1>	Backup server and cloud user are credible .
	<1.1.0>	Backup server is credible , cloud user is not credible.
	<1.0.1>	Backup server is not credible , cloud user is credible.
	<1.0.0>	Backup server and cloud user are not credible.
Backup server S	<1.1.1>	Master server and cloud user are credible.
	<1.1.0>	Master serve is credible, cloud user is not credible.
	<0.1.1>	Master serve is not credible, cloud user is credible.
	<0.1.0>	Master server and cloud user are not credible.
The credible user	<1.1.1>	Master server and backup server are credible
	<1.0.1>	Master server is credible, backup server is not credible.
	<0.1.1>	Master server is not credible, backup server is credible.
	<0.0.1>	Master server and backup server are not credible.

$0.0.0 >>$ or $<< 1.0.0 > < 0.0.0 > < 0.0.0 >>$, it is the condition that a master server is not credible and exits to provide cloud service. We could be known from the above, it is because the credible user's participation, it will make credible state judge more judgment basis, so as to make the right judgment. Cloud users as main object of cloud services, enjoy the authentic judgment has two effects: (1) establish the majority in three or more parties judgment criteria, so to avoid the master server and backup server getting a contradiction; (2)When the cloud user couldn't provide reliable judgment basis for server, namely when cloud users for a triple $S << 0.0.0 >, < 0.0.1 >, < 1.0.0 >>$, the master and backup servers are unable to provide service for the client, so even if there is a contradiction, it won't bring more problems. There are no technical barriers in the credible cloud service model based on behavior Graph and tripartite decision-making mechanism. In this paper, the recommended method is in the main operating agent software for cloud server. At the same time, we choose a number of cloud users machine running in the cloud user installed on the client related to the client proxy software, the main support agent software defined rules. Each entity sends information to each other by means of IP multicast hello message to report the respective state of reliable judgment triples $< M.B.C >$. In order to ensure reliable triples the real-time and reliability of the information exchange, all parties need to maintain a few time variable, including: (1) the hello message sending time interval for the hello - time corresponding to the time t of rule 1, each decision every time period t sends a hello message to the other two entities to send their own reliable judgment of the entire cloud services. (2) S expiration time elements in the item of the ex - time, corresponding rule 1 e in time. If an entity within the prescribed time ex - time didn't receive other entities' reliable judgment state information, then it will set $S < 0.0.0 >$. In the ex - time, for example, if the master server didn't receive a hello message from credible user, so S related item is set to $< 0.0.0 >$. Generally speaking, the ex - time should be greater than the hello - time, because the network is delayed, it is generally believed the latter should be the former three times.

Table 3. Different credible environment of each entity a triple S

The entity	S	Explain
Master sever S	<1.1.1>	Backup server and cloud user are credible .
	<1.1.0>	Backup server is credible , cloud user is not credible.
	<1.0.1>	Backup server is not credible , cloud user is credible.
	<1.0.0>	Backup server and cloud user are not credible.
Backup server S	<1.1.1>	Master server and cloud user are credible.
	<1.1.0>	Master serve is credible, cloud user is not credible.
	<0.1.1>	Master serve is not credible, cloud user is credible.
	<0.1.0>	Master server and cloud user are not credible.
The credible user	<1.1.1>	Master server and backup server are credible
	<1.0.1>	Master server is credible, backup server is not credible.
	<0.1.1>	Master server is not credible, backup server is credible.
	<0.0.1>	Master server and backup server are not credible.

The credible cloud user, as part of the credible judgment entity, it represents all users that enjoy cloud service. For cloud users, they can be generated credible judge triples, according to their own confidence judgment from IP message, all cloud users update the status. Finally, in the tripartite decision-making mechanism, only credible judgment triples for tripartite judgment of selected cloud users is involved in judgment. In addition, we try to avoid a cloud client transfer delay problems, if all cloud users' message in a certain time doesn't transfer success, cloud service considers the cloud client fails. In order to avoid the occurrence of this phenomenon, when we select the cloud users, we should pay attention to this following, Selecting the appropriate number of client cloud users and make sure that these cloud users won't appear problem at the same time. Try to make sure that the cloud users do not connect on the same network access equipment, and avoid handling at same time.

5. MODEL SIMULATION AND RESULT ANALYSIS

5.1. The Simulation Data Collection

The experimental data are from the log files of MyNonCS2KSrv, a non-commercial Web server provided by Microsoft (2017), a variety of data collection tools, laboratory server user behavior in the log audit system and Matlab stochastic simulation data. Behavior of evidence collection tool, Sax2 and Bandwidth Monitor behavior, they are responsible for collecting illegal link count, sensitive port scanning, data throughput, etc. From the server log audit system of behavior include user throughput, sensitive page evidence behavior such as residence time.

5.2. Behavior Data Processing and Construction of Behavior Graphs

We randomly select two groups without overlap from the data set; respectively denote them as Standard user group U1and screening user group U2. U1 are used to construct the ideal cloud user behavior graph, U2 are used to construct screening cloud user behavior graph and choose the most credible cloud user. We need to simulate the behavior of the malicious users in the U2, Specific method is as follows: the malicious user simulates DDoS attacks, we set the interval to send a GET request with some random numbers, the mean value of them is 20ms, and i.e. the transmission rate of HTTP request approximately is 50 / s. The length of attack time is the running time of the cloud service. There are two methods to generate the content of GET request: the first one is to intercept the fragment of a normal user's HTTP request sequence; the second one is to generate the content of each GET request randomly. We use behavioral evidence normalization formula to standardize the behavioral evidence in both groups. There are 6 comparison points in the service. According to the data analysis in U1, contrasted each cloud user's behavior, the cloud user behavior can be divided into: 1) resources occupation attribute the behavior of the evidence, it includes cloud user throughput, IP packet transmission delay, user takes the process time; 2) behavior safety attribute the behavior of the evidence, it includes the user illegal connection times, key port scanning frequency, root access to sensitive times, page retention time. Resources possession attribute indicates whether the cloud service environment safety, Cloud user throughput shows that in unit time through cloud users operating the amount of data, reflecting the current network load; Transmission delay shows that IP packet transmission used in the transmission medium; Process time is used to indicate that the network ever in malicious processes. Behavior safety property is mainly used to determine whether the user behavior in line with the general rules. According to section3, it introduces the analysis method to calculate value comparison cloud user behavior analysis. User behavior pass class hierarchy as shown in Figure 5. At the same time, calculate the relative weight vector for the 6 comparison points: $[W_{vp1}, W_{vp2}, W_{vp3}, W_{vp4}, W_{vp5}, W_{vp6}] = [0.0449, 0.3537, 0.2031, 0.1131, 0.1906, 0.0946]$.

Through the above method, we can get the elements of each element in the set of weights and the weight vectors of behavioral evidence is obtained. $[E_{11}, ..., E_{13}, E_{21}, ... , E_{24}] = [0.0834, 0.0615, 0.0379, 0.2390, 0.13964, 0.1345, 0.1027, 0.3410]$. To collect data by Matlab to establish ideal cloud user behavior graph, credible screening cloud user behavior model graph and credible screening cloud user behavior result graph, as shown in Figure 6 and Figure 7, Figure 8, a path represents cloud users' each time the use of cloud services.

Figure 5. User behavior class hierarchy

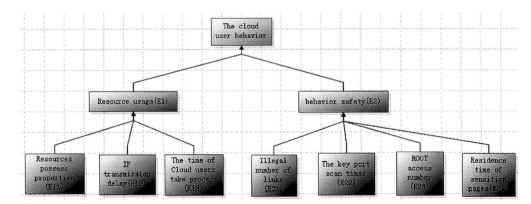

Figure 6. The ideal figure cloud user behavior

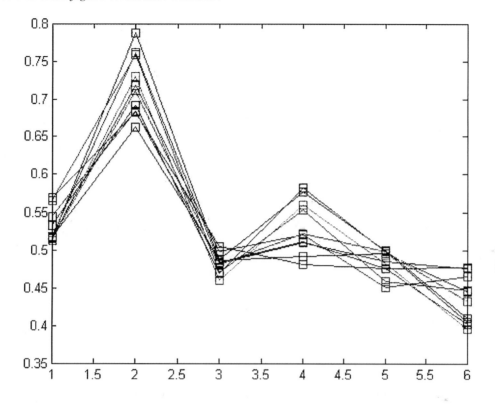

Figure 7. The credibility screening cloud user behavior

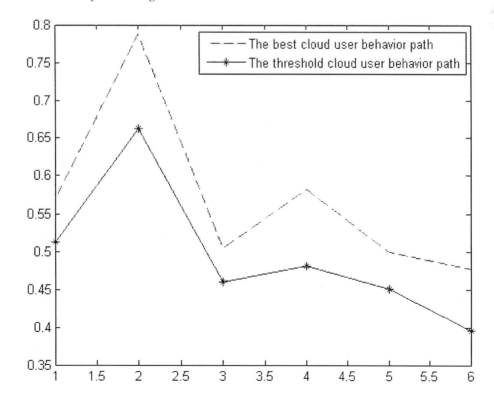

Figure 8. The results of credibility screening cloud user behavior

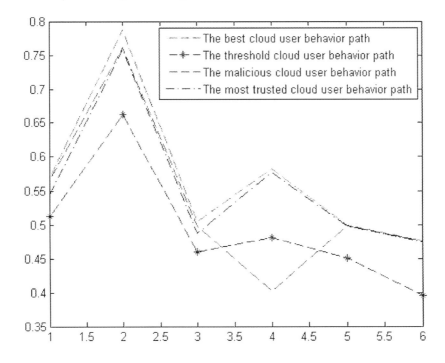

5.3. The Screening Credible Cloud Users by Behavior Data

Through the analysis of the first set of data, comparison points 1 ~ 6 user behavior analysis value range of stability, in turn, are: 0.5120~ 0.5689,0.6627~ 0.7873,0.4601~ 0.5040,0.4815~ 0.5819,0.4509~ 0.4988,0.3950~ 0.4763,We get the behavior of the ideal user behavior graph, a path in this picture shows that users' using a cloud service, because the user behavior analysis of the value, the greater the user behavior, the more credible, therefore the maximum points, connecting the contrast make optimal path, as shown in Figure 9 the green line, Figure 9 red line represents the confidence threshold path, each comparison point has a credible threshold value, as long as there is a comparison point beyond the red line, the total deviation again small is ruled out, finally choose the minimum deviation of cloud users, as shown in Figure 9 the blue line represents the credible cloud users. In anomaly detection, Detection Ratio (DR) and False Positive Ratio (FPR) are two important performance metrics. Detection rate in this experiment is mainly embodied in the credible users of cloud detection rate, and the rate of false positives is mainly manifested in the false positives to credible cloud users. We test the DR and the FPR of the model by changing the proportion of malicious users, and compare it with PTM (Almenares et al., 2004) and MDA (Jang et al., 2011), the results are shown in Figure 9 and Figure 10.

In Figure 9, we find that when the proportion of malicious users is low, the three models all have a higher detection rate (DR>0.9); with the proportion of malicious users increasing, the DR of PTM decreases significantly and the DR of MDA has a small decline, but our model remains a higher DR. In Figure 10, when the proportion of malicious users is low, the three models all have a low FPR (FPR<0.01); with the proportion of malicious users increasing, the FPR of PTM and MDA increases significantly, but our model remains a lower FPR. In the process of service, credible services running time often is an important measure of service performance. Through the experiment, we can use this model and the

Figure 9. The success rate of the three models

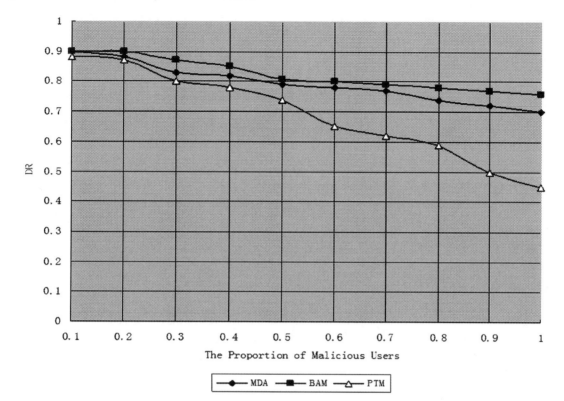

Figure 10. The rate of false positives of the three models

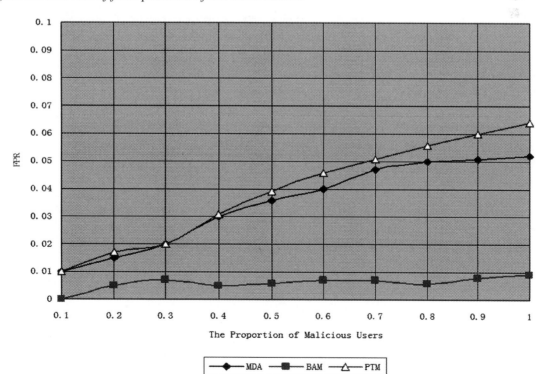

traditional model based on various decision-making double-machine hot backup credible service runtime ratios comparison shows that the result is shown in Figure 11.

The Figure 11 shows that with the traditional double machine hot backup service model, when the proportion of malicious users of cloud is small, in this paper, the model and the traditional model based on various decision-making double-machine hot backup credible service running time is approximately 1, but as a malicious user increases, the proportion of the credible service running time increases with the index grade, it shows that the greater the proportion of malicious cloud users, this model is superior to traditional dual machine thermal Model.

6. CONCLUSION

Model in this paper could ensure the whole cloud service has applied prospect in the respect of high availability, at the same time, it can improve the safety and credibility of cloud service as a whole. We introduce a reliable cloud client reliable judgment of the cloud services, and from a period of time to enjoy the same master for cloud services cloud users, we choose the most credible user. The most credible users of cloud judgment result is an important judgment factor of judging tripartite mechanism, including cloud services master server and backup server and the client, the three comparisons make a comprehensive analysis to judge the state of credible of the cloud services and provide more comprehensive basis. it enhances the credibility of cloud service and availability. Moreover, index (0 ~ 2) method AHP scale than before simple method of AHP scale advantage is: 1) simple judgment information is

Figure 11. The proportion of credible cloud services running time

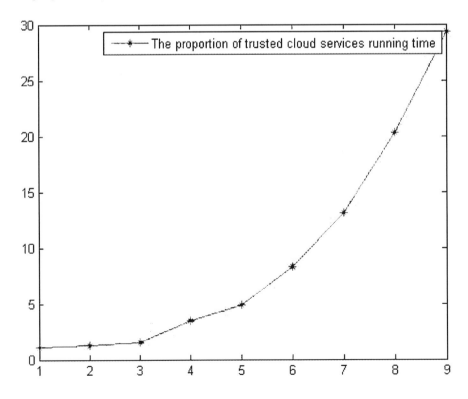

needed, security experts or decision makers could quickly give. 2) network security experts or decision makers by including a vector of parameters can be w, flexible and convenient to adjust a sorting weight value and satisfaction. 3) appropriate choosing a value can improve the consistency of AHP judgment matrix. 4) easy to tabulation collect expert judgment information. A credible cloud service model based on behavior Graphs and tripartite decision-making mechanism, the implementation method is not complicated, flexible configuration, has a good promotion value.

ACKNOWLEDGMENT

This work is supported by the Natural Science Foundation of Hebei province (F2016201244), the Natural Science Foundation of Hebei institution (ZD2015088) and the National Natural Science Foundation of China (Grant No. 61379116).

REFERENCES

Almenarez, F., Marin, A., & Campo, C. (2004). PTM: A pervasive trust management model for dynamic open environments. *Proc of the 1st Workshop on Pervasive Security, Privacy and Trust*. Boston: IEEE Computer Society.

Alzain, M. A., Pardede, E., Soh, B., & Thom, J. A. (2012). Cloud Computing Security: From Single to Multi-clouds. *Proceedings of the 2014 47th Hawaii International Conference on System Sciences* (Vol. 2, pp. 5490-5499). IEEE.

Alzain, M. A., Pardede, E., Soh, B., & Thom, J. A. (2012). Cloud Computing Security: From Single to Multi-clouds. *Proceedings of the 2014 47th Hawaii International Conference on System Sciences* (Vol. 2, pp. 5490-5499). IEEE.

Brosso, I., Neve, A., Bressan, G., & ... . (2010). A continuous authentication system based on user behavior analysis. *Proc of 2010 Int. Conf on Availability, Reliability and Security (pp.* 380-385). Piscataway, NJ: IEEE. 10.1109/ARES.2010.63

Chen Ya Rui, Tian Li Qin, & Yang, Y. (2011). Model and analysis of user behavior based on dynamic game theory in cloud computing. *Acta Electronica Sinica*, 39(8), 1818-1823.

Ding Yan Huai-Min Wang, Shi Peichang, Qing-Bo Wu, Dai Huadong, & Hony, R. (2015). Credible cloud services. *Journal of computers*, 1, 133-149.

Elaine, S., NiuYuan, Jakobsson, M. (2011). Implicit authentication through learning user behavior. *Proc of ISC '10, LNCS* (Vol. 6531). Berlin: Springer.

Khazzar, A., & Savage, N. (2010). Graphical authentication based on user behaviour. *Proc of the 2010 Int Conf on Security and Cryptography (pp.* 86-89). Piscataway, NJ: IEEE.

Liqin, T., Chuang, L., & Tieguo, J. (2006). Quantitative Analysis of Trust Evidence in Internet. *Proceedings of the International Conference on Communication Technology ICCT '06* (pp.1-5). IEEE. 10.1109/ICCT.2006.342023

Liu Gang, Mawhinney, Li Xiaoyong. (2014). Based on various decision-making mechanism of double machine hot backup model. *Computer engineering and design*, 35(9), 3061-3064.

Liu Xiao Meng, & Bi Hong Jun. (2012). Analysis on model of intrusion detection in cloud computing environment. Railway Computer Application.

Lv Yanxia li-qin tian, shan-shan sun. (2013). Cloud computing environment based on FANP credible evaluation and control of the user behavior analysis. *Journal of computer science*, 40(1), 132-135.

Microsoft. (2017). Microsoft How to analyze non-commerce web server log files [EB/OL]. Retrieved from http://support.microsoft.com/kb/293887/zh-cn

Niyato, D., Wang, P., Hossain, E., Saad, W., & Han, Z. (2012). Game theoretic modeling of cooperation among service providers in mobile cloud computing environments. In *Service Provider* (pp. 3128-3133).

Peizhuang, W. (1983). Fuzzy Set Theory and Its Applications. Shang Hai: Shanghai Scientific & Technical Publishers.

Shen, Q., & Dong, B., & Xiao De bao. (2012). Design and implementation of cloud monitoring system based on server clusters. *Computer Engineering & Science*, 34(10), 73–77.

Srinivasan, S. (2012). Cloud computing security. *Revista Economica*, 1, 171-174.

Trostle, J. (2006). Protecting Against Distributed Denial of Service (DDoS) Attacks Using Distributed Filtering. Proceedings of *Securecomm and Workshops '06* (pp. 1–11).

Udoh, E., & Hsu, C.-H. (2013). Cloud computing technology and science. *International Journal of Grid and High Performance Computing*, 5(4), 1–4. doi:10.4018/ijghpc.2013100101

Yang Xiaofen, & Liu Yi. (2012). Dual machine thermal real-time database system for mechanism design and implementation. *Computer engineering and application.*

Xie Li Jun, Zhu Zhi Qiang, Sun, L., & Pan, N. (2013). Research on behavior trust evaluation model of cloud services based on membership theory. *Application Research of Computers*, 30(4), 1051-1054.

Xu, J., Townend, P., & Arshad, J. (2012). Cloud Computing Security: Opportunities and Pitfalls. *International Journal of Grid and High Performance Computing*, 4(1), 52–66. doi:10.4018/jghpc.2012010104

Ze, Jang, Li Shuang qing, Yin Cheng guo. (2011). Evaluating network user behavior trust based on multiple decisions attributes [in Chinese]. *Application Research of Computers*, 28(6), 2289–2293.

Ze-Shui Xu. (1999). Construct the judgment matrix in AHP index (0, 2) scale method. *Journal of Qufu Normal University*, 1, 50-52.

Zhang kai, & Pan Xiao. (2014). Under the cloud computing model of access control based on user behavior trust. *Journal of computer applications*, 34(4), 1051-1054.

This research was previously published in the International Journal of Grid and High Performance Computing (IJGHPC), 8(3); edited by Emmanuel Udoh, Ching-Hsien Hsu, and Mohammad Khan, pages 38-56, copyright year 2016 by IGI Publishing (an imprint of IGI Global).

Chapter 48
Keystroke Dynamics Authentication in Cloud Computing:
A Survey

Basma Mohammed Hassan
Benha University, Egypt

Khaled Mohammed Fouad
Benha University, Egypt

Mahmoud Fathy Hassan
Benha University, Egypt

ABSTRACT

Cloud computing needs a strong and efficient authentication system because the user will access his rented part through a faraway connection and it will make the authentication sensor device besides the user place for identification and verification so how to know the user who claimed himself to be the legal user. Keystroke identification system as a biometric authentication technique is strongly Candidate for the security issues in cloud computing technology. Keystroke dynamics as a security system did not need extra hardware because the authentication device will be the existing keyboard based on everyone has a unique style for writing. The other biometric methods are addressed with each advantage and disadvantage along with keystroke method. In this paper, all known studies about keystroke technique are explained and compared between them according to the classification technique, number of the participated users and each study results then introduces a survey on software and hardware of other biometric authentication techniques and after the literature review is addressed then keystroke as a biometric authentication system is suggested to access cloud computing environment because it has many advantages to being a part of the known security systems which spread in our world.

DOI: 10.4018/978-1-5225-8176-5.ch048

INTRODUCTION

Cloud computing security issues (Paranjape et al., 2013) such as access control, authentication and authorization (Emam, 2013) requires a high-guaranteed security model to increase the quality of service and user confidence (Chang et al., 2011; Kim et al., 2012). The internet, as the backbone, provides many resources as a utility to end-users as and when needed basis (Seminar report, 2006), so how to know that the user who request to access his rented part in cloud computing to be the legal individual without using a firm authentication technique. Personal identification methods are the most common mechanisms for authentication in cloud computing; however, it is not a secure way for authenticating users. Moreover, most of the biometric identification techniques (Babich, 2012) require special hardware, thus complicate the access point and make it costly to the ordinary users or even to the companies.

Keystroke dynamics (Rupinder et al., 2014; Monrose et al., 1999; Messerman et al., 2011; Peacock et al., 2004; Bergadano et al., 2002) is a biometric identification technique which depends on user behavior while typing on a computer keyboard (Kaur et al., 2013). It is more secure and does not need any special hardware to the access point. Keystroke dynamics is the most apparent sort of biometrics available on computer components, but it has not yet led to real hardware security applications for cloud computing technology if compared to other biometric techniques.

SECURITY ISSUES FOR CLOUD COMPUTING ENVIRONMENT

Cloud computing is not secure by nature because the implicit security system is often unaware and less visible, which creates a false sense of security and worry about what is actually secured and controlled (Tin, 2015) and this makes the users have no confidence. As a result, reduce the number of subscribers and users of this technology.

Cloud computing poses privacy concerns because the service provider or any other hackers can access data stored on the cloud server at any time. It could alter or even delete information by accidentally or deliberately ways. Access control and user authentication are considered the security technologies used for platforms and controls a process in the operating system not to approach the area of another process (Mell, 2011) so if companies supplied the users by the devices to access the cloud computing servers for authentication process, how can be authenticate the legal individual from a faraway other than the cost of such devices? The following sections show the different between many biometric identification methods and why we suggest keystroke dynamics to access cloud computing.

BIOMETRICS SYSTEM OPERATION

The biometric system can be operated in two modes: enrollment and authentication modes.

In the enrollment mode, the biometric system converts the person's biometric characteristics into a template or profile then stores this in a storage system (Divya et al., 2015). In the authentication or test mode, the biometric system can be used for verification or identification processes i.e. compare the new features collected to the stored templates of the user. Figure 1 shows the typical enrollment and test mode for a biometric system operation.

A biometric system is an automated system capable of (Chaudhary et al., 2015; Anil, 2004):

Figure 1. Traditional biometric system layout

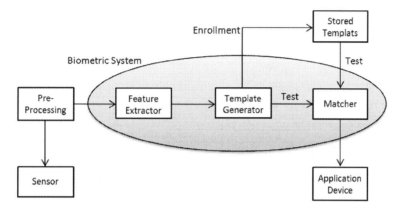

1. Capturing a biometric sample from an end user.
2. Processing and extracting the biometric data from that sample.
3. Storing the extracted information in a database.
4. Comparing the stored data with data contained in reference templates for deciding how well they match and indicating whether or not an identification of identity has been achieved.

WHAT IS BIOMETRICS?

The word "Biometric" is an ancient Greek word which referees to bio means "life" and metric means "measure" (Babaeizadeh et al., 2015). Biometric authentication supports three important factors of information security system. These factors are authentication, identification, and non-repudiation. Authorization and Authentication (Emam, 2013) are kinds of security and privacy issues of cloud computing. A lot of research discussed this problem and tried to introduce many solutions and methods to decrease the gap between security or authentication and cloud computing environment which make effects and prevents the spread of that technology.

Biometrics (Jaiswal et al., 2011) is a set of technologies based on the measurement of unique behavioral or physical characteristics for the purpose of identifying or authentication an individual (Bandara et al., 2015). Biometric authentication systems (BAS) are believed to be effective compared to the traditional authentication methods such as passwords, tokens and PINs (Tin, 2015; Teh et al., 2013) which failed to keep up with the challenges presented because they can be stolen or lost (Lee, 2012) which means an infirm security system. Authentication types can be classified under three different security field (Liu, 2001) as the following:

*   **Something you Know:** Something only you remember like password, PIN, or a piece of personal information (such as where are you born?).

- **Something you Have:** Something only you possess such as a smart card, card key, or a token like a Secure ID card.
- **Something you Are:** Some biometric property.
- Combinations (Multiple factors).

Biometric authentication classifications consist of two types Physical and behavioral biometrics (Jaiswal et al., 2011) as shown in Figure 2.

- **Physiological Biometrics:** based on data derived from direct measurement of a part of the human body and relies on something the users are such as fingerprint (Cao et al., 2013), iris (Li, 2015), face (Aco, 2015; Ghanavati, 2015), hand geometry (Guo, 2012), retina (Kochetkov, 2013; Barrero et al., 2013) as well as Palmprint (Lee, 2012; Wu et al., 2013) recognitions.
- **Behavioral Biometrics:** based on the user's behavior such as signature (Shah et al., 2015), voice (Rudrapal at al., 2012) and keystroke dynamics (Bhatt et al, 2013).

GENERAL DESCRIPTION OF BIOMETRICS TECHNOLOGIES

The following sections address some of biometric authentication techniques with its known advantages and disadvantages features. Figure 3 shows some of the biometric recognition methods:

Finger Recognition

Involves taking a feature pattern of a person's fingertips and records finger characteristics like whorls, arches, and loops (Mell et al., 2009)

Advantages:
1. Very high accuracy

Figure 2. Classification of biometric authentication

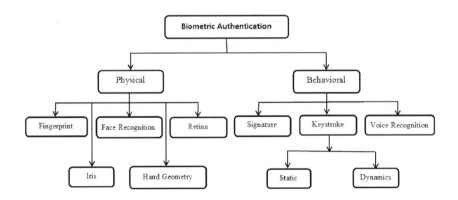

Figure 3. Some of biometric recognition methods

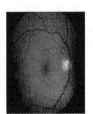
Retina

DNA

Palmprint

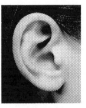
Ear

Face

Fingerprint

Iris

Hand geometry

Keystroke

Signature

Voice

Gait

2. Easy to use.
3. It is standardized.
4. It is one of the most developed biometrics
5. Small storage space needed for the biometric template, reducing the size of the database memory required.
6. Most economical biometric authentication technique.

Disadvantages:

1. It can make mistakes with the dryness or dirty of the finger skin, as well as with the age (is not appropriate with children because the size of their fingerprint changes quickly).
2. Very intrusive because it is still related to criminal identification.

Iris Recognition

It was used specific pattern recognition techniques based on images of the iris of an individual's eyes. Analyzes features like rings, furrows, and freckles existing in the colored tissue surrounding the pupil (Mellor, 2009). This technology was piloted in Saudi Arabia as a method of keeping track of the millions making Haj (Kaur et al., 2013).

Advantages:

1. The eye from a dead person would break up too fast to be useful, so no extra precautions have to be taken with retinal scans to be sure the user is a living human being.
2. Very high accuracy.
3. Verification time is generally less than five seconds.

Disadvantages:

1. Very expensive.
2. Very Intrusive.
3. A lot of memories for the data to be stored.

Face Recognition

Face recognition is a biological characteristics recognition technology, using the inherent physiological features of humans for ID recognition (Banerjee et al., 2014; Kaur et al., 2013).

Advantages:

1. Can identify terrorists, criminals, etc.
2. Can find missing children.
3. Prevents voter fraud.
4. Targets shoppers.

Disadvantages:

1. Isn't always accurate.
2. Hindered by glasses, masks, long hair, etc.
3. Must ask users to have a neutral face when pictures are being taken.
4. Considered an invasion of privacy to be watched.
5. Can easily be mistreated.

Hand Geometry Recognition

A lot of measurements of the human hand can be used as biometric characteristics. These include hand shape, the lengths and widths of the fingers, and the overall size of the hand (Thakur, 2014).

Advantages:

1. Easily integrated into other devices or systems.
2. The amount of data required to uniquely identify a user in a system is the smallest by far, allowing it to be used with Smart Cards easily.
3. It has no public problems as it is associated most commonly with authorized access.

Disadvantages:

1. Very expensive
2. Considerable size.
3. It is not valid for an arthritic person since they cannot put the hand on the scanner properly.
4. Requires special hardware to use.

Retina Recognition

It is the innermost layer of the eye. Compare images of the blood vessels in the back of the eye (Thakur, 2014).

Advantages:
1. There is no known way to replicate a retina.
2. Very high accuracy.
3. The eye from a dead person would damage too fast to be useful, so no extra precautions have to be taken with retinal scans to be sure the user is a living human being.

Disadvantages:
1. Very expensive.
2. It has the stigma of consumer's thinking it is potentially harmful to the eye.
3. Comparisons of template records can take upwards of 10 seconds, depending on the size of the database.
4. Very intrusive.

DNA Recognition

Deoxyribonucleic Acid is the one-dimensional ultimate unique code for one's individuality, except for the fact that identical twins have identical DNA patterns (Thakur, 2014).

Advantages:
1. It is standardized.
2. It impossible that the system made mistakes.
3. Very high accuracy.

Disadvantages:
1. Very expensive.
2. Extremely intrusive.
3. Matching not done in real-time.

Palmprint Recognition

The palms of the hand have patterns of ridges and valleys, similar to those found in fingerprints these features can be used for uniquely identifying a person (Rohit, 2015; Salave et al., 2015; Chaudhary et al., 2015).

Advantages:
1. Fixed line structure.
2. Low intrusiveness.
3. Low-cost capturing device.
4. Low-resolution imaging.

Disadvantages:
1. More processing time.
2. Less tolerant to elastic, rotational, and translational variances and noise within the image.

Signature Recognition

Signature verification analyzes the way a user's signs name. Such systems measure features such as speed, velocity, acceleration and pressure (Shahane et al., 2015).

Advantages:
1. Cheap technology.
2. Reasonably accurate.
3. A Little time of verification (about five seconds).
4. Non-intrusive.
5. Easy to the user.

Disadvantages:
1. Error rate: one in 50.
2. Signature verification is designed to verify subjects based on the traits of their unique signature. As a result, individuals who do not sign their names in a regular manner may have difficulty enrolling and verifying in signature verification.
3. Systems can be fooled by imitation signatures.

Voice Recognition

Behavioral and physiological factors Combine to make speech patterns that can be captured by speech processing technology (Dhobale et al., 2015).

Advantages:
1. Verification time is about five seconds.
2. Non-intrusive.
3. High social acceptability.
4. Cheap technology.

Disadvantages:
1. Low accuracy.
2. A person's voice can be easily recorded and used for unauthorized PC or network.
3. An illness such as a cold can change a person's voice, making absolute identification difficult or impossible.

Keystroke Recognition

Unlike the previous biometric authentication technologies, keystroke recognition technology needs no additional hardware devices. Since the input device is the existing Keyboard, that technology reduced cost compared to expensive biometrics acquisition and sensors devices. Keystroke dynamics is the most apparent sort of biometrics available on computer components, but it has not yet led to real security system applications for cloud computing technology if compared to other used fortunate biometric techniques. However, a keystroke can be an actual tool to help access control systems for computer resources and other related applications like cloud computing environment (Ponkshe et al., 2015).

Advantages:
1. No extra hardware needed other than the keyboard.
2. No specialized training is needed for keystroke as it is a daily activity.
3. Keyboard biometric technique is cheapest as compared to other biometric techniques used for authentication.
4. Keyboard biometric acts as a promising system even if the intruder knows the username and password of the legal user.
5. Can be easily integrated with other, existing authentication systems.

Disadvantage:
1. There is no uniformity in keystroke mechanism like other biometrics. Keystroke biometrics can lead conflict in the typing style due to occasional typing.
2. Using one hand for entering the password.
3. Keyboard layout plays an important role in typing style.
4. Users typing pattern will change over time with injuries, sickness, stress, sleep, etc.

A keystroke can be divided to static and dynamic identification system as the following:

- **Keystroke Static authentication (KSA):** The user is asked to type several times a fixed text, like a password in order to build his profile or template. During the identification stage, the user is supposed to provide the same string captured during his enrollment to verify if this way of typing matches the model stored or not (Babaeizadeh et al., 2014; Bours & Mondal, 2015)
- **Keystroke Dynamic authentication (KDA):** The user is required to provide a free text to create his templates. It isn't important what he is typing, but how he is typing it, so the user didn't need to remember his password every time when access to the system (Babaeizadeh et al., 2014; Bours & Mondal, 2015)

Multimodal Biometric Systems

Multimodal biometric systems combine multiple biometric technologies, such as voice, face and fingerprint technologies to perform a single application (Divya et al., 2015). This creates a more efficient and secures biometric system with a high-level of accuracy.

The Performance of the System of Authentication Biometrics Is Measured Through the Following Definitions

False Rejection Rate (FRR): represents the percentage to reject incorrectly a legitimate user as a result of some variation in his normal type of typing (Tin, 2015) and can be calculated as the following equation (1).

$$\mathrm{FRR}\left(\%\right) = \frac{\text{No. of false Rejected}}{\text{total No. of legal authentiction attempts}} \tag{1}$$

False Acceptance Rate (FAR): represents the percentage of incorrectly acceptance the user Impostors as a legitimate user. This type of error is caused by cheating and imitation on the system (Hassan et al., 2013) and can be calculated as the following equation (2).

$$\mathrm{FAR}\left(\%\right) = \frac{\text{No. of false accepted}}{\text{total No. of impostor authentication attempts}} \tag{2}$$

Equal Error Rate (EER): Represents the percentage of the overall accuracy of the security system against other systems. It may be also referred to as Crossover Error Rate (CER) (Joyce et al., 1990).

MATHEMATICAL APPROACHES

The mathematical approaches to keystroke analysis can be divided into the following techniques. These techniques are not all the existing methods but they explained the terminology of summary of the main research approaches of keystroke in table 1 such as:

- **Statistical Approach:** Statistical methods of keystroke dynamics are the most common study thoroughfare within that field. The basic statistical features like the median, mean and standard deviation (Modi et al., 2006; Revett et al., 2006; Revett et al., 2005) of keystroke timings were used because this method is low overhead, ease of implementation and the simplicity
- **Neural Networks:** is a technique that emulates the biological artificial neuronal network (ANN) for information processing. ANN has used the timing features between successive keystrokes. These keystroke timings are computed through the network comparator to validate the data, in order to determine whether the user is authentic or not (Uzun & Bicakci, 2012). Table 1 illustrates each approach (statistical or neural network) of the studies from (1990 until 2008), classification of the keystroke (static or dynamic) is used in this study, number of the participated users and the percentage of FAR and FRR values.

HISTORY OF KEYSTROKE DYNAMICS

In the early research documented and analysis into keystroke dynamics authentication, the piercing article by Gaines et al., (1980) is especially the turning point to keystroke dynamics definition. Their research showed that the field was effectively initiated during the telegraphy manual phase, where operators had been observed to have a unique tapping style "fist" by that made their friends could often identify them. By induction of that principle, they supposed that a similar signature could arise during regular typing and an initiative analysis was addressed, investigating the relationship and effectiveness of identification of individuals, based upon their unique keystroke signatures. Therefore, research arising in the 1980s and 1990s such as Umphress et al., (1985), Young et al., (1989), Bleha et al., (1990), Joyce & Gupta,

Table 1. Summary of the main research approaches of keystroke

Study	Mathematical Techniques		Users	FAR (%)		FRR (%)	
Joyce & Gupta (1990)	Static	Statistical	33	0.25		16.36	
Leggett et al. (1991)	Dynamic	Statistical	36	12.8		11.1	
Brown & Rogers (1993)	Static	Neural Network	25	0		12.0	
Bleha & Obaidat (1993)	Static	Neural Network	24	8		9	
Napier et al (1995)	Dynamic	Statistical	24	3.8 (Combined)			
Obaidat & Sadoun (1997)	Static	Statistical	Neural Network	15	0.7	0	1.9	0
Monrose& Rubin (1999)	Static	Statistical	63	7.9 (Combined)			
Cho et al. (2000)	Static	Neural Network	21	0		1	
Ord & Furnell (2000)	Static	Neural Network	14	9.9		30	
Bergadano et al. (2002)	Static	Statistical	154	0.01		4	
Guven & Sogukpinar (2003)	Static	Statistical	12	1		10.7	
Sogukpinar & Yalcin (2004)	Static	Statistical	40	0.6		60	
Yu & Cho (2004)	Static	Neural Network	21	0		3.69	
Gunetti & Picardi (2005)	dynamic	Neural Network	205	0.005		5	
Clarke & Furnell (2007)	Static	Neural Network	32	5 (Equal Error Rate)			
Lee & Cho (2007)	dynamic	Neural Network	21	0.43 (Average Integrated Errors)			

(1990), Obaidat et al., (1993) (1994), De Ru et al., (1997), Lin (1997). Monrose et al., (1997), Obaidat et al., (1997) began to explore other methods of keystroke analysis, typically employing a range of novel mathematical analysis techniques, But also differing in the formal data collection method and refer the interested reader to complete surveys such as Ahmed et al., (2013), Pettey et al., (2014) indicated a detailed history of keystroke dynamics. Leggett et al., (1991) in their study are used dynamic keystroke characteristic that allowed continuous verification in real-time through the daily work session. Their study results indicated significant promise for user identification problem.

Brown & Rogers (1993) presented a method to identify users through analyzing keystroke patterns using neural networks and a very simple geometric distance. They created a model of each user's normal typing manner then compared with their later stored profile. Results demonstrated complete exemption of imposters with accepted false alarm rate when the sample text was limited to the user's name. Bleha & Obaidat (1993) used the perceptron algorithm to verify the identity of computer users. By applying real-time of the time durations between the keystrokes entered in the user's password.

The password used was the user's name and decision functions were derived using the data in training stage to compute the weight vectors. Results were achieved FRR of 9%, and FAR of 8%. Napier et al., (1995) proposed new measures of individual provided a means of verifying the identity of the user. Probabilistic efficacy was used to measure the inter-key latencies statistic in individual typing style then tried to eliminate the user occasional keystrokes. The results were indicated that the algorithm achieved combined FAR of 0.9% and FRR of 3.8%. Cho et al., (2000) proposed an autocorrelated neural network that is trained with the set of timing vectors of the user's keystroke dynamics then used to distinguish between the user and an another imposter. This approach can be implemented using a Java applet which used in the World Wide Web.

Ord and Furnell (2000) used PIN-based authentication using a neural network approach for classifying and distinguished between 14 test subjects using 6-digit PIN they achieved FAR of 9.9% and FRR of 30%. This study illustrated the possibility of the use of codes typed on the numeric keypad. User authentication for accessing computers can be more secure using keystroke rhythms as the biometric authentication method. Guven & Sogukpinar (2003) study used a vector based keystroke analysis applied for identification of keystroke patterns. Keystroke identification system is studied to achieve biometric authentication using neurophysical characteristic. Sogukpinar and Yalcin (2004) obtained very attractive results, which was developed from existing algorithms. They tried to research the effect how writing rhythm can change when the people are sleeplessness, nervousness, tiredness, etc. and other physical conditions such as (sitting shape and distance from the keyboard were placed, the way how the hands was typed on keyboard), how make changes the person who writes with left or right hand. This study was considered to be used as an extra security spread that can be seen in password based verifying systems such as banking, e-commerce etc. The study by Clarke and Furnell (2007) developed mathematical and data recording techniques that got employing statistical techniques and neural networks also, trying to fuse data from multiple parallel sensors. Combined not only keystroke analysis but also facial, voice, and fingerprint recognitions. However, such systems required more mobile capabilities (camera or fingerprint reader) and a significant level of processing on the mobile phone and these requirements are available nowadays a lot.

Yu & Cho (2004) proposed solutions for the limitations of previous research such as the long time to train the model, data were before processed internal by a human and a large data set was required with a support vector machine (SVM) detector. Results of the experimental showed that the proposed methods were promising and that the keystroke dynamics is a viable and practical way to add more security to identity verification. So that study is considered to be an additional advantage and increase the possibility of using keystroke technology. In Gunetti and Picardi (2005) presented a method based on dynamic keystroke to compare typing samples of free text that can be used to verify personal identity. They had tested the technique on 205 individuals and obtained an FAR less than 5% and an FAR less than 0.005%. These approaches depend on how the user typed, not what he was typed and this method is very useful in computer security way to user authentication detection. Another study such as Lee and Cho (2007) based on keystroke dynamics and depended on learning vector quantization for detection and retrained support vector data with the impostor patterns. Results of the experimental showed that improved of the retraining authentication performance which used novelty detectors.

HARDWARE/SOFTWARE IMPLEMENTATION OF BIOMETRIC AUTHENTICATION

Authentication in cloud computing environment plays an important role in security. It protects Cloud Service Providers (CSP) against various types of attacks or hackers, where the aim is to verify a user's identity when a user wants to request services from cloud servers. There are multiple authentication technologies that verify the identity of a user before presenting access to cloud computing resources. One of the most interesting studies about keystroke dynamics authentication is cloud computing using mobile presented by Babaeizadeh, Bakhtiari, and Chaudhary et al., (2015). This paper proposed a strong method of authentication in the password authentication method by combining it with keystroke authentication system. Password of legal user they cannot gain access rights on 97.33% of efforts correctly in authenticating mobile's users to access cloud computing. This is because the keystroke duration of each individual depends on his behavioral characteristic ways. Therefore, by applying this method, it becomes very difficult for an attacker to claim as the owner. Hence, this method offers the potential to enhance the security of authentication in MCC.

There is a lot of research also tried to make a hardware implementation of many biometric identification systems on FPGA or DSP such as the following. Prabhakar et al., (2003) proposed an implementation of an algorithm characterization and correlation of templates created for biometric authentication based on iris texture analysis programmed on FPGA. The authentication based on processes like characterization methods based on frequency analysis of the sample and achieved high accuracy of 96.52% and time of 16.11 ms. Wakil, Tariq, Humayun and Abbas (2015) presented an FPGA-based architecture for fingerprint recognition by using Xilinx System Generator which can be further implemented on all Xilinx FPGA gave high accuracy and can be used for high-security issues. Gayathri and Sridhar (2013) proposed and improved fast thinning algorithm for Fingerprint Image implemented in MATLAB and simulation results of Xilinx ISE and Modelsim. Based on two modules (binarization module and thinning module) their Experimental results showed that the algorithm is more efficient than the preferred algorithm systems according to the proposed architecture results.

Fatt et al., (2009) have presented a Digital Signal Processor (DSP) implementation of the iris verification algorithm. Using hamming distance method to extract the iris features based on texture analysis. Experiment results showed that the approach has achieved high accuracy of 98.62% and time of 198.9 ms. Kannavara and Bourbakis (2009) have presented a local-global (LG) graph methodology for iris-based biometric authentication. The global graph of the presented test image was compared with the global graph of the stored reference image and achieved high accuracy of 92% and time of 0.0149 ms. Poinsot et al., (2011) proposed a biometric system combines two modalities Palmprint and face. Hardware implementation of the Texas instrument digital signal processor and Xilinx FPGA platforms using Hamming distance algorithm and score fusion then have time 0.4 ms.

Liu, et al., (2006) proposed a hardware implementation based on FPGA for an iris biometric processor. By this solution, a reduction of the processing time is obtained and security levels of the whole system are increased due to the reduction of software involved and achieved high accuracy of 88% and time of 2.725 ms. Sanchez et al., (2006) provided novel hardware implementations which enabled us to discover that three key portions of an iris recognition algorithm can be parallelized.

The main result is that the implementation on a modest sized FPGA is approximately 9.6, 324, and 19 times faster than a state-of-the-art in their research and achieved a time of 0.002 ms. Vijayalami and Obulesu (2012) presented a generic, flexible parallel architecture, which is suitable for all ranges of object detection applications and image sizes. The proposed architecture implemented the AdaBoost-based detection algorithm, which is one of the most efficient object detection algorithms and achieved minimum period 15.30 ns. In Zhao and Xie (2009) described an embed iris recognition system for the personal identification they used only one DSP core which completed image acquisition, image processing, and communication with the peripheral circuits. The model system not only reduced costs, shorten the development cycle. It also provided a good running platform for the high-speed image processing achieved a time of 471.56 ms.

Vatsa, Singh, and Noore (2009) presented an accurate non-ideal iris segmentation using the modified Mumford-Shah functional. Depending on the type of abnormalities to be encountered during image capture, a set of global image enhancement algorithms was applied to the iris image. While this enhances the low-quality regions, it also added undesirable artifacts in the original high-quality regions of the iris image achieved an accuracy of 97.21% and 1.82 ms. In Hu and Xie (2010) showed a study of Iris Identification in authentication techniques. Most modern iris recognition systems were deployed on traditional sequential digital systems, such as simple DSPs and data matched one by one, which wasted much time. In their study, iris matching considered the executed portion of a modern iris recognition algorithm parallelized on an FPGA system demonstrated a 22 times speedup of the parallelized algorithm on the FPGA system when compared to simple DSPs and got out 32 us and this is a great time different.

Guru Nanak Institute of Technology Student (2012) proposed a hardware implementation of iris matching. They presented a parallel processing alternative using Spartan-3AN field programmable gate arrays (FPGAs) and achieving a significant reduction in execution time when compared to conventional software-based applications. The Hamming distance was employed for classification of iris templates, and two templates were found to match if the hamming distance between them is less than the threshold value.

Sudiro and Yuwono (2012) focused on implementing a part of fingerprint recognition system. Firstly, they developed a simple algorithm to extract fingerprint features and test this algorithm on PC. Secondly, they implemented this algorithm into FPGA devices. Their results are an adaptable fingerprint minutiae extraction algorithm into hardware implementation with 14.05% of EER, better than reference algorithm that they mentioned, which is 20.39%. The computational time is 18 seconds less than a similar method, which took 60-90 seconds just for pre-processing step.

Canyellas et al., (2005) presented a hardware/software implementation of a fingerprint minutiae extraction algorithm. The proposed system consisted of a microprocessor and a coprocessor implemented in an FPGA. In order to develop an efficient implementation, fixed-point computations have been substituted the floating point ones. Due to the low feature requirements the whole system was suitable with embedded flexible hardware. In a first stage, the algorithms optimized in order to reduce the number of floating point operations. It was demonstrated that the operations can be performed with integer numbers without significant changes in the obtained minutiae. In a second stage, a profiling of the software version was located the most critical tasks of the algorithm. These functions were implemented in hardware, with a significant improvement of the biometrics identification time (about 70 ~ 90% of reduction).

Yan (2010) proposed a hardware-software cooperating mechanism because the traditional hardware implementation mechanism was not flexible, configurable, and not easy to expand the functions. Moreover, the traditional software implementation costs higher, and the power consumption is higher compared with a hardware implementation. His research merged the advantages traditional hardware implementation on function, performance, power consumption, cost, and the advantages of a software implementation, flexible, configurable, and easy to expand. The time-cost parts in the proposed system, orientation field and frequency field estimation, and implemented with Very Large Scale Integrated Circuits (VLSI). This research indicated that the biometrics authentication is the most secure mechanism of security authentication techniques because it connected the authentication medium with the user directly,

But it is not suitable to be used in wireless network directly because the transfer medium of wireless network is open when the biometric information was transferred on the wireless network. In this paper, the proposed system connected the authentication medium with the user directly and protected the biometric information transferred on the public wireless channel.

Morizet et al., (2008) presented Principal Component Analysis (PCA) algorithm used in face recognition system and implemented on different architectures for choosing the best solution for designing a real-time face recognition system. Benchmarks and comparisons given for PC, DSP and FPGA and results showed that FPGA soft core was too slow for this computation. An IP solution is the best choice.

But DSP is also a good compromise for implementing easily the algorithm and having acceptable processing time because it offered a good trade-off between processing time and implementation easiness.

Teh et al., (3013) provided a survey on keystroke dynamics biometrics authentication. It covered research performed during the last three decades, as well as proposing some future works in this study. Nauman et al., (2013) proposed a protocol for keystroke dynamics analysis which allowed web-based applications to make use of remote belief and delegated keystroke analysis. Moreover, they presented a prototype implementation of their protocol using Android operating system. Bhatt and Santhanam (2013) have presented a survey paper that explained the researchers work on keystroke dynamics, as well as, they discussed advantages and disadvantages of this research. After storing the values obtained from the mobile device, as shown in Figure 4, inserted values had to compare with the stored values for the next login. A detailed study on the evolution of keystroke dynamics as a measure of authentication was carried out. This paper gave an insight from the infancy stage to the current work done on this domain which can be used by researchers working on this topic.

AUTHENTICATION IN CLOUD COMPUTING ENVIRONMENT

It is widely supposed username and password are not very secure authentication mechanism because it is difficult to confirm that the demand is from the rightful or legal individual. Moreover, commonly users choose easy passwords for a machine to guess. Even the best password can be stolen by dictionary and brute force attacks (Karnan et al., 2011). In cloud computing, the input constraints construct hard for users to input complex passwords, often leading to the employ of short passwords and password managers. In addition, users reuse their passwords for identifying in different servers and they use weak passwords which cause to increase risks to the security of user's shared information (Acer et al., 2013). Authentication is the main part of every security system especially in a widespread network such as CC. It helps protect shared information from unauthorized people and it is a key technology for information security.

The AAA module (Housley & Aboba, 2007) was a management for authentication, authorization, and accounting. When a user tries to access CSP, then AAA checked the user's authentication informa-

Figure 4. Process of comparing values in mobile device with CSP

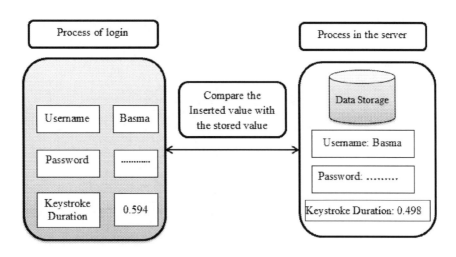

tion. If the user was authenticated, then AAA got the user's access level, which has been most recently generated, by inspecting the user's information in the database. In addition, authentication methods determine who is the legal user? And, is the user really who he claimed to be? In addition, verification of user's identity was the most important goal behind an authentication technique. In other words, an authentication mechanism determined how user identified and verified access to sensitive information (Köse, 2011). Verification means to confirm that demand is from the legal user. Identification implies on determining user's identity by comparing the security question, image, voice, or other information that are available in the database and the templates.

Ziyad and Kannammal (2014) proposed a multifactor biometric authentication system for cloud computing environment. This biometric method was fingerprint and palm vein. The goal was to handle the biometric data in a secure fashion by storing the palm vein biometric data in multi-component smart cards and fingerprint data in the central database of the cloud computing security server.

In this proposed technique, the processes of matching biometric data were performed on the card with Match on Card technology; therefore it helped improve security system.

COMMERCIALIZED SOFTWARE

The commercialized software is available in the market such as BioTracker, KeyTrac, BioChec and much other software shown in Table 2. Unfortunately, the effectiveness and methodology are not publically available due to copyright issues; therefore, it is difficult to evaluate the effectiveness of each system.

CONCLUSION

Despite keystroke dynamics is one of the most appearing biometric authentication systems but it doesn't come to real implementation until now. Cloud computing needs authentication system easy to be used, efficient, doesn't spend a lot of money for maintenances or enchantments in the same time so keystroke will economize a lot of costs. This paper addressed hardware / software implementation of keystroke dynamic and suggests this technique, keystroke dynamics, to be used as a biometric authentication system for accessing cloud computing server because of all its advantage and this technique will be the coming revolution in information security.

Table 2. Market research

Software	Text Authentication	Service Delivery	Comments
Intensity Analytics CVMetrics and Tickstream	Continuous	SaaS or Network server	People type differently based on application
BioTracker	Continuous	Server Side	Mouse clicks
KeyTrac	Continuous	Server Side	Java/C++ Libraries
BehavioSec	Continuous	Server Side	Free Mobile App
BioChec	Static	Server Side	Free SDK(Software development Kit)
DiBiSoft	Static	Client Side	$10-$20

ACKNOWLEDGMENT

The authors would like to thank the anonymous reviewers and the editor for the constructive and helpful comments and suggestions.

REFERENCES

Acar, T., Belenkiy, M., & Kupcu, A. (2013). Single password authentication, *Microsoft Research. IACR Archive, 57*(13), 1–28.

Ahmad, N., Szymkowiak, A., & Campbell, P. Keystroke dynamics in the pre-touch screen era, *Frontiers in Human Neuroscience, Volume 7*, Article 835, 1-10

Anil, K., Ross, A., & Prabhakar, S. (2004). An introduction to biometric recognition. *IEEE Transactions on Circuits and Systems for Video Technology, 14*(1), 1–20.

Babaeizadeh, M., Bakhtiari, M., & Maarof, M. (2014). Authentication method through keystrokes measurement of mobile users in cloud environment. *International Journal of Advance Soft Computing, 6*(3), 94–112.

Babaeizadeh, M., Bakhtiari, M., & Mohammed, A. (2015). Authentication methods in cloud computing: A survey, *Research Journal of Applied Sciences. Engineering and Technology, 9*(8), 655–664.

Babich, A. (2012). Biometric authentication, types of biometric identifiers, *Bachelor's Thesis Degree Programmed in Business Information Technology*, 1-53

Bandara, H., Ravindra, S., Silva, P., & Weerasinghe, P. (2015). The universal biometric system. *Proceedings of the International Conference on Advances in ICT for Emerging Regions*, Colombo, Sri Lanka (pp. 1-6).

Banerjee, S., Gupta, N., & Gupta, V. (2014). Implementation and management of framework for PAAS in cloud computing. *International Journal of Innovations & Advancement in Computer Science, 2*(2), 38–49.

BehavioSec website. (n. d.) Retrieved from http://www.behaviosec.com/mobile-demonstration-video/

Bergadano, F., Gunetti, D., & Picardi, C. (2002). User authentication through keystroke dynamics [TISSEC]. *ACM Transactions on Information and System Security, 5*(4), 367–397. doi:10.1145/581271.581272

Bhatt, S., & Santhanam, T. (2013). Keystroke dynamics for biometric authentication: A survey. *Proceedings of the International Conference on Pattern Recognition, Informatics and Mobile Engineering* (pp. 17-23). IEEE. Retrieved from http://www.biochec.com/DLgallery.php

BioTracker website. (n. d.). Retrieved from http://plurilock.com/products/biotracker

Bleha, S., & Obaidat, S. (1993). Computer user verification using the perceptron. *IEEE Transactions on Systems, Man, and Cybernetics, 23*(3), 900–902. doi:10.1109/21.256563

Bleha, S., Slivinsky, C., & Hussien, B. (1990). Computer access security systems using keystroke dynamics. *IEEE Transactions on Pattern Analysis and Machine Intelligence*, *12*(12), 1217–1222. doi:10.1109/34.62613

Bours, P., & Mondal, S. (2015). Continuous authentication with keystroke dynamics, Norwegian Information Security Laboratory (NISlab), PP. (41-58), GCSR College

Brown, M., & Rogers, J. (1993). User Identification via keystroke characteristics of typed names using neural networks, Studies. *International Journal of Man-Machine*, *39*(6), 999–1014. doi:10.1006/imms.1993.1092

Canyellas, N., Cantu, E., Forte, G., & Lopez, M. (2005). Hardware-Software co-design of a fingerprint identification algorithm. *Audio- and Video-Based Biometric Person Authentication*, LNCS (Vol. 3546, pp. 683-692). Springer-Verlag Berlin

Cao, K., Pang, L., Liang, J., & Tian, J. (2013). Fingerprint classification by a hierarchical classifier. *Pattern Recognition Letters*, *46*(12), 3186–3197. doi:10.1016/j.patcog.2013.05.008

Chang, H., & Choi, E. (2011). User authentication in cloud computing. *Ubiquitous Computing and multimedia applications, Communications in Computer and Information Science* (Vol. 151, pp. 338–342

Chaudhary, S., & Nath, R. (2015). A new multimodal biometric recognition system integrating iris, face and voice. *International Journal of Advanced Research in Computer Science and Software Engineering*, *5*(4), 145–150.

Cho, S., Han, C., Han, D., & Kim, H. (2000). Web-based keystroke dynamics identity verification using neural network. *Journal of Organizational Computing and Electronic Commerce*, *10*(4), 295–307. doi:10.1207/S15327744JOCE1004_07

Clarke, L., & Furnell, M. (2007). Advanced user authentication for mobile devices, *Network Research Group, School of Computing, Communication and Electronic, University of Plymouth. Computers & Security*, *26*(2), 109–119. doi:10.1016/j.cose.2006.08.008

De Ru, W. G., & Eloff, J. H. (1997). Enhanced password authentication through fuzzy logic. *IEEE Transactions on Expert*, *12*(6), 38–45. doi:10.1109/64.642960

Dhobale, R., & Mulik, M. (2015). A survey of voice recognition system and its application. *International Journal of Advance Research in Computer Science and Management Studies*, *3*(3), 38–43.

DiBiSoft website. (n.d.). Retrieved from http://www.morpheusfiles.com/DiBiSoft-publisher-1212368.html

Divya, R., & Vijayalakshmi, V. (2015). Analysis of multimodal biometric fusion based authentication techniques for network security. *International Journal of Security and Its Applications*, *9*(4), 239–246. doi:10.14257/ijsia.2015.9.4.22

Emam, A. (2013). Additional authentication and authorization using registered email-ID for cloud computing. *International Journal of Soft Computing and Engineering*, *3*(2), 110–113.

Fatt, R. N. Y., Haur, T. Y., & Ming, M. K. (2009). Iris verification algorithm based on texture analysis and its implementation on DSP. *International Conference on Signal Acquisition and Processing DSP*, Kuala Lumpur (Vol. 2, pp.198 – 202). 10.1109/ICSAP.2009.9

Gaines, R., Lisowski, W., Press, S., & Shapiro, N. (1980). *Authentication by keystroke timing: Some preliminary results (Technical Report, No 0-8330-0246-5)*. Santa Monica: Rand Corporation.

Gayathri, S., & Sridhar, V. (2013). An improved fast thinning algorithm for fingerprint image. *International Journal of Engineering Science and Innovative Technology*, *2*(1), 264–270.

Ghanavati, B. (2015). Designing a new face recognition system robust to various poses, *Journal of mathematics and computer science*, 15, 32-39

Gomez-Barrero, M., Galbally, J., & Fierrez, J. (2014). Efficient software attack to multimodal biometric systems and its application to face and iris fusion. *Pattern Recognition Letters*, *36*, 243–253. doi:10.1016/j. patrec.2013.04.029

Gunetti, D., & Picardi, C. (2005). Keystroke analysis of free text. *ACM Transactions on Information and System Security*, *8*(3), 312–347. doi:10.1145/1085126.1085129

Guo, J.-M., Hsia, C.-H., Liu, Y.-F., Yu, J.-C., Chu, M.-H., & Le, T.-N. (2012). Contact-free hand geometry-based identification system. *Expert Systems with Applications*, *39*(14), 11728–11736. doi:10.1016/j. eswa.2012.04.081

Guru Nanak Institute of Technology. (2012). Hardware implementation of iris matching. *Research Paper India, 1*(6), 46-48

Guven, A., & Sogukpinar, I. (2003). Understanding users' keystroke patterns for computer access security. *Computers & Security*, *22*(8), 695–706. doi:10.1016/S0167-4048(03)00010-5

Hassan, S., Selim, M., & Zayed, H. (2013). User Authentication with Adaptive Keystroke Dynamics. *International Journal of Computer Science Issues*, *10*(4), 127–134.

Housley, R. & Aboba, B. (2007). Guidance for authentication, authorization, and accounting (AAA) key management, *Network Working Group, the IETF Trust.*

Hu, Z., & Xie, M. (2010). Iris biometric processor enhanced module FPGA-based design. *Second International Conference on Computer Modeling and Simulation* ICCMS '10 (*Vol. 2*, pp. 259 – 262), IEEE Browse Conference Publications.

Intensity Analytics website. (n. d.). Retrieved from http://www.hotfrog.com/business/intensity-analytics/intensity-analytics-products-707237

Jaiswal, S., Bhadauria, S., & Jadon, R. (2011). Biometric: Case study. *Journal of Global Research in Computer Science*, *2*(10), 19–48.

Joyce, R., & Gupta, G. (1990). Identity authentication based on keystroke latencies. *Communications of the ACM*, *33*(2), 168–176. doi:10.1145/75577.75582

Kannavara, R., & Bourbakis, N. (2009). Iris biometric authentication based on local global graphs, an FPGA implementation. *IEEE transaction On Computational Intelligence for Security and Defense Applications,* 4, 1-7.

Karnan, M., Akila, M., & Krishnaraj, N. (2011). Biometric personal authentication using keystroke dynamics: A review. *Applied Soft Computing*, *11*(2), 1565–1573. doi:10.1016/j.asoc.2010.08.003

Kaur, M., & Virk, R. (2013). Security system based on user authentication using keystroke dynamics. *International Journal of Advanced Research in Computer and Communication Engineering, 2*(5), 11–21.

KeyTrac website. (n. d.). Retrieved from https://anytext.keytrac.net/en/tryout

Kim, M., Jeong, H., & Choi, E. (2012). Context-aware platform for user authentication in cloud database computing. *Proceedings of the International Conference on Future Information Technology and Management Science & Engineering, LNIT* (Vol. 14, pp. 170-176).

Kochetkov, A. (2013). Cloud-based biometric services: just a matter of time, *Biometric Technology, 5*, 8–11

Köse, C. (2011). A personal identification system using retinal vasculature in retinal fundus images. *Expert Systems with Applications, 38*(11), 13670–13681.

Lee, H., & Cho, S. (2007). Retraining a keystroke dynamics based authenticator with impostor patterns, Department of Industrial Engineering, Seoul National University, Computers & Security, Republic of Korea, 26(4), 300-310

Lee, J. (2012). A novel biometric system based on palm vein image, *Department of Electrical Engineering. Chinese Naval Academy, 33*(12), 1520–1528.

Leggett, J., Williams, G., Usnick, M., & Longnecker, M. (1991). Dynamic identity verification via keystroke characteristics. *International Journal of Man-Machine Studies, 35*(6), 859–870. doi:10.1016/S0020-7373(05)80165-8

LI, Y. (. (. (2015). Iris recognition algorithm based on MMC-app, *International Journal of Signal Processing. Image Processing and Pattern Recognition, 8*(2), 1–10. doi:10.14257/ijsip.2015.8.2.01

Lin, D. (1997). Computer-access authentication with neural network based keystroke identity verification. *Proceedings of the IEEE International Conference of Neural Network*, Houston, TX *(Vol.* 1, pp. 174–178).

Liu, J., Sanchez, R., Lindoso, A., & Hurtado, O. (2006). FPGA implementation for an iris biometric processor, *IEEE International Conference on Field Programmable Technology*, Bangkok (pp. 265 – 268).

Liu, S., & Silverman, M. (2001). Practical Guide to Biometric Security Technology. *ITS Pro IEEE, 3*(1), 27–32. doi:10.1109/6294.899930

Mell, P., & Grance, T. (2011).The NIST definition of cloud computing, Computer security division information technology laboratory, National Institute of Standards and Technology, Gaithersburg.

Mellor, C. (2009). The open Cloud manifesto: A call to action for the worldwide Cloud community. *The Register*. Retrieved from http://www.theregister.co.uk/2009/03/29/open_cloud_manifesto/

Messerman, A., Mustafic, T., Camtepe, S., & Albayrak, S. (2011). Continuous and non-intrusive identity verification in real-time environments based on free-text keystroke dynamics, *Proceedings of the International Joint Conference on Biometrics*, Washington, DC (pp. 1-8). 10.1109/IJCB.2011.6117552

Modi, S., & Elliott, S. (2006). Keystroke dynamics verification using a spontaneously generated password. *Proceedings of the IEEE International Carnahan Conference on Security Technology (ICCST '06)*, Lexington, KY (pp. 116–121). 10.1109/CCST.2006.313439

Monrose, F., & Rubin, A. (1997). Authentication via keystroke dynamics. *Proceedings of the 4th Conference on Computer and Communications Security*, New York (pp. 48–56). ACM.

Monrose, F., & Rubin, D. (1999). *Keystroke dynamics as a biometric for authentication.* Elsevier.

Morizet, N., Amiel, F., Hamed, I., & Ea, T. (2008). A comparative implementation of PCA faces recognition algorithm. *Proceedings of the14th International Conference on Comparative Implementation of PCA Face Recognition Algorithm* (pp. 865- 868). IEEE

Napier, R., Laverty, W., Mahar, D., Henderson, R., Hiron, M., & Wagner, M. (1995). Keyboard user verification: Toward an accurate, efficient and ecological valid algorithm. *International Journal of Human-Computer Studies, 43*(2), 213–222. doi:10.1006/ijhc.1995.1041

Nauman, M., Ali, T., & Rauf, A. (2013). Using trusted computing for privacy preserving keystroke-based authentication in smartphones. *Telecommunication Systems, 52*(4), 2149–2161. doi:10.100711235-011-9538-9

Obaidat, M., & Macchairolo, D. (1994). A multilayer neural network system for computer access security. *IEEE Transactions on Systems, Man, and Cybernetics, 24*(5), 806–813. doi:10.1109/21.293498

Obaidat, M., & Macchiarolo, D. (1993). An online neural network system for computer access security. *IEEE Transactions on Industrial Electronics, 40*(2), 235–242. doi:10.1109/41.222645

Obaidat, M., & Sadoun, B. (1997). Verification of computer users using keystroke dynamics. *IEEE Transactions on Systems, Man, and Cybernetics. Part B, Cybernetics, 27*(2), 261–269. doi:10.1109/3477.558812 PMID:18255865

Ord, T., & Furnell, S. (2000). User authentication for keypad-based devices using keystroke analysis [MSc Thesis]. *University of Plymouth, UK.*

Paranjape, V., & Pandey, V. (2013). An improved authentication technique with OTP in cloud computing. *International Journal of Scientific Research in Computer Science and Engineering, 1*(3), 22–26.

Peacock, A. K. X., & Wilkerson, M. (2004). Typing patterns: A key to user identification. *IEEE Security and Privacy, 2*(5), 40–47. doi:10.1109/MSP.2004.89

Pettey, C., & Meulen, R. (2008). Gartner says contrasting views on Cloud computing is creating confusion. *Proceedings of the Gartner Symposium/ITxpo, Orlando.* Retrieved from http://www.gartner.com/newsroom/id/766215

Poinsot, A., Yang, F., & Brost, V. (2011). Palmprint and face score level fusion: Hardware implementation of a contactless small sample biometric system. *Optical Engineering (Redondo Beach, Calif.), 50*(2), 1–12. doi:10.1117/1.3534199

Ponkshe, R., & Chole, V. (2015). Keystroke and mouse dynamics: A review on behavioral biometrics. *International Journal of Computer Science and Mobile Computing, 4*(2), 341–345.

Prabhakar, S., Pankanti, S., & Jain, K. (2003). Biometric Recognition, Security and Privacy Concerns. *IEEE Security and Privacy Magazine, 1*(2), 33–42. doi:10.1109/MSECP.2003.1193209

Revett, K., deMagalh~aes, S., & Santos, H. (2005). Password secured sites-stepping forward with keystroke dynamics. *Proceedings of the International Conference on Next Generation* (pp. 1-6)

Revett, K. deMagalh~aes, S., & Santos, H. (2006). Enhancing login security through the use of keystroke input dynamics. Proceedings of Advances in Biometrics, Berlin, Germany (Vol. 3832, pp. 661-667). Springer

Revett, K., deMagalh~aes, S., & Santos, H. (2007). On the use of rough sets for user authentication via keystroke dynamics. *Proceedings of the 13th Portuguese Conference on Progress in Artificial Intelligence*, Guimarães, Portugal (pp. 145–159). Springer. 10.1007/978-3-540-77002-2_13

Rohit, N., Patil, M., Patil, Y., Muske, K., Gudadhe, S., & Umale, J. (2015). Parallel palmprint identification on GPU. *International Journal of Advanced Research in Computer and Communication Engineering*, *4*(1), 261–264. doi:10.17148/IJARCCE.2015.4158

Rudrapal, D., Debbarma, S., & Debbarma, N. (2012). Voice recognition and authentication as a proficient biometric tool and its application in online exam for p.h people. *International Journal of Computers and Applications*, *39*(12), 5–12.

Rupinder, S., & Narinder, R. (2014). Comparison of various biometric methods. *International Journal of Advances in Science and Technology*, *2*(I), 24–30.

Salave, H. & Pable, S. (2015). Improved palmprint identification system. *International journal of scientific & technology research, 4*(3), 180-185.

Seminar Report and PPT. (2006). Retrieved from http://www.seminarsonly.com/computer%20science/Cloud-Computing.php

Shah, A., Khan, M., & Salam, A. (2015). An appraisal of off-line signature verification techniques. *International Journal of Modern Education and Computer Science, 7*(4), 67–75. doi:10.5815/ijmecs.2015.04.08

Shahane, P.R., Choukade, A.S., & Diyewar, A.N. (2015). Online signature recognition using Matlab. *International journal of innovative research in electrical, electronics, instrumentation, and control engineering, 3*(2), 107-112

Sogukpinar, I., & Yalcin, L. (2004). User identification at login via keystroke dynamics. *Journal of Electronic and Electrical Engineering, 4*(1), 995–1005.

Sudiro, S., & Yuwono, R. (2012). Adaptable fingerprint minutiae extraction algorithm based on crossing number method for hardware implementation using FPGA device, *International Journal of Computer Science. Engineering and Information Technology, 2*(3), 1–30.

Teh, S., Teoh, A., & Yue, S. (2013). A survey of Keystroke Dynamics Biometrics. *The Scientific World Journal, 2013*, 1–24.

Thakur, S. (2014). Cloud computing survey and development trend. *Online International Interdisciplinary Research Journal, 4*(Special Issue), 148-156

Tin, H. (2015). The performance evaluation for personal identification using palmprint and face recognition. *Proceedings of the International Conference on Image Processing*, Singapore (pp. 39-44),

Umphress, D., & Williams, G. (1985). Identity verification through keyboard characteristics. *International Journal of Man-Machine Studies*, *23*(3), 263–273. doi:10.1016/S0020-7373(85)80036-5

United States Government Accountability Office (ACO). (2015). Facial recognition technology. Report to the Ranking Member, *Subcommittee on Privacy, Technology and the Law, Committee on the Judiciary, U.S. Senate.*

Uzun, Y., & Bicakci, K. (2012). A second look at the performance of neural networks for keystroke dynamics using a publicly available dataset. *Computers & Security*, *31*(5), 717–726. doi:10.1016/j.cose.2012.04.002

Vatsa, M., Singh, R., & Noore, A. (2008). Improving iris recognition performance using segmentation, quality enhancement, match score fusion and indexing. *IEEE Transactions on Systems, Man, and Cybernetics. Part B, Cybernetics*, *38*(4), 1021-1035. doi:10.1109/TSMCB.2008.922059 PMID:18632394

Vijayalami & Obulesu, B. (2012). Hardware implementation of face detection using AdaBoost algorithm. *Journal of Electronics and Communication Engineering*, *1*(2), 93–102.

Wakil, Y., Gul Tariq, S., Humayun, A., & Abbas, N. (2015). An FPGA-based minutiae extraction system for fingerprint recognition. *International Journal of Computers and Applications*, *111*(12), 31–35. doi:10.5120/19592-1362

Wu, K.-S., Lee, J.-C., Lo, T.-M., Chang, K.-C., & Chang, C.-P. (2013). A secure palm vein recognition system. *Journal of Systems and Software*, *86*(11), 2870–2876. doi:10.1016/j.jss.2013.06.065

Yan, W. (2010). *Software-hardware cooperative embedded verification system fusing fingerprint verification and shared-key authentication. M.Sc. Diploma Work in System-on-Chip Design Area, Royal Institute of Technology.* Shanghai, China: KTH.

Young, J., & Hammon, R. (1989). Method and apparatus for verifying an individual's identity, *U.S. Patent and Trademark Office, Washington, No.* 4805222.

Yu, E., & Cho, S. (2004). Keystroke dynamics identity verification - its problems and practical solutions. *Computers & Security*, *23*(5), 428–440. doi:10.1016/j.cose.2004.02.004

Zhao, X., & Xie, M. (2009). A practical design of iris recognition system based on DSP. *Proceedings of the International Conference of Intelligent Human-Machine Systems and Cybernetics,* Hangzhou, Zhejiang (Vol. 1, pp. 66-70), 10.1109/IHMSC.2009.25

Ziyad, S., & Kannammal, A. (2014). A multifactor biometric authentication for the cloud. *Computational Intelligence, Cyber Security and Computational Models, Advances in Intelligent Systems and Computing* (Vol. 246, 395-403).

This research was previously published in the International Journal of Enterprise Information Systems (IJEIS), 11(4); edited by Madjid Tavana, pages 99-120, copyright year 2015 by IGI Publishing (an imprint of IGI Global).

Section 4
Utilization and Applications

Chapter 49
Cloud Computing and Cybersecurity Issues Facing Local Enterprises

Emre Erturk
Eastern Institute of Technology, New Zealand

ABSTRACT

This chapter sets out to explore new trends in cyber and cloud security, and their implications for businesses. First, the terminology and assumptions related to cloud computing are stated. Next, the chapter reports on contemporary research around the awareness of security issues, and the security processes within the cloud computing realm. Cyber security poses a different challenge to local small and medium sized organizations, which may seem to have less at stake financially. However, they are more vulnerable, due to fewer resources dedicated toward prevention. A series of serious security incidents may even keep them out of business. Furthermore, security needs to be understood and handled differently in a cloud based environment. Therefore, the chapter identifies unique security practices and recommendations for these businesses to run their IT resources safely in the cloud.

INTRODUCTION

First, it is important to define and differentiate certain key terms before the narrower topic of cloud security is investigated. Three traditional terms are frequently used: information security, computer security, and cyber security. Information security involves defending private and sensitive information "from unauthorized access, use, disclosure, disruption, modification, or destruction in order to provide confidentiality, integrity, and availability" (National Institute of Standards and Technology, 2013a, p. 94). This broad definition implies that the information can take any form: physical, print, analog, electronic, digital, etc. In comparison, computer security focuses particularly on protecting computer hardware and the data that the computers hold (Emberton, 2016). Cyber security is "the collection of tools, policies, security concepts, security safeguards, guidelines, risk management approaches, actions, training, best practices, assurance and technologies that can be used to protect the cyber environment and [the] organization and user's assets" (International Telecommunication Union, 2016). This seems to include

DOI: 10.4018/978-1-5225-8176-5.ch049

computers and digital information in general; however, the cyber environment (cyberspace) primarily consists of "the interdependent network of information systems infrastructures including the Internet and telecommunications networks" (National Institute of Standards and Technology, 2013a, p. 58).

One of the early definitions of cloud computing security is "the set of control-based technologies and policies designed to adhere to regulatory compliance rules and protect information, data applications and infrastructure associated with cloud computing use" (Rouse & Cole, 2012). The National Institute of Standards and Technology, i.e. NIST, (2013a) states that cloud computing use entails network access to a shared pool of configurable IT capabilities and resources. Furthermore, according to NIST (2013a, p. 35) the cloud consists of "five essential characteristics (on-demand self-service, ubiquitous network access, location independent resource pooling, rapid elasticity, and measured service); three service delivery models (Software as a Service, Platform as a Service, and Infrastructure as a Service); and four enterprise access models." Another definition of cloud security is "the set of procedures, processes and standards designed to provide information security assurance in a cloud computing environment" (Janssen, 2016).

Cloud security is a recent term, and encompasses issues and protection of a range of online services using any one of the cloud computing delivery models. Therefore, cloud security is a subset of cyber security. Information technology virtualization is an important technology that powers cloud computing. Virtualization enables a piece of hardware (for example, a server) to be segmented and provisioned as multiple devices and resources. The four cloud enterprise access models are Private Cloud, Community Cloud, Public Cloud, and lastly Hybrid Cloud, which is emerging and may offer advantages in terms of security. As opposed to cyberspace in general, "the cloud" and its backup facilities appear to leave less room for certain risks, e.g., destruction of data by insiders within the client business. On the other hand, in cloud computing, shared resources inherently involve various risks such as access control and privacy. These major risks are covered in this chapter, by exploring their prevalence and the applicable solutions.

BACKGROUND

According to Frost & Sullivan's report *State of Cloud Computing New Zealand* as cited in Jeremiah and Clarke (2013), 63% of organizations in New Zealand that use cloud solutions intend to increase their cloud budget. Furthermore, an increasing number of smaller and medium sized enterprises are spending significant amounts of their IT budget (Jeremiah and Clarke, 2013). Software as a Service (for example, email, office productivity software, and customer relationship management applications), and storage space are commonly accessed in the cloud. During this era of growth, there are still challenges such as security threats and integration with legacy applications. According to Phil Harpur as cited in Jeremiah and Clarke (2013), research shows that security is the most important criteria when selecting a cloud vendor, ahead of other important criteria including reputation, support, and price. Aldarbesti, Goutas, and Sutanto (2016) found that security and customization are two main attributes that influence the decision to change from on-premises software to cloud based Software as a Service.

Cloud based IT services involve particular risks and vulnerabilities whereby security and privacy can be compromised. Although a major portion of the literature on cloud computing focuses on multinational or large company cases, this information may not necessarily be relevant or useful to ordinary or small and medium sized organizations. Therefore, it is important to distinguish some of the characteristics of cloud computing adoption and usage among regional and local companies. This will help identify some unique security practices or recommendations for these companies. This research was conducted with local industry representatives and IT professionals in Hawke's Bay, New Zealand.

According to the New Zealand (NZ) Ministry of Business, Innovation and Employment (2014), "a small business is any type of enterprise or firm with fewer than 20 employees" while the category of 'small to medium' is defined as having between 20 to 49 employees. Businesses with fewer than 50 employees typically do not have staff at the same skill and experience level as those of larger businesses. Despite this setback, smaller businesses are reporting commendable use of online channels of communication and ecommerce according to Statistics New Zealand's 2013 Business Operations Survey as cited by the NZ Ministry of Business, Innovation and Employment (2014). In addition, New Zealand has been ranked second in the world for ease of doing business in a recent report by the World Bank (2015). The same World Bank (2015) report has also ranked New Zealand first, for starting a business and getting credit, among 189 economies across the world.

In terms of technology adoption, smaller companies face particular challenges, which include more frequent employee turnover and limited IT budgets (Bradley & Cooper, 2014). Smaller companies are also affected (as much as large companies) by the potential risk of vendor lock-in, which refers to the difficulty or inability to change from one service provider to another. This is an even more important factor if the business relies on multiple service delivery models, for example: not only Software as a Service but also Infrastructure as a Service (provision of cloud based hardware, network, server, and storage resources). This multiple outsourcing aspect also brings unique security implications with it. Another consideration for smaller companies is business continuity and recovery after a disaster or attack, without having abundant backup and redundant resources at their disposal.

Information reflecting current and local cloud computing and security issues has been gathered from an extensive and up-to-date literature review and through meetings and interviews with local companies. This information helps to understand the needs of, and gaps faced by the companies. The suggestions made in this chapter will also be useful for other small and medium sized companies around the world.

Although New Zealand has a small population, it is a relatively ambitious and well-equipped "e-society" (Erturk & Fail, 2013). Although cloud computing services have been adopted by many small and medium sized companies, the majority of them are not yet using the relatively new security tools and procedures such as Cloud Access Security Brokers (CASBs) or are not aware of all of the available practical advice for better managing their cloud resources (Lin, 2016). CASBs are security check points placed between cloud consumers and cloud providers, to consolidate multiple security policies, such as "authentication, single sign-on, authorization, credential mapping, device profiling, encryption, tokenization, logging, alerting, malware detection and prevention" (Gartner, 2016a). While this research aims at assisting industry and IT practitioners, another goal is to inform academic researchers and students by reporting and reflecting on real-world cloud computing and cyber security issues.

ISSUES AND PROBLEMS

Around the world, intermittent high profile attacks continue to remind IT and corporate executives of the importance of cybersecurity. According to a series of IT executive interviews conducted by Costa, Santos, and da Silva (2013) in Portugal (a relatively small European country), Access Control is one of most important criteria for evaluating cloud services along with Availability and Provider Qualifications. In the same study, Google Apps and Office 365 were compared, and it was indicated that Access Control is equally important for both of these major cloud providers. Other earlier studies such as Georgiou and Lambrinoudakis (2014) mention malware, unauthorized use, denial of service attacks, communications interception, and phishing on the list of possible threats for the cloud environment. Despite the serious costs of data loss and damage to any companies' reputation, IT security professionals are not abundant and many businesses are unable to and do not hire dedicated security professionals (King, 2015).

Among the innumerable cloud security breaches, Cusick (2016) listed the following in his presentation during the Cloud Security Session of the Oracle CSO Advisory Board: SQL injection, Cross-site scripting, Cross-site request forgery, and session hijacking. According to IT security expert Kurt Hansen as cited in Henderson (2015), newly released malware code tends to escape detection and removal by obfuscation.

In recent years, there are three particular examples of incidents affecting ordinary regional and small or medium companies in New Zealand that are covered in this chapter. First, as an example of Software as a Service, hackers have recently targeted Office 365 Email (in conjunction with Outlook Web). Secondly, as another example of Software as a Service (SaaS), company websites built on WordPress may also be vulnerable. Third, recent ransomware is also targeting cloud based storage. According to Rich Chetwynd, founder and CEO of ThisData (New Zealand based cloud security company), "a lot of smaller companies are getting target with ransomware probably more than bigger" as cited in Lin (2016). These three types of threats are discussed within this section, including possible solutions and practical recommendations.

Example: Software as a Service and Spoofing

Office 365 is the cloud based version of the popular Microsoft Office Suite, alongside SharePoint, Skype, and other services such as cloud based storage and online collaboration. It is an example of Software as a Service (SaaS), and has a scalable business model in terms of pricing and capacity – according to the cloud customer's needs. The subscription to Office 365 also includes "Outlook on the Web" (formerly known as Outlook Web Access). Session hijacking (also known as cookie hijacking) has been a security concern with Office 365 in recent years (Bowne, 2013).

Microsoft Exchange Server can be deployed on the cloud for any organization or company. Whether this mail server is installed on premise or hosted on the cloud, emails are delivered to employees and other users through Outlook Web Access. A recent example of a vulnerability in Outlook Web Access is Cross-site scripting (Cisco Security, 2013). Generally, this starts with the user following a crafted URL (to the malicious site). This may allow attackers to steal authentication credentials from cookie data and then perform further attacks. In this particular instance, Microsoft has resolved the vulnerability by releasing appropriate software updates and has corrected the manner in which the software handles URLs (Cisco Security, 2013). However, Cross-site scripting (XSS) is still common, and there are different types.

The above is an example of a reflected attack, whereby the malicious code is accessed by clicking on a link in an email and then reflected from an infected web site to the user's browser, which executes the code. According to the Open Web Application Security Project (2016), another type of XSS is a stored or persistent attack, during which the malicious code is permanently injected into a target server such as a database or forum. This way, the malware script can propagate without email as an initial springboard.

The most recent instance of a vulnerability in Microsoft Outlook Web Access is Web Access Spoofing (Cisco Security, 2016; National Institute of Standards and Technology, 2016). This attack is related to Cross-site scripting. However, instead of being limited to malicious HTML, JavaScript, VBScript,

ActiveX, or Flash code, web access spoofing has the potential to conduct an attack even when XSS is not possible in a given application. This may involve altering a string or value in the browser window, and presenting the wrong result or text to the user (hence the name, text injection, rather than script injection).

Example: Software as a Service and Malicious Exploits

Secondly, WordPress is currently popular in New Zealand and around the world for building websites for small and medium sized businesses. This section focuses on websites created using the "wordpress.org" platform, which is different from the "wordpress.com" hosting service, which hosts not only WordPress websites but also sites created with other applications. Various attacks are constantly being devised and launched against WordPress websites (Kemp, 2015). The latest hacking attempts include SQL injections as well as systematic and automated monitoring and infection through Exploit Kits. One of the critical considerations here is to run one or more strong security plugins for the company WordPress website. According to Kemp (2015), another important requirement for securing a WordPress site (regardless of whether it is hosted locally or on the cloud) is to make regular backups so that, in case of a compromise, any corrupt files can be replaced with the correct copies. Additional steps and tools to guard WordPress sites against hacking include using cloud based reverse proxies and firewalls. With a reverse proxy (such as CloudFlare), incoming visitors go through the intermediary server, which screens them against known attacks, before they reach the web site itself. Sucuri CloudProxy Firewall and Ninja Firewall are examples of application firewalls that can be used to protect websites. Although proxies and firewalls can be used together, other than blocking dangerous incoming traffic, reverse proxies can also perform services such as load balancing, compression, encryption, and anonymization before the web site is accessed.

Another way to host a WordPress site is to put it on a virtual private server (VPS), which is sold by a web hosting company as Infrastructure as a Service (IaaS). As a result, in the context of a denial of service or brute force login attack, the VPS is targeted. Although the hosting company will provide the appropriate and requested operating system, processing power, memory, and technical support cost effectively, the customer also manages and is responsible for protecting the virtual machine. Doing so requires technical knowledge and setting up similar measures as outlined in the previous paragraph, but for the VPS.

Hacking threats against WordPress sites continue to mount this year (Goodin, 2016). The attacks involve infecting files on ordinary websites with malicious software such as crypto ransomware and the 'Nuclear Exploit kit' which may in turn infect the visitors of those sites. One of the reasons why the WordPress platform is a common target is its popularity. WordPress is used by an estimated 26% of all websites, and used by almost 60% of websites that are based on a content management system (W3 Techs, 2016). Another reason WordPress is targeted by hackers is the modular design capability with many extensions, themes and plugins available. These components make developing sites on the WP platform productive and quick, but they may also contain unintentional vulnerabilities and expose the site (Handley, 2015). According to data from the WPScan Vulnerability Database as cited on the IP Geo Block (2015) website, only 35% of vulnerabilities are related to WP core functionality (including ones in the older versions of WP), while 53% of vulnerabilities are related to plugins, and 13% are related to themes. It is unrealistic to expect all commercial or free WP extensions to be secured. The web master should check the logs to see if any plugin or theme files have been modified, and remove them in case of a security compromise.

Example: Software as a Service and Ransomware

Third, in recent years, local businesses of different sizes throughout New Zealand have been targeted by ransomware, a malware which encrypts company and user data, and demands payment in return for releasing the data back to the victim. The so-called crypto-ransomware is spread through cyberspace, and continues to evolve in terms of exploiting different platforms and data stores. This may be done by gaining access through mobile devices, for example within the Android operating system (MediaCenter Panda Security, 2015).

NetSafe is an independent and non-profit organization, established with the purpose of helping New Zealanders with common cyber security issues, and providing them with information and support in case of incidents (https://www.netsafe.org.nz/about-netsafe/). Among its numerous efforts, NetSafe maintains a blog named Security Central, which provides information on and how to deal with a wide range of security and privacy issues. According to Security Central (2015), ransomware is currently the most problematic type of malware for small businesses and home users. One tactic is to put malicious links on social media or other websites, which prompts Android users to install a so-called video player to watch content. Once the malware is installed and takes over the mobile device, the user is unable to use the home and back buttons. Worse yet, a lock-screen is displayed, stating that the user has been identified and charged by New Zealand's Security Intelligence Service for downloading illegal content, and is required to pay a fine before they can use their device again (Security Central, 2015). In reality, the proper solution is to remove the malware in the device's safe mode or using an anti-virus solution, just as with personal computer ransomware (Sophos, 2016).

Kharraz, Robertson, Balzarotti, Bilge, and Kirda (2015) have done an in-depth analysis of more than a thousand ransomware samples. The commonly found malicious activities are encrypting files, changing the master boot record (MBR), deleting files, and stealing personal information. Furthermore, according to Kharraz et al.'s research (2015), payment is extracted typically through four means: charging through premium numbers, forced online shopping, online payments or vouchers, and via bitcoin transactions. The sources of ransomware are by no means limited to cloud computing or just the internet. Moreover, additional backups on the cloud can be part a precautionary measure against ransomware. When faced with ransomware (especially the more complicated ones on personal computers), many individuals and businesses have felt desperate and paid an average of 700 NZD, approximately US$ 500 (Morton, 2015). Data loss and corruption are not covered by traditional insurance policies. Instead, new cyber insurance products classify these losses as "extortion expenses". The coverage includes compensation for business interruption and fees paid to IT experts for system repair and data restoration (Delta Insurance, 2015).

Man-in-the-Cloud Attacks

Another example of latest developments is unauthorized access to a user's (i.e., the company's) data on the cloud. As a recent variant of the traditional man-in-the-middle attack, the "man-in-the-cloud" attack is aimed against files stored on Google Drive, OneDrive, Dropbox, Box, and other third-party cloud based data storage services (Imperva, 2015). With the growing use of mobile devices and online services that can be accessed by multiple users, the available "attack surface" for hackers is also significantly bigger. The man-in-the-cloud attack does not steal user names and passwords but steals the synchronization tokens that are used by these cloud storage applications for the purpose of file synchronization. This was initially demonstrated by Imperva (2015) during the Black Hat USA 2015 Conference. Stealing the tokens does not compromise the account as a whole, but provides access to the specific files, which the tokens were created for. There is, however, potential for placing malware or ransomware in the files or folders in question, which can lead to further attacks. Globally, man-in-the-middle attacks against small businesses are prevalent. According to Bradley (2013), many small businesses in the United States are vulnerable against attacks (e.g. man-in-the-middle) aimed at online banking and financial applications.

Cloud based storage is free up to a certain capacity, and is a very convenient tool for small and medium businesses. It is important for ordinary cloud users (and not just IT professionals) to be informed, not only about the common threats discussed in sections 3.1, 3.2, and 3.3, but also about the man-in the-cloud and other hypothetical threats, and to take necessary precautions to protect their business data.

Security and Privacy in the Cloud for Small-to-Medium Businesses

According to the Office of the Privacy Commissioner of New Zealand (2013), personal information is "any piece of information that relates to a living, identifiable human being" including contact details, financial instruments, health information, and purchase records. The International Association of Privacy Professionals or IAPP (2011) defines privacy as "the appropriate use of personal information under the circumstances [which will] depend on context, law, and the individual's expectations; also, the right of an individual to control the collection, use, and disclosure of personal information." On the other hand, many cloud service providers do not necessarily guarantee specific levels of security and privacy in their service level agreements (Gholami & Laure, 2015). Furthermore, the Office of the Privacy Commissioner (2013) has published written guidelines for small businesses on better managing the private information that is stored in the Cloud. Table 1 is a summarized adaptation, but also expands their guidelines.

There are a number of activities that are necessary for security and privacy within cloud computing. Table 2 summarizes these types of activities (National Institute of Standards and Technology, 2013c; Gholami & Laure, 2015). Although these are commonly performed by service providers, it is useful

Table 1. Cloud privacy checklist for small businesses

Guidelines:	Recommended Practices:
Understand that you are responsible for the information you put in the cloud	Make sure that private information is not misused or disclosed to someone else, and information can be removed or corrected immediately
Know your cloud provider's responsibilities, and be ready to ask the provider for more information	Research the provider's technical protections and physical security measures
Be prepared to deal with data theft if it happens	Know how to notify and remedy your customers
Inform your customers if their data will be stored on the cloud (and also offshore if that is the case)	Have a privacy policy (on your website), which explains how you are using the cloud services
Be prepared to address all customer requests	In case of redundancy (i.e. backups), be aware of how long it takes to remove or change all copies
Understand whether (and how) the location of the data will have legal and jurisdictional ramifications	Big providers will multiple data centers can move data around; but they should be able to tell you about the privacy laws of any of those countries
Be aware of potential insider threats or data mining from within the cloud provider itself	Research the provider's authorization and audit trail features. Investigate the provider's internal and third party marketing policies
Be prepared to overcome vendor lock-in, in case you want to change providers or leave the cloud	Find out what will happen to information stored on the provider's server (e.g. deletion) when you leave. Download a copy of the information before changing service providers.

Table 2. Security and privacy protection activities

Security Context:	Description:
Authentication and Authorization	Design and implement identification schemes.
Identity and Access Management	Involves provisioning and de-provisioning users.
Confidentiality, Integrity, and Availability	Control data integrity and modifications to data.
Monitoring and Incident Response	To be performed continuously according to the client's policies and legal auditing requirements
Policy Management	Define and enforce rules for proof of compliance
Privacy	Protect personally identifiable information from phishing, identity theft, and misuse by attackers

for client companies to be aware of them, to be able to speak with their provider about them, and to be to prepared to either carry out some of these activities (or get other assistance) in situations where the provider may not be expected or obligated to do so.

The major cloud providers' standard service level agreements discuss availability and financial credits in cases of downtime, rather than security or privacy, as can be seen from the examples of Google (2015a), Amazon Web Services S3 (2015b), and Microsoft Azure Cloud Services (2016). On the other hand, these major cloud service providers have published about their advanced security practices and capabilities in detail online. Google (2015b), for example, has an information security team of more than 500 experts. Its data center facilities are protected by fencing and biometric access, and monitored 24/7 by cameras and security guards. Data access by Google staff is strictly controlled. Retired hard disks are completely wiped. All online services and APIs (Application program interfaces) are accessed via SSL (Secure Sockets Layer, i.e. an encrypted link between the server and the browser). Google's cloud services use the same encryption standards as Google's own corporate data. End user as well as technical maintenance actions are logged. Google performs intrusion detection and security scanning for common vulnerabilities, such as cross-site scripting (XSS). Furthermore, Google (2015c) operates VirusTotal, a free online service that analyzes files and URLs to identify viruses, worms, and other kinds of malware. In addition to VirusTotal, Google uses multiple anti-virus engines in conjunction with its various products.

Microsoft has also published information online about its cloud security practices and technologies (Microsoft, 2015b). Microsoft complies with international as well as industry-specific standards, and fulfills numerous security audits. In addition, Microsoft aims to provide transparency about its privacy practices, and adheres to a global code of practice for cloud privacy, ISO/IEC 27018. It uses a variety of precautions, e.g. the physical separation of back-end servers from public interfaces (Microsoft, 2014).

Although the cloud provider choices for small and medium businesses are not limited to the biggest vendors, it may be useful to review their market share worldwide and in New Zealand. Amazon Web Services, Microsoft, and Google are consistently among the top five in the Infrastructure as a Service (IaaS) category, and have been the three fastest growing cloud providers worldwide, in both IaaS and PaaS (Platform as a Service) combined, in the last quarter of 2015, according to the Synergy Research Group (2016). In New Zealand, among a number of important global vendors, Microsoft, Google, and Amazon Web Services also tend to dominate in various service categories. Datacom, Inc., an Amazon Web Services (AWS) partner in Southeast Asia and Australasia, is the largest general IT Services (e.g. consultancy) provider in New Zealand, according to market research done by the International Data

Corporation, i.e. IDC, (Krassiyenko & Te Hira, 2015). AWS is a potential cloud computing solution, not just for larger companies, but also can be set up in a beneficial way for small businesses (Mah, 2015).

Amazon Web Services (2015a) has also released a white paper which provides an overview of the AWS security policies and processes. AWS cloud services are continuously audited, with certifications from accreditation bodies. AWS is also compliant with a variety of data protection laws, for example, in the European Union. AWS has a "shared security model," where the provider is responsible for protecting the underlying infrastructure and the user has flexibility to choose and define the security controls for their resources (such as encryption options, denial of service mitigation tools, and monitoring features).

The Cloud Security Alliance has released a draft guidance paper, which includes a simple cloud security management model (Mogull, 2015). This sequential model can be applied to a cloud related project or problem of any size and scope. The following is an adaptation and explanation of Mogull's (2015) work:

- Identify necessary security and compliance requirements.
- Evaluate your provider, service, and deployment models.
- Define the cloud service architecture.
- Assess the provided security controls.
- Identify and document the control gaps.
- Design and implement new controls to solve those gaps.
- Monitor and manage changes over time.

Although the model above requires an IT background with an analytical attitude, it can be practiced by cloud-consuming businesses together with available IT professionals in the region. Simultaneously, it is important to understand that the risks and costs involved in privacy and security go beyond attacks and the corresponding technical and policy controls, as pointed out in the Cloud Security Guide for SMEs by the European Union Agency for Network and Information Security (2015). Table 3 is based on section 4 of the guide by the European Union Agency for Network and Information Security (ENISA).

Finally, there is another potential security risk associated with cloud based applications, whereby data may be accidentally leaked online by end users. This is possible, for example, in the case of "Shadow IT"

Table 3. Potential information security risks and costs

| Software Security Vulnerabilities |
| Management Portal Compromise |
| Network & Direct Attacks |
| Social Engineering Tactics |
| Device Theft or Loss |
| Physical Hazards |
| System Overloads |
| Unexpected Costs |
| Cloud Vendor Lock-in |
| Administrative problems |
| Foreign Jurisdiction Issues |

as noted by the Cloud Security Alliance (2016b). Shadow IT refers to any software applications including cloud based ones, which are used by company employees without the direct approval or knowledge of the company's management. As a result, security advice for these applications may not yet have been devised or communicated to employees.

The Findings of the Local Research

There are three major threats for small and medium sized New Zealand businesses, as discussed in the previous sections, and supported by NetSafe's summary data on reported cybercrimes as cited by Hails (2015): ransomware, intercepted emails, and compromised websites. According to NetSafe (2016), the average financial loss incurred by small New Zealand businesses that reported being involved in scams and security incidents was approximately 13,500 NZD, slightly more than US\$ 9,000. For example, one small business had its website hacked, and the customer data was stolen. The hacker demanded a ransom not to publish the customer data online. The business' staff also had to spend time and money, for cleaning up the compromised site. Other typical scenarios are related to ecommerce fraud, involving payments. The following is an anecdote reported to NetSafe (2015) by a small business that lost 76,000 NZD: "I regularly order items from an [overseas] supplier … an invoice arrived by email with a new account number, we made payment … when the supplier questioned why the funds had not arrived … we realized that the email had been intercepted … the [overseas] company confirmed that their email system had been hacked …"

A survey was prepared and shared with participants from various local organizations in October 2015. It was aimed at understanding these organizations' plans for using cloud based services in the future, their cloud security and privacy policies, their overall reaction to the current threats, and their general trust of the cloud. These survey questions can be found in the Appendix.

The respondents have confirmed that they plan to invest more in cloud computing in the future. Part of this investment will be aimed toward increasing and optimizing the cloud services, that they are already using. The service models in question include Software as a Service (SaaS), Platform as a Service (PaaS), and Infrastructure as a Service (IaaS). A number of respondents have also indicated that they would be interested in Security as a Service (SECaaS). SECaaS is defined as a cloud business model, where a large service provider with advanced infrastructure can combine and offer security services on a subscription basis to individuals and businesses cost effectively without requiring on-premises their own hardware and capital expenditures (Furfaro, Garro, & Tundis, 2014). For the local respondents, web security and email security were mentioned as the main areas where they needed assistance. Other areas identified included business continuity and recovery, data loss prevention, and identity and access management.

Furthermore, the local respondents' answers indicate that they currently trust the cloud more than they used to, 12 months ago. Notwithstanding this confidence, they have also stated that there are a number of necessary security controls that must be in place for a company to migrate to the cloud or to continue to use cloud based services. The controls expected from the cloud service provider include anti-malware solutions, protection of data with encryption, BCP/DR (Business Continuity Planning/Disaster Recovery) practices, transparency about the geographical location of data, and protection from DDoS (Distributed Denial of Service) attacks. These high expectations of cloud consumers are important because they are realistic about their own technical understanding. The respondents see their employees' knowledge of the cloud and the users' awareness of security issues as somewhat informed, rather than well informed.

Finally, research interviews and meetings were also held with local IT professionals between September and November 2015. These cloud computing meetings had a broader agenda than just security matters; the particular question where security and privacy are ranked against other factors can be found in the Appendix. When the professionals were asked which factors are relevant to companies adopting cloud based services, they highlighted service to end users, and security and privacy as extremely important.

FURTHER CONSIDERATIONS AND RECOMMENDATIONS

Although it may have unique risks, cloud computing also brings new solutions with it. Therefore, security of systems (and the perception thereof) may increase as a result of greater virtualization, cloud backups, access to third-party expertise, and improving anonymity in cloud based services. Many IT managers feel that security has improved as a result of running cloud based applications (QuoteColo, 2015). For a small or medium business, this can provide an opportunity for staff to focus more on their core products, and to devote more time toward innovative use of software applications, rather than administering day-to-day IT operations and trouble-shooting (Ghormley, 2012).

A Public Cloud is shared among the clients, who access a continuous service or a capacity but without having their own dedicated physical assets, e.g. any guarantees as to where their data would be stored (Gartner, 2016c). This flexibility allows higher scalability and greater economies of scale for the service provider. This leads to better prices for the clients, who will save money on their capital expenditures. On the other hand, a Private Cloud environment is "used by only one organization," and "ensures that an organization is completely isolated from others" in terms of dedicated resources (Gartner, 2016b). The Hybrid Cloud model is often a combination of the private and public enterprise deployment models, offering the benefits of both. The hybrid model can mean the ability to use collocation or dedicated services alongside public cloud resources, possibly from multiple service providers.

A Hybrid Cloud system extends the capacity or the capability of a cloud service through integration with another cloud service, while seeking to maintain control and security. A business may store its sensitive data in a secure in-house or private-cloud space but may also need to interface that data with a business intelligence application provided as a public cloud software service (Moore, 2014). Another example of a hybrid cloud is when a business may use public cloud computing resources, in order to meet temporary needs that exceed their private cloud or in-house infrastructure capacity (Bittman, 2012).

According to Kevin Jones (2012), former Vice President of Infrastructure and Cloud Computing Services at Dell (currently Senior Vice President, Hewlett Packard), there are two approaches to cloud adoption. With the revolutionary approach, an organization may move to cloud based resources and applications rapidly and on a whole scale. The evolutionary approach involves a case-by-case evaluation of portfolio items and a step-by-step implementation, and the organization may possibly stop at any point in time. On one hand, small and medium businesses are not burdened by large scale legacy applications and large past investments in their own IT infrastructure and systems, and may more easily undertake a revolutionary approach. However, the evolutionary approach has its unique advantages whereby a business can gradually pick and adopt only those services, which they can afford and have the basic technical know-how necessary to realize the potential benefits.

There are IT companies that specialize in providing cloud computing solutions to small and medium sized businesses in New Zealand. Microsoft Office 365 and remote technical support are a few of the popular services, for example, ComputerCare (2015). According to another company providing such services, Softsource (2016), a hybrid cloud infrastructure also offers benefits to smaller businesses, including cost-effective scalability, ability to match changes in system load, and greater security. In addition to private security companies, it is important for the government and non-profit bodies to advise and assist businesses from all sectors of the economy in cyber security matters.

Small businesses are part of social fabric of their respective cities and communities, and any negative impact of cybercrime will also have unfavorable repercussions for large businesses (Das & Nayak, 2013). Furthermore, many IT security services companies are themselves small and medium sized businesses. Therefore, government cooperation and support for those security companies can be viewed as a very beneficial public policy (Department for Business, Innovation & Skills, 2015). Roberts and Wolfe (2015) conducted an extensive survey across New Zealand with organizations of various sizes regarding their experiences with and attitudes toward cyber security. One key finding was that many organizations believe the government is not providing enough resources and information to help businesses with protecting themselves in the cyber environment. Another finding was that most of the organizations believe that will cybercrime will increase in the next 24 months.

Next, it is also important to carefully select vendors and to understand which applications and data are sensitive. In Software as a Service, the business can only control a small set of user specific configuration settings. The business's own efforts may be concentrated on protecting the usernames, passwords, and browser sessions of the users via the appropriate endpoint security measures. According to Trend Micro (2012), a leading global security software vendor, the business relies on the software service provider to manage security. Another important consideration is clarifying and negotiating who (i.e., the client or the provider) has responsibility for the security of the middleware in a hybrid cloud (Ghormley, 2012). The interfaces and touch points between the components are the potential sources of risk. A breach in the public cloud could provide a way for unauthorized access to a business's other applications (Cloud Standards Customer Council, 2016). Therefore, a potential challenge of the hybrid model is the higher complexity of design and integration (He & Wang, 2015).

According to Gretchen Marx (2013), IBM's Security Portfolio Strategy Director, the security perimeter of the company network is not clear-cut, and there are many possible points of entry in a cloud computing environment. With the proliferation of company mobile devices, growing use of BYOD (Bring Your Own Device), and new interfaces to external stakeholder systems, data protection with the help of network firewalls and intrusion detection systems is not enough. It is important to ensure that the mobile devices used for work have the latest software updates, and to separate the business data from personal data. User access to business data needs to be managed according to the user's location and the device being used (Marx, 2013). Furthermore, the formulation of organizational policies for data protection, and the installation of security software are necessary measures (Georgiou & Lambrinoudakis, 2014). According to Vitti, dos Santos, C. B. Westphall, C. M. Westphall, and Vieira (2014), data backup, verification of data integrity, and recovery planning are recommended, not only for providers, but also for the cloud users.

Systems security and the integration of applications need to be handled differently in a cloud based environment. Businesses should focus more on the particular data that are exchanged between their different applications (Rossi, 2016), and then work to make that data more secure using encryption and other means. Improving security is worth the extra time, money and effort, even for smaller businesses.

CONCLUSION AND FUTURE RESEARCH DIRECTIONS

Increasingly, small businesses around the world are using cloud computing services. Cloud services expenditures among small and medium businesses in the US are growing at an average rate of 40% every year, according to Compass Intelligence, as cited in a Forbes article by Columbus (2015). This is also the case globally, where the cloud service market is expected to grow at a rate of 17.2% each year until 2018, according to Odin Research (2015). Furthermore, hybrid cloud services are used by 18% of small and medium businesses with fewer than 100 employees (Columbus, 2015). As cited in the same article by Columbus (2015), 78% of these businesses are also expected to be cloud operational by 2020, especially in terms of financial management, email, collaboration, e-commerce, and office applications. The Cloud does not only provide technology resources but is also a catalyst for improving a company's business model (Glass & Schiff, 2013; Aldarbesti, Goutas, & Sutanto, 2016).

As cloud services adoption grows, the trust in the security of these services is also improving as cloud service providers make their security measures stricter and more compliant. Times have changed, and the fears and doubts are being contained as providers have invested significant resources to implement, test, and strengthen their security measures (Gasiorowski-Denis, 2015). Despite the growing confidence, it is still important for clients to implement additional measures such as strong encryption on their data (Trend Micro, 2012). The Hybrid Cloud model, combined with the evolutionary adoption approach, can allow businesses to surpass the level of security of a public cloud as well as a traditional IT environment. Nevertheless, in addition to encryption and stronger user passwords, businesses with hybrid clouds can also consider using an additional facility, for example, a VPN (Virtual Private Network) between the on-premises component and the public cloud environment (Cloud Standards Customer Council, 2016).

Another aspect of the current environment has to do with the clients' behavior on the cloud and to what extent the clients are aware of the risks associated with the cloud. The professional participants of this research project in Hawke's Bay indicate that they foresee continued investment in cloud IT services in the near future. According to Odin (2015), there are two paths: cloud leapers that will move straight to the cloud, and cloud converters that will switch from locally installed software and hardware to remote services at the next opportunity. Regardless of the path selected, it is crucial for local organizations to help make their employees savvy about cloud security. The up-and-coming workforce is already familiar with some cloud based applications, e.g. Google Drive (Erturk, 2016). So the next level of training should involve business owners and employees obtaining privacy and general security related knowledge.

While the typical risks to regional businesses are not limited to these attacks above, the scope of this chapter has been limited to summarizing the sample case studies above with particular cyber security scenarios. There are other scenarios and solutions that can be featured in research articles in the future. Government agencies are increasingly adopting cloud computing, and also need up-to-date information. (New Zealand Government CIO, 2015). Another interesting research opportunity would be through the analysis of current cyber threat data feeds and how Big Data may help combat threats (Souza, 2016). From a technical perspective, a certain attack can be selected and analyzed in depth. Furthermore, future studies can continue formulating and elaborating security policies and best practices that will build on the existing cloud computing and cybersecurity literature.

Smartphones constantly access the cloud; as a result, future mobile security expertise needs to cover both mobile and cloud related aspects (NZ Ministry of Business, Innovation, and Employment, 2015).

Aside from cloud based business services on computers and mobile devices, further studies on cyber security can focus on the Internet of Things (IoT). IoT refers to the rapidly growing network where "a large number of embedded devices employ communication services offered by the Internet protocols [and these] smart objects are not directly operated by humans, but exist as components in buildings or vehicles, or are spread out in the environment" according to the Internet Architecture Board's guiding document drafted by Tschofenig, Arkko, Thaler, and McPherson (2015).

The rise of cloud computing has been a prerequisite for the Internet of Things. Security and privacy are among the pressing challenges as noted by the Internet Society (Rose, Eldridge, & Chapin, 2015). Cloud computing leverages remote and networked IT resources, and allows small and distributed devices to interact with powerful servers which have control and data analysis capabilities. Instances of Device-to-Cloud communications include pushing software updates to the objects. Examples for these objects are ones that transfer data to the cloud infrastructure, which in turn relays that information to the remote users' devices.

Security is more complicated in this IoT connectivity model, for example, since there are two types of credentials: the credentials for wireless network access, and those for cloud access (Tschofenig, Arkko, Thaler, & McPherson, 2015). Studies on IoT and interconnected objects and sensors have started being published in recent years. Nevertheless, new research of greater relevance to home and small business IoT users would be very helpful, especially if they address the emerging security and privacy issues and solutions.

REFERENCES

W3 Techs. (2016). *Usage Statistics and Market Share of Content Management Systems for Websites, May 2016.* Retrieved from https://w3techs.com/technologies/overview/content_management/all

Aldarbesti, H., Goutas, L., & Sutanto, J. (2016). The Building Blocks of a Cloud Strategy: Evidence from Three SaaS Providers. *Communications of the ACM, 59*(1), 90–97.

Amazon Web Services. (2015a). *Introduction to AWS Security.* Retrieved from https://d0.awsstatic.com/whitepapers/Security/Intro_to_AWS_Security.pdf

Amazon Web Services. (2015b). *Amazon S3 Service Level Agreement.* Retrieved from https://aws.amazon.com/s3/sla/

Bittman, T. (2012, September 24). *Mind the Gap: Here Comes Hybrid Cloud.* Retrieved from http://blogs.gartner.com/thomas_bittman/2012/09/24/mind-the-gap-here-comes-hybrid-cloud/

Bowne, S. (2013). *Cookie Re-Use in Office 365 and Other Web Services.* Retrieved from https://samsclass.info/123/proj10/cookie-reuse.htm

Bradley, D., & Cooper, J. (2014). Cloud Computing's Selection and Effect on Small Business. *Entrepreneurial Executive, 19,* 87–94.

Bradley, S. (2013). *Protecting Small Business Banking.* Retrieved from https://www.sans.org/reading-room/whitepapers/threats/protecting-small-business-banking-34277

Cisco Security. (2013). *Microsoft Exchange Outlook Web Access Cross-Site Scripting Vulnerability.* Retrieved from https://tools.cisco.com/security/center/viewAlert.x?alertId=31974

Cisco Security. (2016). *Microsoft Exchange Server Outlook Web Access Spoofing Vulnerability.* Retrieved from https://tools.cisco.com/security/center/viewAlert.x?alertId=42911

Cloud Security Alliance. (2016a). *The Treacherous 12: Cloud Computing Top Threats in 2016.* Retrieved from https://downloads.cloudsecurityalliance.org/assets/research/top-threats/Treacherous-12_Cloud-Computing_Top-Threats.pdf

Cloud Security Alliance. (2016b). *Mitigating Risk for Cloud Apps.* Retrieved from https://www.survey-monkey.com/r/cloud-apps

Cloud Standards Customer Council. (2016). *Practical Guide to Hybrid Cloud Computing.* Retrieved from http://www.cloud-council.org/deliverables/CSCC-Practical-Guide-to-Hybrid-Cloud-Computing.pdf

Columbus, L. (2015, May 4). *Roundup of Small & Medium Business Cloud Computing Forecasts and Market Estimates, 2015.* Retrieved from http://www.forbes.com/sites/louiscolumbus/2015/05/04/roundup-of-small-medium-business-cloud-computing-forecasts-and-market-estimates-2015/#4c19adec1646

ComputerCare. (2016). *OneCare.* Retrieved from http://www.computercare.co.nz/onecare.html

Costa, P., Santos, J. P., & Da Silva, M. M. (2013). Evaluation Criteria for Cloud Services. In *Proceedings of the 2013 IEEE Sixth International Conference on Cloud Computing.* Retrieved from https://www.researchgate.net/publication/261436007_Evaluation_Criteria_for_Cloud_Services

Cusick, J. (2016). *Considerations for Cloud Security Operations.* New York, NY: Oracle CSO Advisory Board Cloud Security Session. Retrieved from https://www.researchgate.net/publication/291522793_Considerations_for_Cloud_Security_Operations

Das, S., & Nayak, T. (2013). Impact of Cyber Crime: Issues and Challenges. *International Journal of Engineering Sciences & Emerging Technologies, 6*(2), 142–153.

De Souza, E. (2016, April 19). *Resurrecting CHAOS (Controlling Havoc and Overhauling Security) for Today's CIOs and CISOs.* Retrieved from http://cloudtweaks.com/2016/04/controlling-havoc-and-overhauling-security/

Delta Insurance. (2015). *Safeguarding Business from Cyber Threats: Embracing Cyber Risk Management.* Retrieved from http://www.deltainsurance.co.nz/Portals/71/Delta_Cyber.pdf

Department for Business Innovation & Skills. (2015). *Policy Paper – 2010 to 2015 Government Policy: Cyber Security.* Retrieved from https://www.gov.uk/government/publications/2010-to-2015-government-policy-cyber-security/2010-to-2015-government-policy-cyber-security

Emberton, N. (2016). *Computer Security.* Retrieved from http://www.computerhope.com/jargon/c/compsecu.htm

Erturk, E. (2016). Using a cloud based collaboration technology in a systems analysis and design course. *International Journal of Emerging Technologies in Learning, 11*(1), 33–37. doi:10.3991/ijet.v11i01.4991

Erturk, E., & Fail, D. (2013). Information technology in New Zealand: Review of emerging social trends, current issues, and policies. *International Journal of Emerging Trends in Computing and Information Sciences, 4*(1), 46–52.

European Union Agency for Network and Information Security. (2015). *Cloud Computing Security Risks and Opportunities for SMEs.* Retrieved from https://www.enisa.europa.eu/activities/Resilience-and-CIIP/cloud-computing/security-for-smes/cloud-security-guide-for-smes

Furfaro, A., Garro, A., & Tundis, A. (2014). Towards Security as a Service (SecaaS): On the Modeling of Security Services for Cloud Computing. *International Carnahan Conference on Security Technology (ICCST).* Retrieved from http://ieeexplore.ieee.org/xpl/articleDetails.jsp?arnumber=6986995

Gartner. (2016a). *Cloud Access Security Brokers (CASBs).* Retrieved from http://www.gartner.com/it-glossary/cloud-access-security-brokers-casbs/

Gartner. (2016b). *Private Cloud Computing.* Retrieved from http://www.gartner.com/it-glossary/private-cloud-computing/

Gartner. (2016c). *Public Cloud Computing.* Retrieved from http://www.gartner.com/it-glossary/public-cloud-computing/

Gasiorowski-Denis, E. (2015). *Trust and Confidence in Cloud Privacy.* Retrieved from: http://www.iso.org/iso/news.htm?refid=Ref1921

Geo Block, I. P. (2015, April 18). *Why so many WordPress plugins vulnerable?* Retrieved from http://www.ipgeoblock.com/article/why-so-vulnerable.html

Georgiou, D., & Lambrinoudakis, C. (2014). A Security Policy for Cloud Providers: The Software-as-a-Service Model. *Ninth International Conference on Internet Monitoring and Protection.* Retrieved from https://www.researchgate.net/publication/266391150_A_Security_Policy_for_Cloud_Providers_The_Software-as-a-Service_Model

Gholami, A., & Laure, E. (2015). Security and Privacy of Sensitive Data in Cloud Computing - A Survey of Recent Developments. *Fourth International Conference on Software Engineering and Applications.* Retrieved from http://arxiv.org/ftp/arxiv/papers/1601/1601.01498.pdf

Ghormley, Y. (2012). Cloud Computer Management from the Small Business Perspective. *International Journal of Management & Information Systems, 16*(4), 349–356.

Glass, H., & Schiff, A. (2013). *Application of ICTs in the NZ Services Sector.* Retrieved from http://www.productivity.govt.nz/sites/default/files/Sub%20105%20-%20Sapere%20Research%20Group%20and%20Covec%20PDF%20-%20%20768Kb.pdf

Goodin, D. (2016, February 5). *Mysterious Spike in WordPress Hacks Silently Delivers Ransomware to Visitors.* Retrieved from http://arstechnica.com/security/2016/02/mysterious-spike-in-wordpress-hacks-silently-delivers-ransomware-to-visitors/

Google. (2015a). *Google Compute Engine Service Level Agreement (SLA).* Retrieved from https://cloud.google.com/compute/sla

Google. (2015b). *Security and Compliance on the Google Platform.* Retrieved from https://cloud.google.com/security/

Google. (2015c). *Google Security Whitepaper.* Retrieved from https://cloud.google.com/security/white-paper

Hails, C. (2015, June 23). *The Top 3 Cyber Security Threats for NZ Small Businesses: #ConnectSmart.* Retrieved from http://blog.netsafe.org.nz/2015/06/23/the-top-3-cyber-security-threats-for-nz-small-businesses-connectsmart/

Handley, J. (2015, August 9). *Why do WordPress websites get hacked?* Retrieved from https://getflywheel.com/layout/why-do-wordpress-websites-get-hacked/

He, W., & Wang, F. (2015). A Hybrid Cloud Model for Cloud Adoption by Multinational Enterprises. *Journal of Global Information Management, 23*(1), 1–23. doi:10.4018/jgim.2015010101

Henderson, J. (2015, January 29). *Check Point: Top 7 security issues impacting NZ businesses in 2015.* Retrieved from http://www.computerworld.co.nz/article/564941/check-point-top-7-security-issues-impacting-nz-businesses-2015/?fp=4&fpid=2117013083

Imperva. (2015). *Man in the Cloud (MITC) Attacks: Hacker Intelligence Initiative Report.* Retrieved from https://www.imperva.com/docs/HII_Man_In_The_Cloud_Attacks.pdf

International Association of Privacy Professionals. (2011). *IAPP Information Privacy Certification: Glossary of Common Privacy Terminology.* Retrieved from https://iapp.org/media/pdf/certification/CIPP_Glossary_0211updated.pdf

International Telecommunication Union. (2016). *Definition of Cybersecurity.* Retrieved from http://www.itu.int/en/ITU-T/studygroups/com17/Pages/cybersecurity.aspx

Janssen, C. (2016). *What Is Cloud Computing Security?* Retrieved from https://www.techopedia.com/definition/25114/cloud-computing-security

Jeremiah, D., & Clarke, A. (2013). *Frost & Sullivan: New Zealand Organisations Steadily Embracing Cloud Computing for IT Solutions.* Retrieved from http://www.frost.com/prod/servlet/press-release.pag?docid=288172988

Jones, K. (2012, May 24). *The Evolutionary vs. Revolutionary Approach to Cloud Computing.* Retrieved from http://www.theguardian.com/media-network/media-network-blog/2012/may/24/evolutionary-revolutionary-cloud-approach-business

Kemp, B. (2015, July 7). *How to Secure WordPress Against Hacking.* Retrieved from https://www.the-seoguy.co.nz/wordpress-security-hardening-securing-wp/

Kharraz, A., Robertson, W., Balzarotti, D., Bilge, L., & Kirda, E. (2015). Cutting the Gordian Knot: A Look Under the Hood of Ransomware Attacks. *12th International Conference on Detection of Intrusions and Malware & Vulnerability Assessment (DIMVA).* Retrieved from http://www.seclab.nu/static/publications/dimva2015ransomware.pdf

King, J. (2015, December 9). *Forecast 2016: Security Takes Center Stage.* Retrieved from http://www.computerworld.com/article/3012135/security/forecast-2016-security-takes-center-stage.html

Krassiyenko, D., & Te Hira, A. (2015, May 18). *New Zealand Businesses Head to the Cloud.* Retrieved from https://www.idc.com/getdoc.jsp?containerId=prNZ25627915

Lin, T. (2016, February 12). *Cloud Security Broker ThisData Helping Businesses Stay Safe in the Cloud.* Retrieved from http://www.stuff.co.nz/business/76826663/cloud-security-broker-thisdata-helping-businesses-stay-safe-in-the-cloud

Lucas, E., Drain, D., & Mckenzie, C. (2014). *New Zealand Insights from PwC's 2014 Global Economic Crime Survey.* Retrieved from http://www.pwc.co.nz/PWC.NZ/media/pdf-documents/publications/pwc-global-economic-crime-survey-new-zealand-supplement-feb-2014-final2.pdf

Lucas, E., Drain, D., & Mckenzie, C. (2016). *Global Economic Crime Survey 2016: New Zealand Insights.* Retrieved from http://www.pwc.co.nz/PWC.NZ/media/pdf-documents/forensic-services/pwc-global-economic-crime-survey-2016-new-zealand-insights.pdf

Mah, P. (2015). *How to Set up Amazon Web Services for Your Small Business.* Retrieved from http://www.cio.com/article/2934791/cloud-computing/how-to-set-up-amazon-web-services-for-your-small-business.html

Marx, G. (2013). *Can Cloud Computing Be Secure: Six Ways to Reduce Risk and Protect Data.* Retrieved from http://www.theguardian.com/media-network/media-network-blog/2013/sep/05/cloud-computing-security-protect-data

MediaCenter Panda Security. (2015). Retrieved from http://xdaplay.blogspot.com/2015/06/mediacenter-panda-security_1.html

Microsoft. (2014). *Windows Azure Privacy Overview.* Retrieved from http://download.microsoft.com/download/7/5/9/759E2283-F517-430E-84AF-0151988C117A/WindowsAzurePrivacyOverview.pdf

Microsoft. (2015a). *Microsoft Responses to Cloud Computing Information Privacy and Security Considerations.* Retrieved from https://www.microsoft.com/en-us/TrustCenter/Compliance/NZCC

Microsoft. (2015b). *Ensuring Security and Privacy in the Trusted Cloud: Microsoft Azure Complies with Global Security Standards.* Retrieved from https://www.microsoft.com/en-us/TrustCenter/Security/AzureSecurity

Microsoft. (2015c). *Trusted Cloud: Microsoft Azure Security, Privacy, and Compliance White Paper.* Retrieved from http://download.microsoft.com/download/1/6/0/160216AA-8445-480B-B60F-5C8E-C8067FCA/WindowsAzure-SecurityPrivacyCompliance.pdf

Microsoft. (2016). *SLA for Cloud Services.* Retrieved from https://azure.microsoft.com/en-us/support/legal/sla/cloud-services/v1_1/

Mogull, R. (2015). *Cloud Computing Concepts and Architectures.* Retrieved from https://github.com/cloudsecurityalliance/CSA-Guidance/blob/master/Domain%201-%20Cloud%20Computing%20Concepts%20and%20Architectures.md

Moore, J. (2014, June 4). *Business Intelligence Takes to Cloud for Small Businesses.* Retrieved from http://www.cio.com/article/2375744/business-intelligence/business-intelligence-takes-to-cloud-for-small-businesses.html

Morton, J. (2015, January 19). *114 Kiwis Hit in Web Attacks.* Retrieved from http://www.nzherald.co.nz/business/news/article.cfm?c_id=3&objectid=11388277

National Institute of Standards and Technology. (2013a). *Glossary of Key Information Security Terms.* Retrieved from http://nvlpubs.nist.gov/nistpubs/ir/2013/NIST.IR.7298r2.pdf

National Institute of Standards and Technology. (2013b). *NIST Special Publication 500-299: Cloud Computing Security Reference Architecture.* Retrieved from http://collaborate.nist.gov/twiki-cloud-computing/pub/CloudComputing/CloudSecurity/NIST_Security_Reference_Architecture_2013.05.15_v1.0.pdf

National Institute of Standards and Technology. (2013c). *NIST Special Publication 500-291: NIST Cloud Computing Standards Roadmap.* Retrieved from http://www.nist.gov/itl/cloud/upload/NIST_SP-500-291_Version-2_2013_June18_FINAL.pdf

National Institute of Standards and Technology. (2016). *Vulnerability Summary.* Retrieved from https://web.nvd.nist.gov/view/vuln/detail?vulnId=CVE-2016-0032

NetSafe. (2015). *Digital Challenge and New Zealanders: A Focus on Reports Made to NetSafe in 2014.* Retrieved from https://www.netsafe.org.nz/safer-internet-day/documents/SID-2015-Internet-Challenges-Report-WEB.pdf

NetSafe. (2016). *Digital Challenge and New Zealanders: A Focus on Incident Reports and Queries Made to NetSafe in 2015.* Retrieved from https://www.netsafe.org.nz/safer-internet-day/documents/SID2016_DigitalChallengesReport2015.pdf

New Zealand Government CIO. (2015). *Cloud Computing Risk and Assurance Framework.* Retrieved from https://www.ict.govt.nz/guidance-and-resources/information-management/requirements-for-cloud-computing/

NZ Ministry of Business Innovation and Employment. (2014). *The Small Business Sector Report.* Retrieved from http://www.mbie.govt.nz/info-services/business/business-growth-agenda/pdf-and-image-library/2014/The%20Small%20Business%20Sector%20Report%202014%20-PDF%208.8%20MB-1.pdf

NZ Ministry of Business Innovation and Employment. (2015). *Information and Communications Technology.* Retrieved from http://www.mbie.govt.nz/info-services/business/business-growth-agenda/sectors-reports-series/pdf-image-library/information-and-communications-technology-report/2015%20Information%20and%20Communication%20Technology%20report.pdf

Odin. (2015). *SMB Cloud Insights: Global.* Retrieved from http://www.odin.com/fileadmin/parallels/documents/smb-reports/2015/SMB_Global_EN_web_20150602.pdf

Office of the Privacy Commissioner. (2013). *Cloud Computing: A Guide to Making the Right Choices.* Retrieved from: https://privacy.org.nz/assets/Files/Brochures-and-pamphlets-and-pubs/OPC-Cloud-Computing-guidance-February-2013.pdf

QuoteColo. (2015). *Cloud Computing in 2015: Infographic.* Retrieved from https://bsdmag.org/cloud_inf/

Roberts, D., & Wolfe, H. (2015). Cybercrime Concerns and Readiness for New Zealand Businesses 2014-2015. *Proceedings of the 6th Annual Computing and Information Technology Research and Education New Zealand (CITRENZ) Conference.* Retrieved from http://www.citrenz.ac.nz/conferences/2015/pdf/2015CITRENZ_1_Roberts_Cybercrime_v2.pdf

Rose, K., Eldridge, S., & Chapin, L. (2015). *The Internet of Things: An Overview. Understanding the Issues and Challenges of a More Connected World.* Retrieved from http://www.internetsociety.org/sites/default/files/ISOC-IoT-Overview-20151022.pdf

Rossi, B. (2016, February 29). *Why Organisations Must Approach Integration and Security in the Cloud Differently.* Retrieved from http://www.information-age.com/technology/cloud-and-virtualisation/123461013/why-organisations-must-approach-integration-and-security-cloud-differently

Rouse, M., & Cole, B. (2012). *What Is Cloud Computing Security?* Retrieved from http://searchcompliance.techtarget.com/definition/cloud-computing-security

Security Central. (2015). *Dealing with 'Police' ransomware on your Android device.* Retrieved from http://www.securitycentral.org.nz/cybersecurity-for-home-internet-users/dealing-with-police-ransomware-on-your-android-device/

Softsource. (2015). *Cloud Computing.* Retrieved from http://www.softsource.co.nz/technologies/cloud-computing.aspx

Sophos. (2016). *Information on Malware Known as Ransomware.* Retrieved from https://www.sophos.com/en-us/support/knowledgebase/119006.aspx

Synergy Research Group. (2016, February 3). *AWS Remains Dominant Despite Microsoft and Google Growth Surges.* Retrieved from https://www.srgresearch.com/articles/aws-remains-dominant-despite-microsoft-and-google-growth-surges

The Open Web Application Security Project. (2016). *Cross-site Scripting (XSS).* Retrieved from https://www.owasp.org/index.php/Cross-site_Scripting_%28XSS%29

Trend Micro. (2012). *Virtualization and Cloud Computing: Security Threats to Evolving Data Centers.* Retrieved from http://www.trendmicro.co.nz/cloud-content/us/pdfs/security-intelligence/reports/rpt_security-threats-to-datacenters.pdf

Tschofenig, H., Arkko, J., Thaler, D., & McPherson, D. (2015). *Architectural Considerations in Smart Object Networking.* Retrieved from https://www.rfc-editor.org/rfc/rfc7452.txt

Vitti, P., Dos Santos, D., Westphall, C. B., Westphall, C. M., & Vieira, K. (2014). Current Issues in Cloud Computing Security and Management. *Eighth International Conference on Emerging Security Information, Systems and Technologies: SECURWARE 2014.* Retrieved from https://www.researchgate.net/publication/266141881_Current_Issues_in_Cloud_Computing_Security_and_Management

World Bank. (2015). *Doing Business 2015: Going Beyond Efficiency.* Retrieved from https://openknowledge.worldbank.org/bitstream/handle/10986/20483/DB15-Full-Report.pdf?sequence=1

This research was previously published in Cybersecurity Breaches and Issues Surrounding Online Threat Protection edited by Michelle Moore, pages 219-247, copyright year 2017 by Information Science Reference (an imprint of IGI Global).

APPENDIX

A. The Cloud Security Survey Questions

1. Please indicate your company size?
2. How many cloud services are you aware of being used within your organization?
3. Do you expect to increase your investment in the cloud?
4. What areas do you plan to invest in?
5. If you plan to make an investment in Security-as-a-Service, in what areas will they likely be?
6. Do you trust cloud computing more than you did 12 months ago?
7. What do you feel is needed to trust cloud more in the future?
8. What security controls do you cite as the most important when assessing a public or private cloud provider?
9. Do you think the users within your company understand what the cloud is?
10. How well do you think most consumers understand the security implications of storing their personal data in the public cloud?
11. Do you think consumers are more open to storing personal data on the cloud vs. others? (Personal data includes the following: contacts, photos, financial files, work files, etc.)
12. How much cloud usage do you believe occurs in your company without the knowledge of the IT organization?
13. When do you think 80% of your IT budget will be comprised of cloud computing services?
14. Do you think consumers are hesitant to use the cloud?

B. Cloud Computing Interview Item 2

- Is the Hybrid Cloud Model the wave of the future (growing more than public or private models)?
- [In particular] Are small and medium companies adopting hybrid cloud services in Hawke's Bay?
- Alternatively, are they using homogenous solutions, fully off-site or fully on-site?

B. Cloud Computing Interview Item 3

- How can "vendor lock-in" concerns be addressed, to allow better portability?

C. Cloud Computing Interview Item 4

The following factors are relevant to companies that are adopting cloud based services. Can you rate the importance of each, in terms of your past experience and perception?

On a scale of 1 to 3:

1 = less important
2 = average importance
3 = extremely important

Industry Suitability. Rating:
Financial Benefit. Rating:
Better Management. Rating:
Service to End Users. Rating:
Reliability and Trust. Rating:
Security and Privacy. Rating:
Explain the answers you have given above, especially where you have rated "1" or "3".

Chapter 50

Data Security and Privacy Assurance Considerations in Cloud Computing for Health Insurance Providers

Amavey Tamunobarafiri
Concordia University of Edmonton, Canada

Shaun Aghili
Concordia University of Edmonton, Canada

Sergey Butakov
Concordia University of Edmonton, Canada

ABSTRACT

Cloud computing has been massively adopted in healthcare, where it attracts economic, operational, and functional advantages beneficial to insurance providers. However, according to Identity Theft Resource Centre, over twenty-five percent of data breaches in the US targeted healthcare. The HIPAA Journal reported an increase in healthcare data breaches in the US in 2016, exposing over 16 million health records. The growing incidents of cyberattacks in healthcare are compelling insurance providers to implement mitigating controls. Addressing data security and privacy issues before cloud adoption protects from monetary and reputation losses. This article provides an assessment tool for health insurance providers when adopting cloud vendor solutions. The final deliverable is a proposed framework derived from prominent cloud computing and governance sources, such as the Cloud Security Alliance, Cloud Control Matrix (CSA, CCM) v 3.0.1 and COBIT 5 Cloud Assurance.

INTRODUCTION

Cloud computing aims to incorporate the evolutionary development of many existing computing approaches and technologies such as distributed services, application, information and infrastructure consisting of a pool of computers, network, information, and storage resources (Meli & Grance, 2011; Gavrilov & Trajkovik, 2012; Takabi & Joshi, 2012). Although cloud computing is still evolving, it has

DOI: 10.4018/978-1-5225-8176-5.ch050

shown potential to enhance collaboration, agility, scale, and availability, although its definitions, issues, underlying technologies, risks, and values need to be carefully considered (Gavrilov & Trajkovik, 2012). According to the National Institute of Standards and Technology (NIST), cloud computing is defined as "a model for enabling ubiquitous, convenient, on-demand network access to a shared pool of configurable computing resources that can be rapidly provisioned and released with minimal management effort or service provider interaction." Cloud computing has five essential characteristics: on-demand self-service, broad network access, resource pooling, rapid elasticity, and measured services. It is also made up of three service models: Software as a Service (SaaS), Platform as a Service (PaaS), and Infrastructure as a Service (IaaS). Cloud computing can further be broken down into four deployment models, namely private, public, community, and hybrid cloud (Meli & Grance, 2011).

For healthcare, cloud computing provides opportunities such as reduced IT service costs, optimizing resources, and improving clinical and quality of service for patients (Ahuja, Mani, & Zambrano, 2012). The Cloud Standards Customer Council (CSCC, 2017) described the benefits of cloud computing in healthcare from different perspectives including economic, operational, and functional advantages, consisting of reduced costs, scalability, ability to adjust to demand rapidly, a potential for broad inter-operability, and integration. Kuo (2011) also discussed opportunities for cloud computing with management, legal, technology, and security considerations. Opportunities include increase in scalability, flexibility, and cost-effectiveness of infrastructure. Despite the benefits of cloud computing, there are security and privacy issues that should be considered when adopting cloud computing, particularly when dealing with healthcare data. Protecting healthcare data is crucial because it involves the collection, storage, and use of personally identifiable health information, according to the Institute of Medicine (IOM, 2009). Insurance providers pay part or all of the expenses when one visits a healthcare professional, spends time in a hospital, or purchases covered health care services or products (CLHIA). In order for a health insurance company to process medical claims, personally identifiable information is obtained from its customers. Ensuring the protection of personal data is crucial; because if exposed, it can cause financial loss and damages to the healthcare provider's reputation, as well as aggravation to the patients. Common related fraud schemes may range from prescription fraud to identity theft, and impersonation of the victim for healthcare insurance benefits, as healthcare information also contains government-issued ID numbers (Mennes, 2016).

A case in point is that of Anthem Inc., the second largest healthcare insurer in the United States in 2015, which experienced a breach of a database involving 80 million customer records. The records contained sensitive information such as emails, medical IDs, names, insurance membership numbers, income data, and social insurance numbers, although there were no actual medical or financial records stolen. The breach was caused by a compromised login credential exploited by cyber-attackers to gain unauthorized access to Anthem's IT system. It was later discovered that Anthem failed to encrypt their files (InfoSec Institute, 2017). The breach cost Anthem Inc., 115 million dollars in settlement (REUTERS, 2017). To avoid attacks, the healthcare industry needs increased security and privacy levels when considering cloud computing. Cloud computing can improve the performance of healthcare organizations, but cloud infrastructures require a highly suitable and auditable computing platform to meet statutory and regulatory requirements governing the handling of protected health information (Intel IT Center, 2013).

According to Identity Theft Resource Centre (2017), over twenty-five percent (25%) of data breaches in the US have targeted the healthcare industry. The HIPAA Journal (2017) reported an increase in the number of healthcare data breaches in the US in 2016, exposing over 16 million health records. The growing number of attacks on the healthcare industry are compelling health insurance providers to implement appropriate mitigating controls for effective and efficient data security and privacy management.

As such, the objective of this research was to develop an assessment tool that can be used by health insurance providers as a guide for cloud service provider selection. It can also be used as a guide for Service-level Agreement (SLA) requirement drafting and/or evaluation.

To further elaborate, the research's final deliverable is an assessment tool derived from prominent cloud computing and governance sources and documents such as the Cloud Security Alliance, Cloud Control Matrix v 3.0.1, and COBIT 5 Cloud Assurance. The tool identifies and lists appropriate controls by the service model (IaaS, SaaS, PaaS) based on risk factors.

LITERATURE REVIEW

Cloud computing is a critical paradigm that organizations can use to increase their operating efficiencies and reduce costs through optimization. The Cloud Standards Customer Council (2017) illustrated how the use of cloud computing by healthcare providers offers greater benefits than in-house, client-server systems. The advantages also include economic, operational, and functional advantages. The economic benefits are reduced IT costs, including lower costs for IT staff resources as the cloud service provider will cover many responsibilities. The operational advantages include scalability, the ability to adjust to demand quickly, increased privacy and security for healthcare information, and health systems and security controls including encryption of data and log-in access. The advantages of healthcare functionalities are enhanced by cloud systems which offer potential for deep integration and inter-operability. The services of cloud computing are based on the internet and use standard protocols in healthcare, so the connection to other systems is straightforward. Cloud computing offers a wide range of new capabilities with added potential to healthcare staffs. Adding to the CSCC (2017), Intel IT Centre (2013) also discussed cloud computing advantages for healthcare as delivery of services and medical processes using the centralized nature of cloud computing can improve the management of data and access and reduce processing times for patient enrolment. Efficient, scalable, and agile healthcare IT is also improved with cloud computing. Finally, by providing around-the-clock availability of information, reducing IT costs, and scalable healthcare services, cloud computing can improve the management of healthcare data and system efficiency (Sajib & Abbas, 2016).

Due to the sensitive nature of healthcare data, it is essential to understand security concerns or challenges that can arise from the use of cloud computing in healthcare industries. While cloud computing presents a range of benefits, it can also pose a risk for healthcare organizations. Looking at cloud computing security and privacy concerns from a general view, Takabi, James, & Gail-Joon (2010) discuss cloud computing as a critical paradigm that organizations can use to increase their operating and economic efficiencies and reduce costs through optimization remarkably. The authors also discuss security and privacy issues that affect the adoption of cloud computing, as well as, the various approaches that can be used in addressing these issues. Some of the security and privacy challenges discussed include authentication and identity management, secure-service management, trust management and policy integration, access control, and privacy and data protection. The research focused on general cloud computing issues; however, the issues discussed also apply equally to healthcare cloud computing.

Kuo (2011) evaluated the challenges of cloud computing in healthcare from four aspects namely legal, technology, security, and management. The management challenges include lack of trust in the privacy and security of data by users, organizational immobility, loss of control, and uncertainly regarding provider compliance with policies and procedures. The technological challenges include exhaustion of resources, performance uncertainty, lock-in of data, transfer of data bottlenecks, and multi-tenancy. The security challenges are attacks from hackers, network breaks, separation failure, public management interface, weak encryption, key management, and privilege abuse, while legal challenges include contract law, data jurisdiction, and privacy.

Zhang & Liu (2010) described security issues shared by healthcare cloud applications. Issues such as ownership of information, authenticity, authentication, non-repudiation, patient consent, and authorization, integrity, confidentiality, availability, and utility of data were discussed. The authors used a methodical approach to inquire into security models and security requirements for healthcare applications that are stored in the cloud. After identifying healthcare security and privacy requirements, an electronic security reference model of health records for healthcare cloud applications was proposed. This reference model helps in determining the security and privacy issues from both the patients' and health practitioners' viewpoints. For health practitioners, security and privacy issues were categorized into two concerns: How are patients' electronic health records retrieved securely from the cloud, and how to validate the authenticity of electronic health records acquired from diverse care delivery organizations, as well as any information gained from the patient upon authorization. These issues are connected to the problem of secure storage and management of electronic health records in the cloud. Although the authors proposed a reference model that can be used to identify security and privacy issues, the identified issues focused only on identity and access management of information in the cloud. Therefore, the authors proposed solutions such as selection of encryption scheme, secure key management, and the use of digital signatures for providing authenticity, integrity, and non-repudiation.

Shariati, Abouzarjomehri, & Ahmadzadegan (2015) discussed data security and privacy protection, particularly risk related to user privileged access, system availability, regulatory compliance, location of data, support for investigation, segregation of data, recovery, data loss/leakage, malicious insiders, flooding attacks, IP spoofing, and distributed denial of service. Different users have different levels of access to the cloud, and it is essential to define who are the privileged users. If access is not accurately controlled data leakage or unauthorized exposure of information stored in the cloud could occur as it is transferred. There is also the possibility of the provider's services being disrupted or made unavailable. Regulatory compliance with policies is also necessary, as well as how and where data is stored, since data could travel to different areas at once and lead to unauthorized access if laws for data protection are not strict in a particular location. Segregation of data can pose a threat to information in the cloud because several people could own different kinds of data. Recovery is vital in case of a natural disaster or an attack, and unavailability of a backup system can lead to total loss of information. There is also a possibility of data transfer to a location not on the client's computer could occur if the cloud storage limit is reached. If the transfer of data to a different location is not properly managed, it could lead to data leakage or loss of data. Robust policies and procedures must also in place to prevent malicious activity by employee access data stored in the cloud. Flooding attacks is another potential problem: As transfer of information is done online by sending requests to retrieve data in the cloud, an attacker could exploit this feature by sending a malicious request to the server instigating a denial of service attack. IP spoofing occurs when an attacker impersonates another user in order to launch an attack against a host by creating malicious IP packets with a deceptive source IP address. Distributed Denial of service attacks (DDoS) carried out using different computers at once by sending a particular request at simultaneously is another concern. The servers get busy with replies and the main request is not answered. Although

Shariati, et. al. (2015) discussed the challenges of cloud computing, no recommendations or solutions to these challenges were presented.

Cloud security in healthcare applications can be assessed by identifying the risks involved, as seen in Daman, Tripathi, & Mishra (2016). The risks presented include issues related to policies changes and violations, ethical and privacy laws, differences in geographical or jurisdictional laws, security loopholes by various cloud providers, XML signature attacks/flooding, failure of cloud access tools/communication media, flooding attacks by viruses, malware programs, DDoS attacks, bad IPs, technical failures/downtime, unauthorised access, and IP & port scanning. Although the paper presented recommendations on considerations prior to adopting cloud computing, no solutions or mitigating controls presented for the risks were identified.

The Intel IT Centre (2013) in the Industry brief on healthcare cloud security also looked at security issues facing the healthcare industry, such as access and identity management, protection of data, compliance, trust, and security architecture. For access, authentication and identification frameworks and standards may not expand to the cloud if they are made of a combination of unique passwords and usernames for each application. This creates a weak link in the security chain. Protection of data is critical and, due to the multitenant nature of cloud computing, it is vital to ensure that healthcare information stored in the cloud is encrypted at rest and in transit. Compliance also poses an issue because privacy laws and regulations differ in different countries and regions which. Compliance with various laws requires the cloud infrastructure to be auditable for features such as controls, security, encryption and geographical locations. Direct control of health information is shifted to the cloud service provider, which involves trust. The cloud service provider must provide tools for data management and provide clarity over the cloud to ensure that agreed-upon policies are being enforced. Secured architecture means the cloud must be made less attractive to cybercriminals. Rootkits and malware can infect hypervisors, BIOs, and operating systems, which are components of the cloud. It is essential that the identities of users and their access to the cloud is properly managed to avoid such attacks.

Gbadeyan, Butakov & Aghili (2017) looked at how to mitigate cloud computing risk from an IT governance perspective for healthcare providers. The paper highlighted security and privacy risks such as multitenancy, unauthorized disclosure of personal health information, repudiation, privacy loss, theft of identity, loss of integrity of personal health information, personal health information unavailability, attack by malicious insiders, as well as IT governance associated with the adoption of cloud computing by the healthcare industry in Canada. The research focused on highlighting individual areas for risk assessment in adopting cloud computing in the Canadian healthcare industry and recommended mitigation of risk strategies in cloud computing using information technology governance practices in Alberta as a guideline. The authors used Alberta's privacy impact assessment requirement and the *COBIT 5 for Risk* professional guide as their research deliverable building blocks. With a focus on healthcare information privacy in the cloud computing models, individual areas for risk assessment were highlighted and mapped to corresponding components of cloud architecture. To propose IT governance and management level of risk mitigation *COBIT 5 for Risk* professional guide was used. The research covered only information risk scenario categories; it did not address other cloud computing risk scenarios.

Sajib & Abbas (2016) in their paper carried out a review on privacy issues that can affect patient information in the cloud by asking two important research questions leading to a successful research study. The paper presents thirteen (13) healthcare patient information privacy issues; namely, integrity, data management, confidentiality, access control, Search pattern privacy, anonymity, authenticity, accountability, non-repudiation, collusion resistance, client platform security, unlink ability and audit-ability. The research also included a general review of solutions for the aforementioned privacy issues.

Issues related to protection of privacy risks in cloud computing were also discussed by Shariati, Abouzarjomehri, & Ahmadzadegan (2015). The privacy and security issues presented in the research paper included: a) Loss of control: when data is transferred to the cloud, total control of the information is given to the cloud service provider, and if this information is not managed correctly, this can lead to loss of data, exposure of data or unauthorized access to the stored information. As such, before the transfer of information to the cloud, it is essential to know the policies and procedures in place for the protection and management of data. b) Access control: the control of access to information stored in the cloud is important to avoid unauthorized access by unauthorized users. c) Data center: Backup made by cloud service providers of information in the cloud should be appropriately protected to avoid theft of the information; and, d) Data protection: ensuring that proper mechanisms are in place to protect information stored in the cloud.

Ravi & Sankar (2015) in the paper entitled *Measuring the security compliance using cloud control matrix (CCM)* discussed how to implement the cloud control matrix. "The cloud control matrix is a baseline set of security controls to help enterprises assess the risk associated with the cloud service provider." It provides various controls that should be implemented by a cloud service provider to control risk related to the service provided. It also includes a list of controls spread across sixteen domains namely, application and security of interface, Audit Assurance and Compliance, Business Continuity Management, Change Control Management, Data Security and Lifecycle Management, Data Center Security, Encryption Key Management, Risk Management, Human Resources Security, Identity and Access Management, Infrastructure and Virtualization, Interoperability, and finally Mobile Security. The cloud service provider uses the CSA cloud control matrix in security risk assessment in a cloud service. Cloud control matrix has several industries accepted regulations, standards and frameworks mapped to it that vendors must follow, including ISO 27001/27002, ISO 27017/27018, NIST 800-53 Rev 4, HIPPA/HITECH Act, etc. For this research, the CSA CCM v 3.0.1 was used. The CSA CCM v3.0.1 contains three new control domains namely management of supply chain, mobile security, interoperability and accountability, portability and transparency.

METHODOLOGY AND DISCUSSION OF RESULTS

The proposed research focused on identifying data security and privacy issues of cloud computing in healthcare that may affect health insurance providers. These issues were then mapped to risk factors by the cloud computing service model. The risk factors are then mapped to appropriate controls from the CCM. The research creates an evaluation template for cloud provider selection. It can also be used as a guide for service level agreement (SLA) drafting and/or requirements by health insurance providers when choosing cloud service providers.

As with most research projects, the proposed framework has a number of limitations. To begin, the research provides a theoretical framework that will require actual implementation/testing in an actual healthcare cloud setting for further validation. A second limitation of this proposed framework is that it is based primarily on two seminal guidance documents; namely, *COBIT 5, Assurance in the cloud* and the *Cloud Security Association's Cloud Control Matrix v. 3.0.1* (2017). However, both guidance documents are in turn based - and thus mappable - to several industry accepted security standards, regulations, and control frameworks. The CCM is a baseline set of security controls to help enterprises assess the risks associated with the cloud service provider. Our research aimed at addressing two primary questions:

1. What are the major security and privacy concerns that may affect cloud computing implementation by health insurance providers?
2. What are the mitigating controls can be implemented to address the privacy and security issues in cloud computing by health insurance providers?

In building the research deliverable, the following steps were taken: 1) A literature review review was conducted aimed at identifying and compiling a list of data security and privacy issues in cloud computing from related works; 2) The identified data, security, and privacy issues identified in Step 1 were subsequently mapped to risk factors by cloud service model (IaaS, SaaS, PaaS) using the *COBIT 5 Controls and Assurance in the Cloud*; 3) The identified risk factors from step 2 were then further mapped to appropriate controls in the CSA CCM v 3.0.1. Finally, an evaluation template was created for cloud provider selection to be used as a guide for healthcare cloud service provider selection; or, as a guide for SLA drafting and requirements when choosing a healthcare cloud service provider. The created evaluation template is documented in the Appendix section of this paper.

Four risk events that can affect two types of assets (data and application/processes) are presented in Table 1. For example, unavailability of data can disrupt activities. For health insurance providers, this can mean disruption of insurance activities such as clients accessing insurance when needed. Loss of data/application can disrupt operations, which can lead to the possibility of partial loss of the information/data. This research has been able to identify risk events that will be affected by each security and privacy issue if exploited. The risk events are associated with the risk factors identified from COBIT 5, Assurance in the cloud.

According to ISACA (2012), Information assets are categorized as data, application, and processes, and these assets are subject to the following risk events:

-   **Unavailability:** The asset is unavailable and cannot be used or accessed by the enterprise. The cause can be accidental, intentional, or legal;
-   **Loss:** The asset is lost or destroyed. The cause can be accidental, for example natural disaster, wrongful manipulation, or an intentional or deliberate destruction of data;

Table 1. High-level impact of the four risk events on assets

Type	Unavailability	Loss	Theft	Disclosure
Data	Disruption of activities, lack of resources to keep on with *business as usual*, possibility of data poisoning	Interruption of operations, required activation of backup restore procedures (DRP); possibility of partial loss of the asset (depending on the recovery point objective (RPO); financial loss associated with recovery efforts	Business competitive disadvantage, possibility of blackmail, loss of credibility with customers/ clients	Damage to company reputation or image, the possibility of regulatory sanctions, financial impact
Application/ Processes	Disruption of activities, lack of resources to keep on with *business as usual*		Higher risk/threat of more selective attacks on data	

- **Theft:** The asset has been intentionally stolen and is now in possession of another individual/ enterprise. Theft is a deliberate action that can involve data loss;
- **Disclosure:** The asset has been released to unauthorized staff/enterprises/organizations or the public. Exposure can be accidental or deliberate. This also includes the undesired, but legal, access to data due to different regulations across international borders.

The proposed assessment tool incorporates security and privacy issues of cloud computing in healthcare and risk factors connected to each security and privacy issue to controls that are in place to mitigate those risk factors. Having confirmed that managing security and privacy is a significant challenge for adopting cloud computing, there is a need for security and privacy assurance. Our research presents an assessment tool in the form of a template that can be used by health insurance providers before adopting cloud computing vendor solutions.

A sample of the actual template is presented in Table 2, which shows identified security and privacy issues of cloud computing in healthcare that may affect health insurance providers. Risk factors from the *COBIT 5, Assurance in the cloud* document have been mapped to the identified security and privacy issues. Applicable control requirements under the sixteen domains of the CSA CCM are mapped to the specific risk factors identified. Finally, analyses of security and privacy parameters defined from the controls of the CSA CCM were also presented.

As shown in Table 2, security and privacy concerns such as identity and access management are relevant in IaaS and SaaS. These are mapped to risk factors such as S1. H – Physical security, S1. D – Legal trans-border requirements, and S3. F – Identity and Access Management (IAM), and the identified risk factors with risk related ranging from theft, disclosure, to financial loss, and even damage of reputation

Table 2. Sample of the evaluation template particular to the issue of identity and access management

Security and Privacy Issues	Description	Risk Factors From the COBIT 5 for Assurance in the Cloud			Cloud Control Matrix V 3.0.1	Recommendation for Analysis
		Risk Factor	Code	Risk Related	Control ID	
Identity and Access Management	Security technique used to regulate who or what can view or use resources in a computing environment. In the case where access is not controlled, we will have the case of unauthorized access to personal healthcare information	Physical Security	S1. B	Theft, disclosure	IAM-02, IAM-04, IAM-05	Are user access policies and procedures established? Are there considerations of higher levels of assurance and multi-factor authentication secrets, e.g., key generation, remote access, and segregation of duties? Is access to data properly segmented? Are there policies and procedures for identity trust verification? Are there proper policies and procedures in place to manage identity and access to data? Are there policies in place to restrict users as per defined segregation? Do these policies and procedures adhere to applicable legal, statutory or regulatory compliance obligations?
		Legal trans-border requirements	S1. D	Disclosure		
		Identity and access management (IAM)	S3. F	Loss, theft, disclosure		

for both the cloud service provider and the customer. If access is not adequately controlled/managed by the cloud service provider, the lack of control will create vulnerabilities which could lead to unauthorized access. It is also important for the cloud service provider to be compliant with jurisdictional laws if data is traveling trans-border, to avoid unauthorized access due to relatively looser laws in a particular jurisdiction. Different customers in the cloud share space, applications, and servers; this is due to the multitenant nature of cloud computing. It is therefore essential for the cloud service provider to ensure proper management of access, otherwise information can be obtained by unauthorized users. Moreover, due to the nature of personally identifiable information health insurance providers possess, it is essential to make sure identity and access management are adequately addressed.

To mitigate these issues, the CSA requires specific IAM control requirements such as IAM-02, IAM-04, IAM-05 (presented in Table 3) to be implemented by a cloud service provider and the service customer. To help define and ensure proper authentication, access control, and management of the digital credential lifecycle of an assured identity whether human, device or process (Priya & Prabakaran, 2012). As a recommendation for analysis, health insurance companies should question whether proper authentication processes are in place, how access is controlled and managed, whether the appropriate policies are in place for compliance, what measures are in place to restrict access, who in the cloud has access to data, whether processes and procedures in place for identity verification, and so forth. Health insurance providers should implement strong password policies, perform regular vulnerability assessment, and train employees on the importance of security and privacy.

Table 5 in Appendix A contains the full table of the evaluation template that contains security and privacy issues, risk factors, mitigating control requirements, and recommendations for analysis of security and privacy parameters.

The identified risk factors were mapped to their individual security and privacy issues. Table 3 contains a snippet of Table 6 in Appendix B. Using Table 2 as an example, the risk factors identified for each security and privacy issue, identity and access management are:

Table 3. Sample of Appendix B with risk factors mapped to security and privacy issues of cloud computing for issues particular to identity and access management

Risk Factors	Risk Related	Description
Physical security	Theft, disclosure	In an IaaS model, physical computer resources are shared with other entities in the cloud. If physical access to the CSP's infrastructure is granted to one entity, that entity could potentially access information assets of other entities. The CSP is responsible for applying physical security measures to protect assets against destruction or unauthorized access.
Legal trans-border requirements	Disclosure	CSPs are often trans-border, and different countries have different legal requirements, especially concerning personal private information. The enterprise might be violating regulations in other countries when storing, processing, or transmitting data within the CSP's infrastructure without the necessary compliance controls. Furthermore, government entities in the hosting country may require access to the enterprise's information with or without proper notification
Identity and access management (IAM)	Loss, theft, and disclosure	To maximize their revenues, CSPs offer their services and applications to several customers concurrently. Those customers share servers, applications, and, eventually, data. If data access is not adequately managed by the CSP application, one customer could obtain access to another customer's data.

S1. H – Physical security: If physical assess is not adequately controlled by a cloud service provider, access granted to one entity can be used to access the information of other customers, which can lead to unauthorized access.

S1. D – for legal trans-border requirements: Since there are different legal requirements from various countries concerning personal information, not having compliance controls might lead to unauthorized access.

S3. F – for IAM: Since cloud service providers offer cloud spaces to different customers at the same time, customers can share servers, application, and data. If access is not adequately managed by the cloud service provider, one customer might have unauthorized access to another customer's information in the cloud. Table 3 also identifies related risks, if the issue is not handled correctly. Related risks ranged from theft and disclosure to loss. Appendix B contains the full table of risk factors and related risk mapped to specific privacy and security risk.

A sample of Table 7 in Appendix C containing mitigation control requirements from the CSA CCM v 3.0.1 is presented in Table 4. Using Table 2 as a point of departure, after identifying risk factors and risk related by the security and privacy issues of cloud computing in healthcare, the risk factors S1. H – Physical security; S1. D – for legal trans-border requirements; and S3. F – for IAM were mapped

Table 4. Sample of Appendix C with mitigating control requirements from the CSA CCM for identity and access management issues

Control Domain	Control Specification
Identity & Access Management Credential Lifecycle/ Provision Management	User access policies and procedures shall be established, and supporting business processes and technical measures implemented, for ensuring the appropriate identity, entitlement, and access management for all internal corporate and customer (tenant) users with access to data and organizationally-owned or managed (physical and virtual) application interfaces and infrastructure network and systems components. These policies, procedures, processes, and measures must incorporate the following: • Procedures, supporting roles, and responsibilities for provisioning and de-provisioning user account entitlements following the rule of least privilege based on job function (e.g., internal employee and contingent staff personnel changes, customer-controlled access, suppliers' business relationships, or other third-party business relationships) • Business case considerations for higher levels of assurance and multi-factor authentication secrets (e.g., management interfaces, key generation, remote access, segregation of duties, emergency access, large-scale provisioning or geographically-distributed deployments, and personnel redundancy for critical systems). • Access segmentation to sessions and data in multi-tenant architectures by any third party (e.g., provider or other customer (tenant). • Identity trust verification and service-to-service application (API) and information processing inter-operability (e.g., SSO and federation) • Account credential lifecycle management from instantiation through revocation. • Account credential and/or identity store minimization or re-use when feasible. • Authentication, authorization, and accounting (AAA) rules for access to data and sessions (e.g., encryption and strong/multi-factor, expirable, non-shared authentication secrets). • Permissions and supporting capabilities for customer (tenant) controls over authentication, authorization, and accounting (AAA) rules for access to data and sessions. • Adherence to applicable legal, statutory, or regulatory compliance requirements.
Identity & Access Management Policies & procedures	Policies and procedures shall be established to store and manage identity information about every person who accesses IT infrastructure and to determine their level of access. Policies shall also be developed to control access to network resources based on user identity.
Identity & Access Management Segregation of duties	User access policies and procedures shall be established, and supporting business processes and technical measures implemented, for restricting user access as per defined segregation of duties to address business risks associated with a user-role conflict of interest.

to mitigating controls requirements from the CSA CCM v 3.0.1. The control requirements represented by their control ID include IAM-02, which requires the cloud service provider to establish policies and procedures to ensure identity and access are adequately managed. IAM-02 incorporates guidelines on what the policies and procedures should contain. IAM-04 deals with the management of identities—it requires the cloud service provider to establish policies and procedure to manage identities of everyone who will have access to the information stored in the cloud system and should also determine their level of access. Policies and procedures should be established to manage access to network resources: IAM-05 requires the cloud service provider to develop policies and procedures to manage access to each of the isolations created. Since every customer has its section of storage in the cloud, this control requirement ensures that rules are in place to manage each separation.

CONCLUSION

Cloud computing in healthcare provides economic, operational, and functional advantages, but the continued rise of attacks targeting the healthcare industries has raised concerns about security and privacy of information in a cloud infrastructure controlled by a cloud service provider. This rise in attacks has necessitated the use of an assessment tool prior to cloud service adoption in the industry. It is therefore of utmost importance for cloud service providers to implement security controls for the identified security and privacy concerns of the healthcare industry and to ensure transparency to gain users' trust.

This research presented a study of critical security and privacy issues that affect the confidentiality, integrity, and availability of user applications and data in healthcare cloud computing. The research identified the features, capabilities, and advantages of cloud computing in healthcare by conducting a literature review. While conducting this review, security and privacy issues in healthcare cloud computing were identified and subsequently mapped to risk increasing and decreasing factors from the *COBIT 5, Assurance in the cloud*. The risk factors were then mapped to control requirements from the CSA cloud control matrix (CCM) to mitigate each of the risks identified.

This study has been able to develop an assessment tool which can be used by health insurance companies as a guide for service level agreement (SLA) drafting and/or requirements by health insurance providers when choosing a cloud service provider.

As previously mentioned in the methodology section, the scope of this research was limited to major security and privacy issues in cloud computing for healthcare industries identified from the study of related works. As cloud computing evolves, more security issues and risks may arise, especially since the healthcare industry has started embracing cloud technology to an even greater extent. This continuing trend will force cloud service providers to be prepared to confront emerging security issues by identifying more cutting edge mitigating control.

REFERENCES

Accenture. (2015). *The Revenue Risk and Human Impact of Healthcare Provider Cyber Security Inaction.*

Ahuja, S. P., Mani, S., & Zambrano, J. (2012, November 2). A Survey of the State of Cloud Computing in Healthcare. *Canadian Center of Science and Education, 1*, 8.

Becker, J. D., & Bailey, E. (2014). A Comparison of IT Governance & Control Frameworks in Cloud Computing. In *Twentieth Americas Conference on Information Systems (AMCIS)* (pp. 1825–1840). Savanah: Association for Information Systems (AIS).

Canadian Life Health Insurance Association (CLHIA). (n.d.). *A guide to supplementary health insurance.*

Cloud Standards Customer Council. (2017, February). Impact of Cloud Computing in Healthcare IT. *Cloud Standards Customer Council, 2*, 20–35.

Daman, R., Tripathi, M. M., & Mishra, S. K. (2016). Security Issues in Cloud Computing for Healthcare. In *2016 International Conference on Computing for Sustainable Global Development (INDIAcom).*

Gatewood, V. (2013). Aspirations to Reality: Filling the Cloud Computing Performance Gap. *ISACA, 2*, 6–9.

Gavrilov, G., & Trajkovik, V. (2012). Security and Privacy Issues and Requirements for Healthcare Cloud Computing. In *ICT Innovations 2012 proceedings.*

Gbadeyan, A., Butakov, S., & Aghili, S. (2017, June). IT governance and risk mitigation approach for private cloud adoption: Case study provincial health providers. *Annales des Télécommunications, 72*(5–6), 347–357. doi:10.100712243-017-0568-5

Hassan, T., James, B. J., & Gail-Joon, A. (2010, December 03). Security and Privacy Challenges in Cloud Computing Environments. *IEEE Security and Privacy, 8*(6), 24–31. doi:10.1109/MSP.2010.186

Identity Theft Resource Center. (2017). *Data Breaches increase by 40 percent in 2016.* Identity Theft Resource Center.

Infosec Institute. (2017). *The Breach of Anthem Health-The largest healthcare breach in history.* Infosec Institute.

Institute of Medicine (US) Committee on Health Research and the Privacy of Health Information. (2009). The Value and Importance of Health Information Privacy. In J. N. Sharyl, A. L. Laura, & O. G. Lawrence (Eds.), *Beyond the HIPAA Privacy Rule: Enhancing Privacy, Improving Health Through Research. Washington, DC*: National Academies Press.

Intel IT Center. (2013, January). Healthcare Cloud Security. *Intel IT Center: Industry Brief*, 10–15.

ISACA. (2012). Security Considerations for Cloud Computing. *ISACA*, 50–80.

HIPAA Journal. (2017, Jan 4). *Largest Healthcare Data Breaches Of 2016.* Retrieved from https://www.hipaajournal.com/largest-healthcare-data-breaches-of-2016-8631/

Kuo, A. M.-H. (2011, September 21). Opportunities and Challenges of Cloud Computing to Improve health care services. *Journal of Medical Internet Research*, 13. PMID:21937354

Meli, P., & Grance, T. (2011, September). The NIST Definition of Cloud Computing. *NIST Special Publication, 15*, 7.

Mennes, F. (2016, June 2). The Impact of Data Breaches Within the Healthcare Industries. *Vasco Worldwide.*

Priya, C., & Prabakaran, N. (2012, October). Security Management in Inter-cloud. *International Journal of Emerging Trends of Technology in Computer Science, 1*(3), 233–235.

Ravi, T., & Sankar, S. (2015). Measuring the Security Compliance Using Cloud Control Matrix. *Middle East Journal of Scientific Research.*

Reuters. (2017, June 23). *Anthem to Pay Record $115M to Settle Law Suits Over Data Breach.* Retrieved November 2017, from https://www.nbcnews.com/news/us-news/anthem-pay-record-115m-settle-lawsuits-over-data-breach-n776246

Sajib, A., & Abbas, H. (2016). Data Privacy in Cloud-assisted Healthcare Systems: State of Art and Future Challenges. *Journal of Medical Systems, 40*(155). PMID:27155893

Shariati, S. M. & Ahmadzadegan, M. H. (2015). Challenges and Security Issues in Cloud Computing from two Perspectives: Data Security and Privacy Protection. Tehran, Iran: IEEE.

Takabi, H., James, B., & Ahn, G.-J. (n.d.). Security and Privacy Challenges in Cloud Computing Environments. *University of Pittsburgh.*

Takabi, H., & Joshi, J. B. (2012). Policy Management as a Service: An Approach to Manage Policy Heterogeneity in Cloud Computing Environment. In *2012 45th Hawaii International Conference On System Sciences.*

Theoharidou, M., Papanikolaou, N., Pearson, S., & Gritzalis, D. (2013). Privacy Risks, Security Accountability in the Cloud. In *5th IEEE Conference on Cloud Computing Technology and Science* (pp. 177-184). United Kingdom: IEEE Press. 10.1109/CloudCom.2013.31

Wan, D., Greenway, A., Harris, J. G., & Alter, A. E. (2010). *Six questions every health industry executive should ask about cloud computing.* Accenture. Retrieved from http://newsroom.accenture.com/images/20020/HealthcareCloud.pdf

Wang, C., Ren, K., Lou, W., & Li, J. (2010, July/August). Toward Publicly Auditable Secure Cloud Data Storage Services. Retrieved from http://ieeexplore.ieee.org/stamp/stamp.jsp?tp=&arnumber=5510914

Xiao, Z., & Xiao, Y. (2013, June). Security and Privacy in Cloud Computing. *IEEE Communication surveys & tutorials, 15*(2).

Zhang, R., & Lui, L. (2010). Security Models and Requirements for Healthcare Application Clouds. In *IEEE 3rd International Conference on Cloud Computing* (pp. 268–275). Miami, Florida: IEEE.

This research was previously published in the International Journal of Monitoring and Surveillance Technologies Research (IJMSTR), 5(4); edited by Nikolaos Bourbakis and Konstantina S. Nikita, pages 1-22, copyright year 2017 by IGI Publishing (an imprint of IGI Global).

APPENDIX A

Table 5. Mapping of risk factors to mitigating controls using the Cloud Control Matrix (CCM) creating an assessment tool

Security and Privacy Issues	Description	Risk Factors From the COBIT 5 for Assurance in the Cloud			Cloud Control Matrix V3.0.1	Recommendation for Analysis
		Risk Factor	Code	Risk Related	Control ID	
Identity and Access Management	Security technique used to regulate who or what can view or use resources in a computing environment. In the case where access is not controlled, we will have the case of unauthorized access to personal healthcare information	Physical Security	S1.H	Theft, disclosure	IAM-02, IAM-04, IAM-05	Are user access policies and procedures established? Are there considerations of higher levels of assurance and multifactor authentication secrets e.g. key generation, remote access, segregation of duties? Is access to data properly segmented? Are there policies and procedures for identity trust verification? Are there proper policies and procedures in place to manage identity & access to data? Are there policies in place to restrict users as per defined segregation? Do these policies and procedures adhere to applicable legal, statutory ore regulatory compliance obligations?
Data protection	Laws and policies designed to protect personal information that is collected, processed and stored by an automated means, such as the cloud.	Browser vulnerabilities	S3. K	Theft, disclosure	DSI-01 DSI-02 DSI-07 HRS-06 GRM- 04	Is the data in the cloud is encrypted at rest and in transit? Are the communication channels secure? Are the data's stored assigned classifications by data owner, type, sensitivity and criticality? Are there policies and procedures in place for secure disposal and complete removal of data in the cloud?
Regulatory compliance/ Legal obligations	Adherence to laws, policies, regulations, guidelines, and specification relevant to the security of data. Privacy laws and regulations differ at national, regional and local levels, making compliance a potentially complicated issue for cloud computing.	Legal trans-border requirements	S1. D,	Disclosure	AAC-01 AAC-02 AAC-03 STA- 09 SEF– 03 HRS-10	Will the cloud service provider be prepared to allow external audits for regulatory purposes? Are independent reviews and assessment conducted at least annually to address policies, standards, procedures and compliance obligations? Is there a control framework to capture standards, regulatory, legal and statutory requirements? Is the CSP compliant with information security and confidentiality and access control?
		Ease to contract SaaS	S3. I,	Loss, theft, disclosure, unavailability		
		Lack of visibility surrounding technical security measures in place	S1. F	Loss, theft, disclosure, unavailability		
Multitenancy/ data segregation	A cloud computing architecture that allows, customers, to share computing resources in a public or private cloud. The failure of mechanism separating storage, memory, routing, and reputation among different tenants of the shared infrastructure.	Multitenancy and isolation failure	S1. E	Theft, disclosure	IVS-09 DSI- 01	What is put in place to ensure that data collected from each customer is appropriately segregated? Are there established policies and procedures to properly segment user access? Is the data segmented in compliance to legal, statutory and regulatory compliance obligations? Is the data classified by the owner based on data type, value, sensitivity and criticality?
Secured Architecture	Virtualized cloud infrastructures offer an even larger potential attack surface. Malware and rootkits can easily infect hypervisor, BIOS and operating systems spread throughout the environment.	Lack of visibility surrounding technical security measures in place	S1. F	Loss, theft, disclosure, unavailability	AIS-01, IVS-07	Are the systems hardened to suit business needs? What are the security measures in place to protect the architecture? Is the cloud architecture designed, developed and deployed using leading industry standards? Does the architecture adhere to applicable legal, statutory or regulatory compliance obligations?
		Lack of visibility into Software Development Lifecycle (SDLC)	S3. E	Loss, theft, disclosure, unavailability		

continued on following page

Table 5. Continued

Security and Privacy Issues	Description	Risk Factors From the COBIT 5 for Assurance in the Cloud			Cloud Control Matrix V3.0.1	Recommendation for Analysis
		Risk Factor	Code	Risk Related	Control ID	
Data Jurisdiction	Due to laws in different jurisdiction, it is challenging for data usage compliance to be checked. i.e. to pinpoint where your data is at a time, and if a cloud service provider is compliant with those laws.	Legal trans-border requirements	S1. D	Theft, disclosure	SEF-01 AIS- 04	What are the policies or procedures in place for data security to include confidentiality, integrity and availability in different jurisdictions to prevent improper disclosure, alteration or destruction? Are points of contacts for applicable regulatory authorities, national and local enforcements, and other legal jurisdictional authorities maintained and regularly updated? Has direct compliance liaison been established? Do these policies and procedures adhere to applicable legal, statutory ore regulatory compliance obligations?
Vendor Lock-in / Portability issues	A customer no being able to move from one provider to the other. Lack of interoperability of interfaces associated with cloud services ties the customer to a provider.	Exit strategy	S3. G	Loss, unavailability	IPY-01, IPY-03, IPY-04, IPY-05	Does the system support interoperability? What is the process in place to ensure a safe migration if needed? Does the CSP use open and published APIs to ensure support for interoperability between components to facilitate migration application? Are there secure standardized network protocols in place to import and export data? Do these policies and procedures adhere to applicable legal, statutory ore regulatory compliance obligations?
Loss of Governance / Control or Ownership of information	Control information is ceded to the cloud service provider, due to lack of appropriate internal security.	Application disposal	S2. D,	Theft, disclosure	GRM-09 GRM-10	Has the ownership of data been defined?
		Data ownership	S3. C	Loss, disclosure, unavailability		
Data management	The software and technologies designed for operations and monitoring applications, data and services in the cloud. For healthcare deploying data management tools that provide visibility across the cloud to ensure agreed-to policies is essential.	Data disposal	S3. D,	Theft, disclosure	AIS-02, AIS-03, AIS-04, DSI- 02, DSI-03, DSI- 07, EKM- 03, EKM- 04, BCR- 11, HRS- 06	In case of termination of a contract, have there been defined process on how data will be disposed of? Are their policies and procedures in place for using encryption in the protection of sensitive data? Are there policies and procedures in place for the use of encryption protocols for protection of sensitive data in the cloud? What kind of platform and data appropriate encryptions are being used? Are policies and procedures in place for defining and adhering to retention period of any critical asset? Do these policies and procedures adhere to applicable legal, statutory ore regulatory compliance obligations?
		Data ownership	S3.C	Loss, disclosure, unavailability		
Unauthorized Disclosure	A process where data in the cloud is disclosed due to unauthorized access to others using the cloud.	Multitenancy and isolation failure	S1. E	Theft, disclosure	AIS-02, AIS-03, AIS-04, DSI- 02, DSI-03, EKM- 03, EKM- 04, GRM- 04, HRS- 06	What are the policies and procedures in place to prevent unauthorized disclosure? How often are the policies and procedures updated? What are the procedures in place for proper data disposal to avoid unauthorized disclosure?
		Data Disposal	S1. I	Disclosure		
		Data Disposal	S3. D	Theft, disclosure		
Distributed denial of service (DDoS)	Distributed Denial of Service attacks aims at overloading a resource (network or service interface) by flooding it with requests from many sources spread across a wide geographical or topological area so that the legitimate users are unable to use the resource as intended.	Scalability. / Elasticity	S1. A	Unavailability	IVS-13	What are the procedures and policies in place to prevent DDoS? Are defence-in-depth techniques applied to detect and respond timely to network based attacks?
Recovery	In the case of a natural disaster or an attack, unavailability of a backup system can lead to total loss of information stored in the cloud	Absence of DRP and Backup	S1. G,	Unavailability, loss	BCR- 11	In the case of a disaster, what is the process for recovery? What happens to the user information in the case of disaster?
		Disaster recovery and backup	S1. B	Unavailability, loss	BCR-11	

APPENDIX B

Table 6. Specifications of risk factors mapped to identified security and privacy issues as described in the Cobit 5 controls and assurance in the cloud

Risk Factor	Code	Risk Related	Description
Infrastructure as a Service (IaaS)			
Scalability/ elasticity	S1. A	Unavailability	Lack of physical resources is no longer an issue. Due to the scalable nature of cloud technologies, the CSP can provide capacity on demand at low cost to support peak loads (expected or unexpected). Elasticity eliminates overprovisioning and under provisioning of IT resources, allowing better cost optimization. This becomes a great advantage for resilience when defensive measures or resources need to be expanded quickly (e.g., during DDoS attacks).
Disaster recovery and back up	S1. B	Unavailability, loss	CSPs should already have in place, as common practice, disaster recovery and backup procedures. However, recovery point objective (RPO), recovery time objective (RTO), and backup testing frequency and procedures provided by the CSP should be consistent with the enterprise security policy.
Legal trans-border requirements	S1. D	Disclosure	CSPs are often trans-border, and different countries have different legal requirements, especially concerning personal private information. The enterprise might be committing a violation of regulations in other countries when storing, processing or transmitting data within the CSP's infrastructure without the necessary compliance controls. Furthermore, government entities in the hosting country may require access to the enterprise's information with or without proper notification.
Multitenancy and isolation failure	S1. E	Theft, Disclosure	One of the primary benefits of the cloud is the ability to perform dynamic allocation of physical resources when required. The most common approach is a multi-tenant environment (public cloud), where different entities share a pool of resources, including storage, hardware and network components. All resources allocated to a tenant should be "isolated" and protected to avoid disclosure of information to other tenants. For example, when allocated storage is no longer needed by a client, it can be freely reallocated to another enterprise. In that case, sensitive data could be disclosed if the storage has not been scrubbed thoroughly (e.g., using forensic software).
Lack of visibility surrounding technical security measures in place	SI. F	Loss, theft, disclosure, unavailability	For any infrastructure, intrusion detection systems (IDS)/intrusion prevention systems(IPS) and security incident and event management (SIEM) capabilities must be in place. It is the responsibility of the CSP to provide these capabilities to its customers. To ensure that there are no security gaps, the security policy and governance of the CSP should match those of the enterprise.
Absence of DRP and backup	SI. G	Unavailability, loss	The absence of a proper DRP or backup procedures imply a high risk for any enterprise. CSPs should provide such basic preventive measures aligned with the enterprise's business needs (in terms of RTO/RPO).
Physical security	SI. H	Theft, disclosure	In an IaaS model, physical computer resources are shared with other entities in the cloud. If physical access to the CSP's infrastructure is granted to one entity, that entity could potentially access information assets of other entities. The CSP is responsible for applying physical security measures to protect assets against destruction or unauthorized access.
Data disposal	SI. I	Disclosure	Proper disposal of data is imperative to prevent unauthorized disclosure. If appropriate measures are not taken by the CSP, information assets could be sent (without approval) to countries where the data can be legally disclosed due to different regulations concerning sensitive data. Disks could be replaced, recycled or upgraded without proper cleaning so that the information remains within storage and can later be retrieved. When a contract expires, CSPs should ensure the safe disposal or destruction of any previous backups.

continued on following page

Table 6. Continued

Risk Factor	Code	Risk Related	Description
Application disposal	S2. D	Theft, disclosure	If current applications are not perfectly aligned with the capabilities provided by the CSP, additional undesirable features (and vulnerabilities) could be introduced.
Data Ownership	S3. C	Unavailability, loss, disclosure	The CSP provides the applications and the customer provides the data. If data ownership is not clearly defined, the CSP could refuse access to data when required or even demand fees to return the data once the service contracts are terminated.
Data disposal	S3. D	Theft, disclosure	In the event of a contract termination, the data fed into the CSP's application must be erased immediately using the necessary tools to avoid disclosures and confidentiality breaches (forensic cleaning may be required for sensitive data).
Lack of visibility into SDLC	S3. E	Unavailability, theft, loss, disclosure	Enterprises that use cloud applications have little visibility into the software SDLC. Customers do not know in detail how the applications were developed and what security considerations were considered during the SDLC. This could lead to an imbalance between the security provided by the application and the security required by customers/users.
Identity and access management (IAM)	S3. F	Theft, loss, disclosure	To maximize their revenues, CSPs offer their services and applications to several customers concurrently. Those customers share servers, applications and, eventually, data. If data access is not properly managed by the CSP application, one customer could obtain access to another customer's data.
Exit strategy	S3. G	Unavailability, loss	Currently, there is very little available in terms of tools, procedures or other offerings to facilitate data or service portability from CSP to CSP. This can make it very difficult for the enterprise to migrate from one CSP to another or to bring services back in-house. It can also result in serious business disruption or failure should the CSP go bankrupt, face legal action, or be the potential target for an acquisition (with the likelihood of sudden changes in CSP policies and any agreements in place). If the customer-CSP relationship goes sour and the enterprise wants to bring the data back in-house, the question of how to securely render the data becomes critical because the in-house applications may have been decommissioned or "sunsetted" and there is no application available to render the data.
Ease to contract SaaS	S3. I	Unavailability, theft, loss, disclosure	Business organizations may contract cloud applications without proper procurement and approval oversight, thus bypassing compliance with internal enterprise policies.
Browser vulnerabilities	S3. K	Theft, disclosure	As a common practice, applications offered by SaaS providers are accessible to customers via secure communication through a web browser. Web browsers are a common target for malware and attacks. If the customer's browser becomes infected, the access to the application can be compromised as well.

APPENDIX C

Table 7. Specification of control requirements from the Cloud Control Matrix V 3.0.1 mapped to identified risk factors Cobit 5 for assurance in the cloud document

Control Domain	CCM V3.0 Control ID	Specification
Audit Assurance & Compliance Audit Planning	AAC- 01	Audit plans shall be developed and maintained to address business process disruptions. Auditing plans shall focus on reviewing the effectiveness of the implementation of security operations. All audit activities must be agreed upon prior to executing any audits.
Audit Assurance & Compliance Independent Audits	AAC- 02	Independent reviews and assessments shall be performed at least annually to ensure that the organization addresses nonconformities of established policies, standards, procedures, and compliance obligations.
Audit Assurance & Compliance Information Systems Regulatory Mapping	AAC- 03	Organizations shall create and maintain a control framework which captures standards, regulatory, legal, and statutory requirements relevant for their business needs. The control framework shall be reviewed at least annually to ensure changes that could affect the business processes are reflected.
Application & Interface Security Application Security	AIS-01	Applications and programming interfaces (APIs) shall be designed, developed, deployed, and tested in accordance with leading industry standards (e.g., OWASP for web applications) and adhere to applicable legal, statutory, or regulatory compliance obligations.
Application & Interface Security Customer Access Requirements	AIS -02	Prior to granting customers access to data, assets, and information systems, identified security, contractual, and regulatory requirements for customer access shall be addressed.
Application & Interface Security Data Integrity	AIS-03	Data input and output integrity routines (i.e., reconciliation and edit checks) shall be implemented for application interfaces and databases to prevent manual or systematic processing errors, corruption of data, or misuse.
Application & Interface Security Data Security / Integrity	AIS-04	Policies and procedures shall be established and maintained in support of data security to include (confidentiality, integrity, and availability) across multiple system interfaces, jurisdictions, and business functions to prevent improper disclosure, alteration, or destruction.
Business Continuity Management & Op Resilience	BCR-11	Policies and procedures shall be established, and supporting business processes and technical measures implemented, for defining and adhering to the retention period of any critical asset as per established policies and procedures, as well as applicable legal, statutory, or regulatory compliance obligations. Backup and recovery measures shall be incorporated as part of business continuity planning and tested accordingly for effectiveness.
Data Security & Information Lifecycle Management Classification	DSI- 01	Data and objects containing data shall be assigned a classification by the data owner based on data type, value, sensitivity, and criticality to the organization.
Data Security & Information Lifecycle Management Data Inventory / Flows	DSI-02	Policies and procedures shall be established, and supporting business processes and technical measures implemented, to inventory, document, and maintain data flows for data that is resident (permanently or temporarily) within the service's geographically distributed (physical and virtual) applications and infrastructure network and systems components and/or shared with other third parties to ascertain any regulatory, statutory, or supply chain agreement (SLA) compliance impact, and to address any other business risks associated with the data. Upon request, provider shall inform customer (tenant) of compliance impact and risk, especially if customer data is used as part of the services.

continued on following page

Table 7. Continued

Control Domain	CCM V3.0 Control ID	Specification
Data Security & Information Lifecycle Management Ecommerce Transactions	DSI-03	Data related to electronic commerce (ecommerce) that traverse's public networks shall be appropriately classified and protected from fraudulent activity, unauthorized disclosure, or modification in such a manner to prevent contract dispute and compromise of data.
Data Security & Information Lifecycle Management Secure Disposal	DSI-07	Policies and procedures shall be established with supporting business processes and technical measures implemented for the secure disposal and complete removal of data from all storage media, ensuring data is not recoverable by any computer forensic means.
Encryption & Key Management Sensitive Data Protection	EKM-03	Policies and procedures shall be established, and supporting business processes and technical measures implemented, for the use of encryption protocols for protection of sensitive data in storage (e.g., file servers, databases, and end-user workstations), data in use (memory), and data in transmission (e.g., system interfaces, over public networks, and electronic messaging) as per applicable legal, statutory, and regulatory compliance obligations.
Encryption & Key Management Storage and Access	EKM-04	Platform and data-appropriate encryption (e.g., AES-256) in open/validated formats and standard algorithms shall be required. Keys shall not be stored in the cloud (i.e., at the cloud provider in question), but maintained by the cloud consumer or trusted key management provider. Key management and key usage shall be separated duties
Governance and Risk Management Program	GRM-04	An Information Security Management Program (ISMP) shall be developed, documented, approved, and implemented that includes administrative, technical, and physical safeguards to protect assets and data from loss, misuse, unauthorized access, disclosure, alteration, and destruction. The security program shall include, but not be limited to, the following areas insofar as they relate to the characteristics of the business: • Risk management • Security policy • Organization of information security • Asset management • Human resources security • Physical and environmental security • Communications and operations management • Access control • Information systems acquisition, development, and maintenance
Governance and Risk Management Policy Review	GRM- 09	The organization's business leadership (or other accountable business role or function) shall review the information security policy at planned intervals or as a result of changes to the organization to ensure its continuing alignment with the security strategy, effectiveness, accuracy, relevance, and applicability to legal, statutory, or regulatory compliance obligations.
Governance and Risk Management Risk Assessment	GRM- 10	Aligned with the enterprise-wide framework, formal risk assessments shall be performed at least annually or at planned intervals, (and in conjunction with any changes to information systems) to determine the likelihood and impact of all identified risks using qualitative and quantitative methods. The likelihood and impact associated with inherent and residual risk shall be determined independently, considering all risk categories (e.g., audit results, threat and vulnerability analysis, and regulatory compliance).
Human Resources Non-Disclosure Agreements	HRS-06	Requirements for non-disclosure or confidentiality agreements reflecting the organization's needs for the protection of data and operational details shall be identified, documented, and reviewed at planned intervals.
Human Resources User Responsibility	HRS- 10	All personnel shall be made aware of their roles and responsibilities for: • Maintaining awareness and compliance with established policies and procedures and applicable legal, statutory, or regulatory compliance obligations. • Maintaining a safe and secure working environment

continued on following page

Table 7. Continued

Control Domain	CCM V3.0 Control ID	Specification
Identity & Access Management Credential Lifecycle / Provision Management	IAM-02	User access policies and procedures shall be established, and supporting business processes and technical measures implemented, for ensuring appropriate identity, entitlement, and access management for all internal corporate and customer (tenant) users with access to data and organizationally-owned or managed (physical and virtual) application interfaces and infrastructure network and systems components. These policies, procedures, processes, and measures must incorporate the following: • Procedures, supporting roles, and responsibilities for provisioning and de-provisioning user account entitlements following the rule of least privilege based on job function (e.g., internal employee and contingent staff personnel changes, customer-controlled access, suppliers' business relationships, or other third-party business relationships) • Business case considerations for higher levels of assurance and multi-factor authentication secrets (e.g., management interfaces, key generation, remote access, segregation of duties, emergency access, large-scale provisioning or geographically-distributed deployments, and personnel redundancy for critical systems) • Access segmentation to sessions and data in multi-tenant architectures by any third party (e.g., provider and/or other customer (tenant)) • Identity trust verification and service-to-service application (API) and information processing interoperability (e.g., SSO and federation) • Account credential lifecycle management from instantiation through revocation • Account credential and/or identity store minimization or re-use when feasible • Authentication, authorization, and accounting (AAA) rules for access to data and sessions (e.g., encryption and strong/multi-factor, expire able, non-shared authentication secrets) • Permissions and supporting capabilities for customer (tenant) controls over authentication, authorization, and accounting (AAA) rules for access to data and sessions • Adherence to applicable legal, statutory, or regulatory compliance requirements
Identity & Access Management Policies and Procedures	IAM-04	Policies and procedures shall be established to store and manage identity information about every person who accesses IT infrastructure and to determine their level of access. Policies shall also be developed to control access to network resources based on user identity.
Identity & Access Management Segregation of Duties	IAM-05	User access policies and procedures shall be established, and supporting business processes and technical measures implemented, for restricting user access as per defined segregation of duties to address business risks associated with a user-role conflict of interest.
Interoperability & Portability APIs	IPY-01	The provider shall use open and published APIs to ensure support for interoperability between components and to facilitate migrating applications.
Interoperability & Portability Policy & Legal	IPY-03	Policies, procedures, and mutually-agreed upon provisions and/or terms shall be established to satisfy customer (tenant) requirements for service-to-service application (API) and information processing interoperability, and portability for application development and information exchange, usage, and integrity persistence.
Interoperability & Portability Standardized Network Protocols	IPY-04	The provider shall use secure (e.g., non-clear text and authenticated) standardized network protocols for the import and export of data and to manage the service, and shall make available a document to consumers (tenants) detailing the relevant interoperability and portability standards that are involved.
Interoperability & Portability Virtualization	IPY-05	The provider shall use an industry-recognized virtualization platform and standard virtualization formats (e.g., OVF) to help ensure interoperability, and shall have documented custom changes made to any hypervisor in use and all solution-specific virtualization hooks available for customer review.

continued on following page

Table 7. Continued

Control Domain	CCM V3.0 Control ID	Specification
Infrastructure & Virtualization Security Network Security	IVS-06	Network environments and virtual instances shall be designed and configured to restrict and monitor traffic between trusted and untrusted connections. These configurations shall be reviewed at least annually, and supported by a documented justification for use for all allowed services, protocols, and ports, and by compensating controls.
Infrastructure & Virtualization Security OS Hardening and Base Controls	IVS-07	Each operating system shall be hardened to provide only necessary ports, protocols, and services to meet business needs and have in place supporting technical controls such as: antivirus, file integrity monitoring, and logging as part of their baseline operating build standard or template.
Infrastructure & Virtualization Security VM Security – Data Protection	IVS- 09	Multi-tenant organizationally-owned or managed (physical and virtual) applications, and infrastructure system and network components, shall be designed, developed, deployed, and configured such that provider and customer (tenant) user access is appropriately segmented from other tenant users, based on the following considerations: • Established policies and procedures • Isolation of business critical assets and/or sensitive user data, and sessions that mandate stronger internal controls and high levels of assurance • Compliance with legal, statutory, and regulatory compliance obligations
Infrastructure & Virtualization Security VM Security - Data Protection	IVS-10	Secured and encrypted communication channels shall be used when migrating physical servers, applications, or data to virtualized servers and, where possible, shall use a network segregated from production-level networks for such migrations.
Infrastructure & Virtualization Security Hypervisor Hardening	IVS-11	Access to all hypervisor management functions or administrative consoles for systems hosting virtualized systems shall be restricted to personnel based upon the principle of least privilege and supported through technical controls (e.g., two-factor authentication, audit trails, IP address filtering, firewalls, and TLS encapsulated communications to the administrative consoles).
Infrastructure & Virtualization Security Network Architecture	IVS-13	Network architecture diagrams shall clearly identify high-risk environments and data flows that may have legal compliance impacts. Technical measures shall be implemented and shall apply defense-in-depth techniques (e.g., deep packet analysis, traffic throttling, and black-holing) for detection and timely response to network-based attacks associated with anomalous ingress or egress traffic patterns (e.g., MAC spoofing and ARP poisoning attacks) and/or distributed denial-of-service (DDoS) attacks.
Threat and Vulnerability Management Vulnerability / Patch Management	TVM-02	Policies and procedures shall be established, and supporting processes and technical measures implemented, for timely detection of vulnerabilities within organizationally-owned or managed applications, infrastructure network and system components (e.g., network vulnerability assessment, penetration testing) to ensure the efficiency of implemented security controls. A risk-based model for prioritizing remediation of identified vulnerabilities shall be used. Changes shall be managed through a change management process for all vendor-supplied patches, configuration changes, or changes to the organization's internally developed software. Upon request, the provider informs customer (tenant) of policies and procedures and identified weaknesses especially if customer (tenant) data is used as part the service and/or customer (tenant) has some shared responsibility over implementation of control.

APPENDIX D

Table 8. Summary of literature review and identified gaps from the related works

Topic	Relevant Work Done	Gap Analysis	References
Challenges and Security Issues in Cloud Computing from two perspectives: Data security and privacy protection.	Discussed the advantages of adopting cloud computing and analyzed the issues related to cloud computing regarding security and privacy of user's data in the cloud	Recommendations or mitigation control requirements for the issues found were not discussed. Issues of data Jurisdiction were not discussed.	(Shariati, Abouzarjomehri, & Ahmadzadegan, 2015)
Security Models and Requirements for Healthcare Application Clouds	Discussed essential concepts related to electronic health record sharing and integration of healthcare cloud computing. Analysed security and privacy issues in management and access to electronic health records.	The research focused on security& privacy issues affecting the identity and access management of information in the cloud. Solutions proposed focused only on issues affecting identity and access management.	(Zhang & Liu, 2010)
Data Privacy in cloud-assisted healthcare system: state of the art and future challenges	A systematic literature review was carried out to identify privacy concerns of personal health information in the cloud.	The paper focused mainly on privacy concerns and did not extensively cover other significant security issues.	(Sajib & Abbas, 2016)
Security and Privacy Challenges in Cloud computing environment	The authors discussed security and privacy issues that affect the adoption of cloud computing and various approaches that can be used in addressing these problems	Challenges were based on general cloud computing	(Takabi, Joshi, & Gail-Joon, 2010)
Measuring the Security Compliance Using Cloud Control Matrix	Overview of the implementation of cloud security alliance Cloud control matrix(CCM)	No recommendation or specific controls for security issues in the cloud control matrix.	(Ravi & Sankar, 2015)
Opportunities and challenges of cloud computing to improve healthcare services.	Opportunities and challenges of cloud computing in healthcare are looked at from 4 different aspects namely: security, technical, legal and economic.	No solution/mitigating controls proposed for the challenges of cloud computing.	(Kuo, 2011)
Security Issues in Cloud Computing for Healthcare	They came up with possible risks in cloud computing for healthcare applications	No solution// mitigation controls recommended for the risks identified Issues of data jurisdiction, availability, data segregation are not discussed	Daman, R., Tripathi, M. M., & Mishra, S. K. (2016)
Industry brief of healthcare cloud computing	Provides an overview of the benefits and security challenges of cloud-based infrastructures for healthcare organizations.	Issues of data jurisdiction, availability, data segregation are not discussed	(Intel IT Center 2013)
IT governance and risk mitigation approach for private cloud adoption: case study of provincial healthcare provider	Looked at how to mitigate cloud computing risk from an IT governance perspective for healthcare providers. Using Alberta Health as a case study, with a focus on Alberta Heath's IT Governance	Focused on information risk scenarios only but did not address other cloud computing risk scenarios categories such as regulatory compliance, architecture, software, etc	Gbadeyan, Butakov, & Aghili (2017)

Chapter 51

Identification of Various Privacy and Trust Issues in Cloud Computing Environment

Shivani Jaswal
Chandigarh University, India

Manisha Malhotra
Chandigarh University, India

ABSTRACT

Cloud computing is a rising paradigm in today's world. In this, users can send his or her request to any CSP, i.e., cloud service provider, of their choice. In return, the CSP reverts him back with that particular service. Now, while communicating from various two locations, the data transferred is not passed through that much amount of security and privacy as expected. So, there are lots of parameters in the environment that are taken care of while sending, receiving or just passing data over the network. This chapter presents various security issues that are underlying in cloud computing. This chapter has illustrated various issues such as Trust, Encryption, Authenticity, Confidentiality and Multi Tenancy. Also, some of the proposed solutions have also been discussed later in the chapter.

INTRODUCTION

Cloud Computing has emerged as a latest domain in terms of technology as well as research. It works basically on the principle of 'pay as per the use model". Cloud computing is a fifth generation computing truly based on service provisioning based on virtualization. This model believes in providing various benefits like speedy deployment, pay as per the usage, economical in costs, scalable, rapid in approving requests, long lasting network access, greater resiliency, hypervisor security against system assaults, lower in cost in context of disaster recovery on-request security controls, continuous recognition of framework altering and quick re-constitution of administrations (Armbrust, et al, 2010).

Cloud computing services can be categorized into three categories: Software as a Service (SaaS), Platform as a Service (PaaS) and infrastructure as a Service (IaaS).

DOI: 10.4018/978-1-5225-8176-5.ch051

Here, SaaS facilitates to the clients that wants to access provider's software applications which is going to run on a cloud infrastructure (Aljawarneh,et al, 2016). Applications are managed and controlled by cloud service provider. Customersneed not to buy the software but instead they can use those services by using web API. For example, Google Docs purely relies its working on JAVA Script, which further runs in the Web browser (Bonatti et al, 2000).

One of thecategories of cloud service is Platform-as-a-service (PaaS). It is a service that delivers application.In this, the client can utilize the cloud specialist co-op's applications to send their applications by utilizing different programming dialects and devices bolstered by the supplier. The service provider does not need to deal with the basic cloud framework but rather shows the control over the sent application (Aberer, et al., 2001). A common example of PaaS is Google App Engine that facilitates the developer to run program on Google's Infrastructure.

Another type of cloud service model is known as Infrastructure-as-a-service (IaaS). In this, virtual machine images are provided as a service and machines generally contains what developers actually want. Rather than acquiring servers, programming, server farm assets, arrange hardware, and the skill to work them, clients can purchase these assets as an outsourced benefit conveyed through the system cloud. Also, the user can increase or decrease the quantity of virtual machines as per their increasing or decreasing requirements. For example, host firewalls.

CLOUD COMPUTING ARCHITECTURE

The working of Cloud computing is generally divided into two parts: backend and frontend (Armbrust, et al., 2009). Here, Frontend is basically a "user section" and backend is a "cloud section".Also, there is a server which works in centralized manner which is further helpful in administering the system and checks whether the system is running smoothly or not, by fulfilling the client's demands. The proper functioning of the environment is taken under some set of rules and protocols that uses special software known as middleware (Singh et al, 2014).

Figure 1. Architecture of high-level cloud middleware

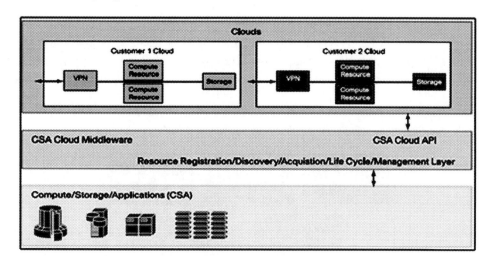

Cloud middleware is also known as Cloud OS, which helps in controlling the services. Networked computers can communicate with each other with the help of middleware. For example: Google App Engine and Amazon EC2/S3.

In an improved vision of the cloud computing, Client sends benefit solicitations to the server. Then system management finds appropriate resources. After the computing resources are found, then the request which was made by client is executed. Finally, the found results are forwarded to clients as a service (Zhang et al, 2010).

INTRODUCTION TO CLOUD COMPUTING CHALLENGES

Over the most recent couple of years, the engaging elements of cloud computing have been filling the incorporation of cloud conditions in the business, which has been therefore inspiring scholarly community and enterprises to proceed onward the way of research (Beth, et al., 1994). Notwithstanding its focal points, the move to this registering worldview raises security concerns, which are the subject of a few reviews. Other than of the issues gotten from Web advancements and the Internet, mists present new issues that ought to be gotten out first keeping in mind the end goal to additionally enable the quantity of cloud arrangements to increment.

The new worldview of Cloud Computing has extreme security dangers to its adopters because of the circulated way of Cloud Computing situations which make them a rich focus for vindictive people. Cloud lives with a completely virtual framework which is, undetectable to the client. This characteristic deliberation guarantees that an application or business administration is not straightforwardly fixing to the basic equipment framework, for example, servers, stockpiling or systems. This permits business administration's to move progressively crosswise over virtualized foundation assets in an exceptionally productive way. In any case, the virtualization strategies utilized as a part of Cloud have various security dangers and assaults (Singh et al, 2015).

As compared to dedicated resource, a Cloud environment which is fully on partially shared, faces a greater risk of attack as compared to dedicated resource environment. Cloud Instances (CIs) are more likely to be got attacked as their task is to move between public and private cloud. Moreover, the easiness of cloning a virtual machine instance leads to propagation of security vulnerabilities and configuration errors. Cloud Consumers run numerous applications/scripts in order to complete their computing tasks. Most of them are too complex and complicated to trust. Even while accessing the source code, it is quite difficult to look after the security of these applications (Rizwana et al, 2012). They might generate codes such as viruses, worms, Trojan horses, bugs that are exploitable to the input generated. It is essential that

Figure 2. Security challenges under the services of cloud computing

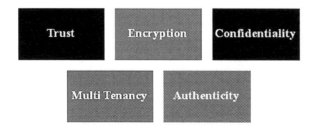

instead of just relying on conventional defense techniques, the next generation of system software must be designed from the ground up to provide stronger isolation of services running on computer systems.

The users and cloud stores sensitive as well as confidential information on to the cloud service provider to reduce cost financially by giving up the control of data of unnecessary data. Therefore, data over the network can be leaked or attacked by the hacker those results in loss of confidential data (Staab et al, (2004).

TRUST

Cloud computing has turned into a conspicuous worldview of registering and IT benefit conveyance. A user can often ask, "Can this model be trusted?" Furthermore, what exactly is the meaning of "trust" in the area or field of cloud computing? What is the ground nature of that trust? (Beth et al, 2004). On this basis of what attributes a client should trust? Who will be the assigned authorities to check, verify, validate or assess cloud attributes? The answers to all the trust based questions are mandatory to be answered so that cloud computing can be adopted widely and finally be helpful in trustworthy computing paradigm (Singh et al, (2016).

Also, instead of informal trust mechanisms, decisions needs to be based on formal trust mechanisms which further helps in making the "official" type of assessment in the society.

Advancement of trust between any cloud specialist co-op and a client goes about as a most compelling motivation of concern now a days. It generally remains an issue of test for a client which cloud specialist co-op he ought to trust upon and whether his information over the system will stay free from gatecrashers or not.To solve this problem, a type of agreement is signed between the cloud service provider and the user. This agreement is known as Service Level Agreement i.e. SLA. It is a legal contract signed among the client (who will be suing the services of cloud) and the CSP (who will be providing services to the user) (Vaquero et al, 2011).

Basically we can divide the challenge of "Trust" into four broader sections i.e.

- Semantics of Trust
- State of the art trust
- Policy based trust judgment
- Evidence based trust

Figure 3. Broader sections of trust

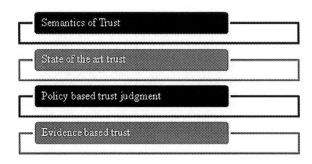

SEMANTICS OF TRUST

Broadly two types of trust can be identified, based on the expectancy of the trustor: *trust in performance* which purely depends upon the performance of the trustee whereas *trust in belief* depends upon the kind of belief a trustee holds. The trustee's execution could be reality of what the trustee says or the accomplishment of what the trustee does (Shaikh et al, 2012).

A trust in performance relationship,

t r u s t _p(d,e, x,k),

Here, trustor = d

trustee = e

performance = x

Above written relationship shows that if e believes x then d also believes x.

trust_b(d,e,x,k)≡believe(e,k⊃ x)⊃believe(d,k⊃)trust_b(d,e,x,k)≡believe(e,k⊃x)⊃believe(d,k⊃x).

Therefore, we can say that "Trust in belief" is transitive whereas trust in performance is not. Also, trust in performance can move through trust in belief. From the definition above, the trustor's mental condition of faith in his hope on the trustee is subject to the confirmation about the trustee's competency, trustworthiness, and goodwill. This prompts sensible structures of thinking from confidence in proof to faith in hope (Jingwei et al, 2013).

STATE OF THE ART TRUST

It can be studied under as:

- Reputation based trust
- SLA verification based trust.

REPUTATION BASED TRUST

Trust and reputation are interrelated, but different in some context. Basically, trust is between two substances; whereas reputation is the compiled opinion of a community towards that substance. We can say that, a community having higher level of reputation is trusted by another number of entities. Also, one who wants to make judgment can make use of calculation and estimation analysis. Here, reputation plays a vital role in choosing any service in some manner. In particular, by the time, a user becomes successful in gaining experience with service.

These sorts of frameworks are broadly utilized as a part of online business and P2P systems. The notoriety of cloud administrations or cloud specialist co-ops will without a doubt affect cloud clients' decision of cloud administrations; thus, cloud suppliers attempt to construct and keep up higher notoriety. Actually, notoriety based trust goes into the vision of making trust judgment in distributed computing (Bonatti et al, 2005).

Reputation plays a key role while choosing a service for the first time. Particularly, while using a service, a user gains experience afterwards, new trust is built regarding service service based on performance or reliability requirements. A specific use cannot trust 100% on any CSP but just taking reputation factor into an account.

SLA VERIFICATION BASED TRUST

"Trust, however confirm" is a solid counsel for managing the connections between cloud clients and cloud specialist co-ops. In the wake of building up the underlying trust and utilizing a cloud administration, the cloud client needs to confirm and reconsider the trust. A service level agreement (SLA) is a legal agreement which is signed between a cloud client and a cloud service provider (Aberer, Ket al, 2001). Therefore, quality of service (QoS) monitors and verification of SLA are an important basis of trust management for cloud computing. A number of models have been proposed that derive trust from SLA verification.

Now, arises the major issues. Sometimes, SLA just focuses on "visible" elements of the service and neglects the "invisible" elements of the services. Also, sometimes, many users do not have capability as well as knowledge regarding monitoring of Quality of Service and SLA verification.

In this way, an expert outsider is expected to give these administrations. In a private cloud, there might be a cloud representative or a trust specialist that is confided in the trust space of the private cloud; so the trusted dealer or trust expert can give the clients in the private cloud the administrations of QoS checking and SLA confirmation. In hybrid clouds, a client inside a private cloud may in any case depend on the private cloud trust expert to lead QoS checking and SLA confirmation; be that as it may, in an open cloud, singular clients and some little associations without specialized ability may utilize a business proficient cloud substance as trust dealer.

POLICY BASED TRUST

This type of trust plays a key role in architecture of open and distributed services as it act as a solution to the problem of authorizing access of control in an open system. The main focus lies on the trust management mechanisms which employ various languages based on policies and various engines that specify reasoning on rules for trust establishment. Here the goal is to think whether an unknown user can be trusted fully or partially, specifically based on credentials and policies (Grandison et al, 2002).

Presently, policy based trust involves various access control decisions. For specifying access control conditions, declarative policies are very well suited that further generates a Boolean decision (in which resources are either granted or denied). Various systems that enforces policy based trust use languages with well defined semantics and further make decisions based on "non subjective" attributes (e.g. address, age etc) which are certified by certification authorities (e.g. digital signatures etc). Generally, policy based trust is developed for the system having strong requirements for protection, for systems having complex rules or for the systems having exact authorization process.

EVIDENCE BASED TRUST

From the meaning of trust given in § 'Semantics of trust', a trustor's faith in the normal conduct of trustee depends on the proof about the trustee's traits of competency, goodwill, and trustworthiness, as for that desire. Formally, we could express a general type of proof based trust as takes after:

believe(u,attr1(s,v1))∧...∧believe(u,attrn(s,vn))→trust_*(u,s,x,c)

which expresses that if an individual u trusts a subject s has property a t r1 with esteem v1,..., trait a t r n with esteem v n, then u trusts (either confide in conviction or trust in execution) s as for x, the execution of s or data made or accepted by s, in a particular setting.

TRUST MODEL

Numerous endeavors have been done in setting of creating trust. A trust model is displayed into upgrade the security and interoperability of distributed computing condition. Imposing Healthcare Social Cloud introduces a trust rating instrument to secure the cloud condition in a joint effort with web-based social networking. SLA Framework is utilized as a part of to propose a trust administration display for security in cloud condition (Edna et al, 2012).

Assessing a cloud benefit security is the need for any association moving towards the cloud. We have distinguished a far reaching rundown of security parameters that are vital and adequate to quantify security as for distributed computing condition. These parameters are consolidated in our trust show and trust esteem is the result. Trust esteem can be a solitary esteem giving the idea of general security of a cloud benefit. It can likewise be separated to different parts of security in light of the parameters and spoken to as a vector. A client can choose a cloud benefit in light of its necessity and requests either for character, information security or whatever other measure recorded in the trust esteem vector (Hamid et al, 2013). Trust demonstrate comprises of different parameters that rely on upon sub parameters and capacities. Capacities are non-flimsy and can be utilized for estimation of quality. Figure 1 shows the theoretical structure of the trust display with the individual parameters expounded with their sub parameters and capacities.

IDENTITY MANAGEMENT-IDM-A

IDM is a key component of the security eco-framework for cloud, and when all is said in done for any web applications. Each cloud benefit has a procedure of creating characters for the cloud clients. This procedure can be inspected to decide security quality related with it. It frames one of the trust segments

Figure 4. Parameters of trust model

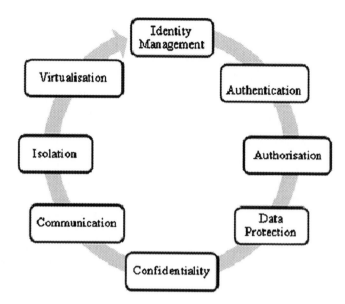

as IDM quality. Different parameters pertinent to the IDM procedure incorporate personality creation, stockpiling and the life cycle administration of the character. These procedures can be measured against the IDM quality segment of the trust demonstrate.

Authentication-B

To expand client certainty at the season of login and character confirmation handle, validation check is required. It is a two sided handle, for client getting to an administration from credible supplier and for supplier to offer administrations to the authentic client. Consequently, genuine utilization of cloud administration by a honest to goodness supplier can be dictated by the quality of verification that structures one of the segments of the trust demonstrate. It quantifies the procedure given by a cloud administration to validation check for client and also benefit (Muchahari et al, 2012).

Authorization-C

A client ought not to have the capacity to utilize any activities not approved for. This property can be checked against the approval quality. An activity including administration get to, playing out any operations, and all information/yield related exercises requires approving clients at these stages. A cloud benefit gives approval by utilizing different strategies. The viability of the strategy is measured regarding the approval quality. It is measured as for the put away ACL (Access Control Strength) trustworthiness, Presence of PMI (Privilege Management Information) and the way toward performing approval check of client.

Data Protection-D

The significant resource of a client and also any association proceeding onward to the cloud is information. Information security issues are at awesome concerns while moving information to and from cloud condition. An information insurance component show by different administrations has qualities that should be measured while assessing the information assurance quality. These can be measured by the information insurance trust esteem part of the model. Information Confidentiality, Integrity and Availability can be measured as for the information assurance quality.

Confidentiality-E

A cloud administration ought to ensure the mystery of the correspondence between a cloud client and supplier and every single other activity performed in different exercises. This property can be measured by privacy parameter. Methods for accomplishing protection of the information, message, Identity era and every other correspondence amongst supplier and client can be measured concerning the classification quality given by the administration.

Communication-F

Information or messages gone in the distributed computing condition inclined to listening in or spillage. The correspondence quality measures the arrangement given by the cloud benefit at the season of information or message transmission. Along these lines the correspondence quality measures quality of norms utilized for message transmission and correspondence.

Isolation-G

Multitenant highlights of distributed computing framework prompts the issue of confinement of assets among numerous clients. Security breaks and infringement are the key variables that are brought on basically because of disengagement. Cloud benefit detachment quality decides the level of assurance given to wipe out the security breaks and limit client get to ranges. The separation quality measured by the trust display, decides the level of security at asset, application and information that is given by the cloud benefit (Shekarpour et al, 2010).

Virtualization-H

The idea of cloud computing is deficient without the virtualization included. A virtualized framework is more inclined to assaults then the physical one. Procedures ought to be given to secure the virtualized condition. The parameter that measures the viability of the security connected to ensure the virtualized condition is virtualization. It decides the security thought at virtualization layer of a distributed computing engineering. It incorporates quality of VM (Virtual Machine), VMM (VM Monitor), Guest VM insurance quality and other checking apparatuses.

Compliance-I

In this, the security can be determined by getting various certifications from various communities and standards.

All the above parameters cover almost all the aspects of cloud security. These parameters are measured individually and the overall sum generates the strength of a service offered by cloud computing

For example

S1(Any cloud service) can have A(Strength value) = 0.8

S2(Any cloud service) can have B(Strength value) = 0.7

Note: The values of Trust evaluated so far just gives an idea of static trust. If a user wants to keep dynamic trust into consideration then it should be made more realistic.

The parameter is shown by the tree structure dictated by the root name. Level alongside root demonstrates sub parameters and leaf hub shows capacities. Hubs speak to parent-tyke relationship. Parent hub can be the weighted whole of its kid hubs. The weights are distinctive for various levels and are talked about in each of the parameters depictions. These weights are chosen in light of the kind of capacity utilized and time to break the accomplished security utilizing them. The genuine parameters are depicted as a gathering of weighted aggregate of its relating sub parameters and capacities. At long last the root hub which demonstrates trust esteem is the vector entirety of the considerable number of parameters.

ARCHITECTURE OF CLOUD USING TRUST MODEL

Various components are required to prepare trust calculation environment. A structure is designed so that trust can be calculated with multiple services provided by cloud service provider. The architecture in figure shows the various components of trust evaluation in cloud environment.

Major components are:

Figure 5. Tree structure of parameters of trust model

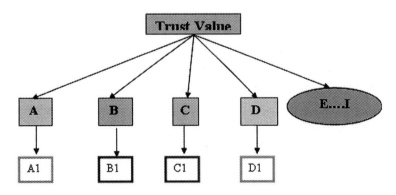

CLOUD SERVICE MANAGER

It plays a vital role in trust model. It provides various specific details such as type of service. It provides details about a specific cloud service like type of service. It also contains information about the specific users associated with that particular service. Also, this kind of information is present remains present with Cloud Service Manager in an updated format. Now, particularly, Cloud Service Manager further contains two types of trust value i.e. Static trust value and dynamic trust value. Here, static trust value is a value which is associated with cloud service which is going to be in use for the first time. Dynamic trust value is calculated with the help of parameters (Pearson et al, 2010).

TRUST EVALUATOR

It is an evaluator that calculates static or dynamic trust values on the basis of various service details available. It also makes use of service log and web for its calculation.

SERVICE LOG

It is a kind of database or log book that contains various information about any service provided by a cloud. It contains information such as number of successful and unsuccessful transactions, response time, waiting time, throughput time and so on. These details are then transferred to the trust model to calculate trust value.

WEB RESEARCH

It helps in drawing conclusions about dynamic trust values of cloud services by collecting various user feedback and comment. Now, if a cloud user want ot utilise one of the service, then he will contact with cloud service manager. Before providing the service, a cloud service manager will take all the possible details into consideration.

CONFIDENTIALITY

It means to prevent the disclosure of private and confidential information. As it is already known that information on any cloud is stored on dispersed locations, so confidentiality becomes an area of concern.

It assures that the consent is given to authorise users for it access. Here, data confidentiality refers to keep data secure from unauthorized access when it is in safe state as well as when the data is in transit state. While ensuring the confidentiality, some additional dimensions are need to be considered viz. user privacy and access privacy. Privacy is considered as one of the primary requirements for achieving security. User privacy is ensuring when he tries to fetch or manipulate data.

Data confidentiality is considered as one of the arising challenge in the ongoing research in Cloud computing. To ensure confidentiality, data is first encrypted and then transferred to the service provider. To continue with this process, external service provider is taken into account. In this, control is outsourced from the third service provider to ensure the maintainability of the confidentiality. Various cryptographic techniques are considered as an existing solution. Also, Storage as a service is generally used by small scale business which is unable to take overheads of capital budget. Many commercial and legal regulations are demanding the need to develop trustworthy solutions for protecting confidential as well as sensitive data whenever it is saved, processed or communicated among the external parties.

Cryptography algorithms are the most efficient tool to ensure the security of data storage in the cloud. Indeed, there are many encryption algorithms that can encrypt the data and convert them into incomprehensible format, in order to ensure their confidentiality (Kalpana et al, 2017).

In an insecure environment like the public cloud, sensitive data must be secured. Regarding the storage service, data must be encrypted before sending them to the cloud server, using the symmetric key cryptosystems such as: Blowfish, etc. But, to ensure the confidentiality of data storage and their treatments, the cloud providers must adopt techniques that can ensure the confidentiality of this type of service. Indeed, researchers stressed a useful encryption technique in this type of environment: Homomorphic Encryption (HE). This technique is able to ensure the confidentiality of data storage and their treatments, located in cloud servers (Yuefa et al, 2009).

The Homomorphic Encryption cryptosystems are asymmetric key, which use different keys for data encryption and decryption.

These algorithms are divided into two categories: symmetric and asymmetric key. The asymmetric key techniques performance is very slower than the symmetric key techniques, and used in general to exchange the keys of symmetric key algorithms. The symmetric key algorithms are a form of encryption that use same key to encrypt and decrypt the data, and are divided into block ciphers and steam ciphers. The input of block cipher when the data is encrypted or decrypted is in block of the fixed data size. This size is depending on the encryption algorithm used. But, in the case of stream cipher the data are encrypted/ decrypted one bit or one byte of data at that's why this cipher type is more efficient for real time processing. In this section, we focus on symmetric key algorithms which can be adopted by cloud providers to ensure the confidentiality of the data storage.

PRINCIPLES OF SYMMETRIC KEY CRYPTOSYSTEMS OPERATION

The philosophy of symmetric key cryptosystems when adopted to encrypt data in the cloud environment is somewhat different to other use cases. Generally, symmetric key techniques were created to encrypt messages, to ensure confidentiality of communication between the sender and the recipient over internet and network applications. The secret key is shared between them to encrypt and decrypt these messages. In cloud case these cryptosystems are used to ensure confidentiality of data, when transferred and when stored in cloud servers. Only the client can have the key. Thus, the data remains confidential and unreadable even to the cloud provider. The principles of operation of the symmetric key cryptosystems in cloud are as follows, and as shown in Figure3. Key Generation: The client generates private– key (PK). Encryption: The client encrypts data with– PK and sends the encrypted data to the Cloud server. Storage: The encrypted data are stored in the– cloud database. Decryption: The client decrypts data after– retrieve them from the cloud, using PK.

MULTI TENANCY

In a cloud environment, various resources and services re shred by various applications at various geographic locations. This is being carried out to resolve the issue of resource insufficiency and to eliminate the cost which is main purpose of cloud. Data and applications are stored on virtual servers as well as on actual hardware.

If these are stored on virtual servers, then their chances that a single virtual machine can have a malicious application which further affects the performance of their machines.

If these are stored on actual hardware, then there can be issues of multi-core processing. The typical solution to this kind to problem is employment of Intrusion Detection Systems to keep their customers and their information safe in cloud environment. Another method being used is Trusted Cloud Computing Platform i.e. TCCP which is designed to provide better security of the virtual machines.

To create secure and exclusive virtual computing environment, a tenant is considered as an application either inside or outside and enterprise. Basically, this environment works on all or some of the selected layers of the an architecture of enterprise i.e. from user interface to storage. All these applications must be multi-user in nature (Gonzalez et al, 2012).

Multi tenancy is considered as a common key attribute which is applicable to all types of the cloud i.e. public, private or hybrid. It is also applicable to the service models i.e. SaaS, PaaS or IaaS. Multi tenancy is also applies to a new service model i.e. ITaaS.

In general terms, the term "software multitenancy" is considered as an architecture in which a single instance of software runs on a single server which further helps in serving multiple tenants.A tenant is referred as a group of several users who shares some common access to a software with specific privileges. In case of multi tenant architecture, an application of software is designed so that a dedicated instance among some users is shared. Along with this instance, its data, user management information, its properties (functional or non functional) are also shared. Here, it is also known that multi instance is totally different from multi tenancy.

Multi tenancy can further be divided into two levels i.e.

- Hypervisor level isolation.
- DB level isolation.

HYPERVISOR LEVEL ISOLATION

It is applicable to low level layer of any software which maps a physical machine with virtual machine on which a particular operating system is run. When this operating system send request to the virtual machine, it is firstly accepted by the hypervisor. Here, this hypervisor isolation also provides the some operating functions such as process scheduling to know which kind of virtual machine is to be run.

An extra layer of indirection is introduced by hypervisor. If a virtual machine is required than a lesser capacity then a hardware partitioning is done to improve the efficiency of the service. This helps in lessen of security concerns.

DB LEVEL ISOLATION

In this isolation, various applications are run by tenant, only difference is the type of data stored by each tenant. So to make this bifurcated, a special id i.e. "t_id" is associated with the each table. Each and every query is executed with the help of this "t_id".

In this approach, rewritten query is done to make degree of isolation more efficient. This is much easier way than hypervisor level.

One of the advantage of DB level isolation is that there is no use of virtual machine overheads which further compiles to lesser economic value to tenant.

SELECTING OUT OF HYPERVISOR AND DB LEVEL ISOLATION

In hypervisor isolation, tenant is given a choice of selecting a service that will serve to its applications and other IT skills. But, to apply this, efficient system administrators are required to be hired for the maintenance of technology stack.

- In DB level isolation, a tight coupling is created between tenant and Cloud service provider. Also, in this the degree of freedom is also limited.
- In case of hypervisor isolation, no reuse of application is allowed. Tenants are required to create their technology stack and further write their own application logic.
- In case of DB level approach, a set of templates is pre defined by the cloud service provider. It purely focuses on operation of a business.

For example, Amazon AWS lies in the category of hardware level in which many users share a physical machine. On another, Force.com lies in the category of DB level in which many users share common database and tables (Subashini et al, 2011).

Therefore, we can say that hypervisor and DB isolation are valid in different context and is applicable to different set of users.

DEGREE OF MULTI TENANCY

It is commonly defined as the tendency of SaaS layer which is to be designed which is too shared among the various tenants.

The degree of multi tenancy is followed in the below written way:

Table 1. Degree of multi tenancy

S. No.	Level	Applicable to Multi Tenancy
1.	Highest degree	IaaS, PaaS and SaaS are fully supportive.
2.	Middle degree	IaaS, PaaS and small SaaS are fully supportive.
3.	Lowest degree	IaaS, PaaS fully supportive.

ADVANTAGES OF MULTI TENANCY OVER SINGLE TENANT APPLICATION

- **Lower Cost:** In case of multi tenant environment, new users as well as old users get access to basic (same) software so in that case scaling requires lesser infrastructure.
- **Sharing:** Medium sized business don't need data centers if they are using Software as a Service. Also, SaaS allows organizations to share all facilities at operational costs.
- **Maintenance and Updates:** While using cloud services, end users are not required to pay maintenance as well as updation fees. Updates and new features are automatically updated by subscription and are paid to the vendors by the users.
- **Configurable:** As we know that services provided by cloud highly configurable that supports multi tenancy. It is so that users can make their application perform as they want, without making any change in underlying code on backend data structure. As the code will remain unchanged, so they can be updated easily.

AUTHENTICATION

Authentication is the demonstration of affirming reality of a quality of a solitary bit of information (a datum) asserted valid by a substance. Conversely with distinguishing proof, which alludes to the demonstration of expressing or generally showing a claim purportedly validating a man or thing's personality, verification is the procedure of really affirming that character. It may include affirming the character of a man by approving their personality records, checking the credibility of a site with a computerized endorsement, deciding the age of a curio via cell based dating, or guaranteeing that an item is the thing that its bundling and naming case to be. At the end of the day, verification frequently includes confirming the legitimacy of no less than one type of recognizable proof (Puttaswamy et al, 2011).

In private as well as public networking environments, authentication is basically done through the use of username and password. Authentication part is cleared when the user inputs the correct username and password.

In the beginning, a user is required to make him registered with some initial stage password. But the biggest disadvantage is that, these passwords can be easily stolen, can be revealed or can be forgotten. To change password of authentication, previously declared must be remembered (Aljawarneh et al, 2017).

These systems and techniques are not optimized enough to make any authentication secure enough to withstand every type of security breach, which points towards the necessity of more secured and fool proof authentication technique.

There are various ways out of which authentication can be categorized:

On the Basis of Factors of Authentication

- Something that user knows.
- Something that user has.
- Something that covers range of elements to verify user's identity.

On the Basis of Ownership

Something that user possess (like ID cards, wrist band, security tokens, software tokens, phone tokens etc)

On the Basis of Factors of Knowledge

Something user knows i.e. passwords, PIN, challenge response etc.) (Aljawarneh et al, 2016).

On the Basis of Factors of Inherence

Something that user does (renal pattern, finger print, face recognition, voice recognition, bio meteric etc.)

Even these represent general scenario of authentication covering basic definition. Over the years many different methods have been proposed to solve this problem or to reduce it to a considerable extent, but still some flaws always occur in each one of them. So to provide a better insight into this problem of secured authentication, we propose a technique which might put an enormous hold over the topic of secured user authentication and access control. Basically user authentication is not the only step or process, it incorporates three A's i.e.

- Authentication
- Authorization
- Auditing.

In this work our main stress is toward these three A's and towards the security of critical data associated with CSP (like password storing files or access control files etc).

- Methods Providing Secured Access Control
- Message Authentication and one time password generation
- Authentication using Private-key Ciphers
- Hashing Functions
- Digital Signature Scheme

Important points to be stressed upon in this research is related to secured user authentication and making sure that the intended hacker or cryptanalyst acting as intended/genuine customer is not able to access any of critical data/information belonging to CSP (such as passwords file or access control related information). And approach used to make it happen is elaborated in proposed schemata.

DIGITAL SIGNATURE AND RSA ENCRYPTION ALGORITHM FOR ENHANCED DATA SECURITY IN CLOUD

In cloud computing platform there are many problems of security like host security, network traffic, backups and critical user data security. A digital signature is a scheme based on mathematical model which demonstrates the authenticity of message or document encrypted with either RSA algorithm or any other algorithm like MD5/SHA etc. If a digital signature is valid it gives an impression to the recipient that message or document was created by a known and legitimate sender and was not altered in between the process of transferring. One can use digital signature and RSA scheme combined together to ensure the data security over cloud. RSA is the most recognizable asymmetric (i.e. requiring two different keys) algorithm. RSA was created by Ron Rivest, Adi Shamir, and Leonard Adleman in 1978 . In digital signature technique the process is that the data is crunched down in few lines using some kind of hashing algorithm which is a called as message digest. Then message digest is encrypted with private key and decrypted using pair of recipient's private key and public key of sender. Digital signature scheme can be used for distributing data over a network just like cloud where it is compulsory to detect forgery and tampering as cloud provides services like pay per use basis and on demand access to services of CSP. So it might prove to be an asset to implementing better security methods over a cloud.

KEY MANAGEMENT

The technique of managing cryptographic keys in a cryptosystem is known as key management. It includes various functions such as generating keys, storing them, using and replacing them. Whole functions are performed on the basis of protocols only.

This technique concerns with the keys at user level either among users or systems.

Successful key management is often critical for the security of a cryptosystem. Practically, it is the most difficult to implement cryptography because it involves training of users, organizational and departmental interactions and coordination among all of the elements (Singh e al, 2015).

Cryptographic is one of the security mechanisms that protect information from unauthorized confession. It can be used to provide security for data storage to protect its integrity while storing data on Cloud paradigm. Cryptographic key management is the most important element of cryptographic system as effective use of cryptographic system requires proper management of cryptographic key. To date, cryptographic key security has been ensured to protect it from vulnerability and security breaches. However, the use of cryptographic key in online or Cloud based applications has prompted large fraction of information security attacks since the consumer of Cloud does not have access to the physical storage servers. Cloud Security Alliance (CSA), the global leaders in Cloud security, has identified that the cryptographic key management at Cloud is a challenge (Gavriloaie et al, 2004).

They recommended that cryptographic keys should be stored on enterprise domain due to their sensitive nature. However, searching of encrypted data from a large data set is problematic on Cloud storage while cryptographic keys are stored at enterprise premises. Furthermore, these limitations of encrypted data restrict Cloud users and they cannot utilize all benefits of Cloud paradigm. All these concerns require a strong cryptographic key management system that can reduce the intricacy of operation on Cloud stored data by processing them on same platform. This research provides an effective and robust security protocol for symmetric cryptographic key management in Cloud that attempts to resolve the above mentioned issues. This thesis contributes in following aspects; Secure Data Storage on Cloud: This part of research offers a mechanism for secure storage of sensitive data on Cloud. This storage scheme can be further utilized in any type of data storage. Using secure protocol user can share cryptographic key with Cloud to manipulate encrypted data. Symmetric Cryptographic Key as a Service: Our second part of research provides Symmetric Cryptographic Key as a service and user may embed this service in other utilities such as mobile/PDAs digital signature utilities etc. Secure Data Access: On the fly computation of cryptographic key will ensure key access security. Proposed protocol is based on secret splitting and use enhanced Shamir's algorithm for cryptographic key splitting. Furthermore, this protocol distributes cryptographic key components to various Cloud servers. That ensures cryptographic key protection, even if the security on one of the Cloud server is compromised. All data transfer between Clouds is done through pkcs#7 protocols that provides data enveloping and de-enveloping during data travelling in insecure environment. In addition to this, SSL protocol is also used which connect end user browser to an application server securely.

As security is delicate issue in distributed computing .the information are originating from cloud utilizing open system (web) there are opportunities to hack the information (Armbrust et al, 2009). There have been parcel of work done on security issues and difficulties yet at the same time there is not 100% full confirmation arrangement. There are numerous physical and some other assault on information that decimate information on server. one answer for that is scattered the information on more than one server rather than one server .yet this not take care of issue totally in light of the fact that information put away in encoded mode utilizing encryption scratch .the aggressors assault on key and might be hack the information.

Attackers attack on data which is placed on same server. So presently ongoing solution is creating multiple copies of same data and that data is to be placed on multiple servers. But again, data is encrypted by an encrypted key. Further, attackers may attack on that encrypted key which further reveals date to the attackers. The solution of this problem is instead of keeping multiple copies of data on various serverson which we can apply Shamir's secret sharing on key. The encrypted key is divided into number of modules and to store them on different server. But again, if any of the attacker attacks on one of the server then that module or part of key is lost but still they can be reconstructed using Shamir's threshold scheme.

Secret Sharing Scheme

The most famous and perfect secret sharing scheme is (k,n)- threshold scheme which was proposed by Shamir in 1979. In this, a key can be reconstructed again and again with minimum number of secrets that are kept on various servers, even if attacked by an attacker. This scheme also overcomes the problem of key exchange. Division of keys is done with the range of polynomial (Aberer 2001).

Also, in this method secret is distributed among all the participants of the group. This secret can only be reconstructed or restructured when a number of shares are combined together. Individual secrets with a single sharing scheme, there are number of players associated with a single dealer. This dealer allocates a secret to a player after the completion of some conditions. In this, it is kept in mind that group of 't' (threshold) can together reconstruct a secret but no group of members less than 't' can reconstruct it. This system is sometimes known as (k-n) threshold scheme).

CONCLUSION

This chapter explains the concept of cloud and various other security issues related to cloud. This chapter has helped in throwing light on some of the major concerns of security i.e. Trust, multitenancy etc. Also, it has explained various solutions that are available till date in the market. As, we know, data security is one of the important issue in cloud computing. In any case, cloud specialist organizations are as yet utilizing customary symmetric key calculations for information security and not giving much straightforwardness on the security calculations being sent. It has also explained the concept of trust with the help of various parameters which are implemented in the trust model. Various key management mechanisms, authentication techniques have been explained in detail. This chapter has illustrates various cryptographic key management schemes (like Shamir secret sharing) used for sending data from one server to another. Also, the future work is concentrating on providing more and more solutions to the cloud computing security issues.

REFERENCES

Abdul-Rahman, A., & Hailes, S. (2000). Supporting trust in virtual communities. *Proceedings of 33rd Hawaii International Conference on System Sciences*, 777-780.

Aberer, K. (2001). P-grid: A self-organizing access structure for p2p information systems. *Proceedings of Ninth International Conference on Cooperative Information Systems*, 179-194.

Aberer, K., & Despotovic, Z. (2001). Managing trust in a peer-2-peer information system. *Proc. of 10th International Conference on Information and Knowledge Management*, 310-317. 10.1145/502585.502638

Aljawarneh, S., Aldwairi, M., & Yassein, M. B. (2017). Anomaly-based intrusion detection system through feature selection analysis and building hybrid efficient model. *Journal of Computational Science*. doi:10.1016/j.jocs.2017.03.006

Aljawarneh, S., Yassein, M.B., & Talafha, W.A. (2017). A multithreaded programming approach for multimedia big data: encryption system. *Multimed Tools Appl*. doi:10.100711042-017-4873-9

Aljawarneh, S. A., Alawneh, A., & Jaradat, R. (2017). Cloud security engineering: Early stages of SDLC. *Future Generation Computer Systems*, *74*, 385–392. doi:10.1016/j.future.2016.10.005

Aljawarneh, S. A., Moftah, R. A., & Maatuk, A. M. (2016). Investigations of automatic methods for detecting the polymorphic worms signatures. *Future Generation Computer Systems*, *60*, 67–7. doi:10.1016/j.future.2016.01.020

Aljawarneh, S. A., Vangipuram, R., Puligadda, V. K., & Vinjamuri, J. (2017). G-SPAMINE: An approach to discover temporal association patterns and trends in internet of things. *Future Generation Computer Systems*, *74*, 430–443. doi:10.1016/j.future.2017.01.013

Armbrust, M., Fox, A., Griffith, R., Joseph, A., Katz, R., Konwinski, A., . . . Stoica, M. (2009). Above The Clouds: A Berkeley View of Cloud Computing. UC Berkeley Reliable Adaptive Distributed Systems Laboratory, 1-23.

Armbrust, M., Fox, A., Griffith, R., Joseph, A. D., Katz, R. H., & Konwinski, A. (2010). A view of cloud computing. ACM Communication, 53(4), 50–58. doi:10.1145/1721654.1721672

Atallah, M., Frikken, K., & Blanton, M. (2005). Dynamic and Efficient Key Management for Access Hierarchies. *Proceedings of ACM Conference Computer Communication Security*, 190–202. 10.1145/1102120.1102147

Banirostam, H., Hedayati, A., Zadeh, A. K., & Shamsinezhad, E. (2013). A Trust Based Approach for Increasing Security in Cloud Computing Infrastructure. *15th International Conference on Computer Modelling and Simulation*, 717-721. 10.1109/UKSim.2013.39

Beth, T., Borcherding, M., & Klein, B. (1994). Valuation of trust in open networks. In *Proc. of the 3rd European Symposium on Research in Computer Security*. Springer-Verlag.

Bonatti, P., & Samarati, P. (2000). Regulating service access and information release on the web. *Proc. of the 7th ACM conference on computer and communications security*, 134-143. 10.1145/352600.352620

Bonatti, P. A., & Olmedilla, D. (2005). Driving and monitoring provisional trust negotiation with metapolicies. In *IEEE 6th International Workshop on Policies for Distributed Systems and Networks (POLICY)*. Stockholm, Sweden: IEEE Computer Society. 10.1109/POLICY.2005.13

Bonatti, P. A., Shahmehri, N., Duma, C., Olmedilla, D., Nejdl, W., Baldoni, M., . . . Fuchs, N. E. (2004). Rule-based policy specification: State of the art and future work. *Report I2:D1, EU NoE REWERSE*, *2*(14), 10.

Canedo, E. D. (2012). Trust Model for Private Cloud. *IEEE International Conference on Cyber Security, Cyber Warfare and Digital Forensic (CyberSec)*, 380-389.

Caronni, G. (2000). Walking the web of trust. *Proceedings of 9th IEEE International Workshops on Enabling Technologies (WETICE)*, 153-158.

Duma, C., Shahmehri, N., & Caronni, G. (2005). Dynamic trust metrics for peer-to-peer systems. *Proc. of 2nd IEEE Workshop on P2P Data Management, Security and Trust*, 776-781.

Gavriloaie, R., Nejdl, W., Olmedilla, D., Seamons, K. E., & Winslett, M. (2004). No registration needed: How to use declarative policies and negotiation to access sensitive resources on the semantic web. In *1st European Semantic Web Symposium (ESWS 2004)*. Springer. 10.1007/978-3-540-25956-5_24

Gonzalez N, Miers C, Redigolo F, Jr M, Carvalho T, Naslund M & Pourzandi M (2012). A quantitative analysis of current security concerns and solutions for cloud computing. *Journal of Cloud Computing: Advances, System and Applications*, 1-11.

Goyal, O., & Pandey, A. (2006). Attribute-based encryption for fine-grained access control of encrypted data. *ACM Conference Computer Communication Security*, 89–98.

Grandison, T., & Sloman, M. (2002). Specifying and analysing trust for internet applications. In Towards The Knowledge Society: eCommerce, eBusiness, and eGovernment. In *The Second IFIP Conference on E-Commerce, E-Business, E-Government (I3E 2002), IFIP Conference Proceedings*. Lisbon, Portugal: Kluwer.

Hossein, R., Elankovan, S., Zulkarnain, M. A., & Abdullah, M. Z. (2013). Encryption as a service as a solution for cryptography in cloud. *International Conference on Electrical Engineering and Informatics indexed in Science Direct*, 1202-1210.

Huang, J., & Nicol. (2013). *Trust mechanisms for cloud computing*. Retrieved from http://www.journalof-cloudcomputing.com/content/2/1/9

Jungwoo, R., Syed, R., William, A., & John, K. (2013). *Cloud Security Auditing: Challenges and Emerging Approaches*. IEEE Security and Privacy.

Kalpana, G., Kumar, P. V., Aljawarneh, S., & Krishnaiah, R. V. (2017). Shifted Adaption Homomorphism Encryption for Mobile and Cloud Learning. *Computers & Electrical Engineering*. doi:10.1016/j.compeleceng.2017.05.022

Krumm, J. (2009). A survey of computational location privacy. *Personal and Ubiquitous Computing*, *13*(6), 291–399. doi:10.100700779-008-0212-5

Li, Chinneck, Wodside, & Litoiu. (2009). Fast scalable optimization to configure service system having cost and quality of service constraints. *IEEE International Conference on Autonomic System Barcelona*, 159-168. 10.1145/1555228.1555268

Li, N., Mitchell, J. C., & Winsborough, W. H. (2002). Design of a role-based trust-management framework. In *Security and Privacy, 2002. Proceedings. 2002 IEEE Symposium on*. IEEE.

Muchahari, M. K., & Sinha, S. K. (2012). A New Trust Management Architecture for Cloud Computing Environment. *IEEE International Symposium on Cloud and Services Computing (ISCOS)*, 136-140. 10.1109/ISCOS.2012.30

Paper, W. (2010). *Introduction to Cloud Computing*. Retrieved from http://www.thinkgrid.com/docs/computing-whitepaper.pdf

Pearson, S., & Benameur, A. (2010). Privacy, security and trust issues arising from cloud computing. *Proceedings of the 2nd IEEE International Conference on Cloud Computing Technology and Science*, 693-702. 10.1109/CloudCom.2010.66

Putri & Mganga. (2011). *Enhancing Information Security in Cloud Computing Services using SLA Based Metrics*. School of Computing, Blekinge Institute of Technology.

Puttaswamy, K. P. N., Kruegel, C., & Zhao, B. Y. (2011). Silverline: Toward Data Confidentiality in Storage-Intensive Cloud Applications. *Proc. Second ACM Symp. Cloud Computing (SOCC '11)*, 10:1-10:13. 10.1145/2038916.2038926

Rizwana Shaikh, M. (2012, April). Cloud Security issues: A Survey. *International Journal of Computers and Applications*.

Sapuntzakis, C., Brumley, D., Chandra, R., Zeldovich, N., Chow, J., Lam, M., & Rosenblum, M. (2008). Virtual appliances for deploying and maintaining software. *17th USENIX Conference on System Administration*, 181–194.

Shaikh & Sasikumar. (2012). Trust Framework for Calculating Security Strength of a Cloud Service. *IEEE International Conference on Communication, Information & Computing Technology (ICCICT)*, 1-6.

Shekarpour, S., & Katebi, S. D. (2010). Modeling and evaluation of trust with an extension in semantic web. *Journal of Web Semantics*, *8*(1), 26–36. doi:10.1016/j.websem.2009.11.003

Singh, A., Juneja, D., & Malhotra, M. (2015). A Novel Agent Based Autonomous Service Composition Framework for Cost Optimization of Resource Provisioning in Cloud Computing. In JKSU-CIS. Elsevier.

Singh, A., & Malhotra, M. (2015). Analysis of security issues at different levels in cloud computing paradigm: A review. *Journal of Computer Networks and Applications*, 2(2), 41–45.

Singh, A., & Malhotra, M. (2015). Evaluation of a Secure Agent based optimized Resource Scheduling Framework in Cloud Environment. IJCAR, 188-198.

Singh, A., & Malhotra, M. (2016). Hybrid Two Tier Framework for Improved Security in Cloud Environment. India-Com., 1601-1606.

Singh, A., & Malhotra, M. (n.d.). A Novel Agent Based Framework for Cost Optimization in Cloud Computing Environment. *International Journal of Cloud Applications*, 53–61.

Staab, Bhargava, Lilien, Rosenthal, Winslett, Sloman, … Kashyap. (2004). The pudding of trust. *IEEE Intelligent Systems, 19*(5), 74–88.

Staab, S., Bhargava, B. K., Lilien, L., Rosenthal, A., Winslett, M., Sloman, M., ... Kashyap, V. (2004). The pudding of trust. *IEEE Intelligent Systems, 19*(5), 74–88. doi:10.1109/MIS.2004.52

Subashini, S., & Kavitha, V. (2011). A survey on security issues in service delivery models of cloud computing. *Journal of Network and Computer Applications, 34*(1), 1–11. doi:10.1016/j.jnca.2010.07.006

Vaquero, L. M., Rodero-Merino, L., & Morán, D. (2011). Locking the sky: A survey on IaaS cloud security. *Computing, 91*(1), 93–118. doi:10.100700607-010-0140-x

Yang, Jia, Ren, Zhang, & Xie. (2013). DAC-MACS: Effective Data Access Control for Multiauthority Cloud Storage Systems. *IEEE Transaction on Information Forensics and Security*, 1790-1801.

Yang, H., & Tate, M. (2009). Where are we at with Cloud Computing?: A Descriptive Literarure Review. *Proceedings of 20th Australasian Conference on Information Systems*, 807-819.

Yuefa, D., Bo, W., Yaqiang, G., Quan, Z., & Chaojing, T. (2009). Data security model for cloud computing. *International Workshop on Information Security and Application*, 141-144.

Zhang, Q., & Cheng, L. (2010). Cloud computing: state-of-the-art and research challenge. *Raouf Boutaba J Internet Serv Appl*, 7-18.

This research was previously published in Critical Research on Scalability and Security Issues in Virtual Cloud Environments edited by Shadi Aljawarneh and Manisha Malhotra, pages 95-121, copyright year 2018 by Information Science Reference (an imprint of IGI Global).

Chapter 52
Cryptographic Cloud Computing Environment as a More Trusted Communication Environment

Omer K. Jasim
Alma'arif University College, Iraq

Safia Abbas
Ain Shams University, Egypt

El-Sayed M. El-Horbaty
Ain Shams University, Egypt

Abdel-Badeeh M. Salem
Ain Shams University, Egypt

ABSTRACT

Cloud Communication Environment is an internet-based computing, where shared resources, software, and information are provided with computers and devices on-demand. They guarantee a way to share distributed resources and services that belong to different organizations. In order to develop cloud computing applications, security and trust to share data through distributed resources must be assured. This paper offers a study of the different mechanisms used in open cloud environments such as keys generation and management, and encryption/decryption algorithms. In addition, the paper proposes a new cryptographic environment, annotated as "CCCE" that deploys the combination between quantum key distribution mechanisms (QKD) and advanced encryption standard (AES), and demonstrates how quantum mechanics can be applied to improve computation.

DOI: 10.4018/978-1-5225-8176-5.ch052

INTRODUCTION

Recently, Cloud computing (CC) (Ateniese, Kamara, 2012) has widely been applied in several industrial fields such as Google, Facebook, Amazon, and (e-business, e-learning... etc.) and is considered a new communication technique that combines multiple disciplines such as parallel computing, distributed computing and grid computing. In return, it provides Virtualization, utility computing, and other multiple services for client enterprise (Ateniese, Kamara, 2012; CCA, 2013).

Basically, cloud computing main principles are based on sharing resources among separately distributed servers and individual clients. This sharing is performed by enabling free accessing of the stored files and data for all clients (CSA, 2013).

Despite the free data accessing is considered an advantage; it has several drawbacks such that any cloud client can manipulate any file transferred through cloud communication. Consequently, many companies have explored the critical areas in a CC environment.

CSA (2013) is an example of those companies, which delivers a package that contains cloud provider, clients and considers the security model. The CSA security model has the ability to interrupt the intruder, who is responsible for destroying and interrupting the original data files and communications.

Later on, the security guarantee issue in cloud communication environment has become a challenge and which attract many studies, such as Hail et al. (1999), who discuss the technical security issues arising from side channel - attacks, browser attacks, browsers' related attacks, and authentication attacks.

Moreover, Jensen et al. (2009) discuss the security vulnerabilities existing in the cloud platform. They grouped the possible vulnerabilities into technology-related, cloud characteristics-related and security controls- related.

In spite of different studies' attempts to solve the security problem in cloud communications, many gaps and threads are still uncovered or handled. In the meantime, all proposed attempts consider the main three building modules in the cloud communication architecture [see Figure 1]. However, none of these attempts care about the whole performance of the interaction between the constituent modules, which in turn, caused data transformation delaying (IDC, 2011; John, Ingo, 2010) and provide a high chance for the attackers to discover the main encryption key and intrude the data streams in the transferred files.

This paper proposed a secured cloud computing environment annotated as "CCCE" in which, a hybrid technique is used in the encryption and decryption processes. The proposed hybrid technique combines the Advanced Encryption Standard Algorithm (AES) and QKD that generates the keys used for the encryption process randomly.

The rest of the paper is organized as follows: the second section shows the CC architecture and implication security, the third section describes the CC precaution, the various types of attacks that threaten the CC data transformation are discussed in the fourth section, the models of cloud encryption files are explained in the fifth section, the sixth section proposes the CCCE architecture and discusses in detail its main building modules including an illustrative example that represents the main functions used through the interaction between the main modules, the seventh section provides the analytical analysis for the proposed model and finally, the eighth section presents the conclusion.

CC ARCHITECTURE AND SECURITY IMPLICATIONS

A cloud computing environment, architecture can be basically divided into three layers, the characteristics layer, the model layer, and the deployment layer (Kun, Qin, 2013). The characteristic layer contains four phases (on demand service, broad network, resource pooling & Rapid elasticity, measured services), see Figure 1. Firstly, the character layer aims to (i) develop and adopt the rapidly evolving of cloud technology, (ii) abstract the details of inner implementations, and (iii) facilitate the information retrieving service anywhere, anytime(Lohr, 2009; Kun, 2013).

Second, the model layer consists of three models arranged as follows:

1. **Infrastructure as a Service (IaaS):** This is a providing services in which the provider is responsible for providing housing, running and maintaining the equipment used to support operations including storage, hardware, servers and networking components. The Amazon web service (S3) is an example for IaaS;
2. **Platform as a Service (PaaS):** This service enables the users to use virtualizes servers and associated services for running existing applications or developing and testing new ones, Google Apps are an example for the PaaS;
3. **Software as a Service (SaaS):** This service aims to run software on the provider's infrastructure and provide licensed applications to enable users to use the services. Moreover, SaaS offers more transparent to the end user. An example of SaaS is the Salesforce.com CRM application.

Each service delivery model has different possible implementations. However, the degree of control by providers is low and they are only responsible for the availability of their services. But user's responsibility is high and they are responsible of confidentiality, data privacy and integrity. Figure 2 shows the cloud provider's responsibility in securing cloud service models.

Figure 1. Cloud environment architecture

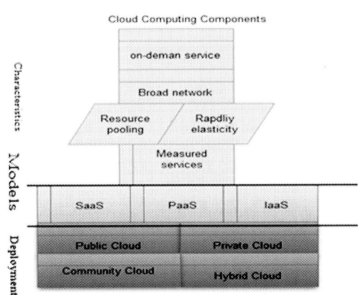

Figure 2. Cloud provider responsibilities

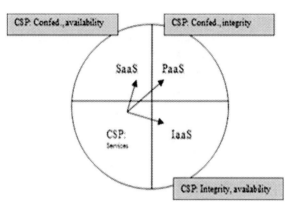

Finally, the cloud deployment layer that includes public, private, community, and hybrid clouds (see Grobauer, Walloshcek and Stocker, 2009). A public cloud supplies an off-site infrastructure over the Internet that lead to efficiency in shared resources as well as vulnerable level of security than private clouds (Mandeep & Manish, 2013).

A private cloud is maintained on a private network and offers a greater level of security and control (Kandukuri & Ramakrishna, 2009).

A community cloud is a semiprivate cloud that is used by a defined group of tenants with similar backgrounds and requirements (Lohr, Steve, 2009). Hybrid clouds are a combination of private and public cloud. They combine on-demand external capacity with on-premises resources and in-house compliance (Mohit & Prem, 2012).

The enclosed cloud environment's components sustain the security criteria in each layer such as authentication, integrity and availability to guarantee the reliable communication. However, to assure the security criteria, strong encryption algorithms are used. These algorithms are usually implemented using key generation, which in turn, caused data transformation delaying (Jensen, Schwenk, Gruschka & Iacono, 2009; John, Ingo, 2010) and provide a higher chance for the attackers (timing or quantum attack) to discover the main encryption key and intrude the data streams in the transferred files. In order to overcome such problem, we propose a model based on key availability and key distribution mechanism associated with QKD techniques to increase the consistency/reliability between the different layers.

CC CRYPTOGRAPHY PRECAUTIONS

Trust, security, and privacy are some of the challenges existing in cloud computing, they have become a major barrier to the rapid growth of cloud computing applications. This section discusses encryption as a countermeasure for the security issue, instantiated in the "Data Leakage", "Data Encryption Based Quantum", and "Customer Identification" mechanisms, in order to aid in providing more secure cloud environments.

DATA LEAKAGE

Security and privacy are the major factors related to cloud computing. Although cloud computing environments are multi domain environment in which various resources are shared, sharing hardware and placing data seem to be risky as any unauthorized person can easily hacked either accidentally or due to malicious attack (Patil & Akshay, 2012; CSA, 2013).

To overcome this, a sensible strategy to ensure data security and privacy is performed based on encryption technique. Accordingly, data should be encrypted from the start so there is no possibility of data leakage (Singh, 2012). Moreover, the user should have been controlling not over the secured data, but also over the keys used for decryption. From the security point of view, this one is the best equivalent approach for securing data at your premises (Singh, 2012).

CLOUD DATA ENCRYPTION BASED QUANTUM

Cloud data encryption based quantum technology platform dispels all security fears through cloud data transmission. This technology offer: (i) simple, low-cost for the data protection, (ii) tools and security services integration, and (iii) an efficient disaster recovery.

Quantum technology solves one key challenge in distributed computing. It can preserve data privacy when users interact with remote computing centers (Kollmitzer & Pivk, 2010). Other quantum tact comes in cryptography, the art of encrypting data, usually called Quantum Cryptography or Quantum Key Distribution (QKD) (Taih & Jasim, 2011), which is illustrated in Figure 3.

Data are encoded based on prepared states, which are known as photons, these photons are then sent as "keys" for encryption/ decryption secured messages (Stipcevic & Medved, 2007; Hirvensalo, 2013). The advantage of using such photons in data transmission lays in the no-cloning theorem (the quantum state of a single photon cannot be copied).

Figure 3. Schematic of QKD

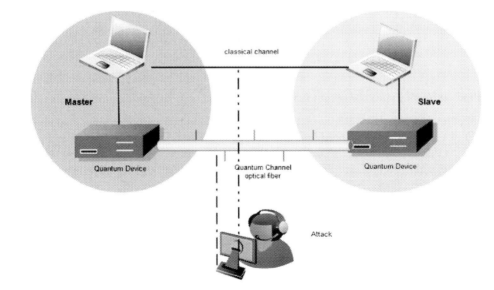

Rawal et al (2012) looks for the perfect alliance between cloud computing and quantum computing, which guarantees data protection for hosted files on remote computers or servers. He encrypted heavy duty of data by using the data processing servers as a quantum computer, which hides input, processing and output data from malicious and attacks.

CUSTOMER IDENTIFICATION

Customer identification is another factor for ensuring security in cloud computing. The encrypted data can be vulnerable by any customer in your organization, if in case your files are pooled. Anyone among your organization can easily get that access to your personal data as there are no restrictions made between the organizations. Accordingly, anyone can delete it or can easily make that change to it (Rukhin, Soto & Nechevatal, 2010).

Customer identification is an important aspect of cloud computing. Due to this only authorized user have been writing and authority to gain access to data and to modify the contents in it. Therefore, the authorization manner with the encryption provision, give a secure environment for data resident in the cloud. Without user "id" verification the system will not allow any of the requests made to allow some transactions, which will ultimately help in data privacy and security.

CC ATTACKS

Despite the usage of cloud computing environments getting more popular, its main risk is the intrusion caused by the attackers. In this section, we discuss the most known attack mechanisms in a cloud computing environment, such as denial-of-service, side-channel, authentication attack and man-in-the-middle attacks.

DENIAL-OF-SERVICE (DoS)

Acts a process that the users or the organization confronts a deprivation of the services of a resource they would normally expect to have. Some security professionals have argued that the cloud is more vulnerable to DoS attacks because it is shared by many users, which makes DoS attacks much more damaging. For example, Twitter suffered a devastating DoS attack during 2010(Subashini & Kavitha, 2012). However, many security techniques have been provided in order to avoid the DoS attackers as discussed later in Sections 5.

SIDE-CHANNEL

An attacker could attempt to compromise the cloud by placing a malicious virtual machine in close proximity to a target cloud server and then launching a side channel attack. Side-channel attacks have emerged as a kind of effective security threat targeting system implementation of cryptographic algorithms (Parsi & Sudha, 2012).

AUTHENTICATION ATTACK

Authentication is a weak point in hosted and virtual services and is frequently targeted. There are many different ways to authenticate users. The mechanisms used to secure the authentication process and the methods used are a frequent target of attackers (Popvic & Hocenski, 2010). Most user-facing services, today still use a simple username and password, type of knowledge-based authentication, with the exception of some financial institutions which have deployed various forms of secondary authentication (such as site keys, virtual keyboards, shared secret questions, etc.) to make it a bit more difficult for popular attacks (Jasim, 2012).

MAN-IN-THE-MIDDLE

This attack is carried out when an attacker places himself between two users at any time the attackers can place themselves into the communication's path in order to intercept and modify communications (see Figure 4). To avoid this type of attacks, some kinds of techniques are used that rely on assumptions combined with quantum cryptography concepts see (Taih & Jasim, 2011).

CLOUD ENCRYPTION MODELS

The two most important processes for information security in cloud environment are encryption and authentication. Generally, the encryption mechanism has become one basic priority in maintaining the data security in the cloud. Whereas, the Authentication mechanism is the process of insuring that both connection sides "service provider side and the end user side" are trusted. The following subsections describe two popular models based on data encryption and authentication mechanisms.

CIPHER CLOUD

Cipher Cloud provides a unified cloud encryption gateway with award-winning technology to encrypt sensitive data in real-time before it's sent to the cloud. It also protects enterprise data using formatting and operations-preserving encryption and tokenized in any private or public cloud environment without affecting functionality, usability, or performance (Cipher Cloud website, 2013).

Figure 4. Schematic of man-in-the-middle attack

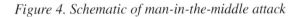
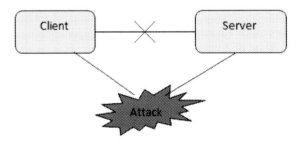

Cipher cloud is considered a new model for encrypted data in the cloud. Users probably have data stored in multiple clouds such as Google, Amazon, Azure, and many others. As an in-line security gateway that sits among users and cloud applications, cipher cloud applies encryption on the fly before sensitive data leaves the enterprise. It offers multiple AES-compatible encryptions and tokenized options, including format and function-preserving encryption algorithms. Users see the real data when gaining access to an application through the Cipher Cloud security gateway, but the data stored in a cloud application is encrypted (CSA, 2012),to understand this model see Figure 5.

By applying encryption in a cloud security gateway, cipher cloud eliminates the inherent security, privacy, and regulatory compliance risks of cloud computing. The cipher cloud security gateway uses flexible, configurable policies to identify sensitive data and automatically encrypt/decrypt data between users and the cloud using encryption keys that remain under the control at all times.

Cipher Cloud reverses the process when employees access cloud applications through the appliance decrypting data in real time, so that users see the actual data rather than the encrypted version that resides within the cloud.

CRYPTOGRAPHIC CLOUD STORAGE

Patil and Akshay (2012) proposed a virtual private storage services that would satisfy the standard requirements (Confidentiality, integrity, Authentication...etc.).

Most of the requirements are obtained by encrypting the documents stored in the cloud, but encryption makes it very hard to search through such documents or to collaborate in real time editing. This model introduced an architecture for a cryptographic storage service that would solve the security problems of "backups, archives, health record systems, secure data exchange and e-discovery".

This architecture is based on three components see Figure 6:

1. **Data Processor (DP):** Processes the data before sending it to the cloud;
2. **Data Verifier (DV):** Verifies data's integrity;
3. **Token Generator (TG):** Generates tokens allowing the service provider to retrieve documents.

Figure 5. Cloud encryption model

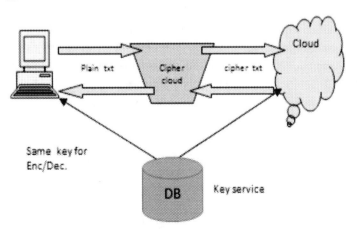

Figure 6. Cryptographic cloud storage architecture

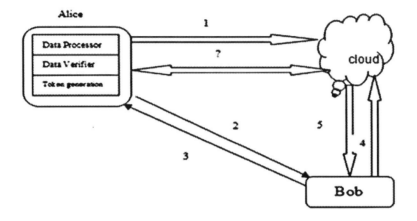

The consumer solution involves using a local application that has the three above mentioned components. Before uploading data to the cloud, Alice uses the data processor to encrypt and encode the documents along with their meta-data (tags, time, size, etc.), then she sends them into the cloud. When she wants to download some documents, Alice uses the TG to generate a token and a decryption key. The token is sent to the storage provider to select the encrypted files to be downloaded. After that, the DV is invoked to verify the integrity of the data using a master key. The document is decrypted using the decryption key.

Generally, the encryption process strategy in cloud environments, mainly depends on encrypting the data in two different phases; (a) in the transmission process before sending the data to the cloud and (b) in the storage process after the transmission and before the storing process.

Despite the encryption process uses complex techniques for random key generation based on mathematical models and computations, its encryption strategy considered vulnerable. So, if the intruder is good enough in the mathematical computation field, he/she can easily decrypt the cipher and retrieve the original transmitted or stored documents.

PROPOSED MODEL

This section show, in detail, the main building modules of the CCCE followed by an illustrative example of the interaction between the performed functions embedded in the different modules of CCCE. Our environment generates the encryption keys based on quantum mechanics instead of mathematics and computations, which in turn, provides unbroken key and eavesdropper detection. Most positive criteria associated with CCCE came from the nature of quantum system work.

CCCE MAIN BUILDING MODULES

CCCE combines cipher cloud model and cloud data encryption based quantum cryptography, aiming for two things.

First, deploy the key generation and key management techniques based on QKD to improve the availability and the reliability of the cloud computing encryption and decryption mechanisms, and second, manipulate heavy computing processes that cannot be executed using personal computers.

Numbers of computations are done in the proposed model before the data flying to the cloud environment. These computations are going to be discussed later in this section in detail.

The environment contains three basic phases with two suggested modes:

1. **Online Mode:** In this mode, clients directly negotiate with the quantum cipher cloud server, to get a final secret key, which used with AES algorithms to encrypt files;
2. **Offline Mode:** The quantum cipher cloud server negotiates with internal server to find the keys and store it in the secret database, next deploy this key to the guests as a genuine random number, it uses with AES algorithm to encrypt files.

With these two ways, the environment contains enterprise, QKD, and open cloud phase as shown in Figure7.

ENTERPRISE CONTROL

In this phase, clients perform some pre-processing operations on the input data before sending to the cloud environment using the following steps consequently:

Figure 7. Main building architecture

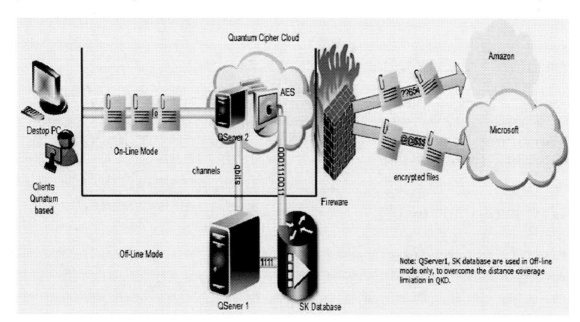

1. On-line:
   a. **Customer side:** Ambit of end user, enterprise, and remote mobile;
   b. Randomly, generate number of qubits are used in the encryption / decryption process;
2. Off-line:
   a. **Customer side:** Ambit of end user, enterprise, and remote mobile;
   b. **Cipher Cloud:** Embracing the encryption/decryption issues for the data or attached files.

This is bolstered by using one type of encryption algorithms such as AES.

QKD

This is the most important phase in the proposed model, it is responsible of key generation, key management and distribution. QKD is a powerful secure technique in which all tasks are computed by quantum physics and computing theory. It is not pure mathematical evolution, but it is a combination of conventional cryptography, information theory and quantum mechanics. Here, photons and spin particles are involved to implement QKD schemes (Lydersen, Wiechers, Wittman, Elser, Skaar, & Makarov, 2009). Moreover, it solves the complexity of the computational design that is associated with the conventional cryptography (Kollmitzer, 2010).

OPEN CLOUD PHASE

This is the beefiest phrase used to absorb and share the documents, the applications or the attachment files over the internet, such as Google Apps., Amazon EC2.

AN ILLUSTRATIVE EXAMPLE (ON-LINE MODE)

Figure 8 is a simple example that illustrates the sending and downloading operations done by the model using online connection and explains the corresponding results and actions taken by the system. The system interactions are written in normal font, the user behaviors are in bold, and our illustrations to some actions will be in capital letter.

ANALYSIS OF CCCE MODEL

In this section, the proposed model is analyzed based on the security management and the integration between the QKD and AES (cipher cloud container).

Figure 8. Sending and downloading operations using online connection

First: - *Sending Data to the Cloud Environment*
   THE SYSTEM ASKS THE USER TO LOG IN OR REGISTER IF IT IS HIS FIRST TIME.
System>> sign in or register as a new user
User >> customer_id
User>> ********
THE CUSTOMER_ID AND THE USER PASSWORD WILL BE SAVED IN THE DATABASE
System _{client}>> welcome "customer_id"; this is a new page for you.
System _{client}>> your account is ready for sending documents and files.
User>> beginning send the query to the system based on client screen.
System _{cloud provider}>> Received the query from the end user,
System _{cloud provider}>> Reply the trusted IP to the user.
System _{client and cloud provider} >> Invokes QKD to starting the key generation process
User>> turn-on client screen to start negotiation with a cloud provider
System _{client and cloud provider} >> generates the own key (Ks).
IN THIS CASE, THE SYSTEM DETERMINES THE FINAL SECRET KEY BASED ON BB84 PROTOCOL.
System _{client and the cloud provider} >> prepares the AES-128, 192, 256.
User>> choose the type of operation from the client screen choices
IN THIS CASE, USER CHOOSE THE TYPE OF ENCRYPTION (FILE, DOCUMENT)
User>> beginning choose the document (d) , choose the AES
System _{client}>> used the AES encryption algorithm to encrypt the documents (d).
EN (d, k) =d'
   SYSTEM COMPLETES THE DOCUMENTS ENCRYPTION.
User>> send the documents (d') to the system _{cloud provider}
User>> wait some seconds based on the internet connections speed.
System _{cloud provider}>> receive the encrypted document, decrypted it based on the own secret key
DE (d', k) =d
System >> files have been sent successfully.
User>> sign out from the system.
***Second:** - Download Data from the Cloud*
User>> sign in
User>> customer_id
User>> *******
SYSTEM>> Verifying the "customer_id" and the password.
System >> welcome "customer_id".
THE SYSTEM PREPARES THE GENERAL INFORMATION FOR THE USER SUCH AS (REMAINDER SPACE, NUMBERS OF FILES
STORED IN HIS ACCOUNT, PREVIEW THIS FILE FOR DOWNLOADING)
System _{cloud provider}>> Reply the trusted IP to the user.
System _{client and cloud provider} >> Invokes QKD to starting the key generation process
User>> turn-on client screen to start negotiation with a cloud provider
System _{client and the cloud provider} >> generate the own key (KS).
IN THIS CASE, THE SYSTEM DETERMINE THE FINAL SECRET KEY BASED ON BB84 PROTOCOL.
User _{client screen}>> send query to retrieve the documents (d).
System _{client and the cloud provider} >> prepares the AES-128, 192, 256.
System _{cloud provider}>> receive the query, encrypted document based on the own secret key
En (d, k) =d'
System _{cloud provider} >> sending the unknown file (d') to authorized users.
System _{client}>> used the AES encryption algorithm to decrypt documents (d').
DE (d', k) =d
User>> download the files and browse them.
System >> files have been sent successfully.
User>> sign out from the system.
AFTER THE SYSTEM FINISHES THE DOWNLOAD MECHANISM, IT WILL BE READY TO PERFORM ANY NEW OPERATION.

SECURITY MANAGEMENT

The rapid growth of cloud computing usage leads to more complications in the security management task that is mainly responsible for providing a secured environment for both the user and the provider. Confidentiality is one of the security management complications that can be assured by encrypting data, processes and communications using many encryption techniques (either symmetric or asymmetric), however, the key management problems (Taih & Jasim, 2011) are still the main limitation for the encryption techniques.

The proposed model has overcome the key availability problem by deploying a new hybrid technique that combines the AES algorithm and the QKD technique. This hybrid technique cultivates the following security management points:

1. Supports scalability in dynamic key distribution;
2. Defeats the most types of attack such as (man-in-the-middle-attack) see (Taih, Jasim, 2011);
3. Provides independent and trusted for each user "send or received" data to/from the cloud.

AES AND QKD INTEGRATION

In order to gain more secured internet communications, the technology environments based internet communications main concerns are the secret key (renewal rate) and the secret communication link. The key renewal rate influences the security of the encrypted data.

In this paper the key renewal influence will be annotated as the Key Encrypted Factor (KEF), which in turn going to be used in the proposed model to answer the following questions: How often secret session keys should be changed? And what is the impact of the classical message passing scheme on the global security?

The answers to the above two questions basically depend on the proposed environment in which the QKD is installed as the main server in the enterprise control phase (see Figure7.) associated with the AES, that is logically used as an encrypted for side-channel cryptanalysis protection. It is known that, in the heavy communication environments the key renewing process based AES algorithm causes collision- rated problem with "2 block length /2" rate (Sıddıka, Frank, Elisabeth & Bart, 2011).

To avoid such collisions, the proposed environment uses a hybrid technique that combines both the AES and the QKD. This combination should enhance the performance of the encryption/decryption process as follows:

If the rate of the key renewing = "$2^{block\ length/2}$", *then the QKD will supply the remaining final secret key.*

If the rate of the key renewing < "$2^{block\ length/2}$", *it is expected that the QKD will provide more new keys in a few seconds periodically.*

Or fully based on the keys are generated from QKD technique

For more clarification, in paper (Sıddıka, Frank, Elisabeth, & Bart, 2011; Eran, Dag, & Adi, 2010) the vulnerabilities of the AES implementation to side channel attacks are explained showing the stringent need for key renewal rate. These attacks can successfully break unprotected AES implementations after the acquisition of 100 process traces, while roughly 50000 power traces are needed to break protected implementations of AES. This result indicates that, in order to guarantee the security in the context of embedded systems, in which trust in the environment cannot be guaranteed, very fast key renewal is a necessity.

CONCLUSION

This paper proposed a new cloud computing environment "CCCE", which integrates and deploys both the AES based cipher cloud and QKD in a hybrid technique aiming to (i) provide more flexibility and secured communication environment, (ii) improve the performance of the encryption/decryption process, and (iii) support more secured data transmission process using less computational time.

Since any existing cloud computing environment depends on either QKD, or AES algorithms for encryption/ decryption process which protect users' data from hacking as much as possible. Our attempt proposes a hybrid technique that combines both the AES and the QKD to build more secured channels for data transmission. The encryption/ decryption process based the hybrid technique will be done before the storage and retrieval phases and after the user authentication phase.

Our attempt enjoys certain advantages when compared with the others, especially with respect to the secret key generation used in the encryption/ decryption process. It can be considered as the first cloud environment that integrates both the cipher cloud gateway and the QKD mechanisms. The preliminary study of the proposed model shows promising results where it shows the availability and the reliability of the secret key generation can be easily achieved based on two main modes, On-line and Off-line mode.

REFERENCES

Ateniese, G., Kamara, S., & Katz, J. (2012). Proofs of storage from holomorphic identification protocols. In Advances in Cryptology (ASIACRYPT '09) (Vol. 5912, Lecture Notes in Computer Science, pp. 319-333).

Cipher cloud gateway architecture. (n.d.). Retrieved from www.ciphercloud.net

Cloud Security Alliance (CSA). (n.d.). Retrieved from http://www.cloudsecurityalliance.org/

Ferrie, P. (2007). Attacks on virtual machine emulators, White Paper. *Symantec Corporation, 3*(12).

Grobauer, B., Walloschek, B., & Stöcker, E. (2009). Understanding cloud-computing vulnerabilities. *IEEE Security and Privacy, 99*, 23–39.

Hail, K., & Chau, H. (1999). Unconditional security of quantum key distribution over arbitrary long distances. *Science, 283*(5410), 2050–2056. doi:10.1126cience.283.5410.2050 PMID:10092221

Hirvensalo, M. (2013). *Quantum computing. Encyclopedia of sciences and religions* (pp. 1922–1926). Springer; doi:10.1007/978-1-4020-8265-8_1230

IDC. (2011). *IDC ranking of issues of cloud computing model*. Retrieved from http://blogs.idc.com/ie/?p=210

Jasim, O. (2012). The goals of parity bits in quantum key distribution system. *International Journal of Computers and Applications, 56*(18), 975–8887.

Jensen, M., Schwenk, J., Gruschka, N., & Iacono, L. (2009). On technical security issues in cloud computing. In IEEE ICCC (pp. 109-116). doi:10.1109/CLOUD.2009.60

John, M., & Ingo, L. (2010). An analysis of the cloud computing security problem. *APSEC 2010 Proceeding Cloud Workshop*, Sydney, Australia.

Kandukuri, R., & Ramakrishna, R. (2009). Cloud security issues. In *Proceedings of the 2009 IEEE International Conference on Services Computing* (pp. 517-520). 10.1109/SCC.2009.84

Kollmitzer, W., & Pivk, E. (2010). *Applied quantum cryptography*. Lecture Note in Physics ISSN 0075-8450, Springer Heidelberg, library of Congress Control Number:2010920541.

Kun, G., Qin, W., & Lifeng, X. (2013). Redact algorithm based execution times prediction in knowledge discovery cloud computing environment. [IAJIT]. *The International Arab Journal of Information Technology*, *10*(13), 47–56.

Lohr, T., & Steve, G. (2009). Cloud computing and EMC deal. *The New York Times*.

Lydersen, L., Wiechers, C., Wittman, C., Elser, D., Skaar, J., & Makarov, V. (2009). Hacking commercial quantum cryptography systems by tailored bright. *IJQS*, *2*(9), 67–80.

Mandeep, T., & Manish, Y. (2013). Using encryption algorithms to enhance the data security in cloud computing. *International Journal of Communication and Computer Technologies*, *1*(12), 78–89.

Markoff, T., & John, N. (2001). An internet critic who is not shy about ruffling the big names in high technology. *New York Times*.

McAllister, R. (2008). Server virtualization. *InfoWorld*, *3*(12), 34–51.

Mohit, E., & Prem, A. (2012). To enhance the data security of cloud in cloud computing using RSA algorithm. *International Journal of Software Engineering*, *1*(1).

Parsi, N., & Sudha, J. (2012). Data security in cloud computing using RSA algorithm. *International Journal of Research in Computer Communication Technology*, *1*(4), 23–37.

Patil, D., & Akshay, R. (2012). Data security over cloud emerging trends in computer science and information technology. In *Proceedings of the International Journal of Computer Applications* (pp. 123-147).

Popovic, K., & Hocenski, Z. (2010). Cloud computing security issues and challenges. In *Conference on Advances in Human-oriented and Personalized Mechanisms, Technologies, and Services* (pp. 344-349).

Rawal, V., Dhamija, A., & Sharma, S. (2012). Revealing new concepts in cpytography & clouds. *International Journal of Scientific & Technology Research*, *1*(7).

Rukhin, A., Soto, J., & Nechvatal, J. (2010). A statistical test suite for random and pseudorandom number generators for cryptographic applications. *IJCA*, *2*(5), 78–90.

Sherif, M., & Hatem, G. (2012). Modern encryption techniques for cloud computing. In *Proceedings of the 2nd International Conference on Communication and Information Technology*.

Singh, B. (2012). Enhancing security in cloud computing using public key cryptography with matrices. *International Journal of Engineering Research and application, 2*(4).

Stipčević, R., & Medved, Y. (2007). Quantum random number generator based on photonic emission in semiconductors. *Review of Scientific Instruments, 78.* 045104 _2007, doi:10.1063/1.2720728

Subashini, T., & Kavitha, V. (2012). A survey on security issues in service delivery models of cloud computing. *Journal of Network and Computer Applications, 2,* 90–101.

Taih, S., & Jasim, O. (2011). Reducing the authentication cost in quantum cryptography. ISBN: 978-1-902560-25-0 © 2011 PGNet- Liverpool, UK.

This research was previously published in the International Journal of Grid and High Performance Computing (IJGHPC) edited by Emmanuel Udoh, Ching-Hsien Hsu, and Mohammad Khan, pages 38-51, copyright year 2014 by IGI Publishing (an imprint of IGI Global).

Chapter 53

Solutions for Securing End User Data over the Cloud Deployed Applications

Akashdeep Bhardwaj
University of Petroleum and Energy Studies (UPES), India

ABSTRACT

With more and more organizations working on the cloud over unsecure internet, sharing files and emails and saving them on cloud storage imperative. Securing the end user sensitive data in transit has thus started to get maximum priority to protect it from Cloud company staff, hackers and data thieves. In this study, an attempt is made to review the research of end user data security. There is an urgent need for solutions for end users' data protection, privacy and during the times when migrating from one Cloud service provider to other. This chapter identifies end user data challenges and issues on cloud and presents use of Public Key Cryptography, Multi Factor Authentication and use of Cloud Aware applications as possible solutions.

INTRODUCTION TO END USER COMPUTING

Cloud based services provide flexible, scalable, pay-per-use, short term contract model for the IT Services make Cloud based services an efficient, affordable and easy to implement option reducing capital expenditure involving IT hardware, licenses, office space, computing power and bandwidth. Security of user data needs to be in place more so in today's context with Cloud based application being hosted on the service provider premise as well as the end user residing in a remote data center, well outside the user's control.

As per a recent survey conducted by International Data Group (IDG), the top three challenges for implementing cloud based security strategy differs between IT and the line-of-business (LOB). A survey conducted by International Data Corporation (IDC) declares that 47% IT Heads are highly concerned about security threats in cloud computing. In a recent survey conducted by Cisco, two thirds of the respondents acknowledged that security and privacy are the top two security issues for cloud consumers.

DOI: 10.4018/978-1-5225-8176-5.ch053

This chapter reviews the challenges in Cloud computing services regarding end user data, analyzing the issues face and presents solutions to overcome them (Schutz et al., 2016). The end user data required to be protected is of four types ranging from usage data which is the information collected from computer systems, then is the sensitive information on health and bank accounts, then is the Personally identifiable information; information to identify an individual and finally is the Unique device identity information that is uniquely traceable like IP addresses, unique hardware identities (MAC address).By using solution paths such as digital keys, multi factor authentication and cloud aware applications.

When there is a need to provide End users with the right type of IT resources to enable them to perform their tasks, usually we do not emphasize on importance of securing the end user data (Bouchana et al., 2015). End user data for end user functionalities such as support, buying hardware, software and licenses, then plan endlessly for installation, support, maintenance as well as worry about capacity planning, creating IDs, configuring profiles or sit on a budgeted pile of money waiting for hiring to be completed.

1. **Web Based Services:** Internet email services (Gmail, Yahoo, and Hotmail), Online stores (Amazon, Fab furnish, Jabong), Web hosting (NetMagic, Tulip). These have been around for many years.
2. **Distributed Computing:** Splitting the processing workload among multiple systems usually connected at the same sites like being done in Parallel and Grid computing technologies.
3. **Datacenters:** Single application being hosted in one location (over single or even multiple servers) does not qualify as a Cloud. Cloud computing leverages pooled hardware resources, automation services involving great deal of virtualization hosted across datacenters.

In these avenues, there are different types of security challenges and versatile solutions for each of the cloud deployment models and also overcome them as well.

1. Software as a Service (SaaS) is pay on demand where users accessing over the cloud some of the examples such as On-Demand CRM Salesforce, Google Apps, Microsoft Office 365, Microsoft Sky Drive.
2. Platform as a Service (PaaS) provides end users with complete environment so that developers can deploy their apps, perform testing and hosting of web applications and databases and that provides virtual servers, OS, development framework and coding apps. Examples are Google apps, Azure from Microsoft, Rack Space.
3. Infrastructure as a Service (IaaS) provides hardware and computing power to end user to provision and harness resources from computing, network devices, storage or servers where the customers pay only for the amount of infrastructure used and not worry about buying hardware, maintaining or upgrading issues. Infrastructure can be scaled up or down dynamically based on application resource and market demands. Some of the examples are Amazon EC2, Rack Space, Attenda RTI, Eucalyptus (Open source).

BACKGROUND

During the 1950-1960s, computer belonged primarily inside government and business establishments and were highly centralized consisting of mainframes in form of large, powerful computer systems, capable of processing high volumes, store large number of records in databases in Data Processing departments. This was primarily for payroll and transaction processing.

The 1960-1970s witnessed the first baby steps towards decentralized computing. Terminals came into the MIS departments with keyboard and VGA monitors connected to mainframes. These had no processing powers of their own and are what is termed as 'dumb terminals'. All the processing was performed on the mainframe.

The 1980s and 1990s saw the growth of decentralized computing. The main reasons for this change was the large number of backlog of application requests for new mainframe programs, increase in knowledge workers able to design and write new programs directly with systems and do more efficient jobs, hardware costs around the globe declined with desktop systems being available for as low as $2000, easy availability of inexpensive software packages like WordStar, dBase, VisiCalc and Lotus-1-23 and moving from user typed commands at a terminal to point and click mouse friendly Graphical User Interface which made the processing programs much easier to use than that the command oriented mainframe programs.

The late 1990s and 2000s further enhanced the goal of making the employees more productive, which meant decentralized end user computing moved to use of distributed networked systems impacting end users in office and homes. The legacy data processing department moved on to become Information Technology Services with newer applications like ERP and CRM. Small but more powerful computing systems (Servers) started to be used resulting in Client Server Computing in which some data and processing was performed on the client and some on the central system which became the data storage processing system (Salvi et al., 2015).

In recent years, Cloud computing and Virtualization has changed the way of work totally. Now remote, work from home or during travel has become possible over smart phones, iPads and Tabs. Modern information threat vectors for end user data have risen in the recent years, these ranges from hackers on hire seeking to steal end user intellectual property data to employees unaware about data security and protection (Fallon & O'Sullivan, 2014). Proper data protection systems need to be in place and a culture of security awareness needs to be a high priority goal of the information security team. European Network and Information Security Agency (ENISA) having identified thirty-five security risks, further subdividing them into policy organizational risks, legal risks, technical risks and non-cloud related.

From these risks, the ENISA identified eight most important risks, five of which directly or indirectly relate to data confidentiality risks. These risks include isolation failure, malicious insider threats, data protection, insecure data deletion and management interface compromise. Similarly, Cloud Security Alliance (CSA) identifies the thirteen kind of risks related to the cloud computing. From among the thirteen risks, CSA declares seven high priority risks, five of which are directly or indirectly involved with data confidentiality which includes: malicious insiders, insecure application programming interfaces, traffic hijacking and account service and data losses.

1. S. Jegadeeswari, P. Dinadayalan and N. Gnanambigai (2015) suggested a new cloud security model related to quality of Service(QoS) for end user data regarding confidentiality to the outsources data on the cloud in form of a Neural Data Security model. This ensured security and high confidentiality using RSA security algorithm (S. Jegadeeswari et al., 2015).

2. Jun Hu et al. addresses data security access control model for secure data access based on MAC control for government cloud platform model. This model includes necessary technical strategies to ensure data security during access. These reviewed relationships between risk factors and expected

solutions. Data access security model with a 3-stage control technology was proposed and high reliability for data displayed (Hu, 2013).

3.   A review of data security issues in cloud computing environment presented by Sahil Zatakiya et al. as a unique cloud computing pattern with resources being provided on demand via internet medium (Zatakiya & Tank, 2013). Security and privacy issues related with cloud and its data storage are analyzed in the paper along with various attacks on cloud computing. Challenges like security issues, data challenges were identified along with solutions regarding the security issues.

4.   N. Hemalatha et al. addresses a comparative analysis of encryption techniques and data security Issues in cloud computing. In this cloud computing technologies regards to delivery models, cloud classification and encryption mechanisms are discussed (Hemalatha et al., 2014). A comparative study is made based on the encryption techniques to maintain the security and confidentiality over a cloud. Cloud computing is classified in various parts regards to data storage, integrity, backup and recovery, security and confidentiality. The importance of data privacy and security is analyzed and encryption techniques used in cloud environment are compared.

5.   Zhang Xin et al (2012) addresses a research on cloud computing data security model based on multi dimensions (Zhang Xin et al., 2012). A complete data security three-layer defense model based on multi dimension is proposed. User authentication and Unauthorized user access is discussed. Every layer has their own role yet combine with each other to data security in cloud computing environments.

6.   Faraz Fatemi M. et al proposed an efficient scalable user authentication model scheme for cloud computing environments by designing user authentication and access control model to enhance the rate of trust and reliability (Fatemi et al., 2014). Separate server systems to stores authentication and cryptography resources from the real time servers are proposed, these help decrease the user authentication dependency and encryption process on the main authentication server.

7.   Data security and authentication hybrid cloud computing model is presented by Jingxin Wang and Xinpei Jia (2012) Various methods to protect user data are discussed regards to security which includes single encryption, multilevel virtualization and authentication interface based on PKI and CA model for better performance (Jingxin & Xinpei, 2012).

END USER APPLICATIONS

End user Applications make a tremendous impact on employee productivity and working culture in form of specialized designed application packages, some of them are mentioned below.

Email and Instant Messaging

Email application enables home and corporate users to contact and communicate with each other and is one of the most commonly used business and personal application package on end user desktops/laptops today. Computer systems need to be connected to a network or the internet for sending and receiving e-mails. The emails are composed using a word processor front end by typing texts and then transmitting that in form of email and receiving messages and attachments. These can be added to the email in form of a document, email itself, worksheets, photographs or other files from an application program—usually WinZip (Feifei & Liping, 2015). Instant messaging or chat is an online communication between multiple users connected to the Internet in real time. This application notifies the user when the others are online so that chat session can be initiated and users can interact. Typical examples are Microsoft Outlook as part of Office 2013 suite package.

Web Browsers

Web browser enables internet users to search and view web information from the Internet. Web pages of information hosted on servers are transmitted over Internet in form of Hypertext Markup Language (HTML) or Java codes. Once the user inputs the web site name or address, the Web browser retrieves the web page to display on the user's PC. Internet has a host of online sites which provide all the information that is required by the user during his browsing session. In the last 5-6 years due to the enormous popularity of the World Wide Web as an information retrieval for home and business users alike, this application has become one of the most popular packages. Typical examples are Internet Explorer, Mozilla Firefox

Document Processing

Word-processing software enables end users to edit, store, format or print information in form of a document. Many word processors also permit users to integrate graphics, numbers, and footnotes easily into a document. Because most clerical, administrative, and managerial employees produce letters, memos, papers, reports, and other printed documents, word processors are one of the most frequently used software applications among end users. Most widely used package is Microsoft Office suite which includes Word as the document processing application.

Spreadsheets

Because clerical, administrative, and managerial employees frequently work with numeric information in addition to texts data for preparing budgets, financial statements, forecasts among others reports in which numeric data is structured as rows and columns in the worksheet to produce meaningful results, graphs and analyzed data. These are again an integral part of Microsoft Office suite.

Database Management Systems

The database management program allows end users to enter, update, store, format and generate reports from data stored as set of records inside tables in the databases. Client and Mailing lists, Employee records, office inventories and class rosters are examples of common databases. Home users at times utilize the database management applications to organize their personal data such as a club roster, or lists, such as an inventory of antique collectibles. Database package is often included in office "suites" of programs to sophisticated enterprise wide database packages (Fidas et al., 2015). Some sophisticated database software includes a data mart, which is a user-friendly front-end that allows employees to extract and analyze data from a database without programming skills. Microsoft SQL and Oracle are two well-known DBMS systems in this domain.

Graphical

Users often need to organize and summarize information in the form of pictures, charts, or drawings. This helps users create illustrations, photographs and charts that summarize large data, analyze trends or show relationships and create presentations in form of slide shows with charts, text, pictures and diagrams for sales, training, lectures, or other similar events requiring visual information. Although specialized software applications are designed for high end graphical usage in engineering design and complex simulation activities, many word-processor, spreadsheet, and database packages sold today also include some graphics capabilities. Adobe Photoshop and Corel Draw are the well-known graphical packages.

Planning and Scheduling

Corporate employees spending sizable office time plan for their assigned tasks, projects and monthly work by carefully scheduling the individual tasks and team projects. Software packages for planning and scheduling which help business and end users maintain an electronic calendar, a to-do list, and an address book. For collaborative projects, scheduling is used for arranging calling, meetings at times convenient for all members in a group. These also help project managers to monitor, plan, and schedule tasks and resources in a group project. Microsoft Project is one such package useful.

Desktop Publishing

This package is a combination of word processor and graphics software. Desktop publishing helps end users design the lay out and prepare quality brochures, documents, newsletters, posters, computer manuals and material which might otherwise be required to be typeset and designed on a printing press system by professionals. Desktop publishing gives the end user more control over typographical add-on features to generate superior what you see is what you get features, preview on the screen before going for printing.

Web Development

Web site development is useful for professionals and home users to design, code and develop the enterprise and personal sites hosted over internet. Web site development packages create, maintain and update portal pages which include text and graphics. The site can incorporate e-mail links, chat rooms, blogs, video streaming. Packages for web development range from word processing to sophisticated packages for professional Web programmers.

Educational and Entertainment

These provide end user learners starting from with basic exposure to detailed experience supplementing over the web with an instructor's lectures or distributed materials. Educational software can also test and provide response on learners' understanding of concepts or on their ability to solve problems. Tutorial software is also available to help computer users learn new software packages. Computer games are, of course, a significant portion of the entertainment industry.

END USER CHALLENGES IN CLOUD

While the Confidentiality, Integrity and Availability triad is the most critical in development, maintenance and availability of cloud application during regular execution for any business enterprise, check on unauthorized users using organization email or sharing critical end user documents or financial data is essential to be performed on regular basis. Another critical gap could be the application data stored in business users' computers – this leads to confidentiality issue (Tzeremes & Gomaa, 2016). At times the End User Computing configuration items typically reside and stored on user local system or in shared drives, not following the right change management processes. Also lack of access control leads to accidental and intentional manipulation of the end user data or their application configuration items which ends up causing availability and integrity issues (Hylli et al., 2014). Risk assessment control areas can be defined which need to include Input, Output/Edits, Data processing, Report, Output file, Backups, Business continuity plans, Change management, Incident, Problem management, Access provisioning, Data privacy, Monitoring, Disposal of end user computing application and Disposal of end user data.

Benefits enjoyed are more often than not accompanied by new set of problems that organizations need to address. The issues can result from an environment in which high end computing system tools are being used by a large number of employees. There is a good chance that end users will encounter one or more of these problems in the course of their work or home computing experience.

Wastage

Refers to the use of money, time, or other resources that do not pay back directly or provide any add-ons to the increased user productivity, or may even result in lower productivity. End users with their limited computer system trainings and skills as compared to computer professionals, often lack skills for performing cost-effective procurements regarding computing hardware network and peripherals or application software. For example, end users who are not knowledgeable about using optimized hardware and software computing, end up purchasing that does not operate (or operate efficiently) on their hardware configurations. If the software an end user purchases operates inefficiently or causes the user's system to crash frequently, the result is often frustration and lower user productivity. Waste also occurs when a software purchase does not meet the required anticipated needs or the software actually costs more than a similar package for a lot less. Another form of waste is employee time spent viewing information over internet, reading or sharing e-mail or social networking messages that are non-productive.

User Mistakes

End users who are careless or ill trained tend to make slipups when using sophisticated software. For example, a project manager estimating a project costs and timelines could inadvertently enter the wrong formula or data for critical calculations. The user may not understand the importance of testing even simple spreadsheet formulas for correctness and tend to assume that results prepared on a computer, are 100% accurate. However, if a formula or number is entered incorrectly, then the results will be incorrect. Another common mistake is a user's failure to make backups of important information. Computer mistakes can be extremely costly, especially in high-stakes business situations.

Cyber Crimes

Although waste and mistakes are usually unintentional, computers are also used to commit intentional crimes. For example, an employee may have access to company information that would be potentially valuable to a competitor, and may try to profit from the sale of the information. Information theft, identity theft, fraud, sabotage is performed over web using computer systems. These crimes are not unique to end-user computing; they emerged very early in the use of mainframe computers. However, the number of personal computer users, the lack of security measures and access to information double the potential for computer crimes among end users.

Computer Piracy

This involves illegal copying, distribution, or use of computer programs or information. Because floppy disks and CDs are simple to copy, software theft is frequent. For example, employees might take the legally bought software application packages to install them on home computers. Legal or illegal? The answer depends on the software vendor's license agreement and on the employer's policies. Sharing software among home users is a similar problem, and also illegal. In fact, software piracy costs software companies billions of dollars in lost sales (Yao et al., 2014). Because pirated software is also a source of computer viruses, the costs in lost productivity are substantially higher than the loss of sales revenue among vendors.

Data Loss

Many end users at home or even in corporate offices do not backup the data as often as they should or as per the company policy, even as a lot of critical information is stored on their workplace and home systems. Consequently, when hardware, software, or a network fails, they risk losing data. Loss of critical data can be expensive because lost data is sometimes impossible to replace. Manual re-entry of destroyed data is expensive and time-consuming, and may contribute to a business failure as compared to recovery of data from a disk or tape.

Virus

A computer virus is a program created with the intent to manipulate and destroy information, erase or corrupt other software and data, or adversely affect computer operations infected by the virus program. Viruses are transmitted from computer to computer via networks over the Internet via data being exchanged by emailing or copying or even use of disk disks, CDs media or USB removable disks and backup tapes). In a networked environment, such as an instructional computer lab at a school or a training department in an organization, the spread of computer viruses is a frequent problem for computer facilities managers. Anti-virus services are expensive and need to be kept updated for defending against new versions of viruses. However, the cost to an individual or an organization of virus attacks, removal, and data restoration can be many times the cost of an antivirus utility program.

Privacy

Another form of computer crime is invasion of privacy; whereby unauthorized parties exploit personal information. This problem occurs because vast amounts of information about employees, clients, patients, and students is often stockpiled in computer systems drives. Without proper policies and security codes of conduct safeguards, authorization access from external or internal sources can cause immense privacy and identity theft issues.

Health

One major source of misuse that may not even be apparent to computer users is the physical environment where systems are operated. Without proper lighting, space, furniture, and environmental safeguards, physical injury to end users can result. Without proper operating procedures and techniques, an appropriate work environment, periodic breaks, and corrective eyewear, employees may subject themselves to a variety of physical ailments (Vollala et al., 2014). Common ailments include headaches, nausea, eyestrain, hand or wrist pain and back and neck aches. Other longer-term health impacts due to extensive computer use, are consequences the medical profession doesn't yet fully understand or know how to treat. Ergonomics is an area that designs workspace to promote employee health, safety, and productivity. Many common ailments can be avoided by paying attention to ergonomics. Employees who provide technical support to end users often confront these problems. Similarly, a technical support job may include providing end users with solutions to many of these same problems. End users typically face the following challenges in Cloud Computing:

1. Limited support for customization can be done for Cloud applications and services to suit end user specific requirements.
2. **Constraints on Features:** Cloud apps tend to be less feature rich as compared to their on-site or in-house counterparts because of in-built capabilities.
3. **Application Latency:** Latency becomes a major factor for Cloud apps that are dependent on transfer of large volumes or time sensitive data.
4. **Statelessness:** Performance issues arise for Cloud apps as the communication is unidirectional, single requests and responses from end users traveling to and from a service provider experience drops or disconnects travel over different paths/routes tend to arrive out of sequence.
5. **Legal Restrictions:** At times force organizations to secure and control its data in a specific geographical location for the Cloud provider's data center.
6. Security of end user data is the most critical issue, depends on Cloud provider's architecture and model, cloud vendors are primarily responsible for managing environmental and virtualization security ensuring Security, Authentication, Integrity and Privacy for data stored on their sites or in transit over unsecure internet links. Here data breaches, compromised credentials/broken authentication, hacked interfaces and APIs, system vulnerabilities due to Zero Day attacks, Account hijacking, Malicious insider threats, Advanced persistence threats, permanent data loss, inadequate compliance checks, DDoS attacks and use of shared resources and storage are among the most critical security issues plaguing end users and their data (Qin Liu et al., 2015).

Below are some of the concerns that are regularly raised by End users and Cloud service consumers to Cloud Service Providers or CSPs. The remaining section presents proposed solutions for resolving these data security issues for the end users.

1.   How Cloud Service Providers instill Confidentiality and Integrity for end user data?
2.   How should the CSPs protect stored data from attacks which is in their cloud data centers?
3.   How to change CSPs and be able to move and migrate from one CSP to another?

SOLUTIONS AND RECOMMENDATIONS: PROPOSED SOLUTIONS FOR RESOLVING CLOUD DATA SECURITY ISSUES

End User Security Using Public Key Cryptography

For Authentication and Integrity issues faced in cloud computing, by implementing Public Key Cryptography seems to be the right approach as shown in the Figure 1. When data is in transit over unsecure internet circuits, unauthorized access of end user data is the main security issue faced by one and all when utilizing Cloud computing services.

To resolve the Cloud Service Providers Security issue of Authentication and Integrity Public Key Cryptography should be used, this is for encryption and decryption of data on the cloud. Encryption is the process of conversion of data into seemingly random, incomprehensible data which ensures that data remains jumbled to everyone for whom it is not intended, even if the intended user has access to the encrypted data. Using the PKI framework which internally has security policies, communication protocols, and procedures to enable secure and trusted communication between cloud service providers or CSPs and the end users over unsecure internet circuits and Cloud computing environments inside as well as outside the organization.

The Public Key Infrastructure is on the hybrid mode encryptions like Symmetric and Asymmetric. The only option for transforming the user data back into intelligible form is to reverse the encryption or decryption using single secret key or two secret keys (Public and Private). The Public Key is available to everyone via a public repository or directory while the Private Key remains confidential to its

Figure 1. Encryption-decryption process

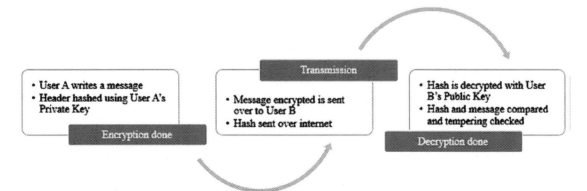

respective owner. Since the key pairs are related mathematically, whatever is encrypted with a Public Key can be decrypted by the corresponding Private Key or vice versa. Public Key Crypto is enabled in the Cloud by means of the following:

1. Each entity encrypts data using their own private keys.
2. All systems and elements in the system like data center units, infrastructure platforms, virtualization systems and other tools entities that are involved, and have their own keys.
3. While fulfilling information exchange and processing functions, then systems and elements will use public and private keys to perform authentication first.
4. Events that occur in the cloud computing are also assigned a unique key.
5. Then the crypto cloud assures security and credibility for the information exchange.

To reap the advantages of Cloud Computing, Services Providers are best advised to go for the following practices and design features of PKI that can further enhance the security:

1. Key Management Server (KMS) should be implemented inside the organization, for the enterprise data stored in the Cloud requires Encryption Keys to decrypt as end-user request, which only the key management server provides them. The Encryption Keys for decrypting data from cipher text to the original plain text should not be on the cloud virtual machines and security process be implemented so that these keys should reside in-memory for a few seconds.
2. Any data moving out or coming in of the data centers can be encrypted and decrypted respectively.
3. The Virtual Machines hosted in the Cloud provider's environment should be encrypted at all point of times in order to protect any kind of data loss in case the virtual snapshot is compromised.
4. In case data encryption is not required, the service provider should revoke any keys associated so that even any sort of data trail remains in the system, it cannot be decrypted.
5. Storage of keys should be done using Hardware Security Model or HSM for performing encryption and decryption.
6. Unsecure encryption algorithms such as RC4, MD5, SHA-1 and Data Encryption Standard (DES) must always be avoided.
7. AES is the symmetric key block cipher algorithm to provide cloud data security. This block cipher uses 128-bit block size and key length can be 128, 192, and 256. Advantages of AES:
   a. Performs in software and hardware platform environments with equal ease.
   b. Inherent process facilities resulting in very good software performance.
   c. Speedy key setup time and good key ability.
   d. Less memory for implementation.
   e. Benefits from instruction level parallelism.
   f. No serious weak keys in AES.

Use Multi Factor Authentication

Multifactor authentication or use of at least two separate identifiers of authentication instead using just an Id and password helps increase security access by adding multiple barriers for inbound user access before actual entry is allowed. In doing so, this reduces the likelihood of an attacker break in plus at the same time makes it harder for anyone with a stolen password gain entry to the system accessing critical data. Protect the users' data stored in cloud servers from external attacks using multi factor authentication, firewalls, and load balancers with specific ports and IDS intrusion detection System.

Establishing robust data center architecture and protection system process for cloud storage systems by applying the following:

- **Multi Factor Authentication (XFC):** This is something the user know (Password) and something the user has been provided by the Cloud provider (RSA Token) or other processes as shown in the Figure 2.
- Security Systems like Firewalls and Load Balancers before the Storage servers which allow only specific ports and data flow inside the Cloud data centers.
- Intrusion Detection System or IDS to detect unauthorized activities in four main areas:
  - **In the Virtual Machine (VM) Itself:** By deploying IDS on the VM, IDS can monitor the system activity to detect and alert on issues that may arise.
  - **In the Hypervisor or Host System:** By having the IDS deployed on the hypervisor host, IDS can monitor the hypervisor as well as traffic between VMs running on the hypervisor. It is a more centralized location for IDS, but there may be issues in keeping up with performance or dropping some information in case the amount of data is huge.
  - **In the Virtual Network:** By deploying the IDS within the host, virtual network monitoring can be done which allows the IDS to monitor the network traffic between the Virtual machines on host systems, as well as the traffic between the host and VMs. This "network" traffic never hits the traditional network.
  - **In the Traditional Network:** Deploying IDS allows IDS to detect and alert regarding the traffic passes from the network devices and infrastructure.
- Using different VLANs and Switches inside data centers for inbound and outbound traffic using
- **Limiting User Access and Separation of Data:** This is done by applying separation for the data that is being stored in servers as per end user profiles i.e. read-only for external level 1 user, read-write for corporate employee as level 2, read-write-delete-modify for enterprise administrators as level 3 users.

Real time examples of multi factor authentication use are Office 365 and Azure MFC. Within Office 365 Exchange, Sharepoint, Lync, Dynamics CRM, Project Management and Office 2013 can be used with multi factor authentication as shown in the Figure 2.

Use of Cloud Aware Applications

Provisioning users migrating from one cloud provider to another and move their Applications, Data and services between Cloud providers by ensuring implementation of cloud aware architectures. This is done be ensuring the applications being built are Cloud-aware and Cloud migration planning is performed for the new Cloud provider's data center. Applications need to be made more Cloud-aware for which there is a need to:

- Review Code and then Architect applications to increase cloud portability.
- Design and Develop open standards for cloud computing.
- Use tools that can work to move applications around clouds without any modifications.

Figure 2. Multi factor authentication overview

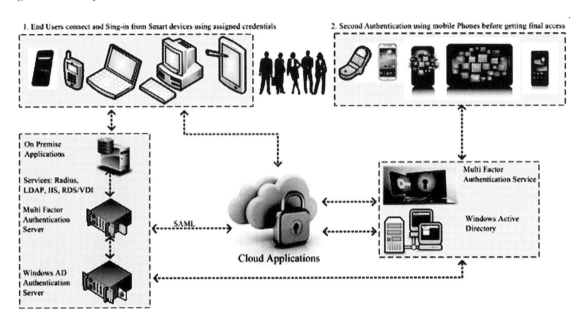

For the Cloud migration planning there is a need to involve the following:

- Discovery of new environment.
- Application, Server and Data migrationn plan.
- Post-migration configuration.
- Verification testing.

During the migration from one Cloud Service Provider to another, users should also include checking on the use of standardized storage protocols for example the ISO standard Cloud Data Management Interface (CDMI) by providers for the Cloud Providers having integration and trust relationship with other providers. Cloud Aware applications have the ability to decrease server count and are able to handle massive work load by virtue of the ability to scale elastically, maximize tenants and minimize idle computing resource. Furthermore, to reduce data transfer costs application developers and data center handlers need to:

1. Minimize payload sizes by using APIs that return only the data required by the consumer needs and perform data compression, reduce CPU computing cost for encoding and decoding.
2. Minimize data transfers by using cache immutable data and seek to replace "chatty" protocols.
3. Instrument code by tracking data transfers throughout an application, which helps identify optimization options and the use of load traffic generation tools which can provide insight into impact of such optimizations.

Cloud Aware Application Maturity Model provides a simple way to assess the level of cloud maturity of an application, just as the Richardson Maturity Model measures the maturity of a REST API. The maturity model suggests changes that can be implemented to increase an application's resilience, flexibility, and scalability in a cloud environment. As listed in Table 1, there are four levels to the maturity model with level 3 representing the highest level of maturity and level 0 representing applications that are not cloud aware.

The author setup web application server using .NET framework 2.0 with Windows 2012 Standard Edition running IIS using HTTPS and SQL Server 2008 as the backend for Admin Portal to setup the multi factor authentication system as a system for user access to the cloud service and created an OTP Client application. The authentication process is defined as follows and described in the Figure 3.

Table 1. Cloud aware application maturity levels

Maturity Level	Application Description
Level 3: Adaptive	Dynamically migrate infrastructure between providers without any service Application can dynamically scale out or scale in based on stimuli
Level 2: Abstracted	Services are stateless Application unaware - unaffected by dependent service failures Application infrastructure agnostic - can run anywhere
Level 1: Loosely Coupled	Application composed - loosely coupled services Application services - discoverable by name Application computing and storage - kept separated Application consumes one of more from compute, storage, and network
Level 1: Loosely Coupled	Application runs - virtualized infrastructure Application can be instantiated - from an image or script

Figure 3. Web application with OTP authentication

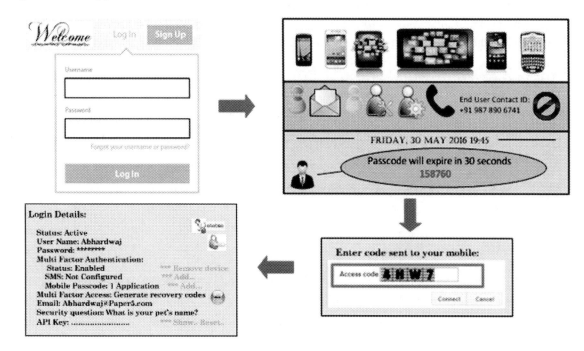

Figure 4. Traffic flow for End User authentication

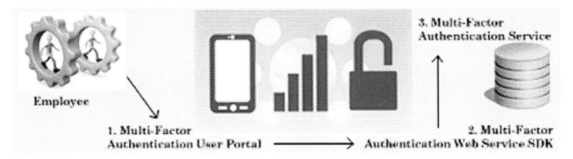

1. User registered and verified end user mobile for receiving SMS.
2. SMS received by the mobile is actually a 4-digit verification code in form of one-time-password (or OTP).
3. To register and verify OTP device, and pair with a cloud account, the OTP Client application to scan and verify the code form.
4. Once done a passcode is generated to enter on the cloud site along with the end user name and password as shown in the Figure 3 and Figure 4.

CONCLUSION

In this chapter the authors identified issues that end users face when using Cloud computing services. Then the authors focused on three specific issues and suggested solutions on making data on the cloud more secure from unauthorized access for integrity during transmission with the Public Key Cryptography, using security systems and solutions to enable end users to have their data interoperate with different cloud providers when migrating from one cloud provider to another. The result analysis is as follows.

*   Public Key Cryptography therefore helps achieve Confidentiality and Data Integrity for end user data over Cloud.
*   With Cloud-aware apps, proper Cloud migration planning and use of standard Cloud storage protocols between the Cloud provider helps achieve application and data migration between providers in a smooth manner.
*   Using multi Factor Authentication along with Intrusion Detection Systems and network traffic routing helps achieve mitigation from attackers for Cloud Computing.

REFERENCES

Bouchana, S., & Abdou Janati Idrissi, M. (2015). Towards an assessment model of end user satisfaction and data quality in Business Intelligence system. *10th International Conference on Intelligent Systems: Theories and Applications* (SITA). doi:10.1109/ICBDSC.2016.7460388

Fallon, L., & O'Sullivan, D. (2014). SECCO: A test framework for controlling and monitoring end user service sessions. *IEEE Network Operations and Management Symposium* (NOMS). doi:10.1109/IADCC.2015.7154830

Fatemi, F., Roshan Ravan, R., Khodadadi, T., Javadianasl, Y., & Halalzadeh, A. (2014). SUAS: Scalable user authentication scheme for secure accessing to cloud-based environments. *IEEE Symposium on Computer Applications and Industrial Electronics (ISCAIE)*.

Feifei, H., & Liping, Z. (2015). Supporting End-User Service Composition: A Systematic Review of Current Activities and Tools, Web Services. *ICWS IEEE International Conference*.

Fidas, C., Sintoris, C., Yiannoutsou, N., & Avouris, N. (2015). A survey on tools for end user authoring of mobile applications for cultural heritage. *6th International Conference on Information, Intelligence, Systems and Applications (IISA)*. 10.1109/IISA.2015.7388029

Hemalatha, N., Jenis, A., Donald, C., & Arockiam, L. (2014). A comparative Analysis of Encryption Techniques and Data Security Issues in Cloud Computing. *International Journal of Computer Applications, 5*(96), 1-6.

Hu, J., Chen, L., Yunhua, W., & Chen, S. (2013). Data Security Access Control Model of Cloud Computing. *IEEE International Conference on Computer Science and Application*. 10.1109/CSA.2013.15

Hylli, O., Lahtinen, S., Ruokonen, A., & Systä, K. (2014). Resource Description for End-User Driven Service Compositions. *2014 IEEE World Congress on Services*. 10.1109/SERVICES.2014.12

Jegadeeswari, Dinadayalan, & Gnanambigai. (2015). A Trust Model based on Quality of Service in Cloud Computing Environment. *International Journal of Database Theory and Application, 5*(8), 161-170.

Jingxin, K., & Xinpei, J. (2012). Data Security and Authentication in Hybrid Cloud Computing Model. *IEEE Global High Tech Congress on Electronics (GHTCE)*.

Qin Liu, Q., Wang, G., Wu, J., & Chang, W. (2015). User-Controlled Security Mechanism in Data-Centric Clouds. *7th IEEE International High Performance Computing and Communications, Symposium on Cyberspace Safety and Security (CSS), 12th International Conference on Embedded Software and Systems (ICESS)*.

Salvi, S., & Sanjay, H. A. (2015). An Encryption, Compression and Key (ECK) management based data security framework for infrastructure as a service in Cloud. *IEEE International Advance Computing Conference (IACC)*.

Schutz, C., Gao, Y., Hau, D., Powers, S., Grimberg, S., & DeWaters, J. (2016). A time series data transformation engine for non-programmer end users. *3rd MEC International Conference on Big Data and Smart City (ICBDSC)*.

Tzeremes, V., & Gomaa, H. (2016). XANA: An End User Software Product Line Framework for Smart Spaces. *49th Hawaii International Conference on System Sciences (HICSS)*. 10.1109/HICSS.2016.721

Vollala, S., Varadhan, V., Geetha, K., & Ramasubramanian, N. (2014). Efficient modular multiplication algorithms for public key cryptography. *IEEE International Advance Computing Conference*. 10.1109/IAdCC.2014.6779297

Yao, X., Han, X., & Xiaojiang, D. (2014). A light-weight certificate-less public key cryptography scheme based on ECC. *23rd International Conference on Computer Communication and Networks*. 10.1109/ICCCN.2014.6911773

Zatakiya, S., Tank, P. (2013). A Review of Data Security Issues in Cloud Environment. *International Journal of Computer Applications, 5*(82), 14-18.

Zhang Xin, Z., Song-qing, L., & Nai-wen, L. (2012). Research on cloud computing data security model based on multi-dimension. *2012 International Symposium on Information Technology in Medicine and Education (ITME)*. 10.1109/ITiME.2012.6291448

This research was previously published in Cybersecurity Breaches and Issues Surrounding Online Threat Protection edited by Michelle Moore, pages 198-218, copyright year 2017 by Information Science Reference (an imprint of IGI Global).

Chapter 54
KIET Framework for Cloud Adoption:
Indian Banking Case Study

Lalit Mohan Sanagavarapu
IIIT Hyderabad, India

Gangadharan G.R.
IDRBT, India

Raghu Reddy Y.
International Institute of Information Technology, India

ABSTRACT

The expenses in the sustenance of IT investments has become a major ledger item in businesses to the extent that in some cases business priorities had to be changed for sustaining IT systems. Cloud computing, a disruptive technology, is changing the sustenance model with on-demand and metered service approach. However, the adoption of this technology has not been consistent across sectors due to fear on loss of control and changes required in application development and deployment. Authors propose KIET (Knowing, Initiating, Evolving and Transforming) framework based on diffusion theory for adoption of cloud computing in organizations that have strong regulatory framework. Authors implemented the proposed framework on the Indian Banking sector, with majority of the banks being in the public sector. After the implementation of the framework, 49.4% of the banks have adopted cloud computing and another 27.8% of the banks have started the initial steps for adoption.

INTRODUCTION

Broad network access, resource pooling, rapid elasticity, measured service and on-demand self-service are the key characteristics of cloud computing. Cloud computing is becoming a 'GOTO' strategy for IT enablement across industries including in government sector. While Infrastructure as a Service (IaaS) continues to dominate, organizations are steadily transferring workloads (Columbus, 2017) to Software

DOI: 10.4018/978-1-5225-8176-5.ch054

as a Service (SaaS) as it brings standardization and cost efficiency. To meet increasing demand and strengthen existing relationships, software virtualization providers, server manufacturers, network providers with advantage of last mile connectivity and existing datacenter space providers have taken the journey of providing cloud services. However, providers like AWS, Microsoft Azure and Google App Engine continue to have larger market share because of their continuous innovations, pricing models and early starter advantage. Some of the Cloud Service Providers (CSPs) have established regions across globe to take the advantage of business potential and cater to data sovereignty requirements. Apart from public CSPs, hybrid and private cloud adoptions are also steadily increasing (Weins, 2017). While there are many successful cloud adoption case studies on cost efficiency, ability to scale on demand and transparency, the adoption has not been consistent across industry sectors due to concerns on security. Some sectors that are heavily regulated have an expectation that the government/regulator would provide a direction, and/or they could wait for someone to make the first call on cloud computing (any emerging technology) has slowed the adoption rate. To address the adoption concern, authors extended the work on Diffusion Theory for Innovation (Rogers, 2010) and Technology Acceptance Model (Tornatzky, Fleischer, & Chakrabarti, 1990) for promoting cloud computing. The extended framework is referred as KIET (Knowing, Initiating, Evolving and Transforming) and has stages for identifying root causes of the concerns in adoption, bringing community together, building awareness, identifying champions in the community, piloting with some of the use cases and steadily guiding for increased adoption. As an implementation of the framework, Indian banking sector is selected as a case study as it is well known fact that banks across the world are the largest users of IT (Sony Shetty, 2017) and are also heavily regulated. If banks adopt an emerging technology, the technology benefits become obvious to their community in specific and other sectors as well in general. Indirectly, implementation of the proposed framework for banking sector leads to improved adoption across other sectors. Involvement of a community (banks) also reduces the degree of uncertainty and perceived risk in the diffusion process; authors involved the community members in the awareness, decision making, execution and feedback on cloud adoption. The community approach is proposed taking cues from the work of McMillan and Chavis (McMillan & Chavis, 1986) that states "…members of a community have a belonging and a feeling that members matter to one another and to the group, and a shared faith that members' needs will be met through their commitment to be together…" In the following sections of the paper, (i) Background on technology adoption in Indian banking sector and various adoption models for emerging technologies are discussed, (ii) framework for implementing cloud adoption sin Banking sector ensuring it is community driven with measurable progress, (iii) results and findings from adoption approach and finally conclusions are elaborated.

BACKGROUND

Technology Adoption in Indian Banks

IT adoption in Indian banks has started only in 1990s with push from banking regulator. Today, some of the Indian banks are leading IT adopters (IDRBT, 2017) across the world. This dramatic transformation in banking is by new regulatory requirements and the technological advancements that aid banks in meeting and exceeding such requirements. Bankers perform complex works such as auditing, account reconciliation, loan underwriting and processing, etc. in a cost-effective manner with IT enablement. Though IT plays the role of a game changer in banking sector, it poses a big challenge for banks as it is ever changing and ever evolving. To address these challenges, phenomenon of cloud computing is found to be the most suited option (Buyya, Broberg, & Gościński, 2011) (Sangavarapu, Mishra, Williams, & Gangadharan, 2014). To understand the perspectives and device an approach for promoting cloud computing, authors conducted a survey with senior executives (Chief Information Officer/IT Head, Chief Information Security Officer) of banks; India has approximately 50 public and private commercial banks and 38 of the executives have responded to the survey (IDRBT, 2016). Based on the number of responses, it becomes apparent that banks are open for technology change and following are the benefits (as shown in Figure 1) that banks hope to obtain with cloud adoption.

Easy to Expand, Increase Agility

In banks, requirements of the computing resources are not static. For instance, during operating hours (generally between 8:30 am – 5 pm India time) of banks, more computing resources are utilized to cater ongoing customer transactions as compared to other time of the day. Also, lot of memory and compute are utilized during end-of-the- day/month /quarter/year in the banks. In the recent times, Government of India has been emphasizing on digital transactions as the burden on printing and managing cash is impeding country's economic and social growth. With cloud computing, banks can add additional processing and storage capability for the surge in digital transactions. Also, this provides small and mid-size banks (SMBs) a level playing field and compete with larger banks because of the transparency in infrastructure pricing and the ability to scale faster.

Accelerating Product Time to Market and Establishment of New Innovative Business

Broad network access and on-demand IT resources availability reduces the lead time for implementation of innovative ideas. This also reduces the gap between large and small banks and the lead time for launching new products and/or providing new services. This need has become more apparent with

Figure 1. Factors favoring Cloud Computing Adoption

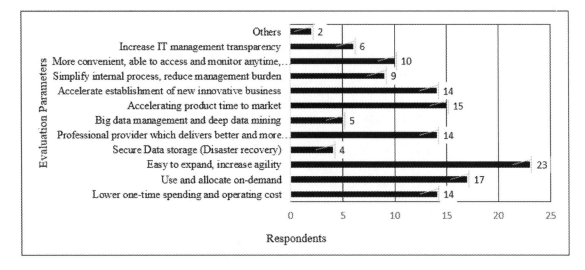

FinTech's (Gulamhuseinwala, Lloyd, Hatch, & Bull, 2017) taking away traditional customers of banks with their innovating products and ease of usability.

Use and Allocate On-Demand

Since, banks can scale their resources on-demand over the cloud, the problems of over/under-utilization can be reduced. Thus, cloud computing helps to minimize the time, effort, and cost required for setting up of resources in the banks including opening new branches.

Lower One-Time Spending and Operating Cost

With the adoption of cloud, banks can reduce the capital expenditure (CapEx on hardware, software, and associated manpower) and thus move to operating expenditure (OpEx). Pay-per-use, a unique feature of cloud computing, helps banks to cut down their initial investment on hardware and software resources drastically as cloud computing allows banks to use the resource and pay accordingly.

Despite the benefits that cloud computing provides, banks have been delaying adoption of this emerging technology across the world. Some of the prominent reasons (as shown in Figure 2) for lack of cloud adoption in Indian banks based on the survey are shown.

Data Security and Confidentiality Issues

As a part of Know Your Customer (KYC) norms, banks capture, store, and process the PII details such as Date of Birth, Tax ID, Phone number, Passport details, etc. The leakage of this confidential data to the external sources due to insider attacks, inconsistent data access policies, compromised security credentials, corruption etc. is a grave threat to bank's reputation and safety. Other issues of security could include data hack, virus attacks by intruders, denial of service attacks, etc. Though likelihood of the occurrence of such breaches is low, ignorance towards such issues is not justifiable. The risk of moving the customers' data to the cloud and losing control over the data make banks hesitant. Although

Figure 2. Factors hindering Cloud Adoption

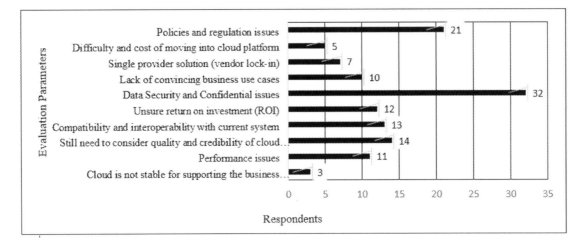

private cloud may be relatively safer than other forms of clouds in these aspects as sphere of control is within bank's management, risks associated with migration still exist. To mitigate the identified security threats in the cloud computing adoption, banks require stringent security measures and ensure that all applications meet the latest rigorous security standards. Like banks' concern, security has been as the paramount concern in cloud adoption across industry sectors (Baiardi & Sgandurra, 2010), (Phaphoom, Wang, Samuel, Helmer, & Abrahamsson, 2015), (Asatiani, 2015), (El-Gazzar, Hustad, & Olsen, 2016) and (Ali, Soar, & Yong, 2016).

Policies and Regulations Issues

As cloud computing is an emerging technology in banks, compliance requirements, jurisdictional laws and other related rules and regulations regarding data storage at service provider facilities are still in formative stage (CSA, 2015). While moving the data from a bank's internal storage to provider's premise, banks closely examine compliance with laws, regulations and auditing requirements. Questions regarding compliance and legal liability of who, how, and where are expected to be answered before taking the first step on any new IT adoption. Thus, considering these regulatory and compliance issues, banks could be hesitating to migrate to the cloud.

Compatibility and Interoperability With Current System

Banks have large monolithic core banking solutions also referred as CBS containing customer and transaction data along with business logic. For an established bank, moving CBS to a cloud environment is a mammoth task due to its dependencies with other interfaces, the volume of data and the possible disruptions. The peripheral systems built around CBS require tighter integration and interoperability for service delivery. CSPs need to review hardware compatibility (commodity x86 vs traditional Unix servers) and software architecture (Monolithic, Tiered, Layered, etc.) to attain this interoperability and integration.

Still Need to Consider Quality and Credibility of Cloud Provider

Vendor lock-in is a situation in which a customer using a product or service from a vendor cannot easily migrate to a competitor's product or service. If a bank tries to migrate from one vendor to another or port an application to cloud, banks like any other customer handling sensitive and critical data would perform several types of compatibilities including interoperability lock-ins, licensing, etc. With increasing cases of mergers and acquisitions of cloud providers, identifying sustainable, credible vendor for an emerging technology service provider is a challenge. Figure 3 details the concerns and expectations that banks have with CSPs.

Safety: Hold Authoritative Security Certification and an Auditable Overall Management and Control

Because of the data sensitivity and the criticality of transactions, banks traditionally use its own employees for most of the operations. However, with the technology efficiencies and improved safety guards, banks have started outsourcing some of their operations. To the extent that for most of the large technology services companies, banking sector has become the major revenue contributor. However, the location of hardware and data was kept in banks' control considering the stringent compliance and most importantly safety and security requirements. With cloud computing, banks are concerned about data protection at CSP site and the access availability for internal/external audit requirements. For banks and other regulated industry sectors, CSPs are expected to have more options for auditing requirements such as allowing the regulator for a physical audit.

Reliability: High Availability and Minimize the Impact on the Business

Most of the banks also have a near DR that provides near zero RTO and RPO, this near DR is connected to bank's primary datacenter through dark fiber cables. This is also a regulatory requirement (Gopalakrishna, 2011) for Indian banks considering the type of transactions (high value and mission critical) being handled for government, industry and capital markets businesses. CSPs while assuring SLAs and building use cases need to understand the service availability requirements and have datacenters/availability zones with 99.999% or above uptime for network and hardware availability.

Services (Accurate, Fast, Focus on Meeting Customers' Requirements)

In interactions with banks and based on industry data, it was observed that banks have less than 30% utilization rate of processing and memory capacity. This is intentional to reduce the need for yearly change of hardware based on additional volume and to handle sudden spurts in growth. In November 2016, Indian government demonetized certain currencies and gave benefits to citizens for using digital transactions, this increased the volume of transactions by 31% (NPCI, 2017). Interestingly, during this period there was no additional hardware (servers and storage) procured by banks because of their over-provisioning model. With cloud adoption and pay-for-use pricing model, banks could have obtained additional storage, processing capacity and network bandwidth without any delay and not worry about keeping overcapacity.

Figure 3. Concerns with Cloud Service Providers

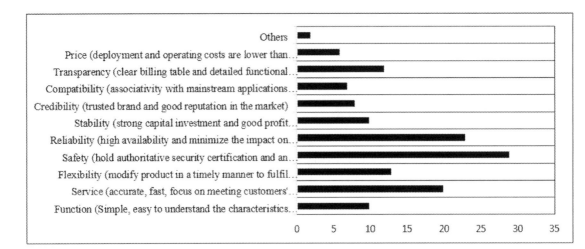

Some of the other perceived concerns that Banks have with CSP are i) Lack of flexibility to modify product in a timely manner to fulfill customer requirements ii) Have not seen stability of CSPs with strong capital investment and good profit growth trend iii) Not a well-established credibility in terms of trusted brand and reputations iv) Compatibility issues associated with mainstream applications and systems v) Complicated pricing models. Apart from the said factors, other issues like technology lock-ins, license related issues, migration costs, huge investment problems, operational stability issues, lack of awareness of services, negative marketing, etc. also act as hindrances to the cloud adoption in the banks. In addition to these, ambiguous service features related to continuity, reliability, availability, support, lack of the monitoring procedures, provider sided SLAs and fear of job losses and control also constitute as factors hindering the adoption of outsourced IT and its enabled services.

EMERGING TECHNOLOGY ADOPTION APPROACHES

Authors reviewed the existing literature on Diffusion Theory and Technology Acceptance Model mechanisms for adoption of newer and emerging technologies such as cloud computing. The literature on the adoption rate in developing and emerging countries and in public sector organizations that have defined hierarchical structure and their own cultural nuances is also studied. Rogers (Rogers, 2010) details the variables that determine the rate of adoption of innovations. Authors extended some of the variables such as trialability and observability for adoption of cloud. Eaton et al. (Eaton & Kortum, 1999) presented a technology diffusion model and identified patterns of diffusion and the rigor of patent protection. While patent protection can be compared to the regulatory constraints, Eaton's model on diffusion was studied only for developed countries that have higher labor cost and deeper technology adoption. Norton et al. (Norton & Bass, 1987) combines Diffusion and Substitution Theory for adoption of newer technologies in the semiconductor industry. However, the work does not distinguish technology adoption for a community/public and the adoption rate was not measured and analyzed. Bayer et al. (Bayer, 1989) have critically scrutinized Diffusion Theory and suggested extensions and modifications to make it applicable for software engineering. From Bayer's research, the effect of mandate and the need for distinguishing adoption at organization vs individual level, etc. are some of the suggested extensions for adopting innovations in the current research paper. Diane et al. (Sonnenwald, Maglaughlin, & Whitton, 2001) proposed five attributes of innovations that influence technology adoption: relative advantage, compatibility, complexity, trialability and observability. They used survey method for innovation adoption and the authors adopted a similar approach conducting an offline and online survey with IT executives of Banks on cloud computing and included their observations for better buy-in. The approach of Rueda et al. (Rueda & Kocaoglu, 2008) combined methods such as Delphi, Bibliometric analysis, and utility to define a global composite indicator that is used as a proxy indicator for the diffusion of the technology. Ross (Ross, 1992) looked at organizational impact due to innovation diffusion and applies to MIS department, measuring the impact may not be directly possible always. Straub (Straub, 2009) reviewed Rogers' Innovation Diffusion Theory, the Concerns-Based Adoption Model, the Technology Acceptance Model (Tornatzky et al., 1990), and the United Theory of Acceptance and Use of Technology. The research incorporates all these models and determines that technology adoption is a complex, inherently social, developmental process; individuals construct unique yet malleable perceptions of technology that influence their adoption decisions. Also, the existing literature of (Dargha, 2012), (Stieninger, Nedbal, Wetzlinger, Wagner, & Erskine, 2014) on cloud adoption methodologies and usage of diffusion theory and Technology Acceptance Model were reviewed to understand the importance of a social group (community). In the recent work, Islam (Islam, 2017) proposes a 'Push and Pull' approach for implementing laboratory innovations in the industry. Authors did not adopt this mandate model as the past experiences of forcing CBS in Indian Banking sector had lot of resistance. It also has set a precedence for some Banks that newer technology can be adopted only if there is a directive by government and/or regulator. Haug et al. (Candel Haug, Kretschmer, & Strobel, 2016) and Oliveira et al. (Oliveira, Thomas, & Espadanal, 2014) reviews cloud adoption across industry sectors and conclude that large (i) firms are early adopters but small firms catch up quickly, in services sector (ii) unregulated market sectors are more cloud adaptive than non-market sectors (iii) cloud adaptiveness can differ significantly within single supply chains. The work of Polyviou et al. (Polyviou & Pouloudi, 2015) and (Sharma, Al-Badi, Govindaluri, & Al-Kharusi, 2016) contributes to the understanding of cloud computing adoption decisions in the public sector and in developed countries. The paper describes job opportunity, trust, perceived usefulness, self-efficacy, and perceived ease of use as reasons for cloud adoption is incorporated in the proposed framework. Briscoe et al. (Briscoe & Marinos, 2009) discusses the importance of openness, community feeling, graceful readiness to failures, convenience and control, environmental sustainability as the primary reasons for the cloud adoption. Authors bank on this community feeling to promote adoption of cloud in banks. Gerard (Garlick, 2011) discusses the advantages of community cloud over public cloud in terms of vendor free, security, and control. The demand for additional involvement of community partners to work a coherent way and the limitations in cost control on capital expenditure and operating expenses are downplayed as against the advantages. Zardari et al. (Zardari, Bahsoon, & Ekárt, 2014) extend goal-oriented requirements engineering and propose Analytical Hierarchy Process for cloud adoption. This adoption approach would be difficult to apply for a community as its members (banks) have different goals though may not be drastically different.

KIET FRAMEWORK FOR CLOUD ADOPTION

Our proposed KIET Framework has 4 stages - Knowing, Initiation, Evolving and Transforming stage for diffusion of cloud computing in banking sector. The authors with the support of IDRBT[1] (Institute for Development and Research in Banking Technology, an organization established by India's central bank – RBI), worked with banking community, CSPs and experts on cloud adoption for the implementation of the framework. The timeline of the framework as shown in Figure 4 was implemented over a period of 4 years (April 2013 - March 2017) to have sustainable adoption at an acceptable pace.

Knowing Stage

In this stage as shown in Figure 5, guideline documents for leveraging cloud services are prepared. To promote cloud computing, authors formed two working groups containing members with expertise in distributed computing and security in March 2013.

Based on the available literature (industry and academic) and NIST guidelines (Mell & Grance, 2011), an initial list of technology benefits and the risks associated with cloud computing was extracted. Authors in their interactions with IT managers from public and private banks formed cloud computing adoption (CCA) working group to discuss on the technology benefits and identify use cases. The use

Figure 4. Timeline for implementation of KIET framework

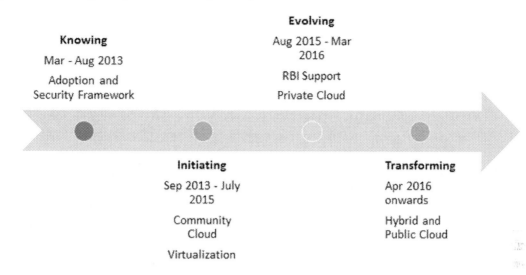

Figure 5. Steps in knowing phase of Cloud Adoption

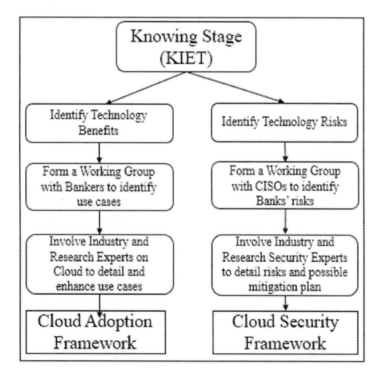

cases identified by CCA working group are further detailed (low/moderate/high critical) with inputs from CBS providers and CSPs (experts). The framework also has an expert involvement for influencing the diffusion, a user base (a community) is formed to realize the advantages of cloud - emerging technology for better acceptance. Service providers were not included in the working groups so that banks (consumers) can express their views without any pressure. Some of the most suitable applications that can be deployed to the cloud environment based on inputs from CCA working group and survey results are documented in a FAQ document (P Kumar & S Mohan, 2017). Some of the applications suited for cloud computing are listed as follows.

Non-Banking Non-Critical Applications

- **Human Resources Operations:** Human resource applications like recruitment, payrolls, compensation management, etc. are required for running a bank and these applications do not have transactional and customer data;
- **Email Services and Learning Management System:** Email services can migrate to cloud environment as most of the users already have public email IDs. Apart from email services, the other identified use cases are Learning Management systems (having seasonal usage and contain heavy learning material), Intranet portal, IT project management tools, Development and Test environment;
- **Applications used by mobile employees (relationship managers that are on the field):** To store their activities and time recordings.

Banking and Non-Critical Applications

- **Customer Relationship Management (CRM) and Analytics:** CRM is an application that is deployed on the cloud and many banks are exploring its implementation on cloud. As most service providers select multichannel access to CRM services, it is beneficial for banks (customers) as services can be accessed from day one onwards, thus, resulting in no latency;
- **Mobile Banking and other Digital Channels:** Banks are offering mobile applications for the customers like online banking application, balance checking application, fund transfer application, requisition of new cheque book, etc.

Since the operations of analytics and reporting platforms are almost uniform or flat throughout the day except at end of the day, it is advisable to adopt the cloud computing for information management system along with CRM deployment.

Banking and Critical Applications

- Applications Related to CBS: CBS is the toughest one to migrate over the cloud considering the dependencies, data criticality and availability requirements. However, a fraction of CBS can be migrated to the cloud like, KYC validation, anti-money laundering regulatory, etc. The interesting fact about these applications is that their workloads reach at peak point only at a time in a day and remains very low for the rest of the time. Small banks and cooperative banks that are lean in IT manpower could adopt CBS on cloud (Alshamaila, Papagiannidis, & Li, 2013), this also provides them to have better safety and security measures;
- Asset management, funds management, and online banking are critical and contain confidential data. Deploying such applications on to a cloud is difficult. They would be migrated only if strict laws and security regulations come into force.

Authors formed a Cloud Computing Security (CCS) working group with Chief Information Security officers of Banks to identify the technology and other operational risks associated with adoption of cloud computing. The CCS working group studied various security guidelines and standards including cloud computing security related documents from NIST (Jansen & Grance, 2011), PCI and PA-DSS (Council, 2013), ISO 27001:2015 (ISO-27001, 2013) guidelines, RBI's Gopalakrishna Committee (Gopalakrishna, 2011) recommendations to prepare a Cloud Security Framework for Indian banks. The document covers security framework for IaaS, PaaS and SaaS services offered through public, private and hybrid cloud deployment models. At the end of Knowing stage, a comprehensive document on cloud security and adoption (Gangadharan, 2013) to provide guidance on cloud computing was released on August 2013 by Governor of RBI (Business Standard, 2013). Working group members from banks identified non-banking non-critical (Intranet, Email, etc.) applications that could leverage cloud services in the initial phase.

Initiation Stage

This stage, authors planned for banks to experiment or setup cloud infrastructure. Authors divided this stage into two waves applying the strategy mentioned as mentioned by Dargha (Dargha, 2012). Authors planned this phase to be longer period to ensure that the first real implementations are without any issues. The two waves give importance on building 'Know and How' on technology, technology management and security of cloud environment:

Wave 1: A cloud set-up using open source Eucalyptus[2] community edition was established in September 2013. After building sufficient knowledge involving researchers and the professional Eucalyptus team, authors demo'ed the set-up to CCA working group members. Based on the developed understanding in Knowing stage, two members of the community volunteered to host their non-banking non-critical applications – Intranet and HelpDesk. These applications require 4GB RAM, 2 Cores and 100 GB storage with Fedora Linux environment, authors connected these applications to Bank datacenter using Virtual Private Network over internet, these workloads ran on trial basis with no charges. Leveraging the industry and research expert panel, a 3 days training program on 'Virtualization and Cloud Computing' was also started. Authors included virtualization topic in the training curriculum as it is the basis for cloud architecture and the adoption of virtualization is validated across sectors. In the training program, two members of the banking community hosted applications on IDRBT's cloud and shared their experiences. Following the training program, other members of CCA have taken initial steps to implement virtualization.

Wave 2: The adoption of virtualization and training programs have spread the awareness on cloud computing and the underlying virtualization technology. To improve the cloud diffusion rate, bring community together and based on the survey participants responses (shown in Figure 6), a community cloud was established on chargeable basis in May 2014 at IDRBT premises. Establishing community cloud (a public cloud in all forms except for the type of tenants) is expected to reduce most of the concerns on adoption of cloud.

The community cloud security architecture is based on the CCS working group requirements. As per NIST definition, community cloud has consumer base with similar functional, compliance and regulatory requirements. The trust and services of the community cloud differentiate it from the public cloud providers. Based on the feature comparison, flexibility to change components, roadmap and available

Figure 6. Preference on Cloud Deployment Model

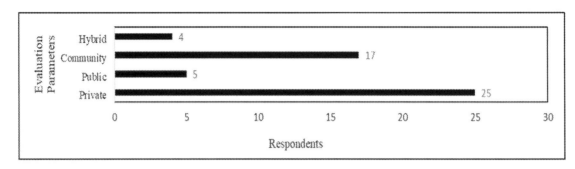

community support, Openstack[3] distribution is selected for building scalable community cloud. The initial set-up with Ecualyptus stack was sunset as its roadmap was unclear with HP's takeover (Holderness, 2014). The research from Liu et al. (Liu, Vlassov, & Navarro, 2014) and Zhang et al. (Zhang, Patwa, Sandhu, & Tang, 2015) also reiterated the decision on Openstack selection for hierarchical multi-tenancy and scalability.

Evolving Stage

While the ideal evolved stage would be full adoption of cloud computing across banking community, this stage is to take the early adopters to more usage and providing new entrants tools and mechanisms for adoption. Building community cloud has identified more banking use cases and has given impetus for using SaaS for eLearning, Email, Payment Channels, etc. With increased momentum of adoption, the community cloud offering has been hived off as a separate organization, IFTAS[4] to run as a services organization rather a R&D organization in July 2015. Though authors did not measure the organizational impact directly based on cloud adoption; however, the number of 'Requests for Proposal for Private Cloud' has increased across Banks and adoption of Community cloud also has increased. RBI has encouraged small cooperative banks to use community cloud for hosting CBS and is also providing financial support for the set-up. This announcement was made in RBI's bi-monthly 'Monetary and Credit Information Review' announcement (Killawala, 2016) stating the prominence and acceptance of cloud by the regulator. The cooperative banks that were struggling to find skilled people have seen this as an opportunity to bridge the gap with a transparent pricing model.

The CCA working group worked with banks to extend their virtualization environment into a private cloud. Banks have also seen this as an opportunity to reduce the number of IT tenders and the related waiting period for shortlisting and procurement of IT infrastructure. Simultaneously, new banks that were following the success stories of virtualization have leapfrogged into private cloud. Also, the 'Virtualization and Cloud Computing' training calendar days has increased from 3 to 5 days to give more importance on cloud set-up with reduced focus on virtualization. CCA working group document is being used by banks in framing their cloud policy document and an assessment tool based on business, technology and operational readiness is prepared for evaluating application readiness for cloud hosting (Sattiraju, Mohan, & Mishra, 2013). Apart from interactions with local service providers and banking community, Authors also collaborated with CSA to obtain global trends and concerns on cloud adoption. For sharing security information, Cloud Information Sharing Center (CISC) established by CSA is leveraged to obtain cloud related incidents/threats/vulnerabilities with its members through IB-CART[5] portal.

Transforming Stage

A quote from Socrates, a great Greek philosopher said, "The secret of change is to focus all of your energy, not on fighting the old, but on building the new…" is still accurate even today. Emerging technologies could be disruptive and/or transformative. Some of the transformative examples on cloud computing has been in ecommerce, social media and roll-out of government programs across the world. The payments system (National Electronic Fund Transfer and Real Time Gross settlement) is offered as a service on community cloud set-up by and for Banks. This brought a transformative change (A. K. Sharma, 2016) for cooperative banks that were using sub-membership and/or could not provide digital (Mobile and Internet) services to customers due to heavy IT infrastructure and the security requirements. The benefits are being realized by some of the banks (Shamarao Vithal Bank, Saraswat Bank and Cosmos Bank) and they have extended themselves from offering traditional banking business to providing cloud services to other smaller banks. Also, State Bank of India[6], India's largest bank transformed itself to provide some of the massive citizen services on Direct Benefit Transfer and No Frill Account Opening (Jan Dhan Yojana) using private cloud. With increased understanding on SLAs, security set-up and pricing models, private banks have started using cloud for analytics and data crunching during off peak hours to take benefit on pricing. National Payments Corporation of India that manages India's retail payments has launched BHIM (Bharat Interface for Money) application for all India citizens in a record 3 week due to its private cloud adoption. With some of these transformational instances, the percentage of banks adopting cloud has increased to 49.4% and another 27.8% banks are in the process formalizing their cloud strategy, shown in Figure 7. However, 22.8% of the banks have not made any progress on cloud adoption.

During this period, the startup ecosystem specifically FinTechs have emerged strong to fill usability and process gaps in banking system. This surge also transformed banks to look for cloud option for IT enablement in an agile mode. One of the newly formed bank, opened 600+ branches (BusinessLine, 2014) on their first day of business leveraging CBS on cloud. The number of banks using community cloud has also increased to 20+ by end of 2016 and is going strong with increased offerings to cooperative societies that are at the grassroot level in Banking. From zero acceptance stage, IDRBT and banks have also started collaborating directly with Industry bodies such as CCICI including giving a keynote talk (CCICI, 2016) on adoption in a joint workshop with NIST. Large CSPs (Microsoft India, 2018) such as AWS, IBM SoftLayer, Microsoft Azure, etc. seeing the potential and adoption rate have set-up availability zones in India and are providing access to their datacenters for third party and regulatory audits, complying CCS working group requirements. This removes the major concerns on data sovereignty and auditory requirements of banks and is expected to transform Indian banking to be future ready.

CONCLUSION

KIET Framework is collaborative (research, industry and consumers) without false sense of urgency and worked with the community to understand pitfalls/value in the emerging technology adoption. As the framework is implemented for a community (Indian banks), authors understood concerns better and measure progress of the results. The effectiveness of the framework is obvious from the change in

Figure 7. Cloud Adoption in Indian banks

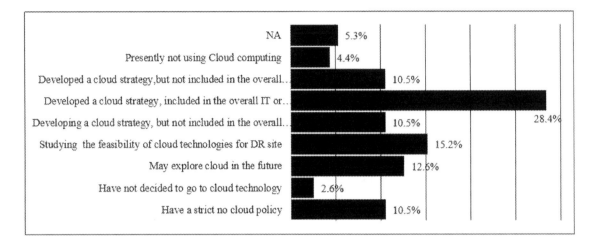

procurement pattern of banks; the number of requests for procurement of regular physical servers has reduced whereas the procurement requests for virtualization and private cloud have increased. Though the initial focus has been public sector, the diffusion effect is felt in cooperative and private banks as well. The cloud training program that started in 2013 is continuing indicating that there are still some banks that are yet to adopt and provides an insight that KIET approach is working for cloud adoption. The framework can be extended to other industries and upcoming disruptive technologies as it involves a community of the sector in building use cases and identifying operational risks, identifies and works with community champions, leverages these champions success stories in enhancing and transforming the sector in a progressive approach. As implementation is done for a highly regulated and IT intensive sector like banking, the implementation of this framework in other sectors could be faster. Authors plan to implement the framework for other similarly regulated sectors like insurance and capital markets. Authors are also exploring options to fine tune the framework and look for early indicators of success.

ACKNOWLEDGMENT

Authors acknowledge Chief Information Security Officers, CIO/IT Heads of Banks, Cloud Service Providers, Cloud Computing Innovation Council of India and other cloud experts for their valuable guidance and involvement in the implementation of the framework.

REFERENCES

Ali, O., Soar, J., & Yong, J. (2016). An Investigation of the Challenges and Issues Influencing the Adoption of Cloud Computing in Australian Regional Municipal Governments. *Journal of Information Security and Applications*, 27–28, 19–34. doi:10.1016/j.jisa.2015.11.006

Alshamaila, Y., Papagiannidis, S., & Li, F. (2013). Cloud Computing Adoption by SMEs in the North East of England. *Journal of Enterprise Information Management*, 26(3), 250–275. doi:10.1108/17410391311325225

Asatiani, A. (2015). Why Cloud? - A Review of Cloud Adoption Determinants in Organizations. In *Proceedings of the 23rd European Conference on Information Systems (ECIS)* (pp. 1–17).

Baiardi, F., & Sgandurra, D. (2010). Securing a Community Cloud. In *Proceedings - International Conference on Distributed Computing Systems* (pp. 32–41). 10.1109/ICDCSW.2010.34

Bayer, J., & Melone, N. (1989). A Critique of Diffusion Theory as a Management Framework for Understanding Adoption of Software Engineering Innovations. *Journal of Systems and Software*, 9(2), 161–166. doi:10.1016/0164-1212(89)90018-6

Briscoe, G., & Marinos, A. (2009). Digital Ecosystems in the Clouds: Towards Community Cloud Computing. In Digital Ecosystems in the Clouds: Towards Community Cloud Computing (pp. 103-108).

Business Standard. (2013). IDRBT Community Cloud. Retrieved May 3, 2018, from http://www.business-standard.com/article/finance/idrbt-sets-up-info-assurance-centre-113080201137_1.html

BusinessLine. (2014). Bandhan Bank Appoints FIS Intl to Develop Core Banking Tool. Retrieved May 3, 2018, from http://www.thehindubusinessline.com/money-and-banking/bandhan-bank-appoints-fis-intl-to-develop-core-banking-tool/article6485160.ece

Buyya, R., Broberg, J., & Gościński, A. (2011). *Cloud computing : Principles and Paradigms*. Wiley. doi:10.1002/9780470940105

Candel Haug, K., Kretschmer, T., & Strobel, T. (2016). Cloud Adaptiveness within Industry Sectors - Measurement and Observations. *Telecommunications Policy*, 40(4), 291–306. doi:10.1016/j.telpol.2015.08.003

CCICI. (2016). Speakers. In *CCICI-NIST-Workshop*. Retrieved May 3, 2018, from https://ccici.in/

Columbus, L. (2017). Roundup Of Cloud Computing Forecasts. Retrieved May 3, 2018, from https://tinyurl.com/ForbCloud

Council, C. (2013). Information Supplement: PCI DSS Cloud Computing Guidelines. *Security Standard Council*, (February). Retrieved from https://www.pcisecuritystandards.org/pdfs/PCI_DSS_v2_Cloud_Guidelines.pdf

CSA. (2015). Cloud Security Alliance - New Survey Finds Companies are in the Dark on Shadow IT Usage. Retrieved May 3, 2018, from https://cloudsecurityalliance.org/media/news/cloud-security-alliance-new-survey-finds-companies-are-in-the-dark-on-shadow-it-usage/

Dargha, R. (2012). Cloud Computing: From Hype to Reality. In *Proceedings of the International Conference on Advances in Computing, Communications and Informatics - ICACCI '12*.

Eaton, B. J., & Kortum, S. (1999). International Technology Diffusion : Theory and Measurement. *International Economic Review*, 40(3), 1–47. doi:10.1111/1468-2354.00028

El-Gazzar, R., Hustad, E., & Olsen, D. H. (2016). Understanding Cloud Computing Adoption Issues: A Delphi Study Approach. *Journal of Systems and Software*, 118, 64–84. doi:10.1016/j.jss.2016.04.061

Gangadharan, G. R. (2013). IDRBT Cloud Security Framework. Retrieved May 3, 2018, from http://idrbt.ac.in/assets/publications/Best Practices/Cloud Security Framework (2013).pdf

Garlick, G. (2011). Improving Resilience with Community Cloud Computing. In *Proceedings of the 6th International Conference on Availability, Reliability and Security, ARES 2011* (pp. 650–655). 10.1109/ARES.2011.100

Gopalakrishna, G. (2011). Working Group on Information Security, Electronic Banking, Technology Risk Management and Cyber Frauds. Retrieved May 3, 2018, from https://rbi.org.in/Scripts/PublicationReportDetails.aspx?UrlPage=&ID=609

Gulamhuseinwala, I., Lloyd, J., Hatch, M., & Bull, T. (2017). EY FinTech Adoption Index. Retrieved May 3, 2018, from http://www.ey.com/gl/en/industries/financial-services/ey-fintech-adoption-index

Holderness, K. (2014). HP Acquires Eucalyptus to Accelerate Hybrid Cloud Adoption in the Enterprise. *HP News*. Retrieved July 31, 2017, from http://www8.hp.com/in/en/hp-news/press-release.html?id=1790521#.WX9gLulm3Dc

IDRBT. (2016). IDRBT Cloud Survey. Retrieved May 3, 2018, from https://docs.google.com/forms/d/e/1FAIpQLScOnHvTWFVkSnFW3PyYPGKrhTl_YJZR838B14zStZclw24Rlg/viewform

IDRBT. (2017). Banking Technology Report. Retrieved May 3, 2018, from www.idrbt.ac.in/assets/publications/BT Awards Review/BTR_2017.pdf

Islam, N. (2017). Crossing the Valley of Death — An Integrated Framework and a Value Chain for Emerging Technologies, *64*(3), 389–399.

ISO-27001. (2013). ISO/IEC 27001 Information security management. Retrieved May 3, 2018, from https://www.iso.org/isoiec-27001-information-security.html

Jansen, W., & Grance, T. (2011). Guidelines on Security and Privacy in Public Cloud Computing. *NIST SP 800--144, 144*(December), 6028.

Killawala, A. (2016). Monetary and Credit Information Review. Retrieved May 3, 2018, from https://rbi.org.in/Scripts/PublicationsView.aspx?id=16968

Kumar, P. S., & S Mohan, L. (2017). FAQs on Cloud Adoption for Indian Banks - Updated. Retrieved May 3, 2018, from http://idrbt.ac.in/bestpractices.html

Liu, Y., Vlassov, V., & Navarro, L. (2014). Towards a Community Cloud Storage. In *Proceedings - International Conference on Advanced Information Networking and Applications* (pp. 837–844). 10.1109/AINA.2014.102

McMillan, D. W., & Chavis, D. M. (1986). Sense of Community: A Definition and Theory. *Journal of Community Psychology*, *14*(1), 6–23. doi:10.1002/1520-6629(198601)14:1<6::AID-JCOP2290140103>3.0.CO;2-I

Mell, P., & Grance, T. (2011). The NIST Definition of Cloud Computing. *National Institute of Standards and Technology, Information Technology Laboratory, 145*, 7. Retrieved from http://csrc.nist.gov/publications/nistpubs/800-145/SP800-145.pdf

Microsoft India. (2018). Microsoft Cloud for BFSI Sector. Retrieved May 3, 2018, from https://www.microsoft.com/india/datacenter/bfsi.aspx

Norton, J. A., & Bass, F. M. (1987). A Diffusion Theory Model of Adoption and Substitution for Successive Generations of High- Technology Products. *Management Science, 33*(9), 1069–1086. doi:10.1287/mnsc.33.9.1069

NPCI. (2017). Statistics. Retrieved May 3, 2018, from https://www.npci.org.in/statistics

Oliveira, T., Thomas, M., & Espadanal, M. (2014). Assessing the Determinants of Cloud Computing Adoption: An Analysis of the Manufacturing and Services Sectors. *Information & Management, 51*(5), 497–510. doi:10.1016/j.im.2014.03.006

Phaphoom, N., Wang, X., Samuel, S., Helmer, S., & Abrahamsson, P. (2015). A Survey Study on Major Technical Barriers Affecting the Decision to Adopt Cloud Services. *Journal of Systems and Software, 103*, 167–181. doi:10.1016/j.jss.2015.02.002

Polyviou, A., & Pouloudi, N. (2015). Understanding Cloud Adoption Decisions in the Public Sector. In *Proceedings of the Annual Hawaii International Conference on System Sciences* (pp. 2085–2094). 10.1109/HICSS.2015.250

Rogers, E. M. (2010). *Diffusion of Innovations*. Simon and Schuster.

Ross, J. W. (1992). MIS as Change Agent: an Extension of Innovation Diffusion Theory. *Proceedings of ACM SIGCPR Conference on Computer Personnel Research* (pp. 241–249). 10.1145/144001.144076

Rueda, G., & Kocaoglu, D. F. (2008). Diffusion of Emerging Technologies: An Innovative Mixing Approach. In Proceedings of Portland International Center for Management of Engineering and Technology (pp. 672–697).

Sangavarapu, L., Mishra, S., Williams, A., & Gangadharan, G. R. (2014). The Indian Banking Community Cloud. *IT Professional, 16*(6), 25–32. doi:10.1109/MITP.2014.97

Sattiraju, G., Mohan, S. L., & Mishra, S. (2013). IDRBT Community Cloud for Indian Banks. In *2013 International Conference on Advances in Computing, Communications and Informatics (ICACCI)* (pp. 1634–1639). IEEE. 10.1109/ICACCI.2013.6637426

Sharma, A. K. (2016). Why Shivalik Cooperative Bank is on Cloud 9. Banking Frontiers. Retrieved May 3, 2018, from http://bankingfrontiers.com/why-shivalik-cooperative-bank-is-on-cloud-9/

Sharma, S. K., Al-Badi, A. H., Govindaluri, S. M., & Al-Kharusi, M. H. (2016). Predicting Motivators of Cloud Computing Adoption : A Developing Country Perspective. *Computers in Human Behavior, 62*, 61–69. doi:10.1016/j.chb.2016.03.073

Sonnenwald, D. H., Maglaughlin, K. L., & Whitton, M. C. (2001). Using Innovation Diffusion Theory to Guide Collaboration Technology Evaluation : Work in Progress. In *Proceedings of the 10th IEEE International Workshops on Enabling Technologies: Infrastructure for Collaborative Enterprises* (pp. 114–119). 10.1109/ENABL.2001.953399

Sony Shetty. (2017). Gartner Says IT Spending in the Banking and Securities Industry in India to Reach $8.9 Billion in 2017. Retrieved May 3, 2018, from http://www.gartner.com/newsroom/id/3606117

Stieninger, M., Nedbal, D., Wetzlinger, W., Wagner, G., & Erskine, M. A. (2014). Impacts on the Organizational Adoption of Cloud Computing: A Reconceptualization of Influencing Factors. *Procedia Technology*, *16*, 85–93. doi:10.1016/j.protcy.2014.10.071

Straub, E. T. (2009). Understanding Technology Adoption: Theory and Future Directions for Informal Learning. *Review of Educational Research*, *79*(2), 625–649. doi:10.3102/0034654308325896

Tornatzky, L. G., Fleischer, M., & Chakrabarti, A. K. (1990). *The processes of Technological Innovation.* Lexington Books. Retrieved from https://tinyurl.com/TechInno

Weins, K. (2017). Cloud Computing Trends: 2017 State of the Cloud Survey. Retrieved May 3, 2017, from https://www.rightscale.com/blog/cloud-industry-insights/cloud-computing-trends-2017-state-cloud-survey

Zardari, S., Bahsoon, R., & Ekárt, A. (2014). Cloud adoption: Prioritizing obstacles and obstacles resolution tactics using AHP. In *Proceedings of the ACM Symposium on Applied Computing* (pp. 1013-1020). 10.1145/2554850.2555067

Zhang, Y., Patwa, F., Sandhu, R., & Tang, B. (2015). Hierarchical Secure Information and Resource Sharing in OpenStack Community Cloud. In *IEEE 16th International Conference on Information Reuse and Integration* (pp. 419-426).

ENDNOTES

[1]   http://idrbt.ac.in/
[2]   https://github.com/eucalyptus/eucalyptus/wiki
[3]   https://www.openstack.org/
[4]   http://iftas.in/
[5]   http://idrbt.ac.in/ib-cart.html
[6]   https://www.sbi.co.in/

This research was previously published in the International Journal of Cloud Applications and Computing (IJCAC), 8(4); edited by B. B. Gupta and Dharma P. Agrawal, pages 72-87, copyright year 2018 by IGI Publishing (an imprint of IGI Global).

Chapter 55
Vehicular Cloud Computing Challenges and Security

Sunilkumar S. Manvi
REVA University, India

Nayana Hegde
Sri Krishna Institute of Technology, India

ABSTRACT

Vehicular Cloud Communication (VCC) is the latest technology in intelligent transport system. Vehicular cloud (VC) facilitates the customers to share resources ranging from storage to computing power to renting it to other users over the Internet. Security of VANET cloud covers various aspects of security, social impact, cost effective communication. Chapter highlights a cost effective, hassle free and secure communication between the cloud and moving vehicles. Communication is established via Network as a Service (Naas). The goal of this chapter is to give a broad overview of Vehicular cloud computing, vehicular cloud applications, mobile computing, and recent literature covering security of vehicular cloud.

INTRODUCTION

Vehicular cloud computing is a new technological model which combines the advantages of cloud computing with vehicular ad hoc network to serve the drivers at low cost and with pay as you go model. Minimize travel time, reduce traffic congestion, provide good computational power at low cost to drivers, reduce environmental pollution, reduce road accidents and make travel more enjoyable are the few objectives of VCC.

According to Whaiduzzaman (2014), the underutilized computing power, memory, sensing and internet connectivity, of large number of autonomous vehicles on roads, parking lots and streets can be coordinated and allocated to other authorized users. Internet access, computing power and storage capabilities can be rented to drivers and other customers exactly as similar to usual cloud computing service. Vehicular Clouds are technologically feasible and economically viable and will be the next paradigm shift. They will provide many benefits, including societal and technological impacts. Vehicular cloud scenario is shown in Figure 1.

DOI: 10.4018/978-1-5225-8176-5.ch055

Figure 1. Vehicular cloud

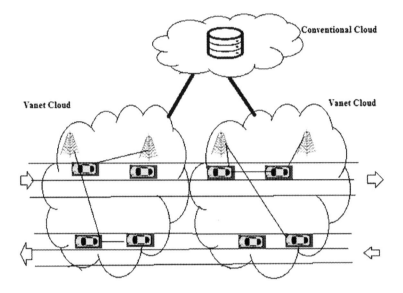

In the figure a group of vehicles are forming the cloud. This vehicular cloud can connect to the internet cloud.

Vehicular cloud is union of vehicular network, cloud computing and mobile computing. Figure 2(a) and Figure 2(b) shows cloud computing and mobile cloud computing. These are explained as follows:

Vehicular Network

In recent past, smarter vehicles have provided the travel experience with safer and delightful driving. Now a day's almost all vehicles are provided with cameras, GPS system, on board computers, small-scale

Figure 2. (a) Cloud computing, (b) mobile cloud computing

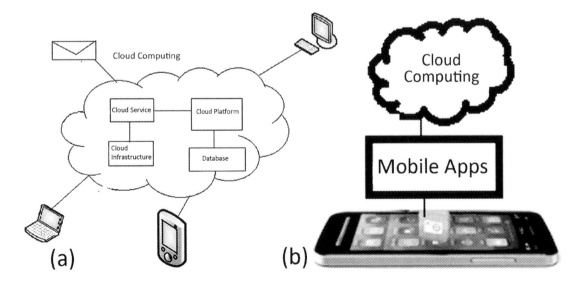

collision radars, various sensors and radio transceivers. Different sensors are used to measure vehicle and road safety conditions, to alert drivers. It also takes care of mechanical malfunctions of vehicles. These vehicles when travel on road make ad hoc network by communicating with each other by wireless communication technology.

Cloud Computing

Cloud computing provides users with the computing, storing capability on demand. Advantage here is users need not invest for computation or storage but he/she can take it on rent from internet. The ever increasing demand for computing and storage has given rise to cloud computing. Customers rent processing, storage, networking and other fundamental computing resources for all purposes to authorized users.

Mobile Cloud Computing

Mobile cloud computing is combination of mobile communication and cloud computing. The drivers use their mobile devices (smart phones) and connect to the cloud via internet. Using mobile communication they can send safety related messages to other drivers and share data. But disadvantage of mobile computation is it suffers from battery constraint, resource limitations. Vehicular cloud overcomes this disadvantage as power is generated when vehicle moves. So we consider VCC more advantageous in adhoc networks.

Need of Vehicular Cloud Computing

Vehicles represent an increasingly important source of computing and sensing resources for drivers as well as for urban communities. The concept of vehicular cloud computing borrows its architecture from mobile cloud computing. Modern day vehicular network needs to evolve as internet of vehicles. It uses intenet to keep the nodes connected while they travel. The advantage of VCC over mobile cloud computing is it has no power constraints. The strength of vehicular cloud is not only due to the computing resources they carry, but also due to the sensors available. Ideally vehicles are major sources of observation and can collect and store enourmous amount of local information. The ability to colect sensor information which is of local relevance is biggest advantage of vehicular cloud. This information is shared between the connected vehicles. It saves lot of time for upload and download of informaion from the internet. It saves cost of connecting to internet cloud.

Vehicular Cloud Computing Types

Vehicular Cloud can be formed by V2V communication and V2I to promote sharing information between vehicles. There are two different types of VCC, Roadside cloud and Central cloud. They are explained as follows.

Roadside Cloud

A network between base station or Road Side Units (RSUs) is known as Roadside cloud. Roadside cloud is mainly used for intermediator work. It does take care of communication between vehicular cloud and central cloud infrastructure. It takes care of inter-vehicle communication broadcasting. RSUs process data collected from moving vehicle to provide convenience to vehicles and it takes care of issueing session keys for secured cmmunication.

Central Cloud

The cloud that is formed by the service provider is known as Central Cloud. The authentication related data of the driver is stored in this cloud. When driver requests, service is provided by roadside cloud to the right driver. A role of intermediator is played by central cloud for trusting relationship for RSU and vehicle. (Altayeb, 2013), (Jungho, 2015) .

Comparision Between VCC and CC

In this section we give a comparision of cloud computing and vehicular cloud computing. (Whaiduzzaman, 2015) summarized that both in CC and VCC services, applications and resources are accessed on demand. Several requestes can be run by one m/c and pretend to be as separate m/c. Payment is done only for the services used.VCC services are temporary but CC services are always available. Network as a Service is available in both model. Storage as a Service is avalable in both model. Cooporation as a Service is possible in CC and it is one of the main aim of VCC. Commercials, infotainment, information for drivers, planed and unplaned disaster management using roads and vehicles is an important application of VCC where as these applications are technically feasible for CC. VCC model can be described as moving network pool. Automatic cloud formation is possible in VCC and it is not possible in CC. One more advantage of VCC is cloud formation takes place autonomously for a vehicle and a running or standing vehicle. Also in VCC vehicle can provide service while it is moving. The VCC is based on CC and mobile computing architecture and it is a better network among the ad hoc networks. The Figure 3 shows the comparison of Vehicular Cloud and Cloud Computing in terms of resources and technologies.

Figure 3. Comparison between CC and VCC

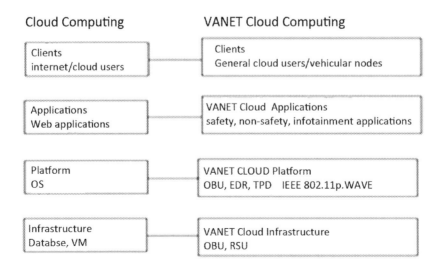

Communication Model in Vehicular Cloud

There are two types of commnication in VANET, Vehicle to Vehicle (V2V) and Vehicle to Infrastructure (V2I) communication. Data is exchanged between vehicle and infrastructure. Base station or RSU and location based service providers are connected to cloud storage. Figure 4. shows the communication model of vehicular cloud.

In V2V communication data is collected by sensors and processed by OBU and shared between other vehicles.In V2I communication CA authenticates the vehicles and LSP collects the location details of the vehicle. RSU connects vehicle to the cloud.

There are three layers of communications in VANET clouds. At three different levels it incorporates different entities

- First layer *is sensor layer* or inside car layer. -This layer deals with sensors, GPS, actuators, RADAR and wireless sensor network.
- Second layer is *vehicle to vehicle layer* or we call it as OBU – OBU or OBU-RSU layer. It uses IEEE 802.11p communication protocol.
- Third layer is *cloud layer*, where communication takes place between gateway to gateway.

Figure 5 gives details of the communication architecture of vehicular cloud. Communication in the first layer uses Wi-Fi or CAN. Inter-car level is second level of communication. In this level vehicles communicate with each other so called as OBU-OBU level. This communication can be either V2V or V2I by using IEEE 802.11p (WAVE) standard. Third level communication enables vehicles to communicate at cloud level. This level uses vehicles or RSUs to serve as gateways. The nomination of vehicle or RSU as gateway will depend upon the underlying framework of VANET cloud.

Figure 4. Block diagram of vehicular cloud communication

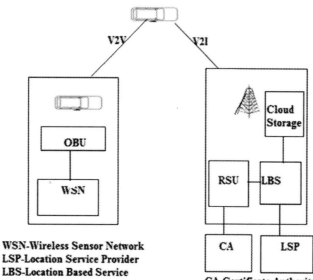

Figure 5. Communication architecture of vehicular cloud layers

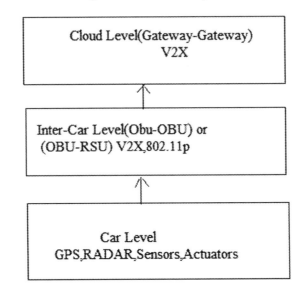

Architecture of Vehicular Cloud Computing

Xi Chen (2015) and Khaleel Mershad (2013) explains VANET cloud service architecture which is popular as Network as a Service (NaaS), Storage as a Service (STaaS), and Cooperation as a Service (CaaS). These three services are explained next. Platform as a Service (PaaS) is not very popular in Vehicular clouds. Figure 6 shows the different layers of service architecture of VC.

1. **Network as a Service or NaaS (Internet Access):** Some smart vehicles will have a permanent Internet access through a cellular network. This helps other vehicles which don't have that facility to share the net by paying fee to it by such vehicles.

2. **Storage as a Service or SaaS (Virtual Network Hard-Disk):** Some smart vehicles will have high on-board storage capacity, which is not completely utilized. But others vehicles which have less storage facility may need it. This case can occur if several users are using a vehicle's hardware at the same time. Some users prefer to have backup of their data on an external harddisk for safety. The user pay nominal rate for the amount of data storage he uses for required amount of time to owner of the renting vehicle and make use of this service. (Arif, 2012).

3. **Data as a Service or DaaS (Virtual Data Provider):** Instead of requesting Internet access to view a website or work on a web application, a user in a smart vehicle may require specific data: for example, a video file, a city map, latest news, road conditions, etc. So vehicular cloud acts as data provider for travel related things like, nearest fuel stations, hotels, etc for requesting drivers.

Applications of Vehicular Cloud Computing

Applications of vehicular cloud are: Airport as a Data Centre, Shopping mall as a data cloud, Traffic light management, and Traffic safety message. Some of the applications of vehicular cloud are discussed in detail.

Figure 6. Service architecture in VANET clouds

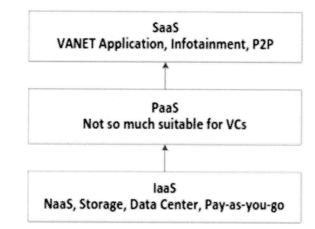

Mallissery (2015) proposed that the concept of VANET cloud is used for helping the regulatory authorities in identifying the vehicles violating the traffic rules through sensors included as part of On Board Unit (OBU). When the vehicle is on fly the sensor values are periodically transferred to the cloud, controlled by the traffic police. So it is used for Transport and Traffic Rule Violation Monitoring Service in ITS. It is a Secured VANET Cloud Application.

Vignesh (2014) explains about stationary cloud to utilize the idle vehicle resources in cities. Vehicles parked at city railway station reach account of nearly 1200 during weekends. These vehicles have very good processing capability and resource poverty can be eliminated by utilizing these vehicular resources.

In a shopping mall if any incident occurred has to be traced with the help of Closed circuit television (CCTV) then lot of processing is required. For that computational ability of the vehicles in parking lot can be utilized.

Saini (2015) proposed a cloud based middleware framework for infotainment application in vehicular network. In this application a service based architecture deligates data fusion and data filtering functionalities to cloud environment. Since most of the processing is done on the cloud it reduces the resources for internet and platform inside the vehicles.

Mallissery (2014) proposed concept of vehicles using cloud(VuC). Here the cloud provides two services: Application as a Service (AaaS) and Storage as a Service (STaaS). It is assumed that all the vehicles are registered with the public cloud through the Certification Authority (CA). The use of public cloud will provide better storage facility; secure accessibility and easy availability of messages, public keys and certificates involved in VANET communication. The proposed system also addresses security attacks in VANET and reduces the overhead involved in communication.

Alazawi (2012) proposed a disaster management system which includes intelligent transport system, mobile cloud computing and VANET. Transportation and telecommunications play a critical role in disaster response and management in order to minimize loss of human life, economic cost and disruptions.

Jelassi (2015) explained an innovative solution in order to provide a satisfactory video streaming quality over a cloud-based VANET architecture. The improvement of video streaming delivery conditions over VANET is realized using cloudlets installed across roads and highways deployed by roadside infrastructure providers.

The main objective of this chapter is to highlight on the security of VCC. The recent works done in the area of security of VCC are listed in the section of literature survey. Next section explains the threat model of VCC which is followed by issues of VCC and challenges of VCC. Security scheme for VCC is explained in detail. The proposed model of secure data storage is explained.

Literature Survey of Vehicular Cloud Computing Security

Suqing Lin (2015) constructed a symmetric-key encryption scheme and a commitment scheme. According to their solution, hybrid encryption and a commitment can be used to add verification to the outsourced decryption more efficiently and a proper verification algorithm should be defined as a constraint during the final decryption for the data receiver.

Yu-Hsun Lin (2013) proposed a Private Circular Query Protocol with cross like search mechanism is proposed to simultaneously accomplish the location-based-NN query and the location privacy preservation, in a novel way.

Ning Cao(2011) proposed privacy-preserving multi-keyword ranked search over encrypted data in cloud computing (MRSE). They chose the efficient similarity measure of "coordinate matching," i.e., as many matches as possible, to capture the relevance of data documents to the search query.

M.Raya (2010) explains the importance of data aggregation and group communication. Here data aggregation is used to secure the communication VANET security. They used symmetric, asymmetric and hybrid cryptography in their work. Symmetric key encryption is used for inter vehicle communication. Efficiency of performance and security both are proved better.

R. Hussain (2014) Presents a less expensive and efficient method for secure and privacy procedure for route tracing and revocation mechanism which is based on the multiple pseudonym.

D. Huang (2011), proposed pseudonymous authentication-based conditional privacy (PACP) scheme. Pseudonyms are generated by roadside unit before communication. The pseudonyms are known only to the vehicles and no other participants in the network. In addition to this the proposed scheme gives a useful procedure for revocation of users.

Jian Shen (2016) proposed a novel lightweight authentication-based access control scheme, which is designed by exclusive-or operations, string concatenation and hash functions. Therefore, this scheme has lower computation cost. Moreover, the main computing work is transferred to the authorized agency, hence, the computation of the user side and the server side is lower than the related authentication scheme for cloud.

Security of Vehicular Cloud

Security Requirement of Vehicular Cloud

Security and privacy are two major challenges faced by all wired or wireless networks who share their resources as explained by (Md Waiduzzam, 2014). Wireless sensor network layer, Wireless communication architecture layer and cloud computing layer are the 3 layers of vehicular cloud architecture. Collecting information and events from the environment is the task of first layer. Second layer takes care of transferring transferring the data from etwr to the cloud through an access point. Storage and service is provided by the cloud layer. Security of vehicular cloud netwrok is depending the imlementation of security of these 3 layers.

Threats for Vehicular Cloud

Zeadally (2012) discussed on security of VANET cloud, as the usage of vehicular cloud service increases, the security requirements increases. Major thearts for vehicular cloud services are:

- Denial of services,
- Identity spoofing,
- Modification repudiation,
- Repudiation,
- Sybil attack, and
- Information disclosure.

To provide secure environment for vehicular cloud services following requirements should be considered:

- Confidentiality,
- Integrity,
- Availability,
- Authentication,
- Privacy,
- Real time constraints.

As per Mahmoud (2010) just like any other wireless networks, different types of attacks can happen on VANET. A vehicle is said to be adversary if it tries to harm or attempts to introduce any kind of misbehaviour in the network by causing problem to any other node, and thereby causing malfunctioning of the network. There are several types of attackers and each has different level of impact on the network. Some attackers are discussed in detail:

- **Drivers Looking Only for Their Interest:** A vehicle driver can send false message to all other vehicles as a road being blocked in order to clear vehicles in his destination road.
- **Users Who Misuse VCC:** A person can use VANET cloud to find out a place where there are no cars (means no people) in order to rob/theft a house in that area.
- **People from within the Industry:** Manufacturers of vehicles know about the security of the vehicles and can steal information.
- **Malicious Attackers:** This is considered to be very dangerous category because it can cause severe damage to the network.

The Table 1 give the summary of attacks and their impacts on VC.
Most common attacks of vehicular cloud network:

- **Denial of Service:** Overload the communication channel by sending continuous messages from a node, in order to make network not available for other nodes to do communication.
- **Interception:** Some nodes act as man in middle so that all important information are passed through the nodes and they can get information that are intended for other destination.

Table 1. Summary of attacks on VC

Type of Attack	Description	Impact
Access	Unauthorized person attempts to obtain information	Network confidentiality affected
Modification	Unauthorized person trying to alter the information	Network integrity affected
Denial of Service	Access or service not available for the legitimate/authorized user.	Network availability affected
Repudiation	Incorrect information was given or deny the occurrence of event	Accountability affected.

- **Fabrication:** Some nodes send false information about traffic condition in order to get some information in the network.
- **Impersonation:** Adversary gives false identity to gather specific information in the network.
- **Alteration and Suppression of Data:** A malicious node receives data, alters it and resends it. A malicious node can send some false data between two nodes and destroy the communication and cause confusion.
- **The Sybil Attack:** A malicious node gives multiple identity of itself and it tries to get control over the network by destroying the communication.
- **Tampering:** A malicious node alters or modifies the data in the network.
- **Identity Spoofing:** Unauthorized user pretends as legitimate user and access the information from the network.
- **Information Disclosure:** A malicious node hides the identity of the node by an adversary in order to get some information forging from the network.

Vehicular Cloud Computing Issues

Architectural Issues

To accommodate the changing demands of the applications the resource availability is a problem and it caused due to high mobility of the nodes. The layered communication network like TCP/IP has been proved not efficient for the emerging technologies and applications.

Functional Challenges

Vehicular cloud is formed by cyber and physical resources. It is important to develop the trustworthy, efficient communication protocol and data processing methods in dynamic environment.

Policy Related Challenges

Standardization of setup, control access, establishment rules are still challenging and needs more attention from Researchers.

Security and Privacy Issues

In VCC communication takes place within vehicles, vehicle to vehicle and vehicle to infrastructure. These communications are either wired or wireless in nature. So there is requirement of security and privacy in all the 3 layers of communication of vehicular cloud system.

Single User Interface

Single-user access interface is another challenge to VCs. When the number of service accesses in a cloud increases, the number of VMs that provide the service will increase to guarantee quality of service. More VMs will be created and assigned. With the increase in VMs, security concerns grow as well.

Heterogeneous Network Nodes

Conventional cloud computing and fixed networks often have homogeneous end users. As it turns out, vehicles have a large array of (sometimes) vastly different onboard devices. Some high-end vehicles have several advanced devices, including a Global Positioning System (GPS) receiver, one or more wireless transceivers, and onboard radar devices. In contrast, some economy models have only a wireless transceiver. Some other vehicles have different combinations of GPS receivers, wireless transceivers, and radar. Different vehicle models have different device capabilities such as speed of processor, volume of memory, and storage. These heterogeneous vehicles as network nodes create difficulties to adapting security strategies as explained by (Gongjun,2012).

Scalability

Security schemes for VCs must be scalable to handle a dynamically changing number of vehicles. Security schemes must handle not only regular traffic but special traffic as well, e.g., the large volume of traffic caused by special events.

Vehicular cloud thus has many challenges and issues as listed above. In this chapter we concentrate on the security of VCC. So we elaborate on one of the issue that is security and privacy of vehicular cloud computing. Important security and privacy issues faced by the VCC are listed and discussed.

Security and Privacy Challenges of VCC

Authentication of High Mobility Nodes

The authentication in VC contains verifying the authentication of users and the integrity of messages. The VC environment is more challenging than vehicular network and cloud computing, due to the high mobility of nodes.

Secure Location and Localization

Location information plays a vital role in VC to transmit data and create connections because most applications in vehicular systems rely on location information such as traffic status reports, collision avoidance, emergency alerts, and cooperative driving. Therefore, the security of location information and localization should be provided among vehicles

Key Management

VCC is decentralized model of cloud computing. Key management is extremely important for mobile nodes. Most of VCC security solution depends on the Vehicular Public Key Infrastructure (VKPI).

Securing Vehicular Communication

Providing secure communication plays very important role in VCC. There is no centralized system in VCC. Communication is V2V or V2I and it is wireless mode. The attack is mostly possible in these layers of VCC. Mainly encryption is used for securing communication.

Data Security

VCC supports Storage as a Service (SaaS) and Cooperation as a Service (CaaS). Both services based on huge amount of Information exchange. This needs data security and integrity. All the sensitive data are encrypted at OBU using vehicle's public key so that data is not accessed by unauthorized users.

When static cloud is formed at a parking lot for temporarily data can be stored in vehicle's memory. Before vehicle moves out of the parking lot data should be backed up. VM should provide the isolation between the applications run on cloud, and users using it. When back up is taken the optimized usage of physical resources should be done. Data backup and recovery process should be simple and it should be secured.

Since we have discussed about the issues and challenges of VCC, now we present some of the solutions to the above discussed problem under the section scheme to protect vehicular communication. It discusses many security related solutions that are used to protect the attacks and threats of security as discussed above.

Schemes to Protect Vehicular Communication

Symmetric Key Approaches

Symmetric key systems were the first type of encryption system used to provide security to user's data. In this system node will have to first have an agreement for sharing of keys and then it should communicate on messages. There are few hybrid communication systems where both symmetric and public key crypto systems both are used for securing the system. As suggested by Brumister and Christolopous (2008) symmetric key algorithm should not be used for authentication as, it may prevent the non-repudiation. Also it is used to suggest the use of 1024 length of key for (AES) for encryption.

Vehicular Public Key Infrastructure

Public key schemes were used prior to the identity based encryption. The use of public key cryptography with manageable and robust PKI since symmetric key cryptography does not support accountability. Authentication is performed by digital signatures of communicated messages: The use of elliptical curve cryptography is done as it reduces processing time. Many vehicles are registered under different states registrations. Each registration authority has its own unique id. Based on their unique id we can identify, which vehicle is registered under which certificate authority. These vehicles will be travelling in different regions beyond their registered regions. So it becomes very important to manage these vehicles. Vehicle public key infrastructure manages the job of managing the vehicles in this way. It mainly consists of three steps.

1. **Key Assignment by Certificate Authority:** In this phase public key and private key are issued by certificate authority. Key assignment for each vehicle is based on the unique id of the vehicle and expiration date is decided by the certification authority.
2. **Key Verification:**
   a. Public Key verification can be done by the certificate authority. It can be explained by steps as follows:
   b. Vehicle 'X' requests for public key from Certificate authority 'Y' (CAy).
   c. Public key for vehicle 'X' (PUx) will be is issued by CAy.
   d. 2. d. Certificate for this vehicle (Cert(X)) is calculated using PUx and Unique id of the CAy

(Cert(X))=PUx| SignPry(PUx|IDCAy).

3. **Certification Revocation:** Certificate revocation is one of the most significant ways to protect information from the attackers. Generally, when the attacker certification is detected or the certification of one node is exposed by attackers, the certificate should be revoked. As explained (Housley R 2002) The Certificate Revocation List (CLR) that is the most important revocation methods in a vehicular network. The CRL contains a list of the most recently revoked certificates which is broadcast among vehicles immediately. However, CLRs has several drawbacks: the length of list can be very long and the lifetime of certificates can be very short.

Pseudonym Based Approaches for Privacy

In a novel approach as explained by (Raya et al., 2006) for privacy preservation proposed by using a set of anonymous keys which have short life time. They have previously amount of time. Once a key is used it cannot be used again. All keys distribution and management is provided by the CA of the network. The stress is given on the point that these keys have to be traceable to the driver only in the case of emergencies and authority requirements.

Pseudonymous Authentication

(Park, 2015) explains some of the privacy preserving vehicle authentications. These schemes are designed on the basis of pseudonym-based techniques. It combines group signature based schemes and pseudonym-based algorithms. Conditional privacy preservation can be built using group signatures. In this method the signature size and computation costs are relatively long and high. In pseudonym-based technique widely used in vehicular networks, each vehicle possesses a lot of unlink able pseudonym certificates and frequently changes its pseudonyms to avoid tracking from global eavesdropper. One drawback of this system is revocation list is very large. Thus, the size of revocation list becomes getting longer depending on not the number of vehicles but the number of pseudonyms in the system.

Identity Based Cryptography

Recently the identity (Mahmoud Al-Q) based signature has become very important for security of VANET applications. This security framework is considered to be good choice due to unique characteristics of VANET. Earlier used symmetric key cryptography and public key cryptography methods are not suitable for VANET security applications. Since VANET is infrastructure less, public key cryptography needs infrastructure for key management and key distribution. Use of keys and its size in public key cryptography pose a constraint on the bandwidth usage of the dynamic wireless networks. Due to real time applications and delay constraints in the communications symmetric key cryptography is also not considered to be good solution. Therefore, Identity based cryptography is considered to be a viable solution for security of VANET.

Identity Based Signatures

As explained by (Shamir, 1984) identity based signature does not use any public key infrastructure like public/private key pairs. Instead it uses a cryptosystem which is built upon public key systems. Here public key is not generated but a general string that uniquely identifies the user is used to encrypt the data. Third Trusted Party will issue the private key to the user. It needs a random seed for generating public and private key pairs.

Signing and Verifying is done in 4 steps:

1. **Setup:** Third Trusted Party creates its own pair of private and public keys using the parameters given by the user. It distributes the public keys to users.
2. **Extraction:** The signer authenticates him/her to the TTP and then requests for his private key from TTP.
3. **Signing:** User after receiving the private key signs the message using the private key and then sends the message to the destination.
4. **Verifying:** Upon receiving the signed text the verifier uses public key of his and public key of TTP to verify the signature.

Identity Based Encryption

Identity based encryption was developed in 2001 and it was based on Elliptical Curve Cryptography. The encryption process is performed in 4 steps:

1. **Setup:** The TTP generates its own pair of public and private key pairs and distributes it within the network.
2. **Extraction:** The sender authenticates himself with the TTP and requests for private key from TTP. TTP generates the private key and gives it to sender.
3. **Encryption:** The sender uses the public key and uses public key of the TTP to encrypt the messages and send it to the receiver.
4. **Decryption:** Upon receiving the encrypted message receiver uses its private key to decrypt the message.

Strength of the identity based encryption:

1. It states the strength of the public key cryptosystem.
2. All level of secrecy is maintained in TTP.
3. Authentication is provided before the private key issued to the sender.
4. The method of calculation of private key is kept secret.

Attribute Based Encryption

Attribute based encryption is a public key encryption. In this algorithm secret key of user and cipher text is based on some attributes. Examples like University name, department name, designation of user etc. In this algorithm decryption of the cipher text is done only after matching the attributes of secret key with attributes of cipher text. An important property of ABE with respect to its security aspect is collusion-resistance. If an adversary has multiple keys, then user should be able to guess crucial security aspect of Attribute-Based Encryption is collusion-resistance: An adversary that holds multiple keys should only be able to access data if user grants permission. The concept of attribute-based encryption was first proposed by Amit Sahai and Brent Waters and later by Vipul Goyal, Omkant Pandey, Amit Sahai and Brent Waters. Recently, several researchers have further proposed Attribute-based encryption with multiple authorities who jointly generate users' private keys.

(Li, 2016) proposed a cipher text policy attribute based encryption (CP-ABE). In this scheme an efficient t user revocation policy is for cloud storage system. A user group is introduced and in this concept and user revocation is efficiently solved with this scheme. After a user leaves the group manager of the group updates all private keys. Additionally, CP-ABE scheme has heavy computation cost, as it grows linearly with the complexity for the access structure. To reduce the computation cost, they proposed outsource of high computation load to cloud service providers without leaking file content and secret keys. Notably, this scheme can withstand collusion attack performed by revoked users cooperating with existing users. They proved the security of scheme under the divisible computation Diffie-Hellman (DCDH) assumption.

Elliptical Curve Cryptosystem for Vehicular Cloud Security

As per (Sharma, 2015) Elliptic Curve Cryptography used for secure communication in the network that also ensures the security requirements such as confidentiality, integrity, privacy etc. The proposed scheme ensures the mutual authentication of both sender and receiver that wants to communicate. The scheme uses additional operation such as one-way hash function and concatenation to secure the network against various attacks i.e. spoofing attack, man-in-the-middle attack, replay attack etc. The effectiveness of the proposed scheme is evaluated using the different metrics such as packet delivery ratio, throughput and end-to-end delay and it is found better where it is not applied. Elliptical curve cryptography is used for authorization of users in vehicular cloud or cloud services (Singh, 2015; Divya, 2014).

Elliptical Curve Arithmetic

As explained by (Darrer, 2013) Elliptical curve cryptography is based on the points on curves. Cryptography is branch of mathematics that converts plaintext into cipher text. There are many algorithms to encrypt data and generate digital signatures. Elliptic Curve Cryptography (ECC) is very important among them. In 1985 a new cryptosystem was developed by Miller and Kolbitz which is dependent on the finite theory of and discrete logarithm problem. Elliptic curve cryptographic schemes can provide the same functionality as RSA schemes which are public-key mechanisms. Due to the reason of discrete logarithm property the key length of the elliptical curve cryptography system is smaller than the RSA. Advantage of ECC is, it gives same level of security to that of RSA and at the same time it has smaller key size compared to RSA. Other important features which make ECC popular for implementation is: it consumes low power, it is faster in computations. Since key size length is small, it takes smaller power and uses less bandwidth.

Wireless devices and smart cards present a good example for the constrained devices with limited resources. Arithmetic in elliptic curves requires a number of modules to calculate ECC operations:

- Modular multiplication,
- Modular division, and
- Modular addition/subtraction operations

The most critical operation, which is computationally expensive, is modular division. There are many applications using ECC as an authentication for encryption, transactions or signature for secure messaging.

Mathematics of Elliptical Curve Cryptography

Definition: An elliptic curve E over a field K is defined by an equation.

Mathematical details of Elliptical Curve Cryptography are given in Figure 7 with an example.

Elliptic Curve Digital Signature Algorithm

Authentication of a message or application in electronics and communication can be done using Digital Signature Algorithm (DSA). DSA has its own unique properties. Private Key in this signature is produced by one single individual. The produced key is verified by any recipient. If 'X' wants to send a message to Y, X should sign the message using her private key. By signing the message X will authenticate the message. Verification of the signature can be done using public key of X. Thus if Y is aware of X's public key, Y can verify the signature and confirm that it has come from authenticated user. Another version of DSA which works on elliptical curve theory is Elliptic Curve Digital Signature Algorithm (ECDSA).

Pairing Based Cryptosystem

The main concept of PBC is constructing a mapping between two suitable cryptographic groups. Then reduce the complexity of one of the group to match with another group. This method produces sufficient cryptographic schemes. DDHP and DLP can be solved with pairing methods. Examples of such pairings are Weil pairings and Tate pairings (Kristin,2004).

Chaos Theory Based Security for Vehicular Cloud

Chaos theory includes the properties of theory of nonlinear dynamics. In this theory simple deterministic equations help to predict the random events. Chaos means lack of orderliness and somewhat unpredictable behavior. They don't obey any rules or behaviors. Chaos theory is a very important theory for securing data on vehicular cloud. (Bahrami, 2016) proposed a scheme for security of cloud service which scrambles data on each multiple fields of a database. The proposed system uses predefined chaos based system to store data on the database. Main advantage of this scheme is data is scrambled and stored in database, so database users, authorized or unauthorized users or cloud administrators cannot get the original data.

Figure 7. Elliptical curves

$$E : y^2 + a_1 xy + a_3 y = x^3 + a_2 x^2 + a_4 x + a_6$$

where $a_1, a_2, a_3, a_4, a_6 \in K$ and $\Delta \neq 0$, where Δ is the *discriminant* of E and is defined as follows:

$$\begin{aligned}
\Delta &= -d_2^2 d_8 - 8d_4^3 - 27d_6^2 + 9d_2 d_4 d_6 \\
d_2 &= a_1^2 + 4a_2 \\
d_4 &= 2a_4 + a_1 a_3 \\
d_6 &= a_3^2 + 4a_6 \\
d_8 &= a_1^2 a_6 + 4a_2 a_6 - a_1 a_3 a_4 + a_2 a_3^2 - a_4^2.
\end{aligned}$$

If L is any extension field of K, then the set of *L-rational points* on E is

$$E(L) = \{(x, y) \in L \times L : y^2 + a_1 xy + a_3 y - x^3 - a_2 x^2 - a_4 x - a_6 = 0\} \cup \{\infty\}$$

where ∞ is the *point at infinity*.

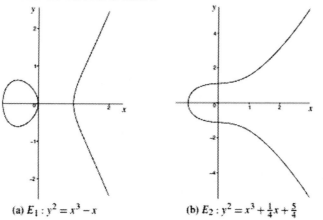

(a) $E_1 : y^2 = x^3 - x$ (b) $E_2 : y^2 = x^3 + \frac{1}{4}x + \frac{5}{4}$

Proposed Idea

In this section we present some of the ideas which will be implemented in VCC and beneficial for the society. These proposals are mainly for focused on the travelers and drivers.

Secure Storage Service for Vehicular Cloud Environment

Some of the vehicles have plenty of storage facility in their OBU and other vehicles which don't have storage facility may require it. It is predicted that vehicles will have multiple tera bytes of memory and they can be rented for other vehicles. The difference between the conventional cloud and VCC based SaaS is that, in VCC the service may be available for less time.

IoV (Internet of Vehicles)

By combining the emerging technology of Internet of Things (IoT) and VANET an autonomous framework can be formed which will be used for maintaining the network between the moving vehicles, hospitals and ambulances. These will help drivers and passengers in the emergency and accident places. It will save time of arrival of ambulances and saves lives.

Environment Sensing on Wheel

The sensors mounted on the vehicles can sense the pollution of the environment. So instead of deploying permanent infrastructure for environment pollution monitoring at large geographical area, the vehicles moving in that area can be used. The collected data can be uploaded to cloud or pollution control board for further processing.

Intelligent Transportation and Connected Vehicles

Intelligent Transportation helps users with the application like safety system, toll collection, trip planning, travel assistance, passenger information and intermodal communication. Communication is possible through IEEE 802.11u, 3G/4G, Wi-Fi, Hotspot, femtocells.

Open Research Issues

1. **Architectural Formation of Vehicular Cloud:** Due to the mobility of host and heterogeneity of nodes it is very difficult to manage computing, communication and storage facilities.
2. **Security and Privacy Issues:** VC is predicted to face same security issues like CC. This is because vehicles which are nodes of network share computational capability power, storage area, and internet facility from CC.
3. **Policy and Operational Management Issues:** There are no proper rules and regulations for setting up of VC and control structure of operation of VC. There is need for establishment of managing system for decision support at local and global level. Rules for incentive payment for vehicles participating in VC should be made.

CONCLUSION

Vehicular cloud has emerged due to high vehicle's computation and storage resources, sensing capabilities and traditional cloud computing. The VCC is considered as a complementary of traditional cloud computing but with more services and applications. In this chapter we presented introduction to vehicular cloud, architecture of vehicular cloud, applications of VC. The chapter gives details of vehicular cloud computing challenges and security. It focuses on security requirement, security threats and challenges. We also presented schemes for secure communications in VC. Secure data storage scheme is proposed. This chapter discusses many beneficial information about vehicular cloud computing and hope it motivates readers about VCC and its implementation about real time.

REFERENCES

Al-Quteyri. (2010). *Security and Privacy of Intelligent VANET*. Computational Intelligence and Modern Heuristics.

Alazawi, Z., Abdljabar, M. B., & Altowaijri, S. (2012). ICDMS: An Intelligent Cloud Based Disaster Management System for Vehicular Networks. *LNCS, 7266*, 40–56.

Altayeb, M., & Mahgoub, I. (2013). A survey of vehicular ad hoc networks routing protocols. *International Journal of Innovation and Applied Studies, 3*(3), 829–846.

Arif, S., Olariu, S., Wang, J., Yan, G., Yang, W., & Khalil, I. (2012). Datacenter at the airport: Reasoning about time-dependent parking lot occupancy. *IEEE Transactions on Parallel and Distributed Systems, 23*(11), 2067–2080. doi:10.1109/TPDS.2012.47

Auter. (2004). The Advantages of Elliptic Curve Cryptography For Wireless Security. *IEEE Wireless Communications*.

Bahrami, M., & Singhal, M. (2016). A light -weight Data Privacy schema for cloud based Databases. *International Conference on Computing, Networking and Communications*. 10.1109/ICCNC.2016.7440634

Cao, N., Wang, C., Li, M., Ren, K., & Lou, W. (2014, January). Privacy-Preserving Multi-Keyword Ranked Search over Encrypted Cloud Data. *IEEE Transactions on Parallel and Distributed Systems, 25*(1), 222–224. doi:10.1109/TPDS.2013.45

Chen, X., Rao, L., Yao, Y., Liu, X., & Bai, F. (2015). The Answer is Rolling On Wheels: Modelling and Performance Evaluation of in-cabin Wi-Fi Communications. *Vehicular Communications, 2*(1), 13–26. doi:10.1016/j.vehcom.2014.10.001

Divya, S. V. (2014). Security in Data Forwarding Through Elliptic Curve Cryptography in Cloud. *International Conference on Control, Instrumentation, Communication and Computational Technologies*.

Eltoweissy, M., Olariu, S., & Younis, M. (2010). Towards Autonomous Vehicular Clouds. *LNICST, 49*, 1–16.

Gerla, M. (2012). Vehicular Cloud Computing. *IEEE Vehicular Communications and Applications Workshop*.

Hankerson, Menezes, & Vanstone. (n.d.). *Guide to Elliptic Curve Cryptography*. Academic Press.

Housley, R., Polk, W., Ford, W., & Solo, D. (2002). *Internet X. 509 public key infrastructure certificate and certificate revocation list (CRL) profile*. RFC 3280.

Huang, D., Misra, S., Verma, M., & Xue, G. (2011, September). Pacp: An efcient pseudonymous authentication-based conditional privacy protocol for vanets. *IEEE Transactions on Intelligent Transportation Systems, 12*(3), 736–747. doi:10.1109/TITS.2011.2156790

Hussain, R., & Oh, H. (2014, October). A Secure and Privacy-Aware Route Tracing and Revocation Mechanism in VANET-based Clouds. *Journal of The Korea Institute of Information Security and Cryptology, 24*(5), 795–807. doi:10.13089/JKIISC.2014.24.5.795

Jelassi, S. (2015). QoE-Driven Video Streaming System over Cloud-Based VANET. *LNCS, 9066*, 84–93.

Kang & Park. (2015). *Design of Secure Protocol for Session Key Exchange in Vehicular Cloud Computing*. Advances in Computer Science and Ubiquitous Computing.

Lee & Chen. (2013). Cloud Server Aided Computation for ElGamal Elliptic Curve Cryptosystem. *IEEE 37th Annual Computer Software and Applications Conference Workshops*.

Li, J. (2016). *Flexible and Fine-Grained Attribute-Based Data Storage in Cloud Computing. IEEE Transactions on Services Computing.*

Lien & Lin. (2013). A Novel Privacy Preserving Location-Based Service Protocol With Secret Circular Shift for k-NN Search. *IEEE Transactions on Information Forensics and Security, 8*(6).

Lin, Zhang, Ma, & Wang. (2015). Revisiting Attribute-Based Encryption With Verifiable Outsourced Decryption. *IEEE Transactions on Information Forensics and Security, 10*(10).

Mallissery, S., Manohara, P. M. M., Ajam, N., Pai, R. M., & Mouzna, J. (2015). Transport and Traffic Rule Violation Monitoring Service in ITS: A Secured VANET Cloud Application. *Annual IEEE Consumer Communications and Networking Conference.* 10.1109/CCNC.2015.7157979

Mallissery, S., Manohara, P. M. M., & Pai, R. M. (2014). Cloud Enabled Secure Communication in Vehicular Ad-hoc Networks. *International Conference on Connected Vehicles and Expo* 2014.

Mershad & Artail. (2013). *Finding a STAR in a Vehicular Cloud. IEEE Intelligent Transport on System Magazine.*

Park, Y. (2015). *Pseudonymous authentication for secure V2I services in cloudbased vehicular networks. J Ambient Intell Human Comput.*

Raya, M., Aziz, A., & Hubaux, J.-P. (2010). Efficient secure aggregation in Vanets. *Proceedings of the 3rd international workshop on Vehicular ad hoc networks.*

Saini, Alam, & Guo. (2015, December). InCloud: a cloud-based middleware for vehicular infotainment systems. *Multimed Tools Appl.*

Sharma, M. K., Bali, R. S., & Kaur, A. (2015). Dynamic key based authentication scheme for Vehicular Cloud Computing. *International Conference on Green Computing and Internet of Things (ICGCIoT).* 10.1109/ICGCIoT.2015.7380620

Shen, J. (2016). *An Authorized Identity Authentication-based Data Access Control Scheme in Cloud.* ICACT.

Sherali Zeadally, S. C. A. I. A. H. (2012). Vehicular ad hoc networks (VANETs): Status, Results and Challenges. *Telecommunication Systems, 50*(10), 217–241. doi:10.100711235-010-9400-5

Singh, S., & Kumar, V. (2015). Secured User's Authentication and Private Data Storage- Access Scheme in Cloud Computing Using Elliptic Curve Cryptography. *International Conference on Computing for Sustainable Global Development.*

Vignesh, N., Shankar, R., & Sathyamoorthy, S. (2014). Value Added Services on Stationary Vehicular Cloud. *LNCS, 8337*, 92–97.

Whaiduzzaman, M., Sookhak, M., Gani, A., & Buyya, R. (2014). A Survey On Vehicular Cloud Computing. *Journal of Network and Computer Applications, 40,* 325–344. doi:10.1016/j.jnca.2013.08.004

Yan, G., Wen, D., Olariu, S., & Weigle, M. C. (2012). Security Challenges in Vehicular Cloud Computing. *IEEE Transactions on Intelligent Transportation Systems.*

This research was previously published in the Handbook of Research on Recent Developments in Intelligent Communication Application edited by Siddhartha Bhattacharyya, Nibaran Das, Debotosh Bhattacharjee, and Anirban Mukherjee, pages 344-365, copyright year 2017 by Information Science Reference (an imprint of IGI Global).

APPENDIX

Table 2. List of Acronyms

AVS	Autonomous Vehicular Cloud
CA	Certificate Authority
CaaS	Cooperation as a Service
CC	Cloud Computing
CRL	Certificate Revocation List
CRM	Customer Relationship Management
DoS	Denial of Services
DRP	Distributed Revocation Protocol
EBS	Elastic Book Store
EDR	Event Data Recorder
GPS	Global Positioning System
IaaS	Infrastructure as a Service
ITS	Intelligent Transportation Systems
SaaS	Software as a Service
STaaS	Storage as a Service
V2I	Vehicle to Interface
V2V	Vehicle to Vehicle
VANET	Vehicular Adhoc Network
VC	Vehicular Cloud
VCC	Vehicular Cloud Computing
V-Cloud	Vehicular Cloud
VM	Virtual Machine
VPKI	Vehicular Public Key Infrastructure
WSN	Wireless Sensor Network

Chapter 56
A Randomized Cloud Library Security Environment

A. V. N. Krishna
PujyaShri Madhavanji College of Engineering & Technology, India

ABSTRACT

Cloud computing is leading the technology development of today's communication scenario. This is because of its cost-efficiency and flexibility. In Cloud computing vast amounts of data are stored in varied and distributed environments, and security to data is of prime concern. RSA or Elliptic Curve Cryptography (ECC) provides a secure means of message transmission among communicating hosts using Diffie Hellman Key Exchange algorithm or ElGamal algorithm. By having key lengths of 160 bits, the ECC algorithm provides sufficient strength against crypto analysis and its performance can be compared with standard algorithms like RSA with a bit length of 1024 bits. In the present work, the plain text is converted to cipher text using RSA or ECC algorithms. As the proposed model is intended to be used in Cloud environment, a probabilistic mathematical model is also used. While the data is being retrieved from the servers, a query is being used which uses the mathematical model to search for the data which is still in encryption form. Final decryption takes place only at user's site by using the private keys. Thus the security model provides the fundamental security services like Authentication, Security, and Confidentiality to the transmitted message and also provides sufficient strength against crypto analysis in Cloud environment.

INTRODUCTION

Cloud computing is the use of computing resources (hardware and software) that are delivered as a service over a network (typically the Internet). The name comes from the use of a cloud-shaped symbol as an abstraction for the complex infrastructure it contains in system diagrams (see Figure 1). Cloud computing entrusts remote services with user's data, software, and computation.

Today many of the largest software companies operate almost entirely in the cloud, the top five software companies by sales revenue all have major cloud offerings, and the market as a whole is predicted to grow at a very fast pace. Yet, despite the trumpeted business and technical advantages of cloud

DOI: 10.4018/978-1-5225-8176-5.ch056

Figure 1. Cloud computing environment

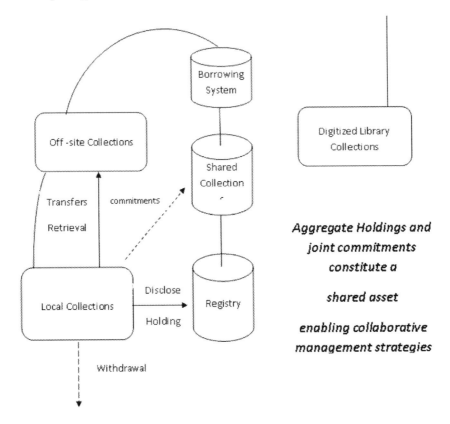

computing, many potential cloud users have yet to join the cloud, and those major corporations that are cloud users are for the most part putting only their less sensitive data in the cloud.

Mell and Grance (2012) define the "security" concerns that are preventing companies from taking advantage of the cloud as:

- Traditional Security
- Availability
- Third-Party Data Control

Traditional Security

These concerns involve computer and network intrusions or attacks that will be made possible or at least easier by moving to the cloud. Cloud providers respond to these concerns by arguing that their security measures and processes are more mature and tested than those of the average company.

Availability

These concerns center on critical applications and data being available. Well-publicized incidents of cloud outages include G mail, Amazon.

Third-Party Data Control

The legal implications of data and applications being held by a third party are complex and not well understood. There is also a potential lack of control and transparency when a third party holds the data. Part of the hype of cloud computing is that the cloud can be implementation independent, but in reality regulatory compliance requires transparency into the cloud.

All this is prompting some companies to build private clouds to avoid these issues and yet retain some of the advantages of cloud computing.

Digital library automation solutions provide timely, efficient and effective enterprise library management services, complete with easy-to-use library and knowledge management functionality. These transformative library services remove information access barriers, such as proprietary information silos, to seamlessly make information access equitable. The end result is open access throughout the organization to information services and resources such as: electronic journals, lab notes, databases or other knowledge assets.

- **Delivery of Core Library Services:** Making them more efficient and accessible.
- **User Satisfaction:** Due to improved information access and knowledge management.
- **Library Operations:** Making them more streamlined and less costly.
- The library's ability to provide for future growth and changing information demands.

Privacy-Enhanced Business Intelligence

The report ("Privacy in Cloud," 2009) finds that for some information and for some business users, sharing may be illegal, may be limited in some ways, or may affect the status or protections of the information shared. A different approach to retaining control of data is to require the encryption of all cloud data. The problem is that encryption limits data use. In particular searching and indexing the data becomes problematic. For example, if data is stored in clear-text, one can efficiently search for a document by specifying a keyword. This is impossible to do with traditional, randomized encryption schemes. State-of-the-art cryptography may offer new tools to solve these problems. Thus Cloud security is an evolving area in the field of information security. In library Information systems utilizing cloud structure, Virtualization forms an integral and intermediate layer between providers and customers of the cloud. It alters the relationship between OS and underlying hardware. This virtualization needs to be protected and secured.

Much like other security systems Library cloud also focuses on primary security services like Authentication, Security and Confidentiality of Data Cryptographers have recently invented versatile encryption schemes that allow operation and computation on the ciphertext. For example, searchable encryption allows the data owner to compute a capability from his secret key (Brakerski & Vaikuntanathan, 2011). A capability encodes a search query, and the cloud can use this capability to decide which documents match the search query, without learning any additional information. Other cryptographic primitives such as homomorphic encryption and Private Information Retrieval perform computations on encrypted data without decrypting.

Historically, encryption schemes were the first central area of interest in cryptography (Stallings, 2006). They deal with providing means to enable private communication over an insecure channel. A sender wishes to transmit information to a receiver over an insecure channel that is a channel which may be tapped by an adversary. Thus, the information to be communicated, which we call the plaintext, must be transformed (encrypted) to a cipher text, a form not legible by anybody other than the intended receiver. The latter must be given some way to decrypt the cipher text, i.e. retrieve the original message, while this must not be possible for an adversary. This is where keys come into play; the receiver is considered to have a key at his disposal, enabling him to recover the actual message, a fact that distinguishes him from any adversary. An encryption scheme consists of three algorithms: The encryption algorithm transforms plaintexts into cipher texts while the decryption algorithm converts cipher texts back into plaintexts. A third algorithm, called the key generator, creates pairs of keys: an encryption key, input to the encryption algorithm, and a related decryption key needed to decrypt.

Any symmetric encryption scheme uses a private key for secure data transfer. In their work on "A simple algorithm for random number generation, the authors presented a simple algorithm which generates random numbers (Krishna & Vinaya, 2009). Krishna, Vinaya, and Pandit (2007) presented a probabilistic algorithm which generates multiple cipher texts for one plain text which is relatively free from chosen cipher text attack. Most of the products and standards use public-key cryptography for encryption and digital signatures. As these cryptographic techniques mature, they may open up new possibilities for cloud computing security use RSA today. Recently, Elliptic Curve Cryptography has begun to challenge RSA (Stallings, 2006). The principal attraction of ECC compared to RSA, is that it appears to offer better security for a smaller key size, thereby reducing processing overhead. Figure 2 shows the rates of challenges for cloud computing (Mell & Grance, 2010).

SECURITY MODEL

In Cryptography, encryption is the process of encoding messages (or information) in such a way that eavesdroppers or hackers cannot read it, but that authorized parties can. In an encryption scheme, the message or information (referred to as plain text) is encrypted using an encryption algorithm, turning it

Figure 2. Rate of challenges to cloud on demand

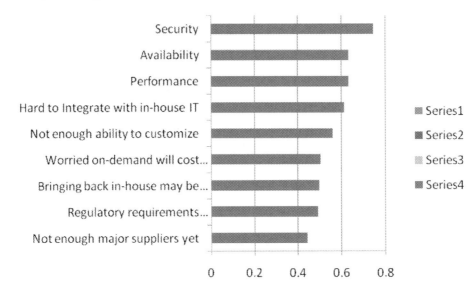

into an unreadable cipher text. This is usually done with the use of an encryption key, which specifies how the message is to be encoded. Any adversary that can see the cipher text should not be able to determine anything about the original message. An authorized party, however, is able to decode the cipher text using a decryption algorithm that usually requires a secret decryption key that adversaries do not have access to. For technical reasons, an encryption scheme usually needs a key-generation algorithm, to randomly produce keys. There are two basic types of encryption schemes Symmetric Key and Public key Encryption.

Symmetric-key algorithms ("Symmetric Key," n.d) are a class of algorithms for cryptography that use the same cryptographic keys for both encryption of plain text and decryption of cipher text. The keys may be identical or there may be a simple transformation to go between the two keys. The keys, in practice, represent a shared secret between two or more parties that can be used to maintain a private information link. This requirement that both parties have access to the secret key is one of the main drawbacks of symmetric key encryption, in comparison to Public key Encryption.

Symmetric-key encryption can use either stream cipher or block cipher.

- Stream ciphers encrypt the digits (typically bits) of a message one at a time.
- Block ciphers take a number of bits and encrypt them as a single unit, padding the plaintext so that it is a multiple of the block size. Blocks of 64 bits have been commonly used. The Advanced Encryption Standard (AES) algorithm approved by NIST in December 2001 uses 128-bit blocks.

Public-key cryptography ("Public Key," n.d) refers to a cryptographic system requiring two separate keys, one of which is secret and one of which is public. Although different, the two parts of the key pair are mathematically linked. One key locks or encrypts the plain text, and the other unlocks or decrypts the cipher text. Neither key can perform both functions by itself. The public key may be published without compromising security, while the private key must not be revealed to anyone not authorized to read the messages.

Public-key cryptography uses asymmetric key algorithms (such as RSA), and can also be referred to by the more generic term "asymmetric key cryptography." The algorithms used for public key cryptography are based on mathematical relationships (the most notable ones being the integer factorization and discrete logarithm problems) that presumably have no efficient solution. Although it is computationally easy for the intended recipient to generate the public and private keys, to decrypt the message using the private key, and easy for the sender to encrypt the message using the public key, it is extremely difficult (or effectively impossible) for anyone to derive the private key, based only on their knowledge of the public key. This is why, unlike symmetric encryption algorithms; a public key algorithm does not require a secure initial exchange of one (or more) secure keys between the sender and receiver. The use of these algorithms also allows the authenticity of a message to be checked by creating a digital signature of the message using the private key, which can then be verified by using the public key. In practice, only a hash of the message is typically encrypted for signature verification purposes.

Public-key cryptography is a fundamental, important, and widely used technology. It is an approach used by many cryptographic algorithms and cryptosystems. It underpins such Internet standards as Transport Layer Security (TLS),]PGP, and GPG. There are three primary kinds of public key systems: public key distribution systems, digital signature systems, and public key cryptosystems, which can perform both public key distribution and digital signature services. Diffie-Hellman Key exchange is the most widely used public key distribution system, while the Digital Signature Algorithm is the most widely used digital signature system.

The distinguishing technique used in public-key cryptography is the use of asymmetric key algorithms, where the key used to encrypt a message is not the same as the key used to decrypt it. Each user has a pair of cryptographic keys – a public encryption key and a private decryption key. The publicly available encrypting-key is widely distributed, while the private decrypting-key is known only to its proprietor, the recipient. Messages are encrypted with the recipient's public key, and can be decrypted only with the corresponding private key. The keys are related mathematically, but the parameters are chosen so that determining the private key from the public key is either impossible or prohibitively expensive. The discovery of algorithms that could produce public/private key pairs revolutionized the practice of cryptography, beginning in the mid-1970s.

In contrast, symmetric key algorithms variations of which have been used for thousands of years– use a single secret key, which must be shared and kept private by both the sender and the receiver, for both encryption and decryption. To use a symmetric encryption scheme, the sender and receiver must securely share a key in advance.

Because symmetric key algorithms are nearly always much less computationally intensive than asymmetric ones, it is common to exchange a key using a key exchange algorithm, then transmit data using that key and a symmetric key algorithm. PGP and the SSL /TLS family of schemes use this procedures, and are thus called hybrid crypto systems.

Description

The two main uses for public-key cryptography are:

- **Public-Key Encryption:** A message encrypted with a recipient's public key cannot be decrypted by anyone except a possessor of the matching private key – it is presumed that this will be the owner of that key and the person associated with the public key used. This is used to attempt to ensure confidentiality.
- **Digital Signatures:** A message signed with a sender's private key can be verified by anyone who has access to the sender's public key, thereby proving that the sender had access to the private key and, therefore, is likely to be the person associated with the public key used. This also ensures that the message has not been tampered with. An analogy to public-key encryption is that of a locked mail box with a mail slot. The mail slot is exposed and accessible to the public – its location (the street address) is, in essence, the public key. Anyone knowing the street address can go to the door and drop a written message through the slot. However, only the person who possesses the key can open the mailbox and read the message.

An analogy for digital signatures is the sealing of an envelope with a personal wax seal. The message can be opened by anyone, but the presence of the unique seal authenticates the sender.

A central problem with the use of public-key cryptography is confidence (ideally, proof) that a particular public key is correct, and belongs to the person or entity claimed (i.e., is "authentic"), and has not been tampered with, or replaced by, a malicious third party (a "man-in-the-middle"). The usual approach to this problem is to use a Public Key Infrastructure (PKI), in which one or more third parties – known as certificate authorities– certify ownership of key pairs. PGP, in addition to being a certificate authority structure, has used a scheme generally called the "Web of thrust", which decentralizes such authentication of public keys by a central mechanism, and substitutes individual endorsements of the link between user and public key. To date, no fully satisfactory solution to this "public key authentication problem" has been found

When using symmetric algorithms, both parties share the same key for en- and decryption. To provide privacy, this key needs to be kept secret. Once somebody else gets to know the key, it is not safe any more. Symmetric algorithms have the advantage of not consuming too much computing power. A few well-known examples are: DES, Triple-DES (3DES), IDEA, CAST5, BLOWFISH, and TWOFISH.

Asymmetric algorithms use pairs of keys. One is used for encryption and the other one for decryption. The decryption key is typically kept secretly, therefore called "private key" or "secret key," while the encryption key is spread to all who might want to send encrypted messages, therefore called "public key." Everybody having the public key is able to send encrypted messages to the owner of the secret key. The secret key can't be reconstructed from the public key. The idea of asymmetric algorithms was first published 1976 by Diffie and Hellmann.

Asymmetric algorithms seem to be ideally suited for real-world use: As the secret key does not have to be shared, the risk of getting known is much smaller. Every user only needs to keep one secret key in secrecy and a collection of public keys that only need to be protected against being changed. With symmetric keys, every pair of users would need to have an own shared secret key. Well-known asymmetric algorithms are RSA, DSA, and ELGAMAL.

However, asymmetric algorithms are much slower than symmetric ones. Therefore, in many applications, a combination of both is being used. The asymmetric keys are used for authentication and after this have been successfully done; one or more symmetric keys are generated and exchanged using the asymmetric encryption. This way the advantages of both algorithms can be used. Typical examples of this procedure are the RSA/IDEA combination of PGP2 or the DSA/BLOWFISH used by GnuPG.

The work is broadly divided into three modules.

- Plain text to be converted to cipher text using RSA or ECC algorithm.
- Probabilistic Model being used to generate Basin values.
- Output of RSA or ECC is scalar multiplied with the value of basins generated from mathematical model to be stored in cloud server.

The RSA Algorithm

The RSA algorithm involves three steps:

1. Key Generation
2. Encryption
3. Decryption ("Public Key," 2000)

Key Generation

RSA involves a public key and a Private Key. The public key can be known to everyone and is used for encrypting messages. Messages encrypted with the public key can only be decrypted using the private key. The keys for the RSA algorithm are generated the following way:

1. Choose two distinct prime numbers p and q.
   a. For security purposes, the integer's p and q should be chosen at random, and should be of similar bit-length.
2. Compute n = pq.
   a. n is used as the modulus for both the public and private keys. Its length, usually expressed in bits, is the key length.
3. Compute ?(n) = (p?–?1)(q?–?1), where ? is Euler's totient function.
4. Choose an integer e such that 1 < e < ?(n) and greatest common divisor gcd(e, ?(n)) = 1; i.e., e and ?(n) are co prime.
   a. e is released as the public key exponent.
   b. e having a short bit length and small Hamming weight results in more efficient encryption – most commonly 216 + 1 = 65,537.
5. Determine d as d ??e?1 (mod ?(n)), i.e., d is the multiplicative inverse of e (modulo ?(n)).
   a. This is more clearly stated as solve for d given de ? 1 (mod ?(n))
   b. This is often computed using the extended Euclidian algorithm.
   c. d is kept as the private key exponent.

By construction, d?e ? 1 (mod ?(n)). The public key consists of the modulus n and the public (or encryption) exponent e. The private key consists of the modulus n and the private (or decryption) exponent d, which must be kept secret. p, q, and ?(n) must also be kept secret because they can be used to calculate d.

Encryption

Alice transmits her public key (n, e) to Bob and keeps the private key secret. Bob then wishes to send message M to Alice.

He first turns M into an integer m, such that 0 ??m < n by using an agreed-upon reversible protocol known as a padding scheme. He then computes the cipher text c corresponding to:

c=me (mod n)

This can be done quickly using the method of exponentiation by squaring. Bob then transmits c to Alice.

Decryption

Alice can recover m from c by using her private key exponent d via computing:

m=cd (mod n)

Given m, she can recover the original message M by reversing the padding scheme.

Elliptic Curve Cryptography

Elliptic Curve Cryptography (Cilardo, Coppolino, Mazzocca, & Romano, 2006) makes use of elliptic curves in which the variables and coefficients are all restricted to elements of a finite field. In ECC we normally start with an affine point called Pm(x,y). These points maybe the Base point (G) itself or some other point closer to the Base point. Base point implies it has the smallest x, y co-ordinates, which satisfy the EC. A character in a message is first transformed into an affine point of the elliptic curve by using it as a multiplier of Pm. That is, if the ASCII value of a character is A, then we determine P0 m=A (Pm). This is one step towards introducing sophistication and complexity in the encryption process. The newly evaluated P0 m is a point on the EC, determined by applying the addition and doubling strategy of ECC technique. Then as per ECC algorithm, P0 m is added with kPB, where k is randomly chosen secret integer and PB is the public key of user B, to yield (P0 m+ kPB). This now constitutes the second part of the encrypted version of the message. The other part, namely, kG, which is the product of the secret integer and the Base point, constitutes the first part. Thus the encrypted message is now made up of two sets of coordinates, namely, (kG, P0 m+ kPB). In this paper we have assigned kG=(x1,y1) and (Pm+kPB)=(x2,y2).

An example of indirect data-mining that might be performed by a cloud provider is to note transactional and relationship information. For example, availability also needs to be considered in the context of an adversary whose goals are simply to sabotage activities. Increasingly, such adversaries are becoming realistic as political conflict is taken onto the Web, and as the recent cyber attacks on Lithuania confirm. An example of indirect data-mining that might be performed by a cloud provider is to note transactional and relationship information. For example, the sharing of information by two companies may signal a merger is under consideration.

Homomorphic encryption (Craig, 2010) schemes that allow simple computations on encrypted data have been known for a long time. For example, the encryption systems (Goldwasser & Micali, 1982) support either adding or multiplying encrypted ciphertexts, but not both operations at the same time. In a breakthrough work, (Stehlé & Steinfeld, 2010) constructed a fully homomorphic encryption scheme (FHE) capable of evaluating an arbitrary number of additions and multiplications (and thus, compute any function) on encrypted data.

Broadly this work deals with the importance of security aspects in Cloud computing in the present day scenario. The very important feature with Cloud is security to data stored and security to data transmitted. To maintain security to data the best technique that can be employed is encryption. Encryption to data supports the very important features like security, confidentiality to data and authentication of users.

The organization of our work is as follows. The work started with discussing the features of RSA and Elliptic Curve Cryptography. In the following sections the concepts of probabilistic model are discussed.

We review here only some of the most important facts about elliptic curve cryptography. Let $p > 2$ be a prime number and let q = pm, for some m in N. Let Fq(also written as GF(q)) be a finite field of q elements. If q is prime, we can think of Fq as the set of integers modulo q (Zq).

Let a1; a2; a3; a4; a6 in Fq.

We say that the elliptic curve over Fq is the set of solutions (x; y) in Fq for the Weierstrass equation

E: y2 + a1xy + a3y = x3 + a2x2 + a4x + a6

in background together with a special point O, called the point at infinity. After a change of variables, equation above can be simplified to the

Following forms (known as simplified Weierstrass form for curves of characteristic p):

E: y2 + xy = x3 + ax2 + b if p = 2

y2 = x3 + ax2 + bx + c if p = 3

y2 = x3 + ax + b if p > 3

When p = 2 we need b = 0, when p = 3 we need a2 (b2 /4ac) b3 = 0 and when p > 3 we need 4a3 + 27b2 = 0 to ensure that E has no multiple roots, so it is possible to draw a tangent line in any point of the curve. It is well known that the points of an elliptic curve define a group law, with O as the identity element. We now define some useful concepts in elliptic curves:

Point multiplication (scalar point multiplication): let s be an integer and P an elliptic curve point. We define [s] P as the sum of P with itself s times. There are well defined formulae for adding two points P and Q of an elliptic curve (R = P + Q) or for computing the scalar point doubling. We remark that [s] P can be efficiently computed (i.e., computed in polynomial time) using double-and-(add or subtract) algorithm and curve order (#E): is the number of points of a given curve E.

The Weiestrass equation defining an elliptic curve over GF (p), for q > 3, is as follows: y2 = x3 + ax + b, where x, y are elements of GF (p), and a, b is integer modulo p, satisfying 4a3 + 27b2 = 0 mod p.

Here p is known as modular prime integer. An elliptic curve E over GF (p) consist of the solutions (x, y) defined by Equations 1 and 2, along with an additional element called O, which is the point of EC at infinity. The set of points (x, y) are said to be affine coordinate point representation. The basic Elliptic curve operations are point addition and point doubling. Elliptic curve cryptographic primitives [13] require scalar point multiplication. Say, given a point P(x, y) on an EC, one needs to compute kP, where k is a positive integer. This is achieved by a series of doubling and addition of P. Say, given k = 20, entails the following sequence of operations P, 2P, 3P, 6P, 12P, 24P, 48P, 96P, 192P, 193P, 386P.

Let us start with P (xP, yP). To determine 2P, P is doubled. This should be an affine point on EC. Use the following equation, which is a tangent to the curve at point P.

S = [(3x2P + a)/2yP] mod p

Then 2P has affine coordinate's xR, yR given by:

xR = (S2 ? 2xP) mod p

yR = [S(xP ? xR) ? yP] mod p

Now to determine 3P, we use addition of points P and 2P, treating 2P = Q. Here P has coordinates (xP, yP) and Q = 2P has coordinates (xQ, yQ).

Then: xR = (S2 ? xP ? xQ) mod p

yR = (S(xP ? xR) ? yP] mod p

Therefore we apply doubling and addition depending on a sequence of operations determined for k. Every point xR, yR evaluated by doubling or addition is an affine point (points on the Elliptic Curve).

Implementation Details of ECC: Once the defining EC is known we can select a base point called G. G has [x, y] coordinates which satisfy the equation y2 = x3 +ax+b (Ramasamy, Prabakar, Devi, & Suguna, 2009). The base point has the smallest x, y values which satisfy the EC.The ECC method requires that we select a random integer k(k < p), which needs to be kept secret. Then kG is evaluated, by a series of additions and doublings, as discussed above. For purpose of this discussion we shall call the source as host A, and the destination as host B. We select the private key of the host B, called nB. k and nB can be generated by random number generators to give credibility. That would be digressing away from the main discussion. Hence we make suitable assumptions for these two parameters. The public key of B is evaluated by PB = nBG. [3] Suppose A wants to encrypt and transmit a character to B, he does the following. Assume that host A wants to transmit the character 'm'. Then the ASCII value of the character 'm' is used to modify Pm as follows: P0m= mPm. Pm we said is an affine point. This is selected different from the Base point G, so as to preserve their individual identities. P0m is a point on the EC. The coordinates of the P0m should fit into the EC. This transformation is done for two purposes. First the single valued ASCII is transformed into a x,y co-ordinate of the EC. Second it is completely camouflaged from the would-be hacker. This is actually intended to introduce some level of complexity even before the message is encrypted according to ECC. As the next step of ECC, we need to evaluate kPB, here PB is a public key of user B. Determining this product involves a series of doubling and additions, depending on the value of k. For a quick convergence of the result, we should plan for optimal number of doubles and additions. The encrypted message is derived by adding P0m with kPB, that is, P0m+kPB. This yields a set of x2, y2 coordinates. Then kG is included as the first element of the encrypted version. kG is another set of x1, y1 coordinates. Hence the entire encrypted version for purposes of storing or transmission consists of two sets of coordinates as follows: Cm = (kG, P0m + kPB), where kG =(x1, y1), (P0 m + kPB) = (x2, y2).

Probabilistic Model

With probabilistic encryption algorithms, a crypto analyst can no longer encrypt random plain texts looking for correct cipher text (Krishna, Vinaya, & Pandit, 2007). Since multiple cipher texts will be developed for one plain text, even if he decrypts the message to plain text, he does not know how far he had guessed the message correctly. To illustrate, assume a crypto analyst has a certain cipher text ci. Even if he guesses the message correctly, when he encrypts the message the result will be completely different cj. He cannot compare ci and cj and so cannot know that he has guessed the message correctly. Under this scheme, different cipher texts will be formed for one plain text. Also the cipher text will always be larger than plain text. This develops the concept of multiple cipher texts for one plain text. This concept makes crypto analysis difficult to apply on plain text and cipher text pairs.

In the ECC algorithm, a random value is used in encryption process. The cipher text is generated as C1 and C2 where C1 gives (Pm+k*G*Pb) and C2 gives k* G where Pm refers to plain text, G is a global parameter; Pb is the public key of receiver and kis the random value. The cipher text is generated as C1 and C2 to provide for decryption process. This makes for more data overhead and more computing overhead during the encryption and decryption process. In the present work, a probabilistic model is used at both sender and receiver which generate the random value which is used in C1. Since a probabilistic model is used, this work does not need the generation of C2 which reduces data and computation overhead.

Probabilistic features are incorporated in the output of ECC model to make it free from chosen cipher text attack.

It involves following steps:

1. Algorithm for generating sequence.
2. Generating Basins with unequal values based on equality of values.
3. Mapping the basin value in the output of ECC.

Algorithm for Generating the Sequence:

1. Consider the sequence for 0 to n values where n is a positive integer.
2. Convert each element of the sequence into ternary form of a given digit number.
3. Represent the values of step 2 in a matrix form of (n+1) * (digit number).
4. Subtract 1 from each element of the matrix specified in step 3.
5. Consider a random matrix key of size (digit number*digit number).
6. Multiply the output of step 4 with the output of step 5.
7. Convert all positive values of matrix to 1, negative values to -1 and zero by 0.
8. Add 1 to each element of output of step 7.
9. Convert ternary values of step 8 into decimal form. A sequence is generated.

Algorithm for Generating Basins from Sequence Generated:

1. Consider the sequence of values starting from 0 to n where n be an integer.
2. Read the sequence generated from algorithm 1.
3. Read the starting element of step 1 and store the first element of step 1 and the corresponding first element of step 2 in a separate basin.
4.1 Compare the element of step 3 with the elements of step 2. If there is a match, store the corresponding elements of step 1 in the basin specified in step 3. Neglect already visited elements.
4.2 Repeat step 4.1 with the remaining elements of the basin of step 3 and store them in the same basin. This will form one basin.
5. Go to next element of step 1 which is not visited earlier.

In cloud computing, querying is processed on the encrypted data. Without decrypting the data, the query needs to be processed and output is transmitted to users in encrypted form only. In the present work, a new mathematical model is used which uses a nonce value and a dynamic time stamp to generate a distributed sequence. This sequence is used as key to generate indexed encrypted values of stored data in the server of the Cloud environment. When a query is to be processed, this mathematical model is used to decrypt the index values of stored encrypted data. Thus known the index values to encrypted message, data is identified and used for transmission to intended users.

IMPLEMENTATION DETAILS

Example of RSA Encryption and Decryption

Choose two distinct prime numbers, such as:

p=61 and q=53.

1. Compute n = pq giving

n=61*53=3233.

2. Compute the totient of the product as $?(n) = (p???1)(q???1)$ giving
3. Choose any number 1 < e < 3120 that is coprime to 3120. Choosing a prime number for e leaves us only to check that e is not a divisor of 3120.

e=17.

4. Compute d, the modular multiplicative inverse of e (mod ?(n)) yielding d=2753.

The public key is (n = 3233, e = 17). For a padded plain text message m, the encryption function is m17 (mod 3233).

The private key is (n = 3233, d = 2753). For an encrypted cipher text c, the decryption function is c2753 (mod 3233).

For instance, in order to encrypt m = 65, we calculate:

c=6517=2790 (mod 3233).

To decrypt c = 2790, we calculate:

M=27902753=65 (mod 3233).

Example for ECC Algorithm

The Elliptic Curve is y2 mod 13 = (x3 ? 5x + 25) mod 13. The base point G is selected as (4, 11). Base point implies that it has the smallest x, y co-ordinates which satisfy the EC. Pm is another affine point, which is picked out of a series of affine points evaluated for the given EC. We could have retained G itself for Pm. However for the purpose of individual identity, we choose Pm to be different from G. Let Pm= (6, 4). The choice of Pm is itself an exercise involving meticulous application of the ECC process on the given EC, the secret integer k, and the private key nB of the recipient B. In the present work we use the basin say, b (2) to consider the values.

Example With Probabilistic Features

Random Value to Be Generated from Probabilistic Model

Step 1: Consider a ternary vector at 81 values (i.e., from 0 to 80).
Step 2: Representing them in matrix form (see Table 1.)
Step 3: $r = r - 1$ (see Table 2)
Step 4: Consider a 4 X 4 matrix (see Table 3)
Step 5: A X r= (see Table 4)
Step 6: $r = $ Sign (A*r) (see Table 5)
Step 7: $R = r+1$ (see Table 6)
Step 8: Converting output of step 7 to integer form as: (see Table 7)
Step 9: Model for generating Basins:
    1.   n [81]= 0 1 2 3 4 5…80
    2.   r [81] = output of step 8.
    3.   Read n[0]=0. Store the values of n[0],r[0] in a basin.

Table 1.

0	0	0	0
0	0	0	1
0	0	0	2
0	0	1	0
0	0	1	1
0	0	1	2
.	.	.	.
.	.	.	.
.	.	.	.
2	2	1	2
2	2	2	0
2	2	2	1
2	2	2	2

Table 2.

−1	−1	−1	−1
−1	−1	−1	0
−1	−1	−1	1
−1	−1	0	−1
.	.	.	.
.	.	.	.
.	.	.	.
.	.	.	.
1	1	0	1
1	1	1	−1
1	1	1	0
1	1	1	1

Table 3.

$$A = \begin{vmatrix} 1 & 5 & -6 & 1 \\ 2 & 1 & 3 & 2 \\ 3 & -2 & -3 & 3 \\ 4 & 2 & 4 & 4 \end{vmatrix}$$

Table 4.

$$\begin{vmatrix} -1 & -8 & -1 & -14 \\ 0 & -6 & 2 & -10 \\ 1 & -4 & 5 & -6 \\ -7 & -5 & -4 & -10 \\ \cdot & \cdot & \cdot & \cdot \\ \cdot & \cdot & \cdot & \cdot \\ \cdot & \cdot & \cdot & \cdot \\ \cdot & \cdot & \cdot & \cdot \\ 7 & 5 & 4 & 10 \\ -1 & 4 & -5 & 6 \\ 0 & 6 & -2 & 10 \\ 1 & 8 & 1 & 14 \end{vmatrix}$$

Table 5.

$$\begin{vmatrix} -1 & -1 & -1 & -1 \\ 0 & -1 & 1 & -1 \\ 1 & -1 & 1 & -1 \\ -1 & -1 & -1 & -1 \\ \cdot & \cdot & \cdot & \cdot \\ \cdot & \cdot & \cdot & \cdot \\ \cdot & \cdot & \cdot & \cdot \\ \cdot & \cdot & \cdot & \cdot \\ 1 & 1 & 1 & 1 \\ -1 & 1 & -1 & 1 \\ 0 & 1 & -1 & 1 \\ 1 & 1 & 1 & 1 \end{vmatrix}$$

Table 6.

$$\begin{vmatrix} 0 & 0 & 0 & 0 \\ 1 & 0 & 2 & 0 \\ 2 & 0 & 2 & 0 \\ 0 & 0 & 0 & 0 \\ \cdot & \cdot & \cdot & \cdot \\ \cdot & \cdot & \cdot & \cdot \\ \cdot & \cdot & \cdot & \cdot \\ \cdot & \cdot & \cdot & \cdot \\ 2 & 2 & 2 & 2 \\ 0 & 2 & 0 & 2 \\ 0 & 2 & 0 & 2 \\ 2 & 2 & 2 & 2 \end{vmatrix}$$

Table 7.

$R = r(4,1) + 3 * r(3,1) + 9 * r(2,1) + 27 * r(1,1).$

0	33	60	0	0	6	0	9
20	54	57	60	0	0	40	0
19	20	54	54	60	54	54	74
9	20	20	33	60	60	0	6
26	9	20	26	57	60	61	0
40	80	19	20	23	54	6	71
54	74	80	20	20	47	60	60
71	6	26	26	20	26	26	60
61	80	40	80	80	20	23	26
61	71	80	74	80	80	20	47
80							

4.1and 4.2 Step 4.1 is repeated with other elements of basin

b (0) = (0, 3, 4, 6, 12, 13, 15, 30, 39, 5, 31, 57, 10, 36)

The basins formed with corresponding elements:

b (1) = (9, 54, 7, 24, 33, 18, 19, 21, 22, 45, 48, 1, 27, 16, 42)

b (2) = (20, 60, 8, 17, 25, 26, 34, 43, 51, 54, 69, 78, 2, 11, 28, 29, 37, 46, 54, 55, 63, 72, 32, 35, 58, 59, 61, 62, 71, 9, 18, 19, 21, 22, 45, 48, 38, 64, 47, 56, 73, 7, 24, 33, 16, 42, 53, 79, 1, 27)

b (3) = (23, 74, 44, 70, 49, 75)

b (4) = (40, 14, 66)

b (5) = (80, 41, 50, 65, 67, 68, 76, 77)

Step 10: Mapping the basin values to the output of ECC:

The values of any basin may be considered as 'k' of the encryption and decryption process of ECC. This is again encrypted by the output of mathematical model to generate final encrypted data to be stored in the Cloud server. Consider a case where basin b(2) is considered for identifying the value used in encryption process. Hence we shall assume that k = 20, and nB = 16. Plaintext is "m", which is made equivalent to 22. Therefore,

PB = nBG = 16(4, 11) = (8, 3)

P0m = 22(4, 11) = (6, 4)

kPB = 20(8,3) = (4,2)

P0m + kPB = (2, 10) + (4, 2) = (4, 2)

Encrypted version of the message 'm' is (11, 1);

CRYPTO ANALYSIS

Encryption and decryption of data is done at two levels.

Encryption:

Level 1: Encryption of data is done using RSA or ECC algorithm.
Level 2: The model also uses probabilistic model to generate random values used in encryption process.

Table 8. NIST recommended key sizes

Symmetric Key Size (bits)	RSA and Diffie-Hellman Key Size (bits)	Elliptic Curve Key Size (bits)
80	1024	160
112	2048	224
128	3072	256
192	7680	384
256	15360	521

Level 3: Decryption of data is done at server level using Basin values of Mathematical model.

Level 4: Decryption of data of level 1 is done at user's site using their private keys.

1. It uses probabilistic features to generate cipher text which makes it relatively free from chosen cipher text attacks. If a simulation game, Game 2 to be generated, then each plain text character must be mapped by 3-450 combinations of cipher text which gives sufficient strength against crypto analysis. The complexity of the model is increased by O (Number of basins formed (number of values of each basin)).

2. Thus the complexity of the proposed model (see Table 8) is exponential in nature.

To use RSA or Diffie-Hellman to protect 128-bit AES keys one should use 3072-bit parameters: three times the size in use throughout the Internet today. The equivalent key size for elliptic curves is only 256 bits. One can see that as symmetric key sizes increase the required key sizes for RSA and Diffie-Hellman increase at a much faster rate than the required key sizes for elliptic curve cryptosystems. Hence, elliptic curve systems offer more security per bit increase in key size than either RSA or Diffie-Hellman public key systems.

CONCLUSION

This work discusses the measures to provide security to data in a Cloud environment. ECC or RSA algorithms are discussed for security in a Cloud environment. ECC itself is a very secure algorithm for encryption. A plaintext character 'S' is taken for implementing the algorithm proposed in this paper. Each character in the message is represented by its ASCII value. Each of these ASCII value is transformed into an affine point on the EC, by using a starting point called Pm. This Pm may be selected to be different from the Base point G. The purpose of this transformation is twofold. Firstly a single digit ASCII integer of the character is converted into a set of coordinates to fit the EC. Secondly the transformation introduces non-linearity in the character thereby completely camouflaging its identity. This transformed character of the message is encrypted by the ECC technique. However, in ECC the cipher text is represented as C1 and C2 to accommodate random values which give strength against crypto analysis. This work also discusses a probabilistic model which generates random values which are used in encryption of data. So this system generates cipher text as C1 only which provides for lesser data and computing overhead on the transmitting medium. This model generates multiple cipher texts for one plain text. Any one cipher text can be used for secured data transfer. The advantage with this model is, it is not only free from linear and differential cryptanalysis but also free from chosen cipher text attacks. Thus the given model supports the important properties like authentication, security and confidentiality and resistance against Chosen cipher text attacks at less computing resources when compared to algorithm like RSA. It provides sufficient security for the same key length at reduced computing and data over head in a Cloud environment.

REFERENCES

Cilardo, A., Coppolino, L., Mazzocca, N., & Romano, L. (2006). Elliptic curve cryptography engineering. *Proceedings of the IEEE, 94*(2), 395–406. doi:10.1109/JPROC.2005.862438

Cloud Computing Security. (2009). *FTC questions cloud computing security.* Retrieved from http://news.cnet.

Craig, G. (2009). Fully homomorphic encryption using ideal lattices In M. Mitzenmacher (Ed.). In *Proceedings of STOC '09 the 41st Annual ACM Symposium on Theory of Computing* (pp. 169-174). New York: ACM.

Craig, G. (2010, August 15-19). Toward basing fully homomorphic encryption on worst-case hardness. In T. Rabin (Ed.), *CRYPTO: Proceedings of the 30th Annual Cryptology Conference (2010).* Santa Barbara, CA (LNCS 6223, pp 116-137).

Diffie, W. (1988). The first ten years of Public Key cryptography. [). New York: IEEE.]. *Proceedings of the IEEE, 76,* 560–577. doi:10.1109/5.4442

Goldwasser, S., & Micali, S. (1982). Probabilistic encryption and how to play mental poker keeping secret all partial information. In *Proceedings of STOC '82 the 14st Annual ACM Symposium on Theory of Computing* (pp. 365-377). New York: ACM.

Krishna, A. V. N., Vinaya, A. B., & Pandit, S. N. N. (2007). A generalized scheme for data encryption technique using a randomized matrix key. *Journal of Discrete Mathematical Sciences and Cryptography, 10*(1), 73–81. doi:10.1080/09720529.2007.10698109

Mell, P., & Grance, T. (2010). *Effectively and securely using the cloud computing paradigm.* Retrieved from http://www.csrc.nist.gov/groups/SNS/cloud-computing/cloud-computing-v26.ppt

Privacy in Cloud. (2009). *Risks to privacy and confidentiality from cloud computing.* Retrieved from http://www.worldprivacyforum.org/pdf/WPF_Cloud_privacy_Report.pdf/

Public Key cryptography. (2000). *Standard Specifications for Public Key Cryptography.* Retrieved from http://www.Stanadard Specifications for Public Key cryptography, IEEE Standard

Public Key. (n.d). Public key algorithm. *Retrieved from* http:// wikipedia.org/wiki/Public-key_cryptography

Ramasamy, R. R., Prabakar, M. A., Devi, M. I., & Suguna, M. (2009). Knapsack based ECC encryption and decryption. *International Journal of Network Security, 9*(3), 218–226.

Stallings, W. (2006). *Cryptography and Network Security* (4th ed.). Upper Saddle River, NJ: Prentice Hall.

Stehlé, D., & Steinfeld, R. (2010, December 5-9). Faster fully homomorphic encryption. In M. Abe (Ed.), *ASIACRYPT: Proceedings of the 16th International Conference on the Theory and Application of Cryptology and Information Security (2010).* Singapore (LCNS 6477, pp 377-394).

Symmetric key. (n.d). *Symmetric key algorithm.* Retrieved from http://wikipedia.org/wiki/Symmetric-key algorithm/

ADDITIONAL READING SECTION

Aydos, M., Yanik, T., & Kog, C. K. (2001). High-speed implementation of an ECC-based wireless authentication protocol on an ARM microprocessor. *IEEE Proceedings of Communication, 148*(5), 273-279.

Boneh, D., Goh, E. J., & Nissim, K. (2005, February 10-12). Evaluating 2-DNF formulas on ciphertexts. In *Proceedings of the 2nd Theory of Cryptography Conference, (TCC 2005).* Cambridge, MA (LNCS 3378, pp. 325-341).

Brakerski, Z., & Vaikuntanathan, V. (2011). Fully homomorphic encryption from ring-LWE and security for key dependent messages. In *Proceedings of the 31st Annual Cryptology Conference.* Santa Barbara, CA (LCNS 6841, pp. 505-524).

Chen, G., Bai, G., & Chen, H. (2007). A high-performance elliptic curve cryptographic processor for general curves Over GF(p) based on a systolic arithmetic unit. *IEEE Transactions on Circuits and Wystems. II, Express Briefs, 54*(5), 412–416. doi:10.1109/TCSII.2006.889459

Cheng, R. C. C., Baptiste, N. G., Luk, W., & Cheung, P. Y. K. (2005). Customizable elliptic curve cryptosystems. *IEEE Transactions on VLSI Systems, 13*(9), 1048–1059. doi:10.1109/TVLSI.2005.857179

Krishna, A. V. N. (2005). A simple algorithm for random number generation. *Journal of Scientific and Industrial Research, 64*, 794–796.

Krishna, A. V. N. (2011). A new nonlinear model based encryption scheme with time stamp and acknowledgement support. *International Journal of Network Security, 13*(3), 202–207.

Krishna, A. V. N., & Pandit, S. N. N. (2004). A new algorithm in network security for data transmission. *Acharya Nagarjuna International Journal of Mathematics and Information Technology, 1*(2), 97–108.

Krishna, A. V. N., & Vinaya, B. A. (2006). Web and network communication security algorithm. *Journal on Software Engineering, 1*(1), 12–14.

Krishna, A. V. N., & Vinaya, B. A. (2009). Training of a new probabilistic encryption scheme using an optimal matrix key. *Georgian Electronic & Scientific Journal, 2*(19), 24–34.

Krishna, A. V. N., & Vinaya, B. A. (2010a). A new model based encryption scheme with time stamp and acknowledgement support. *International Journal of Network Security, 11*(3), 172–176.

Krishna, A. V. N., & Vinaya, B. A. (2010b). A new nonlinear, time stamped and feedback model based encryption mechanism with acknowledgement support. *IJANA, 21-24.*

Lauter, K. (2006). The advantages of elliptic cryptography for wireless security. *IEEE Wireless Communications*, *11*(1), 62–67. doi:10.1109/MWC.2004.1269719

Lee, J., Kim, H., Lee, Y., Hong, S. M., & Yoon, H. (2007). Parallelized scalar multiplication on elliptic curves defined over optimal extension field. *International Journal of Network Security*, *4*(1), 99–106.

Moon, S. (2006). A binary redundant scalar point multiplication in secure elliptic curve cryptosystems. *International Journal of Network Security*, *3*(2), 132–137.

Paillier, P. (1999, May 2-6). Public-key cryptosystems based on composite degree residuosity classes. In *Proceedings of the International Conference on the Theory and Application of Cryptographic Techniques*. Prague, Czech Republic (LNCS 1592, pp. 223-238).

Raines, A., & Potoczny, H. B. (2006). Cryptanalysis of an elliptic curve cryptosystem for wireless sensor networks. *International Journal of Security and Networks*, *2*(3/4), 260–271.

Shi, Z. H., & Yan, H. (2008). Software implementation of elliptic curve cryptography. *International Journal of Network Security*, *7*(2), 157–166.

Smart, N. P., & Vercauteren, F. (2010. May 26-28). Fully homomorphic encryption with relatively small key and ciphertext sizes. In *Proceedings of the 13th International Conference on Practice and Theory in Public Key Cryptography*. Paris (LNCS 6056, pp. 420-443).

Sweeny, L. (1997). Weaving technology and policy together. *The Journal of Law, Medicine & Ethics*, *25*, 2–3.

Wang, H., Sheng, B., & Li, Q. (2006). Elliptic curve cryptography-based access control in sensor networks. *International Journal of Security and Networks*, *1*(3/4), 127–137. doi:10.1504/IJSN.2006.011772

Yongliang, L., Gao, W., Yao, H., & Yu, X. (2007). Elliptic curve cryptography based wireless authentication protocol. *International Journal of Network Security*, *4*(1), 99–106.

KEY WORDS AND DEFINITIONS

Asymmetric Encryption: Public-key cryptography refers to a cryptographic system requiring two separate keys, one of which is secret and one of which is public. Although different, the two parts of the key pair are mathematically linked. One key locks or encrypts the plaintext, and the other unlocks or decrypts the cipher text. Neither key can perform both functions by itself. The public key may be published without compromising security, while the private key must not be revealed to anyone not authorized to read the messages.

Cloud Computing: Is the concept of using someone else's computer equipment instead of your own. It allows a person or a business to forget about technical details like whether a hard drive is big enough and puts that concern on another party. Sometimes those third parties charge for the use of the equipment or computer programs, which they are making available for you to use. Other times, the service is available as a public service.

Cloud Computing Security: (Sometimes referred to simply as "cloud security") Is an evolving sub-domain of information security. It refers to a broad set of policies, technologies, and controls deployed to protect data, applications, and the associated infrastructure of cloud computing. Cloud security is not to be confused with security software offerings that are "cloud-based."

Homomorphic Encryption: Is a fully homomorphic encryption scheme (FHE) capable of evaluating an arbitrary number of additions and multiplications that is compute any function on encrypted data.

Probabilistic Encryption: Is an encryption process which generates multiple cipher texts for one plain text. This encryption is free from chosen cipher text attacks.

Symmetric Encryption: A class of algorithms for cryptography that use the same cryptographic keys for both encryption of plain text and decryption of cipher text. The keys may be identical or there may be a simple transformation to go between the two keys. The keys, in practice, represent a shared secret between two or more parties that can be used to maintain a private information link.

ENDNOTES

[1.] ECC Algorithm: Elliptic Curve Cryptography Algorithm.

[2.] Mod: Modular Function.

[3.] RSA Algorithm: Rivest-Shamir-Adleman Algorithm.

This research was previously published in Cloud Computing and Virtualization Technologies in Libraries edited by Sangeeta N. Dhamdhere, pages 278-296, copyright year 2014 by Information Science Reference (an imprint of IGI Global).

Index

T

U

V

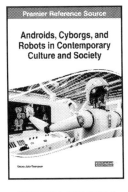

Ensure Quality Research is Introduced to the Academic Community

Become an IGI Global Reviewer for Authored Book Projects

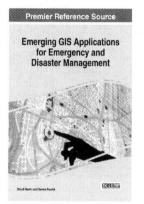

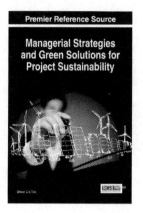

The overall success of an authored book project is dependent on quality and timely reviews.

In this competitive age of scholarly publishing, constructive and timely feedback significantly expedites the turnaround time of manuscripts from submission to acceptance, allowing the publication and discovery of forward-thinking research at a much more expeditious rate. Several IGI Global authored book projects are currently seeking highly qualified experts in the field to fill vacancies on their respective editorial review boards:

Applications may be sent to:
development@igi-global.com

Applicants must have a doctorate (or an equivalent degree) as well as publishing and reviewing experience. Reviewers are asked to write reviews in a timely, collegial, and constructive manner. All reviewers will begin their role on an ad-hoc basis for a period of one year, and upon successful completion of this term can be considered for full editorial review board status, with the potential for a subsequent promotion to Associate Editor.

If you have a colleague that may be interested in this opportunity,
we encourage you to share this information with them.

Printed in the United States
By Bookmasters